THE GREENWOOD ENCYCLOPEDIA OF

African American Literature

THE GREENWOOD ENCYCLOPEDIA OF
African American Literature

VOLUME II

D–H

Edited by
Hans Ostrom and J. David Macey, Jr.

GREENWOOD PRESS
Westport, Connecticut • London

Library of Congress Cataloging-in-Publication Data

The Greenwood encyclopedia of African American literature / edited by Hans Ostrom and J. David Macey, Jr.
     p. cm.
    Includes bibliographical references.
    ISBN 0–313–32972–9 (set : alk. paper)—ISBN 0–313–32973–7 (v. 1 : alk. paper)—
ISBN 0–313–32974–5 (v. 2 : alk. paper)—ISBN 0–313–32975–3 (v. 3 : alk. paper)—
ISBN 0–313–32976–1 (v. 4 : alk. paper)—ISBN 0–313–32977–X (v. 5 : alk. paper) 1. American
literature—African American authors—Encyclopedias. 2. African Americans—Intellectual life—
Encyclopedias. 3. African Americans in literature—Encyclopedias. I. Ostrom, Hans A.
II. Macey, J. David.
PS153.N5G73   2005
810.9'896073—dc22   2005013679

British Library Cataloguing in Publication Data is available.

This book is included in the *African American Experience* database from Greenwood Electronic Media.
For more information, visit www.africanamericanexperience.com.

Library of Congress Catalog Card Number: 2005013679
ISBN: 0–313–32972–9 (set)
     0–313–32973–7 (vol. I)
     0–313–32974–5 (vol. II)
     0–313–32975–3 (vol. III)
     0–313–32976–1 (vol. IV)
     0–313–32977–X (vol. V)

First published in 2005

Greenwood Press, 88 Post Road West, Westport, CT 06881
An imprint of Greenwood Publishing Group, Inc.
www.greenwood.com

Printed in the United States of America

The paper used in this book complies with the
Permanent Paper Standard issued by the National
Information Standards Organization (Z39.48–1984).

10 9 8 7 6 5 4 3 2 1

CONTENTS

LIST OF ENTRIES

TOPICAL LIST OF ENTRIES

The following list of entries, organized according to topical categories, includes a complete list of author entries and provides a comprehensive overview of the *Encyclopdedia*'s coverage of the literary, critical, historical, cultural, and regional contexts of African American literature. Please consult the Index for assistance in locating discussions of specific literary texts and other topics.

Athletes and Sports

Ali, Muhammad (born 1942)

Basketball

Campanella, Roy (1921–1993)

Carter, Rubin "Hurricane" (born 1937)

Johnson, Jack (1878–1946)

Jordan, Michael Jeffrey (born 1963)

Louis, Joe (1914–1981)

Mays, Willie Howard, Jr. (born 1931)

Robinson, Jackie [Jack Roosevelt] (1919–1972)

Authors

Abernathy, Ralph David (1926–1990)

Adams, Jenoyne (born 1972)

Adoff, Arnold (born 1935)

Ai (born 1947)

Albert, Octavia Victoria Rogers (1853–1889)

Aldridge, Ira (1807–1867)

Alers, Rochelle (born 1943)

Alexander, Elizabeth (born 1962)

Alexander, Lewis (1900–1945)

Allen, Jeffrey Renard (born 1962)

Allen, Richard (1760–1831)

Allen, Samuel Washington (born 1917)

Allison, Hughes (1908–c. 1974)

Als, Hilton (born 1961)

Amos, Robyn (born 1971)

Anderson, Garland (1886–1939)

Anderson, Mignon Holland (born 1945)

Brown, Wesley (born 1945)

Brown, William Wells (1815–1884)

Browne, Theodore (c. 1910–1979)

Bryan, Ashley (born 1923)

Buchanan, Shonda (born 1968)

Buckley, Gail Lumet (born 1937)

Bullins, Ed (born 1935)

Bunkley, Anita Richmond (born 1944)

Burrill, Mary ("Mamie") Powell (c. 1882–1946)

Burroughs, Margaret Taylor Goss (born 1917)

Burton, Annie Louise (1860–?)

Bush-Banks, Olivia Ward (1869–1944)

Busia, Akosua (born 1966)

Bussey, Louré (born c. 1971)

Butcher, Philip (born 1918)

Butler, Octavia E. (born 1947)

Butler, Tajuana "TJ" (born 1971)

Byrd, Adrianne (born c. 1976)

Cain, George (born 1943)

Caldwell, Ben (born 1937)

Campbell, Bebe Moore (born 1950)

Campbell, James Edwin (1867–1896)

Carmichael, Stokely (1941–1998)

Carroll, Vinnette (1922–2003)

Carter, Charlotte (born 1943)

Carter, Stephen L. (born 1954)

Cartiér, Xam Wilson (born 1949)

Cary, Lorene (born 1956)

Cary, Mary Ann Camberton Shadd (1823–1893)

Cassells, Cyrus (born 1957)

Chambers, Veronica (born 1971)

Charles, Kraal (Kayo) Y. (born 1975)

Chase-Riboud, Barbara (born 1939)

Chennault, Stephen D. (born 1940)

Chesnutt, Charles Waddell (1858–1932)

Childress, Alice (1916–1994)

Christian, Marcus Bruce (1900–1976)

Clair, Maxine (born 1939)

Clarke, Breena

Cleage [Lomax], Pearl Michelle (born 1948)

Cleaver, Eldridge (1935–1998)

Cleaver, Kathleen Neal (born 1946)

Cliff, Michelle (born 1946)

Clifton, Lucille (born 1936)

Clinton, Michelle T. (born 1954)

Cobb, Ned (1885–1973)

Cobb, William Jelani (born c. 1972)

Coffin, Frank B[arbour] (1871–1951)

Cole, Harriette (born c. 1963)

Coleman, Anita Scott (1890–1960)

Coleman, Evelyn (born 1948)

Coleman, Wanda (born 1946)

Collier, Eugenia (born 1928)

Colter, Cyrus (1910–2002)

Cone, James H. (born 1939)

Cooper, Anna Julia Haywood (1858/1859–1964)

Cooper, Clarence, Jr. (1934–1978)

Cooper, J[oan] California (born 193?)

Coppin, Fanny Marion Jackson (c. 1837–1913)

Corbin, Steven (1953–1995)

Cornish, Sam[uel] James (born 1935)

Cornish, Samuel Eli (c. 1790–1858)

Corrothers, James (1869–1917)

Cortez, Jayne (born 1936)

Cose, Ellis (born 1950)

Cotter, Joseph Seamon, Jr. (1895–1919)

Historical and Cultural Figures

Literary Movements, Schools, and Organizations

Music and Musicians

D

Dandridge, Raymond Garfield (1882–1930). Poet, lyricist, and artist. Raymond Garfield Dandridge was known in Cincinnati, Ohio, according to Calvin Dill Wilson's foreword to *Zalka Peetruza and Other Poems* (1928), as the "Paul Laurence Dunbar of Cincinnati." More than that, Dandridge was viewed as an inspiration to those who knew him for his indefatigable will to write and support himself despite his debilitating paralysis, and a man whose poetic output bridged the dialect tradition and the concerns of the **New Negro** movement (*see* **Harlem Renaissance**). Born to Raymond and Ella Carter Dandridge in Cincinnati on April 8, 1882, Dandridge attended Cincinnati public schools, including Hughes Night High School, while he held down a number of odd jobs, including working as a porter at the local YMCA. Described as an outstanding student who also excelled at track and swimming, Dandridge demonstrated an interest in and aptitude for art during his school days as well. His family, including a brother, Oscar William Dandridge, purchased a house in the Price Hill district of Cincinnati in 1908, and it was here that, in 1911, Dandridge was stricken with a fever from which he seemed to recover, only to be confined to bed by paralysis on July 4, 1912. Losing the use of both legs and his right arm, the bedridden Dandridge nonetheless maintained his spirit of perseverance—a note to his first published volume of poems, *Penciled Poems* (1917), quotes him as saying, "'Tis good to make the best of it"—taking up writing and finding employment selling coal by phone. Local newspaper clippings discuss Dandridge's inspirational story, describing how he dialed the phone with a pencil tip held in his mouth, and in one article he was dubbed a "coal dealer poet"—reminiscent, perhaps, of the dubbing of **Langston Hughes** as the "bus boy poet" early in his career. More important, Dandridge taught himself to write with his left hand and, with "dark and luminous eyes that suggest the poet" (according to Wilson), he began to look at the world with poetic vision.

In his poetry, Dandridge employs the tradition of Negro **dialect poetry** made famous by **Paul Laurence Dunbar**, most frequently in a humorous ("'Ittle Touzle Head") or sentimental ("Fren'ship") vein. The poems sometimes suffer from the outlandish, exaggerated misspellings that plague dialect poetry, but also offer some very warm and poignant portraits and lessons in homespun expression. But we also find tributes to national figures such as Abraham Lincoln, **Booker T. Washington**, and Theodore Roosevelt; local benefactors Mr. and Mrs. Roger Kemper Rogan (president of the Laboiteaux Co.); and clergy and acquaintances Cardinal Mercier, Father Clarence Joseph Schmitt, and Mrs. Mary Howdon, along with references to his Price Hill ("Price Hill") neighborhood and the local **NAACP** ("Supplication") among his poems in Standard English. His first volume, *Penciled Poems* (1917)—dedicated to his mother—contains fifty-one poems, none of which appear in his second volume, *The Poet and Other Poems* (1920), dedicated to his deceased brother Oscar. However, twenty poems from the first volume are revised and included among the eighty-six poems in his final book, *Zalka Peetruza and Other Poems* (1928), which was dedicated to the Rogans.

The breadth of subjects in Dandridge's poems is notable—the art and nature of poetry, religion, family, patriotism, love, morality, nature, the meaning of life, and children are among the topics confronted—and Dandridge employs a variety of stanzaic patterns, including rhymed couplets, alternating rhymes, quatrains, **sonnets**, **blank verse**, **free verse**, and stanzas with refrains. Significantly, Dandridge wrote a number of poems that dealt with the African American experience (sometimes in assertive, politically conscious terms), including "Time to Die," "To an Unhanged Judas," "Decreed," "Toussaint," "Supplication," "Opportunity," "Censored," "Brother Mine," "Toil Created," "Arise," "Facts," "My Grievance," "Zalka Peetruza," and "Color Blind." Poems such as "De Drum Majah" seem to look forward to poems that celebrate individual style and flare such as **Sterling A. Brown**'s "Puttin' on Dog" and "Sporting Beasley," while "Zalka Peetruza" anticipates the exoticism and tone of **Claude McKay**'s "Harlem Dancer" and **Langston Hughes**'s poems dealing with the blighted lives of misunderstood women. While few, if any, readers would claim that Dandridge is a poetic genius, his lyrics as crafted poetry are frequently musical, heartfelt, and interesting, though occasionally bathetic, and the range of his subject matter is notable. The revisions to the poems from *Penciled Poems* (twenty) and *The Poet and Other Poems* (thirty-six) that reappear in *Zalka Peetruza and Other Poems*, if done by Dandridge, indicate that he was conscious of the crafting of his poems, down to careful alterations in spelling and punctuation in his dialect work. During his lifetime, Dandridge's poems appeared, besides in local papers and his published volumes, in the anthologies *The Book of American Negro Poetry* (1922; 1931), *Negro Poets and Their Poems* (1923; 1935), and *An Anthology of Verse by American Negroes* (1924).

Dandridge was conscious of the monetary value of his poetry as well. He published a number of his poems on small cards for sale, and had poems published with sheet music as well. Additionally, Dandridge was an illustrator whose drawings "Jim Crow Bird" and "Out of the Frying Pan" delivered pointed political messages in the papers in which they appeared. Besides his acknowledgment in the local press, among Dandridge's papers at the Cincinnati Historical Society are a letter from France regarding a poem of his included in *Friends' Intelligences*, a letter mentioning him and addressed to his mother from the Franklin Delano Roosevelt White House from 1936, and a February 27, 1930, obituary from the *Catholic Telegraph*, appearing just three days after his death. The poem he dedicated to his brother, "Gone West," can perhaps apply to his own life, too: when he asks if his brother hears the cannon fire of violence among the living, he seems to hear back from him that "toil and pain and woe/And care and strife—ah! Yes, and death/Were left behind, below."

Resources: Sterling Brown, *Negro Poetry and Drama* (1937; repr. New York: Atheneum, 1972); William Coyle, ed., *Ohio Authors and Their Books, 1796–1950* (Cleveland, OH: World, 1962); Raymond Garfield Dandridge: *Penciled Poems* (Cincinnati: Powell and White, 1917); *The Poet and Other Poems* (Cincinnati: Powell and White, 1920); *Zalka Peetruza and Other Poems* (Cincinnati: McDonald, 1928); Robert B. Eleazer, *Singers in the Dawn: A Brief Anthology of American Negro Poetry* (Atlanta: Conference on Education and Race Relations, 1934); Joanne V. Gabbin, "Raymond Garfield Dandridge," in *Dictionary of Literary Biography*, vol. 51, ed. Trudier Harris (Detroit: Gale, 1987); James Weldon Johnson, *The Book of American Negro Poetry* (New York: Harcourt, Brace, 1922); Robert T. Kerlin, *Negro Poets and Their Poems* (Washington, DC: Associated Publishers, 1923); Jean Wagner, *Black Poets of the United States: From Paul Laurence Dunbar to Langston Hughes*, trans. Kenneth Douglas (Urbana: University of Illinois Press, 1973); Newman Ivey White and Walter Clinton Jackson, eds., *An Anthology of Verse by American Negroes* (Durham, NC: Trinity College Press, 1924).

Steven C. Tracy

Danner, Margaret Esse Taylor (1915–1984). Poet, editor, and community activist. Danner is considered an important figure in the **Black Arts Movement** of the 1960s but was active in literary circles well before that decade. She was born in Kentucky but relocated to **Chicago, Illinois**, before moving to **Detroit, Michigan**. While in Chicago, Danner worked for *Poetry: The Magazine of Verse* from 1951–1957, as an editorial assistant and an assistant editor; there, she worked with Karl Shapiro and Paul Engle, who both nurtured her creativity as a poet. In 1961, Danner moved to Detroit, where she became the first poet-in-residence at Wayne State University. Significantly, she established a community arts center, Boone House Writers (1962–1964), before traveling to Africa, and met such notable poets as **Dudley Randall**, **Robert Hayden**, **Naomi Long Madgett**, and **Owen Dodson**, and the innovative thinker and critic **Hoyt Fuller**. Together, Boone House and **Broadside Press**, founded by Randall in

1965, made Detroit a key part of the Blacks Arts Movement, and made Danner's poetry a central focus in the movement. As one of the twenty-eight Broadside Series poets, Danner published five volumes of poetry in which she writes of Africa and protests against White racism and its effects on African Americans, treating subjects ranging from the **civil rights movement**, to old age, to Black heritage. Broadside Press published her first three works: *To Flower* (1962), *Poem Counterpoem* (with Dudley Randall, 1966), and *Impressions of African Art Forms* (1960), which set the tone of her career as a poet. Her other volumes include *Iron Lace* (1968) and *The Down of a Thistle: Selected Poems, Prose Poems and Songs* (1976), dedicated to Robert Hayden. Danner also edited two anthologies of students' verse: *Brass Horses* (1968) and *Regroup* (1969). In 1973, Danner was among eighteen prominent Black women poets invited to read from her works at the Phillis Wheatley Poetry Festival, organized by the poet and novelist **Margaret Walker** and held at Jackson State College (now University). Writing over several decades, before she died in Chicago in 1986, Danner was a poet ahead of her time who made a significant contribution to African American literature and to the Black Arts Movement. The spokesperson for the Black Arts Movement, **Addison Gayle, Jr.**, called Danner a "literary godparent" (Carson, 199). And, like the works of **Gwendolyn Brooks**, **Mari Evans**, **Nikki Giovanni**, **Sonia Sanchez**, and **Langston Hughes**, her works continue to address issues that connect to African heritage and culture.

Resources: June M. Aldridge, "Margaret Esse Danner," in *Dictionary of Literary Biography*, vol. 41, *Afro-American Poets Since 1955*, ed. Trudier Harris and Thadious M. Davis (Detroit: Gale, 1985), 84–89; Leonard Pack Bailey, ed., *Broadside Authors and Artists: An Illustrated Biographical Directory* (Detroit: Broadside, 1974); Sharon Carson, "Danner, Margaret Esse," in *The Oxford Companion to African American Literature*, ed. William L. Andrews, Frances Smith Foster, and Trudier Harris (New York: Oxford University Press, 1997), 199–200; Margaret Esse Taylor Danner: *The Down of a Thistle: Selected Poems, Prose Poems, and Songs* (Detroit: Broadside Press, 1976); *Impressions of African Art Forms* (Detroit: Broadside Press, 1968); *To Flower* (Detroit: Broadside Press, 1962); Margaret Esse Taylor Danner and Dudley Randall, *Poem Counterpoem* (Detroit: Broadside Press, 1966); Don L. Lee, "Toward a Definition: Black Poetry of the Sixties (After Leroi Jones)," in *The Black Aesthetic*, comp. Addison Gayle, Jr. (Garden City, NY: Doubleday, 1971), 222–233; Haki Madhubuti (Don L. Lee), *Dynamite Voices*, vol. 1, *Black Poets of the 1960's* (Detroit: Broadside, 1971); Dudley Randall, *The Black Poets* (New York: Bantam, 1971).

Loretta G. Woodard

Danticat, Edwidge (born 1969). Writer and professor. Danticat was born in Port-au-Prince, **Haiti**. She moved to **Brooklyn, New York**, when she was twelve. Her writing often reflects on the life of the refugee/exiled immigrant. Her father immigrated to the United States for economic and political reasons in 1971, followed two years later by her mother. Raised by her aunt, and speaker of Kréyol until she moved to America to reunite with her parents, Danticat published her first English writings at age fourteen, including newspaper articles about her migration that inspired *Breath, Eyes, Memory* (1994). Her books, essays, and editorial work also reflect on this conundrum of identity for the Haitian national—torn between the country that defines her identity and the revolutionary movement that defines Haiti's place in the **diaspora**, she depicts the human striving for hope.

Danticat graduated with a degree in French literature from Barnard College and received her M.F.A. from Brown University. Her short stories have appeared in twenty-five periodicals, and her books have been translated into Korean, Italian, German, French, Spanish, and Swedish. She is currently a visiting professor of creative writing at New York University and the University of Miami.

Danticat, who was the American Book Award winner for *The Farming of Bones* in 1999, and was National Book Award finalist for *Krik? Krak!* in 1995, also won the Fiction Award from *The Caribbean Writer* in 1994. In 1995 she won the Woman of Achievement Award and the Pushcart Short Story Prize. In 1996 Danticat received the Best Young American Novelist Award from GRANTA for *Breath, Eyes, Memory*, and in 1999 she won the International Flaiano Prize for Literature for *Farming of Bones*.

In addition to *Farming of Bones, Krik? Krak!*, and *Breath, Eyes, Memory*, Danticat has written *After the Dance: A Walk Through Carnival in Jacmel, Haiti* (2002), and *Behind the Mountains* (2002, her first book for young readers). She has edited *The Butterfly's Way: Voices from the Haitian Dyaspora in the United States* (2001) and *The Beacon Best of 2000: Great Writing by Men and Women of All Colors and Cultures* (2000). Her latest book is *The Dew Breaker* (2004).

Each of Danticat's works reflects on Haiti's bloody past, and notes how the scars of the present are merely markers of memory for those Haitians who dealt with the dictatorships and revolutions that erupted in Haiti and the Dominican Republic in the 1930s. Hers is a postcolonial, feminist perspective with the issues of strained migration experiences, broken family life, suppressed human sexuality, and **gender** roles as main themes for her texts. She explores the relationship between mother and daughter in a deconstructionist fashion, keeping in mind the political underpinnings that sometimes play just under that characterization (*see* **Deconstruction**). Her personal experience plays a part in her politics as a writer and in her young female characters' inner lives. With a voice that bores into these young girls' psyches, Danticat's place as the writer is that of the eyewitness, using the Haitian tradition of storytelling as the medium through which to purge the experiences of those who suffered through the torture of living under siege.

Danticat's most recent book, *The Dew Breaker*, is written in vignettes that focus on the central character, Ka Bienaimé, and the macoute who is her father, named the "Dew Breaker" for his tendency to come early and strike swiftly in matters of torture and killing. Ka is a sculptress who captures in her art what she has learned of her father's experiences in prison—little knowing that her father was, in fact, a government-sanctioned torturer. The vignettes swing back to her father's past and forward through characters affected by torture and migration, coming to Ka's father's confession, and the place her mother has in this revelation. The book is a study in the temporality of trauma and the remorse of a man haunted by a past filled with the blood of others. Danticat based the novel on stories inspired by sightings in Brooklyn of a former leader of the Haitian paramilitary group that in the early 1990s terrorized and killed Jean-Bertrand Aristide supporters.

In *The Farming of Bones* Danticat focuses on the 1937 massacre in the Dominican Republic of Haitians commonly attributed to Generalissimo Rafael Leonidas Trujillo. Trujillo was the Dominican dictator widely praised initially for his reforms and economic stabilization of the Dominican Republic. He was trained as a member of the Dominican Republic National Guard by the United States and ultimately feared as an unruly killer and leader of that guard. The title of the book reflects doubly on the bones of those left in the cane fields following those massacres and the actual farming of those fields; in this way she comments on the politics of the era in the context of those left to cope with the trauma of loss. Danticat uses the interwoven lives of two characters who might be seen as representatives of both sides of Hispaniola—Señora Valencia and Amabelle, who both view this time period through the lens of love and family.

Breath, Eyes, Memory is Danticat's most personal exploration of migration. Sophie, the main character, bears some resemblance in her experience to that of the author, insofar as separation of family and difficulty in adjustment to immigrant life are concerned. In this narrative Danticat reflects on the body as a site of trauma, noting the experience of the childless mother in exile and the motherless child with whom she is reunited in the United States. Escape from psychological and physical harm is the theme of the storytelling present in this text through the matriarchal figures who influence Sophie's break with her and her mother's past, rooted in the act of rape. A product of rape, Sophie in some ways represents the Haitian diaspora.

Krik? Krak! is a collection of nine stories about life under Haiti's dictatorships. Highlighted is the terrorism of the Tonton Macoutes and the national psyche with regard to this, as well as the issues unique to migration. Her first young reader's novel, *Behind the Mountains*, focuses on Haiti during election time and highlights the upheaval that forces migration. *After the Dance: A Walk Through Carnival in Jacmel* is Danticat's perspective on her first experience of carnival after years of being afraid to attend. (*See* **Creole**.)

Resources: Edwidge Danticat: *After the Dance: A Walk Through Carnival in Jacmel, Haiti* (New York: Crown Journeys, 2002); *Behind the Mountains* (New York: Orchard Books, 2002); *Breath, Eyes, Memory* (New York: Soho Books, 1994); *The Dew Breaker* (New York: Knopf, 2004); *Farming of Bones* (New York: Vintage, 1998); *Krik? Krak!* (New York: Soho Books, 1995); Edwidge Danticat, ed., *Beacon Best of 2000: Great Writing by Women and Men of All Colors and Cultures* (Boston: Beacon Press, 2000); *The Butterfly's Way: Voices from the Haitian Dyaspora in the United States* (New York: Soho Press, 2001).

Elizabete Vasconcelos

Darden, Christopher (born 1957). Attorney and novelist. Born in Martinez, California, Darden received his B.S. in criminal justice administration from San Jose State University and his J.D. from the Hastings College of Law, University of California. After serving with the National Labor Relations Board, Darden joined the Los Angeles County District Attorney's office. He became nationally known when he served as one of the prosecuting attorneys in the trial of O. J. Simpson in 1995 for the murder of his wife, Nicole Brown Simpson, and her friend Ronald Goldman. Shortly after the trial, Darden joined the faculty at Southwestern University School of Law. In 1999, he left the university and established his own legal firm, Darden and Associates, specializing in criminal defense and civil litigation. He has become a frequent television commentator, a speaker at universities and corporate gatherings, an actor in television dramas and films, and an author.

Written with Jess Walter, Darden's first book, *In Contempt* (1996), is his account of the Simpson trial. The book provides a frank appraisal of why the prosecution lost the case and an often moving account of how the racial issues surrounding the case affected Darden. He has subsequently written a series of mystery novels with Dick Lochte. *The Trials of Nikki Hill* (1999) and *L.A. Justice* (2000) focus on the professional and personal crises of Nikki Hill, a prosecutor with the Los Angeles District Attorney's office. In *Last Defense* (2002) and *Lawless* (2004), the central character is Mercer Early, a young African American defense lawyer. All of these novels are set in **Los Angeles, California**, and demonstrate Darden's firsthand knowledge of the forces that have generated the city's volatile energy. (*See* **Cose, Ellis**.)

Resources: Christopher Darden and Dick Lochte: *L.A. Justice* (New York: Warner Books, 2000); *Last Defense* (New York: New American Library, 2002); *Lawless* (New York: New American Library, 2004); *The Trials of Nikki Hill* (New York: Warner Books, 1999); Christopher Darden and Jess Walter, *In Contempt* (New York: Regan Books, 1996); John Gregory Dunne, "The Slam Dunk," *The New Yorker*, Apr. 15, 1996, pp. 40–43; Adam Hochschild, "Closing Argument," *New York Times Book Review*, Apr. 28, 1996, p. 14.

Martin Kich

Dasein Literary Society (1958–1960). The Dasein Literary Society generally refers to a poetry collective formed by a handful of students at Howard University in the late 1950s. This designation, however, is not wholly accurate. The original collective consisted of six young Black men who called themselves the Howard Poets, but are often referred to as the Dasein Poets because of the title of the journal they published, *Dasein*. The Dasein Literary Society more properly refers to the poets published in the issues of *Dasein*, rather than being limited to the Howard Poets (Napier, 57).

The Howard Poets have been recognized as representing "one of the toughest intellectual strains in contemporary [B]lack poetry" (Redmond, 314). Indeed, it has been suggested that in the wake of the 1954 rulings of *Brown v. Board of Education*, the poets "actively sought to demonstrate that the [B]lack man was a serious intellectual contender" (Napier, 57). Initiated by Oswald Govan and Percy Johnston, the collective began forming in the fall of 1958. They were joined by Walter De Legall, Alfred Fraser, LeRoy Stone, and Joseph White. Stone christened the group the Howard Poets in an article he wrote for the student newspaper, *The Hilltop*, in May 1959. During the following year, the group grew in popularity both on and off campus.

The environment at Howard was significant in developing their sensibilities as poets and intellectuals. Among the faculty, **Sterling A. Brown** and **Toni Morrison** (then known as Antonia Wofford) were especially supportive (Napier, 58). Although the Howard Poets did not adhere to a single theme, they did share interests in philosophy and **jazz**. They all studied philosophy and appreciated jazz as a Black musical form that related directly to their poetry, in both form and content. These interests often combined with their social concerns, producing work that foreshadowed the **Black Arts Movement** both thematically and aesthetically.

Despite their popularity and the supportive environment, the Howard Poets would soon split. In April 1960, Johnston and Stone read at a campus event without the other poets, hoping to begin their careers away from the group. The resulting tension and jealousy effectively broke up the collective. By May, Stone and White had left Howard.

Later that year, Johnston began work on publishing a literary journal. The first issue of *Dasein* appeared in March 1961 and was attributed to the Dasein Literary Society of Howard University (this may be what triggered the confusion in names). With the exception of White, each of the Howard Poets contributed to the first issue, which also included work from, among others, Delores Kendrick and **Lance Jeffers**. Johnston published *Dasein* for more than a decade, the final issue appearing in 1973.

While there has been some critical investigation of them, the Howard Poets have largely been ignored and excluded from anthologies. Unfortunately, this is the norm for many of the Black artist collectives of the time. Critical emphasis is often placed on the more recognizable names of the Black Arts Movement, overshadowing the work that came before it.

Resources: Walter De Legall et al., *Burning Spear: An Anthology of Afro-Saxon Poetry* (Washington, DC: Jupiter Hammon Press, 1963); Winston Napier, "The Howard Poets," in *Washington and Washington Writing*, ed. David McAleavey (Washington, DC: Center for Washington Area Studies, 1986), 57–67; Aldon Lynn Nielsen, *Black Chant: Languages of African-American Postmodernism* (Cambridge: Cambridge University Press, 1997); Eugene Redmond, *Drumvoices: The Mission of Afro-American Poetry* (New York: Anchor Books, 1976).

Raquel Rodriguez

Dash, Julie (born 1952). Film director, film producer, screenwriter, novelist, and nonfiction writer. Dash is best known for writing and directing the acclaimed independent film *Daughters of the Dust* (January 1992), which concerns the African American Peazant family, who live on an island (Dawtah) off the coast of South Carolina and are part of the Gullah subculture, but who must move to the mainland. The story is set in 1902 and features several complex female characters. Dash became the first African American female director to have a full-length feature film distributed nationwide (also known as "general release"), and the film drew widespread critical acclaim. She later wrote a book about how the film was made. In 1997 Dash published a novel with the same title and based on the same material. Born in New York City, Dash earned a B.A. in psychology from the City College of New York (CCNY) and also studied at the David Picker Film Institute in the Leonard Davis Center for the Performing Arts (CCNY) ("Julie Dash"). She was awarded a fellowship in writing and producing at the American Film Institute in **Los Angeles, California**, and, in 1986, received an M.F.A. in motion picture and television production at UCLA. Dash has directed a number of feature films and movies for television: *Subway Stories: Tales from the Underground* (1997), *Incognito* (1999), *Funny Valentines* (1999), *Love Song* (2000), and *The Rosa Parks Story*, starring Angela Bassett (2002). She also has directed music videos and, at this writing, is at work on another novel as well as on motion picture projects ("Julie Dash"). *Filmmakers* magazine listed *Daughters of the Dust* as among the fifty most important independent American films ("Julie Dash").

Resources: Julie Dash: *Daughters of the Dust* (New York: Dutton, 1997); *Daughters of the Dust: The Making of an African American Woman's Film* (New York: New Press, 1992); Julie Dash, director and screenwriter, *Daughters of the Dust* (1992; New York: Kino International, 1996 [VHS]; 2000 [DVD]); Julie Dash, director, *The Rosa Parks Story* (Los Angeles: Xenon Entertainment, 2003 [DVD]); "Julie Dash," Geechee Girls Productions Web site, http://www.geechee.tv/julieinfo/bio2.html.

Hans Ostrom

davenport, doris (born 1949). Teacher, feminist, and poet. davenport (who prefers to spell her name without capitalization) is an important feminist writer and a poet who, among other things, gives voice to lesbian experience. doris davenport was born January 29, 1949, in Gainesville, Georgia. The oldest of six daughters and one son, she grew up in nearby Cornelia, Georgia. It was there, between the ages of eleven and twelve, that she began writing short stories. This rustic setting at the foot of the Appalachian Mountains and her experiences as an "Affrilachian" (an African American from the Appalachians) provides the source material for much of her writing. (*See* **Affrilachian Poets.**)

davenport attended Paine College in Augusta, Georgia, graduating cum laude in 1969. She went on to obtain her M.A. in English from the State University of New York at Buffalo in 1971 and her Ph.D. from the University of Southern California in 1991, with a dissertation titled "Four Contemporary Black Women Poets: Lucille Clifton, June Jordan, Audre Lorde & Sherley Anne Williams."

In 1980 davenport self-published *it's like this*, a book of poetry. Her second self-published work, *eat thunder and drink rain* (1982), takes on the stricture of the so-called straight community as well as the presumed expanded borders of the lesbian community (Montgomery, 157). In 1981 her work appeared in *This Bridge Called My Back: Writings by Radical Women of Color*, edited by Cherríe Moraga and Gloria Anzaldúa. Her other works include an Italian translation of *eat thunder and drink rain* (1988), and *voodoo chile/slight return* (1991). Additionally, davenport has published essays in many Black and feminist publications as well as having poems published in *Listen Here: Women Writing in Appalachia*, edited by Sandra L. Ballard and Patricia L. Hudson (2003).

In the spring of 1991 davenport received the Kentucky Foundation for Women Grant, which allowed her to live and work in northern Italy. She has also received been listed in *Who's Who Among American Teachers* (2002) and has received the Georgia Council for the Arts Individual Artist Award (1993), the Syvenna Foundation for Women Residency (1993), the North Carolina Arts Council Writing Fellowship (1992), the Writers' Workshop/Asheville First Prize in Poetry (1992), and the Kentucky Foundation for Women Grant (1991).

Her upcoming works include *Madness like Morning Glories: Poems*, to be published by Louisiana State University Press in 2005. She has been an assistant professor of English at Stillman College, Tuscaloosa, Alabama, since August 2002.

Resources: Sandra I. Ballard and Patricia L. Hudson, eds., *Listen Here: Women Writing in Appalachia* (Lexington: University of Kentucky Press, 2003); doris davenport: *eat thunder and drink rain* (self-published, 1982); *it's like this* (self-published, 1980); *Madness Like the Morning Glories: Poems* (Baton Rouge: Louisiana State University Press, 2005); personal communications with Denisa Chatman-Riley (Aug. 7–22, 2004); *voodoo chile/ slight return* (self-published, 1991); James A. Miller, "Coming Home to Affrilachia: The Poems of doris davenport," in *Her Words: Diverse Voices in Contemporary Appalachian Women's Poetry*, ed. Felicia Mitchell (Knoxville: University of Tennessee Press, 2002); Helena Louise Montgomery, "doris davenport," in *Contemporary Lesbian Writers of the United States: A Bio-Bibliographical Critical Sourcebook*, ed. Sandra Pollack and Denise D. Knight (Westport, CT: Greenwood Press, 1993), 155–159.

Denisa Chatman-Riley

Davis, Angela Y. (born 1944). Theoretician, civil rights activist, and advocate for prison reform. Davis is arguably one of the most radical African American cultural philosophers to emerge in the 1960s. Prior to leaving Birmingham, Alabama, to pursue higher education in New York, Massachusetts, Germany, and California, she embraced ideals put forth by her parents (both teachers and activists), ideals that led to an awareness of global politics. As an undergraduate at Brandeis University, Davis studied Marxist philosophy under Herbert Marcuse before leaving the country in 1965 to study in Frankfurt under Theodor Adorno and Jürgen Habermas. While word of the growing Black Liberation Movement reached her overseas, Davis participated in the German student movement's "determined campaign to attack the fascist and racist attitudes which had become so deeply embedded" (Davis, *Autobiography*, 138).

When she returned to the United States in 1967 (to finish her doctorate under Marcuse at the University of California), Davis affirmed her ideologies with the Che-Lumumba Club, an exclusively African American faction of the Communist Party. After joining both the Communist Party and the **Black Panther Party** in 1968, Davis was under surveillance by the Federal Bureau of Investigation (FBI) for radical anti-Americanism. In 1969, she was dismissed from the Philosophy Department at UCLA as a result of her activism, publicly ousted by Ronald Reagan, then governor of California, for being a Communist. Her relationships with activists such as **Huey Newton**, **Eldridge Cleaver**, and George Jackson led the media to portray Davis as one of the most notorious advocates of Black Liberation.

A poster calling for the release of Angela Davis, 1971. Courtesy of the Library of Congress.

The third woman in U.S. history to make the FBI's Most Wanted List after being targeted for her affiliation with the Soledad Brothers, Davis was charged in the conspiracy to free George Jackson in 1970 after a shootout and a failed kidnapping in the Marin County Hall of Justice on August 7, 1970 (Nadelson, 58). The judge for Jackson's trial and three other people were killed. Davis was not at the scene, but the police and prosecutors implicated her because they claimed weapons used in the shootout were registered to her. Davis went underground but was captured less than a month later in New York City. She was subsequently charged with a list of offenses including conspiracy, kidnapping, and homicide. She spent a year and a half in prison but eventually was found not guilty on all charges by an all-White jury.

Not long after, Davis published *If They Come in the Morning: Voices of Resistance* (1971), a collection of essays on Marxist and race-related ideologies, and resumed her teaching career at San Francisco State University. After cofounding the National Alliance Against Racism and Political Repression in 1972, she committed herself to relating personal experiences with discrimination and captivity. Joy James clarifies why Davis tactically "evokes" the Roman god of doors (Janus) in *Angela Davis: An Autobiography* (1974) by explaining that "For activist-intellectuals, such as Davis, who struggled with exclusionary but overlapping worlds shaped by **race**, class, sex, **gender** and violence, Janus in its positive manifestation represents the opportunity to confront the contradictory existence of abrogated freedom within the world's most powerful nation-state" (2). An unsuccessful run for vice president of the United States on the Communist Party ticket prompted Davis to continue exploring culturally pressing topics in such pivotal works as *Women, Race and Class* (1981), *Women, Culture and Politics* (1989), *Blues Legacies and Black Feminism: Gertrude "Ma" Rainey, Bessie Smith, and Billie Holliday* (1998) and *The Angela Y. Davis Reader* (1998). Davis maintains careers as a professor, theorist, public speaker, and an organizer while continuing to contribute to audio compilations, magazines, and journals. A recent work is *Are Prisons Obsolete?* (2003). (*See* **Marxism**.)

Resources: Angela Y. Davis: *Angela Davis: An Autobiography* (New York: Random House, 1974); *Are Prisons Obsolete?* (New York: Seven Stories Press/Open Media Series, 2003); *Blues Legacies and Black Feminism: Gertrude "Ma" Rainey, Bessie Smith, and Billie Holiday* (New York: Pantheon, 1998); *If They Come in the Morning: Voices of Resistance* (New York: Third Press, 1971); *Women, Culture, and Politics* (New York: Random House, 1989); *Women, Race, and Class* (New York: Random House, 1981); Joy James, ed., *The Angela Y. Davis Reader* (Oxford: Blackwell, 1998); Reggie Nadelson, *Who Is Angela Davis? The Biography of a Revolutionary* (New York: P. H. Wyden, 1972).

Stephen M. Steck

Davis, Arthur P. (1904–1996). Literary critic, anthologist, and educator. Arthur Paul Davis, a revered pioneer in African American literary study and criticism, was born in Hampton, Virginia. As valedictorian of his class, he received a high school diploma from Hampton Institute (now Hampton University) and matriculated at Howard University for one year. He accepted a scholarship to Columbia University and moved to New York City during the earlier years of the **Harlem Renaissance**; there he met **Langston Hughes**, **Countee Cullen**, and other key figures of the **New Negro** movement. At Columbia, Davis was elected to Phi Beta Kappa and earned a B.A. (1927), M.A. (1929), and Ph.D. (1942). He was the first African American to receive a doctorate in English from Columbia.

Davis, who began his distinguished career as an educator in 1927, taught at North Carolina College (now North Carolina Central University), Hampton Institute's summer school, and Virginia Union University, where in 1929 he taught his first course in African American literature. During this time, few African American colleges, and apparently no White colleges, offered Black literature courses; thus Davis was a pioneer in teaching African American literature at the college level. In 1944, he joined the faculty at Howard University as a full professor and taught at Howard for thirty-six years, until his retirement in 1980. At Howard, Davis inspired generations of African American scholars and authors, including **Amiri Baraka**, **Houston A. Baker, Jr.**, and Paula Giddings.

Davis wrote a newspaper column, "With a Grain of Salt," for the *Norfolk Journal and Guide* (1933–1950) and penned scholarly essays for such publications as the *CLA Journal*, **The Crisis**, *Journal of Negro Education*, *Journal of Negro History*, *Middle-Atlantic Writers Association Review*, **Opportunity**, and **Phylon**. With **Sterling A. Brown** and Ulysses G. Lee he edited the landmark publication *Negro Caravan* (1941), the first comprehensive collection of African American literature and an excellent example of intelligent, insightful editing. *Isaac Watts: His Life and Works* (1943), Davis's seminal work on the English hymnologist, was republished in England in 1948 to commemorate the 200th anniversary of Watts's death. *Cavalcade: Negro American Writing from 1760 to the Present* (1971), edited by Davis and **J. Saunders Redding**, was one of the most critically acclaimed Black anthologies, as well as required reading in many university-level African American literature courses during the 1970s and 1980s. *The New Cavalcade: African American Writing from 1760 to the Present*, edited by Davis, Redding, and **Joyce Ann Joyce**, was published in 1991 (vol. 1) and 1992 (vol. 2). Davis also published *The New Negro Renaissance: An Anthology* (1975), edited with Michael W. Peplow, and *From the Dark Tower: Afro-American Writers (1900 to 1960)* (1974), which *Choice* selected as one of the outstanding books of 1974–1975. Among Davis's honors are a Doctor of Letters honorary degree conferred by Howard University (1984) and awards from the **College Language Association** (1975), Howard University's College of Liberal Arts (1979), the Middle-Atlantic Writers Association (1982, 1988), and the District of Columbia Public Library (1992). The Arthur P. Davis Papers are housed in the Moorland-Spingarn Research Center's Manuscript Division at Howard University.

Resources: Sterling Brown, Arthur P. Davis, and Ulysses G. Lee, eds., *Negro Caravan: Writings* (New York: Dryden Press, 1941); Arthur P. Davis, *Isaac Watts: His Life and Works* (New York: Dryden Press, 1943); Arthur P. Davis, ed., *From the Dark*

Tower: Afro-American Writers (1900 to 1960) (Washington, DC: Howard University Press, 1974); Arthur P. Davis and Jill Nelson, "When I Came to Howard in 1944, Howard Had the Finest, Most Impressive Cadre of Black Intellectuals to Be Found Anywhere in the World," *Washington Post Magazine*, July 5, 1987, p. 26; Arthur P. Davis and Michael W. Peplow, eds., *The New Negro Renaissance: An Anthology* (New York: Holt, Rinehart, and Winston, 1975); Arthur P. Davis and J. Saunders Redding, eds., *Cavalcade: Negro American Writing from 1760 to the Present* (Boston: Houghton Mifflin, 1971); Arthur P. Davis, J. Saunders Redding, and Joyce Ann Joyce, eds., *The New Cavalcade: African American Writing from 1760 to the Present* (Washington, DC: Howard University Press, 1991); Jennifer Jordan, "Arthur P. Davis: Forging the Way for the Formation of the Canon," *Callaloo* 1, no. 2 (1997), 450–460; Sharon Malinowski, ed., *Black Writers: A Selection of Sketches from Contemporary Authors*, 2nd ed. (Detroit: Gale, 1994), 166–167; Jeanne-Marie A. Miller, "A Tribute to Dr. Arthur P. Davis (1904–1996)," *CLA Journal* 40 (1996), 109–111; Ann Allen Shockley and Sue P. Chambers, *Living Black American Authors: A Biographical Directory* (New York: Bowker, 1973), 38.

Linda M. Carter

Davis, Bridgett M. (born 1960). Filmmaker, novelist, and professor. Davis was born and grew up in the University District of **Detroit, Michigan**, where she attended Cass Technical High School (Spratling). She earned a B.A. from Spelman College in 1982. Davis gained national attention in 1996 with the release of an independent film she wrote, directed, and coproduced: *Naked Acts*, the story of a young African American actress who is required to appear nude in an independent art film and who has to come to terms with her past. In 2004 Davis published *Shifting Through Neutral*, a novel about a middle-class African American family in Detroit. The story is told from the perspective of Rae. It concerns not only Rae's maturation but also a complex, dysfunctional family (Westervelt). The novel is set in the neighborhood in which Davis grew up (Spratling). At this writing, Davis teaches creative writing and journalism at Baruch College in the City University of New York.

Resources: Bridgett M. Davis, *Shifting Through Neutral* (New York: Amistad/HarperCollins, 2004); Bridgett M. Davis, screenwriter and director, *Naked Acts* (1996; MTI Video, 2001 [VHS and DVD, 2001]); Cassandra Spratling, "Detroit Stars in Tale of a Tragic Family," *Detroit Free Press*, June 6, 2004, p. A12, review of *Shifting Through Neutral*; Amy Westervelt, "Review of *Shifting Through Neutral*," *San Francisco Chronicle*, May 30, 2004, p. M-4.

Hans Ostrom

Davis, Daniel Webster (1862–1913). Poet and historian. Often compared with **Paul Laurence Dunbar** for his use of **dialect poetry** to re-create an idealized plantation life, Davis has almost disappeared from the literary canon. Born on a North Carolina farm, he moved with his family to Richmond, Virginia, after the **Civil War**. After graduating from high school he taught in the Richmond colored public schools and became an ordained Baptist minister in 1895.

As a preacher, Davis won renown for his **sermons**. He worked tirelessly in Richmond, serving on the boards of numerous organizations as a representative of his race. He also found time to write *The Life and Public Service of Reverend William Washington Browne* (1910) and *The Industrial History of the Negro Race in the United States* (1911), which was used as a textbook in the Richmond public schools. However, he is best remembered for his poems.

His two volumes of poetry, *Idle Moments* (1895) and *'Weh Down Souf and Other Poems* (1897), are distinguished by their conciliatory and deferential air and use of dialect. Davis is often denounced for his minstrel show characters, who reinforce the negative stereotypes held of Blacks. His dialect poems, with titles such as "Bakin' an' Greens," "Hog Meat," and "Hants," are criticized for their focus on plantation life and the customs and superstitions that accompanied it. Many of his poems feature characters who are buffoons and accommodating lackeys, but they also include stories of African American achievers such as **Booker T. Washington**. Davis wrote Standard English poems that were highly moralistic and encouraged his African American readers to put their faith in God and to work hard for a better future.

Resources: Daniel Webster Davis: *Idle Moments* (Baltimore: The Educator of Morgan College, 1895); *The Industrial History of the Negro Race in the United States* (Richmond, VA: Negro Education Association, 1911); *The Life and Public Service of Reverend William Washington Browne* (Richmond, VA: M. A. Browne-Smith, 1910); *'Weh Down Souf and Other Poems* (Cleveland, OH: Helman-Taylor, 1897); Joan R. Sherman, *Invisible Poets: Afro-Americans of the Nineteenth Century*, 2nd ed. (Urbana: University of Illinois Press, 1989), 172–186; Jean Wagner, *Black Poets of the United States*, trans. Kenneth Douglas (Urbana: University of Illinois Press, 1973), 138–141.

Patricia Kennedy Bostian

Davis, Frank Marshall (1905–1987). Poet, journalist, and autobiographer. Davis's poetry focuses on the urban life of South **Chicago, Illinois**—its people and its struggles. Davis gave up his journalism career to move to Hawaii in 1948, but his work was rediscovered in the 1960s by the **Black Arts Movement**. On a college speaking tour, he was hailed as "the long lost father of modern Black poetry" (Tidwell, 60).

Although praised for his strong imagery and powerful voice, Davis is also criticized for being overly pedantic, strident, and propagandistic. *Black Man's Verse* (1935), Davis's first publication, brings together his interest in **jazz** and social oppression. Carl Sandburg's influence is seen in "Chicago's Congo," a reply to Sandburg's "Chicago." The section "Ebony Under Granite" is compared with Edgar Lee Masters's *Spoon River Anthology* in its portrayals of a town's citizens, both rich and poor. The volume was widely praised by reviewers (Tidwell, 63). Between 1935 and 1947 Davis served as executive editor for the Associated Negro Press in Chicago.

In *I Am the American Negro* (1937), Davis employs **free verse** in an attack against Jim Crow laws. He felt free verse, along with jazz, represented a break with regular rhymed poetry, and it helped him achieve his goal of exposing racial injustice.

Through Sepia Eyes (1938) was a limited edition Christmas publication—its poems were republished in *47th Street: Poems* (1948). This volume explores the life of Southside Chicago's multicultural mix and shows Davis focusing more on issues of class than on **race**, as had been the case in his earlier books. *47th Street* attracted the positive interest of reviewers for its portraits of Black life. It also attracted the interest of the House Un-American Activities Committee for its sympathies with the proletariat. (*See* **Cold War, The**.)

Livin' the Blues: Memoirs of a Black Journalist and Poet (1992), edited by John Edgar Tidwell from Davis's manuscripts, details Davis's early life growing up in a racially oppressive America and his experiences as a journalist.

Black Moods: Collected Poems (2002) includes all of Davis's extant publications, including his final volume, *Awakening, and Other Poems* (1978), and other previously unpublished work. At the time of his death, Davis was working on a manuscript titled "That Incredible Waikiki Jungle."

Resources: Frank Marshall Davis: *Awakening, and Other Poems* (Chicago: Black Cat, 1978); *Black Man's Verse* (Chicago: Black Cat, 1935); *Black Moods: Collected Poems*, ed. John Edgar Tidwell (Urbana: University of Illinois Press, 2002); *47th Street: Poems* (Prairie City, IL: Decker, 1948); *I Am the American Negro* (Chicago: Black Cat, 1937); *Livin' the Blues: Memoirs of a Black Journalist and Poet*, ed. John Edgar Tidwell (Madison: University of Wisconsin Press, 1992); *Through Sepia Eyes* (Chicago: Black Cat, 1938); John Edgar Tidwell, "Frank Marshall Davis," in *Dictionary of Literary Biography*, vol. 51, *Afro-American Writers from the Harlem Renaissance to 1940* (Detroit: Gale, 1987), 60–66; James O. Young, *Black Writers of the Thirties* (Baton Rouge: Louisiana State University Press, 1973).

Patricia Kennedy Bostian

Davis, Ossie (1917–2005). Actor, producer, director, playwright, novelist, screenwriter, memoirist, and political activist. Davis has been regarded as one of the most eminent and respected African Americans in the entertainment industry since the 1940s. He had a long résumé as an actor, producer, and director. Less well known is his long career as a writer in virtually every genre, except poetry. In the 1998 memoir, *With Ossie & Ruby*, Davis details his life as an aspiring writer, emphasizing how, as a boy, he escaped into a life of the imagination to distance himself from the ugly realities of racism he experienced growing up in rural Georgia in the Jim Crow era. (Ruby in the title of the book refers to Davis's wife, actress Ruby Dee.) Davis loved language so much that he decided to be an English major at Howard University, awestruck by **Sterling A. Brown** and **Alain Locke** there. But Davis spent many frustrating hours attempting to establish a career as a novelist before admitting defeat and embarking on an acting career immediately after **World War II**. He gained sufficient confidence in his writing talent in the 1950s, and it came to fruition with the successful autobiographical play *Purlie Victorious* (first staged in 1961 and filmed in 1963). He acknowledged his debt to *A Raisin in* *the Sun*, by **Lorraine Hansberry**, for empowering his own quest for personal theatrical expression.

Davis considered his writing as a product of what he called "The Struggle" for African American civil rights and equality. He also admitted that writing was a form of therapy for his deep-seated anger as a Black man. Therefore, Davis's writing choices were most directed since the 1970s toward popularizing African American history for young people, as well as educating them about Black cultural heroes to inspire their own dreams of success. In the play *Escape to Freedom* (1976), Davis scripted a highly ritualized, but very accessible, biographical work about Douglass overcoming enforced illiteracy. Davis combined choral song with spoken narrative and dialogue to dramatize Douglass's heroic efforts to gain his full humanity. In the novel *Just Like Martin* (1992), the teenage protagonist, Isaac Stone, learns the message of peaceful political activism from **Martin Luther King, Jr.**'s example in the wake of the 1963 Birmingham church bombing. Davis's 1982 play about **Langston Hughes** aims to introduce young people to the life

Ossie Davis as Gabriel in *The Green Pastures*, 1951. Courtesy of the Library of Congress.

of the poet and his centrality in Black history from Harpers Ferry (one of Hughes's relatives died in the raid by **John Brown** there) to the **Harlem Renaissance**.

Davis garnered numerous awards throughout his long career, culminating in the National Medal of Arts in 1995. For his writing, he won the American Library Association's Coretta Scott King Award and the Jane Addams Children's Book Award for *Escape to Freedom*. He was also nominated for an Emmy for his teleplay *Teacher, Teacher*, written with Allan Sloan and broadcast on the *Hallmark Hall of Fame* in February 1969. As late as 2002, Davis was performing in movies, costarring in the film *Bubba Ho-Tep*, in which he played President John F. Kennedy.

Resources: Don Coscarelli, *Bubba Ho-Tep* (Metro Goldwyn Mayer, 2002, DVD); Ossie Davis: *Escape to Freedom: A Play About Young Frederick Douglass* (New York: Viking, 1976); *Just Like Martin* (New York: Simon and Schuster, 1992); *Langston: A Play* (New York: Delacorte, 1982); *Purlie Victorious: A Comedy in Three Acts* (New York: Samuel French, 1961); Ossie Davis and Ruby Dee, *With Ossie & Ruby: In This Life*

Together (New York: William Morrow, 1998); Sara J. Ford, "Ossie Davis," in *Dictionary of Literary Biography*, vol. 249, ed. Christopher Wheatley (Detroit: Gale, 2002), 69–74; Lewis Funke, *The Curtain Rises: The Story of Ossie Davis* (New York: Grosset & Dunlap, 1971); Michael E. Greene, "Ossie Davis," in *Dictionary of Literary Biography*, vol. 38, ed. Thadious M. Davis and Trudier Harris (Detroit: Gale, 1985), 80–86.

David A. Boxwell

Davis, Thulani N. (born 1949). Playwright, novelist, journalist, and poet. Thulani Davis is a writer whose work finds voice in many expressive forms: opera, plays, poetry, novels, journalism. Much of her work is in the genre of **historical fiction** and engages the political aspects of the Black experience and everyday life.

Davis was born in Virginia in 1949. As a youth, she was part of the effort to desegregate Virginia schools; she integrated her high school when she was fourteen years old. Civil rights activist **Malcolm X** was an early influence on her; she admired his boldness and eloquence, and consequently her early poetry was written in a social protest style. Her early influences and experiences are evident in her work as an adult. Davis attended Barnard College in the late 1960s, and in the 1970s, she was writing and performing with **Nto-zake Shange** and Jessica Hagedorn. Davis worked in the theater in New York and eventually became a writer for *The Village Voice* starting in 1985, first writing music and theater reviews and later covering politics.

In 1985, Davis wrote a libretto for *X: The Life and Times of Malcolm X*. Her cousin Christopher Davis wrote the story line for the opera, and her cousin Anthony Davis composed the music. The opera is based on the life of her early hero, Malcolm X. It focused on Malcolm X's youth, the murder of his father and insanity of his mother, his early criminal activity, his reform from crime, his preaching in **Harlem, New York**, and his service to the **Nation of Islam**, his transformation during his pilgrimage to Mecca, and finally his assassination.

In addition to writing a libretto in 1985, Davis also published a collection of poems, *Playing the Changes*. The poems are an impressionistic interpretation of city life and evoke feelings of violence and danger.

Davis' first novel was published in 1992. Titled *1959*, the text, which is semiautobiographical, is set in the small town of Turner, Virginia. It is a historical drama and **coming-of-age** story set (appropriately) in 1959, and tells the story of Willie Tarrant, the twelve-year-old daughter of a college professor. Willie is chosen to give **Martin Luther King, Jr.**, a tour of the local Black college and is later selected to desegregate the local schools. Through Willie's eyes readers see how the town reacts to social changes as protests and boycotts begin in response to segregation.

In 1993, Davis collaborated with Howard Chapnick in publishing *Malcolm X: The Great Photographs*. Davis wrote the text accompanying a compilation of photographs that documented Malcolm X's life.

Davis's second novel, *Maker of Saints*, was published in 1996. It is an urban mystery novel that is loosely based on the scandalous death of a Manhattan artist, Ana Mendieta, allegedly at the hands of her husband. In the text, the protagonist, Cynthia "Bird" Kincaid, investigates the suspicious death of her friend, performance artist Alex Decatur. The police rule Decatur's death a suicide, but Bird believes her art critic boyfriend is the culprit. Bird goes through her friend's videotaped diaries and possessions in an attempt to discover the truth of what happened . She learns unexpected secrets about her friend's life and work, as well as about herself.

In 1997, Davis wrote the libretto for *Amistad*, working again with her cousin Anthony Davis. *Amistad* is based on a historical incident where Africans took over a slave ship, killed the crew, stood trial, and were determined to be free.

Davis wrote an original, full-length play, *Everybody's Ruby*, in 1998. The play is set in the 1950s and dramatizes the historical murder case of a thirty-seven-year-old mother of four, Ruby McCollum, who stood trial for killing a wealthy White man. The play is set in Florida, and in the play, writer **Zora Neale Hurston** comes to cover the trial. The drama reveals how the different characters react to the death and the trial.

Resources: Thulani Davis: *All the Renegade Ghosts Rise* (Washington, DC: Anemone Press, 1978); *Everybody's Ruby* (New York: Samuel French, 2000); *Maker of Saints* (New York: Scribner's, 1996); *1959: A Novel* (New York: H. Hamilton, 1992); *Playing the Changes* (Middletown, CT: Wesleyan University Press, 1985); *X: The Life and Times of Malcolm X* (libretto) (New York: Nani Press, 1986); Thulani Davis and Howard Chapnick, *Malcolm X: The Great Photographs* (New York: Stewart, Tabori & Chang, 1993); Thulani Davis and Anthony Davis, *Amistad: An Opera in Two Acts* (New York: G. Schirmer, 1997); Thulani Davis and Anne LeBaron, *The E. & O. Line: An Electronic Blues Opera: After the Story of Orpheus and Eurydice* (Musical Score, 1991); Eric Ledell Smith, "Thulani Davis," in *Blacks in Opera: An Encyclopedia of People and Companies, 1873–1993* (Jefferson, NC: McFarland, 1995); "Thulani Davis," in *Black Writers: A Selection of Sketches from Contemporary Authors*, 3rd ed. (Detroit: Gale, 1999); "Thulani Davis," in *Contemporary Authors*, vol. 182 (Detroit: Gale, 2000).

Kimberly Black-Parker

Dean, Phillip Hayes (born 1937). Playwright and actor. *The Owl Killer*, one of Dean's earlier works, introduces the reader to the plight of the Black working man in industrialized an urban setting, a theme Dean revisits in later works. Noah, an abused worker in Moloch, a small city north of **Detroit, Michigan**, in turn abuses his family, with tragic results. Dean was born in **Chicago, Illinois**, but grew up in Pontiac, Michigan. He rose to national attention with his 1971 play *Sty of the Blind Pig*, which was produced by the Negro Ensemble Company. The play was singled out by *Time* magazine as one of ten best plays of the year. The production featured veteran performers Mary Alice as Alberta and Richard Ward as Blind Jordan. The action of the play takes place in Chicago, where Alberta, a single, attractive, but cloistered young woman lives with her mother, Weedy. They are visited by a mysterious blind stranger who is a catalyst for explosive changes. Dean received the Drama Desk Award for most promising playwright and the Dramatists' Guild's Hull-Warriner Award. The play was adapted for television by Dean and aired in 1974, directed by Ivan Dixon. *Freeman* continues Dean's exploration into failed dreams of the urban Black male. The play was later taped for television and aired in 1977, directed by Lloyd Richards and with Dick Anthony Williams in the title role. Dean's play *Robeson* premiered on Broadway in 1978 and featured James Earl Jones. It was directed by Lloyd Richards with original staging by Charles Nelson Reilly. The play, although well received by many, was embroiled in a hailstorm of protest led by **Paul Robeson**'s son, Robeson's contemporaries, and other prominent members of the African American community. The protesters contended that the play deemphasized Robeson's political activism. A public television version featuring Jones, directed by Lloyd Richards, was aired in 1978. A subsequent production featuring Avery Brooks returned to Broadway in 1988 and 1995 and was directed by Harold Scott. By then, the controversy had subsided and the play was met with critical acclaim.

Dean has written for the television series *On Being Black* and has worked as a director and stage manager. Other plays include *Dink's Blues*, *The Minstrel Boy*, and *The Last American Dixieland Band*. Dean has acted on Broadway in *The Wisteria Trees* with Helen Hayes and Walter Matthau. He also worked with the influential director Herbert Bergof in the all-Black Broadway revival of *Waiting for Godot*. His plays have been presented at the Crossroads Theatre, the American Place Theater, the Chelsea Theatre, the St. Louis Black Repertory, and many regional and university theaters.

Resources: Phillip Hayes Dean: *The Bird of Dawning Singeth All Night* (New York: Dramatists' Play Service, 1998); *Every Night When the Sun Goes Down* (New York: Dramatists' Play Service, 1998); *Freeman* (New York: Dramatists' Play Service, 1973); *Moloch* (New York: Dramatists' Play Service, 1998); *Robeson* (1978; New York: Dramatists' Play Service, 1997); *The Sty of the Blind Pig and Other Plays* (1972; Indianapolis, IN: Bobbs-Merrill, 1973); Paul Carter Harrison and Gus Edwards, eds., *Classic Plays from the Negro Ensemble Company* (Pittsburgh, PA: University of Pittsburgh Press, 1995); Woodie King and Ron Milner, eds., *Black Drama Anthology* (New York: New American Library, 1971); "Paul Robeson's Legacy Traced in Play," *Philadelphia Tribune*, Feb. 2, 1997, p. A15; "Wrestling over Robeson," *Forward*, June 28, 1998, pp. 35–41.

Joan F. McCarty

DeBerry, Virginia (born c. 1962) and Donna Grant (born c. 1963). Collaborative authors of a series of novels with romantic themes. However, their collaboration actually started well before they conceived the idea of writing novels together.

DeBerry attended Fisk University and completed a degree in education at the State University of New York at Buffalo. She then taught for ten years in Buffalo area schools. Grant attended Barnard College and graduated from New York University. She then worked for the *New York Daily News*. Friends of both women urged them to try plus-size modeling. Although they signed with different agencies and were sometimes competing for the same assignments,

DeBerry and Grant became acquainted, and their acquaintance gradually developed into a friendship. Although both women had very successful modeling careers, they realized that modeling was not a long-term option. DeBerry shifted her focus to representing models as an agent and eventually became a vice president with the agency BB/LW. When she was offered the chance to be the fashion editor of the newsletter *Great Dimensions*, she discovered that Grant had earlier become the celebrity-focus editor of the newsletter. The two women found that they shared common interests and worked well together. After a period with *Maxima* magazine, where DeBerry was editor and chief and Grant was managing editor, they collaborated on their first novel.

DeBerry and Grant's novels have included *Tryin' to Sleep in the Bed You Made* (1997), *Far from the Tree* (2000), and *Better Than I Know Myself* (2004). Each novel has been more successful commercially and critically than the previous one. For *Better Than I Know Myself*, DeBerry and Grant received the African American Literary Award Show Open Book Award for Best Contemporary Fiction and Author of the Year—Female.

Although DeBerry and Grant have continued to exploit certain elements of the **romance novel** formula, each of their novels has had a distinct focus. Within the framework of a lovers' triangle, *Tryin' to Sleep in the Bed You Made* explores the very different ambitions of two young women who are such close friends that they might almost be siblings. *Far from the Tree* concerns two sisters with very different lives who travel with their mother to a property in North Carolina that they have inherited from their father. The trip and the events associated with the property become connected thematically as well as dramatically as the sisters rediscover who they are through a fuller knowledge of the circumstances that have shaped their family history. *Far Better Than I Know Myself* presents a contemporary, African American version of Mary McCarthy's *The Group*, focusing on three very different young women who inexplicably become very close friends while attending Columbia University.

Resources: Virginia DeBerry and Donna Grant, *Better Than I Know Myself* (New York: St. Martin's Press, 2004); *Far from the Tree* (New York: St. Martin's Press, 2000); *Tryin' to Sleep in the Bed You Made* (New York: St. Martin's Press, 1997); "Twice the Magic," *Black Issues Book Review* 6 (Nov. 2004), 58–59; Sharon Fitzgerald, "Partners in Their Prime," *Black Issues Book Review* 2 (Sept./Oct. 2000), 64–66; Kalyn Johnson, "Review of *Better Than I Know Myself*," *Black Issues Book Review* 6 (May/June 2004), 46; Yvette Russell, "Word Star," *Essence* 27 (Feb. 1997), 56.

Martin Kich

Deconstruction. One of the most influential movements of post-1965 philosophy and literary theory, deconstruction is a way of reading and analyzing texts that has had profound implications for understandings of Western metaphysics, the relationship of language and text to knowledge and reality, and the mutual articulation of identity and difference.

Deconstruction was conceived by the French linguist and philosopher Jacques Derrida. For Derrida, the Western philosophical tradition had continually made a series of evaluative—though often unnamed—assumptions about meaning and its relationship to the world. The project of deconstruction is to unmask these assumptions and trace the ways in which they often contradict the intent of their authors. One of the most important assumptions Derrida took to task, especially as it relates to literature, is the claim that there exists a transcendental knowledge of reality unmarked by writing, that there is a clear demarcation between "language" and "reality." Claims that reality is unmediated, and that it can be understood and transmitted in unmediated ways, were false for Derrida. To the contrary, writing—or more broadly what Derrida called "text"—is a constant mediator. All knowledge passes through text, Derrida claimed; every text, by the very fact that a text requires language to communicate meaning, is interconnected with every other text. And the sign systems used in the process of making language are themselves mediated by cultural, historical, social, and other influences, all of which are in constant states of flux, states that in themselves can be articulated only through further textual representation. In short, as Derrida famously claimed in his groundbreaking work *Of Grammatology* (trans. 1976), "There is nothing outside the text" (158).

While Derrida and others are notoriously uneasy with simplifying the practice of deconstruction into a static system one can simply apply, there tend to be three basic moves made in a deconstructive reading. The first locates in the text under analysis an underlying binary opposition that provides the text's structure. That binary opposition inevitably privileges one term by placing it at the center of the text, and in the process silences its opposite. Key examples for Derrida of such hierarchical binaries include presence over absence, fullness over emptiness, identity over difference. The second move inverts this binary to hypothesize what the effects on the text would be if the silenced term were privileged and centralized, and the formerly privileged term were cast out. The bulk of deconstructive work attends to this challenge of inversion. But contrary to what is often claimed—that deconstruction is simply about the inversion of binaries—the third move, having already located a central binary and reworked it, attempts to move beyond it. Instead of leaving the formerly silenced term in the privileged space of the center, the third move attempts to imagine a text without a center. To make that move, conceptually the most radical one, requires locating what is mutual in elements belonging to the binary relationship. Each term requires the other in order to carry meaning, in other words. One cannot have presence without absence, identity without difference, fullness without emptiness, and vice versa.

The antifoundationalist standpoint of deconstruction suggests that there are no grounding static truths accessible through language, but rather that knowledge is always circulating and mediated, built differentially through decentered systems of language. This standpoint has made deconstruction popular with cultural and literary critics invested in destabilizing traditional hierarchies. Systems structured through unequal power relations, such as patriarchy, racial supremacy, capitalism, and **colonialism**, can be deconstructed to show the ways in which binary oppositions such as man over woman, White over Black, rich over poor, and West over East are often unspoken assumptions whose effects must be traced in order to understand how each mutually defines the other.

Since the mid-1980s, deconstructive work has left a significant mark on African American literary studies. Taking as its starting point that knowledge can be represented only through inherently unstable texts, theorists such as Houston A. Baker in *Blues, Ideology, and Afro-American Literature* (1987) and Henry Louis Gates, Jr., in *The Signifying Monkey* (1988) attend to the texture of Black representation. Unlike writers who posit an essential or transcendent African American identity (a claim often made in **multicultural theory**), Baker and Gates locate **vernacular** tropes, or modes of expression, whose history can be traced into the production of African American knowledge. For example, Baker turns to the **blues** as a conceptual framework because of the ways in which it refuses stability by constantly placing the protagonist at a "crossroads." Gates utilizes the Yoruban tradition developed in Nigeria called **"signifyin(g),"** in which narrative tropes are repeated, but repeated differently through irony, revision, and improvisation. Both the blues and signifying are self-reflexive frameworks, rooted in history, that attempt to eschew transcendent identity categories that are not connected to historical change.

Deconstruction generally, and the deconstructive practices of the likes of Baker and Gates in particular, have drawn criticism for being politically naïve, divorced from the material conditions of lived experience, trapped in the world of text. That is, a Marxist approach, for example, might insist there are certainly economic and political realities outside "the text." However, if one takes a main claim of deconstruction seriously—that there is no outside to the text—then the continual instability offered by deconstructive practice assures that the logics that structure the hierarchies of power which buttress violence and oppression remain in constant states of revision and, perhaps eventually, dissolution. Therefore, deconstruction does not necessarily preclude the possibility of social or economic change. (*See* **Marxism**.)

Resources: Houston A. Baker, Jr., *Blues, Ideology, and Afro-American Literature: A Vernacular Theory* (Chicago: University of Chicago Press, 1984); Homi K. Bhabha, *The Location of Culture* (New York: Routledge, 1994); Jonathan Culler, *On Deconstruction: Theory and Criticism After Structuralism* (Ithaca, NY: Cornell University Press, 1982); Jacques Derrida: *Dissemination* (Chicago: University of Chicago Press, 1981); *Of Grammatology* (Baltimore: Johns Hopkins, 1976); Henry Louis Gates, Jr., *Black Literature and Literary Theory* (New York: Methuen, 1984); *The Signifying Monkey: A Theory of Afro-American Literary Criticism* (New York: Oxford University Press, 1988); Henry Louis Gates, Jr., ed., *"Race," Writing and Difference* (Chicago: University of Chicago Press, 1986); Abdul R. JanMohammed and David Lloyd, eds., *The Nature and Context of Minority Discourse* (New York: Oxford University Press, 1990); Barbara Johnson, *A World of Difference* (Baltimore: Johns Hopkins University Press, 1987); Christopher Norris, *Deconstruction: Theory and Practice*, 3rd ed. (New York: Routledge, 2002).

Keith Feldman

Delaney, Lucy A. (c. 1828–?). Autobiographer. Delaney's only published work, an **autobiography** titled *From the Darkness Cometh the Light; or, Struggles for Freedom* (1891), is a **slave narrative** that uses the trope of the courtroom in order to establish the moral and legal rights of Black women. Delaney also emphasizes the strength of maternal instincts, which are able to transcend human cruelty.

Women play strong roles in this autobiography. Delaney's father is sold south, but Delaney's mother, Polly, and her sister Nancy both escape from slavery. Polly returns in order to protect Lucy from being punished, then successfully sues for her own freedom, because she had been born free and brought into slavery through kidnapping. She then takes legal action to secure Lucy's release. Similar role models within her own family seem to have provided Delaney with a sense of identity that she transformed into the ability to write her story. Verner D. Mitchell notes that unlike many other slave narratives, Delaney's does not contain "an authenticating preface" that would serve as a means "to verify the truthfulness of the author's story" (Mitchell, 98). Delaney appears to have decided that she was capable of authenticating her own story. Although, as Mitchell points out, she deprecates her ability to write such a work, the narrative provides ample evidence of Delaney's fortitude; she stands up to slave owners who threaten to whip her, and she endures seventeen months in prison while waiting for her legal case to be heard. Moreover, although Delaney's four children all died—two in childhood and the others in their twenties—her sorrow is overlaid with joy that they lived and died free and that neither their lives nor hers was shadowed with the possibility of being torn apart from one another and enslaved (Delaney, 58).

Delaney's legal battle for her freedom is the centerpiece of the work. Lindon Barrett argues that although Delaney's concerns are similar to those in other antebellum slave narratives, their placement within a courtroom "dramatizes the convergence of the scriptive and the prescriptive, the private and the public, the individual and the social" (Barrett, 105). By taking on the "scriptive" position of self-authorship, and denying external (prescriptive) definitions of the African American self, Delaney is not merely undergoing an ordeal in order to secure a basic human right, but deliberately assumes the role of author in order to testify to her experience in her own words. The courtroom can also be read as a site of racial and **gender** struggle, for both the persecutors and the supporters of Delaney and her mother are White men. Although forced to work within a legal and social system in which she was a dual minority, Delaney succeeds, demonstrating that neither slavery nor enforced silence can triumph over the strength of Black women.

Resources: Lindon Barrett, "Self-Knowledge, Law, and African American Autobiography: Lucy A. Delaney's *From the Darkness Cometh the Light*," in *The Culture of Autobiography: Constructions of Self-Representation*, ed. Robert Folkenflik (Stanford, CA: Stanford University Press, 1993), 104–124; Lucy A. Delaney, *From the Darkness Cometh the Light; or, Struggles for Freedom* (1891), in *Six Women's Slave Narratives* (New York:

Oxford University Press, 1988); Deborah Garfield, "Lucy A. Delaney," in *The Oxford Companion to African American Literature*, ed. William L. Andrews et al. (New York: Oxford University Press, 1997); Verner D. Mitchell, "Lucy A. Delaney," in *African American Authors, 1745–1945: A Bio-Bibliographical Critical Sourcebook*, ed. Emmanuel S. Nelson (Westport, CT: Greenwood Press, 2000).

Tracey S. Rosenberg

Delany, Martin R. (1812–1885). Author, editor, orator, and politician. Martin Robison Delany was born free in Charles Town, Virginia (now Charleston, West Virginia), to Pati and Samuel Delany, a free Black woman and her slave husband. In 1822 Delany's mother moved the family to Chambersburg, Pennsylvania, fleeing Virginia authorities who had threatened to imprison her for teaching her children how to read and write. In 1823, after purchasing his own freedom, Delany's father joined the family in Pennsylvania. At the age of nineteen, Delany walked the 150 miles from Chambersburg to **Pittsburgh, Pennsylvania**, where he attended Lewis Woodson's school at Bethel African Methodist Church. After five years of schooling, Delany began studying medicine with Dr. Andrew M. McDowell, eventually setting up his own medical practice as a "cupper, lecher [*sic*], and bleeder" in 1836. Delany's early years in Pittsburgh were marked by his participation in a number of societies and organizations dedicated to the abolition of **slavery** and the elevation of the African American masses. He founded the Theban Literary Society in 1832 and the Young Men's Literary and Moral Reform Society of Pittsburgh in 1837. Delany also helped to organize the State Convention of the Colored Freedmen of Pennsylvania in 1841. His years in Pittsburgh were also marked by the first of his many travels, nationally and internationally. In 1836 he attended a Black conference in New York City, and in 1839 he traveled through **Texas** and the Southwest, scouting possible locations for Black settlement.

In March 1843 Delany married Catherine A. Richards. They had eleven children, seven of whom survived into adulthood. All the sons were named after prominent African American leaders and revolutionaries: Toussaint L'Ouverture (founder of **Haiti** and Black military hero), Charles Lenox Redmond (abolitionist), Alexander Dumas (author), Saint Cyprian (the sanctified Christian bishop), Faustin Soulouque (emperor of Haiti), and Ramses Placido (the ruler of ancient Egypt, and the poet and martyred hero of Cuba). They named their one daughter, born in 1864, Ethiopia Halle Amelia for the land of Delany's ancestors.

The 1840s marked Delany's entry into publishing, first in 1843 as the editor of *The Mystery*, one of Pittsburgh's African American **newspapers**, and in 1847 as coeditor of *The North Star*, the newspaper of **Frederick Douglass**. As coeditor of *The North Star*, Delany became subject to Douglass's influence and spent much of 1848 touring the Midwest delivering antislavery lectures, visiting free Black communities, and soliciting subscriptions. In 1849 Delany ended his association with Douglass, retired as coeditor of *The North Star*, and returned to Pittsburgh to resume his medical practice close to his family. He attended Harvard Medical School during the fall of 1850, but he was expelled following petitions from White medical school students to Dean Oliver Wendell Holmes. Delany returned to publishing in 1856 as contributing editor to the *Provincial Freeman* of Chatham, Ontario, Canada, and again in 1875 as editor for several months of the *Charleston Independent*.

In the 1850s Delany pursued two closely related facets of his life: his own literary production as an author of fiction and nonfiction and his interest in Africa. In 1852, Delany published *The Condition, Elevation, Emigration, and Destiny of the Colored People of the United States*. This was followed in 1853 by *The Origin and Objects of Ancient Freemasonry*, a work derived from Delany's own participation in **Prince Hall** Freemasonry and augmented by his desire to see African American traditions of Freemasonry regarded as authentic. In 1859, while Delany traveled to Liberia to meet with other members of the Niger Valley Exploring Party (experiences chronicled in *Official Report of the Niger Valley Exploring Party*, 1861), portions of his serialized novel *Blake; or, The Huts of America* appeared in *The Anglo-African Magazine* from January to July 1859. Although the magazine continued to publish after that time, no more installments of Delany's novel appeared. Probably the installments were delayed by the onset of the **Civil War**. The entire novel was not printed until the fall of 1861. *The Weekly Anglo-African* ran a complete version of *Blake* in consecutive weekly installments from November 26, 1861, until around May 24, 1862; the novel likely contains six chapters that remain missing, although they probably were published in the first four issues of *The Weekly Anglo-African* in May 1862. The novel follows the slave Henry Holland, who has escaped from Colonel Francks's Southern plantation after sending his son north to Canada. Henry spends the bulk of the novel wandering around **the South**, disguised, visiting with slaves on various plantations, inquiring as to their treatment there, and meeting with the most trustworthy and reputable of them. He talks of his plans for a general slave rebellion and mentions a two-year time frame. The first part of the novel ends with Henry successfully escorting the remaining slaves from the Franckses' farm to the safety of Canada. In the second part of the novel, Henry is hired out to some Whites heading to Cuba. There, he continues to visit slaves, gathering information about their status. Before departing, he meets his cousin, the Cuban poet Placido. The slaves throughout Cuba begin their planned revolt, but the government steps in and stops their plans. In the remainder of the novel, Blake sails on a slaver for Africa, with the intention of seizing the boat at sea, but instead does nothing, and the novel ends in its current incomplete state, without the threatened slave revolt across the Americas. Though incomplete, *Blake* remains significant for its imagining of an organized slave rebellion and its promise of retribution for the evils of **slavery**.

In addition to his editorial work and literary production, Delany is best remembered as a nascent Black Nationalist and budding politician. During the Civil War, he recruited Black troops for the Union Army, eventually meeting with President Lincoln and becoming the first commissioned Black major in the Union Army in February 1863. Following the Civil War, Delany worked with the Freedmen's Bureau in the South to guarantee the rights of recently emancipated African Americans. His involvement in politics continued as he sought, among other things, appointment as the first Black minister to the Republic of Liberia. Delany's last decade was occupied with African resettlement plans. He worked with the Liberian Exodus Joint Stock Steam Ship Company in 1877. When their ship, the *Azor*, sailed from South Carolina and Georgia to Africa in 1878, the company was consumed by debt. Delany worked unsuccessfully to raise funds to save the ship from being sold at auction. Before his death in 1885, Delany campaigned for Virginia Republican congressional candidate John F. Dezendorf, unsuccessfully sought a civil service appointment in **Washington, D.C.**, and worked for a **Boston, Massachusetts**, firm as its agent to South America. (*See* **Back-to-Africa Movement**; **Black Nationalism**.)

Resources: Martin R. Delany: *Blake; or the Huts of America*, intro. Floyd J. Miller (Boston: Beacon Press, 1970); *The Condition, Elevation, Emigration, and Destiny of the Colored People of the United States* (Philadelphia: Martin R. Delany [self-published], 1852); *Official Report of the Niger Valley Exploring Party* (New York: T. Hamilton, 1861); *The Origin and Objects of Ancient Freemasonry; Its Introduction into the United States, and Legitimacy among Colored Men*, 2nd ed. (Xenia, OH: A. D. Delany, 1904); Cyril E. Griffith, *The African Dream: Martin R. Delany and the Emergence of Pan-African Thought* (University Park: Pennsylvania State University Press, 1975); Frank A. Rollin, *Life and Public Services of Martin R. Delany* (New York: Arno Press, 1969); Dorothy Sterling, *The Making of an Afro-American: Martin Robison Delany, 1812–1885* (Garden City, NY: Doubleday, 1971); Victor Ullman, *Martin R. Delany: The Beginnings of Black Nationalism* (Boston: Beacon Press, 1971).

Matthew R. Davis

Delany, Samuel R. (born 1942). Writer and professor. Delany is a prolific **science fiction** writer, memoirist, self-described "pornographer," literary critic, and social commentator. Since the publication in 1962 of his first book, *The Jewels of Aptor*, he has published numerous novels, short stories, essays, interviews, cultural commentary, and memoirs. What is most remarkable about this prolific output is its consistent quality, wide range, and continual development. Despite his numerous works in other genres, Delany has always strongly identified himself as a science fiction writer. But his work has always pushed at and expanded the boundaries and conventions of the field, constantly seeking out new forms, ideas, and themes. Indeed, his work has become more challenging and complex, and in some ways more difficult, over the course of his career.

Delany has also been an important figure in opening up the once almost exclusively White male world of science fiction to minority voices, both by being one of the first Black science fiction writers and by writing about the experiences of non-White characters of all hues and backgrounds, of women, and of gay and bisexual characters. Almost none of his protagonists are heterosexual White men, but the racial identity of his characters is not made an issue in his books. He creates worlds in which race as we understand it is not a significant category, and thus implicitly critiques our society's obsession with **race** and racial categorization. Delany has been a trailblazer for such later Black writers as **Octavia E. Butler** and **Stephen Emery Barnes**, who have used science fiction as an arena in which to explore racial questions in a speculative and imaginative manner.

Samuel Ray Delany, Jr., was born in 1942 and raised in **Harlem, New York**'s Black middle class. His position as both marginal (as a Black man and a gay man) and privileged (in the economic and social opportunities available to him) is a major influence on his work. Delany graduated from the prestigious Bronx High School of Science and attended the City College of New York, though he did not take a degree. He has traveled and lived in Europe and Turkey, and for many years made his living as a writer. Since 1988 he has been a professor at the University of Massachusetts at Amherst, the State University of New York at Buffalo, and currently at Temple University. However, he still makes his permanent home in his native New York City, to which he has a great attachment and about which he has written powerfully and evocatively, most recently in his book-length essay *Times Square Red, Times Square Blue* (1999).

The power of language to shape human reality has been a strong theme of Delany's work since the beginning of his career. Much of his later work explicitly refers to literary and cultural theorists such as Roland Barthes, Jacques Derrida, and Michel Foucault, who sought to reveal and undo assumptions about language and communication. For such theorists, language is not a passive tool but an active social force. But Delany's work has always demonstrated a strong literary and linguistic awareness and even self-consciousness, both in its style and in its subject matter. He has always been fascinated by language's influence on the way we perceive and conceive of the world and ourselves. This may be related to his dyslexia, which he has said heightened his sense of the material reality of language. *Babel-17* (1966) centers on the efforts of a poet to crack what is believed to be a military code used by an alien race with which Earth is at war. What she finally discovers is that this code is in fact a highly exact and analytical language that has no word for "I", and thus no concept of individual identity. The novel examines the capacity of culture and language not only to control the way people see the world but also to determine who they are as persons.

Dhalgren (1974), which is simultaneously Delany's most "difficult" and his most popular novel, is about the efforts of a nameless bisexual amnesiac to find his identity in the course of his wanderings through a postapocalyptic American city. He can find such an identity only by constructing one, and one of the ways he does so is through writing. By the end of the book (whose final phrase loops back to its opening words), the reader is left with the strong implication that the protagonist has written the novel that we have just finished reading about him. The novel is an enactment of the ways in which we create ourselves through our language and our ideas about ourselves. Delany had earlier explored this idea of self-creation through self-narration in *The Einstein Intersection* (1967), a retelling of the ancient Greek **myth** of the poet Orpheus set in the far distant future. In the original myth, Orpheus descends into the underworld to bring his dead wife back to life by the power of his song, only to lose her again because of his own doubts. Delany's protagonist is a member of an alien race that has come to earth long after humanity has departed. These aliens live out human myths and stories in an attempt to understand what it meant to be human, trying to make sense of the world they have inherited. By the end of his quest, the protagonist realizes that he and his people must create their own stories, rather than live out secondhand versions of someone else's. He must be a new Orpheus, one who no longer sings the dead songs. Thus the novel is also an allegory about the power of art to create new realities.

Delany's work argues against the notion of a single, unified human nature. Instead, it celebrates difference, exploring the wide range of human possibilities that different languages and cultures can produce. However, Delany's work also delves into the complications and difficulties (up to and including war) that can result from such differences, especially when they are not acknowledged or recognized. His novel *Stars in My Pocket Like Grains of Sand* (1984) is largely about a clash of cultures, the conflict of incompatible assumptions about the universe and about people—including who and what (in a universe occupied by many different intelligent species) get to be defined as "people." In this book, the conflict between a social ideal based on exclusion and hierarchy and an ideal based on inclusion and free choice ends almost with the destruction of a planet. The implication is that differences, even or especially the most radical differences, must be accepted if humanity is to survive, let alone to thrive. On a smaller scale, the antihero of *Trouble on Triton* (originally published in 1976 under the title *Triton*) makes himself and those around him miserable because he cannot reconcile his rigid, sexist ideas of the ways in which people should live and think with the variety and openness of his utopian society.

Delany's celebration of difference particularly focuses on the celebration of sexual difference. Many of his protagonists are women, and most of his male protagonists are gay or bisexual. The exploration of sexuality is central to Delany's work. In his fiction, he not only presents universes in which homosexuality is completely accepted and women are fully equal members of society, but he also presents universes in which our familiar sexual categories do not apply. In his Nebula Award-winning short story "Aye, and Gomorrah" (1967), those people who are physically capable of deep space travel are neither male nor female, and are eagerly sought after as sexual partners. In *Trouble on Triton*, it is as easy to change one's gender or one's sexual orientation as it is to change one's hair color.

Delany further explores the various ways and means of sexuality in the four-volume "Return to Nevèrÿon" series: *Tales of Nevèrÿon* (1979), *Neveryóna*

(1983), *Flight from Nevèrÿon* (1985), and *Return to Nevèrÿon* (originally published in 1987 under the title *The Bridge of Lost Desire*). Rather than being set in the future, these books are set in the distant past, in a world in which the rulers are dark-skinned and the barbarian lower classes are blonde and blue-eyed. These books are a deliberate revision of the sword and sorcery genre of which the Conan the Barbarian series is the most famous example. In them, Delany investigates the complex and contradictory realities of such a fantasized primitive world, examining the development of civilization in order to uncover the historical roots of our own culture. Among the topics these ambitious books address are the origins and development of language, the family, sexuality, **gender** roles, private property, commerce, social hierarchy, and the interconnections of sex and power and of language and power. **Slavery** is a major theme of the series, with clear references to American history. The protagonist of the series is a former slave who rises to power and abolishes slavery. He is also a gay man whose sexual desires are all sadomasochistic, based on submission and domination. This is an example of the difficulty of separating sexuality and power in a hierarchical society in which, like our own, not all people are equal or equally free: slavery is both a sociopolitical phenomenon and a state of mind. But by making a mutually consenting game out of the power some people exercise over others, Delany's protagonist is able to defuse it to an extent, and to create pleasure out of pain. In the third book of the series, Delany makes explicit the parallels between the ancient world he has created and our contemporary world by juxtaposing a plague that affects only homosexuals in his fictional world with the AIDS epidemic in 1980s New York City. In so doing, he directly addresses questions of homophobia and social stigma.

As is confirmed by his many awards, Delany has gained recognition and acclaim not only in the science fiction, but also in literary theory, **gay literature**, and **lesbian literature**. Despite controversies regarding the intellectual and stylistic challenges of some of his work, and the graphic sexual content of novels such as *The Mad Man* (1994) and *Hogg* (1998), his reputation as an important writer and thinker is secure and growing. (*See* **Queer Theory**.)

Resources: Primary Sources: *Fiction:* Samuel R. Delany: *Atlantis: Three Tales* (Middletown, CT: Wesleyan University Press, 1995); *Aye, and Gomorrah* (New York: Vintage, 2003); *Babel-17* (Boston: Gregg Press, 1966); *The Ballad of Beta-2* (Boston: Gregg Press, 1965); *The Bridge of Lost Desire* (New York: Arbor House, 1987) (reprinted as *Return to Nevèrÿon*); *The Complete Nebula Award-Winning Fiction* (New York: Bantam, 1986); *Dhalgren* (Boston: Gregg Press, 1974); *Distant Stars* (New York: Ultramarine, 1981); *Driftglass* (Garden City, NY: Doubleday, 1971); *The Einstein Intersection* (London: Gallancz, 1967); *Empire: A Visual Novel* (New York: Berkeley, 1978); *Empire Star* (Boston: Gregg Press, 1966); *The Fall of the Towers* (trilogy: *Out of the Dead City, The Towers of Toron*, and *City of a Thousand Suns*) (Boston: Gregg Press, 1970); *Flight from Nevèrÿon* (Middletown, CT: Wesleyan University Press, 1994); *Hogg* (New York: Talman, 1995); *The Jewels of Aptor* (London: Gallancz, 1962); *The Mad Man* (New York: Richard Kasak Books, 1994); *Neveryóna* (New York: Bantam, 1983);

Nova (New York: Doubleday, 1968); *Stars in My Pocket Like Grains of Sand* (New York: Bantam/Dell, 1984); *Tales of Nevèrÿon* (New York: Bantam, 1979); *They Fly at Ciron* (New York: St. Martin's Press, 1993); *The Tides of Lust* (New York: Lancer Books, 1973) (reprinted as *Equinox*); *Triton* (New York: Bantam, 1976) (reprinted as *Trouble on Triton*). Nonfiction: *The American Shore* (Elizabethtown, NY: Dragon Press, 1978); *Bread and Wine* (New York: Juno Books, 1999); *Heavenly Breakfast* (New York: Bantam, 1979); *The Jewel-Hinged Jaw* (New York: Ultramarine, 1977); *Longer Views: Extended Essays* (Middletown, CT: Wesleyan University Press, 1996); *The Motion of Light in Water* (New York: Masquerade Books, 1988); *1984: Selected Letters* (Middletown, CT: Wesleyan University Press, 2000); *Shorter Views* (Middletown, CT: Wesleyan University Press, 2000); *Silent Interviews* (Middletown, CT: Wesleyan University Press, 1994); *Starboard Wine* (New York: Ultramarine, 1984); *The Straits of Messina* (New York: Serconia Press, 1989); *Times Square Red, Times Square Blue* (New York: New York University Press, 1999). **Secondary Sources:** Douglas Barbour, *Worlds Out of Words: The SF Novels of Samuel R. Delany* (Frome, UK: Bran's Head Books, 1979); Richard Bleiler, ed., *Science Fiction Writers: Critical Studies of the Major Authors from the Early Nineteenth Century to the Present Day*, 2nd ed. (New York: Scribner's, 1998); Damien Broderick, *Reading by Starlight: Postmodern Science Fiction* (New York: Routledge, 1995); Robert Elliott Fox, *Conscientious Sorcerers: The Black Postmodernist Fiction of Leroi Jones/Amiri Baraka, Ishmael Reed, and Samuel R. Delany* (Westport, CT: Greenwood Press, 1987); Seth McEvoy, *Samuel R. Delany* (New York: Ungar, 1984); James Sallis, ed., *Ash of Stars: On the Writing of Samuel R. Delany* (Jackson: University Press of Mississippi, 1996); George Edgar Slusser, *The Delany Intersection: Samuel R. Delany Considered as a Writer of Semi-Precious Words* (San Bernardino, CA: Borgo, 1977); Jane Branham Weedman, *Samuel R. Delany* (Mercer Island, WA: Starmont House, 1982).

Reginald Shepherd

DeLoach, Nora (1940–2001). Novelist and social worker. DeLoach is best known as the author of the "Mama" series of detective novels. She was born and grew up in Orlando, Florida. Her name was Nora Frazier until she married William DeLoach in 1963. They had two sons and a daughter. DeLoach died June 19, 2001, a few weeks after a diagnosis of leukemia. Before her death she had lived in Decatur, Georgia.

DeLoach's novels are reminiscent of Agatha Christie's novels featuring Miss Marple, and of Sir Arthur Conan Doyle's Sherlock Holmes tales. DeLoach suggested that the character Mama is not based on herself or any other mystery writer's characters, but is influenced by the work of Pearl S. Buck, an early twentieth-century novelist, some of whose books are set in China (*Contemporary Black Biography*, 51). The series consists of eight novels: *Mama Solves a Murder* (1994), *Mama Traps a Killer* (1995), *Mama Saves a Victim* (1997), *Mama Stands Accused* (1997), *Mama Stalks the Past* (1997), *Mama Rocks the Empty Cradle* (1998), *Mama Pursues Murderous Shadows* (2000), and DeLoach's last published novel, *Mama Cracks a Mask of Innocence* (2001).

The first four novels were published by Holloway House, and Bantam Books published the subsequent novels. Her readership grew because, published by

Bantam, her books were introduced to a larger, more diverse audience. De-Loach's version of the fictional detective can be compared with detectives created by other contemporary Black American authors, such as **Hugh Holton, Valerie Wilson Wesley, Terris McMahan Grimes,** and **Gar Anthony Haywood,** all of whom have published series of novels featuring a sleuth.

DeLoach's style is known to readers of mystery fiction as "cozy" because the crimes are solved in conventional ways and because neither violence nor sex figures significantly in the plots. Most of the main characters in DeLoach's novels are African American, and the setting is usually a small town in **the South.** The amateur detective "Mama" works with her daughter, Simone, to solve crimes. Mama, called "Candi" by her friends and neighbors, is Grace Covington; her husband, James; their two sons, Will and Rodney; and their daughter Simone make up the Covington family.

Other works by DeLoach include *Silas,* a novel (1991), and *How to Write and Sell Genre Fiction* (1994). (*See* **Crime and Mystery Fiction.**)

Resources: Nora DeLoach: *How to Write and Sell Genre Fiction* (Orlando, FL: Rotuma, 1994); *Mama Cracks a Mask of Innocence* (New York: Bantam Books, 2001); *Mama Pursues Murderous Shadows* (New York: Bantam Books, 2000); *Mama Rocks the Empty Cradle* (New York: Bantam Books, 1998); *Mama Saves a Victim* (Los Angeles: Holloway House, 1997); *Mama Solves a Murder* (Los Angeles: Holloway House, 1994); *Mama Stalks the Past* (New York: Bantam Books, 1997); *Mama Stands Accused* (Los Angeles: Holloway House, 1997); *Mama Traps a Killer* (Los Angeles: Holloway House, 1995); *Silas* (Los Angeles: Holloway House, 1991); Ashyia Henderson, ed., *Contemporary Black Biography,* vol. 30 (Detroit: Gale, 2001), 50–52; Carolyn Tillery, "The Fiction of Black Crime: It's No Mystery," *American Visions,* Apr./May 1997, 18–21.

Deloice Holliday

Demby, William (born 1922). Novelist. William Demby spent the majority of his creative life working and writing as an expatriate in Italy, where he was employed for a number of years as a translator of screenplays and as a scriptwriter in the Italian film industry. Though often an expatriate, and though his work is concerned with "American" themes, especially **race,** Demby's fiction more broadly addresses the inherent injustices, absurdities, and troubling complexities of the human condition. Demby was born on Christmas Day, 1922, in **Pittsburgh, Pennsylvania,** and he studied as an undergraduate at West Virginia State University until his schooling was interrupted when he left to fight in **World War II,** during which he was stationed in Italy and North Africa. When he returned from the war, he completed his undergraduate education at Fisk University in **Nashville, Tennessee.** While there, he studied creative writing under the poet **Robert Hayden.** He graduated from Fisk in 1947 and then returned to Italy to study art history at the University of Rome. Demby lived in Italy until 1969, when he returned to the United States to teach at College of Staten Island in New York City. Demby has written three novels: *Beetlecreek* (1950), *The Catacombs* (1965), and *Love Story Black* (1978), which many critics viewed as a reversion from *The Catacombs* to a simpler, less interesting style.

Of his three works, *The Catacombs* is widely considered to be Demby's best and most important; it is also his most experimental and overtly self-referential. The novel is set in Rome and its primary narrator is Bill Demby, a Black writer who has been living abroad for some time with his wife, but who soon begins a romance with a young Black actress, Doris, who is also having an affair with an Italian count. The novel's rather small-scoped plot concerns the love triangle—including Doris's mysterious, prematurely ended pregnancy (the reader is never sure if it was a miscarriage or an abortion)—that develops between these main characters. But more than simply the drama that plays out among these characters, *The Catacombs* is an examination of human morals and attitudes of the time. Interspersed throughout the narrative are brief, montage-like news flashes that announce mostly disturbing happenings (deaths, disasters, upheavals) from around world, and it is ultimately this broader setting that buttresses the novel's foreboding, brooding tone. The novel ends on a note of loneliness and despair, with the count crying out for Doris into the darkness of the place of the novel's title. Although the three characters betray and fail each other, when set against the existential despair of the times, the novel is more a lamentation for them, and for humanity in general, than it is a damning, final judgment; in a dangerous, sad world, humans can, and will, treat each other poorly and unjustly.

This theme is also apparent in Demby's more naturalistic, tragic first novel, *Beetlecreek*, in which the main characters, a young Black boy, Jimmy, and an old White recluse, Bill Trapp, fail to achieve friendship despite the immense enjoyment each finds in the other's company, and despite sharing the common bond of leading marginal, displaced lives (Jimmy has just moved from Pittsburgh, and Bill doesn't blend into the all-Black village of Beetlecreek). Although Demby goes to great lengths to establish the rich goodness and depth of these characters' interior lives, their individual goodness does not sustain them in a society that discourages openness and sincere investigations of—and, indeed, is frightened by—otherness and difference.

Resources: Robert Bone: *The Negro Novel in America*, rev. ed. (New Haven, CT: Yale University Press, 1965); "William Demby's Dance of Life," *TriQuarterly*, Spring 1969, 127–141; William Demby: *Beetlecreek* (New York: Rinehart, 1950); *The Catacombs* (New York: Pantheon, 1965); *Love Story Black* (New York: Reed, Cannon & Johnson, 1978); Edward Margolies, "The Expatriate as Novelist: William Demby," in his *Native Sons: A Critical Study of Twentieth-Century Negro American Authors* (Philadelphia: Lippincott, 1968), 173–189; Roger Whitlow, *Black American Literature: A Critical History* (Chicago: Nelson Hall, 1973), 122–125.

Joel Anderson

Dent, Thomas Covington (1932–1998). Poet, playwright, historian, and journalist. Dent was born in **New Orleans, Louisiana**. His death on June 6, 1998, marked the end of a literary career that lasted four decades. His death was also a significant loss for Southern literature.

Tom Dent was a socially committed writer whose central concerns were civil rights, and individual and racial identity. He explored these themes in his poetry, *Magnolia Street* (1976) and *Blue Lights and River Songs* (1982); in his plays, especially the classic *Ritual Murder* (unpublished at this writing); and in numerous articles and essays. Dent's sense of commitment did not end with his writing.

After earning a B.A. at Morehouse College (1952), Dent did graduate work at Syracuse University before joining the Army (1957–1959). He moved to New York City in 1959, worked for the **NAACP** Legal Defense Fund, and founded, with **Calvin Coolidge Hernton** and **David Henderson**, the legendary **Umbra Workshop**, which was Dent's introduction to the **Black Arts Movement**.

In 1965, Dent returned to New Orleans, where he worked with the **Free Southern Theatre** (FST) and served as the executive director of the New Orleans Jazz and Heritage Foundation. Dent's most significant contributions were his encouragement of younger artists through the FST's Writers' Workshop (BLKARTSOUTH), the Congo Square Writers Union, the Southern Black Cultural Alliance, and his roles in literary journals such as **Nkombo** and **Callaloo.**

Dent's final project, which allowed him to indulge his passion for writing and oral tradition, was *Southern Journey: A Return to the Civil Rights Movement* (1997), a reevaluation of the **Civil Rights Movement**, a collection of interviews with individuals who played vital roles in the movement. "Driven by the conviction that the strength, beauty, and pitfalls of existence must be transmitted to the young, Dent's life and works are exemplary of what it means to be a Southern humanist" ("In Memoriam," 231).

Resources: Tom Dent: *Southern Journey: A Return to the Civil Rights Movement* (New York: William Morrow, 1997); "Two Views of New Orleans," *African American Review* 27, no. 1 (Summer 1993), 52; "In Memoriam: Thomas Covington Dent, 1932–1998," *The Mississippi Quarterly* 52, no. 2 (1999), 213; Kalamu ya Salaam, "Enriching the Paper Trail: An Interview with Tom Dent," *African American Review* 27, no. 1 (Summer 1993), 327–344; Jerry W. Ward, Jr.: "Tom Dent," in *The Oxford Companion to African American Literature*, ed. William L. Andrews, Frances Smith Foster, and Trudier Harris (New York: Oxford University Press, 1997), 209–210; "Thomas C. Dent: A Preliminary Bibliography," *Obsidian II* no. 4 (Winter 1989), 103–112.

John Greer Hall

Derricotte, Toi (born 1941). Memoirist and poet. Derricotte's work often transcends traditional generic classifications—such as poetry, **autobiography**, and prose fiction—and uses specific scenes derived from her own life to uncover general truths about how individuals experience **race** and **gender**, color and class, private recollection and public record.

Born to middle-class parents near **Detroit, Michigan**, Derricotte received a bachelor's degree in special education from Wayne State University in 1965 and a master's degree in creative writing and English literature from New York University in 1984. She has twice been awarded poetry fellowships by the

National Endowment for the Arts (1985 and 1990), and she has been awarded a Pushcart Prize (1989) and the Folger Shakespeare Library Poetry Book Award (1990). A professor in the English Department at the University of Pittsburgh, Derricotte also curates an online exhibit on the Academy of American Poets Web site and sits on the board of Cave Canem, a nonprofit organization dedicated to assisting African American poets through retreats, workshops, prizes, and anthologies, which she cofounded with **Cornelius Eady**.

Like **Richard Wright** and **Nella Larsen** before her, Derricotte depicts the danger of accepting an identity bestowed by society, which often leads to an internalization of racism; she then contrasts this threat with language's ability to articulate experience, to erase the loneliness that comes from silence, and to create a stronger, more honest community. In *The Black Notebooks* (1997), a series of vignettes taken from her journals over a span of more than twenty years, Derricotte, a light-skinned Black woman capable of **passing** for White, explores how "Blackness" exists as a color, as a feeling, as a race, as a social mandate that signifies a set of behaviors and traits, as something "both real and unreal" (182). The *New York Times* named it a notable book of 1998. (*See* **Color of Skin**.)

Derricotte's four books of poetry—*The Empress of the Death House* (1978), *Natural Birth* (1983), *Captivity* (1989), and *Tender* (1997)—also investigate "the integral connection between beauty, function, and drama," another objective of *The Black Notebooks* (19). Formally, the postconfessional poems privilege wordplay, varying line lengths, collages of styles, and anaphora (repetition of words at the beginnings of lines). More original, however, is Derricotte's deft description of frequently marginalized subjects, including female sexuality, childbirth, domestic violence, child abuse, **slavery**, dislocation, and racial prejudice. For her, the writer must mark down memories; putting the past—either one's own or that of one's community—into clear particulars combats the erasures of incidents that go against the accepted, repressive version of history. As she explains in the preface to *Tender*, "the job of the artist . . . is to hold complexities, to see and make clear" (ix).

Resources: Toi Derricotte: *The Black Notebooks: An Interior Journey* (New York: Norton, 1997); *Captivity* (Pittsburgh, PA: University of Pittsburgh Press, 1989); *The Empress of the Death House* (Detriot: Lotus Press, 1978); *Natural Birth* (Ithaca, NY: Firebrand Books, 2000); *Tender* (Pittsburgh, PA: University of Pittsburgh Press, 1997); Calvin Hernton, *The Sexual Mountain and Black Women Writers: Adventures in Sex, Literature, and Real Life* (New York: Anchor Books, 1987); Charles H. Rowell, "Beyond Our Lives: An Interview with Toi Derricotte," *Callaloo* 14, no. 3 (1991), 654–664); Loretta G. Woodward, "Toi Derricotte," in *African-American Autobiographers: A Sourcebook*, ed. Emmanuel S. Nelson (Westport, CT: Greenwood Press, 2002), 90–94.

Jessica Allen

Detroit, Michigan. When twelve-year-old Denise moves to the city of Detroit from rural Virginia in **A. J. Verdelle**'s 1995 novel, *The Good Negress*, her arrival constitutes not just a geographical change but also a more metaphorical passage into national belonging. The movement of Southern African Americans to the industrial North, as Verdelle represents it, is analogous to the passage of Europeans to American shores. Thus, when Denise's teacher, Missus Pearson, insists that the girl unlearn the Southern **vernacular** that defines her speech, the teacher's adamancy turns on the faith that only through the mastery of Standard English will Denise move beyond her Southern Black "immigrant" status to attain full citizenship and share in American promise in Detroit.

Historically, African Americans moved to Detroit in pursuit of greater political or economic freedom. The first notable wave of Black migration to the city occurred in the 1840s, after Michigan outlawed **slavery** in its state constitution of 1837. Previously, Black migration to Detroit had been inhibited by events such as the Blackburn Riot of 1833, an uprising among the Black population provoked by a city court's decision to support the arrest of fugitive slaves Thornton and Ruth Blackburn by Kentucky slave hunters (*see* **Race Riots**). The riot led to the more militant regulation of African Americans under the mantle of an 1827 Black Code, and prompted what is likely the first race riot commission in American history. Between 1840 and 1850, however, the Black population in Detroit tripled, from 193 to 587. More important, African Americans formalized their community through the emergence of Black churches and political efforts such as the 1843 Michigan State Colored Convention. The city's proximity to Canada also made it a key station on the **Underground Railroad**, and prominent antislavery advocates including William Lambert, George DeBaptiste and **Henry Bibb** were active in aiding the passage of fugitive slaves to freedom via Detroit. Following the **Civil War**, the city's Black population rose steadily throughout the rest of the century. Though Black Detroiters numbered 4,111 by 1900, the city's African American population was still proportionately small compared with Southern cities such as Birmingham, Alabama, or **Atlanta, Georgia**, or other Northern cities such as New York City and **Philadelphia, Pennsylvania**.

However, in the early twentieth century, the rise of the automobile industry dramatically increased the demand for laborers and made Detroit an attractive destination for Southern Blacks amid the **Great Migration**. Early on, the integration of migrant workers into the auto industry was superintended by African American ministers and representatives from the Urban League. This careful intervention by religious and political leaders allowed a skilled company of Black laborers to secure employment. Later, the depletion of White personnel during **World War I**, and a rising need for workers willing to assume service jobs or potentially dangerous positions, stimulated growth of the Black workforce all the more. These factors inspired remarkable demographic changes in Detroit in the first third of the twentieth century. Between 1916 and 1926, for example, African American employment at the Ford Motor Company rose from 50 to 10,000. More generally, the city's Black population increased by nearly 2,000 percent between 1910 and 1930, rising from 5,741 to 120,066.

Yet the ostensible optimism of these demographic changes was diminished by the persistence of racial inequality and conflict outside the workplace.

Black migrants faced continual housing shortages, and those who were able to secure accommodations in existing Black neighborhoods were burdened by high rents and, at times, virtually unlivable conditions. Moreover, African Americans who were solvent enough to seek housing outside the city's East Side ghetto found themselves at peril. In the famous "Sweet case" of 1925, for example, a black dentist named Ossian Sweet was threatened by a violent White mob (numbering in the hundreds) after Sweet moved his family to the otherwise **"White"** Garland Avenue. When shots fired from the Sweet home killed one White man in the mob and wounded another, the dentist and his family were tried for murder. The Sweets were defended by famed criminal lawyer Clarence Darrow, acting at the request of the **NAACP**, and were eventually acquitted, but the details of the case epitomized interracial tensions in Detroit between the wars. Equally meaningful was the city's substantial Ku Klux Klan membership, a contingent that tried to intimidate other upwardly mobile Blacks from moving into White neighborhoods.

While the threat of White racism in the guise of mob rule and Klan action was consistent and palpable for Black Detroiters in the first half of the twentieth century, the city's predominantly White police force also proved to be an enduring menace as the century wore on. As early as 1926, a mayoral committee reported that Detroit's poor race relations were likely exacerbated by the unfair and overly violent actions of the police (Thomas, 165). Moreover, police discrimination and brutality were conspicuous in Detroit's major race riots of 1943 and 1967. The 1943 uprising began on a hot Sunday in summer, when a series of skirmishes between Blacks and Whites at Belle Isle Park ignited into mob violence citywide. City police were devastatingly partial to White rioters during the disturbance, ultimately shooting seventeen African Americans amid the violence. By the time the riot was suppressed by federal troops, thirty-four people had been killed, twenty-five of them Black. City police provoked the July 1967 riot when officers raided an illegal after-hours drinking establishment on Twelfth Street, in the heart of an all-Black neighborhood. Late in the evening, as police detained the saloon's clientele, bystanders became enraged and hurled debris and shouted condemnations of inequality. The tensions on Twelfth Street escalated into one of the most brutal uprisings in American history, resulting in forty-three deaths (thirty of them at the hands of law enforcement personnel) and more than 7,000 arrests over five days of violence. One of the most unsettling reports from the 1967 riot was the Algiers Motel incident, in which law enforcement officers allegedly murdered three Black men and tortured nine others during "interrogations" at the Algiers Motel. The event stands as an apocalyptic marker from Detroit's summer of 1967, when long-deferred African American hopes materialized into citywide rebellion.

African American writers from Detroit have been sharp in registering how the promise of early twentieth-century Black migration ultimately went unrealized in the city. In Anthony Butts's "Detroit, One a.m.," for example, Black employees at an all-night restaurant confront the incongruity between past hopes and present dejection. In **Robert Hayden**'s "Elegies for Paradise Valley," a suite of poems composed for the predominantly Black, East Side section of Detroit where Hayden grew up, the specter of racism and the impenetrability of American inequality are juxtaposed against scenes of urban decay.

Similarly, in a reminiscence published in his *Collected Prose*, Hayden acknowledges the vitality of the Black community in Paradise Valley, only to concede that remembering Detroit leaves him with an overwhelming sense of bereavement. For Hayden, Paradise Valley's redeeming qualities (such as occasional performances by Bessie Smith at the Koppin Theater, visits from the boxing champion Joe Louis, or Black civil rights rallies organized by followers of **Marcus Garvey**) are effectively diminished by the area's status as a site of disillusionment. As Hayden writes of himself, "This was no sentimental trek back into the past. He felt no nostalgia, no longing for the good old days. . . . He knew that the good old days in the Detroit slums had never been good" (20). In **Al Young**'s poem "City Home/Detroit," the speaker reaches a similarly grim conclusion in revisiting his hometown after time away.

While Butts, Hayden, and Young offer literary manifestations of Black Detroit's disenchantment, other African American writers from outside the city have used its history as a metonymic example of a broader Black American frustration. For instance, in **Michael S. Harper**'s poems "Song: *I Want a Witness*" and "A Mother Speaks: The Algiers Motel Incident, Detroit," the Detroit riot of 1967 represents the effects of American race relations on the African American psyche, in both collective and individual contexts. "Song: *I Want a Witness*" takes a panoramic view of the Twelfth Street uprising, while "A Mother Speaks" depicts the personal trauma of that historical moment through compelling first-person testimony. In both poems, Harper documents the Detroit rebellion as an urgent call to awareness of enduring racial divide in the United States, and of the need for that discord's reparation.

Yet it would be misleading to suggest that African American literature has represented Detroit exclusively in critical or melancholy terms. For example, Al Young's meditation "Détroit Moi" begins by revisiting the city's difficult history of conflict and disappointment, but builds to a celebration of the city's diversity ("When they ask/and you can't identify the hometowns of colorful Americans, say Detroit"), that culminates in a litany of Black and White Detroit cultural heroes ranging from Robert Hayden, **Malcolm X**, and **Toi Derricotte**, to Elmore Leonard and Michael Moore. The vitality that Young celebrates is apt, given Detroit's numerous and varied cultural contributions. In African American literature, this energy is, of course, evident in the work inspired by Detroit noted here, but also in the city's notable literary activities beyond the page: the founding of the influential **Broadside Press** by **Dudley Randall** in the 1960s, for instance, or in the anthologies published recently by the Detroit Black Writers' Guild.

Resources: Anthony Butts, "Detroit, One a.m.," in *Giant Steps: The New Generation of African American Writers*, ed. Kevin Young (New York: Perennial, 2000), 40–41;

Detroit Black Writers' Guild: *Before I Wake and Other Tales* (Detroit: Detroit Black Writers' Guild, 1990); *Inner Visions: A Poetry Anthology* (Detroit: Detroit Black Writers' Guild, 1994); *Paradise Valley Days: A Photo Album Poetry Book* (Detroit: Detroit Black Writers' Guild, 1998); Michael S. Harper: "A Mother Speaks: The Algiers Motel Incident, Detroit" (1970), in his *Songlines in Michaeltree: New and Collected Poems* (Urbana and Chicago: University of Illinois Press, 2000), 27; "Song: *I Want a Witness*" (1972), in his *Songlines in Michaeltree: New and Collected Poems* (Urbana and Chicago: University of Illinois Press, 2000), 57; Robert Hayden, "Elegies for Paradise Valley," in his *Collected Poems*, ed. Frederick Glaysher (New York: Liveright, 1996), 163–171; "From *The Life*: Some Remembrances," in his *Collected Prose*, ed. Frederick Glaysher (Ann Arbor: University of Michigan Press, 1984), 17–27; John Hersey, *The Algiers Motel Incident* (1968; Baltimore: Johns Hopkins University Press, 1998); David M. Katzman, *Before the Ghetto: Black Detroit in the Nineteenth Century* (Urbana: University of Illinois Press, 1973); August Meier and Elliot Rudwick, *Black Detroit and the Rise of the UAW* (New York: Oxford University Press, 1979); Thomas J. Sugrue, *The Origins of the Urban Crisis: Race and Inequality in Postwar Detroit* (Princeton, NJ: Princeton University Press, 1996); Richard W. Thomas, *Life for Us Is What We Make It: Building Black Community in Detroit, 1915–1945* (Bloomington: Indiana University Press, 1992); Heather Ann Thompson, "Rethinking the Politics of White Flight in the Postwar City: Detroit, 1945–1980," *Journal of Urban History* 25, no. 2 (1999), 163–198; A. J. Verdelle, *The Good Negress* (Chapel Hill, NC: Algonquin Books, 1995); Al Young: "City Home/ Detroit," in his *Geography of the Near Past* (New York: Holt, Rinehart and Winston, 1976), 46; "Détroit Moi," in his *The Sound of Dreams Remembered: Poems 1990–2000* (Berkeley, CA: Creative Arts, 2001), 20–22; *Snakes: A Novel* (New York: Holt, Rinehart and Winston, 1970).

Michael Borshuk

Dett, R[obert] Nathaniel (1882–1943). Poet, composer, and pianist. Robert Nathaniel Dett was one of a growing number of individuals in the 1900s to arrange and adapt African American **spirituals** and folk melodies. He is also noteworthy for having created compositions that merged traditional African American musical forms with conventional classical music. Dett was heavily influenced by his mother, who made him recite Bible passages and poems by Tennyson, Longfellow, and Shakespeare, and his grandmother, who sang spirituals in their home (McBrier, 175). After receiving a rigorous education in music, Dett taught at several colleges. He is most known for his achievements at Hampton Institute in Virginia, where he served as choir director, founded the Hampton Choral Union and the Musical Arts Society, and established and directed the School of Music and the Hampton Institute Choir.

The works of Nathaniel Dett include "five piano suites; eight Bible vignettes; forty or more choral works; two oratorios; twenty-four vocal solos; one violin solo; and two collections of Negro spirituals" (McBrier, 176). He compiled many of the spirituals and folksongs used in his collections and compositions from African American churches. He is most known for "Juba" from *In the Bottoms* (1913) and "Listen to the Lambs" (1914) (McBrier, 176).

"Juba" is "considered by many critics to be one of the best evocations of Black folk dance in the classical literature" (Bustard). He also published poetry and wrote accounts of the musical tours he took in Europe.

Prior to the efforts of individuals, including Dett, who sought to preserve spirituals and folk songs, America's exposure to traditional African American music chiefly came by way of minstrel shows (*see* **Minstrelsy**). Minstrel shows often featured White performers in black makeup (blackface); they performed African American songs but usually in a derisive manner. Dett desired to redefine the image of spirituals. He also desired to preserve what he believed to be a dying art form. Although evidence existed in his time of a burgeoning body of literature on spirituals, Dett continued to believe that Americans were indifferent to African American music, and that literature on African American themes and competent African American composers were lacking (Spencer, 134).

Resources: Clark Bustard, *Robert Nathaniel Dett* (2002), http://www.timesdispatch.com; R. Nathaniel Dett: *Album of a Heart* (Jackson, TN: Mocowat-Mercer, 1911); *The Collected Piano Works of R. Nathaniel Dett* (Evanston, IL: Summy-Birchard, 1973); *In the Bottoms: Characteristic Suite for Piano* (1913; repr. Boca Raton, FL: Masters Music, 2000); *Listen to the Lambs* (New York: G. Schirmer, 1913); "Negro Music," in *The International Cyclopedia of Music and Musicians*, 6th ed., ed. Oscar Thompson (New York: Dodd, Mead, 1952), 1243–1246; *Negro Spirituals* (London: Blandford, 1959); R. Nathaniel Dett, ed., *The Dett Collection of Negro Spirituals* (Chicago: Hall & McCreary, 1936); Natalie Hinderas, *Piano Music by African American Composers*, CD-ROM (New York: CRI, 1992); Moses Hogan, ed., *The Oxford Book of Spirituals* (New York: Oxford University Press, 2002); Vivian McBrier, "Nathaniel Robert Dett," in *Dictionary of American Negro Biography*, ed. Rayford W. Logan and Michael R. Winston (New York: Norton, 1982); Anne Key Simpson, *Follow Me: The Life and Music of R. Nathaniel Dett* (Metuchen, NJ: Scarecrow Press, 1993); John Michael Spencer, "R. Nathaniel Dett's Views on the Preservation of Black Music," *The Black Perspective In Music* 10 (1982), 132–148.

Gladys L. Knight

Detter, Thomas P. (c. 1826–?). Journalist, essayist, and short story writer. Thomas Detter is one of the earliest known African Americans on the western frontier to publish a work of fiction. Born in Maryland, Detter began a life of adventure, activism, entrepreneurship, and literary achievement when he moved to California in 1852 in search of gold, opportunity, and freedom. He would later travel throughout the West: Nevada, Idaho, and the Pacific Northwest, dwelling in "various mining camps and frontier settlements" (Foster, 212). During these travels, Detter joined in committees and organizations to fight for "public education," "voting rights," and "admission of testimony by African Americans in court cases" (Foster, 211). Moreover, Detter, "along with poet **James Monroe Whitfield** (1822–1871), [was] one of the first African Americans to serve on a jury in Nevada" (Foster, 211). Detter was also an accomplished orator, speaking at rallies and at the fifth anniversary celebration for the Fifteenth Amendment (1870). The Fifteenth Amendment gave all people, regardless of race or color, the right to vote. Detter served as an African Methodist Episcopal minister, invented and sold his patented cough syrup and hair restorer, and owned the Silver Brick Shaving Saloon and Bathing Establishment.

Detter's literary contributions include commentaries, essays, and one book of fiction, *Nellie Brown; or, The Jealous Wife with Other Sketches* (1871). He wrote articles for the *San Francisco Elevator* and the *Pacific Appeal* on "national and local social and political issues" (Foster, 211). He also wrote in an effort to persuade African Americans to move west. *Nellie Brown* consisted of a novella, short stories, and essays. It was republished in 1996. In the introduction, Frances Smith Foster, professor at Emory University, illustrates the significance of the work to African American literary tradition. According to Foster, *Nellie Brown*, the novella within the book, is "one of the early examples of 'divorce fiction' that was developing in nineteenth-century American literature and as such represents a singular innovation in the African American literary tradition" (212). Foster also states that Detter's work offers a glimpse into the lives of African Americans during a pivotal period in America's history ("Who Is the First?").

Resources: Thomas Detter, *Nellie Brown; or, The Jealous Wife with Other Sketches* (1871; repr. Lincoln: University of Nebraska Press, 1996); Frances Smith Foster, "Thomas Detter," in *The Oxford Companion to African American Literature*, ed. William L. Andrews, Frances Smith Foster, and Trudier Harris (New York: Oxford University Press, 1997), 211–212; Elmer R. Rusco, *"Good Time Coming?" Black Nevadans in the Nineteenth Century* (Westport, CT: Greenwood Press, 1975); "Who Is the First Black Novelist of the American West?" *Africana*, Oct. 1, 2004, http://www.africana.com/research/blackfacts/bl_fact_78.asp.

Gladys L. Knight

DeVeaux, Alexis (born 1948). Poet, playwright, educator, essayist, novelist, short fiction writer, and author of children's stories. DeVeaux, the daughter of Richard Hill and Mae DeVeaux, was born September 24, 1948, in New York City. She received a B.A. from Empire State College in 1976, and both an M.A. (1989) and a Ph.D. (1992) from the State University of New York at Buffalo. DeVeaux has published for both youth and adult audiences. In the children's book *Na-ni*, she addresses the dream deferred (in the words of **Langston Hughes**) of a poor girl who, when her family's welfare check is stolen, is unable to get a new bicycle. Likewise, in the novel *Spirits in the Street*, DeVeaux focuses on the **Harlem, New York**, community of the 1970s, which is plagued by domestic abuse, death, drug abuse, and social workers' mistreatment of poor Blacks.

The **coming of age** of women, their treatment, and the choices they make in order to be autonomous Black women is also a recurring theme. The plays *Circles* (1973), *The Tapestry* (1976), and *The Fox Street War* (1979) place Black women at the forefront. In *Circles* and *The Tapestry* the protagonists learn to break away from the pressures of society as it seeks to define their womanhood. In *The Fox Street War*, DeVeaux again represents Black women as vehicles of change as they ultimately force the landlord to make necessary changes in their living environment.

In more recent work, such as the prose poem "Sister Love" (1983), De-Veaux makes women her focal point through an examination of the ways in which Black women silence one another. She envisions a world free from labels and projects a community that will not be guided and influenced by homophobia.

DeVaux's work is both domestic and international in scope. Her essays "Zimbabwe: Woman Fire," "Southern Africa: Listening for the News," and "Blood Ties" show her political attachment to women's liberation, a theme that manifests itself in her work on American Black women.

DeVeaux is currently an associate professor of Women's Studies at the State University of New York at Buffalo and the poetry editor of *Essence* magazine.

Resources: Primary Sources: Alexis DeVeaux: "Blood Ties," *Essence* 13 (Jan. 1983), 62–64, 121; *Circles* (New York: Frederick Douglass Creative Arts Center, Mar. 1973); *Don't Explain: A Song of Billie Holliday* (New York: Harper & Row, 1980); *Li Chen/Second Daughter, First Son* (New York: Ba Tone Press, 1975); *Na-ni* (New York: Harper & Row, 1973); *A Season to Unravel* (New York: St. Marks Playhouse, Jan. 25, 1979); "Sister Love," *Essence* 14 (Oct. 1983), 83–84, 150, 155; "Southern Africa: Listening for the News," *Essence* 12 (Mar. 1982), 168; *Spirits in the Street* (Garden City: Anchor, 1973); *The Tapestry*, in *9 Plays by Black Women*, ed. Margaret B. Wilkerson (New York: Mentor Books, 1986), 135–195; "Zimbabwe: Woman Fire," *Essence* 12 (July 1981), 72–73, 111–112. **Secondary Sources:** Ronda Glikin, "Alexis De Veaux," in her *Black American Women in Literature: a Bibliography, 1976–1987* (Jefferson, NC: McFarland, 1989), 41–45; Linda Metzger, ed., *Black Writers: A Selection of Sketches from Contemporary Authors* (Detroit: Gale, 1989), 151–152; Priscilla Ramsey, "Alexis DeVeaux," in *Afro-American Writers After 1955: Dramatists and Prose Writers*, ed. Thadious M. Davis and Trudier Harris (Detroit: Gale, 1985), 92–96; Claudia Tate, "Alexis DeVeaux," in *Black Women Writers at Work*, ed. Claudia Tate (New York: Continuum, 1983), 49–59; Margaret Wilkerson, "Music as Metaphor: New Plays of Black Women," in *Making a Spectacle: Feminist Essays on Contemporary Women's Theatre*, ed. Lynda Hart (Ann Arbor: University of Michigan Press, 1989), 61–75; Dana A. Williams, *Contemporary African American Female Playwrights: An Annotated Bibliography* (Westport, CT: Greenwood Press, 1998), 38–39.

Brandon L. A. Hutchinson

Dialect Poetry. Written in what are known as "nonstandard" forms of English, African American dialect poetry has a long and controversial history. Some of the earliest examples of African American **vernacular** literature presented in lyric form can be found in songs from the **slavery** era, such as in the recurring phrase "Coming for to carry me home" in the spiritual "Swing Low, Sweet Chariot" or in the lines "We bake de bread/Dey gib us de crust" from a secular song exposing the injustices of slavery rather than expressing a hope for release. By contrast, the first published African American poets—**Phillis Wheatley** is an example—employed a lofty Standard English and wrote in traditional forms of English poetry. It was not until the later 1800s that black dialect (real or invented) was used regularly in poetry by White and Black Americans. African American poets at first adopted and modified the White poetic traditions for representing Black dialect in verse, only to move away from the use of dialect around 1920 and later. Black vernacular English has regained much of its status and popularity in African American poetry since the 1960s.

After the **Civil War**, dialect poetry began to enjoy widespread and enthusiastic acceptance in part because of the growing demand for literary realism and local color writing. Most dialect poetry in this period was written by White authors who were generally less concerned with presenting authentic Black speech patterns than with creating specific moods or atmospheres in their works. In what is now commonly called the plantation tradition, White authors used invented Black dialects to paint a nostalgic picture of a rapidly disappearing way of life, a change signaled by the decline of plantation culture and an increase of schooling among blacks in **the South**. Examples of the plantation tradition in verse include poems by Irwin Russell and Sidney Lanier and minstrel songs by Stephen Collins Foster. A few White poets have used Black dialect for other purposes. John Greenleaf Whittier's poem "At Port Royal" (1862) includes an effort to render Black dialect in the service of abolitionism, for instance, and the White literary avant-garde incorporated Black dialect in their poems well into the twentieth century, as evidenced in Vachel Lindsay's "Congo: A Study of the Negro Race" (1914) and John Berryman's *The Dream Songs* (1964).

An early instance of Black vernacular used by an African American poet in the era of **Reconstruction** is **Frances E. W. Harper**'s *Sketches of Southern Life* (1872), which includes six poems narrated by Aunt Chloe and presents both the **autobiography** of a former slave and an oral history of the eras of slavery and Reconstruction. The speech in these poems sounds more genuine than the dialect used by a number of other Black poets—such as **Daniel Webster Davis**, **James Edwin Campbell**, and **James D. Corrothers**—whose poems often appeared in White publications and adhered to the conventions of the plantation tradition. Two of the most notable late nineteenth-century poets writing in this tradition are **Paul Laurence Dunbar** and **James Weldon Johnson**. Dunbar mixed Standard English and dialect poems in *Majors and Minors* (1895) and his best-selling volume *Lyrics of Lowly Life* (1896); in the introduction to the latter work, the influential White critic William Dean Howells praised the dialect poems above the others in the volume, although Dunbar had had little direct contact with rural speakers of Black dialect, learning what he knew secondhand from his parents, and was influenced primarily by White American and British poets such as Poe, Longfellow, Tennyson, Shelley, and Shakespeare. Dunbar nonetheless succeeded in producing some of the most sophisticated and musical of the dialect poems written in this period. Fearing he would be remembered only as a writer of dialect poetry, he expressed remorse that his most serious poetry had not received the same attention and praise as his dialect poetry, which he disparaged in "The Poet" (1903) as "a jingle in a broken tongue."

Dunbar has been criticized as a supporter of negative racial stereotypes, but he was by all accounts a positive influence on subsequent generations of Black poets. **Langston Hughes** gave him thoughtful attention in his essay "The Negro Artist and the Racial Mountain" (1926), as did **Sterling A. Brown** in his study *Negro Poetry and Drama* (1937). Subsequent generations of Black poets have located in Dunbar the beginnings of an authentic Black voice in American poetry; he has been the subject of a number of studies since the later 1960s, and his collection of poems was reissued in 1967 and, in expanded form, in 1993. The poetry of Johnson, Dunbar's contemporary and close friend, similarly included pieces written in strongly inflected Black dialect, such as "Sence You Went Away" (1900), alongside others in spoken Black English, such as "The Creation" (1920), or in elevated forms of Standard English, such as "Lift Ev'ry Voice and Sing" (1921).

By the early 1920s, the tide was turning against dialect poetry. In his preface to *The Book of American Negro Poetry* (1922), James Weldon Johnson characterized the African American vernacular as a softened, and thus more musical, form of English, and commented positively on the dialect poetry of **Claude McKay**, John W. Holloway, **James Edwin Campbell**, and **Daniel Webster Davis**, yet Johnson ultimately rejected this artistic mode as fundamentally limited to the expression of humor and pathos. The problem for Johnson lay not in the dialect itself but in its seemingly inextricable ties to the long-standing plantation tradition of White authors using invented Black speech to present romanticized accounts of the slavery-era South. **Countee Cullen** echoed this judgment in his preface to the poetry anthology *Caroling Dusk* (1927), characterizing dialect poetry as a "fast-dying medium" that had offered only a limited range of poetic expression and had mostly been the province of White poets.

The minstrel and plantation traditions had indeed burdened the literary use of Black dialect with racial stereotyping. By the 1920s, Claude McKay had moved away from his poems in Jamaican English, as presented in his two early collections *Songs of Jamaica* (1912) and *Constab Ballads* (1912), and toward the loftier forms and language of traditional English poetry, particularly the **sonnet**. Several other of the most significant writers of the **Harlem Renaissance**, however, purposefully and effectively used Black dialect verse in their works. **Zora Neale Hurston** included examples of song lyrics and poems employing the Black vernacular in her essay "Characteristics of Negro Expression" (1934) as well as in her collection *Mules and Men* (1935) and her autobiographical *Dust Tracks on a Road* (1942), and **Jean Toomer** incorporated African American dialect into his **prose poems** in *Cane* (1923). More extensive use of Black vernacular was made by Langston Hughes and Sterling

A. Brown, both of whom demonstrated a strong interest in the spoken language of working-class African Americans.

Hughes' poetry was strongly influenced by Dunbar and frequently made innovative use of dialect alongside African American musical traditions, including the **blues**. For example, Hughes' first collection of poetry, *The Weary Blues* (1926), contains a number of poems written in Black dialect and structured according to the three-line blues stanza. Brown's poetry offers an even more complete fusion of artistic and popular concerns; for example, the title poem of *Southern Road* (1932) combines the work song, blues form, and Black dialect to tell the powerful story of a man convicted of murder and sentenced to work on a chain gang. Engagement with this compelling poetry by Brown and Hughes prompted Johnson to reevaluate his statements on the limitations of dialect and to publish a new preface to the 1931 edition of *The Book of American Negro Poetry*, in which he praised the use of "genuine folk stuff" and the representation of "the common, racy, living, authentic speech of the Negro."

Hughes, in particular, was a strong influence on two prominent African American poets of the 1940s, **Margaret Walker** and **Gwendolyn Brooks**. Walker's poem "Poppa Chicken," appearing in *For My People* (1942), strongly resembles the vernacular poems by Hughes. Brooks's early poems, by contrast, reflect Hughes's humor and melodies but not his use of dialect. In 1967, the year of Hughes's death, Brooks met Imamu **Amiri Baraka** and other young, engaged writers of the **Black Arts Movement** at a writers' conference; only after this meeting did she begin to blend urban Black dialect with the language of traditional poetry, as evidenced in her poem "The Third Sermon on the Warpland" (1969) and elsewhere.

Hoyt Fuller's "Toward a Black Aesthetic" (1968), an important manifesto of the Black Arts Movement, called for a new Black Poetry that was relevant and revolutionary in both content and style. In keeping with this new aesthetic, Black English permeates the poetry from this period and is frequently presented alongside (although not always clearly distinguishable from) the many other ways of speaking in contemporary American culture. Baraka's words in *Preface to a Twenty Volume Suicide Note* (1961) and subsequent volumes bridge the gap between the Beats and the Blacks (*see* **Beat Movement**); **Etheridge Knight**'s *Poems from Prison* (1968) speak in the various voices of America's street, drug, and prison cultures; and **Gil Scott-Heron**'s recorded poem "The Revolution Will Not Be Televised" (1970) opposes the chatter of White media culture with a call for militancy in the Black vernacular. In comparison, a number of the poems by Black women writers who regularly employ Black vernacular in their work—such as **Sonia Sanchez**'s "Summer Words of a Sistuh Addict" (1966), **Nikki Giovanni**'s "Beautiful Black Men" (1968), and **Carolyn M. Rodgers**'s "Jesus Was Crucified" (1969)—often present a voice that is more unified and intimate but no less capable of recording conflict, resistance, and resilience.

The poems written after the waning of the Black Arts Movement in the mid-1970s are too numerous and too varied to allow for a full account of the uses of Black English, even if one arbitrarily excludes spoken word poetry and **rap** lyrics from the discussion. In any case, the use of Black vernacular English is found in much contemporary poetry, and important critical studies in recent years—such as Aldon Lynn Nielsen's *Black Chant: Languages of African-American Postmodernism* (1997) and **Fahamisha Patricia Brown**'s *Performing the Word: African American Poetry as Vernacular Culture* (1999), have maintained that the spoken (rather than the written) word has long been the base unit of African American poetry. (*See* **Folklore**; **Folktales**; **Peformance Poetry**; **Slang**; **Smitherman, Geneva**.)

Resources: John Berryman, *The Dream Songs* (New York: Farrar, Straus and Giroux, 1969); Fahamisha Patricia Brown, *Performing the Word: African American Poetry as Vernacular Culture* (New Brunswick, NJ: Rutgers University Press, 1999); Sterling A. Brown, *Southern Road* (New York: Harcourt, Brace, 1932); Countee Cullen, ed., *Caroling Dusk* (New York: Harper & Bros., 1927); Paul Laurence Dunbar, *The Complete Poems of Paul Laurence Dunbar* (New York: Dodd, Mead, 1913); Rachel Blau DuPlessis, *Genders, Races, and Religious Cultures in Modern American Poetries, 1908–1934* (New York: Cambridge University Press, 2001); Susan Gubar, *Racechanges: White Skin, Black Face in American Culture* (New York: Oxford University Press, 1997); Langston Hughes, *The Weary Blues* (New York: Knopf, 1926); Vachel Lindsay, *Collected Poems* (New York: Macmillan, 1925); Claude McKay, *The Dialect Poetry of Claude McKay* (Salem, NH: Ayers, 1987); Aldon Lynn Nielsen, *Black Chant: Languages of African-American Postmodernism* (New York: Cambridge University Press, 1997); *Reading Race: White American Poets and the Racial Discourse in the Twentieth Century* (Athens: University of Georgia Press, 1988); Michael North, *The Dialect of Modernism: Race, Language, and Twentieth-Century Literature* (New York: Oxford University Press, 1998); Hans Ostrom, "Audience," "Black Dialect," and "Poetics," in his *A Langston Hughes Encyclopedia* (Westport, CT: Greenwood Press, 2002), 12–14, 38–40, 306–308; Steven C. Tracy, *Langston Hughes and the Blues* (Urbana: University of Illinois Press, 1988).

James B. Kelley

Diaspora. From the Greek for "a scattering or sowing of seeds," diaspora refers to a people or ethnic population that has been forced or induced to leave its homeland and settle in other parts of the world. This exile, removal, dispersal, or migration entails that population's keeping alive certain "native" traditions and cultural practices in new social contexts. Diaspora originally referred to the resettlement of the Jewish people outside of Palestine after the Babylonian exile. In the twentieth century, the term has signified the processes of resettlement and cultural survival for groups, especially people of African descent whose ancestors were forced into **slavery** and those who have become refugees or noncitizens in the wake of nationalist conflict. This expanded meaning of diaspora has proven extremely useful for African Americanist scholarship across the disciplines, which now more than ever engages with cultures, languages, and texts that originate from outside the borders of the United

States in its efforts to theorize and account for the modern Black experience in the Americas.

In a way, this shift in critical perspective, led by studies such as **Paul Gilroy**'s *The Black Atlantic* (1993) and **Hazel V. Carby**'s *Cultures in Babylon* (1999), is in line with the emergence and development of African American letters, for the literary field has always intuited itself as part of what might be called a diasporic consciousness. **William L. Andrews** and **Henry Louis Gates, Jr.**'s revisionary collection of eighteenth-century **slave narratives**, *Pioneers of the Black Atlantic* (1998), demonstrates how the undeniable violence and terror of the transatlantic slave trade enabled the writing of the Africa diaspora. Narratives by **John Marrant**, John Jea, **James Albert Ukawsaw Gronniosaw**, and Ottabah Cugoano deal variously with the universalist Christian impulse toward slave liberation, the creolization of European sensibilities in the Caribbean, and African contact with Indians in the Americas. The most famous of the early black slave narratives, **Olaudah Equiano**'s *Interesting Narrative* (1789), features a narrator whose adventurous crisscrossing of the **Middle Passage** entails inhumane suffering and degradation at first but also offers opportunities for capitalist trade and, indeed, the eventual purchase of his freedom. Gilroy has appropriated the metaphor of Equiano's seamanship to theorize the cultural richness and political insurgency of what he terms the **"Black Atlantic,"** which is informed by, but not reducible, to the transatlantic slave trade.

Nineteenth-century abolitionists were no less interested in Africans' dispersed presence in the world, given the entrenchment of the institution of slavery in the United States (*see* **Abolitionist Movement**). **David Walker**'s *Appeal* (1829) recognizes slavery as an international concern, and he speaks out passionately against the further displacement of African populations by colonization schemes. After the passage of the Fugitive Slave Law as part of the Compromise of 1850, which had signaled the North's complicity in **the South**'s slavery interests, the prominent activist **Martin R. Delany** qualified Walker's assessment in *The Condition, Elevation, Emigration, and Destiny of the Colored People of the United States* (1852). Here Delany makes the provocative claim that colonization is absolutely necessary, but that Africa's geography and climate in general, and Liberia's "burlesque" of self-government in particular, are not fit for African Americans; he proposes instead a free Black nation in Spanish-speaking Latin America, in "Nicaragua and New Grenada." **Alexander Crummell** was more sympathetic to the American Colonization Society's former colony, and he pushed for missionary settlement of Liberia in *The Future of Africa* (1862).

The incipient **Black nationalism** of the abolitionists was transformed into full-fledged, participatory Pan-Africanism by the likes of the American intellectual **W.E.B. Du Bois**, the Trinidadian intellectual C.L.R. James, the Jamaican activist **Marcus Garvey**, Senegalese poet Léopold Sédar Senghor, and the Martinican poet Aimé Césaire. Du Bois's *The Souls of Black Folk* (1903) and James's *The Black Jacobins* (1938) stand as the two most significant works of black social critique, cultural theory, and radical historiography in the twentieth century. Founded in 1914, Garvey's Universal Negro Improvement Association (UNIA) updated the colonization debate to meet the independent **"New Negro"** sensibilities of the **Harlem, New York**, political elite. His Black Star steamship line proved especially attractive to the UNIA's 2 million members worldwide. In the 1930s Senghor and Césaire founderd **Négritude**, a revolutionary political and aesthetic movement that encouraged Black artists to forsake "European" judgment and taste and to embrace their spiritual and cultural "Africanness." Many of these African anglophone and francophone artist–activists helped coordinate a series of global forums that sought to consolidate the political and cultural forces of the African diaspora. The Pan-African Conference of 1900 took place in London and served as the precursor to the five Pan-African Congresses that met in the great cosmopolitan centers of the Western world after **World War I: Paris, France**, in 1919; London, Paris, and Brussels in 1921; London, Paris, and Lisbon in 1923; New York City in 1927; and, most notably, Manchester, England, in 1945.

During the **Harlem Renaissance** and in the years immediately following **World War II**, African American literature and culture were profoundly affected by migrations to and emigration from the United States. **Langston Hughes** composed some of his most radical verse in the Soviet Union between 1932 and 1933. The globetrotter and consummate provocateur **Claude McKay** wrote romanticizing **dialect poetry** about his native Jamaica; his novels *Home to Harlem* (1928), *Banjo* (1929), and *Banana Bottom* (1933) are set in the United States, France, and Jamaica, respectively. Even the quintessential African American folk romance *Their Eyes Were Watching God* (1937) was written by **Zora Neale Hurston** while she conducted ethnographic research in **Haiti**; *Tell My Horse* (1938) is the vibrant account of her fieldwork. This diasporic mode of literary production also characterizes the way in which postwar expatriates established or extended their literary careers in continental Europe. **James Baldwin** wrote his most moving essays and narratives—*Go Tell It on the Mountain* (1953), *Notes of a Native Son* (1955), and *Giovanni's Room* (1956)—after moving to Paris in 1948. While he was an expatriate, **Chester Himes** was commissioned by a French publisher to create his renowned Harlem series of detective fiction featuring Coffin Ed Johnson and Grave Digger Jones. **Richard Wright** had already published *Native Son* (1940) and *Black Boy* (1945) by the time he exiled himself and his family from the United States in 1947. The years he spent living in and traveling from France produced a number of radically new aesthetic and political choices: *The Outsider* (1953), *Savage Holiday* (1954), and *The Long Dream* (1958) are heady philosophical novels, and his sojourn in the Gold Coast colony in Africa (later Kwame Nkrumah's Ghana) is memorably documented in the protonationalist *Black Power* (1954).

In the 1960s Black nationalism took up the banner of Pan-Africanism in more militant tones. African decolonization, the **Vietnam War**, and students' and workers' protests the world over led to African American appeals for

Third World solidarity, which were frequently made by the activist and spiritual leader **Malcolm X** and the poet and playwright LeRoi Jones (**Amiri Baraka**). Equally important to note is how black nationalism's notorious misogyny and sexism were rigorously critiqued by radical Black feminists such as **Angela Y. Davis**, a Pan-African internationalist in her own right. In a similar but more indirect vein, third-generation Barbadian **Paule Marshall** has written several novels—Brown Girl, Brownstones (1959); The Chosen Place, the Timeless People (1969); Praisesong for the Widow (1983)—from a Black woman's perspective, connecting West Indian and African American families and histories while exposing the cross-cultural consistency of forms of patriarchal and sexual domination.

Contemporary writers from Jamaica-born romance novelist Colin Channer to Jamaican-descended former U.S. Secretary of State and autobiographer Colin Powell continue to highlight the large extent to which the African diaspora informs Black literature and culture, as well as modern social life more generally. Another development has witnessed Black intellectuals penning memoirs in which they reflect on their African cultural and family heritages: the Ghanaian-descended Kwame Anthony Appiah's In My Father's House (1992) and the Malian Manthia Diawara's In Search of Africa (1998) are exceptional examples. Inspired by Du Bois's unfinished project of similar scope, Appiah and Gates produced the multimedia encyclopedia Africana (1999), which brings together an astounding number of entries on topics of political, historical, geographical, and cultural relevance in all the lands and traditions that constitute the African diaspora. Finally, the awarding of the Nobel Prize for Literature to Nigeria's Wole Soyinka in 1986, St. Lucia's Derek Walcott in 1992, and the United State's **Toni Morrison** in 1993 has definitively linked the African diaspora to the symbolic capital of world literature and global letters.

Working with the vast heterogeneity of the African diaspora poses new questions and challenges for scholars in African American literary and cultural studies. For example, even with shifting topographies and cosmopolitics in mind, a fundamental reorientation of how critics approach their objects of study may be in order. In his pathbreaking comparative analysis of African anglophone and francophone modernisms, The Practice of Diaspora (2003), Brent Hayes Edwards posits that "the cultures of black internationalism can be seen only in translation. It is not possible to take up the question of 'diaspora' without taking account of the fact that the great majority of peoples of African descent do not speak or write in English" (7). Such a claim is at once enabling and daunting, for Edwards's extension of African Americanist scholarship in diasporic terms would practically require transnational, multilingual methodologies and pedagogies, the bulk of which is not necessarily encouraged or supported by dominant institutional structures. To be sure, these are concerns with which all departments of languages and literatures are currently grappling as the U.S. academy adjusts itself to the reconfiguration of intellectual labor brought about by globalization and its concomitant downsizing and outsourcing imperatives. In this regard, the African diaspora is both a centuries-old phenomenon that demands contemporary scholarly attention and a recent product of the reorganization of the disciplines in the global university. (*See* **Creole**.)

Resources: William L. Andrews and Henry Louis Gates, Jr., eds., *Pioneers of the Black Atlantic: Five Slave Narratives from the Enlightenment, 1772–1815* (Washington, DC: Civitas, 1998); Kwame Anthony Appiah, *In My Father's House: Africa in the Philosophy of Culture* (New York: Oxford University Press, 1992); Kwame Anthony Appiah and Henry Louis Gates, Jr., eds., *Africana: The Encyclopedia of the African and African American Experience* (New York: Basic Civitas, 1999); Hazel V. Carby, *Cultures in Babylon: Black Britain and African America* (London: Verso, 1999); Martin R. Delany, *The Condition, Elevation, Emigration, and Destiny of the Colored People of the United States* (1852; New York: Arno, 1968); Manthia Diawara, *In Search of Africa* (Cambridge, MA: Harvard University Press, 1998); Brent Hayes Edwards, *The Practice of Diaspora: Literature, Translation, and the Rise of Black Internationalism* (Cambridge, MA: Harvard University Press, 2003); Michel Fabre, *From Harlem to Paris: Black American Writers in France, 1840–1980* (Urbana: University of Illinois Press, 1991); Frantz Fanon, *The Wretched of the Earth*, trans. Constance Farrington (1961; New York: Grove, 1963); Paul Gilroy, *The Black Atlantic: Modernity and Double Consciousness* (Cambridge, MA: Harvard University Press, 1993); C.L.R. James, *The Black Jacobins: Toussaint L'Ouverture and the San Domingo Revolution*, 2nd ed., rev. (1938; New York: Vintage, 1963); Michelle M. Wright, *Becoming Black: Creating Identity in the African Diaspora* (Durham, NC: Duke University Press, 2004).

Kinohi Nishikawa

Dickerson, Debra J. (born 1959). Memoirist and journalist. Debra Dickerson's nonfiction writings about education, race relations, and her personal struggles place her within rich traditions of African American **autobiography** and sociopolitical essay writing.

In her memoir *An American Story* (2000), Dickerson recalls her upbringing in **St. Louis, Missouri**. Born into a troubled household (her mother fled from Dickerson's abusive father in 1973), Dickerson found solace in authors ranging from Charles Dickens to **Maya Angelou**. In 1980, after failing to take degrees at Florrisant Community College and the University of Missouri–Columbia, Dickerson enlisted in the Air Force. The memoir recounts her two-year stint as a Korean language specialist in South Korea, including the brutal sexual assault she endured there, and her subsequent rise to second lieutenant in **Texas** and then chief of intelligence at Ankara Air Station in Turkey. Along the way, Dickerson earned a B.A. in government from the University of Maryland at College Park (1984) and an M.A. in international relations from St. Mary's University (1988). In 1992, after her discharge from the Air Force, she entered Harvard Law School, a decision she calls her "first consciously political act" (2000, p. 231). She earned a J.D. in 1995.

Dickerson's writing career began with the publication of the award-winning essay "Who Shot Johnny?," about a drive-by shooting that left her nephew paralyzed, in the January 1998 issue of *The New Republic*. Subsequent essays on economic disparities, the politics of race relations, and popular culture have appeared in *US News & World Report*, the *Washington Post*, and *Essence*, among other publications.

Dickerson's book *The End of Blackness* (2004) takes its subtitle, *Returning the Souls of Black Folk to Their Rightful Owners*, from **W.E.B**. **Du Bois**'s 1903 work *The Souls of Black Folk*. Dickerson's work discusses issues such as pride or shame in African heritage, class and assimilation into the "Western" lifestyle, and the implications of racial humor.

Resources: Debra Dickerson: *An American Story* (New York: Pantheon, 2000); *The End of Blackness: Returning the Souls of Black Folk to Their Rightful Owners* (New York: Pantheon, 2004).

Melissa Shields

Dickey, Eric Jerome (born 1961). Novelist and screenplay writer. The author of nine novels and one screenplay, Eric Jerome Dickey is well known for his character-driven stories of contemporary African Americans. Most of his books deal with relationship issues, be they romantic or familial. His most recent novel, *Naughty or Nice* (2003), which was number 14 on the November 16, 2003, *New York Times* Best-Sellers List (*Eric*), concerns three sisters who reunite during the Christmas holidays. Each is struggling with a romantic crisis. Camilli, in a review of this novel, states that "Dickey's holiday gift to readers follows his usual sure-fire formula of African-American sex, love, infidelity and redemption," as seen in his previous novels *Sister, Sister* (1996), *Cheaters* (1999), and *The Other Woman* (2003) (Camilli, 59). However, Dickey does employ a more somber style in some of his work. For example, in *Thieves' Paradise* (2002), nominated for a 2003 **NAACP** Image Award, the main character, Dante Brown, an ex-con, laid-off computer technician, fights to get his life in order and capture the attention of Pam, who is only looking for a man of means. Concerning this novel, Dickey has said that it shares characteristics of the noir style of writing, and of all his novels, "the characters with the inner conflict are the most interesting" (Daniels). Dickey, a young and prolific author, shares his stories with a wide and devoted audience of fans and critics alike. In an article for *Ebony* magazine, Foston asserts that Dickey "creates fiction that is additive," and that he "has received critical acclaim for his ability to navigate readers through the murky depths of relationships and the issues that bind them or break them" (Foston, 98).

Resources: Sara Camilli, "Review of *Naughty or Nice*," *Publishers Weekly*, Oct. 6, 2003, p. 59; Karu F. Daniels, "Eric Jerome Dickey's Double Duty," *The Ru Report* (Dec. 18, 2003), http://www.eurweb.com/articles/columns/12182003/columns/250312182003 .cfm; Eric Jerome Dickey; *Between Lovers* (New York: Dutton, 2001); *Cheaters: Caught Up in the Game* (New York: Dutton, 1999); *Friends and Lovers* (New York: Dutton, 1997); *Liar's Game* (New York: Dutton, 2000); *Milk in My Coffee* (New York: Dutton, 1998); *Naughty or Nice* (New York: Dutton, 2003); *The Other Woman* (New York: Dutton, 2003); *Sister, Sister* (New York: Dutton, 1996); *Thieves' Paradise* (New York: Dutton, 2002); Web site, http://ericjeromedickey.com; Beth Farrell, "Review of

Cheaters, by Eric Jerome Dickey," *Library Journal*, Oct. 1, 2001, p. 164; Nikitta A. Foston, "Black Male Authors: Smart, Sexy and Successful," *Ebony*, Dec. 2002, pp. 98+; Emily Jones, "Review of *Milk in my Coffee*, by Eric Jerome Dickey," *Library Journal*, Oct. 15, 1998, p. 96; Lillian Lewis, "Review of *Liar's Game*, by Eric Jerome Dickey," *Booklist*, Apr. 15, 2000, p. 1522; "Review of *The Other Woman*, by Eric Jerome Dickey," *Kirkus Reviews*, Apr. 1, 2003, pp. 493+.

Judith M. Schmitt

Dillon, Leo (born 1933) and Diane Dillon (born 1933). Illustrators and writers. For more than forty years, the Dillons have worked in collaboration. The duo, who are married, have illustrated a variety of media, including book jackets, album covers, textbooks, and prints. They have worked on a variety of genres, including **science fiction**, fantasy, Scandinavian mythology, and medieval literature. However, they are best known for their work in **children's literature**, especially African **folktales**. They are the only illustrators to have earned back-to-back Caldecott awards (in 1976 and 1977). Given by the American Library Association, the Caldecott is awarded to writers and illustrators of a single book each year.

Leo Dillon was born March 2, 1933, in **Brooklyn, New York,** to immigrant parents from Trinidad. His father, Lionel, owner of a trucking business, and his mother, Marie, a dressmaker, supported their son's artistic endeavors. Dillon attended the High School of Industrial Design in New York City, then enlisted in the Navy so that he could attend college on the GI Bill. On the advice of a trusted instructor, he enrolled at the prestigious Parsons School of Design. There he met his future wife and partner, Diane, who grew up in Glendale, California. During their time at school, the pair tried to "keep [their] relationship a secret because in those days inter-racial couples were not easily accepted. [They] knew of couples... who had been beaten up walking down the street" (*Fifth Book of Junior Authors*). The couple married in 1957.

The Dillons soon started collaborating on their illustrating work, leading to the existence of what they would call the "third artist." The pair would pass artwork back and forth, each adding to it and commenting on it. Ultimately, it would be difficult to tell who had done what. The Dillons agree that their joint work is better than their work could be individually.

In the late 1950s and early 1960s, the Dillons worked on a variety of material as freelance artists. In 1975, they illustrated their first children's book: Verna Aardema's *Why Mosquitoes Buzz in People's Ears: A West African Tale*. The story includes a wide variety of animals, and the Dillons used bold, colorful illustrations. Their artistry earned them their first Caldecott Award.

Their second Caldecott Award the following year was also for an African-themed book. Margaret Musgrove's *Ashanti to Zulu: African Traditions* (1976) is an alphabet picture book. Each of the twenty-six letters is represented by a different African tribe, and each page provides a bit of information about the pictured tribe. The Dillons tried to include realistic, accurate drawings of the people and their surroundings, and they received praise for their efforts.

In 1985, the Dillons worked with **Virginia Hamilton** to illustrate her *The People Could Fly: American Black Folk Tales*. The pair received acclaim for their cover art as well as for the black-and-white illustrations accompanying the twenty-four animal, supernatural, fantasy, and slave tales.

They received their first Coretta Scott King Award in 1991 for *Aida*, and have received it twice more, for *Her Stories* (1996) and *The People Could Fly*. In 1998 the Dillons edited and illustrated *To Every Thing There Is a Season: Verses from Ecclesiastes*.

After a long and prolific career, the Dillons continue to receive acclaim for their contributions to children's literature. While their artwork addresses a wide variety of topics and themes and is expressed in various media and styles, their contributions to illustrating African American tales have earned them the most praise. (*See* **Children's Literature.**)

Resources: "Dillon, Diana, and Dillon, Leo," *Fifth Book of Junior Authors and Illustrators; Junior Authors Electronic* (New York: H. W. Wilson and Co., 1983; updated 1999), as reprinted in *Biographies Plus Illustrated*, vnweb.hwwilsonweb.com; Leo Dillon and Diane Dillon, *To Every Thing [sic] There Is a Season* (New York: Scholastic, 1998); Byron Preiss, ed., *The Art of Leo and Diane Dillon* (New York: Ballantine, 1981); Barbara Rollock, *Black Authors and Illustrators of Children's Books*, 2nd ed. (New York: Garland, 1992); Anita Silvey, ed., *Children's Books and Their Creators* (Boston: Houghton Mifflin, 1995).

Heidi Hauser Green

Dixon, Melvin (1950–1992). Poet, novelist, and critic. In his life and writing, Dixon insisted upon asserting the representative and complete humanity of African Americans regardless of sexual orientation. His works give voice to the rarely heard African American homosexual man. Born in Stamford, Connecticut, in 1950, Dixon attended school there. He graduated from Wesleyan University, where he studied English and French literature and dance, in 1971. He continued his education at Brown University, where he earned a Ph.D. in English in 1975. A Ford Foundation postdoctoral fellowship allowed him time to research African American writers in **Paris, France**, while on leave from his first teaching position, at Williams College (1976–1980). Dixon later taught at Queens College and the City University of New York Graduate Center (1980–1992). In 1984 he was awarded a National Endowment for the Arts fellowship in poetry, and in 1988 he received an award for fiction from the New York Arts Foundation. During 1985–1986 he held a Fulbright lectureship in Senegal, where he began work on his translation of *The Collected Poems of Léopold Sédar Senghor*, published in 1991. Dixon died at age forty-two, from complications arising from AIDS. *Love's Instruments*, his second collection of poems, was published posthumously.

In *Ride Out the Wilderness: Geography and Identity in African American Literature* (1987), Dixon examines how African American writers have worked with locations and landscapes (the wilderness, the mountaintop, the underground) that are both literal and metaphorical. This study of "symbolic geography" dovetails with Dixon's interest in space and place in his poetry and fiction. *Change of Territory: Poems* (1983) explores Dixon's travels to his parents' and grandparents' home in North Carolina, to Paris, and to West Africa. In the book, Dixon often represents these explorations through the use of poetic personas/masks as well as through autobiographical remembrance. His novel *Trouble the Water* (1989) follows its protagonist, Jordan, on a journey of self-discovery in the Carolina hinterlands of his past. Jordan must confront both the estranged father who is held responsible for his mother's death and the grandmother who wants him to avenge that loss. Influenced by both **James Baldwin**'s searching fictional examinations of familial relations and Southern Gothic traditions of eccentricity and violence, *Trouble the Water* won the Nilon Award for Excellence in Minority Fiction. Dixon's second novel, *Vanishing Rooms* (1991), explores the complex of psychological and sexual spaces inhabited by an interracial homosexual couple in New York City's Greenwich Village. When his White partner is murdered, Jesse seeks to understand the event as well as the nature of their relationship. The story develops through contrasting narrators: Jesse; Ruella, a female friend; and Lonny, a fifteen-year-old White boy from the neighborhood who is one of the murderers. Like Baldwin's *Another Country*, Dixon's *Vanishing Rooms* provides a range of perspectives on **race**, sexuality, love, and homophobia. The poems in *Loves' Instruments*, many of them written after Dixon's AIDS diagnosis, examine loss, loneliness, and anger as well as people and places important to his life as an artist. (*See* **Gay Literature; Gothic Literature; Queer Theory.**)

Resources: Melvin Dixon: *Change of Territory: Poems* (Lexington: University of Kentucky Press, 1983); *Love's Instruments* (Chicago: Tia Chucha Press, 1995); *Ride Out the Wilderness: Geography and Identity in Afro-American Literature* (Urbana: University of Illinois Press, 1987); *Trouble the Water* (Boulder: University of Colorado Press/Fiction Collective II, 1989); *Vanishing Rooms* (New York: Dutton, 1991); Vivian May, "Reading Melvin Dixon's *Vanishing Rooms*: Experiencing the Ordinary Rope That Can Change in a Second to a Lyncher's Noose or a Rescue Line," *Callaloo* 23, no. 1 (Winter 2000), 366–381; Hermine D. Pinson, "Geography and Identity in Melvin Dixon's *Change of Territory*," *MELUS* 21, no. 1 (Spring 1996), 99–111; Jerome de Romanet, "A Conversation with Melvin Dixon," *Callaloo* 23, no. 1 (Winter 2000), 84–109; Maurice Wallace, "The Autochoreography of an Ex-Snow Queen: Dance, Desire and the Black Masculine in Melvin Dixon's *Vanishing Rooms*," in *Novel Gazing: Queer Readings in Fiction*, ed. Eve Kosofsky Sedgwick (Durham, NC: Duke University Press, 1997).

Joseph T. Skerrett, Jr.

Dodson, Howard (born 1939). Social activist, historian, lecturer, nonfiction writer, and research center director. Dodson is, at this writing, chief of the Schomburg Center for Research in Black Culture of the New York Public Library, located in **Harlem, New York**. Under his leadership, the center has developed a comprehensive public research library devoted exclusively to documenting and interpreting the African **diaspora** and African history and culture.

Dodson's policies have increased the number of users of the Schomburg Center from 40,000 to 125,000 annually, and he has established a scholars-in-residence program that has provided fellowships for more than eighty scholars. Dodson has curated such diverse exhibitions as "Censorship and Black America" and "Lest We Forget: The Triumph over Slavery," and has organized major events at Carnegie Hall. In recent years he has secured the private papers of **Alex Haley** and **Malcolm X** for the Schomburg Center's collection.

A specialist in African American history and culture and a prolific scholar, Dodson has published four books and numerous essays and articles. His most recent work, *Jubilee: The Emergence of African American Culture* (2002), chronicles the transatlantic slave trade, one of the most wretched and lamentable chapters in the annals of human existence. Based upon an exhibit at the Schomburg Center to celebrate its seventy-fifth anniversary in 2000–2001, *Jubilee* documents the extent to which the colonization of North and South America depended upon slave labor. It focuses on the cultural, political, economic, and social activities in which enslaved Africans took part to redefine themselves and their world and to reshape their own destiny. Dodson has also published *The Black New Yorkers: The Schomburg Illustrated Chronology* (2000), which documents the African presence in New York City from colonial times until the present day.

Dodson was born in Chester, Pennsylvania, and completed high school in 1957. He received his undergraduate degree in social studies and English from West Chester University in 1961, and earned two masters' degrees from Villanova University in history and political science before joining the Peace Corps. In 1967, after spending three years in Ecuador as the director of credit union educational programs for the National Credit Union Federation, he moved to **Washington, D.C.**, to become the director of minority recruiting and deputy director of campus recruiting for the Peace Corps.

In 1974 Dodson was named executive director of the Institute of the Black World in **Atlanta, Georgia**, and began teaching at Emory University. In 1979 he returned to Washington as a consultant for the National Endowment for the Humanities. He has received the James Weldon Johnson Medal for Cultural Achievement and the New York Association of Black Journalists 2002 Community Leadership Award, and has been appointed to the President's Commission on the National Museum of African American History and Culture.

Resources: Herb Boyd: "Howard Dodson Saluted," *Amsterdam News*, Nov. 16, 2000, p. 9; "Schomburg Designated as Repository for Malcolm X Papers," *Amsterdam News*, Jan. 9, 2003, pp. 1+; Howard Dodson: *The Black New Yorkers: The Schomburg Illustrated Chronolgy* (New York: John Wiley, 2000); *Jubilee: The Emergence of African American Culture* (Washington, DC: National Geographic, 2002); Gerald Horne, "Schomburg Library Chief Discusses the Development of the New CIBC History Book," *Interracial Books for Children Bulletin* 19, no. 1 (1988), 3–5; Thomas Riggs, ed., *St. James Guide to Black Artists* (Detroit: St. James Press, 1997); TaRessa Stovall, "The Power of African American Culture," *The Crisis*, Mar./Apr. 2003, pp. 48+.

Raymond E. Janifer, Sr.

Dodson, Owen (1914–1983). Poet, playwright, and novelist. Dodson's plays, poetry, and novels address a variety of topics; his plays explore subjects ranging from war to comedy, while his novels and poetry discuss spirituality and race. After growing up in **Brooklyn, New York**, Dodson, the youngest of eight children, received a scholarship to Bates College in Lewiston, Maine, where he earned his B.A. in 1936. He went on to Yale University's School of Drama, earning his M.F.A. in playwriting 1939. At Yale, Dodson wrote two plays: *Divine Comedy* (1938) and *The Garden of Time* (1939).

In 1938, while still working on his M.F.A., Dodson went to Spelman College in **Atlanta, Georgia**, to teach drama. From 1938 until 1942, Dodson was an instructor and director of drama at Atlanta University, where his colleagues included **Sterling A. Brown, William Stanley Braithwaite,** and **W.E.B. Du Bois** (Grant, 641). After a brief stint in the Navy in 1942–1943, Dodson wrote and directed *New World A-Coming* (1944) to draw attention to the accomplishments of Blacks in **World War II**. Two years later, he published *Powerful Long Ladder* (1946), his first and best-known book of poetry. From 1947 until 1969, he taught theater and directed plays at Howard University in **Washington, D.C.** In 1951, Dodson turned his attention to fiction and wrote the poetic and semiautobiographical novel *Boy at the Window* (1951), about a boy and his invalid mother ("Owen Vincent Dodson").

Dodson went on to write several more novels: *When Trees Were Green* (1951), *Cages* (1953), *The Confession Stone: Song Cycles* (1970), *Come Home Early, Child* (1977) and *The Harlem Book of the Dead* (1978).

Resources: Owen Dodson: *Boy at the Window* (New York: Farrar, Straus, and Giroux, 1951); *The Confession Stone: Song Cycles* (London: P. Bremen, 1970); *Powerful Long Ladder* (New York: Farrar, Straus, and Co., 1946); Nathan Grant, "Extending the Ladder: A Remembrance of Owen Dodson," *Callaloo* 20 (1998), 640–645; James V. Hatch, *Sorrow Is the Only Faithful One: The Life of Owen Dodson* (Chicago: University of Illinois Press, 1993); "Owen Vincent Dodson," *Literature Resource Center—Author Resource Pages*, University of Central Oklahoma (Oct. 28, 2003), http:// galenet.galegroup.com.vortex2.ucok.edu:2050/servlet/LitRC?vrsn=3&OP=contains& locID=edmo56673&srchtp=athr&ca=1&c=1&ste=6&tab=1&tbst=arp&ai=24714 &n=10&docNum=H1000026029&ST=Dodson%2C+Owen&bConts=10927; Charles H. Rowell, "An Interview with Owen Dodson," *Callaloo* 20 (1998), 627–639; James Van Der Zee, Owen Dodson, and Camille Billops, *The Harlem Book of the Dead* (Dobbs Ferry, NY: Morgan & Morgan, 1978).

Julie Claggett

Dorr, David F. (1827/1828–1872). Travel writer and diary writer. Born to slaves in **New Orleans, Louisiana**, Dorr seems to have been so light-skinned that he was generally able to pass as White. He himself indicated that his owner, a lawyer named Cornelius Fellowes, typically treated him paternally rather than tyranically. Certainly, Fellowes provided Dorr with a very good education. From 1851 to 1854, Dorr accompanied Fellowes on a tour of Europe and the Middle East, during which Dorr was as much a companion as a servant.

Although Fellowes promised to free Dorr when they returned to the United States, he did not keep his word. Subsequently Dorr escaped northward up the Mississippi Valley and ultimately settled in Cleveland, Ohio.

Dorr kept a diary during his travels with Fellowes, and from those notes, he wrote the account that was privately printed in Cleveland in 1858. The book received some good notices in the Cleveland newspapers, and Dorr became a speaker of some repute at local gatherings. The book seems to have gained little broader attention, however.

Dorr enlisted in the Union Army in 1862, and he served for more than a year with the Seventh Ohio Volunteer Infantry. At the battle of Ringgold in Georgia, he received severe wounds in the jaw and right shoulder. Indeed, Dorr's death in 1872 can be attributed to the long-term effects of his wounds, and he apparently spent much of his last decade wrangling for a more generous pension from the War Department. Shortly before his death, he returned to New Orleans to live.

As Malini Johar Schueller argues in her introduction to the University of Michigan Press's recent edition of Dorr's book, Dorr writes about his travels in the manner of a genteel European or Anglo-American traveler, and thereby subverts the usual distinctions of socioeconomic and racial privilege. It is not that he entirely ignores or conceals his racial identity. Rather, he simply does not make it a focal point of the narrative, as if he were emphasizing the oddity of an African American traveler of leisure at a time when most African American travel narratives were accounts of escape. But that uniqueness is precisely what has continued to make his book a historical and a literary curiosity. (*See* **Passing**.)

Resources: David F. Dorr, *A Colored Man Round the World*, ed. Malini Johar Schueller (1858; Ann Arbor: University of Michigan Press, 1999); Malini Johar Schueller, "Introduction," in David F. Dorr, *A Colored Man Round the World*, ed. Schueller (Ann Arbor: University of Michigan Press, 1999), ix–xliii.

Martin Kich

Douglass, Frederick (1818–1895). Abolitionist, orator, author, editor, and politician. Frederick Bailey (he later changed his name) was born to a slave named Harriet Bailey and an unknown White man in February 1818 at Tuckahoe, near the town of Easton, in Talbot County, Maryland. Reared on the plantation of Col. Edward Lloyd, young Frederick Douglass was the property of Capt. Aaron Anthony, the plantation's manager. Having grown up not knowing the identity of his father and having lost his mother (who was sold) near the age of seven, Douglass grew up committed to battling **slavery**, the institution that had deprived him of a father and taken away his mother. Douglass's early years appear to have been relatively free from physical abuse, and his favored status as an intelligent and tractable young man led to his selection, in 1825, to become a servant in the **Baltimore, Maryland**, home of Hugh and Sophia Auld, relatives of his master. In the Auld home, Douglass received rudimentary education in reading and writing from Sophia Auld, until Hugh discovered her teaching and put a stop to the practice. One of Douglass's first acts of rebellion against the dictates of slavery, famously recounted in his autobiographies, was to learn to read and write despite prohibitions to the contrary. As he wrote in his *Narrative* of 1845, hearing that he was barred from furthering his literacy made him see "the pathway from slavery to freedom." Douglass's literacy would become one of his strongest assets later in life, as he was able passionately and articulately to convey the horrors of slavery in his orations, autobiographies, a novella, and countless editorials and articles in support of the antislavery cause.

Following a dispute between Hugh Auld and his brother Thomas, Douglass returned to Maryland as the slave of Thomas Auld, who subsequently hired Douglass out to the notorious Edward Covey, a "slave-breaker." It was under Covey's supervision that Douglass first personally experienced the brutality of the slave system, finding himself subject to frequent and unprovoked physical beatings at the hands of his overseer. Following six months of abuse, Douglass, then sixteen years old, fought back, in a famous scene recounted in his *Narrative*. In his recollection of the fight, Douglass discusses the impact of his resistance, which not only kept him from further beatings by Covey for the remainder of the year he spent with him, but also "rekindled the few expiring embers of freedom, and revived within me a sense of my own manhood. It recalled the departed self-confidence, and inspired me again with a determination to be free" (115). Buoyed by this desire, Douglass made a first, and unsuccessful, attempt to escape from slavery in 1836 as he was being sent back to Baltimore to reside with Hugh and Sophia Auld.

From 1836 to 1838, Douglass learned the caulking trade in the Baltimore shipyards, hiring himself out independently to shipbuilders and returning a prearranged portion of his earnings each week to Hugh Auld. By taking on additional work and negotiating higher wages, Douglass was able to set aside a small portion of his earnings each week. This money later helped him achieve his freedom. On September 3, 1838, Douglass, disguised as a free Black merchant sailor and aided by Anna Murray, took a train from Baltimore to New York City. From New York, he headed to New Bedford, Massachusetts, where he married Anna and selected Douglass as his new last name.

In the years following, Douglass became a regular presence as an articulate and impassioned speaker for the **Abolitionist Movement** against the horrors of slavery. Less than three years following his escape, Douglass was working full-time as a lecturer. During this period, he befriended the noted abolitionist William Lloyd Garrison. The most important document to emerge out of Douglass's collaboration with Garrison was Douglass's *Narrative of the Life of Frederick Douglass, an American Slave* (1845), which he wrote at the urging of Garrison, who published and distributed the book. Released in June 1845 under the aegis of the American Anti-Slavery Society, and subsidized by the Massachusetts Anti-Slavery Society, the *Narrative* sold remarkably well: 4,500 copies in the first five months and 30,000 over the next five years. The success of the *Narrative* propelled Douglass to international celebrity as a speaker against slavery. The *Narrative* was considered so incendiary and inflammatory that Douglass was sent to England as a speaker immediately following its publication, in response to worries that his former master would seek his capture. In anticipation of the publication of his narrative, Douglass sailed to Liverpool, England, on August 16, 1845, to embark upon a lecture tour and to stay clear of those intent on capturing him and returning him to slavery. His success as a speaker and agitator for American abolition during his sojourn in England earned him friends, influence, and investors willing to assist Douglass in the purchase of his freedom from his former master and in the establishment of his own newspaper, *The North Star*.

Shortly after the publication of Douglass's *Narrative*, Douglass and Garrison began a planned two-month speaking tour of Ohio and New York. While the tour was largely successful—speaking to large crowds and converting many to the

Undated portrait of Frederick Douglass. Courtesy of the Library of Congress.

causes of free soil and immediatism—Garrison paid a price for his efforts. In late September, after speaking to crowds at three large meetings in one day in Cleveland, he collapsed from exhaustion. Unable to continue and confined to bed, Garrison left Douglass to continue their engagements in New York, and he traveled alone to Syracuse and Buffalo. When he was finally well enough to return home to **Boston, Massachusetts**, at the end of October, Garrison expressed only one complaint about the experience that had left him near death, far from family and friends—that throughout his convalescence, he had heard nothing from Douglass, and was disappointed to hear secondhand that Douglass was continuing with plans to start a newspaper of his own.

The possibility of Douglass's beginning his own newspaper had first been broached when Douglass returned from his trip to England. British supporters had raised money and negotiated for the purchase of Douglass's freedom, in a complicated transaction that required the transfer of Douglass's ownership from Hugh Auld to his brother. These supporters had also offered Douglass more than $2,000 in the form of an annuity, which would free Douglass from wage earning and give him ample opportunity to promulgate the abolitionist cause. Douglass politely declined the offer, arguing that he was too young to be "superannuated" and suggesting instead that the money be used for the purchase of a printing press and equipment for a Black-run newspaper. Upon

Douglass's return to the United States in 1847, he brought news of the gift from British supporters and asked the American Anti-Slavery Society for its support of another newspaper. The leadership of the American Anti-Slavery Society argued that other antislavery newspapers had been started in his absence, that a Black-run newspaper would reinforce the color distinction, and that Garrison's *The Liberator* was itself having difficulty in retaining Black subscribers. The leadership persuaded Douglass to lay aside the venture for the time being. However, when he ultimately decided to begin his own paper, and word reached Garrison, the effort marked the first of many disagreements that would drive the two men farther and farther apart.

While the founding of Douglass's own newspaper—*The North Star*—in 1847 was instrumental in driving a wedge between Douglass and Garrison, it was not in itself the cause of trouble between the two, but rather a symptom of a larger disagreement developing out of Douglass's sense of his own position within the movement. According to Douglass's biographer William S. McFeely, Douglass "decided to begin his own newspaper . . . to find his own voice." Others have also described Douglass's dissatisfaction with his position relative to Garrisonian abolition in these terms: given that Douglass himself was educated and articulate, he became increasingly frustrated the more he imagined that he was valuable to abolitionists merely as a symbol or a figure, and not as someone with his own ideas and agenda. According to James L. Gray, "William Lloyd Garrison and other abolitionists wanted [Douglass] to appear on the platform to show his whip-scarred back while they talked about the evils of slavery, but Douglass soon decided that he should denounce slavery as well as describe it and become analyst as well as example" (39). In addition to the sense that he was valued more for his physicality than for his opinions, Douglass expressed dissatisfaction with the manner in which he felt himself to be taken as the basis of Garrison's speeches and writing. The establishment of his own newspaper gave him ample opportunity to speak for himself and denounce the wrongs of slavery rather than merely serve as a symbol to an abolitionist cause, a cause he felt was increasingly limiting his ability to voice his own opinions. Douglass continued to publish *The North Star*—later retitled *Frederick Douglass's Paper*—through 1863, contributing nearly all of its content.

In 1853, Douglass published a novella, *The Heroic Slave*, his sole work of fiction. It was written in response to a scheme hatched in 1852 by Julia Griffiths of the Rochester Ladies' Anti-Slavery Society to raise funds for the cause. She asked celebrities to submit antislavery statements that were to be printed along with a facsimile of the author's signature. The entire collection was to be entitled *Autographs for Freedom*. The two-volume collection included assorted entries by individuals such as **Harriet Beecher Stowe**, John Greenleaf Whittier, and William Henry Steward. Most of these entries were brief, but Douglass's contribution was a sixty-five-page novella that Douglass biographer William S. McFeely has described as a "curious mirror of his *Narrative of the Life of Frederick Douglass.*" Douglass's novella fictionalizes the successful 1841 slave revolt led by Madison Washington aboard the American ship *Creole* while it was en route from Virginia to **New Orleans, Louisiana**. After wresting control of the ship from their captors, Washington and his fellow slaves directed the ship to Nassau, where they gained their freedom. Filtered through the remembrances and recollections of both a sailor aboard the *Creole* and Washington's abolitionist friend, Mr. Listwell, Madison Washington emerges as a heroic figure of epic proportions. *The Heroic Slave* is therefore significant not just for being Douglass's sole work of fiction, but also for the manner in which the novella imagines the violent overthrow of slavery through armed resistance. The novella thus presents a more radical stance concerning resistance than Douglass ever took in his multiple autobiographies or in his many speeches and articles.

Douglass's second autobiography, *My Bondage and My Freedom*, appeared in 1855. In some ways an enlarged and expanded version of the 1845 *Narrative*, *My Bondage and My Freedom* also reflected on Douglass's years of freedom and painted a more arresting picture of slavery's evils. The first half of the work, "Life as a Slave," recounts many of the scenes that had so moved readers of his first autobiography—his fight with Edward Covey, the beating of his aunt Esther, and his acquisition of literacy. The second half, "Life as a Freeman," entered new territory. Here Douglass recounted his rising prominence within the abolitionist movement and his decision to go his own way in order to achieve his own voice. Douglass indicates that "it did not entirely satisfy me to *narrate* wrongs; I felt like *denouncing* them" (361–362). He would go on to write one more account of his life, *Life and Times of Frederick Douglass* (1881; revised and expanded in 1892). While these later autobiographies offer significant insights into the life and mind of Frederick Douglass, his first autobiography remains the most significant of these works, marking his emergence as an articulate and thoughtful voice against slavery with national importance.

Following the outbreak of the **Civil War** in 1861, Douglass became increasingly involved in politics, all the while continuing publication of his papers and speaking tours. Douglass lobbied President Abraham Lincoln to let African Americans fight in the Union ranks; later, in 1863, he published an address in *Douglass's Monthly* urging African Americans to enlist in the Union Army. His efforts in lobbying the president and encouraging African Americans toward service were instrumental in the establishment of the Fifty-fourth and Fifty-fifth Massachusetts Regiments of colored soldiers. In 1866, Douglass urged President Andrew Johnson to grant suffrage to newly freed African Americans. In 1871 he visited Santo Domingo as part of a commission tasked with determining the country's attitude toward annexation by the United States. These efforts, combined with Douglass's national stature and continued allegiance and service to the Republican Party, led to a number of political appointments, many of which were firsts for any African American. In 1874 he was named president of the Freedmen's Bureau Bank. In 1877 he was appointed federal marshal and recorder of deeds for **Washington, D.C.**, a post he held until 1881. In 1889 he was named consul to **Haiti**, and in 1893, chargé d'affaires for the Dominican Republic. In 1893 Douglass attended the World's Columbian Exposition in **Chicago, Illinois**, a world's fair held to commemorate the 400th anniversary of Columbus's arrival in the New World. At the exposition, Douglass, along with **Ida B. Wells-Barnett**, circulated a pamphlet, *The Reason Why the Colored American Is Not in the World's Columbian Exposition*, that protested the exclusion of African Americans from displays highlighting America's progress over the past four centuries. Douglass and Wells-Barnett also objected to the limitation of African Americans' presence to ethnographic displays and the tawdry entertainments of the Midway Plaissance.

Douglass died of a heart attack February 20, 1895, at his home at Cedar Hill, Washington, D.C. He is buried alongside his wife and daughter in Mount Hope Cemetery in Rochester, New York, where he lived during much of his life. Douglass's importance to American literature and culture is difficult to overstate. His 1845 *Narrative* stands as one of the finest examples of the **slave narrative** genre and is a testament to Douglass's eloquence and persuasiveness as he combated slavery in particular and racial discrimination in general. Many of the twentieth century's notable African American authors, particularly those writing within the autobiographical tradition, owe a debt to Douglass and his writings (*see* **Autobiography**). These authors include **Booker T. Washington, W.E.B. Du Bois, James Weldon Johnson, Ralph Ellison,** and **James Baldwin**, among many others. While Douglass is best remembered for his efforts to end slavery and to better the situation of African Americans, he was also a passionate voice for the equal rights of women, participating in the 1848 Seneca Falls Convention along with Elizabeth Cady Stanton and Susan B. Anthony to advocate equal rights for women. In fact, Douglass's last public act before his death was to deliver a rousing address at a rally for women's rights.

Resources: Frederick Douglass: *The Heroic Slave*, in *Three Classic African-American Novels*, ed. Williams L. Andrews (New York: Mentor, 1990); *My Bondage and My Freedom*, ed. John David Smith (New York: Penguin, 2003); *Narrative of the Life of Frederick Douglass, an American Slave: Written by Himself*, ed. John W. Blassingame, John R. McKivigan, Peter P. Hinks, and Gerald Fulkerson (New Haven, CT: Yale University Press, 2001); James L. Gray, "Culture, Gender, and the Slave Narrative," *Proteus* 7, no. 1 (Spring 1990), 37–42; Nathan Irvin Huggins, *Slave and Citizen: The Life of Frederick Douglass* (Boston: Little, Brown, 1980); Gregory P. Lampe, *Frederick Douglass: Freedom's Voice, 1818–1845* (East Lansing: Michigan State University Press, 1998); Waldo E. Martin, Jr., *The Mind of Frederick Douglass* (Chapel Hill: University of North Carolina Press, 1984); William S. McFeely, *Frederick Douglass* (New York: W. W. Norton, 1991); Dickson J. Preston, *Young Frederick Douglass: The Maryland Years* (Baltimore: Johns Hopkins University Press, 1980); Benjamin Quarles, *Frederick Douglass* (Englewood Cliffs, NJ: Prentice-Hall, 1968); Eric J. Sundquist, ed., *Frederick Douglass: New Literary and Historical Essays* (Cambridge: Cambridge University Press, 1990); Booker T. Washington, *Frederick Douglass* (Philadelphia: George W. Jacobs, 1907).

Matthew R. Davis

Dove, Rita (born 1952). Poet, novelist, short story writer, and dramatist. Although a versatile writer, Dove is chiefly known for her poetry. Her poems started to appear in major periodicals in the early 1970s. In just over a decade, she became one of the most celebrated poets of her generation with her Pulitzer-winning collection *Thomas and Beulah* (1986). In 1993–1995, she was the youngest Poet Laureate of the United States, and she is also the only African American to date to win that honor. Dove's poetry has been widely praised for its technical sophistication as well as its accessibility. Critics have noted her innovative imagery, her well-controlled syntactic structure, and the complexity and range of her subject matter. In terms of her literary ancestry, Dove has been compared with Emily Dickinson, Robert Frost, **Langston Hughes**, **Zora Neale Hurston**, and **Gwendolyn Brooks**, to name just a few. While Dove's central focus is on her African American heritage and her identity as a woman, she endeavors to speak to the broadest possible spectrum of the reading public. She states, "Obviously, as a black woman, I am concerned with race. . . . But certainly not every poem of mine mentions the fact of being black. They are poems about humanity, and sometimes humanity happens to be black. I cannot run from, I *won't* run from any kind of truth" (Kastor, B2). Currently Commonwealth professor of English at the University of Virginia, Dove continues to lead a productive career as a poet.

Rita Frances Dove was born in Akron, Ohio, on August 28, 1952, to Elvira Elizabeth Hord and Ray Dove, who encouraged their daughter's academic and artistic pursuits. As a young girl, Dove showed a propensity for reading and writing. But she did not realize the full significance of writing in her life until the eleventh grade, when an English teacher took her to a book-signing event featuring the poet John Ciardi. From there, a path in literature opened up in front of the aspiring young Dove. In 1970, Dove enrolled at Miami University in Ohio as a presidential scholar and studied English literature with a secondary focus on German language and literature. She graduated summa cum laude in 1973 and went on to study modern European literature at the University of Tübingen in Germany as a Fulbright scholar. Dove earned an M.F.A. in 1977 from the University of Iowa's Writers' Workshop and married Fred Viebahn, a German novelist, in 1979.

After two early chapbooks (*Ten Poems* in 1977 and *Only Dark Spot in the Sky* in 1980), Dove's first full-length collection, *The Yellow House on the Corner*, appeared in 1980. Based on her master's thesis at Iowa, this collection clearly shows Dove's poetic vision: although deeply affected by such contemporary African American poets as **Haki Madhubuti** (Don L. Lee) and Gwendolyn Brooks, Dove strives to move beyond the **Black Arts Movement** toward a broader vision of humanity. In this volume, surrealist expressions (often cast in the context of dreams) contrast with **slave narratives** grounded in specific experiences of individuals or historical events. This interest in narrative led to her next collection, *Mandolin* (1982), another chapbook that features a seven-poem sequence which a few years later was incorporated into her masterpiece, *Thomas and Beulah* (1986). *Museum* (1983) represents an important stage of development in Dove's career in that it breaks out from the largely autobiographical nature of her previous work. With a broad social, cultural, and historical perspective, *Museum* explores issues of cultural heritage, the dissemination of knowledge, and historical memory. In poems as wide-ranging in time and space as "Tou Wan Speaks to Her Husband, Liu Sheng," "Catherine of Alexandria," and "Parsley," Dove highlights her interest in presenting history and culture from her perspective as a woman as well as an African American.

Rita Dove, 1994. © Christopher Felver/Corbis.

Thomas and Beulah, the most critically acclaimed collection of Dove's work, recreates family history against a backdrop of significant social events from the 1920s to the 1960s. The forty-four-poem volume is divided into two parts: "Mandolin" and "Canary in Bloom." "Mandolin," which more than triples the original version of seven poems, recounts in fictionalized form the experiences of Dove's maternal grandfather, Thomas Hord, who moved from his native Tennessee to Akron, Ohio, in 1921. Thomas, an expert mandolin player, is haunted all his life by the loss of his dear friend at the start of his journey north ("The Event"). Even his marriage to Beulah and their family life cannot completely assuage his remorse and pain ("Nothing Down"); he dies alone in his car, unable to get his medication ("Thomas at the Wheel"). "Canary in Bloom" commemorates Dove's maternal grandmother, who died in 1969, and had its genesis in a poem titled "Dusting," which first appeared in *Museum*. According to Dove, at first she did not envision parallel stories about her grandparents in *Thomas and Beulah*, which started out as her account of the story her grandmother told about her grandfather. "Then this poem 'Dusting' appeared, really out of nowhere. I didn't realize that this was Thomas's wife saying 'I want to talk. And you can't do his side without doing my side'" (Kitchen and Rubin, 236). The result is a life balanced between the weight of domesticity ("Daystar") and the yearning for love ("Recovery" and "Company").

Dove's later collections of poetry, including *Grace Notes* (1989), *Mother Love* (1995), and *On the Bus with Rosa Parks* (1999), continue to consolidate her reputation as one of America's leading poets today. (A selection from her previous published work appeared as *Selected Poems* in 1993.) *Grace Notes* is more personal than any of her earlier work; she allows the reader glimpses of her new role as a mother and of her career as an academic. Section three deals primarily with maternal life, including breast-feeding ("Pastoral") and changes in her body brought on by childbirth ("Genetic Expedition"). "After Reading *Mickey in the Night Kitchen* for the Third Time Before Bed" is a mother's candid lesson in sex education to her three-year-old daughter. In *Mother Love*, Dove continues the maternal theme but adapts the **sonnet**, a form traditionally devoted to romantic idealizations, to portray the tension between mother and daughter through a reworking of the classic myth of Demeter and Persephone. *On the Bus with Rosa Parks* returns to personal and social history, beginning with a section depicting African American life titled "Cameos," set in the 1920s through the 1940s, and closing with the title section that commemorates the civil rights pioneer. As Dove notes, the collection's title is a phrase uttered by her daughter in reference to the fact that they were riding on the same bus with Mrs. Parks during a conference in 1995 (91).

Just as Dove resists any preconceived notion of what her poetry ought to be like, so she does not restrict herself to one mode of literary expression. In 1985, her first collection of short stories, *Fifth Sunday*, appeared. It consists of eight stories and concerns young, often female characters who find themselves in conflict with social conventions. As Dove explains, the stories in this book "feature individuals who are trying to be recognized in a world that loves to pigeonhole and forget" (Rubin and Kitchen, 13). Dove's 1992 novel, *Through the Ivory Gate*, is motivated by a similar impulse. Virginia King, a young Black college graduate not unlike Dove herself, returns to her native Akron, Ohio, where she feels alienated from her family and romantic love. In an interview, Dove discussed the difficulty of moving from poetry to fiction (Ostrom). In 1994, Dove published a verse play, *The Darker Face of the Earth*, which reworks the classic tragedy of *Oedipus the King*. Dove's play follows the classic model in its plot of mistaken identity and incest, but her story is set on a South Carolina plantation where slavery and miscegenation are the key factors for the identity confusion.

Resources: **Primary Sources:** *The Darker Face of the Earth: A Verse Play* (Brownsville, OR: Story Line, 1994); *Fifth Sunday* (Lexington: University of Kentucky Press, 1985); *Grace Notes* (New York: Norton, 1989); *Mandolin* (Athens, OH: Ohio Review, 1982); *Mother Love* (New York: Norton, 1995); *Museum* (Pittsburgh, PA: Carnegie-Mellon University Press, 1983); *On the Bus with Rosa Parks* (New York: Norton, 1999); *The Only Dark Spot in the Sky* (Phoenix, AZ: Porch, 1980); *Selected Poems* (New York: Pantheon, 1993); *Ten Poems* (Lisbon, IA: Penumbra, 1977); *Thomas and Beulah* (Pittsburgh, PA: Carnegie-Mellon University Press, 1986); *Through the Ivory Gate* (New York: Pantheon, 1992); *The Yellow House on the Corner* (Pittsburgh, PA: Carnegie-Mellon University Press, 1980). **Secondary Sources:** Grace Cavalieri, "Rita Dove: An Interview," *American Poetry Review* 24, no. 2 (1995), 11–16; Susan Davis, "Entering the World Through Language," in *Conversations with Rita Dove*, ed. Earl G. Ingersoll (Jackson: University Press of Mississippi, 2003), 38–52; Akasha Hull, "Review of *Selected Poems*," *Women's Review of Books* 11, no. 8 (1994), 6–7; Elizabeth Kastor, "The Poet, the Biographer, and the Pulitzer Glow," *Washington Post*, Apr. 17, 1987, pp. B1–B2; John Keene, "Rita Dove's *The Darker Face of the Earth*: An Introductory Note," *Callaloo* 17, no. 2 (1994),

371–373; Judith Kitchen and Stan Sanvel Rubin, "A Conversation with Rita Dove," *Black American Literature Forum* 20, no. 3 (1986), 227–240; Adele S. Newson, "Review of *On the Bus with Rosa Parks*," *World Literature Today* 74, no. 1 (2000), 165–166; Hans Ostrom, "Interview with Rita Dove/Review of *Through the Ivory Gate*," *Soundlife* (Sunday suppl.), *Tacoma News Tribune*, Nov. 29, 1992, p. 11; Stan Sanvel Rubin and Judith Kitchen, "Riding That Current as Far as It'll Take You," in *Conversations with Rita Dove*, ed. Earl G. Ingersoll (Jackson: University Press of Mississippi, 2003), 3–14; John Shoptaw, "Review of *Thomas and Beulah*," *Black American Literature Forum* 21, no. 3 (1987), 335–341; "Twentieth-Century Demeter," *The New Yorker*, May 15, 1995, pp. 90–92; Helen Vendler, "Identity Markers," *Callaloo* 17, no. 2 (1994), 381–399.

Wenxin Li

Drake, David (c. 1800–c. 1870). Potter and poet. Although Drake was born into **slavery** and was forced to remain a slave for almost his entire life, he became a supremely accomplished potter who inscribed his own short poems on some of the clay containers he produced. Pieces of Drake's pottery, at this writing, in some cases sell at auction for tens of thousands of dollars. One example of his epigrammatic poetry, this one inscribed on an earthenware jar from 1862, is as follows: "I made this jar all of cross/If you dont [*sic*] repent, you will be lost" ("Stoneware Jar").

Drake's pottery is valued chiefly because of the accomplished workmanship and unusual glazing, but also because it was, like his poetry, produced in circumstances hostile to artistic achievement. Indeed, slaves were in general prohibited from learning to read and write, so to some extent Drake camouflaged his poetry with his pottery. He was born and spent almost his entire life in and around Edgefield, South Carolina. The exact dates of his birth and death are not known, but he lived several years after the Emancipation Proclamation and the **Civil War**, and so he was able to experience life as a free man. In 2001 Samuel J. Hardman published an edition of poetry from Drake's pottery.

Resources: Tom Fox, "From Freedom to Manners: African American Literacy in the Nineteenth Century," in *Contested Terrain: Diversity, Writing, and Knowledge*, ed. Phyllis Kahaney and Judith Liu (Ann Arbor: University of Michigan Press, 2001); Sammy J. Hardman, *Dave's Poems: The Poetry of Enslaved African-American Poet David Drake* (Commerce: North Georgia Literary and Folk Arts Society, 2001); "Stoneware Jar 1862 [by David Drake]," *Dave the Potter*, http://www.usca.edu/aasc/davepotter.htm.

Hans Ostrom

Drama. The consensus is that African American drama, or literature for the stage, essentially begins with **William Wells Brown**, who usually is also identified as the first African American novelist. Brown wrote two plays, *Experience; or, How to Give a Northern Man a Backbone* (1956) and *The Escape; Or, A Leap for Freedom* (1857). The former is linked to concerns of the **Abolitionist Movement**, of which Brown was a part; the play's protagonist is a minister from the North who supports **slavery** but who is, as fate would have it, sold into slavery himself, whereupon he changes his view of the institution. As one might guess, the latter play, *The Escape*, concerns an escape from slavery and draws on conventions of **slave narratives**, which often feature dramatic tales of fleeing slavery. As early as the 1820s, a writer now known as Mr. Brown (his first name is disputed) created a play titled *The Drama of King Shotaway*, which was produced in New York City in 1923. The play concerns a rebellion on the Caribbean Island of St. Vincent. (Brown was a native of the West Indies and a former sailor.) In addition to *The Drama of King Shotaway*, there were also performative, dramatic elements in much African American **folklore** and in African American folk music, such as work songs, which sometimes featured a dramatic "call and response" element. Also, the form of stage entertainment known as **minstrelsy** featured dramatic sketches and skits as well as short melodramatic performances. Nonetheless, William Wells Brown is viewed as the first African American to become a bona fide dramatist.

Later in the nineteenth century, **Pauline E. Hopkins** wrote the play *Peculiar Sam; or, the Underground Railroad*, a drama combining music with historical elements based on the **Underground Railroad**. It was first staged in **Boston, Massachusetts**, in 1880.

Among the important signposts in the progress of African American drama is the play *Rachel*, by **Angelina Weld Grimké**; it was arguably the first widely successful, genuinely popular play by an African American playwright and performed by African Americans; it was first produced in 1916, in **Washington, D.C.**, and it dramatized the impact of **lynching** on an African American family. Although **Paul Laurence Dunbar** is known chiefly for his poetry, he also wrote plays, including the one-act *Winter Roses* (1899), a love story. Just after the turn of the century, **Joseph Seamon Cotter, Sr.**, wrote *Caleb, The Degenerate* (1903), which Peterson and others see as dramatizing "the industrial education and work philosophy of Booker T. Washington" (Peterson, "Drama," 229).

Between the era of Hopkins, Grimké, Cotter, and Dunbar and the era of the **Harlem Renaissance**, African American drama continued to grow slowly but steadily. **W.E.B. Du Bois** wrote and produced *The Star of Ethiopia* in 1913, and **Mary ("Mamie") Powell Burrill**, a Washington, D.C., writer, published *They That Sit in Darkness* and *Aftermath* in 1919; the former concerns birth control, and the latter concerns an African American soldier who had served in **World War I**. Two of the most prolific playwrights of this era were **Willis Richardson** and **Randolph Edmonds**. Richardson's *The Chip Woman's Fortune* (1923) is considered the first dramatic play by an African American to be produced on Broadway. Richardson wrote dozens of other plays and also edited anthologies of African American drama. Edmonds is known for his numerous one-act plays, which were collected in such volumes as *Shades and Shadows* (1930) and *Six Plays for a Negro Theatre* (1934). Richardson and Edmonds are especially important figures because playwriting was their main focus, whereas some earlier writers, including Du Bois and Dunbar, wrote drama only occasionally. Additionally, Richardson made African American drama more visible by means of his anthologies, and Edmonds, a professor, taught playwriting and established theater companies affiliated with colleges. Thus both men helped to expand the audience for African American drama.

The Harlem Renaissance in particular, and the decades of the 1920s and 1930s generally, were crucial to African American drama, which took a great leap forward then, especially with regard to the volume and quality of plays created and the variety of dramatic forms in which African American writers worked (*see* Krasner). **Harlem, New York**, became an active site for theater; the magazines *The Crisis* and *Opportunity* offered awards for playwriting; and playwriting was among the arts that Du Bois, **Alain Locke**, and other "architects" of the Harlem Renaissance supported as part of a larger plan to cultivate the **Talented Tenth**. The musical play/revue *Shuffle Along*, by Noble Sissle and Eubie Blake, debuted in 1921, starring **Josephine Baker** and **Paul Robeson**. It took Broadway by storm, and became a symbol of the Roaring Twenties. Writers connected with the Harlem Renaissance who wrote plays include **Garland Anderson, Frank Wilson, Wallace Thurman, Georgia Douglas Johnson, John F. Matheus**, and **Eulalie Spence**. **Zora Neale Hurston**'s play *Color Struck* was published in the magazine *Fire!!* (1926). In Washington, D.C., **May Miller** was beginning what was to become a prolific career as both playwright and poet; she received encouragement from **Willis Richardson**, Mary Burrill, and others. Her plays include *Scratches* (1929) and *Stragglers in the Dust* (1930). She also edited the anthology *Negro History in Thirteen Plays* (1934) with Richardson.

In 1930 **Langston Hughes** and Zora Neale Hurston began a promising but ill-fated collaboration on a musical and comedic play, *Mule Bone*, which drew on Hurston's short story "Bone of Contention" and, like the short story, was set in rural Florida. Unfortunately, an irreparable quarrel occurred, springing in part from their different relationships to a patron of the arts, Charlotte Osgood Mason, and in part from a personality conflict. In any event, they abandoned the collaboration even though they had made considerable progress on the manuscript, and *Mule Bone* was not produced until 1991, long after both writers had died and legal issues had been sorted out. *Mule Bone* debuted on Broadway in February 1991, with music composed by Taj Mahal, who set some of Hughes's poetry to music for the production. The play was also published in 1991, accompanied by a full account of the controversy in 1930.

After the *Mule Bone* collaboration disintegrated, Hughes wrote the tragic play *Mulatto* in 1931. Four years later, while he was traveling in Mexico, a theatrical agent produced the play in upstate New York, drew interest from investors, and arranged for the play to be produced on Broadway, all unknown to Hughes (Ostrom, 260–261). Producer Martin Jones rewrote the third act, making it more melodramatic, without Hughes's permission. The play opened on Broadway on October 24, 1935, but met with harsh reviews. It was later restored to its original form and published in *Five Plays by Langston Hughes* (1963). Hughes's short story "Father and Son," included in the collection *The*

Ways of White Folks (1934), uses the same characters and conflict as those in *Mulatto*.

In 1938 Hughes helped establish the avant-garde Harlem Suitcase Theatre at 317 West 125th Street in Harlem (Ostrom, 154). Actors, writers, and others associated with the group included Louise Thompson, Mary Savage, Grace Johnson, Dorothy Peterson, Toy Harper, Alta Douglas, **Gwendolyn Bennett**, Waring Cuney, Dorothy Maynor, and Robert Earl Jones (the father of James Earl Jones, who became a renowned theater and motion picture actor). Among the plays produced by the Harlem Suitcase Theatre was Hughes's *Don't You Want to Be Free?*

Although Hughes is known primarily as a poet, he produced many kinds of drama over the course of his career. In 1932 he published the one-act play *Scottsboro Limited*, concerning the **Scottsboro Boys**, and in 1938 he wrote *Angelo Herndon Jones*, which concerned the arrest and trial of labor activist Angelo Herndon in **Atlanta, Georgia**. Hughes's comedic plays include *Little Ham* (1936) and *When the Jack Hollers* (1936), written with **Arna Bontemps**. His musical plays include *Tambourines to Glory* (1963); *Simply Heavenly* (1959), which is based on a character from his short fiction, Jesse B. Simple; and *Black Nativity: A Christmas Song Play* (1961), which is still produced frequently. With Elmer Rice and Kurt Weill, he collaborated on the opera *Street Scene* (1946), based on Rice's play of that title. He collaborated with Jan Meyerowitz on two operas—*The Barrier* (1950, based on Hughes's play *Mulatto*) and *Esther* (1957), based on the biblical character—as well as the oratorio *Five Foolish Virgins* (1954) and the Easter cantata *The Glory Around His Head* (1955). With **William Grant Still**, Hughes collaborated on the opera *Troubled Island* (1938), set in Haiti and based on Hughes's play of the same title. With **James P. Johnson**, composer of the famous 1920s song "Charleston," Hughes collaborated on a **blues** opera, *De Organizer* (1940). Other plays by Hughes include *Soul Gone Home* (1937), *The Road* (1935), *Jericho-Jim Crow* (1963), *The Sun Do Move* (1942), *Prodigal Son* (1965), and *Front Porch* (1938).

In addition to the energy supplied by the Harlem Renaissance, the Federal Theatre Project (FTP), one of the New Deal programs of Franklin D. Roosevelt's administration, also gave a boost to African American drama in the 1930s, and its creative energy carried into the 1940s (Fraden). Directed by Hallie Flanagan, the FTP included several subgroups known as **Negro units**, that were devoted to developing African American drama. **Abram Hill**, Willis Richardson, Georgia Douglas Johnson, **Richard Wright**, Frank Wilson, **Theodore Ward**, **Theodore Browne**, **Hughes Allison**, **Owen Dodson**, and Rose McClendon were among those involved, in varying degrees, with the FTP, which also sponsored the famous production of an African American version of Shakespeare's *Macbeth*, produced and directed by John Houseman and Orson Welles. (Welles and Houseman also produced a stage version of Richard Wright's novel *Native Son* on Broadway in 1941.) Negro units existed in every region of the United States and in cities such as New York; Seattle, Washington; Cleveland, Ohio; **Chicago, Illinois**; Indianapolis, Indiana; and

Atlanta. An archive of the FTP is held in the library at George Mason University. (*See also* **Federal Writers' Project**.)

In addition to Hughes, playwrights active in the 1950s included **Alice Childress, Ossie Davis**, and **Loften Mitchell**, who later wrote an important critical book (*Black Drama*, 1967). Arguably the two most important African American plays of the decade were **James Baldwin**'s *Amen Corner* (1955), concerning a Black female minister in Harlem, and **Lorraine Hansberry**'s *A Raisin in the Sun* (1959), a realistic drama about a Black family that takes its title from a poem ("Harlem") by Langston Hughes. With *A Raisin in the Sun*, Hansberry became the first African American female playwright to have a play produced on Broadway, and also created one of the most significant, widely produced, and critically acclaimed works of American drama in the twentieth century. Her achievement symbolized how far African American theater had come in 100 years.

The **Black Arts Movement** of the 1960s ushered in the next great era of African American drama. Probably the most influential figure in black theater in the 1960s was LeRoi Jones, later known as **Amiri Baraka**. His plays, which include *Dutchman* (1964), *The Slave* (1964), and *The Toilet* (1964), are unvarnished, provocative dramatizations of racism, race relations, class conflict, and intersections between sexuality and **race**. Baraka also founded the **Black Arts Repertory Theatre/School**, an influential drama group in Harlem. **Adrienne Kennedy, Ed Bullins, Ben Caldwell, Ron Milner, Douglas Turner Ward, Vinnette Carroll**, and **Thomas Covington Dent** are among the playwrights associated with this politically charged, artistically adventurous period of African American drama. As a playwright, teacher, and supporter of community theater, **Rob Penny** was an important figure in **Pittsburgh, Pennsylvania**, during this period.

In the latter third of the twentieth century, many important African American playwrights emerged. **Charles Gordone** won the Pulitzer Prize in drama in 1971 for his play *No Place to Be Somebody* (1969); he was the first African American playwright to win the Pulitzer in drama. **Melvin Van Peebles, Phillip Hayes Dean**, Richard Wesley, **J. E. Franklin, Joseph A. Walker, Charles H. Fuller, Jr., Samm-Art Williams, Jeff Stetson**, and **George C. Wolfe** were among the other award-winning dramatists of this period. **Ntozake Shange** won critical acclaim with the enormously popular dramatic work, *for colored girls who have considered suicide/when the rainbow is enuf* (1975). **Suzan Lori Parks** has been another dynamic young voice in African American and American theater, winning the Pulitzer Prize in 2002 for her play *Topdog/Underdog* (2001). However, the most influential and widely acclaimed African American playwright of the period was **August Wilson**. Wilson's evocative, historically alert, and enormously innovative plays include *Ma Rainey's Black Bottom* (1982), which won a Drama Critics Circle Award; *Fences* (1986), which won a Pulitzer Prize in 1987; and *The Piano Lesson* (1990). By the time Shange, Parks, and Wilson had achieved their place of prominence in American theater, African American drama had come of age in every dramatic subgenre and theatrical venue, from musical plays and comedy to realistic drama, tragedy, and avant-garde theater, and from community theater and college drama programs to regional theater, off-Broadway, Broadway, and the international stage.

Resources: Esther Spring Arata and Nicholas John Rotoli, *Black American Playwrights, 1800 to the Present: A Bibliography* (Metuchen, NJ: Scarecrow Press, 1976); Thadious M. Davis and Trudier Harris, eds., *Dictionary of Literary Biography*, vol. 38, *Afro American Writers After 1955: Dramatists and Prose Writers* (Detroit: Gale, 1985); Harry J. Elam, *Taking It to the Streets: The Social Protest Theater of Luis Valdez and Amiri Baraka* (Ann Arbor: University of Michigan Press, 1997); Harry J. Elam and Robert Alexander, eds., *Colored Contradictions: An Anthology of Contemporary African-American Plays* (New York: Plume, 1996); Harry J. Elam and David Krasner, eds., *African American Performance and Theater History: A Critical Reader* (New York: Oxford University Press, 2001); Federal Theatre Project materials [archive], George Mason University Library, Washington, DC, http://www.gmu.edu/library/specialcollections/federal.html; Rena Fraden, *Blueprints for a Black Federal Theatre, 1935–1939* (Cambridge: Cambridge University Press, 1994); Christy Gavin, ed., *African American Women Playwrights: A Research Guide* (New York: Garland, 1999); Samuel A. Hay, *African American Theatre: An Historical and Critical Analysis* (Cambridge: Cambridge University Press, 1994); Errol G. Hill and James V. Hatch, *A History of African American Theatre* (Cambridge: Cambridge University Press, 2003); Langston Hughes: *The Collected Works of Langston Hughes*, ed. Arnold Rampersad, 16 vols. (Columbia: University of Missouri Press, 2001–2004), esp. vols. 5 and 6; *Five Plays by Langston Hughes*, ed. Webster Smalley (Bloomington: Indiana University Press, 1963); Zora Neale Hurston and Langston Hughes, *Mule Bone: A Comedy of Negro Life*, ed. George Houston Bass and Henry Louis Gates, Jr. (New York: HarperPerennial, 1991); David Krasner, *A Beautiful Pageant: African American Theatre, Drama, and Performance in the Harlem Renaissance, 1910–1927* (New York: Palgrave Macmillan, 2002); Loften Mitchell, *Black Drama: The Story of the American Negro in the Theatre* (New York: Hawthorn Books, 1967); Hans Ostrom, *A Langston Hughes Encyclopedia* (Westport, CT: Greenwood Press, 2002); Bernard L. Peterson: *A Century of Musicals in Black and White: An Encyclopedia of Musical Stage Works by, About, or Involving African Americans* (Westport, CT: Greenwood Press, 1993); *Contemporary Black American Playwrights and Their Plays: A Biographical Directory and Dramatic Index* (Westport, CT: Greenwood Press, 1988); "Drama," in *The Oxford Companion to African American Literature*, ed. William L. Andrews, Frances Smith Foster, and Trudier Harris (New York: Oxford University Press, 1997), 228–234; *Early Black American Playwrights and Dramatic Writers* (Westport, CT: Greenwood Press, 1990); Charlie Reilly, ed., *Conversations with Amiri Baraka* (Jackson: University Press of Mississippi, 1994); Willis Richardson and May Miller, eds., *Negro History in Thirteen Plays* (Washington, DC: Associated Publishers, 1935); Taj Mahal, *Mule Bone: Music Composed and Performed by Taj Mahal/Lyrics by Langston Hughes* [compact disc] (Santa Monica, CA: Grammavision/Rhino Records, 1991); Allen L. Woll, *Dictionary of the Black Theatre: Broadway, Off-Broadway, and Selected Harlem Theatre* (Westport, CT: Greenwood Press, 1983).

Hans Ostrom

Drumgoold, Kate (c. 1858–?). Writer and teacher. Drumgoold is best remembered as the author of a **slave narrative**, *A Slave Girl's Story; Being an Autobiography of Kate Drumgoold* (1898). The child of slave parents, she performed domestic work, saved money to attend school, was a devout Christian, and worked to uplift the newly emancipated African Americans during the post-**Reconstruction** period in the United States. Born in Virginia, Drumgoold was one of twenty-two children (she had one brother and twenty sisters). Her mother was sold away from her children in Richmond, Virginia, to a man in Georgia. After the end of the **Civil War** she returned and managed to claim all of her living daughters (four had died). Kate's brother, James, was forced to fight in his master's place during the war.

Drumgoold suffered from poor health but maintained strong religious beliefs. In 1866, as a result of the preaching of Rev. David Moore, of the Washington Avenue Baptist Church in **Washington, D.C.**, Drumgoold was "saved," in the parlance of Christian conversion. She was encouraged in her Christian beliefs by her nearly 100-year-old grandmother. Drumgoold subsequently persuaded a woman from the church to teach her to read.

It was Drumgoold's greatest desire to be able to go to a "pay school"—one she could attend full time, undisturbed. Contracting smallpox forced her school plans to be postponed for three or four years. After discovering that some teachers were killed in **the South** for trying to educate Negroes, Drumgoold vowed, "I would die to see my people taught" (23).

Drumgoold attended Wayland Seminary in Washington, D.C., and an unnamed school in the Blue Ridge Mountains. She moved to **Brooklyn, New York**, and taught there from 1886 until typhoid fever forced her to stop teaching. The year of her death is not known.

Resources: William L. Andrews, *To Tell a Free Story: The First Century of Afro-American Autobiography, 1760–1865* (Urbana: University of Illinois Press, 1986); John W. Blassingame, ed., *Slave Testimony: Two Centuries of Letters, Speeches, Interviews, and Autobiographies* (Baton Rouge: Louisiana State University Press, 1977); Joanne M. Braxton, *Black Women Writing Autobiography: A Tradition Within a Tradition* (Philadelphia: Temple University Press, 1989); Kate Drumgoold, *A Slave Girl's Story; Being an Autobiography of Kate Drumgoold* (1898), in *Six Women's Slave Narratives* (New York: Oxford University Press, 1988), 3–62; Darlene Clark Hine, Wilma King, and Linda Reed, eds., *"We Specialize in the Wholly Impossible": A Reader in Black Women's History* (Brooklyn, NY: Carlson, 1995); Darlene Clark Hine and Kathleen Thompson, *A Shining Thread of Hope: The History of Black Women in America* (New York: Broadway Books, 1998); Tera A. Hunter, *To 'Joy My Freedom: Southern Black Women's Lives and Labors After the Civil War* (Cambridge, MA: Harvard University Press, 1997).

Regina V. Jones

Du Bois, W.E.B. (1868–1963). Scholar, activist, author, and editor. Renowned for his work as an activist and scholar, William Edward Burghardt Du Bois (usually pronounced *do-boyz*, as opposed to the French pronunciation) wrote with prophetic passion and published in a wide range of genres. Fully aware that his words affected readers emotionally as well as intellectually, Du Bois drew upon the duality of his personal experiences as a Black writer raised in an Episcopalian family in rural Great Barrington, Massachusetts, to create works that explore the question of what it means "to be black and to be an American." His *The Souls of Black Folk* (1903) reveals the tragedy of the Black experience in America and has been said by some to be to Black literature what *The Adventures of Huckleberry Finn* is to the canon of Anglo-American literature. In 1933, **James Weldon Johnson** wrote that the impact of *Souls* was "greater upon and within the Negro race than any other single book published in this country since *Uncle Tom's Cabin*." The concept of "double consciousness" articulated in the book remains a potent idea in **Black Studies**. It concerns the extent to which, because of historical and social circumstances, African Americans are virtually forced to be conscious of themselves as individuals but simultaneously and constantly as Black Americans, thereby being "doubly conscious" in ways White Americans rarely experience.

Du Bois, the first Black to graduate from Harvard University with a Ph.D., completed his dissertation, *The Suppression of the African Slave Trade to the United States of America, 1638–1870*, in 1895. With *The Souls of Black Folk* he began to develop the distinctive voice that would later define him as an outspoken activist and as the leader of the National Association for the Advancement of Colored People (**NAACP**). Du Bois was the only Black man elected to the board of directors of the NAACP when it was founded, in 1910; among other duties as director of research and publications, he would edit and write for the organization's magazine, **The Crisis**.

Du Bois had already founded and edited the monthly journal *Horizon* (1907–1910) as part of the Niagara Movement, which had been organized from a meeting in 1905 of twenty-nine Black leaders to protest for Black civil and political rights. As editor of *The Crisis*, during the **Harlem Renaissance**, Du Bois sought to publish works of literature that were set in Black life but not so directly propagandistic that they ignored the principles of art. Under Du Bois's leadership, *The Crisis* became the primary vehicle in the nation for literary art and criticism written by Black Americans, a position it maintained until **Opportunity: A Journal of Negro Life** began publication in 1923. Among many intellectuals, editors, and writers responsible for the Harlem Renaissance, Du Bois was arguably the most influential figure, articulating views about the **New Negro** and the **Talented Tenth**, cultivating support for the arts and developing personal relationships with writers including **Langston Hughes, Countee Cullen**, and **Jessie Redmon Fauset**. (Cullen was married briefly to Du Bois's daughter, Yolanda.) In this era especially, Du Bois's assertive political stance was often perceived to be in contrast to that of **Booker T. Washington**, who tended to emphasize economic self-reliance over political activism.

A prolific writer, Du Bois wrote the short story "The Coming of John"; a biography, *John Brown* (1909); and poems including "A Litany of Atlanta," "A Hymn to the People," "Christ of the Andes," "The Prayer of the Bantu," and

"The Prayers of the God," most of which were first published in *Horizon*. His novels, *The Quest of the Silver Fleece* (1911) and *Dark Princess: A Romance* (1928), are written in the drawing-room **vernacular** of Black America's intelligentsia, to which Du Bois belonged. Although Du Bois felt that his writings and political activism could change the fate of Black America, he later became disillusioned with America. In 1961 he joined the Communist Party and moved to Accra, Ghana, where he obtained citizenship, and died on August 27, 1963, on the eve of the civil rights march on **Washington, D.C.**

W.E.B. Du Bois, 1919. Courtesy of the Library of Congress.

Du Bois's other writings include *The Philadelphia Negro* (1899); *The Star of Ethiopia* (1913); *The Negro* (1915); an open letter to President Woodrow Wilson (1916); essays in *The Crisis* on Blacks in the war in Europe (1919); *Dark Water: Voices from Within the Veil* (1920); *The Brownies' Book* (1920), a magazine for black children; *The Gift of Black Folks: The Negroes in the Making of America* (1924); "A Lunatic or Traitor" (1924); "The Negro Mind Reaches Out" (1925); *Black Reconstruction* (1935); a weekly column in the **Pittsburgh Courier** (1936–1938); *Black Folk Then and Now* (1939); *Dusk of Dawn* (1940); columns for the **Chicago Defender** (1945–1948); *Encyclopedia of the Negro and Democracy: Colonies and Peace* (1945); *The World and Africa* (1947); *The Ordeal of the Mansart* (1957); and *Black Flame* (1957). He began work on the *Encyclopedia Africana* project in 1961.

Resources: Williams L. Andrews, ed., *Critical Essays on W.E.B. Du Bois* (Boston: G. K. Hall, 1985); Herbert Aptheker, *The Literary Legacy of W.E.B. Du Bois* (White Plains, NY: Kraus International, 1989); Houston A. Baker, Jr., "The Black Man of Culture: W.E.B. Du Bois and 'The Souls of Black Folk,'" in Baker's *Long Black Song* (Charlottesville: University Press of Virginia, 1972); Keith Byerman, *Seizing the Word: History, Art, and the Self in the Work of W.E.B. Du Bois* (Athens: University of Georgia Press, 1994); W.E.B. Du Bois: *Black Reconstruction* (New York: Harcourt, Brace, 1935); *Dark Princess: A Romance* (New York: Harcourt, Brace, 1928); *The Negro* (New York: Holt, 1915); *The Ordeal of Mansart* (New York: Mainstream Publishers, 1957); *The Philadelphia Negro: A Social Study* (Philadelphia: University of Pennsylvania Press, 1899); *The Quest of the Silver Fleece: A Novel* (Chicago: A. C. McClurg, 1911); *The Souls of Black Folk* (Chicago: A. C. McClurg, 1903); *The World and Africa* (New York: Viking, 1947); Gerald Early, ed., *Lure and Loathing: Essays on*

Race, Identity, and the Ambivalence of Assimilation (New York: Allen Lane, 1993); Dale Peterson, "Notes from the Underworld: Dostoyevsky, Du Bois, and the Discovery of Ethnic Soul," *Massachusetts Review* 35 (Summer 1994), 225–247; Arnold Rampersad, *The Art and Imagination of W.E.B. Du Bois* (New York: Schocken, 1990).

Imelda Hunt

Duckett, Larry (1953–2001). Musician, actor, poet, and playwright. Although other Black gay male writers and performers, such as **Essex Hemphill**, Marlon Riggs, **Joseph Beam**, and Blackberri, achieved wider acclaim in the 1980s and 1990s, Larry Duckett (or Duckette, as he was often known as a performer) was nevertheless an important contributor to the Black gay literary and artistic renaissance that developed at that time. (*See* **Gay Literature**.)

Duckett grew up in Capitol Heights, Maryland, and graduated from Virginia State University in 1976 with a bachelor's degree in applied music. He received his start in **Washington, D.C.**'s Black arts scene through being what he described as a "hired extra" in Station to Station, an African American poetry collective (Beemyn 1999). Duckett's work in the group brought him to the attention of Essex Hemphill, who recruited Duckett to be the second male voice in "Brass Rail," a performance poem Hemphill was writing (named for a seedy Black gay bar in the capital).

They first performed the work at the ENIK Alley Coffeehouse, a carriage house in northwest Washington that had been converted into a Black LGBT performance venue. The success of "Brass Rail" led Hemphill in 1983 to invite Duckett and another Black gay artist, Wayson Jones, to create Cinque, a regular performance group named for the leader of the *Amistad* slave uprising. With its vivid imagery about Black gay life, cutting-edge political verse, and tightly woven harmonies, Cinque quickly developed a large following beyond the Coffeehouse. Touring brought Cinque wider acclaim, and its poetic style became nationally known after the group's work was featured in Marlon Riggs's 1989 film *Tongues Untied*.

Although Cinque disbanded after a few years, Duckett continued to work with Hemphill and other local artists, including Michelle Parkerson and Chris Prince. He performed as an actor and musician at the Painted Bridge Arts Center in **Philadelphia, Pennsylvania**; The Kitchen in New York City; and the Kennedy Center and the National Theatre in Washington. He also assisted Riggs with his last documentary, *Black Is ... Black Ain't* (1995).

In 1997, Duckett staged *We Heard the Night Outside*, his play based on his ten-year collaborative relationship with Hemphill, who had died two years earlier. The play was presented in **Chicago, Illinois**, in 1998 by A Real World, the city's African American LGBT performance ensemble. Duckett also staged the work as a solo piece before he became too sick to perform.

Duckett was diagnosed in the early 1990s with multiple sclerosis, which became progressively worse over the decade. He died on September 26, 2001, in a fire in his Washington apartment. He apparently fell asleep while smoking in bed.

Resources: Brett Beemyn: "'It Was like the Sun Rose': The Coffeehouse and the Development of a Black LGB Community in Washington, D.C.," presented at The Future of the Queer Past Conference, University of Chicago, 2000; telephone interview with Larry Duckett, Oct. 5, 1999; Kara Fox, "Artist Larry Duckett Dies," *Washington Blade*, Oct. 5, 2001, p. 35.

Brett Beemyn

Due, Tananarive (born 1966). Science fiction novelist and short story writer. Due's first novel, *The Between*, was nominated for the Bram Stoker Award for Superior Achievement in a First Novel by the Horror Writers Association, and her writing since then has continued to garner critical acclaim as she weaves realism and the supernatural into fantastic **science fiction** tales. Due is the daughter of civil rights activist Patricia Stephens Due, who spent forty-nine days in jail rather than pay a fine for sitting at the segregated lunch counter of a Woolworth's store in 1960. Due has a bachelor's degree in journalism from Northwestern University and a master's degree in English literature from the University of Leeds in England, where she was a Rotary Foundation Scholar. Due has been a columnist for the *Miami Herald* and has taught at writing workshops throughout the country, including the Clarion Science Fiction and Fantasy Writers Workshop.

My Soul to Keep (1998) is, at this writing, in feature-film production by actor and producer Blair Underwood. In 2000, Due published *The Black Rose*, a fictionalized account of the life of Madame C. J. Walker, America's first Black female millionaire, philanthropist, and president of a Black beauty supply company. Walker was a key figure in the **Harlem Renaissance**. The outline for the novel was written by **Alex Haley** before his death in 1992, and the completed novel was nominated for an **NAACP** Image Award.

To commemorate her mother's civil rights activism, Due authored *Freedom in the Family: A Mother–Daughter Memoir of the Fight for Civil Rights*, with her mother in 2003. Through alternating chapters, both women detail their perspectives on the **Civil Rights Movement**, and the book features interviews with civil rights leaders such as **Stokely Carmichael** and ordinary people who made their own contributions to the movement.

Due is married to the novelist and television writer **Stephen Emory Barnes**, whom she met in 1997 at a writer's conference at Clark Atlanta University.

Resources: Tananarive Due: *The Between: A Novel* (New York: HarperCollins, 1995); *The Black Rose* (New York: Ballantine, 2000); *The Good House: A Novel* (New York: Atria Books, 2003); *The Living Blood* (New York: Washington Square Press, 2002); *My Soul to Keep* (New York: Eos, 1998); Tananarive Due and Patricia Stephens Due, *Freedom in the Family: A Mother–Daughter Memoir of the Fight for Civil Rights* (New York: Ballantine, 2003).

Roxane Gay

Duke, Lynne (born 1956). Journalist. Duke's book, *Mandela, Mobutu, and Me: A Newswoman's African Journey* (2003) springs from her experiences as a journalist-observer in South Africa. Born and raised in **Los Angeles, California**, Duke began writing at an early age. As the youngest child in a family of four spirited children, she struggled to be heard. Thus, it became a habit for her to vent through writing when she felt no one was listening to her. As a way of claiming her voice, at about the age of ten she began to keep a series of journals and diaries, a practice that would stand her in good stead in her future endeavors. She continued writing throughout out her years at Windsor Hills Elementary School and Crenshaw High School in Los Angeles. At Crenshaw, one of her teachers recognized her writing skill and encouraged her to develop it.

Duke started out as a theater major at the University of California, Los Angeles. She interrupted her college education in order to work in New York City, where she took a night job transcribing news for the Columbia Broadcasting System and fell in love with the news business. After completing an undergraduate major in political science at Columbia, she went on to earn a master's (with honors) from Columbia's Graduate School of Journalism.

That experience and training led her to her present position as a staff writer with the *Washington Post*, where, at this writing, she has worked for more than seventeen years. Before joining the staff of the *Post*, Duke wrote briefly for the *Miami Herald*, gaining some recognition there; in 1988, she was a finalist for a Pulitzer Prize. She has written on issues as varied as Clarence Thomas's Supreme Court appointment, the Sudanese refugees, Martha Stewart, Pete Rose, "White flight" from cities to suburbs, sexual abuse of Harlem Boys' Choir members, and of course, politics in Africa.

As a correspondent for the *Washington Post*, Duke was assigned to South Africa. Her first visit to the continent was in 1990, shortly after Nelson Mandela's release from his twenty-eight-year imprisonment. She traveled in and out of southern and central Africa over the next nine years, serving as bureau chief in Johannesburg for five of those years.

Duke's book is the result of her observations over that period of time. The storytelling ability that she developed early in life infuses this book. It is not simply a journalistic documentation of events but an account of those events as seen through the lens of her association with the people involved in those events. The book exhibits a compassion for the people but also a brutal honesty, as when Duke reports on the trial of Winnie Mandela.

Resource: Lynne Duke, *Mandela, Mobutu, and Me: A Newswoman's African Journey* (New York: Doubleday, 2003).

Yvonne C. Williams

Dumas, Henry (1934–1968). Short story writer, poet, and civil rights activist. Henry Dumas participated in the **Civil Rights Movement, Black Power Movement**, and **Black Arts Movement**, until he was killed by a New York City Transit policeman in a **Harlem, New York**, subway on May 23, 1968. The details of his death remain unclear, but his talent and his literary legacy have been recognized thanks in large part to his colleague, friend, and literary executor **Eugene B. Redmond**, who has edited and published several collections of Dumas's poetry and prose since his death. Dumas's work has been celebrated by the Dumas "cult" or "movement," which includes such literary and cultural notables as **Quincy Thomas Troupe**, **Maya Angelou**, **Gwendolyn Brooks**, **Toni Morrison**, and **Amiri Baraka**. Beginning with his early years in Sweet Home, Arkansas, where he was born July 20, 1934, Dumas' many experiences influenced his writing, which has been praised for its authentic voice, its mixture of natural and supernatural phenomena, its **blues** and **gospel music**, and its revolutionary politics.

At the age of ten, Dumas moved to **Harlem, New York**, where, in 1953, he graduated from Commerce High School and began studying at City College. He left college, however, to join the Air Force. After four years in the Air Force, including a year in the Arabian Peninsula, he attended Rutgers University part-time and was a full-time husband and father, supporting two sons. He operated printing machines, was a social worker for the state of New York, and served as assistant director of Upward Bound at Hiram College. During this period, he helped to develop little magazines including *Umbra*, *Camel*, *American Weave*, and **Negro Digest**, and he was active in the Civil Rights Movement. In 1967 Dumas began to work as a teacher–counselor and director of language workshops at Southern Illinois University's Experiment in Higher Education in East St. Louis, Missouri, where he met Redmond. Although Dumas contributed to the "little magazines" that he edited, published, and helped to distribute, he did not live to see his writing published in book form. Since his death in 1968, his work has continued to appear in such anthologies as *The Second Set: The Jazz Poetry Anthology*, vol. 2, and several volumes of his poems and stories have been published: *Ark of Bones and Other Stories* (1971), *Play Ebony: Play Ivory* (1974), *Rope of Wind and Other Stories* (1979), *Goodbye, Sweetwater* (1988), *Knees of a Natural Man: The Selected Poetry of Henry Dumas* (1989), and *Echo Tree: The Collected Short Fiction of Henry Dumas* (2003).

According to Redmond, Dumas's interests included religion and music. Carolyn Mitchell notes that religion and music "are intertwined as theme and motif in Dumas's fiction and poetry." Dumas was praised as "the most original Afro-American poet of the sixties" in a *New York Times Book Review* (Lester), and Clyde Taylor wrote that "Dumas aspired to the oldest, most honored version of poet/prophet to his people. He sought to incarnate their cultural identity, values, and mythic visions as well as codify and even reshape those myths into modalities of a more soulful existence." According to Redmond, Dumas is reminiscent of **James Baldwin**, **Ernest J. Gaines**, **Alice Walker**, **Toni Morrison**, **Ralph Ellison**, **Sherley Anne Williams**, and **Lance Jeffers** "in his earth lore, his cultural reclamations and his creative far reach," although there is "a mellowed-down freshness in Dumas...he is both ancient and contemporary" (iv).

Resources: Henry Dumas: *Ark of Bones, and Other Stories*, ed. Hale Chatfield and Eugene Redmond (Carbondale: Southern Illinois University Press, 1971); *Goodbye Sweetwater: New and Selected Stories*, ed. Eugene Redmond (New York: Thunder's

Mouth Press, 1988); *Knees of a Natural Man: The Selected Poetry of Henry Dumas*, ed. Eugene Redmond (New York: Thunder's Mouth Press, 1989); *Play Ebony: Play Ivory*, ed. Eugene B. Redmond (New York: Random House, 1974); *Poetry for My People*, ed. Hale Chatfield and Eugene Redmond (Carbondale: Southern Illinois University Press, 1970); *Rope of Wind and Other Stories*, ed. Eugene B. Redmond (New York: Random House, 1979); Eugene B. Redmond: "The Ancient and Recent Voices within Henry Dumas," introduction to *Goodbye, Sweetwater* (New York: Thunder's Mouth Press, 1988); "Introduction," in *Ark of Bones and Other Stories* (Carbondale: Southern Illinois University Press, 1974), i–xviii; "Introduction," in *Knees of a Natural Man* (New York: Thunder's Mouth Press, 1989); Clyde Taylor, "Henry Dumas: Legacy of a Longbreath Singer," *Black World*, Sept. 24, 1975.

Deborah Brown

Dunbar, Paul Laurence (1872–1906). Poet, essayist, fiction writer, playwright, and songwriter. Paul Laurence Dunbar was the first African American author to gain national acclaim before the **Harlem Renaissance**. He was born in Dayton, Ohio, to former Kentucky slaves, Matilda and Joshua Dunbar. His father escaped **slavery** by fleeing to freedom in Canada, then returned to the United States and joined the Massachusetts 55th Regiment and the 5th Massachusetts Colored Cavalry during the **Civil War**. Matilda, a widow with two sons, was freed after the Civil War. During Dunbar's childhood years, his father told him plantation stories, and his mother recited poetry to him. Although Dunbar himself had not been enslaved, he interacted with the last generation of African Americans who were slaves. This early influence shaped his renowned Southern plantation Negro **dialect poems**. At age six he composed his first poem (Cunningham, 10). In developing his own poetic voice, Dunbar read the works of Oliver Wendell Holmes, Henry Wadsworth Longfellow, John Keats, and Alfred Lord Tennyson. His mother supported Dunbar throughout his writing career and ensured that he received his education, despite the family's poverty. The only African American student at Dayton Central High, Dunbar excelled in academics and extracurricular activities. He served as editor of the school's newspaper, was president of the Literary Society, and was a member of the debating team. He and a classmate, Orville Wright, edited a short-lived community Black newspaper, the *Dayton Tattler*.

After he graduated from high school in 1891, racial discrimination prevented Dunbar from attending college. He took a job in Dayton's Callahan Building as an elevator operator. When he wasn't running the elevator, he wrote poetry. He also published essays in local newspapers and magazines. Dunbar became locally known after James Newton Mathews invited him to recite his poetry at the Western Association of Writers yearly meeting in Dayton. Financial backing from Mathews allowed Dunbar to publish his first book of poetry, *Oak and Ivy*, in 1893. Also that year, he attended the World's Columbian Exposition, worked as a clerk for the Haitian Pavilion, and met **Frederick Douglass**. Douglass referred to Dunbar as "one of the sweetest songsters his race has produced of whom I hope great things" (Cunningham, 105).

Paul Laurence Dunbar, 1890. Courtesy of the Library of Congress.

In 1895, Dunbar moved to Toledo, Ohio, with the help of a psychiatrist, Dr. H. A. Tobey, and a lawyer, Charles Thatcher, both fans of his work. They arranged opportunities for Dunbar to recite his poems publicly, and they financially backed his second book, *Majors and Minors* (1896). The "majors" were Dunbar's poems written in Standard English verse, while his "minors" were poems written in Southern plantation Negro dialect. "*Majors and Minors* [became] the most notable collection of poems ever issued by a Negro in the United States" (Brawley, 40). During this time, Dunbar began corresponding with Alice Ruth Moore, a light-skinned teacher and writer from **New Orleans, Louisiana**. In 1897, he traveled to London on a poetry recitation tour. Upon returning to the United States, he married Alice and worked as a reading room assistant in the Library of Congress until 1898. However, Dunbar's health declined, possibly because of exposure to dust while working in the library. He developed tuberculosis and drank alcohol to cure it. From 1898 to 1900, he collaborated with Will Cook on Black musical plays. He separated from Alice in 1902 and continued to write until his death in 1906.

A versatile writer, Dunbar published short stories, novels, theatrical contributions, song lyrics, and articles. His novels include *Folks from Dixie* (1898), *Sport of the Gods* (1902), *The Strength of Gideon & Other Stories* (1900), and *The Fanatics* (1901). His theatrical contributions include *Clorindy, or the Origin of the Cakewalk* (1898) and *In Dahomey: A Negro Musical Comedy* (1902).

It was rare during this time for a Black writer to achieve notoriety in such mainstream magazines as the *Saturday Evening Post*, *Harper's Weekly*, and *The Atlantic Monthly*. Dunbar marked a place in African American history by being the first Black author to be read by Blacks and Whites before the Harlem Renaissance. Prominent White author and literary critic William Dean Howells praised *Majors and Minors* in an 1896 book review in *Harper's Weekly*. Although this review propelled Dunbar into national recognition, his work, specifically the dialect pieces, garnered both acclaim and criticism. Blacks accused him of conceding to racist ideals in his dialect pieces. He often struggled between being a martyr for the African American plight and being accepted by White audiences. Since Dunbar's dialect pieces attracted more attention from the mainstream, he will always be remembered as a prominent African American dialect writer.

Resources: Primary Sources: Paul Laurence Dunbar: *Clorindy, or the Origin of the Cakewalk*, music by Will Marion Cook and lyrics by Paul Laurence Dunbar (New York: Witmark Music, 1898); *The Collected Poetry of Paul Laurence Dunbar*, ed. Joanne Braxton (Charlottesville: University Press of Virginia, 1993); *Dream Lovers: An Operatic Romance*, with music by Samuel Coleridge-Taylor (London: Boosey, 1898); *Folks from Dixie* (New York: Dodd, Mead, 1898); *In His Own Voice: The Dramatic and Other Uncollected Works of Paul Laurence Dunbar*, ed. Herbert Woodward Martin and Ronald Primeau (Athens: Ohio University Press, 2002); *Lyrics of Love and Laughter* (New York: Dodd, Mead, 1903); *Lyrics of Lowly Life* (New York: Dodd, Mead, 1896); *Lyrics of Sunshine and Shadow* (New York: Dodd, Mead, 1905); *Lyrics of the Hearthside* (New York: Dodd, Mead, 1899); *Majors and Minors* (Toledo, OH: Hadley & Hadley, 1895); *Oak and Ivy* (Dayton, OH: United Brethren Publishing House, 1893); *Poems of Cabin and Field* (New York: Dodd, Mead, 1899); *The Sport of the Gods* (New York: Dodd, Mead, 1902); *When Malindy Sings* (New York: Dodd, Mead, 1903). **Secondary Sources:** Robert Bone, *Down Home: A History of Afro-American Short Fiction from Its Beginnings to the End of the Harlem Renaissance* (New York: Putnam's, 1975); Benjamin G. Brawley, *Paul Laurence Dunbar: Poet of His People* (Chapel Hill: University of North Carolina Press, 1936); Virginia Cunningham, *Paul Laurence Dunbar and His Song* (New York: Dodd, Mead, 1947); Christopher C. DeSantis, "The Dangerous Marrow of Southern Tradition: Charles W. Chesnutt, Paul Laurence Dunbar, and the Paternalist Ethos at the Turn of the Century," *Southern Quarterly* 38 (Winter 2000), 79–97; James Weldon Johnson, *The Book of American Negro Poetry* (New York: Harcourt, Brace, 1922; rev. ed., 1931); Jay Martin, ed., *A Singer in the Dawn: Reinterpretations of Paul Laurence Dunbar* (New York: Dodd, Mead, 1975); William M. Ramsey, "Dunbar's Dixie," *Southern Literary Journal* 32 (1999), 30–45; J. Saunders Redding, *To Make a Poet Black* (Chapel Hill: University of North Carolina Press, 1939); Peter Revell, *Paul Laurence Dunbar* (Boston: Twayne, 1979); Jean Wagner, *Black Poets of the United States, from Paul Laurence Dunbar to Langston Hughes* (Urbana: University of Illinois Press, 1973); Lida Keck Wiggins, *The Life and Works of Paul Laurence Dunbar* (Naperville, IL: J. L. Nichols, 1907).

Shawntaye M. Scott

Dunbar-Nelson, Alice Moore (1875–1935). Short story writer, poet, journalist, and dramatist. Alice Dunbar-Nelson was the only African American woman to publish a collection of short stories as part of the vastly popular local color movement of the nineteenth century (Menke, 78). This noteworthy milestone in American literary history, though, did not guarantee widespread recognition or appreciation of her writing. As a matter of fact, it was just in the last decade or two of the twentieth century—and in no small part due to the efforts of the scholar **Gloria Hull**—that scholars and critics have begun to look more closely and seriously at Dunbar-Nelson's literary output.

A small volume titled *Violets and Other Tales*, containing romantic poems, sketches, and sentimental short stories, was published under her maiden name,

Alice Ruth Moore, in 1895. It received pleasant but moderated response from reviewers. Many critics at the time were predisposed to consider women's writing as little more than a nicety. Nevertheless, one admiring reader, **Paul Laurence Dunbar**, felt it provided glimpses of a talent very much akin to George Washington Cable's. (The comparison to Cable has continued to this day and is understandable, given that both he and Dunbar-Nelson were from **New Orleans, Louisiana**, and given his place in the local color tradition.) Dunbar corresponded with Alice Moore for a couple of years, and the two were married in 1898.

The collection *The Goodness of St. Rocque and Other Stories* (1899) came out the year following their marriage and was dedicated to Paul Laurence Dunbar. (The couple separated a few years later, and she wed the journalist Robert J. Nelson in 1916, after a marriage to a teaching colleague, Henry Callis, was dissolved.) Rich in atmosphere and scenery, the short stories in this second collection are much more than entertaining diversions and light reading in the local color vein. The stories grapple with serious issues such as immigration, labor strife, poverty, and, in a subtly covert way, **race**. While most of the stories have **White** characters and Creoles of indeterminate ancestry, "Mr. Baptiste," for example, illustrates how race hatred exacerbates a workers' riot. Additionally, the story "Sister Josepha" engages in considerations of uncertain racial identity in a world where certainty was required. For the most part, however, it was possible for middle-class, White readers to overlook race and racial **passing**, subjects many of them found unseemly for literature, and instead to dwell on the parade of White characters in their sultry settings and with their quaint, exotic ways.

These casts of White characters appear in more than just the two published collections. The novella *A Modern Undine*, written sometime around 1900, was never published. In the novella, an aristocratic White Southern woman marries a successful White Northern man. The issue of race never enters into this novella; it is far more concerned with the tightly circumscribed role for women at the turn of the century. Similarly, a group of short stories (only a couple of which were ever published) that Dunbar-Nelson worked on during the first decade of the 1900s and that she planned to gather in a collection to be titled *The Annals of 'Steenth Street*, highlights economic hardships and class issues among European immigrants in New York City.

Scholars have noted the irony of this African American woman writing so many pieces populated by White characters. To some, it seems as if she were trying to sidestep matters of race or separating herself from the plight of Black people. Dunbar-Nelson was an extremely light-skinned, reddish-haired woman of mixed Caucasian, African American, and Native American ancestry. She also relished her **Creole** heritage. But whether she succumbed to her own type of intraracial bigotry or conformed to the reading public's demands, we may never know with certainty what motivated her artistic decisions concerning the complexion of her characters. Whatever the case, race and racism in the United States were not ignored by Alice Dunbar-Nelson. She campaigned for the ill-fated Dyer Anti-Lynching Bill debated in Congress in 1922 (*see* **Lynching**).

Dunbar-Nelson used her positions in education and in women's clubs to fight for racial justice. In 1914 she gathered, edited, and published a group of speeches to commemorate the fiftieth anniversary of the Emancipation Proclamation. This anthology, titled *Masterpieces of Negro Eloquence, 1818–1913*, represents her attempt to compile exemplary orations by African Americans for future generations of Black children. Finally, in her own writing, her most explicit work dealing with the issue of race can be found in her journalism and essays. For example, her journalistic piece from the late 1920s, "Brass Ankles Speaks," expresses her outrage at dark-skinned African Americans' bias against lighter-skinned Blacks. Her short story "The Stones of the Village" and her three-act play *Gone White*—both of which were written in the early 1900s and remained unpublished in her lifetime—deal with racial passing.

Resources: Violet Harrington Bryan, "Race and Gender in the Early Works of Alice Dunbar-Nelson," in *Louisiana Women Writers: New Essays and a Comprehensive Bibliography*, ed. Dorothy H. Brown and Barbara C. Ewell (Baton Rouge: Louisiana State University Press, 1992), 121–138; Alice Dunbar-Nelson: *Give Us Each Day: The Diary of Alice Dunbar-Nelson*, ed. Gloria T. Hull (New York: Norton, 1984); *The Works of Alice Dunbar-Nelson*, ed. Gloria T. Hull, 3 vols. (New York: Oxford University Press, 1988); Alice Dunbar-Moore, ed., *Masterpieces of Negro Eloquence, 1818–1913* (Mineola, NY: Dover, 2000); Jürgen Grandt, "Rewriting the Final Adjustment of Affairs: Culture, Race, and Politics in Alice Dunbar-Nelson's New Orleans," *Short Story* 9, no. 1 (2001), 46–57; Charmaine N. Ijeoma, "Alice Dunbar-Nelson: A Biography," *Collections* 10 (2000): 25–54; Pamela Glenn Menke, "Behind the 'White Veil': Alice Dunbar-Nelson, Creole Color, and *The Goodness of St. Rocque*," in *Songs of the Reconstructing South: Building Literary Louisiana, 1865–1945*, ed. Suzanne Disheroon-Green and Lisa Abney (Westport, CT: Greenwood Press, 2002), 77–88.

Timothy K. Nixon

Duncan, Thelma Myrtle (born 1902). Playwright. Duncan, the author of at least seven one-act plays in diverse settings and about diverse subjects, has gained recognition as an early twentieth-century forerunner of African American woman playwrights such as **Lorraine Hansberry**, **Alice Childress**, and **Suzan-Lori Parks**.

Thelma Duncan was born in **St. Louis, Missouri**, and received her higher education at Howard University in **Washington, D.C.**, and New York's Columbia University. Her first play, *The Death Dance* (1923), written while a student in Montgomery Gregory's drama class at Howard, was published in the 1927 collection *Plays of Negro Life*. In the play, one of the first performed by the Howard University Players, Duncan uses the story of a young West African warrior accused of stealing gold to explore universal themes of loyalty, guilt, and rebellion against corrupt authority. Her second published play, *Sacrifice* (1930), explores similar themes in a contemporary urban setting. In this drama, a young African American student named Billy faces the consequences of stealing a chemistry exam, with the help of his friend Ray. Duncan's play *Black Magic* was published in the 1931 collection

Yearbook of Short Plays, edited by Claude Merton Wise and Lee Owen Snook.

Duncan's unpublished plays include *Driftin'*, a three-character drama set in a bar that explores the dynamics of African American romantic relationships; *Jinda*, a play set in India with Indian protagonists; and *Payment*, a drama about race relations that features both African American and Caucasian characters.

In later life, Duncan worked as a music teacher and continued to write. In 1932, she married and moved to Alberquerque, New Mexico. Howard's Moorland-Spingarn Research Center preserved the original manuscripts of her unpublished works.

Resources: Kyleelise Holmes, "Duncan, Thelma Myrtle," in *Black Drama* [electronic database], http://www.alexanderstreetz.com (Alexandria, VA: Alexander Street Press, 2004); Alain Locke, ed., *Plays of Negro Life: A Source-Book of Native American Drama* (New York: Harper & Bros., 1927); Willis Richardson, ed., *Plays and Pageants from the Life of the Negro* (Jackson: University Press of Mississippi, 1993); Claude Merton Wise and Lee Owen Snook, eds., *The Yearbook of Short Plays: New Non-Royalty Plays Designed for Study and Production* (Evanston, IL: Row, Peterson, 1931); Scott Zaluda, "Lost Voices of the Harlem Renaissance: Writing Assigned at Howard University, 1919–1931," *College Composition and Communication* 50, no. 2 (Dec. 1998), 232–257, see 249–250.

Melissa Shields

Dunham, Katherine (born 1909). Choreographer, dancer, scholar, writer, and teacher. Dunham is a nationally and internationally acclaimed dancer and choreographer, known especially for her innovations in modern dance. She worked with African Caribbean and African American dance traditions and developed them into her own technique. The vibrant, passionate, and syncopated movements in Dunham's choreography express great energy.

Dunham was born in Joliet, Illinois, and grew up in **Chicago, Illinois**. In the 1930s, Dunham earned degrees from the University of Chicago in anthropology, including a Ph.D. She also studied with Melville Herskovits at Northwestern University. Her background in anthropology inspired her dance performances and choreography. In the late 1930s she founded the Katherine Dunham Dance Company, choreographed for the Negro Federal Theatre Project, and choreographed for the New York Labor Stage. Subsequently, she acted and danced in the films *Cabin in the Sky* (1940) and *Stormy Weather* (1943). With George Ballanchine, she choreographed the dances. (*See* **Federal Writers' Project.**)

In addition to her artistic work, Dunham is the author of *Island Possessed*; *Dances of Haiti*; *Katherine Dunham's Journey to Accompong*; and *A Touch of Innocence*, which is her **autobiography**. *Island Possessed* chronicles her ethnographic experience in **Haiti**.

Dunham has visited, researched, taught and performed in Africa, the West Indies, North America, Europe, Asia, and Latin America. She also served as cultural advisor to Senegal. Besides her books, she has published several scholarly articles.

In 1967, Dunham joined the faculty of Southern Illinois University (SIU) at Edwardsville, and she founded the Performing Arts Training Center at the SIU branch campus in East St. Louis, Illinois. She has received a Guggenheim Award to support her dissertation research, the University of Chicago Alumni Professional Achievement Award, and the Kennedy Center Award. After retiring from SIU, she created her own arts center. At this writing she lives in East Saint Louis, where she is the executive director and founder of the Katherine Dunham Centers for Arts and Humanities.

Resources: Amy Alexander, *Fifty Black Women Who Changed America* (Sacramento, CA: Kensington Press/Citadel Press, 1999); Joyce Aschenbrenner: *Katherine Dunham: A Dancing Life* (Chicago: University of Illinois Press, 2002); "Katherine Dunham," in *Black Women in America*, ed. Darlene Clark Hine (Brooklyn, NY: Carlson, 1993); Katherine Dunham: *Afro-Caribbean Songs and Rhythms* (New York: Decca, 1946), vinyl disc; *Dances of Haiti* (Los Angeles: Center for Afro American Studies, UCLA, 1983); *Island Possessed* (Chicago: University of Chicago Press, 1994); *Katherine Dunham's Journey to Accompong* (New York: Henry Holt, 1946); *A Touch of Innocence: Memoirs of Childhood* (1959; repr. Chicago: University of Chicago Press, 1994); James Haskins, *Katherine Dunham* (New York: Coward, McCann & Geoghegan, 1982); Chris Hegedus, D. A. Pennebaker, and David Hawkins, directors, *Dance Black America*, videorecording (New York: Pennebaker Associates, 1984), includes dance choreographed by Dunham.

Shondrika L. Moss

Katherine Dunham, 1956. Courtesy of the Library of Congress.

Durem, Ray (1915–1963). Poet and political activist. Ray Durem was born in Seattle, Washington; received little formal education; and ran away from home at age fourteen. While still underage, he enlisted in the Navy, and later fought in the Abraham Lincoln Brigade in the Spanish Civil War. Born into a mixed-race family, he had the appearance of a **White** man, but resolutely lived as a Black man. Durem contended that his ability to pass gave him special insight into White racism. This perspective emerged in his poetry, in observations ranging from pithy aphorisms to scathing condemnations. Working on the West Coast in factories, shops, and warehouses, he became a voracious reader. Durem started to write poetry in the 1940s because "My hope is that my poems will play some role in arousing that righteous anger and fury and willingness to die without which no people wins its liberty." Durem's poetry was first published in *The Crusader*, edited by Robert Williams. His poetry attracted the attention of **Langston Hughes**, who introduced his work to the London-based publisher-editor Paul Breman. This contact resulted in a lasting friendship, as well as the publication of a group of Durem's poems in Breman's anthology *Sixes and Sevens* (1962). Other poems by Durem appeared, posthumously, in anthologies and magazines including *Phylon*, *Venture*, the *Herald Dispatch*, *New Negro Poets, U.S.A.* (edited by Langston Hughes, 1964), the *Umbra Anthology* (1967), and *Soulscript*, edited by June Jordan (1970).

Durem's political views as expressed in the aggressively race-oriented aesthetic of his poems made him a precursor of the **Black Arts Movement**. His only poetry collection, *Take No Prisoners* (1971), appeared long after his death. Durem's legacy is his acerbic topical wit as exemplified in frequently quoted poems such as "Award," "Broadminded," and "Reflection," which reads in total: "Sometimes I think, how very odd—/the black man worships the white man's god." Durem's poem "A Decoration for the President," a biting commentary on President Kennedy's Cuban policies, is regarded as the reason that the Umbra Literary Society broke up, due to editorial dissension over whether or not to publish the poem in the aftermath of Kennedy's assassination. Durem died of cancer in 1963. He was a poet ahead of his time, one whose views, in hindsight, anticipated the Black Arts Movement's endorsement of separatism, **Black Nationalism**, and art that calls for radical action.

Resources: Arnold Adoff, ed., *The Poetry of Black America: Anthology of the Twentieth Century* (New York: Harper & Row, 1973); Paul Breman, ed., *You Better Believe It: Black Verse in English* (Harmondsworth, UK: Penguin, 1973); Ray Durem, *Take No Prisoners* (London: Paul Breman, 1971); Langston Hughes, ed., *New Negro Poets, U.S.A.* (Bloomington: Indiana University Press, 1964).

Lauri Ramey

Durham, David Anthony (born 1969). Novelist, short story writer, and educator. David Anthony Durham is the author of two historical novels: *Gabriel's Story* (2001) and *A Walk Through Darkness* (2002) (*see* **Historical Fiction**). *Gabriel's Story* fictionalizes the often overlooked push westward by Blacks following the **Civil War**. *A Walk Through Darkness* is the story of a slave who escapes his master in an attempt to find his spouse and child.

Durham's parents are of African Caribbean ancestry; he was born in New York City but spent his formative years in Trinidad. Durham attended the University of Maryland, receiving his B.A. in 1992 and his M.F.A. in 1996. He has traveled broadly within the United States, and has worked as a whitewater rafting guide, a wilderness course leader for Outward Bound, a substitute teacher in Maryland, a bartender, and a sushi chef. Durham has also traveled extensively outside the United States and has lived in the Caribbean, Central America, and Europe.

Durham's short stories have appeared in the literary journals *Bartleby*, *Catalyst*, *QWF*, and *Staple: New Writing*. Writing awards that Durham has received include the Dolphin Moon Press Prize (1991), the Malcolm C. Braly

Fiction Prize (1991), the Zora Neale Hurston/Richard Wright Fiction Award (1992), the Borders Original Voices Award (2001), the Hurston/Wright Award for debut fiction and the Zora Neale Hurston/Richard Wright Foundation and Borders Books Award for *Gabriel's Story* (2002). Durham now divides his time between the United States and Scotland.

Resources: David Anthony Durham: *Gabriel's Story* (New York: Doubleday, 2001); *A Walk Through Darkness* (New York: Doubleday, 2002); Robert Fleming, "PW Talks to David Anthony Durham," *Publishers Weekly*, Apr. 1, 2002, p. 50; John Lowe, "Exodus, Race, and the American West," *World and I*, Aug. 2001, 218; Paul Spillenger, "First Novels, Lasting Lessons," *Washington Post*, Jan. 8, 2001, p. C5.

Michelle LaFrance

Dyson, Michael Eric (born 1958). Journalist and cultural critic. Like **Henry Louis Gates, Jr.**, **bell hooks**, and **Cornel West**, Michael Eric Dyson is a Black public intellectual whose work has found audiences in the U.S. academy and popular media alike. His criticism has broadened the pedagogical scope of African American cultural inquiry to include not just literature and written expression but also film, television, sport, and popular music. He also has promoted critical analysis of Black political and cultural celebrity from the **Civil Rights Movement** to the present.

Dyson is Avalon Professor in the Humanities at the University of Pennsylvania, where he teaches courses in the Religious Studies Department and in the Afro-American Studies Program. He has also taught at the Chicago Theological Seminary, the University of North Carolina at Chapel Hill, and Brown, Columbia, and DePaul universities. He is a weekly columnist for the *Chicago Sun-Times* and a commentator for **Tavis Smiley**'s National Public Radio program.

Born in **Detroit, Michigan**, in 1958, the second of five sons, Dyson graduated from public school in 1976 after having been expelled from a boarding school for battling with classmates over an issue of prejudice. In the troubled years thereafter, he attended church religiously and became a Baptist minister by the time he was only twenty-one. Recognizing that he needed to continue his education in order to provide material support for his young son, Dyson moved to **the South** and earned his B.A. from Carson-Newman College in Jefferson City, Tennessee, in 1982. Dyson then spent several years as a freelance journalist, contributing music reviews to *Rolling Stone*, and book and film reviews to nationally syndicated newspapers; he also wrote columns for *Christian Century* and *The Nation*. The articles, essays, and reviews Dyson published during this brief but enormously productive period earned him the 1992 Magazine Award from the National Association of Black Journalists. He returned to the academy to earn his M.A. and Ph.D. in religion from Princeton University in 1991 and 1993, respectively.

Dyson's first book, *Reflecting Black* (1993), collects key statements and thought pieces on Black popular culture that he composed as a journalist. The collection was met with enthusiasm, for it signaled a "new direction" in African American critical thought by dealing with precisely those cultural texts that traditional academics and intellectuals did not deem fit for scholarly inquiry. From Michael Jackson's "postmodern spirituality" to the "pedagogy of desire" engendered by **Michael Jordan**'s physique, Dyson combines engaging intellectual discourse with a flair for the popular, identifying the constitutive traits of contemporary Black cultural expression while critiquing their supposed essentialism. He notes, "An oppositional African-American cultural criticism holds that identity is socially and culturally constructed from the raw materials of the individual and social, the private and public, and the domestic and civic. Racial identity is not exhausted by genetic inheritance" (xx). *Reflecting Black* has also received praise for negotiating religious ethics and faith within the putatively secular realm of intellectual discourse. *Between God and Gangsta Rap* (1996) and *Open Mike* (2002) advance Dyson's vision of academic vocation along similar lines.

Making Malcolm (1995) signals Dyson's attempt to cut through the "myth" surrounding **Malcolm X**'s life and teachings so that the civil rights leader's work might be usefully taken up by younger and future generations of activists and concerned citizens. Central to his analysis is a questioning of **Black Nationalism**'s racially essentialist tenets, as well as a critique of the mass media's appropriation of Malcolm X's image to depoliticizing ends. Dyson refers to the particular form of critical writing that he employs in *Making Malcolm* as "biocriticism." This accessible fusion of biography and cultural inquiry informs his studies of a handful of other twentieth-century African American icons: religious and civil rights leader **Martin Luther King, Jr.** (2000); slain **hip-hop** star **Tupac Shakur** (2001); and, most recently, the legendary master of **soul**, Marvin Gaye (2004).

Resources: Sidney I. Dobrin, "Race and the Public Intellectual: A Conversation with Michael Eric Dyson," in *Race, Rhetoric, and the Postcolonial*, ed. Gary A. Olson and Lynn Worsham (Albany: State University of New York Press, 1999), 81–126; Michael Eric Dyson: *Between God and Gangsta Rap: Bearing Witness to Black Culture* (New York: Oxford University Press, 1996); *Holler If You Hear Me: Searching for Tupac Shakur* (New York: Basic Civitas, 2001); *I May Not Get There with You: The True Martin Luther King, Jr.* (New York: Free Press, 2000); *Making Malcolm: The Myth and Meaning of Malcolm X* (New York: Oxford University Press, 1995); *Mercy, Mercy Me: The Art, Loves, and Demons of Marvin Gaye* (New York: Basic Civitas, 2004); *Open Mike: Reflections on Philosophy, Race, Sex, Culture, and Religion* (New York: Basic Civitas, 2002); *Race Rules: Navigating the Color Line* (Reading, MA: Addison-Wesley, 1996); *Reflecting Black: African-American Cultural Criticism* (Minneapolis: University of Minnesota Press, 1993); *Why I Love Black Women* (New York: Basic Civitas, 2003).

Kinohi Nishikawa

Dystopian Literature. The word "dystopia" is of Greek origin and usually means an imaginary "bad place." It signifies the opposite of utopia, and for that reason is sometimes called "anti-utopia." Yet it is important to keep in mind that the utopian and dystopian concepts are relative because they depend largely on the reader's point of view toward social, political, or interpersonal conditions. Sometimes, by extrapolating current political, economic, and social trends to outlandish extremes, writers of dystopian fiction warn about the potential future developments of contemporary society. Dystopian visions are almost always set in the future and portray conditions that are dreadful and undesirable, but not unimaginable in comparison with the current society. The ruling power of the dystopia is often in hands of a totalitarian dictatorship, which is characterized by bureaucracy, suppression of the individual and his or her humanity, instigation of fear, and insistence on total submission of its citizens.

While some of H. G. Wells's early works could be considered dystopian—for example, *The Time Machine* (1895)—dystopian fiction as a genre did not become widely popular until the twentieth century, during which period people experienced the Bolshevik Revolution in Russia, two world wars, the development and delivery of nuclear bombs, the **Cold War**, the expansion of transportation and communication, and rapid technological progress. While people welcomed new inventions and the increased standard of living, they also became concerned about the position of the individual in society, the routinization of work, the growing destructive power of new weapons, and ecological consequences of their fast-paced and industrialized lives. These concerns are reflected in many dystopias. *Iron Heel* (1907), by Jack London, is a narrative of Avis Everhard, the wife of a revolutionary, Ernest Everhard, who participates in preparations for a revolution in order to overthrow the rule of the tyrannical and exploitive Oligarchy, also referred to as the Iron Heel. In 1921, the Czech writer Karel Capek produced his play *R.U.R.: Rossum's Universal Robots*. The play introduced a new word, "robot," and presented a world where humans are destroyed by their machines. Another important dystopian work is the novel *We* (1924), by Eugene Zamyiatin, a book Gorman Beauchamp calls "not only Zamiatin's most important work, but . . . arguably the most effective of all the dystopian depictions of the technological abolition of man" (56).

Brave New World (1932), a novel by Aldous Huxley, increased the popularity of dystopian fiction. As William Matter points out, Huxley began writing the novel as a parody of H. G. Wells's *Men Like Gods* (1923), but produced a "masterpiece of dystopian fiction—an incisive, satiric attack upon twentieth century man's sometimes ingenuous trust in progress through science and mechanization" (94). The story takes place more than 600 years in the future, in the year A.F. 632 (After Ford). Immediately following birth, a person is placed into one of five castes (the Alphas, Betas, Gammas, Deltas, and Epsilons), each programmed through special educational techniques to be satisfied with their status and to lack any desire for change. Bernard Marx, one of the two main characters, is banished to the Falkland Islands, where he is to live in isolation with only a few others who also have shown rebellious characters. The other central figure, John the Savage, takes his own life as he realizes that the choices he is offered—the life in his Indian reservation or the life in the sterile, anonymous, and mechanized brave new world—do not provide more than a choice "between insanity on the one hand and lunacy on the other" (Huxley, viii).

George Orwell, whose real name was Eric Arthur Blair, created an even more terrifying vision than Huxley's in his book *1984* (1949). Where Huxley's brave new world is, at least on the surface, clean, productive, comfortable, and trouble-free, Orwell paints a picture of not-so-distant future in a superstate called Oceania, where all of the citizens are ruled by the Party and the ultimate dictator, Big Brother. The historical data are continuously revised and rewritten, Newspeak (the approved language) has reduced words to a bare minimum, and people are stripped of all luxuries, living in shabbiness and discomfort. The Party's quest for power for power's sake is achieved through the annihilation of individual; thus, sex and personal pleasure are the only ways of subversion. Winston Smith and his lover, Julia, represent two different ways of resistance against the regime. While Winston wishes to transform the rules, Julia's ambition is more private; her main goal is only to break the rules. The all-powerful character of the ruling class and its total subjugation of humanity are accentuated by the fact that Winston's and Julia's attempts at defiance result in failure.

There are, of course, many other notable dystopias that followed Huxley's and Orwell's visions of the future. *Fahrenheit 451* (1953), by Ray Bradbury, is the story of a fireman, Guy Montag, whose job is to burn books. As the novel progresses, Montag realizes how empty his life has been, and at the end of the novel, he joins group of rebellious intellectuals who memorize books in hopes that they may be of benefit to humankind in the future. In *Player Piano* (1952), a novel by Kurt Vonnegut, people are divided into two major classes (the managerial and engineering elite and the masses), technology has almost completely taken over humans, and the United States is ruled by an enormous computer named EPICAC XIV. In *Make Room! Make Room!* (1966), a novel by Harry Harrison, overpopulation is the major problem, and people must live in scarcity and constant fear for life. *A Clockwork Orange* (1962), by Anthony Burgess; *Heroes and Villains*, by Angela Carter (1969); *The Handmaid's Tale* (1986), by Margaret Atwood; *He, She, and It* (1991), by Marge Piercy; and *Slow River* (1995), by Nicola Griffith, are yet other examples of dystopias written in the twentieth century.

Postapocalyptic fiction became a specific subgenre of dystopian literature during the Cold War, although some older works could also qualify as postapocalyptic, such as *The Last Man* (1826), by Mary Wollstonecraft Shelley. The typical story usually involves a nuclear war (or another world-scale catastrophe) that wipes out the majority of the population on Earth; savage behavior, violence, and struggle for food and shelter are main characteristics of such narratives. Examples of postapocalyptic fiction include *Earth Abides* (1949), by George R. Stewart; *The Day of the Triffids* (1951), by John Wyndham; *On the Beach* (1957), by Neville Shute; *Alas, Babylon* (1959), by Pat Frank; *Level Seven* (1959), by Mordecai Roshwald; *The Wind from Nowhere* (1962), by J. G. Ballard; *Riddley Walker* (1980), by Russell Hoban; *Fiskadoro* (1985), by Denis Johnson; and *Forever Peace* (1997), by Joe Haldeman.

African American dystopian genre literature is not yet abundant, arguably because African Americans, by necessity, have had to confront the real dystopian past of **slavery** and segregation, as opposed to an imagined dystopian future. Nonetheless, there are undoubtedly considerable dystopian elements in works by **Sutton E. Griggs**, **Samuel R. Delany**, **Stephen Emory Barnes**, and others. **Octavia E. Butler**'s Xenogenesis trilogy—*Dawn* (1987), *Adulthood Rites* (1988), and *Imago* (1989)—does end with a renewed hope for humanity, but it also includes dystopian features. For example, Earth is destroyed by nuclear war, genetic alteration of humans by extraterrestrial beings called Oankali is commonplace, and temporary infertility has been artificially imposed on humans. In her Earthseed books—*Parable of the Sower* (1993) and *Parable of the Talents* (1998)—Butler presents a community transformed by a catastrophe. The group of desperate people led by Lauren Oya Olamina Bankole attempt to start over by changing their ways of living and possibly by leaving the planet Earth. While traveling with her companions and trying to establish a new settlement, Lauren develops a new religion, Earthseed, in hopes that by teaching and following its edicts, people can create a better society and rectify their problems. **LeVar Burton** envisions in his debut novel *Aftermath: A Novel of the Future* (1997) a near-future Earth shaken by race riots, natural disasters, and other problems.

Resources: Primary Sources: Margaret Atwood, *The Handmaid's Tale* (Boston: Houghton Mifflin, 1986); Ray Bradbury, *Fahrenheit 451* (1953; repr. New York: Simon and Schuster, 1967); Anthony Burgess, *A Clockwork Orange* (1962; repr. New York: W. W. Norton, 1986); Angela Carter, *Heroes and Villains* (1969; repr. New York: Penguin, 1983); Nicola Griffith, *Slow River* (New York: Ballantine, 1995); Aldous Huxley, *Brave New World* (New York: HarperCollins, 1998); Jack London, *The Iron Heel* (New York: Grosset & Dunlap, 1907); George Orwell, *1984* (New York: Harcourt Brace Jovanovich, 1949); Marge Piercy, *He, She, and It* (New York: Knopf, 1991); Kurt Vonnegut, Jr., *Player Piano* (1952; repr. New York: Holt, Rinehart and Winston, 1966); H. G. Wells: *Men Like Gods* (New York: Macmillan, 1923); *The Time Machine and The War of the Worlds* (New York: Oxford University Press, 1977); Yevgeny Zamiyatin, *We*, trans. Mira Ginsburg (New York: Viking Press, 1972). **Secondary Sources:** Raffaella Baccolini and Tom Moylan, eds., *Dark Horizons: Science Fiction and the Dystopian Imagination* (New York: Routledge, 2003); Gorman Beauchamp, "Zamiatin's *We*," in *No Place Else: Explorations in Utopian and Dystopian Fiction*, ed. Eric S. Rabkin, Martin Harry Greenberg, and Joseph D. Olander (Carbondale: Southern Illinois University Press, 1983); M. Keith Booker: *The Dystopian Impulse in Modern Literature: Fiction as Social Criticism* (Westport, CT: Greenwood Press, 1994); *Dystopian Literature: A Theory and Research Guide* (Westport, CT: Greenwood Press, 1994); Erika Gottlieb, *Dystopian Fiction East and West: Universe of Terror and Trial* (Ithaca, NY: McGill–Queen's University Press, 2001); Krishan Kumar, *Utopia and Anti-Utopia in Modern Times* (Oxford: Blackwell, 1987); William Matter; "On *Brave New World*," in *No Place Else: Explorations in Utopian and Dystopian Fiction*, ed. Eric S. Rabkin, Martin Harry Greenberg, and Joseph D. Olander (Carbondale: Southern Illinois University Press, 1983).

Iva Balic

E

Eady, Cornelius (born 1954). Poet, playwright, professor, and political activist. Eady is an award-winning poet whose many honors include the Lamont Prize from the Academy of American Poets, fellowships from the National Endowment for the Arts and the Rockefeller and Guggenheim foundations, and the Oppenheimer Award for the best first play by an American playwright. He was born in Rochester, New York, where his parents had moved from Florida in search of steady employment. Eady spent his childhood in a close community of African Americans, where he developed a strong interest in music. He spent hours at the local library listening to **jazz** and **blues** records. He became interested in poetry during his junior high school years. He attended college at Empire State University in Rochester, where he majored in English with an emphasis in creative writing. He has published several volumes of poetry, including *Kartunes* (1980), *Victims of the Latest Dance Craze* (1986), *You Don't Miss Your Water* (1995), and *The Autobiography of a Jukebox* (1996).

Eady's most recent and most celebrated volume of poetry, *Brutal Imagination*, appeared in 2001. It quickly earned several awards and was named a finalist for the 2001 National Book Award. The stage production of *Brutal Imagination* opened soon afterward off-Broadway and garnered Eady his Oppenheimer Award. *Brutal Imagination* is a chilling and powerful cycle of poems told from the point of view of the fictional African American murderer fabricated by Susan Smith of South Carolina, who in 1994 drowned her two children by rolling her car into a lake and then told authorities that they had been kidnapped by a Black man. *Brutal Imagination* makes a bold political statement. Eady both condemns and expresses sympathy for Susan Smith's

475

refusal to accept responsibility for the killing of her sons and for her racial exploitation of a dominantly White society's fear of violence from wrongly demonized African American men.

Eady's most notable achievement, outside of poetry and theater, is Cave Canem, which he founded in 1996 with the poet **Toi Derricotte**. Cave Canem (which means "beware the dog" in Latin) is a retreat at Esopus, on New York's Hudson River, where young African American writers can gather for workshops, offer creative and emotional support, sponsor poetry readings, and spark each other's creativity. Among the many poets Eady cites as his influences are **Yusef Komunyakaa** and **Amiri Baraka**. His poetry often is described as political and musical, drawing on the influences of the jazz and blues records he listened to as a child. About his work, Eady says, " 'I tell my students that it is a thing to face if you are a black poet. People will say your writing is political and that you are writing about race even when you think you're not, even when you think you're just writing about the people you know best' " (Trethewey, 196). Previously the director of the Poetry Center at the State University of New York in Stony Brook, Eady is currently professor of English and creative writing at American University in **Washington, D.C.**, where he is also faculty adviser to *Folio: A Literary Journal at American University*.

Resources: Cornelius Eady: *The Autobiography of a Jukebox* (Pittsburgh: Carnegie-Mellon University Press, 1996); *Brutal Imagination: Poems* (New York: Putnam, 2001); *The Gathering of My Name* (Pittsburgh: Carnegie-Mellon University Press, 1991); *Kartunes* (New York: Warthog Press, 1980); *Victims of the Latest Dance Craze* (1986; Pittsburgh: Carnegie-Mellon University Press, 1997); *You Don't Miss Your Water: Poems* (Pittsburgh: Carnegie-Mellon University Press, 2004); Natasha Trethewey, "About Cornelius Eady," *Ploughshares* 28 (2002), 193–197.

Stephen Roger Powers

Early, Gerald Lyn (born 1952). Essayist, jazz critic, literary and cultural critic, editor, and professor. Gerald Early was born in **Philadelphia, Pennsylvania**. His father died when he was an infant, and his mother, a straight-talking, "indomitable" woman, did not remarry until Early and his two sisters reached adulthood. While he might lay claim to an upbringing steeped in Black middle-class sensibilities (he was raised as a "high" Episcopalian), his family was by no means bourgeois. As a youngster, Early negotiated the fringes of the gang life that defined the boundaries of Philadelphia's neighborhoods.

Such hardships undoubtedly provide the framework for Early's writing. He is, first and foremost, a gifted essayist in the tradition of H. L. Mencken and **James Baldwin**. In fact, his aspiration for his first collection of essays, *Tuxedo Junction* (1989), is summed up in his hopes that the book might be seen as an "American Common Reader" (a play on Virginia Woolf's *The Common Reader*). Early's writings in this book, which won the Whiting Award, as well as those in the 1994 collection *The Culture of Bruising*, winner of the National Book Critics Circle Award, serve broadly as fields in which he elaborates upon the underpinnings of American culture as it influences and is, in turn, permeated by **jazz** and **blues** music, sports (baseball and boxing loom large), family relations, and matters of race. His critiques generally spring from a species of autobiographical confession. He also, in the tradition of essayists, presents ideas in flight: he alights upon point after point until, finally, his essays resemble an intricate web of intellectual dialogue. Although Early is suspicious of most theoretical approaches to literature and culture, and claims he is bored by the triptych of **race, gender**, and class, these issues frame much of his cultural analyses. The Black male in general, and the Black male intellectual more specifically, are topics to which Early routinely turns from his position as a Black male scholar. And he baldly addresses such conundrums as the **"Talented Tenth"** in his introduction to his 1995 book, *One Nation Under a Groove: Motown and American Culture*: "I am by no means bashful about enjoying the perks and privileges, the overall sense of cultivation, of being part of an elite.... I've been working class and I've been middle class and middle class is better" (5). It is indeed Early's unabashed forthrightness that has set him up as a whipping boy for some within the Black Nationalist and Afrocentrist camps. Articles such as "Understanding Afrocentrism" (1995) have earned him the dubious label of "Black conservative" in some quarters. (*See* **Afrocentrism; Black Nationalism**.)

Early has edited numerous collections, the most important of which are *"My Soul's High Song"* (1991); *Speech and Power* (1992–1993); and *Lure and Loathing* (1993). He has published one volume of poetry, *How the War in the Streets Is Won* (1995). His latest book is *This Is Where I Came In* (2003), a slim collection of three lectures in which he returns to the familiar subjects of **Muhammad Ali** and Sammy Davis, Jr., and renews his interest in Black Philadelphia with an essay on Cecil B. Moore. Sounding increasingly more like a cultural historian than a literary critic, Early has titled a forthcoming book *When Worlds Collide: The Korean War and the Integration of the United States.*

Early is currently Merle Kling Professor of Modern Letters at Washington University in **St. Louis, Missouri**, where he is the founding director of the university's Center for the Humanities. Early has twice been nominated for the Grammy Award for Best Album Notes ("Yes I Can: The Sammy Davis, Jr. Story," 2000; and "Rhapsodies in Black: Music and Words from the Harlem Renaissance," 2001). He has served as a consultant on Ken Burns's documentaries on baseball and jazz, and is a regular commentator on National Public Radio. A fellow of the American Academy of Arts and Sciences, he has had an essay, "Life with Daughters," included in *The Best American Essays of the Century.*

Resources: Gerald Early: *The Culture of Bruising: Essays on Prizefighting, Literature, and Modern American Culture* (Hopewell, NJ: Ecco, 1994); *Daughters: On Family and Fatherhood* (Reading, MA: Addison-Wesley, 1994); *How the War in the Streets Is Won: Poems on the Quest of Love and Faith* (St. Louis: Time Being Books, 1995); "Life with Daughters: Watching the Miss America Pageant," in *The Best American Essays of the Century,* ed. Joyce Carol Oates (Boston: Houghton Mifflin, 2001); *One Nation Under* *a Groove: Motown and American Culture* (Hopewell, NJ: Ecco, 1995); *Speech and Power: The African-American Essay and Its Cultural Content, from Polemics to Pulpit*, 2 vols. (Hopewell, NJ: Ecco, 1992–1993); *This Is Where I Came In: Black America in the 1960s* (Lincoln: University of Nebraska Press, 2003); *Tuxedo Junction: Essays on American Culture* (New York: Ecco, 1989); "Understanding Afrocentrism," *Civilization* 2, no. 4 (July–Aug. 1995), 31–39; Gerald Early, ed., *Lure and Loathing: Essays on Race, Identity, and the Ambivalence of Assimilation* (New York: Penguin, 1993); *The Muhammad Ali Reader* (Hopewell, NJ: Ecco, 1998); *"My Soul's High Song": The Collected Works of Countee Cullen* (New York: Doubleday, 1991); *The Sammy Davis, Jr. Reader* (New York: Farrar, Straus, and Giroux, 2001).

Rebecka Rychelle Rutledge

Ebony (1945–present). Magazine. At a time when only literary and political magazines competed for Black consumer attention, *Ebony* magazine transformed the nature of the Black popular audience in the United States, and helped to reshape Black literary culture. By the early 1950s, *Ebony* had become the leading mass-market Black-audience periodical in the United States, reporting a readership of half a million per year. Understanding *Ebony*'s relationship to literary culture depends in part on understanding the nature of the magazine's early success, since this success was simultaneous with the decline of literary and political journals.

As a kind Black American counternarrative to *Life* magazine, *Ebony* expanded the visual vocabulary of "acceptable" race images in U.S. mass culture. The magazine was in many ways typical of the general-interest genre of magazines, featuring stories on celebrities, news, travel, and sports, with the important distinction of its focus on Black America. Yet the magazine has been criticized by Black intellectuals for its willingness to blur the distinction between news and sensationalist gossip, as well as for its reliance on alcohol and tobacco advertising revenues; the magazine appears to undermine the very community it purports to serve, according to such critics. At issue is the question of *Ebony*'s effects. Is it commercial dross, successful because of its appeal to the lowest common denominator through its bathing beauty issues? Or is the very fact of its success a more important indicator of Black social and economic integration into U.S. life?

Few literary magazines survived the **Great Depression**, but 1944 saw the introduction of the short-lived *Negro Story*. Other black-owned periodicals that survived the depression, wartime censorship, and the precarious conditions of Black publishing, included long-running political magazines such as **The Crisis** and **Opportunity**. The only other Black-audience popular magazines in circulation in the 1940s and 1950s were owned by the **Johnson Publishing Company**, and included **Negro Digest** (1942); *Tan* (1950), a "confessional" magazine; *Jet* (1952), a small news magazine; and *Copper Romance* (1953). Johnson's magazines primarily trafficked in broad, sensational themes, alienating the Black intelligentsia even while publishing articles by figures such as **Richard Wright**.

The cover of *Ebony* magazine, "The Schoolmarm Who Glorified Leg Art," January 1947. Yale Collection of American Literature, Beinecke Rare Book and Manuscript Library.

Ebony's success must be understood as part of a larger process; as in the dominant U.S. culture, the readership for literary journals turned to the large glossies and television. But *Ebony*'s success may also be attributed to factors that include the aggressive business practices of its parent company, the increasing censorship (and self-censorship) of Black radicalism in the 1950s, and the increasing opportunities for Black participation in music, radio, television, and film. Literary magazines such as *Negro Story* were arguably destined to decline, subject to larger cultural forces such as television. However, literary magazines held a special role in Black America, and thus it has been suggested that Johnson's brash style exacerbated tendencies present in the culture at large, helping to destroy a valuable component of the Black public sphere at midcentury.

Resources: Langston Hughes, "*Ebony*'s Nativity—An Evaluation from Birth," *Ebony* 21 (Nov. 1965), 27, 40–42; Toni C. King, "'Who's That Lady?' *Ebony* Magazine and Black Professional Women," in *Disco Divas: Women and Popular Culture in the 1970s*, ed. Sherrie A. Inness (Philadelphia: University of Pennsylvania Press, 2003), 87–102; Tom Krannawitter, "*Ebony* Magazine and the Non-Existence of Black Conservatives," *The Claremont Institute for the Study of Statesmanship and Political Philosophy*, http://www.claremont.org/writings/precepts/20010618finch_krannawitter .html.

Valerie Begley

Edmonds, S[heppard] Randolph (1900–1983). Playwright. A prolific playwright, Randolph Edmonds (as he is known) also contributed significantly to drama and theater arts programs at African American colleges and universities. Born in Lawrenceville, Virginia, Edmonds graduated from St. Paul's Normal and Industrial High School as class valedictorian in 1921. He received a scholarship to attend Oberlin College, where he received a B.A. degree in English literature in 1926. His first full-length play, *Rocky Roads* (1926), was produced at Oberlin in 1926. Also during this year Edmonds began teaching English and drama at Morgan State College in **Baltimore, Maryland**, where he formed the Morgan Dramatic Club and, in 1930, the Negro Intercollegiate Drama Association, "the first organization of its kind for black colleges and universities" (Williams, 68). During the summers of 1927–1930, Edmonds attended Columbia University. At this time Edmonds published his first set of plays, *Shades and Shadows* (1930). In 1931, he received his M.A. degree from Columbia University. He also received a Rockefeller Foundation fellowship to Yale University where he studied drama from 1934 to 1935. Edmonds published *Six Plays for a Negro Theatre* (1934) during this time. In 1935, he left Morgan State College to head the Speech and Theater Department at Dillard University in **New Orleans, Louisiana**. The following year he "organized black colleges in the South and Southwest into the Southern Association of Dramatic and Speech Arts (SADSA) and served as its president for seven years" (Williams, 69). Along with James E. Gayle, Edmonds formed the Crescent Concerts Company in New Orleans in 1942, the "first concert company known to have been owned and controlled by blacks" (Williams, 70). Also in 1942 Edmonds's last anthology, *The Land of Cotton and Other Plays*, was published. Edmonds wrote many other plays that have been produced in colleges and universities across the country. In all, he wrote forty-eight plays by the time of his retirement in 1970, along with several essays on theater for leading African American publications.

Resources: Randolph Edmonds: *The Land of Cotton and Other Plays* (Washington, DC: Associated Publishers, 1942); "The Negro in the American Theatre 1700–1969," *Pan-African Journal* 7 (1974), 13–28, 297–322; *Shades and Shadows* (Boston: Meador, 1930); *Six Plays for a Negro Theatre* (Boston: Baker, 1934); Paul David Nadler, "American Theatre and the Civil Rights Movement, 1945–1965," Ph.D. dissertation, City University of New York, 1995; Allen Williams, "S. Randolph Edmonds," in *Dictionary of Literary Biography*, vol. 51, *Afro-American Writers from the Harlem Renaissance to 1940*, ed. Trudier Harris and Thadious M. Davis (Detroit: Gale, 1987).

Ama S. Wattley

Edwards, Grace F[rederica] (born c. 1943). Novelist. Grace F. Edwards was born and reared, and still resides, in **Harlem, New York**. She is the author of six novels, all of which are set in her native Harlem. Edwards takes readers on a political, social, historical, and musical tour of Harlem as the locus of a deep tradition of intellectual, social, and artistic expression, creating a historicized sense of the cultural milieu in which her mysteries and thrillers are based. (*See* **Crime and Mystery Fiction**.)

Edwards's first book, *In the Shadows of the Peacock* (1988), is a historical novel set in 1930s Harlem. She is most widely known for her series of mysteries featuring African American sleuth/protagonist Mali Anderson. Setting her novels in contemporary times, Edwards utilizes the voice of an elder to historicize the setting of Harlem. The first of the series, *If I Should Die*, was published in 1997, and received an Anthony Award nomination for best novel. The second in the series, *A Toast Before Dying* (1998), won the 1999 Fiction Honor Book award from the Black Caucus of the American Library Association. *No Time to Die* (1999) and *Do or Die* (2000) are the most recent publications in the series. In an interview, Edwards stated that the Columbia Broadcasting System has purchased television rights to the series and may produce it, with Queen Latifah in the starring role ("Interview"). Edwards's most recent publication, *The Viaduct* (2004), moves back to the vibrant nightlife of early 1970s Harlem, portraying post-**Vietnam War** Harlem culture in a historical thriller.

Edwards has been a member of the Harlem Writers Guild since the early 1970s. Founded in 1950 by the historian John Henrik Clarke and **Rosa Guy**, **John Oliver Killens**, and Walter Christmas, among others, the Guild is the oldest continuously operating African American writers workshop in the country. It has served not only as a workshop for notable artists such as **Maya Angelou**, but also as the proponent of progressive human rights struggles. Edwards currently is its secretary.

Resources: Grace F. Edwards: *Do or Die* (New York: Doubleday, 2000); *If I Should Die* (New York: Doubleday, 1997); *In the Shadows of the Peacock* (New York: McGraw-Hill, 1988); *No Time to Die* (New York: Doubleday, 1999); *A Toast before Dying* (New York: Doubleday, 1998); *The Viaduct* (New York: Doubleday, 2004); "Interview with Grace F. Edwards," *Bestsellers World*, http://www.bestsellersworld.com/interviews-edwards.htm.

Esther L. Jones

Edwards, Junius (born 1929). Novelist and short story writer. Edwards captures the spirit and experiences of the African American soldier and veteran in his short stories and novels. His work also focuses on African Americans and their life in **the South**, centering on issues that he encountered as a Southern native. He was born in Alexandria, Louisiana, and studied at the University of Chicago and the University of Oslo in Norway. His writing skill brought him a *Writer's Digest* Short Story Contest award (1958) and, like his African American contemporary, the novelist **James Baldwin**, Edwards was awarded the Eugene Saxton fellowship in 1959. The short story that brought him the *Writer's Digest* award was "Liars Don't Qualify." It deals with the Black American soldier and his struggles to handle the racial prejudices of American society after returning from the Korean War. "Liars Don't Qualify" became the foundation for Edwards's novel *If We Must Die*. The novel did not receive much critical acclaim when it was published in 1961, or when it was republished in 1963, because it fails to address many of the issues facing Blacks, such as those connected to the **Civil Rights Movement**. Edwards took his novel's title from a line of poetry by **Claude McKay**. As Australia Henderson states in the *Dictionary of the Literary Biography*, Edwards's novel "has a slight plot and minimal dramatic action" (66). However, it provides "a sympathy for and understanding of the conflicts and obstacles the black soldier confronts," Henderson suggests.

In 1967, Edwards continued highlighting the situation of the Black soldier in his short story "Duel with the Clock," in which he delves into the psychology and personality of the soldier. Later, the poet **Langston Hughes** published the story in *The Best Short Stories by Negro Writers* (1967). Edwards shifts his attention away from the African American soldier in his short story "Mother Dear and Daddy," written in 1966. This story taps into the racial tensions among light- and dark-skinned African Americans in Louisiana and reveals the compassion of children compared with adults in a color-conscious environment. "Mother Dear and Daddy," along with his previous short stories and his novel, make up his short list of published works during the 1950s and 1960s. Edwards eventually went into advertising in New York. His work is included in the anthology *Calling the Wind* (1993).

Resources: Junius Edwards, *If We Must Die* (Washington, DC: Howard University Press, 1984); Australia Henderson, "Junius Edwards," in *Dictionary of Literary Biography*, vol. 33, *Afro-American Fiction Writers After 1955* (Detroit: Gale, 1984), 65–67; Langston Hughes, ed., *The Best Short Stories by Negro Writers: An Anthology from 1899 to the Present* (Boston: Little, Brown, 1967); Clarence Major, ed., *Calling the Wind: Twentieth Century African-American Short Stories* (New York: HarperPerennial, 1993); Donna Olendorf, ed., *Contemporary Authors*, vol. 142 (Detroit: Gale, 1994), 121–122; Australia Tarver, "Junius Edwards," in *The Oxford Companion to African American Literature*, ed. William L. Andrews, Frances Smith Foster, and Trudier Harris (New York: Oxford University Press, 1997), 126.

Brande Nicole Martin

Edwards, Louis (born 1962). Novelist, essayist, and public relations expert. Edwards has fashioned a solid reputation as an inventive novelist whose works have garnered critical acclaim. Edwards's writing is marked by his interests in exploring critical issues regarding racial identity, class, Southern culture, and American society. Raised in Lake Charles, Louisiana, he attended Louisiana State University (LSU) and earned a bachelor's degree in journalism. Edwards then served as a graduate assistant in the English Departments at both LSU and the University of New Orleans. Since 1986, he has worked in the public relations offices for both the New Orleans Jazz and Heritage Foundation and the JCV Jazz Festival–New York. The Black experience in Louisiana life and in **New Orleans, Louisiana,** in particular, factor heavily into the plots and character development in his work. In an interview broadcast on National Public Radio (August 9, 2001) it was noted that Edwards had entered into the "literary tradition" of writers influenced by New Orleans. In his first novel, *Ten Seconds* (1991), Edwards deftly renders the complexity of modern Black male subjectivity through the portrayal of the novel's male protagonist, Eddie, whose youthful potential, human frailty, and deferred dreams are continuously placed in balance with the desire to achieve a more rewarding life. In his support of the book, **Charles R. Johnson** considered the novel as having charted "the broken hearts of modern black men" in a way that rendered the immediacy of Black male experiences tangible to its audience. The novel received critical acclaim and was named one of the year's best by *Publishers Weekly* (1991), and earned the PEN Oakland Josephine Miles Award (1991). Other awards following the novel were a Guggenheim fellowship (1993) and the Whiting Writers Award (1994). In 1995, Edwards used his journalistic and literary background in an interview with **Albert Murray**, in which the two men discussed Murray's work in theorizing African American cultural aesthetics and his relationships with such renowned artists and writers as **Ralph Ellison** and **Romare Bearden**.

Edwards's second novel, *N: A Romantic Mystery* (1997), conjoined various literary genres including mystery, "noir," and the use of an embedded narrative—a story within a story. In this second novel, Edwards constructed a mélange of characters reflecting Black New Orleans. While the premise of the novel centers on a murder investigation by the female protagonist, Aimée DuBois, an educated Creole woman and independent journalist, the novel in actuality is an investigation of class and racial identity in New Orleans with Edwards rendering the city as an integral character rather than merely serving as a setting for the narrative. In its review of the novel, *Publishers Weekly* wrote, "Edwards examines New Orleans as a paradigm of cultural ambivalence and dislocation" (March 3, 1997), while the review in *Library Journal* noted his use of "attention-getting mixed narrative viewpoints and rhythmic, ultimately entrancing prose" in developing the novel (April 1, 1997).

In his third novel, *Oscar Wilde Discovers America* (2003), Edwards creates a metahistory of America, American culture, and transatlantic intercultural contacts among literary figures during the final decades of the nineteenth century. Giving a voice to Wilde's Black valet, who accompanied the author on a publicity tour throughout the United States, the novel possesses an ethnographic quality in its use of history, depiction of real-life political figures, and eloquent discussion of **slavery** as marked by the story of fugitive slaves.

Resources: Louis Edwards: "Albert Murray on Stage: An Interview," in *Conversations with Albert Murray*, ed. Roberta S. Maguire (Jackson: University Press of Mississippi, 1997), 78–93; *N: A Romantic Mystery* (New York: Dutton, 1997); *Oscar Wilde Discovers America* (New York: Scribner's, 2003); *Ten Seconds* (St. Paul, MN: Graywolf Press, 1991); Debbie Elliott, "New Orleans Author Finds New Way to Write About an Old City," *Morning Edition*, National Public Radio, Aug. 9, 2001; Ameena Meer, "Interview with Louis Edwards," *BOMB* 37 (Fall 1991), 14–15; "Review of *N: A Romantic Mystery*," *Library Journal*, Apr. 1, 1997, p. 133; "Review of *N: A Romantic Mystery*," *Publishers Weekly*, Mar. 3, 1997, p. 67; Albert E. Wilhelm, "A Review of *Ten Seconds*," *Library Journal*, May 1, 1991, p. 105.

Robin Goldman Vander

Elam, Patricia (born c. 1971). Novelist, freelance writer, radio and newspaper commentator, and attorney. The daughter of a librarian and **Boston, Massachusetts**, municipal judge, Elam grew up reading, writing, and illustrating her own books, but she did not study creative writing until later in her life. She graduated from Adelphi University, received a J.D. degree from the Northeastern University School of Law, and practiced law for sixteen years. While practicing law, she realized that writing was her true passion. She used her legal expertise to write a commentary on the O. J. Simpson case that aired on National Public Radio (NPR). Her commentary brought her national attention from many major networks, and she has subsequently offered commentaries on the impact of Colin Powell's *My American Journey* (1995), the Clinton impeachment (1996), the controversy over Ebonics (1997), the perils of teen murder (2000), and the emotional turmoil of 9/11 (2002). Although she enjoys writing commentary, Elam, who has gone on to earn an M.F.A. in creative writing at the University of Maryland, prefers to write fiction.

Elam's fiction and nonfiction have been published in newspapers including the *Washington Post* and *Newsday*, as well as such popular magazines as *Epoch*, *Emerge*, and *Essence*. Her short story "A Taxi Ride," published in *New Stories from the South: The Year's Best 1997*, won the 1997 O. Henry Award. She also published a short memoir–essay titled "Dancing on My Father's Shoes" in *Father Songs: Testimonies by African-American Sons and Daughters* (1997), an anthology of moving and deeply personal essays about African American fathers. By 2001, Elam had published her first novel, *Breathing Room*, which was nominated for the 2002 Hurston/Wright Legacy Award. *Breathing Room* addresses such serious real-life issues as single parenting, adultery, interracial relationships, and teen sex. Most recently, Elam published "Scenes from a Marriage" in *Brown Sugar 3: When Opposites Attract* (2004).

Apart from her fiction and commentary, Elam has written on **Black feminism** (1995) and has called for more heroes like Ron Brown (1996) and for recognition of long overlooked black actors (2002). She has written reviews of **Maya Angelou**'s *Song Flung Up to Heaven* and the movie *A Time to Kill*, and she contributes to several Web sites, including www.seeingblack.com. Elam has served on the Maryland State Arts Council and on the board of the Hurston/Wright Foundation, and she continues to serve on the board of the PEN/Falkner Foundation. She is a mentor and teacher at Duke Ellington School for the Arts in **Washington, D.C.**, and has taught in the UCLA Extension Program (online), at the Writer's Center in Bethesda, Maryland, and at Goucher College. Over the years, Elam has received grants from the District of Columbia Commission on the Arts and has won several awards, including the Associated Writing Programs Intro Journal Award for "Young Boyz Drinkin a Forty Out the Bag."

Resources: Commentary on National Public Radio: Patricia Elam: "Commentary: Oscar Nominations and Awards for Black Actors," *Morning Edition*, National Public Radio (Mar. 22, 2002); "Commentator Blasts Caricatures in *A Time to Kill*," *Morning Edition*, National Public Radio (Aug. 26, 1996); "Commentator Says We Need More Heroes like Ron Brown," *Morning Edition*, National Public Radio (Apr. 10, 1996); "Commentator Thanks Colin Powell for Being Black," *Morning Edition*, National Public Radio (Sept. 26, 1995); "Dear Ms. Clinton," *Morning Edition*, National Public Radio (Aug. 28, 1998); "Ebonics," *Morning Edition*, National Public Radio (Aug. 21, 1996); "Impeachment," *Morning Edition*, National Public Radio (Feb. 17, 1999); "Patricia Elam-Ruff Tells How She Helped Her Son," *Morning Edition*, National Public Radio (Nov. 12, 1996); "Washington Mourns Murder of Students," *Morning Edition*, National Public Radio (Feb. 15, 2000). **Commentary in Newspapers:** Patricia Elam: "Fiction," *Washington Post*, Nov. 3, 1996, www.washingtonpost.com; "Letters: A Manifesto of Sorts for a Black Feminist Movement," *New York Times*, Dec. 12, 1995, p. 22; "Longing to Be Safe Again," *The New Crisis* 109, no. 1 (Jan./Feb. 2002), 56; "A Triumphant Last Song," *The New Crisis* 109, no. 3 (June/July 2002), 49. **Books, Anthologies, and Other Publications:** Patricia Elam: *Breathing Room* (New York: Pocket Books, 2001); "Dancing on My Father's Shoes," in *Father Songs: Testimonies by African American Sons and Daughters*, ed. Gloria Wade-Gayles (Boston: Beacon Press, 1997); "Scenes from a Marriage," in *Brown Sugar 3: When Opposites Attract*, ed. Carol Taylor (New York: Washington Square Press, 2004); "A Taxi Ride," in *New Stories from the South: The Year's Best 1997*, ed. Shannon Ravenel (Chapel Hill, NC: Algonquin, 1997).

Candie McKee

Elaw, Zilpha (c. 1790–?). Preacher and autobiographer. Elaw was born free near **Philadelphia, Pennsylvania**. Her *Memoirs of the Life, Religious Experience, and Ministerial Travels and Labours of Mrs. Zilpha Elaw, an American Female of Colour* (1845) recounts her pious upbringing in the free state of Pennsylvania. Having lost her mother at twelve, she was placed by her father with the Mitchell family, Quakers who exposed Elaw to their quiet, inner religion. Unused to their form of worship, Elaw fell to sin, but was later converted following a dream where the angel Gabriel announced the coming of the Day of Judgment, which forced her to realize that she was unprepared to meet and to be judged by God. Attempting find God, Elaw prayed, and in the midst of singing, she had a vision of Jesus, whose "very looks spoke, and said 'Thy prayer is accepted, I own thy name.'" Her memoir was reprinted in an anthology edited by William Andrews (1986).

In 1808, Elaw joined a Methodist group and converted. In 1810, she met Joseph Elaw, a fellow Christian, married him, and moved to Burlington, New Jersey. Two years later, she gave birth to her daughter. Her husband died in 1823, leaving Elaw to work as a domestic in order to raise their daughter. In 1828, Elaw began her itinerant ministry, later traveling south at personal risk, for as a free Black, she could have been arrested and sold into **slavery**, and as a woman preaching to slaves, she was a threat to the cultural and economic institution of oppression. In 1840 she traveled to London, England, where she preached for five years while writing her *Memoirs*, which were published in 1845 and which allude to a desire to return to the United States. Unfortunately, nothing further is known of Elaw following that publication. (*See* **Autobiography**.)

Resources: William Andrews, ed., *Sisters of the Spirit: Three Black Women's Autobiographies of the Nineteenth Century* (Bloomington: Indiana University Press, 1986); Sue E. Houchins, ed., *Spiritual Narratives* (New York: Oxford University Press, 1988).

Pamela Ralston

Elder, Lonne, III (1927–1996). Playwright, screenwriter, and actor. Born in Americus, Georgia, Elder went to live with relatives in New Jersey after losing both parents at an early age. He continued his education at the New Jersey State Teachers College but also was employed as a dock worker, a waiter, and a professional gambler. Upon his discharge from the Army in the early 1950s, he studied acting and worked in summer stock. He became active with the Harlem Writers Guild, where he worked with **Alice Childress**, a noted playwright and actor. Later, he formed a lasting friendship with an aspiring actor/director, **Douglas Turner Ward**, who became his roommate during the late 1950s.

Interested in both writing and performing, Elder made his Broadway debut in the role of Bobo in **Lorraine Hansberry**'s award-winning play, *A Raisin in the Sun*. He traveled with the national tour during 1960 and 1961. He became involved with the Negro Ensemble Company and appeared in Douglas Turner Ward's groundbreaking work *Day of Absence*, in the role of Clem. Elder was the coordinator for the Negro Ensemble Company's program for directors and playwrights, and he attended the Yale University filmmaking program on a Joseph Levine fellowship. His interest in writing did not wane, and he penned more plays, including *A Hysterical Turtle in a Rabbit Race* and *Charades on East Fourth Street*. Elder was a pioneer Black writer for television, writing scripts for *Camera Three* (early 1957), *NYPD* (1967–1968), and *McCloud*. His best-known play, *Ceremonies in Dark Old Men*, produced by the Negro Ensemble Company in 1969, centers on the likable, but deeply conflicted, Parker family. The play won the Outer Critics Circle Award, the Vernon Rice Drama Desk Award, and the **Los Angeles** Drama Critics Award. Elder wrote the teleplay for the ABC television broadcast of the play (1975). To date, it is the only play of Elder's to be published. In 1972, he was nominated for an Academy Award for his screenplay adaptation of the Newbery Award–winning book, *Sounder*. Elder was the first African American to be nominated for an Oscar for a screenplay adaptation. Although he did not win the coveted Oscar, he continued to write screenplays, including *Sounder, Part 2* (1976), *A Woman Called Moses* (1978), and *Melinda*.

Elder died at the Motion Picture and Television Hospital in Woodland Hills, California. A memorial for him was held at the Schomburg in October 1996.

Resources: Lonne Elder III, *Ceremonies in Old Dark Men* (New York: Noonday Press, 1997); Chester J. Fontenot, "Mythic Patterns in *River Niger* and *Ceremonies in Old Dark Men*," *MELUS* 7, no. 1 (Spring 1980), 41–49.

Joan F. McCarty

Elizabeth (1766–1866). Spiritual autobiographer and evangelist. Elizabeth (no surname is recorded) asserted her identity as God's instrument in a society that objectified her. Born in Maryland to slave parents who belonged to a Methodist society, she was converted in 1778 after experiencing visions of hell and heaven. Sold twice, she sought peace through prayer, and "was often carried to distant lands and shown places where [she] would have to travel and deliver the Lord's message."

Set free in 1796, Elizabeth began attending religious meetings but resisted public speaking, reasoning that she lacked the education to "understand the Scriptures." Consulting church leaders, she was told that the Bible did not allow for female ministry. In 1808, convinced of her spiritual authority, she became the first African American woman preacher. Clergymen opposed her relentlessly, dismissing her claim of divine inspiration, rejecting her enthusiastic style, and condemning her violation of Paul's dictum that women should be silent in church.

Although some early nineteenth-century sects and churches, including Methodists and African Methodists, allowed women to engage in public prayer and exhortation, *preaching* from a biblical text to audiences of both sexes was generally forbidden. Ordination, or official recognition, was reserved for men. In the 1830s and 1840s, Methodists and African Methodists joined middle-class denominations in preferring formally educated ministers, a move that further marginalized charismatic women (Brekus, 295–296; Humez, 138–140). Elizabeth persisted in leading meetings in several states and in Canada, sometimes addressing large, racially mixed groups. Defying legal codes that restricted Blacks' rights of assembly and interstate travel, she entered slave territory at great personal risk and denounced **slavery** in Virginia (Moody, 42–43; Brekus, 248–249).

Elizabeth retired in **Philadelphia, Pennsylvania**, in 1853. Her life story, dictated ten years later to an amanuensis, was published as *Memoir of Old Elizabeth, a Coloured Woman* (1866). An anonymous writer later added an account of Elizabeth's final days. This updated memoir, *Elizabeth, a Colored*

Minister of the Gospel, Born in Slavery (1889), was distributed by the Friends Tract Association. A traditional spiritual **autobiography**, Elizabeth's narrative centers on her relationship with God, omits merely personal details, and employs formulaic and biblical phrases. Unlike contemporary autobiographers Jarena Lee and **Zilpha Elaw**, she presents no formal argument for women's ministry. But Galatians 3:28 speaks from her title page: "There is neither Jew nor Greek, there is neither bond nor free, there is neither male nor female: for ye are all one in Christ Jesus."

Resources: Catherine A. Brekus, *Strangers and Pilgrims: Female Preaching in America, 1740–1845* (Chapel Hill: University of North Carolina Press, 1998); Elizabeth, *Memoir of Old Elizabeth, a Coloured Woman with a Short Account of Her Sickness and Death* (Philadelphia: David Heston, 1866), also available as electronic text at the University of North Carolina, Chapel Hill, Library: http://docsouth.unc.edu/neh/eliza1/eliza1.sgml; Jean M. Humez, " 'My Spirit Eye': Some Functions of Spiritual and Visionary Experience in the Lives of Five Black Women Preachers, 1810–1880," in *Women and the Structure of Society: Selected Research from the Fifth Berkshire Conference on the History of Women*, ed. Barbara J. Harris and JoAnn McNamara (Durham, NC: Duke University Press, 1984), 129–143; Joycelyn K. Moody, "On the Road with God: Travel and Quest in Early Nineteenth-Century African American Holy Women's Narratives," *Religion and Literature* 27, no. 1 (1995), 35–51.

Mary De Jong

Ellington, Edward Kennedy "Duke" (1899–1974). Jazz composer, band leader, and pianist. Undoubtedly one of the preeminent **jazz** musicians of the 20th century, Ellington helped to define the genre, captured its nuances, and moved the music from the dance halls of **Harlem, New York**, to Carnegie Hall and the opera houses of the world, while representing a universalized national experience through the sounds of African America.

The son of a butler of some prominence in **Washington, D.C.**, Ellington was early enthralled by artistic production. In 1923, he became a jazz pianist in New York City, and by 1927 the emerging star led his own orchestra in Harlem's famous Cotton Club. In his four years there, he made his name as a composer, arranger, and bandleader by merging **ragtime** rhythms, uptempo **swing** choruses, and what he and trumpeter Bubber Miley called "jungle style," which emphasized the African tribal influences on America's melodies and rhythms.

Commercial success allowed Ellington to begin to push on the boundaries of jazz writing. He began to move away from the exoticized aesthetics of the "jungle" by inserting into more scripted compositions the experiences of contemporary America, what prominent trumpeter Wynton Marsalis calls "America's themes: cities, technology, telephones, trains, airplanes… interpersonal relationships" (151). In these larger pieces, including "Creole Rhapsody," "Reminiscing in Tempo," and "Diminuendo and Crescendo in Blue," Ellington wrote with specific musicians in mind, understanding precisely the mood, technique, and personality that each member of his growing orchestra could add. One such composition that Ellington continually revised during his long career was "Black, Brown, and Beige," originally penned in 1943. Subtitled a "tone parallel to the history of the Negro," the monumental work was first performed at Carnegie Hall in New York City, and utilized the particularities of African American music such as the **blues**, **spirituals**, and sorrow songs to represent the centrality of African American experience to the development of U.S. culture.

Throughout the 1960s and into the early 1970s, Ellington continued to expand on what he portrayed as America's and, later, the world's music. As Albert Murray proclaimed, "No American artist working in any medium whatsoever in any generation has ever fulfilled the vernacular imperatives more completely and consistently" (22). Ellington's **autobiography**, *Music Is My Mistress* (1973), has become a classic of jazz literature. In this subtle and engaging work, the Duke sketches the many close relationships he developed over a sixty-year career, charts his travels as a diplomat for the U.S. State Department around the world, and recenters the question of national identity in the importance of human understanding. (*See* **Vernacular**.)

Resources: Duke Ellington, *Music Is My Mistress* (1973; repr. New York: Da Capo, 1988); Wynton Marsalis and Robert G. O'Meally, "Duke Ellington: Music Like a Big Hot Pot of Good Gumbo," in *The Jazz Cadence of American Culture*, ed. Robert G. O'Meally (New York: Columbia University Press, 1998); Albert Murray, "The Vernacular Imperative: Duke Ellington's Place in the National Pantheon," *Boundary 2* 22, no. 2 (Summer 1995), 19–24.

Keith Feldman

Ellis, Erika (born 1965). Novelist. Born in Plainfield, New Jersey, to well-educated and career-oriented parents, Ellis completed a B.A. at Wellesley College and an M.A. at the University of California, Los Angeles. Like her husband, the novelist **Trey Ellis**, she has an intimate awareness of the issues confronting the upwardly mobile, upper-middle-class African American characters about whom she writes.

Good Fences (1997), Ellis's first novel, traces an African American family's progress toward their realization of the American dream, with a great many ironic and several nightmarish turns along the way. Tom Spader and his wife, Mabel, start out in Lovejoy, Illinois. A light-skinned African American, Tom is an ambitious attorney who seizes the opportunity to practice in New York City. At first the family lives in a multiethnic neighborhood in **Brooklyn, New York**. But then Tom gains a great deal of fame—and subsequently a tremendous increase in his income—when he successfully defends a bigoted White landlord against charges of setting the fire that destroyed one of his tenements and killed two young African Americans asleep in the building. When Tom is appointed to a judgeship, the family leaves Brooklyn behind and relocates to the affluent White suburb of Greenwich, Connecticut.

But instead of enjoying their affluence, the Spaders are oppressed by their awareness that they don't really fit into their new community and by Tom's almost constant admonitions that they have to prove themselves the equals of their neighbors and to preserve every advantage they have gained. Tom never truly represses his nagging awareness that the case that has made his legal career has come at a great cost to his own sense of self and to his broader responsibility to his race. Instead of trying to compensate for his guilt, Tom tries to compensate for his doubt. Ultimately, he takes the lead in an effort to restrict the entry of other non-Whites into his community. Although Tom dominates his family, the novel is told largely from Mabel's point of view, tracing her growing awareness of both her husband's unsettling obsessions and the impact they have had on their children.

Resources: Veronica Chambers, "Meet the Neighbors," *Newsweek*, June 8, 1998, p. 70; Erika Ellis, *Good Fences* (New York: Random House, 1997); Betsy Groban, "Review of *Good Fences*," *New York Times Book Review*, July 5, 1998, p. 14.

Martin Kich

Ellis, Thomas Sayers (born 1965). Poet and editor. Born in **Washington, D.C.**, Ellis created what he calls an "urban naturalist" poetry that explores his home landscape as well as the percussive sounds and visual vibrancy of the African American experience. He attended Paul Laurence Dunbar High School in Washington and did undergraduate work at Harvard University, where he studied with the poets Seamus Heaney, Derek Walcott, and Robert Pinsky. He also worked for two years as a teaching assistant to filmmaker **Spike Lee**, then working with Harvard's African American Studies program. In 1987, while living in Cambridge, Massachusetts, Ellis cofounded the Dark Room reading series. Hosting luminaries such as **Alice Walker** and **Yusef Komunyakaa**, the series began in the house at 31 Inman Street, where Ellis lived. The Dark Room Collective, which grew out of the series, gathered together a group of young, intellectual African American writers to exchange writing and to discuss books and ideas. It included writers **Kevin Young**, **Natasha Trethewey**, and Major Jackson, and its members have gone on to take their place among the most celebrated Black writers currently publishing in American arts and letters. Ellis edited *On the Verge: Emerging Poets and Artists* (1993); he then earned his M.F.A. at Brown University in 1995, studying under **Michael S. Harper**. Ellis's celebrated first book of poetry, *The Good Junk* (1996), was followed by *The Genuine Negro Hero* (2001), which announced his "burning desire . . . to create the kind of compositions that resemble a literary mini–March on Washington" (31). His poems draw equally from music, film, painting, poetry, and the urban landscape, and are as likely to reference painter **Romare Bearden** and the musicians Parliament-Funkadelic as the poets Theodore Roethke and **Sterling A. Brown**. Ellis currently teaches on the English faculty at Case Western Reserve University.

Resources: "The Dark Room Collective: A Special Section," *Callaloo* 16 (1993), 511–555; Thomas Sayers Ellis: *The Genuine Negro Hero* (Kent, OH: Kent State University Press, 2001); *The Good Junk* (St. Paul, MN: Graywolf Press, 1996); "A Loud Noise Followed by Many Louder Ones: The Dark Room Collective (1987–1998)," *American Poetry Review*, Mar./Apr. 1998, 39; *The Maverick Room* (St. Paul, MN:

Graywolf Press, 2005); Thomas Sayers Ellis, ed., *On the Verge: Emerging Poets and Artists* (Boston: Agni Press, 1993); Askold Melnyczuk, "A Costly Telegram to the Dark Room Collective," *Callaloo* 16 (1993), 513–514; Charles H. Rowell, "An Interview with Thomas Sayers Ellis," *Callaloo* 21 (1998), 88–99; Kevin Young, ed., *Giant Steps: The New Generation of African American Writers* (New York: HarperCollins, 2000).

Christy J. Zink

Ellis, Trey (born 1962). Novelist and screenwriter. Born in **Washington, D.C.**, Ellis was educated at Phillips Academy, Andover, and Stanford University. Before writing fiction, he was a professional journalist, writing for *Newsweek* and contributing to publications such as *Playboy* and *The Village Voice*. He published his first novel, *Platitudes*, in 1988. This novel was well reviewed by the *New York Times Book Review*, and it gave Ellis a place among such established African American postmodernist artists as **Ishmael Reed**, **Spike Lee**, and **Darius James**. Structured as an epistolary novel, *Platitudes* is a pastiche of music lyrics, photos, linguistic representations of **jazz**, and television dialogue set within a narrative conceived as a struggle between two authors, Dewayne and Isshee. Their competing stories (within the story of the novel) of the characters Earle and Dorothy, along with their own interactions, create a complex and volatile exploration of the politics of **race** and sexuality, as well as of writing itself. Ellis returned to these themes in his second novel, *Home Repairs* (1993). The satiric *Home Repairs* presents diarylike recordings of the sexual misadventures of the central character, Austin McMillan. Ellis produces a much less bitter, although no less biting, satire in his most recent novel, *Right Here, Right Now* (1999). Widening the scope of his critical eye, Ellis constructs an elaborate story of Ashton Robinson, a well-educated African American who finds himself a TV self-help guru. This novel revisits the author's concerns with social platitudes and sexual relations through a critique of the trappings of wealth, and the hypnotic sway of popular culture.

Ellis's interest in the influence of television and film most likely emerges out of his intimate contact with these worlds. Bothered by the production of his first screenplay, *The Inkwell* (1992), Ellis used the pseudonym Tom Ricostranza in the credits. His relationship with the network Home Box Office (HBO) has been much more amiable; the network has produced his screenplays *Cosmic Slop* (1994) and *The Tuskegee Airmen* (1996), for which he was nominated for an Emmy. In 2003, Showtime aired *Good Fences*, based on a screenplay Ellis adapted from the novel by his wife, Erika Ellis. From *Platitudes* to *Good Fences*, Ellis addresses the lives of the black bourgeoisie with love and humor. Yet, like the writer of *Fences*, **August Wilson**, Ellis refuses to "whitewash" his characters "just because some white people might mistake one man's flaws" for the actions of an entire community ("The New Black Aesthetic," 238). Trey Ellis is a self-proclaimed "thriving hybrid" of the NBA—the New Black Aesthetic (242). His innovative work presents "a politically engaged African-American postmodernism that derails narrative conventions in order to specify a connection between aesthetics and politics" (Lubiano, 161).

Resources: Trey Ellis: home page, http://literati.net/Ellis; *Home Repairs* (New York: Simon and Schuster, 1993); "The New Black Aesthetic," *Callaloo* 38 (Winter 1989), 233–251; *Platitudes* (New York: Vintage, 1988); *Right Here, Right Now* (New York: Simon and Schuster, 1999); Wahneema Lubiano, "Shuckin' off the African-American Native Other: What's Pomo Got to Do With It?" *Cultural Critique*, Spring 1991, 149–186.

Theresa L. Geller

Ellison, Ralph (1914–1994). Novelist and essayist. Ralph Ellison is best known for his novel *Invisible Man* (1952), one of the most enduring, ambitious, and important American novels. He was born on March 1, 1914, in Oklahoma City, **Oklahoma**. He studied classical music at Tuskegee Institute in Alabama from 1933 to 1936, but failed to complete his degree because of financial difficulties. He started his writing career in New York City, beginning with a review published in 1937 in *New Challenge*, a journal edited by **Richard Wright**. He published a number of short stories in the early 1940s prior to his masterwork, *Invisible Man*, which won the National Book Award in 1953. Although he published two collections of essays during his lifetime—*Shadow and Act* (1964) and *Going to the Territory* (1986)—he never managed to complete a second novel, much to the disappointment of the American public who waited eagerly, in vain, for a follow-up to *Invisible Man*. Ellison spent his life composing an enormous work that he never completed. Much of the manuscript for it was destroyed in a fire in 1967, but it is generally agreed that he was simply unable to produce something that would match the power of his first novel. A version of his work-in-progress was published posthumously as *Juneteenth* (1999), to poor reviews.

Published at the beginning of the **Civil Rights Movement**, *Invisible Man* contains elements of protest, especially as it reflects on the meaning of the **Harlem, New York**, **race riots** of the 1930s and 1940s. Yet the more revolutionary Black activists of the 1960s criticized the novel because the narrator refuses to participate fully in those riots. Even the literary critic Irving Howe criticized Ellison for not taking a clear political stand in his works, and for not writing the kind of protest novel that Richard Wright had written, such as *Native Son*. In his essay "The World and the Jug," Ellison defends himself vigorously against Howe's attack, arguing essentially that ideology should not be the driving force behind fiction. Militant activists of the 1960s interpreted the fate of *Invisible Man*'s protagonist–narrator—exile in a hole—as a sign of his cowardice, or as escape from confrontation. Defenders of the novel and Ellison himself saw the narrator as an individualist and a victim of a fate that seems beyond his control. Virtually everything that happens to him in the novel stems from the fact that he was born Black in a world that refuses to recognize him as an individual. His quest to discover his identity cannot be separated from his race, and the injustice of that situation is precisely what sets the narrator in motion and eventually propels him into the hole where he writes the novel. Invisible Man would not be able to tell his story without first reflecting on his experiences, many of which are based on humiliation, abuse, and the loss of self-control.

Invisible Man is a novel of ideas, as surreal as it is emotionally gripping. Like those of a dream, the details of the narrative are clearly symbolic, and the reader is encouraged to figure out what everything means, even though the narrator seems unable to do so. The famous Battle Royal scene, for instance, or the scenes in Liberty Paints and in the hospital afterward are clearly allegorical. They represent some version of America where White men hold the power and Black men who work for them are both invisible and blind. As the narrator describes such scenes, he plays to the reader's confusion. Though he is composing his narration from his well-lit hole in the ground, he brings readers into the perspective of his younger, naïve self, asking them to share his mystification and refusing to interpret the world he describes.

Marking the beginning of his dreamlike journey is an actual dream of his grandfather, an ambiguous figure who seemed mad on his deathbed as he offered contradictory advice to the next generation. In the dream this ex-slave mocks the narrator and gives him a prophetic note that reads, "Keep this nigger-boy running." This written message appears after a watershed moment in the narrator's life: he has received a scholarship to the local Black college after subjecting himself to humiliation and physical abuse at the Battle Royal. There are, in fact, a number of incidents in the novel in which the narrator's identity is controlled by written messages from powerful men: the letters he carries from the college administrator, Bledsoe, to prospective employers in New York, for instance, or the name given to him by Brother Jack when he joins the Brotherhood. He is blind to these messages because he only slowly learns the meaning of his grandfather's dream: that he will keep running until he takes charge of his own destiny.

Part of the narrator's problem is that he does not recognize the nature of power until he has been destroyed by it. Another part is that he too readily accepts the version of success projected by the dominant culture. He is drawn to money and fame, and feels that college is the only way to achieve them. At the same time, he disdains the authentic Black folk history that has partially formed him. The event that ruins his college career demonstrates this division: he is ordered to drive Mr. Norton, a rich, White trustee, to meet Jim Trueblood, a poor, Black sharecropper. Trueblood narrates the story of how he unconsciously impregnated his daughter while Norton listens, fascinated, and the narrator grows distraught at Norton's reaction and at Trueblood's existence, which is a source of shame for the narrator. The forces of Black folk culture and of White power contend throughout the novel, and the narrator is often caught between them and eventually thrust out by them, just as in the Battle Royal.

The individual and the group constitute another pair of antagonistic forces in *Invisible Man*. The pressures to conform to the vision of the college are at war with the narrator's understanding of his own free will. He gets in trouble for following Mr. Norton's orders even though he thought he was doing what

Ralph Ellison, 1966. Courtesy of the Library of Congress.

was expected of him. Bledsoe, the college president, tries to convince the narrator that if he is to have any power at all, he must make decisions according to his own free will while hiding the fact that he has made these decisions. Ironically, Bledsoe undercuts this advice by sabotaging the narrator's progress when he arrives in New York. The same tension is felt when the narrator joins the Brotherhood and is trained to make speeches for their cause. At certain moments during his speeches, his emotions pour out of him, and the Brotherhood—a Communist organization that relies on precision, science, and history rather than the emotions of an individual—reprimands him and takes away what little power he has.

One memorable speech occurs in a large stadium when the narrator falters, recovers, then screams to the audience, "Look at me!" He confesses that a transformation is occurring right there on the stage: "I feel, I feel suddenly that I have become *more human*" (*Invisible Man*, 345–346). The development of his understanding of what it means to be human constitutes the novel's progress, but the movement of the novel is more like a downward spiral than a straight line. In the prologue he describes history as a boomerang that will hit you in the head if you are not careful, and his life reflects a similar pattern. After the stadium speech most of the members of the Brotherhood denounce him for his recklessness, his inattention to history, and his individualistic disregard of the good of the group. Like Bledsoe, they take away the power he has developed by preventing him from making speeches in Harlem. Yet he defies them in a funeral speech following the death of his only friend, Brother Tod Clifton.

Clifton's death provides a challenge for the reader as well as the narrator because he has left his position in the seemingly benevolent Brotherhood to sell racist icons—paper **Sambo** dolls—on the streets. Not only has he become a two-bit hustler, but he has chosen to peddle an object that the narrator considers an "obscenity." Clifton's downward spiral is mystifying, and the narrator recalls how Clifton, confronted by the militant Black activist Ras the Exhorter, suggests that men are tempted to plunge outside history. The narrator, of course, plunges outside history into his hole, so even though he is troubled by Clifton's decision to make money at the expense of the dignity of his race, he chooses to focus on Clifton's humanity in the funeral speech. There is much at stake here, for the narrator comes to realize that history has already left out men like himself and like Clifton, that they are invisible from history's point of view. Clifton surrenders to the condition of invisibility, which is a tragic refusal because he has the opportunity, like Louis Armstrong in the prologue and like the narrator in his writing of the book, to turn that invisibility into art. Despite Clifton's failure, the narrator insists on preserving his friend's dignity after his death by recognizing his essential humanity despite his flaws.

The Brotherhood again condemns the narrator for eschewing their party line, and he is finally able to recognize the hypocrisy of the organization and the contradictions of his role within it. Yet he has nowhere to go, which has been his condition throughout the novel. He tries to return to Harlem, but its streets are now a chaos of riots and madness. Disguising himself in sunglasses, he is mistaken for a man named Rinehart, who is revealed to be a protean **trickster** figure, a preacher, lover, and con man rolled into one. The narrator realizes that becoming Rinehart could benefit him, but he discards the disguise because he realizes that he is not Rinehart: adopting another's identity is not the solution. He is left with the fragments of the facets of his own identity that have been handed to him, and that he has carried around in his briefcase throughout the book, including a bank in the form of a racist depiction of Black people, one of the Sambo dolls Clifton had sold, the name that the Brotherhood gave him, and his scholarship to college. After falling into a hole during the riots, he destroys these items and, through the process of telling his story, begins to discover who he has really been all along.

The self-reliance that the narrator slowly develops is reminiscent of the great American thinkers of the nineteenth century, including Ellison's namesake, Ralph Waldo Emerson. Upon accepting the National Book Award for *Invisible Man*, Ellison highlighted his admiration for American literary tradition: "If I were asked in all seriousness just what I considered to be the chief significance of *Invisible Man* as a fiction, I would reply: Its experimental attitude, and its attempt to return to the mood of personal moral responsibility for democracy which typified the best of our nineteenth-century fiction" (*Shadow*, 102). One of the novel's epigraphs is from Melville's *Benito Cereno*, a work about the failure of this personal moral responsibility with regard to Black people. *Invisible Man*'s strength derives partly from Ellison's understanding of this American literary tradition, coupled with the fact that the African American perspective within it had been underrepresented before the 1950s. The first section of Ellison's essay collection *Shadow and Act* develops this theme as it delves into literary history of the nineteenth and twentieth centuries, scrutinizing individual writers such as **Mark Twain**, Stephen Crane, and Richard Wright. The second section in this collection focuses on music, and Ellison's perspective on jazz and **blues** is as clear and as valuable as his perspective on literature is. Many critics have detailed the connection between music and *Invisible Man*, a novel that reveals a deep knowledge of the blues and its **folklore** and that is structured as a kind of theme-and-variation with a good deal of jazzlike improvisation along the way.

Shadow and Act did not fully placate Ellison's readers, who continued to look for another novel. Interviewers consistently asked Ellison about his progress, and he methodically deflected them. His short fiction, originally published before *Invisible Man*, was also sparse, yet it was collected posthumously and published under the title *"Flying Home" and Other Stories* (1996). Although it contains some masterpieces, including the title story and "King of the Bingo Game" (1944), this collection is generally viewed in relation to *Invisible Man*. The power of Ellison's stories is not lessened by their scope, though: they are as emotionally intense as his grand work and, in some cases, more honest because less ambitious. The story "Mister Toussan" (1941) involves the interplay between history, folklore, and storytelling, but it does not shoulder the burden felt by *Invisible Man* to say something enormous about this interplay.

Ellison's essays, collected in *Going to the Territory* (1986) as well as in *Shadow and Act*, also are frequently seen as potential insights into *Invisible Man*, yet they have merit apart from the novel. Like its predecessor, the latter collection of essays focuses on literature and music, but there is an even greater sense of history in them as well as insightful pronouncements on American government. Ellison also published fragments of what would become *Juneteenth* in his lifetime, but by all accounts the work was chaotic and unfinished despite his four decades of work on it. Ellison's literary executor, John Callahan, pieced together some of these fragments and published them as *Juneteenth* in 1999; the critical reception was hostile, both to the work and to Callahan's attempts to make a coherent story. It is a story of Reverend Hickman and Senator Sunraider, known as "Bliss" as a child. Bliss had been abandoned as a child, following his White mother's false accusation of rape against Hickman's brother. Bliss's transformation into a race-baiting politician and Hickman's continued protection of him despite this act continues, in a way, Invisible Man's realization at Tod Clifton's funeral: racism is part of the American fabric, but forgiveness and healing are possible. The fact that this message is not fully developed in *Juneteenth* does not detract from its power.

Ellison's stature as a public figure and an academic are noteworthy, especially in light of the fact that both he and his famous protagonist did not complete college. In addition to being the first African American to receive the National Book Award, Ellison was the recipient of the Rockefeller Foundation Award and the Prix de Rome fellowship, the Medal of Freedom, and the Chevalier de l'Ordre des Arts et Lettres. He held fellowships and distinguished professorships at the University of Chicago, Rutgers, Yale, and New York University, and received honorary doctorates from many other universities. Far from invisible, he was recognized as one of the great writers of his time despite his relatively small body of published work, and his great novel will continue to make him visible throughout the imaginable future.

Resources: Primary Sources: Ralph Ellison: *The Collected Essays of Ralph Ellison*, ed. John F. Callahan (New York: Modern Library, 1995); *"Flying Home" and Other Stories*, ed. John F. Callahan (New York: Random House, 1996); *Going to the Territory* (New York: Random House, 1986); *Invisible Man* (New York: Random House, 1952); *Juneteenth: A Novel*, ed. John F. Callahan (New York: Random House, 1999); *Living with Music: Ralph Ellison's Jazz Writings*, ed. Robert G. O'Meally (New York: Modern Library, 2001); *Shadow and Act* (New York: Random House, 1964). **Secondary Sources:**

Kimberly W. Benston, ed., *Speaking for You: The Vision of Ralph Ellison* (Washington, DC: Howard University Press, 1987); Harold Bloom, ed., *Ralph Ellison* (New York: Chelsea House, 1986); Robert Bone, *The Negro Novel in America* (New Haven, CT: Yale University Press, 1958); Mark Busby, *Ralph Ellison* (Boston: Twayne, 1991); Robert J. Butler, ed., *The Critical Response to Ralph Ellison* (Westport, CT: Greenwood Press, 2000); Ronald Gottesman, comp., *Studies in "Invisible Man"* (Columbus, OH: Charles E. Merrill, 1971); Maryemma Graham and Amritjit Singh, eds., *Conversations with Ralph Ellison* (Jackson: University Press of Mississippi, 1995); John Hersey, ed., *Ralph Ellison: A Collection of Critical Essays* (Englewood Cliffs, NJ: Prentice-Hall, 1974); Lawrence Jackson, *Ralph Ellison: Emergence of Genius* (New York: John Wiley, 2002); Kerry McSweeney, *Invisible Man: Race and Identity* (Boston: Twayne, 1988); Alan Nadel, *Invisible Criticism: Ralph Ellison and the American Canon* (Iowa City: University of Iowa Press, 1988); Robert G. O'Meally, *The Craft of Ralph Ellison* (Cambridge, MA: Harvard University Press, 1980); Robert G. O'Meally, ed., *New Essays on "Invisible Man"* (Cambridge: Cambridge University Press, 1988); Horace A. Porter, *Jazz Country: Ralph Ellison in America* (Iowa City: University of Iowa Press, 2001); John M. Reilly, ed., *Twentieth Century Interpretations of "Invisible Man"* (Englewood Cliffs, NJ: Prentice-Hall, 1970); Edith Schor, *Visible Ellison: A Study of Ralph Ellison's Fiction* (Westport, CT: Greenwood Press, 1993); Jerry Gafio Watts, *Heroism and the Black Intellectual: Ralph Ellison, Politics, and Afro-American Intellectual Life* (Chapel Hill: University of North Carolina Press, 1994).

D. Quentin Miller

Emanuel, James A. (born 1921). Poet and critic. Although he has been writing poetry since the 1950s, Emanuel is probably best known for his creation of a new poetic genre, jazz **haiku**, which revolutionizes traditional haiku by incorporating rhyme and narrative. As with each of these art forms, his poetry embraces the spontaneity of musical and lyrical expression in its descriptions of African American experiences. While haikus often emphasize the relationship between humanity and **nature**, **jazz**, as Emanuel writes in the preface to *Jazz from the Haiku King* (1999), "spread its gospel of survival through joy and artistic imagination." Influenced strongly by **Langston Hughes**, about whom he has written a critical work, his poetry has a liberal, inclusive approach that strives to break down racial stereotypes and generalizations. The notion of freedom lies at the heart of his work, which aims to transcend social and political boundaries. Jazz haiku lends itself to the live arena, and Emanuel has performed his poetry across the world. A CD, *Middle Passage*, featuring saxophone accompaniment, was released in 2001. Emanuel is also a respected literary critic, publishing numerous critical articles on African American aesthetics and writers, including essays on **James Baldwin**, **Richard Wright**, and **Amiri Baraka**. Born in Alliance, Nebraska, he received his Ph.D. from Columbia University. He has held professorships in the United States, Poland, and France, and has received numerous awards, including a Special Distinction Award from the ***Black American Literature Forum***. He now lives in **Paris, France**.

Resources: James A. Emanuel: *Jazz from the Haiku King* (Detroit: Broadside Press, 1999); *Langston Hughes* (Boston: Twayne, 1967); *Whole Grain: Collected Poems, 1958–1989* (Detroit: Lotus Press, 1991); James A. Emanuel and Theodore L. Gross, eds., *Dark Symphony: Negro Literature in America* (New York: Free Press, 1968); Tyler Stovall, *Paris Noir: African Americans in the City of Light* (Boston: Houghton Mifflin, 1996).

Brian Burton

Epic Poetry/The Long Poem. An epic poem is a long narrative in verse. Historically, epic poems have taken heroes, heroines, gods, or God as their subject; epics often tell stories of wars or quests of great importance, focusing on civilizations or ways of life in profound crisis. Constituting a Western literary tradition stretching from the *Iliad* and the *Odyssey* (c. 800 B.C.E.) through Edmund Spenser's *The Faerie Queene* (1590–1596) and John Milton's *Paradise Lost* (1674), no other literary genre has enjoyed the status of the epic poem.

After Milton, the epic poem in English changed significantly. Mock-epic poems, including those by Alexander Pope, and epic biographical poems such as William Wordsworth's *The Prelude* (1850), began to replace the traditional epic. During the nineteenth century, the novel took the epic poem's central place in European, British, and American literature. In the twentieth century, both poets and critics tended to use the term "long poem" in place of "epic poem," partly because the term "epic" brings with it traditions, assumptions, and conventions that belong to bygone eras.

We have no evidence to suggest that African Americans wrote works of epic poetry between the arrival of the first Black slaves in North America and the nineteenth century, but as African Americans acquired education in literature, sometimes with the help of members of the **Abolitionist Movement**, they encountered epic poems including Dante's *Divine Comedy* (1320) and Milton's *Paradise Lost* (Blackshire-Belay).

The genealogy of the modern African American long poem, of which **Carolivia Herron** has given a noteworthy outline, reached its first milestone with John Boyd's *The Vision*, published in England in 1835, and with the work of **James Monroe Whitfield**. In *America and Other Poems* (1853), Whitfield offers two long poems, "America" and "How Long?," which exemplify the political utility of the genre by presenting a strongly abolitionist perspective. "America," written in iambic tetrameter, takes as its subject American hypocrisy, democracy, and **slavery**; "How Long?" is an extended reflection on the reasons why Blacks are still enslaved. In the work of **James Madison Bell**, the genre's inherent polemical elements emerge with a vociferous argument for and against "American values," including freedom. Bell's long poems include a poem on emancipation (1862), "The Day and the War" (1864), a poem on the death of Lincoln (1865), "Valedictory on Leaving San Francisco" (1866), and "The Progress of Liberty" (1866), on the end of the **Civil War**.

The end of the nineteenth century and the beginning of the twentieth witnessed the publication of the three longest poems ever written by African Americans. Two of these poems were written by **Albery Allson Whitman.**

Whitman's *Not a Man, and Yet a Man* (1877), which includes more than 5,000 couplet verses, concerns the exploits of a Black slave. Whitman also wrote *An Idyl of the South* (1901), an epic poem in two parts; composed entirely in ottava rima, it narrates stories of **the South** in the style of Tennyson. The third long poem is Robert E. Ford's 8,600-word *Brown Chapel, a Story in Verse* (1905).

Other African Americans who contributed to the genre of long poem include James Ephraim McGirt, **George Marion McClellan**, George Hannibal Temple, **George Reginald Margetson**, **Edward Smyth Jones**, **Fenton Johnson**, and Maurice N. Corbett. **James Weldon Johnson** included works by McClellan and Margetson in his anthology *The Book of American Negro Poetry* (1922).

McGirt wrote three epics in the pastoral and military styles of the Latin poet Virgil, including *Avenging the Maine* (1899). McClellan's intricate long poem "The Legend of Tannhauser and Elizabeth," based on Richard Wagner's opera *Tannhäuser* and published in *The Path of Dreams* (1916), is often described as the most accomplished work of nineteenth-century African American narrative epic (Bruce).

Temple wrote *The Epic of Columbus's Bell* (1900), which describes how a bell on Columbus' ship became the centerpiece of an African American church in New Jersey. Johnson self-published the long poem *Visions of the Dusk* in 1915. Corbett wrote *The Harp of Ethiopia* (1914).

In 1904, **Frances Ellen Watkins Harper** published *Moses: A Story of the Nile*, a poem in blank verse akin to that of Milton, and with a similar focus on biblical themes. The narrative suggests how a gifted African American can further the achievements of the race by making contributions to American democracy, technology, and education. Harper's distinctly irregular blank verse represents a significant stylistic innovation.

Harlem Renaissance poet **Countee Cullen**, best known for his lyric poetry, wrote the long poems "Shroud of Color," "Heritage" and "The Black Christ." Cullen's contemporaries **Melvin B. Tolson**, **Jean Toomer**, and **Langston Hughes** also wrote long poems. Tolson won the National Poetry Contest at the American Negro Exposition in **Chicago, Illinois**, for his long poem "Dark Symphony" (1940). In this poem, which employs musical tempos, Negro **spirituals**, and biographical sketches of great Blacks in world history, Tolson praises the achievements of his race while celebrating the **New Negro**. In 1953 Tolson published his *Libretto for the Republic of Liberia*, and *Harlem Gallery: Book I, The Curator* in 1965. In *Libretto*, Tolson draws upon Hart Crane's *The Bridge* (1930) to tell a multilingual history of Liberia that is divided into sections with titles drawn from the notes of an ascending scale (do, re, mi, etc.). In *Harlem Gallery*, Tolson initiates what was to have been a multivolume epic narrative of a Black man in America, but he died before he could complete the epic. Toomer, who is best known for his novel *Cane* (1923), also wrote the long poem "Blue Meridian" (1936).

Langston Hughes's *Montage of a Dream Deferred* (1951) is arguably the most famous African American long poem. Drawing on the **blues**, scat singing, and **jazz**, but also using traditional forms such as the **ballad**, Hughes expresses his vision of **Harlem, New York**, and, indirectly, of African Americans. Many of the poems within the poem are spoken by different imagined citizens of Harlem, giving the long poem a dramatic quality. In 1961 Hughes published the long poem *Ask Your Mama: 12 Moods for Jazz.*

Gwendolyn Brooks's *Annie Allen* (1949) is a formal mock epic with all the standard epic devices, and is reminiscent of Alexander Pope's *The Rape of the Lock* (1714). Playfully known as "The Anniad," *Annie Allen* deals with serious issues such as the doubly subservient position of Black women vis-à-vis Black men and their White oppressors. Brooks pursues her inquiry into the social and spiritual position of Black women in contemporary America in her poem *In the Mecca* (1968), which concerns Mrs. Sallie, who lives in the run-down Mecca Building in Chicago and is searching for her missing daughter, Pepita. On her quest, she encounters an array of urban characters who are generally optimistic about the future of African Americans. Ultimately, however, this bright sense of the future becomes bleak for Mrs. Sallie when she discovers that her daughter has been murdered by one of the poverty-stricken residents of the Mecca.

More recent examples of the African American long poem include *Black Anima* (1973), by N. J. Loftis, which describes from both Black and White perspectives a trip into the hell of historical slavery. **Jay Wright** published the long poem *The Double Invention of Komo* in 1980. He modeled his poem on ancient African rituals such as the Komo initiation rite among the Bambara. The poem celebrates both the pluralism and the unity of African Americans. More recently, **Harryette Mullen** has worked in longer poetic forms (*Sleeping with the Dictionary*, 2002). (*See* **Baraka, Amiri**.)

Resources: Margaret Beissinger, Jane Tylus, and Susanne Wofford, eds., *Epic Traditions in the Contemporary World: The Poetics of Community* (Berkeley: University of California Press, 1999); James Madison Bell, *The Poetical Works of James Madison Bell* (Lansing, MI: Wynkoop, Hallenback, Crawford, 1901); Carol Blackshire-Belay, ed., *Language and Literature in the African American Imagination* (Westport, CT: Greenwood Press, 1992); Gwendolyn Brooks: *Annie Allen* (New York: Harper, 1949); *In the Mecca* (New York: Harper & Row, 1968); Dickson D. Bruce, "George Marion McClellan," in *Dictionary of Literary Biography*, vol. 50, *Afro-American Writers Before the Harlem Renaissance*, ed. Trudier Harris (Detroit: Gale, 1986), 206–212; Frances Ellen Watkins Harper, *Poems* (Philadelphia: Ferguson, 1898); Carolivia Herron, "Early African American Poetry," in *The Columbia History of American Poetry*, ed. Jay Parini and Brett C. Miller (New York: Columbia University Press, 1993), 31–35; Langston Hughes: *Ask Your Mama: 12 Moods for Jazz* (New York: Knopf, 1961); *Montage of a Dream Deferred* (New York: Holt, 1951); Fenton Johnson, *Visions of the Dusk* (New York: Fenton Johnson, 1915); James Weldon Johnson, *The Book of American Negro Poetry* (New York: Harcourt, Brace, 1922); N. J. Loftis, *Black Anima* (New York: Liveright, 1973); George Marion McClellan: *The Path of Dreams* (1916; repr. Freeport, NY: Books for Libraries, 1971); *Poems* (Nashville, TN: A.M.E. Publishing, 1895); Hiram Kelly Moderwell, "The Epic of the Black Man," *The New Republic*, Sept. 1917, 154–155; Harryette Mullen, *Sleeping with the Dictionary* (Berkeley: University of California Press, 2002); Melvin B. Tolson: *Harlem Gallery and*

Other Poems, ed. Raymond Nelson (Charlottesville: University Press of Virginia, 1999); *Libretto for the Republic of Liberia* (New York: Twayne, 1953); James Monroe Whitfield, *Poems* (Buffalo, NY: Leavit, 1853); Albery Allson Whitman: *An Idyl of the South* (New York: Metaphysical Publishing, 1901); *Not a Man, and Yet a Man* (1877; repr. Upper Saddle River, NJ: Literature House, 1970); Jay Wright, *The Double Invention of Komo* (Austin: University of Texas Press, 1980).

Antony Adolf

Epistolary Novel. The epistolary novel is composed to represent some kind of letter format: one long letter, multiple letters by one character in the novel, or several letters that different characters exchange. Some of the earliest works in the tradition of the English novel were epistolary novels, including *Pamela* (1740) and *Clarissa* (1747–1748) by Samuel Richardson.

Elizabeth Campbell has identified several distinct characteristics, in addition to the effect of letters being written by characters in the novel, that define epistolary fiction: "fragmentation, subjectivity, abandonment of chronology; repetitiveness, associative and sometime seemingly illogical connections, and most of all, unconventional use of language" (334–335). Sometimes epistolary novels also lack the sense of closure that other kinds of novels have. Elizabeth MacArthur observes that letter writers "cannot make insinuations about the future . . ., and they cannot explain the significance of present events in relation to a large whole. . . . since the characters themselves cannot write as if they knew the larger shape of the events they are experiencing, their narrations will be unlikely to suggest inexorable progress towards a significant and predetermined end" (9). This unstable closure, along with the other characteristics of the epistolary novel, involves the reader in the narratives differently from the ways other kinds of novels involve the reader.

Most early epistolary novels were written for or by women and were originally categorized as sentimental novels because of their subject matter and because of the function they fulfilled: "Though the epistolary form lent itself to a range of didactic purposes, it was preeminently the favored mode of moral instruction for women" (Gilroy and Verhoeven, 2). Richardson's two famous novels—*Pamela* and *Clarissa*—both purported to be concerned about the virtue of women. While epistolary novels may no longer be solely sentimental in nature, Campbell argues that past and current epistolary novels are nonetheless about "sexual politics." However, she adds that "contemporary ones are more blatantly political in theme and more radical in form" (332). More contemporary epistolary novels portray the wide range of experiences lived by all people, yet most are still written by women and very few appear to be written by ethnic minority writers.

The most often cited epistolary novel within the African American tradition is **Alice Walker**'s *The Color Purple* (1982). This novel also fits within the "mainstream epistolary tradition of a pathetic heroine (like Clarissa or Héloïse) writing to an absent addressee" because Celie addresses her letters first to God and later to her sister, Nettie (Gilroy and Verhoeven, 14). *The Color Purple* also fits within mainstream epistolary fiction because it "documents the commodification of the female body in patriarchal society" (Gilroy and Verhoeven, 14).

Race and the African American tradition, however, are not just background within *The Color Purple*; they strongly influence the novel. According to Gilroy and Verhoeven, "Walker...both invokes and subverts the type of slave narrative that depends on religious transformation. Moreover, other dominant features of slave narratives appear in Celie's letters (sexual and physical assaults, the abduction of children, hard labor), while 'Nettie's letters to Celie memorialize' the slave narrative's focus on escape, freedom, and 'moral uplift'" (14). The ultimate praise of the effects of this novel and its place in literary history come because "Walker creates a generic hybrid whose blending of the epistolary genre with the slave narrative radically revises literary history" (Gilroy and Verhoeven, 14). Linda Kauffman also argues that *The Color Purple* "fuses epistolary with slave narrative" (xvi–xvii) through the use of common motifs: "forced labor, beatings, sexual assaults which result in pregnancy and which lead to the abduction and selling of children" (189). Kauffman, along with Gilroy and Verhoeven, acknowledge Walker's debt not only to **slave narratives** but also to the writing of **Zora Neale Hurston**.

Other examples of epistolary novels within the African American tradition include two young-adult novels: *Color Me Dark: The Diary of Nellie Lee Love*, by **Patricia McKissack**, and *The Ups and Downs of Carl Davis III*, by **Rosa Guy**. *Color Me Dark* is part of the Dear America series published by Scholastic. This series of novels follows young girls living through historical events through their journals. *Color Me Dark* tells the story of a young girl living during, and being part of, the migration of Southern African Americans to **Chicago, Illinois**, in search of better jobs and a better life. *The Ups and Downs of Carl Davis III* is about a young New York City boy who is sent to live with his grandmother in South Carolina. Carl's letters to his parents, in which he expresses his feelings about his new life, including problems with peers and a prejudiced teacher, form the basis of this epistolary novel.

Early criticism of the epistolary novel focused on eighteenth-century examples (including Richardson), but critics today are giving new attention to the epistolary novel, which in turn provides a new narrative of its history. Gilroy and Verhoeven take exception with some of this contemporary criticism: "Criticism on epistolary writing does not seem to have come to grips with those issues of race and post-colonialism that have preoccupied, and continue to preoccupy, broad sections of the academic community;...though American epistolary writing is well-represented, there is little discussion of the work of Hispanic or black Americans" (13). Research bears out the fact that few Hispanic or African American writers have written within the epistolary tradition, which may be one reason they are underrepresented in discussion of epistolary fiction. Why more African American writers have not used this mode to explore issues of race, identity, and colonization (for example) remains an open question, as does the use of the epistolary form in the age of cell telephones, "instant messaging," and E-mail.

Resources: Janet Gurkin Altman, *Epistolarity: Approaches to a Form* (Columbus: Ohio State University Press, 1982); Anne Bower, *Epistolary Responses: The Letter in 20th-Century American Fiction and Criticism* (Tuscaloosa: University of Alabama Press, 1997); Elizabeth Campbell, "Re-visions, Re-flections, Re-creations: Epistolarity in Novels by Contemporary Women," *Twentieth Century Literature* 41 (1995), 332–348; Mary A. Favret, *Romantic Correspondence: Women, Politics, and the Fiction of Letters* (Cambridge: Cambridge University Press, 1993); Amanda Gilroy and W. M. Verhoeven, eds., *Epistolary Histories: Letters, Fiction, Culture* (Charlottesville: University Press of Virginia, 2000); Elizabeth C. Goldsmith, ed., *Writing the Female Voice: Essays on Epistolary Literature* (Boston: Northeastern University Press, 1989); Rosa Guy, *The Ups and Downs of Carl Davis III* (New York: Delacorte, 1989); Linda S. Kauffman, *Special Delivery: Epistolary Modes in Modern Fiction* (Chicago: University of Chicago Press, 1992); Elizabeth J. MacArthur, *Extravagant Narratives: Closure and Dynamics in the Epistolary Form* (Princeton, NJ: Princeton University Press, 1990); Patricia C. McKissack, *Color Me Dark: The Diary of Nellie Lee Love* (New York: Scholastic, 2000); Ruth Perry, *Women, Letters, and the Novel* (New York: AMS Press, 1980); Alice Walker, *The Color Purple* (New York: Harcourt Brace Jovanovich, 1982).

Susie Scifres Kuilan

Equiano, Olaudah (1745–1797). Writer. African-born author of *The Interesting Narrative of the Life of Olaudah Equiano; or, Gustavus Vassa, the African* (1789), Equiano is an important figure of both multiple literary genres and of abolitionism. An Ibo born in Isseke in present-day Nigeria, Equiano begins his narrative with a discussion of Ibo society and his kidnapping into European slavery at age eleven. There is some inconclusive evidence that he was born in South Carolina, but even if this proves true, his *Narrative* remains a foundational work of the African American literary tradition; it sets out most of the arguments against **slavery** and racism that African Americans have developed during the two centuries since its publication. Equiano's *Narrative* holds prominent places in such genres as the **slave narrative**, abolitionist literature, **travel writing, autobiography**, and spiritual/Christian literature.

Equiano's *Narrative* opens by quoting Isaiah, which situates Equiano's work in the biblical tradition of social criticism, the jeremiad. By the end of the first (of twelve) chapters, Equiano has discussed not only Christianity but also geography, anthropology, judicature, comparative cultural analysis, **gender** studies, **race** theory, economics, a comparison of slaveries, African religion, and historical theories on the Jewish **diaspora**. In addition to its diversity of topics, Equiano's *Narrative* recounts the author's travels in Africa, the Caribbean, Mesoamerica, the United States, Europe, Turkey, and even the Arctic. This not only provides an exciting read but also counters the traditional Western triumvirate of travel–knowledge–power associated with "White" men.

Three particularly important themes of the African American tradition in Equiano are the **Middle Passage**, the preference for death over slavery (famously dramatized by **Toni Morrison** in *Beloved*, 1987) and, perhaps most important, the theme of the "talking book." When Equiano acknowledges his

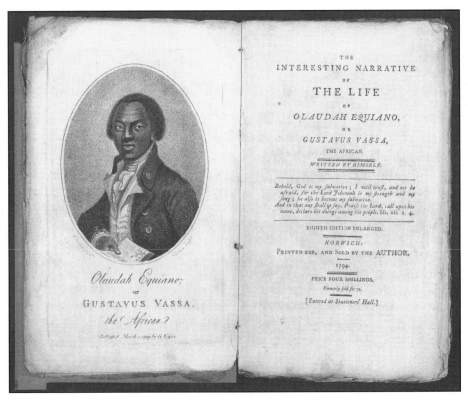

Frontispiece and title page from *The Interesting Narrative of the Life of Olaudah Equiano*, 1794. Courtesy of the Library of Congress.

great desire to "talk to the books" like a European, he acknowledges knowledge and linguistic fluency as a means to power, a paramount theme of African American literature and arts that recurs from **Frederick Douglass** through **Malcolm X** to **rap** artists.

Equiano's *Narrative* shows the author imbued with high educational expectations before his capture. Although Equiano admires European culture, he depicts his native Ibo society as essentially equal to, and in some ways superior to, European society. Thus, when Equiano overcomes multiple injustices to buy himself out of slavery, start a business, join a North Pole expedition, accept a British government appointment to commissary, and even write and publish a book, the implicit argument is not that Africans are merely improvable specimens when exposed to European culture but that Equiano's successes are manifestations of his African heritage.

After publication of *Interesting Narrative*, Equiano married an Englishwoman, Susan Cullen. Before his death, Equiano's *Narrative* had gone through eight English editions and had been translated into Dutch, Russian, and French. Equiano remains one of the most widely read of all African authors.

Resources: Robert J. Allison, "Introduction," in *The Interesting Narrative of the Life of Olaudah Equiano* (Boston: Bedford Books, 1995); Angelo Costanzo, *Surprising*

Narrative: Olaudah Equiano and the Beginnings of Black Autobiography (Westport, CT: Greenwood Press, 1987).

Kevin M. Hickey

Erotica. "Erotica" is a name given to literature in which intimacy and sexuality are the primary, even the exclusive, focus of the writing. This genre of literature has become so popular that major companies publish it in mass-market paperback editions. Warner Books (New York) is one example. The popularity and acceptability of erotica indicate a shift in American culture with regard to what is considered to be taboo. Undoubtedly one precursor to the shift, if not one of its direct causes, was the **sexual revolution** of the late 1960s and early 1970s. Erotica seems to occupy a niche in the literary marketplace between what most people would regard as pornographic, obscene, objectionable material and literature in which sexuality is part of an array of themes the literature addresses. For instance, the writings of **Langston Hughes**, **Richard Wright**, **James Baldwin**, **Toni Morrison**, and **Alice Walker** may include sexuality as a theme, but the writings do not present themselves, nor have they been interpreted as, erotica. At the same time, most literature that presents itself as, or is marketed as, erotica is less graphic than writing that presents itself as, or is marketed as, pornography. From a variety of perspectives—historical, sociological, literary, economic, and moral and ethical—the genre of erotica is a potentially intriguing phenomenon, and it occupies a narrow but nonetheless popular category of literature. African American literary erotica is one of numerous subcategories of erotica, and **Zane**, at this writing, is one of the most popular writers in the subcategory. Much African American erotica appears in anthologies.

Resources: Samiya Bashir, ed., *Best Black Women's Erotica 2* (San Francisco: Cleis Press, 2002); J. H. Blair, ed., *Black Satin: Contemporary Erotic Fiction by Writers of African Origin* (New York: Berkeley Books, 2004); Miriam DeCosta-Willis, Reginald Martin, and Roseann P. Bell, eds., *Erotique Noire/Black Erotica* (New York: Anchor, 1992); Robert Fleming, ed., *After Hours: A Collection of Erotic Writing by Black Men* (New York: Plume, 2002); Jossel Flowers Green, *Twilight Moods* (New York: Writers and Poets, 2002); Kathleen E. Morris, *Speaking in Whispers: African-American Lesbian Erotica* (New York: Third Side Press, 1996); Retha Powers, ed., *Black Silk: A Collection of African American Erotica* (New York: Warner Books, 2002); Blanche Richardson and Iyanla Vanzant, *Best Black Women's Erotica* (San Francisco: Cleis Press, 2001); Carol Taylor, ed., *Brown Sugar: A Collection of Erotic Black Fiction* (New York: Plume, 2001).

Hans Ostrom

Essay. Prose form based in the European tradition of writing by Michel de Montaigne, Francis Bacon, Blaise Pascal, Charles Lamb, William Hazlitt, Leigh Hunt, and Viriginia Woolf. The American essay tradition is shaped by the writings of Thomas Paine, Ralph Waldo Emerson, Henry David Thoreau, and E. B. White. Many critics of the essay identify the writings of Montaigne as one important origin of the modern essay, which is based in the birth of the modern individual and the rise of secularism. The essay is well suited for explorations of specific locations, times, events, and pressing social questions. For example, Montaigne wrote about such diverse topics as the European discovery of the American continents in his essay "Of the Caniballes" (1580), the experience of reading philosophical traditions in "Of Books" (1580), and the worldly human body in "Of Cripples" (1588) and "Of Physiognomy" (1588).

The essay is a highly diverse prose genre marked by flexibility, digression, and openness. It often features meditations on personal experience that question common knowledge or philosophical traditions. Essayists often "speak" in the first person to offer a personal account of familiar experiences or ideas. Essays are also often composed of personal anecdotes, observations, and references to or direct quotation of other writers and well-known figures. Consequently, the essay is often considered an occasional or ephemeral form that must make the particular universal if the individual essay is to survive beyond the immediacy of its chronological or geographical context. In terms of tone and direction, the essay is marked by a digressive, provisional, sometimes wandering speaker seeking innovative ideas, experiences, and ways of viewing common questions or problems. Some locate the essay's exploratory nature in the rise of empiricism and discovery in the writings of scientist–philosophers such as Francis Bacon and New World explorers such as Christopher Columbus. Others turn to the essay as the most formless of prose genres, an open arena that is able to question received knowledge and to renounce dogma by seeking out the evidence of new experience or data. Audience is also a key component of the form, insofar as readers are invited to share in recounted personal experience or observations and since many essayists directly address a particular audience that might be incorporated into the essay itself. In the African American essay tradition, the form often also serves as a vehicle for direct engagement with political and cultural events, thereby bearing affinity to other rhetorical traditions and socially engaged forms such as **sermons**, protest novels, and political speeches.

The African American essay has played a central role in shaping national debates about racism, African American literary traditions, and the limits of American democratic systems for authors and intellectuals, who often hold positions of cultural power as race spokespersons. A significant proportion of African American novelists, dramatists, and poets are also essayists. Important African American essayists include **Booker T. Washington, Anna Julia Haywood Cooper, W.E.B. Du Bois, James Weldon Johnson, Langston Hughes, Zora Neale Hurston, Richard Wright, Ralph Ellison, James Baldwin, Alice Walker, Audre Lorde, June Jordan, Gerald Early, Patricia J. Williams**, and **Stanley Crouch**. These writers' essays are often valued in literary, cultural, and political traditions as much as, or more than, their poetry, fiction, and drama.

The most famous and influential early African American essays are Anna Julia Cooper's long meditation A *Voice from the South* (1892), Booker T.

Washington's political essays "The Awakening of the Negro" (1896) and "Signs of Progress Among the Negroes" (1900), and W.E.B. Du Bois's collection of historical, sociological, and literary essays, *The Souls of Black Folk* (1903). These formative essays shaped the genre as an important venue for African American intellectuals' political commentary and analysis of the meanings of **race**, class, **gender**, and freedom in America. In their essays, Washington, Cooper, and Du Bois seek to represent the concerns of African Americans generally to an American public and to articulate a program for future race relations in America after **Reconstruction**. Washington underscored the importance of basic education and hard work within African American communities that he would fully outline in his autobiography *Up from Slavery* (1901). Cooper emphasized the importance of giving voice to the countless Black women who were largely overlooked in dominant political conversations about race, **the South**, and the challenges of Reconstruction. DuBois outlined a philosophy of racial uplift that included investment in the higher education and leadership of a **"talented tenth"** to represent the general African American population. As these early essayists demonstrated, the African American essay as a form provides the flexibility in speaking position and subject matter by which Cooper, Washington, and Du Bois were able to draw from both particular personal experiences and general experiences of members of the entire race, as well as to address both a White and a Black audience in America, sometimes separately and sometimes simultaneously.

During the literary movement known as the **Harlem Renaissance**, the essay provided a venue for debates about the role of literature and African American artists' multiple responsibilities to art, to politics, and to representations of African American culture and experience. Langston Hughes's "The Negro Artist and the Racial Mountain" (1925) is a central document on the role of race and writing from the Harlem Renaissance. It was written as a kind of response to an essay, "The Negro-Art Hokum," by **George Schuyler**, but also stands alone as an important statement about aesthetics. Since then, nearly all African American writers have had to respond in some way to what James Weldon Johnson called "The Dilemma of the Negro Author" (1928), and the essay is often where African American authors debate the dilemma. Some look to the question of the racial composition of intended and actual audiences, such as in "Our Literary Audience" (1930), by **Sterling A. Brown**, which argued for the crucial role played by great audiences—both White and Black—in making great art, and sixty years later Stan West compared the role of the Black writer to that of a tightrope walker among a racially divided audience in "Tip-Toeing on the Tight Rope: A Personal Essay on Black Writer Ambivalence" (1998). Other writers have responded to Johnson's dilemma by considering what role and form African American fiction should take. Richard Wright laid out a "Blue Print for Negro Writing" (1937) by arguing that African American writers must recognize and use the political messages of art, while **Addison Gayle, Jr.**, argued for a specifically Black aesthetic in African American fiction in his essays that provided the theoretical grounding of the **Black Arts Movement**, including especially "Cultural Strangulation: Black Literature and the White Aesthetic" (1971).

The essay has also served as a key site for authors to create or refuse literary lineages. **Wallace Thurman** traced and evaluated the literary history of African Americans before the Harlem Renaissance by condemning previous writers for working within White literary traditions in his essays "Negro Artists and the Negro" (1927) and "Negro Poets and Their Poetry" (1928). **Alain Locke** provided the de facto manifesto for the Harlem Renaissance by arguing that writers must consciously create a new, specifically African American cultural tradition in his opening essay, "The New Negro" (1925), for the collection of the same name. Ralph Ellison was a key figure in redrawing American literary histories across and outside racial lines in his essay collections *Shadow and Act* (1964) and *Going to the Territory* (1986), especially in the essays "Twentieth-Century Fiction and the Black Mask of Humanity" (1953), "Change the Joke and Slip the Yoke" (1963), and "The Novel as a Function of American Democracy" (1967). Within a specifically African American literary tradition, James Baldwin criticized the representational choices of his literary forefather Richard Wright as Baldwin staked out his own literary territory in his essay collection *Notes of a Native Son* (1955), most notably in his famous essay "Everybody's Protest Novel."

Regarding a specifically female literary tradition, Alice Walker's "Searching for Zora," (1975), originally published in the feminist magazine Ms., was an important catalyst for projects to rescue literary foremothers, such as Zora Neale Hurston, from obscurity. In the essay, Walker recounts her quest to locate and buy a gravestone for Hurston's unmarked grave, a fate that Walker saw as emblematic of the African American woman writer. Walker also reexamined Southern literary histories at large to claim Flannery O'Connor as her literary foremother, and she included both essays in her bestselling collection *In Search of Our Mothers' Gardens* (1983). **Toni Cade Bambara** also participated in the creation of a woman-centered literary and cultural tradition in her groundbreaking collection *The Black Woman* (1970), considered the first major **Black feminist** publication, which brought together essays, as well as short stories and poems, by African American women. June Jordan's *Civil Wars* (1981) is recognized as the first major collection of essays by an African American woman.

Many African American essayists were very conscious of their roles as race spokespersons. In response, many essayists borrowed from the ethnographic study genre, and consequently reflected and criticized contemporary ideas about race and anthropology. **Pauline E. Hopkins** augmented her romance fiction with the essay "The Dark Races of the Twentieth Century" (1905), an early examination of potential kinship based on race in the aftermath of the failures of Reconstruction to create a unified America and amid growing U.S. imperialism. The best known, and most debated, use of ethnographic techniques is in the nonfiction of Zora Neale Hurston. In addition to her folkloric study *Mules and Men* (1935), Hurston penned many essays about African

American **folklore** and culture, most notably "Characteristics of Negro Expression" (1930), informed by her training as an anthropologist by Franz Boaz at Barnard College.

Many African American writers have used the essay as a means of publicly exploring the complex cultural terrain of important African American cities, neighborhoods, and communities. **Paul Laurence Dunbar** and Langston Hughes both wrote essays about **Washington, D.C.**, in order to explore the myth and reality of middle-class and upper-class African American society. James Weldon Johnson, Wallace Thurman, Langston Hughes, and **Arna Bontemps** wrote essays specifically about **Harlem, New York**, during the Harlem Renaissance. James Baldwin examined his experiences in the city of **Paris, France**, as a means of contrasting African American living conditions and ideas about race both in the urban North and the segregated South in his essay collections *Notes of a Native Son* (1955) and *Nobody Knows My Name* (1961). Similarly, LeRoi Jones wrote about politics and life in Cuba to contrast the American political scene in his essay "Cuba Libre" (1961). (*See* **Amiri Baraka**.)

The essay has served as a key site for writers to bring African American experiences and perspectives to major political questions of the day. James Baldwin's best-selling *The Fire Next Time* (1963) helped bring the moral challenge of the **Civil Rights Movement** to a national audience concerned about racial violence and the rise of the **Nation of Islam** and **Black Nationalism**. One of the first paid publications for the young Alice Walker was her essay "The Civil Rights Movement: What Good Was It?" (1967), which won a contest in the *American Scholar*. The essay has brought popular novelists into the realm of public debate—for instance, **Chester B. Himes**'s sardonic call to action in response to segregation during **World War II** in "Negro Martyrs Are Needed" (1943)—and it has brought political activists into conversation with Black artists and traditions, as in **Angela Y. Davis**'s "Billie Holiday's 'Strange Fruit': Musical and Social Consciousness" (1988), which joined a distinguished tradition of essays on Black music, as well as Davis's own widely read essays of political theory in *Women, Race, and Class* (1981). African American intellectuals and academics have come to national prominence by using the essay form to bring personal experience and historical grounding to current topics of fierce public debate, such as legal scholar Patricia J. Williams's critiques of the Clarence Thomas–Anita Hill senate confirmation controversy in "A Rare Case Study of Muleheadedness and Men," and her critiques of multiculturalism and the fate of the Civil Rights Movement in her best-selling essay collection *The Alchemy of Race and Rights* (1991). (*See* **Multicultural Theory**.)

The essay has proven to be a central genre for African American journalistic enterprises and examinations of popular culture. Many African American writers gained a public name by writing for Black-identified magazines such as **Callaloo**, W.E.B. Du Bois's ***The Crisis***, ***Opportunity***, *Obsidian*, **Phylon**, and *Sojourner*, or for popular magazines designed for an African American audience, such as *Essence*, **Ebony**, and *Jet*. Toni Cade Bambara introduced readers of *Essence* to the folk character M'Dear in her essay "Beauty Is Just Care...Like Ugly Is Just Carelessness," which advocated "brainwashing" as a folk remedy for the racist messages permeating popular culture, within a magazine heavily packed with advertisements for Black beauty products. On the other hand, Langston Hughes's later career included regular contributions to the African American newspaper the **Chicago Defender**, both in the form of his Jesse B. Simple tales and of essays, and June Jordan wrote a regular essay column for *The Progressive*, a leftist magazine advocating peace and justice, both internationally and domestically. Many of James Baldwin's essays were commissioned by journalistic publications, most notably his essays about desegregation in the South, such as "Fly in the Buttermilk" (1958), which appeared in *Harper's Magazine*, and about life in Harlem and downtown Manhattan during that same period, which he contrasted in "Fifth Avenue, Uptown: A Letter from Harlem" (1960) and "East River, Downtown: Postscript to a Letter from Harlem" (1961), first published in the *New York Times Magazine* and *Esquire*, respectively. During the rise of Third World nationalism and the Black **diaspora**, journalistic essays proved a particularly important means for African Americans to become familiar with the everyday lives and struggles of Black people around the globe. Angela Davis and Amiri Baraka wrote many political essays in this vein. June Jordan reported from politically volatile countries for various magazines and collected her writings in *On Call: Political Essays* (1985), including her contribution to the growing antiapartheid movement in America with her essay "South Africa: Bringing It All Back Home" (1981), first published in the *New York Times*.

In addition to the European roots of the essay as a genre, it is important to note that African American essayists also draw from rhetorical and generic traditions specific to the African American experience. In addition to generally recognized American masters of the form—Ralph Waldo Emerson, Henry David Thoreau, Henry James, and E. B. White—African American essayists draw from a distinguished rhetorical tradition of African American orators, including **Frederick Douglass**, **Henry Highland Garnet**, **David Walker**, and **Sojourner Truth**. While the essay as a form is marked by its ability to forge a subjective speaking voice, the African American oratory tradition provides essayists with the rhetorical tools to address immediate audiences, often divided along racial lines. The abolitionist oratory tradition especially provides a tradition in which African Americans forged a public voice by claiming and critiquing widely held American beliefs about freedom, independence, and autonomy. African American essayists also draw from a robust Black church tradition, which lends a polemical tone to many essays. Some have discussed the essay as a print version of spaces of public debate, such as a Black pulpit used to launch accusations at its audience (Early, 1993, x), or as a passionate feminist dialogue between women from different backgrounds (Joeres, and Mittman, 1993, 156). The importance of oratorical prowess in contemporary African American essays is evidenced in the writings of **Cornel West** and **Michael Eric Dyson**, academics and essayists also well known as public speakers and influenced by the poetics of oral forms, such as **hip-hop** in Dyson's essays in particular.

Resources: Primary Sources: James Baldwin: *The Fire Next Time* (New York: Dell, 1963); *Notes of a Native Son* (Boston: Beacon Press, 1955); Amiri Baraka, *Home: Social Essays* (New York: Morrow, 1966); Anna Julia Cooper, *A Voice from the South: By a Black Woman of the South* (1892; repr. New York: Oxford University Press, 1988); Angela Y. Davis et al., *If They Come in the Morning: Voices of Resistance* (New York: Third Press, 1971); W.E.B. Du Bois, *The Souls of Black Folk* (Chicago: A. C. McClurg, 1903); Ralph Ellison, *Shadow and Act* (New York: Random House, 1964); Langston Hughes: *Good Morning Revolution: Uncollected Writings of Social Protest by Langston Hughes*, ed. Faith Berry (Seacaucus, NJ: Carol Publishing Group, 1992); *Langston Hughes and the Chicago Defender: Essays on Race, Politics, and Culture: 1942–1962*, ed. Christopher C. De Santis (Urbana: University of Illinois Press, 1995); "The Negro Artist and the Racial Mountain," *Nation* 23 (1926), 692–694; Zora Neale Hurston, "Characteristics of Negro Expression," in *Negro: An Anthology*, ed. Nancy Cunard (London: Wishart, 1934), 39–46; June Jordan, *Some of Us Did Not Die: New and Selected Essays* (New York: Basic/Civitas Books, 2002); Audre Lorde, *Sister Outsider* (Freedom, CA: Crossing Press, 1984); Alice Walker, *In Search of Our Mothers' Gardens* (Trumansburg, NY: Crossing Press, 1984); Richard Wright, "Blueprint for Negro Writing," *New Challenge* 2 (Fall 1937), 58–65. **Secondary Sources:** T. W. Adorno, "The Essay as Form" (Frankfurt Am Main: Suhrkamp Verlag, 1958), trans. Bob Hullot-Kentor and Frederic Will, *New German Critique* 32 (1984), 151–171; Wendy Bishop and Hans Ostrom, eds., *Genre and Writing: Issues, Arguments, Alternatives* (Portsmouth, NH: Boynton-Cook/Heineman, 1997); Alexander J. Butrym, ed., *Essays on the Essay: Redefining the Genre* (Athens: University of Georgia Press, 1989); Gerald Early: *Speech and Power*, vol. 1, *The African-American Essay and Its Cultural Content from Polemics to Pulpit* (Hopewell, NJ: Ecco Press, 1992); *Speech and Power*, vol. 2, *The African-American Essay and Its Cultural Content from Polemics to Pulpit* (Hopewell, NJ: Ecco Press, 1993); Ruth-Ellen Boetcher Joeres and Elizabeth Mittman, eds., *The Politics of the Essay: Feminist Perspectives* (Bloomington: Indiana University Press, 1993); Cristina Kirklighter, *Traversing the Democratic Borders of the Essay* (Albany: State University of New York Press, 2002); Philip Lopate, *The Art of the Personal Essay: An Anthology from the Classical Era to the Present* (New York: Anchor, 1994); Peter Mack, "Rhetoric and the Essay," *Rhetoric Society Quarterly* 23, no. 2 (Spring 1993), 41–49.

Brian J. Norman

Evans, Mari (born 1923). Poet, essayist, playwright, and children's author. Evans is best known for her poetry, but she has also published children's books and plays, and she has edited a critically acclaimed reference guide to African American women authors.

Born and educated in Ohio, Evans pursued fashion design before turning to poetry. Her first collection, *Where Is All the Music?* (1968), concentrates on relationships; only three of the poems give any indication of the activism her later writings embrace. "Black jam for dr. negro" explores the rejection of

White middle-class values by its narrator. A doctor, the speaker embarrasses his partner with his "natural ways": his afro and the way he walks announce him as a Black man who is unwilling to change in order to win approval from others. "Who can be born black" is frequently anthologized and celebrates the African American heritage. Evans' second volume, *I Am a Black Woman* (1970), was named the most distinguished book of poetry by an Indiana writer. The poet shifts from commentary on the struggle for individuals to forge and maintain personal relationships to addressing the needs of the African American community. In the collection's title poem, she moves the reader through history from **slavery**—"I saw my mate leap screaming to the sea and I/with these hands/cupped the lifebreath from my issue in the cane-brake"—to Korea and Vietnam—"I/learned Da Nang and Pork Chop Hill in anguish." The poem ends with the exultant "I am a black woman/tall as a cypress...Look on me and be/renewed." Evans uses "domestic" poems to illustrate the pressing difficulties of the community of women in particular. Two of the poems, "The Great Civil Rights Law A.D. 1964" and "The Emancipation of George Hector (a Colored Turtle)," address the effectiveness of equal rights legislation in the Black community. The social injustices endured by children is also a strong theme in the volume and prefigures her later children's fiction.

In *Nightstar* (1981), Evans's poems fully embrace the concerns of community and seek to shed light on overlooked needs. "Modern American Suite in Four Movements—New York City" juxtaposes the fashion district of New York with the plight of the homeless. After providing images and scenes from both the fashion world and the world on the streets, Evans ends the poem: "This is America to me." Typographically the poem is spread across the page—there are no neat line or stanza breaks. Many of the poems in *Nightstar* are more experimental in their use of typography, African American idiom, and portraits of the characters of the Black community. The poems also take on a **blues** flavor, and some ("Blues in B," "Black Queen Blues," and "Cellblock Blues") are celebrations of blues music itself. (*See* **Black Arts Movement**.)

Evans believes that poets are in a position to be teachers. They are the eyes of their communities, and it is their responsibility to sound the warnings of societal indifference and injustices. Her poetry expresses these warnings, often in direct exhortations to the reader. *A Dark and Splendid Mass*, Evans's 1992 collection, uses the paean, a poetic form of praise, to convey the resilient spirits of victims of abuse and deprivation.

Evans's juvenile fiction addresses the concerns of childhood and the injustices children in the Black community face. *Dear Corinne, Tell Somebody! Love, Annie: A Book about Secrets* (1999) examines the secrets that abused children hold and encourages them to confide in adults. *Singing Black*, published in 1976, is a poetry anthology designed to instill pride in the youngest African American readers.

Along with poetry and children's books, Evans has written and produced plays. Her five-year stint as producer and writer of the well-received television program *The Black Experience* (1968–1973) perhaps gave her insight into the value of the theater as another venue for the discussion of the African American community. *River of My Song* was produced in 1977, and *Eyes*, based on **Zora Neale Hurston**'s *Their Eyes Were Watching God*, followed in 1979. Her most political drama is *Boochie*, also produced in 1979. It is the monologue of an old woman who reveals the negative forces in the Black community (addiction, welfare, violence) as she prepares dinner for her son, Boochie.

One of Evans's most significant contributions is the 1983 *Black Women Writers (1950–1980)*. This critical anthology offers autobiographical statements by women authors as well as critical commentary on their work. She both edited and contributed essays to the anthology.

The winner of many awards, including a Woodrow Wilson grant in 1968, Evans divides her time among teaching, writing, theater work, and community service.

Resources: David Dorsey, "The Art of Mari Evans," in *Black Women Writers (1950–1980)*, ed. Mari Evans (New York: Doubleday, 1984), 170–189; Mari Edwards: *A Dark and Splendid Mass* (New York: Harlem River Press, 1992); *Dear Corinne, Tell Somebody! Love, Annie: A Book about Secrets* (East Orange, NJ: Just Us Books, 1999); *How We Speak* (Chicago: Third World Press, 2003); *I Am a Black Woman* (New York: Morrow, 1970); *I Look at Me!* (Chicago: Third World Press, 1974); *JD* (Garden City, NY: Doubleday, 1973); *Jim Flying High* (Garden City, NY: Doubleday, 1979); *Nightstar: Poems 1973–1978* (Los Angeles: University of California Center for Afro-American Studies, 1981); *Rap Stories* (Chicago: Third World Press, 1974); *Singing Black: Alternative Nursery Rhymes for Children* (East Orange, NJ: Just Us Books, 1976); *Where Is All the Music?* (London: P. Breman, 1968); *Whisper* (Berkeley: University of California Center for African American Studies, 1979); Mari Evans, ed., *Black Women Writers (1950–1980): A Critical Evaluation* (New York: Doubleday, 1984); Wallace Peppers, "Mari Evans," in *Dictionary of Literary Biography*, vol. 41, *Afro-American Poets Since 1955* (Detroit: Gale 1985), 117–123.

Patricia Kennedy Bostian

Everett, Percival (born 1956). Novelist. Everett's prolific and wide-ranging fiction features extensive erudition and prodigious linguistic play as it satirizes contemporary American life. His complex fictions move impishly between categories of identity and genre. They simultaneously complicate the notion of "African American literature," speak from within that category, and engage in **signifying** on the tradition they resist (Russett, 12). Born in Fort Gordon, Georgia, and raised in Columbia, South Carolina, Everett attended the University of Miami and pursued graduate work in philosophy at the University of Oregon. He cites the philosopher Ludwig Wittgenstein as an important influence on his approach to language. He received an M.A. in creative writing from Brown University in 1982. In 1985 Everett began teaching at the University of Kentucky, and subsequently held posts at the University of Notre Dame, the University of California at Riverside, and, since 1999, the

University of Southern California. Since 1994 he has served as an editor at *Callaloo.* Carolyn See characterized Everett's first novel, *Suder* (1983), as "a mad work of comic genius, combining symbols and myths from ancients and moderns, white culture and black, juxtaposing heartbreak with farce" (1). Despite the broad generic and thematic scope of Everett's work, Margaret Russett nevertheless discerns certain recurring features: "straight mimetic realism," in *Cutting Lisa* (1986) and *Walk Me to the Distance* (1985); "rambunctious, pun-drunk parodies of the Western" such as *God's Country* (1994) and *Grand Canyon, Inc.* (2001); "Southern Gothic Science Fiction" in *Zulus* (1990); rewritings of Greek mythology, such as *For Her Dark Skin* (1990) and *Frenzy* (1997); and experiments with metafiction in *Watershed* (1996), *Glyph* (1999), *Erasure* (2001), and *American Desert* (2004) (9–10). Everett has received a Hurston/Wright Legacy Award, a New American Writing Award, and an award for literature from the American Academy of Arts and Letters.

Resources: Percival Everett: *American Desert* (New York: Hyperion, 2004); *Big Picture* (St. Paul, MN: Graywolf Press, 1996); *Cutting Lisa* (London: Ticknor & Fields, 1986; repr. Baton Rouge: Louisiana State University Press, 2000); *Erasure* (Hanover, NH: University Press of New England, 2001); *For Her Dark Skin* (Seattle, WA: Owl Creek Press, 1990); *Frenzy* (St. Paul, MN: Graywolf Press, 1997); *Glyph* (St. Paul, MN: Graywolf Press, 1999); *God's Country* (Boston: Faber & Faber, 1994); *Grand Canyon, Inc.* (San Francisco: Versus Press, 2001); *Suder* (New York: Viking Press, 1983; repr. Baton Rouge: Louisiana State University Press, 1999); *Walk Me to the Distance* (London: Ticknor & Fields, 1985; repr. London: Century Hutchinson, 1986); *Watershed* (St. Paul, MN: Graywolf Press, 1996); *The Weather and Women Treat Me Fair* (Little Rock, AR: August House, 1987); *Zulus* (Sag Harbor, NY: Permanent Press, 1990; repr. Boston: Knightsbridge, 1991); Percival Everett and James Kincaid, *A History of the African American People (proposed) by Strom Thurmond as Told to Percival Everett and James Kincaid* (New York: Akashic Books, 2004); "Percival L. Everett," in *Black Writers*, ed. Sharon Malinowski (Detroit: Gale, 1994), 212–213; Margaret Russett, "Percival Everett: The African-American Novelist Under *Erasure*," United States Consulate (Istanbul) Web site, www.usconsulate-istanbul.org.tr/reppub/newamstud/mrussett.html; Carolyn See, "Review of *Suder*," *Los Angeles Times Book Review*, July 31, 1983, pp. 1, 8.

Alex Feerst

Evers, Medgar (1925–1963). Civil rights activist. In 1954, Evers wrote "Why I Live in Mississippi," which appeared in **Ebony** magazine. In the article, he portrays a **South** filled with potential. The article includes pastoral references to open spaces, cattle raising, and fishing. The article was an explication of why many blacks decided to stay in the South and fight for civil rights when others were migrating north. Evers was field secretary for the National Association for the Advancement for Colored People (**NAACP**) in Jackson, Mississippi, during the **Civil Rights Movement**. His work to register Blacks to vote and desegregate the University of Mississippi resulted in the hatred of many Southern **Whites** and ultimately in his assassination.

Evers's life inspired songs, including Bob Dylan's "A Pawn in Their Game," "Too Many Martyrs ("The Ballad of Medgar Evers") by Phil Ochs and Bob Gibson, and Dick Weismann's "Medgar Evers' Lullaby." His wife, Myrlie, wrote the tribute *For Us the Living*, which was later made into a television movie (1983). His assassination and the subsequent trials of those accused were the subject of the movie *Ghosts of Mississippi* (1996), starring Whoopi Goldberg and Alec Baldwin.

Resources: Taylor Branch, *Parting the Waters: America in the King Years, 1954–63* (New York: Simon and Schuster, 1988); Medgar Evers, "Why I Live in Mississippi," *Ebony*, Nov. 1958, 27–28, reprinted in *Mississippi Writers: Reflections of Childhood and Youth*, vol. 2, *Nonfiction*, ed. Dorothy Abbott (Jackson: University Press of Mississippi, 1986), 210–211; Myrlie B. Evers-Williams and William Peters, *For Us, the Living* (Garden City, NY: Doubleday, 1967); Jack Mendelsohn, *The Martyrs: Sixteen Who Gave Their Lives for Racial Justice* (New York: Harper & Row, 1966); Willie Morris, *Ghosts of Medgar Evers: A Tale of Race, Murder, Mississippi, and Hollywood* (New York: Random House, 1998); Adam Nossiter, *Of Long Memory: Mississippi and the Murder of Medgar Evers* (Reading, MA: Addison-Wesley, 1994).

Gregory W. Fowler

Exoticism. Exoticism is a framework of stereotypes involving licentious sex, primitivism, and mystery, and it ultimately functions to underpin Western colonial pursuits. The definitions of *exotic* in the *Oxford English Dictionary* (*OED*) range from something foreign or "introduced from abroad" to "having the attraction of the strange or foreign." Between the seventeenth century and the twentieth, the definition of exotic shifted from such racially neutral terms as *extrinsic* or *nonindigenous* to more highly charged terms such as *barbarous*, *monstrous*, and *glamorous*. In the eighteenth century, the age of the European Enlightenment and accelerated exploration, the use of *exotic* as both noun and adjective in designating people of foreign origin incorporated overtones of the feral and the fascinating. At the same time, the conception of **race**, with its physical criteria for classifying human groups, began to form in the West, and definitions of race interconnected with definitions of exotic in a web of colonialist representations. Through the travel narratives and curiosity cabinets produced by the adventurers of the 1600s and 1700s, Europeans at home encountered foreign figures and artifacts in exotic contexts that never existed in the first place. As Peter Mason puts it in *Infelicities: Representations of the Exotic*, the exotic "is not something that exists prior to its 'discovery.' Rather it is the very act of 'discovery' that produces the exotic as such" (1–2). Or, in the words of the turn-of-the-century German anthropologist Leo Frobenius: "The idea of the barbarous Negro is a European invention" (Miller, 291). Inseparable from the vocabulary of classification and display, the representation of foreign peoples and their cultures (particularly African and New World) as exotic thus fashioned European and American doctrines of cultural and colonial superiority. Exoticism, then, should be understood as a mode of interpretation by which the Western, Enlightenment self could understand itself as a rational observer of a mysterious other.

By the middle of the twentieth century, the definition of exotic acquired an explicitly sexual meaning: "of or pertaining to strip-tease or a strip-teaser." This development demonstrates the process by which the foreign came to be understood through race, and race through sex, particularly in its unconventional and carnal forms. In other words, the association of so-called primitive peoples with excessive sensuality and nakedness, which coalesced in the Western imagination by the eighteenth century, transformed over the ensuing centuries into a visual and verbal iconography equating dark skin with illicit sexuality. Bound up with this exotic heart of darkness was the sexual liberty that the West believed it had restrained and repressed in itself. Thus, if the term *exotic* came especially to signify Blackness (rather than simply "foreignness"), it also signified sexual intensity and could be used strictly in that sense; as the *OED* notes, "exotic dancer—a euphemism for stripper." The terms that ultimately merged in the meanings of exotic and exoticism included Blackness, spectacle, and sexuality. Consequently, when Sigmund Freud characterized the enigma of female sexuality as psychology's "dark continent," he voiced the tacit configuration of the mysterious as exotic, and the exotic as Black or African and excessively sexual.

The exotic in not merely the foreign, set in opposition to the domestic; it is also inflected with desire and femininity. This inflection or representation has economic and affective advantages, producing the cultural and material authority of the Western and masculine self over the exotic and feminine other. In order to understand such cultural production, it is necessary to define exoticism as analogous to Orientalism and to approach it specifically through the questions Edward Said raises in *Orientalism*: "How did philology, lexicography, history, biology, political and economic theory, novel writing, and lyric poetry come to the service of Orientalism's broadly imperialist view of the world?" (15). What Said calls the "nexus of knowledge and power creating 'the Oriental' and in a sense obliterating him as a human being" (39), illuminates the meaning of exoticism and the transfiguration of Africans and African Americans into sexual, racial and mysterious elements in literature, history, politics.

In "Black Bodies, White Bodies," Sander Gilman similarly concludes that Black sexuality, in particular Black female sexuality, represented, especially in the nineteenth-century colonial mind-set, the antithesis of European sexual mores and civility. Surveying eighteenth- and nineteenth-century narrative paintings, including William Hogarth's *A Rake's Progress* and *A Harlot's Process*, Gilman notes that the mere presence of a Black servant indicates the work's concern with illicit sexual activity. Thus, in Edouard Manet's renowned *Olympia* (1863), the inclusion of the Black woman servant inflects the portrait of the nude White woman with a more "primitive," exotic sexuality. While Olympia may seem placid in her nakedness, beneath her White exterior she is as exotic and voracious as her Black servant, which evokes stereotypes of African carnality. According to Gilman, the sexualization of

Black women culminated in the European fascination with Hottentot features and the association of these features with an exaggerated sexual temperament. What is especially significant about Gilman's argument is that it reveals the conjunction of the exotic, erotic and pathological in Enlightenment Europe's representations of African peoples.

In *Reconstructing Womanhood*, **Hazel V. Carby** discusses the codes of sexuality that consolidated around the figures of the mistress and the slave in nineteenth-century America, demonstrating the pernicious effect of exoticism upon Black women well into the twentieth century. Where Gilman focuses upon class relations and explains, near the end of his article, how stereotypes of Victorian prostitutes incorporated fetishized images of Hottentot women, Carby argues that the institution of **slavery** created a cult of virginal purity that demanded the repression of White female sexuality and the projection of erotic desire onto the figure of the "negress." Thus, like nineteenth-century Europe, antebellum America divided Black and White womanhood across a metaphoric system of purity and promiscuity. This ideology rested upon the scapegoated figure of the Negress, the image of the lascivious, exotic Black woman.

The act of exoticizing a woman as a Negress entails not only a myth of excessive sexual appetite but also of unfathomable essence, as if the woman resembles some kind of rare and unclassified species of animal. For example, in **Nella Larsen**'s novella *Quicksand* the African American or "mulatta" heroine, Helga Crane, is perceived through this myth by her European acquaintances; she is consequently "exhibited" like an exotic object or "strange species of pet dog" in the streets of Denmark (Larsen, 309). Encumbered by the large and glittering jewelry that she concedes to wear, Helga begins to feel "like a veritable savage. . . . This feeling was intensified by the many pedestrians who stopped to stare at the queer dark creature, strange to their city. . . . To them this girl, this Helga Crane, this mysterious niece of the Dahls, was not to be reckoned seriously in their scheme of things. True, she was attractive, unusual, in an exotic, almost savage way, but she wasn't one of them" (310).

This painful combination of exclusion and exoticism is also explored by William Faulkner's *Absalom, Absalom!*, in which the mixed-race and rejected son of Thomas Sutpen, Charles Bon, becomes embedded in narrative sections of sexual longing and exotic fantasy. The process of exoticization, in this case, accompanies the feminization of Charles Bon; he becomes, by virtue of his "black blood" and connections to the imported cultures of **New Orleans, Louisiana**, "catlike," mysterious, and "femininely flamboyant and therefore . . . opulent, sensuous, sinful" (Faulkner, 81, 76). Throughout *Absalom, Absalom!* Charles Bon must struggle against this image in order to be recognized as a member not only of the Sutpen family but also of the human race. While both Larsen and Faulkner explore the tragic effects of burying an individual's humanity under fantasies of exotic excess, **Ishmael Reed** picks up exoticism as a comic trope and, in *Mumbo Jumbo*, turns it against the "Wallflower Order" of Western asceticism. **Harlem, New York**, becomes a "Strange Exotic Island in the Heart of New York" where sex, hoodoo, and mystery return forgotten

African epistemological prototypes to the African Americans who engage in such practices (Reed, 99).

In some cases, exoticism can verge upon idealization, the type of which produced doctrines of the noble savage and visions of Africa as an idyllic paradise. For instance, in *The Conquest of Grenada, Part I* (1669), John Dryden includes the speech of an exotic "savage" who announces that he is, unlike the corrupt Englishmen, "free as Nature first made man" (Aldridge, 601). And, in *Oroonoko* (1688), Aphra Behn uses Oroonoko's irreproachable honor and majestic story to rebuke the hypocrisies of European civilization. Invested with a kind of excessive nobility, Oroonoko becomes an exotic specimen from a golden-age world. As Dickson Bruce shows in *The Origins of African American Literature*, such representations point not only to a penchant for the exotic in the seventeenth and eighteenth centuries but also to what Bruce calls "the counterimagery" of the emerging antislavery cause (24). This counterimagery is evident in *The Natural History of Senegal* (1757), a French travel narrative in which Michel Adanson praises the "the ease and indolence" of Black people and claims that their "simplicity [in] dress and manners" brought to mind "the world at its birth" (Aldridge, 603). While this nostalgic primitivism developed as a narrative against the horrors of the slave trade, it also helped to fashion the exotic into an alluring, illusory figure for the European and Anglo-American imagination.

Resources: A. Owen Aldridge, "Primitivism in the Eighteenth Century," in *The Dictionary of the History of Ideas*, Electronic Text Center, http://etext.lib.virginia.edu, 2003; Aphra Behn, *Oroonoko, and Other Writings*, ed. Paul Salzman (Oxford: Oxford University Press, 1998); Dickson Bruce, *The Origins of African American Literature* (Charlottesville: University Press of Virginia, 2001); Hazel Carby, *Reconstructing Womanhood: The Emergence of the Afro-American Woman Novelist* (Oxford: Oxford University Press, 1987); William Faulkner, *Absalom, Absalom!* (New York: Vintage, 1990); Sander Gilman, "Black Bodies, White Bodies: Toward an Iconography of Female Sexuality in Late Nineteenth-Century Art, Medicine, and Literature," in *"Race," Writing, and Difference*, ed. Henry Louis Gates, Jr. (Chicago: University of Chicago Press, 1986); Nella Larsen, *Quicksand*, in *Classic Fiction of the Harlem Renaissance*, ed. William L. Andrews (New York: Oxford University Press, 1994); Peter Mason, *Infelicities: Representations of the Exotic* (Baltimore: Johns Hopkins University Press, 1998); Christopher Miller, "Theories of Africans: The Question of Literary Anthropology," in *"Race," Writing, and Difference*, ed. Henry Louis Gates, Jr. (Chicago: University of Chicago Press, 1986); Ishmael Reed, *Mumbo Jumbo* (Garden City, NY: Doubleday, 1972); Edward Said, *Orientalism* (New York: Vintage, 1978).

Dana Medoro

Expatriate Writers. An expatriate is someone who takes up residence in a country that is not his or her native land. Unlike exiles, forced by political, ethnic, religious or other reasons to flee their homelands, expatriates are free to return when and if they choose. They leave for various reasons. For some the motivation is philosophical, to demonstrate their disagreement with social or political policies. Others move for the adventure or in search of that special place where they feel they can fulfill their dreams. Still others leave for work, study, or a combination of reasons.

Some of the earliest and best-known African American expatriate authors are **Claude McKay**, **Jean Toomer**, **Countee Cullen**, **Nella Larsen**, **Jessie Redmon Fauset**, **Richard Wright**, **Frank Yerby**, and **James Baldwin**, who lived abroad, mostly in Europe and particularly in France, during the periods just after **World War I** and **World War II**. Many left because they found a personal freedom in Europe that allowed them to practice their craft away from the racial segregation policies, the discrimination, and the violence that many African Americans were subject to.

They were not the first African Americans to choose to leave the United States, yet more than any of those who preceded them, the experiences, exploits, and work produced by these twentieth-century voyagers provided a model, set the tone, and ignited the dreams of many others who followed in their footsteps. One of the earliest emigrations of African Americans happened during the American Revolution when some 30,000 former slaves who had, in exchange for a promise of freedom, escaped across British lines to aid in the fight against the American rebels, were evacuated to Nova Scotia along with the defeated Loyalists. Canada, the terminus for the **Underground Railroad**, was a haven for runaway slaves. Some also escaped to Mexico.

Even during **slavery** there were African Americans who went abroad. Prominent Black members of the **Abolitionist movement** often traveled to England, which was the center of the global antislavery movement. Wealthy free Blacks traveled, too, mostly in England or France, where they often sent their children for education. The artist Henry Ossawa Tanner went to France to study in 1819 and remained there, returning to the United States only for visits. Ironically, even when these countries were practicing slavery in their overseas colonies, Black Americans encountered a more racially tolerant social climate there than what they faced at home.

There was a time when Black Americans were actively encouraged to leave America. The **back-to-Africa movement**, organized in 1816 by the American Society for Colonizing Free People of Color in the United States, commonly known as the American Colonization Society, was led by a group of prominent White men. Members included Rev. Robert Finley, Andrew Jackson, Daniel Webster, and Francis Scott Key. They proposed establishing a colony in Africa for free-born Blacks and emancipated slaves similar to Britain's establishment in 1787 of a colony for free Blacks in the Sierra Leone in West Africa. It was a notion that resulted in an odd marriage between supporters on both sides of the slavery issue. Pro-slavery advocates wanted slavery continued, and saw the presence of free Black people as a threat. Antislavery advocates' support stemmed from belief that even free Black people would never be given parity in America, and thus they would be better off in a country of their own. Prior to this movement, similar sentiments had been advocated and even acted on. Paul Cuffe, a Black Quaker and a ship captain, helped about forty former slaves reach Sierra Leone. In 1819 the U.S. Congress gave the American Colonization Society $100,000, and in 1820 the first ship sailed to West Africa, its destination Liberia. It is estimated that over a period of two decades at least 11,000 Blacks went to Liberia, about half of them newly freed slaves.

The years from the end of the **Civil War** to the turn of the century and just prior to the outbreak of World War I were years of great progress and equally great challenge for African Americans. It was a period marked by the flourishing of creative, economic, educational, and political activity. Great strides were made in Black arts and literature. African American talent such as **Paul Laurence Dunbar**, **Charles Waddell Chesnutt**, and the Fisk Jubilee Singers were introduced to wider audiences at home and abroad. Prominent African American educators and intellectuals were also traveling abroad more.

At the same time, in **the South**, the estimated 4 million newly emancipated slaves were experiencing battles against their recently gained liberty. Defeated White Southerners moved rapidly to reassert supremacy in the face of a drastically altered social order and in the midst of a war-torn economy. In less than a decade, Black southerners would see the gains from the Reconstruction period reversed. Secret societies like the notorious Ku Klux Klan emerged. Jim Crow became law in the South, lynching was a frequent occurrence, and interracial clashes increased as Blacks fought back. In response to this situation and encouraged by stories championed in the active Negro press about abundant job opportunities in the burgeoning factory industry and greater racial tolerance, Black Southerners began to head north, the first wave of the **Great Migration**.

Once they arrived in the North, their dreams often became nightmares. They encountered discrimination in housing and work. There were frequent clashes between these newcomers and the recently arrived White European immigrant skilled laborers with whom they competed for jobs. Hostility often erupted into violence. There were **race riots** from **Atlanta, Georgia**, to **Philadelphia, Pennsylvania**. It would take America's entry into **World War I** (1917) and **World War II** (1941) to catapult the country's racial policies and practices to the top of its domestic agenda and force change as African Americans and organizations fighting for civil rights, such as the National Association for the Advancement of Colored People (**NAACP**) and the National Urban League, vigorously protested the inequalities Black citizens faced at home while America was sending soldiers to fight for democracy in foreign lands.

For African American soldiers, fighting began before they left for the battlefront. There were numerous racial incidents on and off military bases, especially in the South. Some of them were quite bloody, such as the 1917 Houston, **Texas**, riot that left several Whites and Blacks dead and resulted in thirteen Black soldiers being hanged for their participation in the riot and forty-one others sentenced to life in prison. Situations like these further inflamed racial tensions across the country. Some 200,000 African Americans served in World War I, in an army that was strictly segregated. The Marines and the Air Force did not accept Blacks. In the Navy they were allowed only as mess attendants. About 100,000 were sent overseas. While most were assigned support roles, about 40,000 saw combat under French command, where they fought with distinction in a military that treated them as equals.

At the end of the war, liberated by the experience of living in a society that was not defined by racial segregation, some soldiers decided to remain in France. Others returned to the United States determined not to accept being treated as second-class citizens. The soldiers returned to an America that was on the verge of an explosion of change on every level—social, economic, political, intellectual, and artistic—and, given the determination by Black Americans to demand their civil rights, racial changes as well. In the immediate postwar period, racial incidents, including riots, erupted across the United States; there were incidents of Black American soldiers being lynched in uniform. So bloody was the summer of 1919 that the writer **James Weldon Johnson** dubbed it the Red Summer.

The end of World War I coincided with a confluence of social, political, and cultural changes in America and abroad: the Roaring Twenties, the Jazz Age and Prohibition, the spread of Socialist and Communist ideology, new religious and spiritual movements. In the African American enclave known as **Harlem, New York**, a firebrand political nationalist named **Marcus Garvey**, through his Universal Negro Improvement Society, was promoting a new "back to Africa" movement at the same time that an explosion of artistic energy that was so strong it would spread across the country was bursting forth and would become known as the **Harlem Renaissance.**

After the war, American artists started flocking to Europe. **Paris, France**, was the magnet attracting the likes of Ernest Hemingway, Gertrude Stein, F. Scott Fitzgerald, Ezra Pound, and others who became known as "the Lost Generation," many of whom would produce works that remain classics. Paris was also calling African American artists, particularly singers and entertainers, a direct legacy of the war years when African American military bands, such as the renowned band of the 369th Combat Unit (the official name of the regiment known as the Harlem Hellfighters), introduced France to Black American music, especially **jazz**, which was now the rage. African American entertainers were regularly invited to appear in Paris and other European capitals. Some, such as **Josephine Baker**, decided to stay, paving the way for others to follow.

One of the first Black American writers to move overseas was Claude McKay, a leading figure in the Harlem Renaissance, who went to England in 1919 and then to France. He traveled throughout Europe, North Africa, and the Soviet Union, and returned to live in the United States in 1934. In fact, nearly all the key figures of the Harlem Renaissance—among them Jean Toomer, Countee Cullen, Jessie Redmon Fauset, **Zora Neale Hurston**, Nella Larsen, **Arna Bontemps, James Weldon Johnson, Alain Locke, W.E.B. Du Bois**, and **Arthur A. Schomburg**—spent time living in Europe and traveling internationally during these years. **Langston Hughes** was an inveterate traveler, as he recounts in his two autobiographies, *The Big Sea* (1940) and *I Wonder as I Wander* (1956). Hughes first went abroad to Mexico in 1920, when he visited his father, who had moved there supposedly to escape America's racism. He traveled to the Soviet Union in the early 1930s with a group of African Americans to work on a film project that never materialized. He covered the Spanish Civil War for the **Baltimore Afro-American** newspaper, covering the story of the war and the participation of the African Americans who joined in the fight against Fascism by volunteering in the Abraham Lincoln Brigade (Ostrom, 25–28). He also traveled in Africa and the Caribbean. But with the exception of Nella Larsen, Zora Neale Hurston and Jessie Redmon Fauset, these notable expatriates are all male. Historians who have examined this period say that few of the Harlem Renaissance women writers traveled abroad or stayed overseas for any extended period, and that their stays have not been well documented.

The **Great Depression** brought the Roaring Twenties to a halt, but it did not stop the flow of African Americans writers and artists traveling overseas. Some traveled thanks to grant or fellowship funding. For others, the travels were politically connected. This was true for Claude McKay and **Paul Robeson**, both of whom were active in the Communist Party.

America's entry into World War II sent even more African American soldiers overseas—about 1 million served in World War II, again fighting and supporting the fight for democracy abroad as members of a racially segregated military. Following the war, the migration patterns resumed. In America, the second wave of the Great Migration was on, as Southern Blacks in even larger numbers headed north in search of a better life. Domestically, the racial climate was equally charged and racial incidents, including lynching, continued.

It was now becoming more commonplace for African Americans to go to abroad, and some decided to stay. In 1947, Richard Wright, the most celebrated Black writer of the time, was fed up with racism in America and moved to Paris. James Baldwin moved the following year, heading first to Paris and later to Switzerland and Istanbul, then settling in a small town outside Paris. Many other African American artists, entertainers, musicians, writers, and actors traveled and spent time in Europe. They moved in the same circles, and for them, Paris remained the draw owing to the small, but vibrant and solid, African American expatriate artistic core that was there.

In the 1950s, during a period marked by the Korean War and **McCarthyism**, a number of American artists, including African Americans, moved abroad. **Chester Himes** settled in Paris, and Frank Yerby moved to Spain. The 1960s, another period marked by a convergence of social, political, and intellectual fervor, saw more African American writers and artists traveling to Europe and also to some of the newly independent African countries. Paris remained a major stopping place. **Melvin Van Peebles** moved to Paris in the 1960s and stayed for a decade. **Barbara Chase-Riboud** moved to Paris after graduating from Yale University in 1961, and remained there.

Some of those who left the United States, such as Richard Wright, chose to not return. Others, such as Baldwin, who did not come back to the U.S. for ten years, eventually did. "I looked on Paris as a refuge, too," Baldwin said. "I never intended to come back to this country." But he came to realize that he was not just a writer, he was an "American writer and this country is my subject." He said he would have to navigate between continents. "Now," he said, "I imagine I will have to spend the rest of my life as some kind of trans-Atlantic commuter."

Resources: Maya Angelou, *All God's Children Need Traveling Shoes* (New York: Vintage, 1991); Abraham Chapman, ed., *Black Voices: An Anthology of Afro-American Literature* (New York: New American Library, 1968); Michel Fabre, *From Harlem to Paris: Black American Writers in France, 1840–1980* (Urbana: University of Illinois Press, 1991); John Hope Franklin and Alfred A. Moss, Jr., *From Slavery to Freedom*, 7th ed. (New York: McGraw-Hill, 1994); "An Interview with James Baldwin, Studs Terkel/1961," in *Conversations with James Baldwin*, ed. Fred L. Standley and Louis H. Pratt (Jackson: University Press of Mississippi, 1989), 14–15, 83–84; Ty Stovall, *Paris Noir: African Americans in the City of Light* (Boston: Houghton Mifflin, 1998).

Wilma Jean Emanuel Randle

E-Zines, E-News, E-Journals, and E-Collections. The zine world has been evolving since its beginnings in the late 1970s. A zine was originally defined as a not-for-profit newspaper or magazine that was published, written, and distributed by an individual. Often expressing alternative or radical viewpoints, print zines were part of the underground press of the era. The advent of the Internet gave birth to the e-zine, and as technology became more sophisticated many e-zines adopted a glossier, more commercial face. Both zines and e-zines are difficult to track because they appear at the whim of the creator and often are published for just a few issues.

As Web publishing has boomed, the meaning of e-zine has broadened to include any newspaper, magazine, or journal that is free or partly free via the Internet. Although these often disappear or become available only by paid subscription, a few titles have shown staying power. *Black Press USA* identifies itself "your independent source of news for the African American community," offers news and opinion, and is written exclusively by African American journalists. Updated daily, it links to a growing number of newspapers throughout the country that are members of the *BlackUSA Network*, including the **Amsterdam News**, the *Birmingham Times*, and the *Seattle Median*. Black Voices.com is a weekly with a Black international perspective on news, commentaries and culture, and has published since 1996. Seeing Black.com, the "funky, alternative site for Black reviews, opinion & voice," emphasizes arts and entertainment, including book and film reviews, and has appeared since 2001. The current issue is free, and back issues are available for purchase. Black Collegian Online (http://black-collegian.com) is "the career site for students and professionals of color," and provides information on jobs, employers, graduate school, and related issues. Selected articles are available back to 1997.

North Star: A Journal of African-American Religious History is a free peer-reviewed journal from Vassar College that is published twice a year in association with the Afro-American Religious History section of the American Academy of Religion. All articles are available online back to 1997. *Freedom Journal*, the first African American–owned and –operated journal, has achieved e-zine status. Published between 1827 and 1829, all of its issues are available through the Wisconsin Historical Society Web site.

Some libraries subscribe to commercial databases that offer Black literature collections. *Ethnic NewsWatch* provides full text of minority newspapers, magazines, and journals. It includes more than sixty African American and Caribbean titles, such as *Research in African Literatures* and *Black Child*. *JSTOR* offers archival issues for seven Black journals, including *African American Review*, **Black American Literature Forum**, and **Callaloo**. The *African-American Poetry 1760–1900* database and the *Database of Twentieth-Century African-American Poetry* from Chadwyck-Healey provide full text for thousands of poems. The *Black Drama* database is available from Alexander Street Press and has the full text of 1,200 plays from 1850 to the present, about a quarter of them previously unpublished. It includes the complete works of leading playwrights such as **Amiri Baraka** and **Ed Bullins**.

Resources: *African-American Newspapers and Periodicals* (2003), http://www.wisconsinhistory.org/libraryarchives/aanp/; *Black Press USA*, http://www.blackpressusa.com; *Black Voices.com*, http://new.blackvoices.com; *North Star*, Vassar College (Spring 2004), http://northstar.vassar.edu; Suzanne A. Vega Garcia, *Recommended African American Websites Diversity & Ethnic Studies*, Iowa State University (Aug. 6, 2002), http://www.public.iastate.edu/~savega/afr_amer.htm.

Maureen A. Kelly

F

Fabio, Sarah Webster (1928–1979). Poet and literary critic. Sarah Webster Fabio was a poet and literary critic who helped establish the West Coast **Black Studies** and **Black Arts movements** of the late 1960s. Additionally, she taught Black literature at Merritt Junior College, the University of California at Berkeley, Oberlin College, and the University of Wisconsin. Born on January 20, 1928, in **Nashville, Tennessee**, Sarah demonstrated a prodigious intellectual aptitude at an early age that was nurtured by her family. In 1943, she enrolled at Spelman College in **Atlanta, Georgia**. A year before completing her bachelor's degree, she returned to Nashville to attend Fisk University, where she met Cyril Leslie Fabio. Upon graduation in 1946, they were married, and had five children over the next decade.

After the Fabios settled in Palo Alto, California, Sarah had the opportunity to complete graduate school. She attended San Francisco State College from 1963 to 1965, working on an M.A. in language arts and creative writing with a concentration in poetry. While a graduate student, she joined a Black writers' workshop, where she met **Amiri Baraka** and **Ed Bullins**. For Fabio, this encounter solidified her decision to utilize her gift of writing to empower Blacks. Upon receiving her master's degree, she taught at Merritt Junior College in Oakland, California. With the support of black students there, she developed a Black Studies program, which she later established at Berkeley in 1968.

Fabio was a prolific writer. Her initial collections of poetry were *Saga of a Black Man* (1968) and *A Mirror, a Soul: A Two-Part Volume of Poems* (1969). Fabio's **jazz**-inspired poems and academic articles were published in **Negro Digest** and *Black World*, as well as the anthologies *The Poetry of the Negro, 1746–1970* (1970), *The Black Aesthetic* (1971), and *To Gwen with Love* (1971).

By far her most inspirational work is the seven-volume poetry collection *The Rainbow Sign* (1973), published the year following her divorce. After teaching Black literature at Oberlin for two years (1972–1974), Fabio entered the University of Wisconsin to pursue a Ph.D. Not long thereafter, she was diagnosed with colon cancer. Despite her illness, Fabio continued to teach and write, publishing her final collection of poems, *Dark Symphony in Duet*, shortly before her death in 1979. As a prolific poet, educator, and critic, Sarah Webster Fabio remains an important yet underestimated literary figure.

Resources: William L. Andrews, Frances Smith Foster, and Trudier Harris, eds., *The Oxford Companion to African American Literature* (New York: Oxford University Press, 1997); Leaonead Pack Bailey, ed. and comp., *Broadside Authors and Artists: An Illustrated Biographical Directory* (Detroit: Broadside Press, 1974); Sarah Webster Fabio: *A Mirror, A Soul: A Two-Part Volume of Poems* (San Francisco: J. Richardson Associates, 1969); *Race Results, U.S.A., 1966: White Right—A Favorite—Wins; Lurline—A Long Shot—Places; Black Power—A Long Shot—Shows; For Stokely Carmichael* (Detroit: Broadside Press, 1967); *Rainbow Signs: Seven Volumes of Poetry* (Oberlin, OH: New Media Workshop, 1973); Sarah Webster Fabio and Thomas Gayton, *Dark Symphony in Duet: A Celebration of the Word; Seascapes, Love Poems, Tributes, Portraits, Black Talk, Africana* (Seattle, WA: Black Studies Program, University of Washington, 1979); *Saga of the Black Man* (Oakland, CA: distributed by Turn Over Book, 1968); James A. Page, comp., *Selected Black American Authors: An Illustrated Biobibliography* (Boston: G. K. Hall, 1977); Theressa Gunnels Rush, Carol Fairbanks Myers, and Esther Spring Arata, *Black American Writers Past and Present: A Biographical and Bibliographical Dictionary*, 2 vols. (Metuchen, NJ: Scarecrow Press, 1975).

Anthony J. Ratcliff

Fair, Ronald L. (born 1932). Novelist. Fair was born and raised in **Chicago, Illinois**. After serving in the Navy, he returned to Chicago, earned credentials as a stenographer, and from 1955 to 1966, was employed as a court reporter. During this period, he worked on several of the novels that would bring him a great deal of attention. Indeed, the publication of his first two novels, in 1965 and 1966, would lead to his being offered visiting professorships at Columbia College, Northwestern University, and Wesleyan University. Over this half-decade, Fair wrote two more books of published fiction, a pairing of two novellas and his third novel. Then, in 1971, he emigrated from the United States to Finland, and has remained there ever since. Although he has continued to write, his published work has consisted of several collections of poems and has not included any new novels.

Fair's first novel, *Many Thousand Gone: An American Fable* (1965), is his only novel set primarily in the Deep **South**. Fusing literary naturalism with a lyric symbolism, Fair represents the racist excesses of the segregationist South through the microcosm of one small town. Set in contemporary Chicago, his second novel, *Hog Butcher* (1966), is a fictional exposé of police brutality, judicial corruption, and institutionalized racism. Two African American boys witness the shooting by police of a well-known athlete. The novel focuses on the attempts to silence, to discount, and then to discredit their testimony as witnesses against the police. The novel was rereleased in paperback as *Cornbread, Earl, and Me* after the success of a film adaptation with that title. Fair's third novel, *We Can't Breathe* (1972), is essentially a fictionalized memoir treating his experiences while growing up in a segregated Chicago neighborhood in the 1940s. For this novel, Fair received the Best Book Award from the American Library Association.

The two novellas published together as *World of Nothing* (1970) are *World of Nothing* and *Jerome*. Through the eyes of two very poor young men who share an apartment, *World of Nothing* describes the colorful eccentrics and hardened predators who populate an African American neighborhood in Chicago. *Jerome* is a castigation of the church hierarchies that have implicitly condoned in-stitutionalized racism. For this book, Fair received the Arts and Letters Award from the National Institute of Arts and Letters.

In his subsequently published collections of poems, Fair has heightened the lyricism that many reviewers and critics have found to be one of the most remarkable features of his novels, and he has presented the sort of vignettes infused with both irony and sympathy for which **Gwendolyn Brooks** is re-membered. In 1969, Fair's play *Sails and Sinkers* was produced.

Resources: *Excerpts* (London: Paul Breman, 1975); *Hog Butcher* (New York: Har-court, Brace, and World, 1966); *Many Thousand Gone: An American Fable* (New York: Harcourt, Brace, and World, 1965); *Rufus* (Stuttgart, Germany: P. Schlack Verlag, 1977; Detroit: Lotus Press, 1980); *We Can't Breathe* (New York: Harper & Row, 1972); *World of Nothing* (New York: Harper & Row, 1970); Robert E. Fleming, "The Novels of Ronald L. Fair," *College Language Association Journal* 15 (1972), 477–487; Dennis Daley Lynch, "Visions of Chicago in Contemporary Black Literature," in *Minority Literature and the Urban Experience*, ed. George E. Carter, James R. Parker, and Sara Bentley (La Crosse, WI: Institute for Minority Studies, University of Wisconsin–La Crosse, 1978), 25–31.

Martin Kich

Fales-Hill, Susan (born 1962). Memoir writer and television writer. Born in Rome, Fales-Hill is the daughter of the Haitian American actress Josephine Premice and Timothy Fales, a **White** blueblood who can trace his ancestry back to the *Mayflower*. Raised primarily in New York City, Fales-Hill attended Lycée Français de New York and then completed a baccalaureate degree in history and literature at Harvard University. Growing up in a multicultural household and educational environment and taking advantage of her family's frequent travels, particularly to Europe, Fales-Hill became fluent in a number of languages, including French, Italian, Spanish, and Caribbean **Creole**.

Fales-Hill has established herself in the television industry. She wrote for *The Cosby Show* and its spin-off, *A Different World*, and she then earned some credentials as an executive producer of *A Different World* and as a consulting producer of the series *Suddenly Susan*, starring Brooke Shields. In the late 1990s, she served as executive producer and head writer of the cable television series

Linc's, which starred Tim Reid. Married to Aaron Hill, a banker, Fales-Hill has become a prominent socialite, lending her name and her energies to many civic and charitable causes. Most notably, she has served on the board of trustees of the American Ballet Theater and has been an active supporter of the Studio Museum in **Harlem, New York**, and the East Side Settlement House.

Fales-Hill's memoir of her mother, *Always Wear Joy: My Mother Bold and Beautiful* (2003), is notable for its depiction of an interracial marriage at a time when American society, even outside **the South**, was still pointedly segregated. Ironically, while Timothy Fales was socially ostracized by high society for marrying a Black woman, he and his wife became the center of a new circle of diverse figures prominent in the arts. Indeed, Premice herself had been castigated by her own aristocratic family for choosing to pursue a career on the stage. Fales-Hill chronicles her mother's successes in *Jamaica* and *Bubblin' Brown Sugar* and her close friendships with many of the most prominent female African American performers of her time. She explores the ramifications of her mother's sacrificing some of her professional ambitions for a marriage that ultimately failed after several decades. In addition, she emphasizes that her mother's career also suffered because of a conundrum that has shaped some of her own experiences: her mother was thought to be "too Black" for some roles and "not Black enough" for others. In a very real sense, Fales-Hill's book represents a continuation, rather than just a recollection, of her mother's attempts to transcend "color lines."

Resources: Patrick Henry Bass, "Working It!," *Essence*, Dec. 2000, 120–128; Ann Brown and Monique R. Brown, "Learning Lingos: TV Executive Studies Foreign Languages for Fun," *Black Enterprise*, Sept. 2000, 209; Susan Fales-Hill, *Always Wear Joy: My Mother Bold and Beautiful* (New York: HarperCollins/Amistad, 2003); Cathy Horyn, "Can a Smile Bridge the Divide?," *New York Times*, Apr. 27, 2003, sec. 9, p. 1; Suzanne Rust, "Review of *Always Wear Joy: My Mother Bold and Beautiful*," *Black Issues Book Review*, Nov./Dec. 2003, p. 69.

Martin Kich

Farmer, Nancy (born 1941). Children's author and writer of young-adult novels and stories. Although Farmer is not herself an African American, her children's books set in Africa have contributed to young readers' being more aware of Africa and of Africa's influence on African American and American culture. Many of Farmer's works feature African characters and settings in Mozambique and Zimbabwe, where she lived for twenty years. Major genres include fantasy, futuristic, and myth-based fiction (particularly Shona and Norse). Farmer was born in Phoenix, Arizona, and grew up in Yuma, a small town near the Mexican border. A graduate of Reed College (1963), a Peace Corps volunteer in India (1963–1965), and a chemistry student at Merrit College and the University of California at Berkeley (1969–1971), Farmer went to the Lake Cabora Bassa region of Mozambique as a scientist in 1972. In 1975 she moved to Zimbabwe, where she met and married her American-born husband, Harold Farmer (1976) and began freelance writing. Her first novel, published in Zimbabwe, was *Lorelei: The Story of a Bad Cat* (1987). After returning to the United States in 1991, Farmer received a $20,000 grant from the National Endowment for the Arts to complete a children's novel set in Zimbabwe, *Do You Know Me?* (1993). For the next ten years, her juvenile novels continued to feature African protagonists and African settings. The futuristic *The Ear, the Eye, and the Arm* (1994) and the fantasy adventure *A Girl Named Disaster* (1996) were Newbery Honor Books, and *The Warm Place* (1995) won honors at the Zimbabwe International Book Fair. Her award-winning picture book, *Casey Jones's Fireman: The Story of Sim Webb* (1998) preserves the history of a distinguished African American. In her most highly acclaimed novel to date, *The House of the Scorpion* (2002), Farmer constructs a futuristic culture from memories of her Southwestern childhood. Her latest novel, *The Sea of Trolls* (2004), relies heavily on Norse mythology for setting and plot. Her works have been anthologized, dramatized, recorded, and translated into several languages. Film rights to *The House of the Scorpion* were purchased in 2004. Farmer and her husband currently reside in California, where the author continues to devote much of her time to writing. (*See* **Children's Literature**.)

Resources: Jennifer M. Brown, "Voices of Experience: Nancy Farmer," *Publishers Weekly*, July 22, 2002, pp. 154–155; Nancy Farmer: *Casey Jones's Fireman: The Story of Sim Webb* (New York: Fogelman, 1998); *Do You Know Me?* (New York: Orchard, 1993); *The Ear, the Eye, and the Arm* (New York: Orchard, 1994); *A Girl Named Disaster* (New York: Orchard, 1996); *The House of the Scorpion* (New York: Atheneum, 2002); *Lorelei: The Story of a Bad Cat* (Harare, Zimbabwe: College Press, 1987); *Runnery Granary* (New York: Greenwillow, 1996); *The Sea of Trolls* (New York: Atheneum, 2004); *Tapiwa's Uncle* (Harare, Zimbabwe: College Press, 1993); *Tsitsi's Skirt* (Harare, Zimbabwe: College Press, 1988); *The Warm Place* (New York: Orchard, 1995); "Farmer, Nancy," *Contemporary Authors Online* (Gale, 2003); Kathleen T. Horning, "The House of Farmer," *School Library Journal* 49 (Feb. 2003), 48–50; Sara Pendergast and Tom Pendergast, *St. James Guide to Young Adult Writers*, 2nd ed. (Detroit: St. James Press, 1998); "Tapiwa's Uncle," *Stories on Stage: Scripts for Readers Theater*, ed. Aaron Shepard (New York: Wilson, 1993).

Karen Sloan

Fauset, Jessie Redmon (1882–1961). Novelist, poet, essayist, journalist, editor, and teacher. Fauset was born in Camden County, New Jersey, the youngest of seven children of Rev. Redmon Fauset and Annie Seamon Fauset. Both of her parents were well educated and literary, and her experience of an elite African American literary culture is a major theme of her writing. Jessie Fauset grew up in **Philadelphia, Pennsylvania**, and attended the city's public schools. On the basis of her excellent academic record, she was admitted to Cornell University in 1901. Fauset received her B.A. in classical and modern languages in 1905 and was the first African American woman to be elected to the prestigious honor society Phi Beta Kappa. In 1919, she earned her master's degree at the University of Pennsylvania. During 1925–1926, Fauset traveled in Europe and spent six months studying French at the Sorbonne and at the Alliance Française in **Paris, France**.

Fauset wrote numerous essays, poems, and short stories from the 1910s to the early 1930s, publishing in various periodicals as well as in anthologies. At the beginning of the **Harlem Renaissance**, she moved to New York City and worked for *The Crisis*, the official publication of the National Association for the Advancement of Colored People (**NAACP**), then edited by **W.E.B. Du Bois**; she soon became its literary editor, a position she held for seven years (1919–1926). An important novelist herself, Fauset is more often remembered for discovering and publishing young writers, including **Countee Cullen**, **Nella Larsen**, **Jean Toomer**, **Claude McKay**, and **Langston Hughes**, who described Fauset as one of "the three people who midwifed the so-called New Negro Literature into being" (*The Big Sea*, 113).

Fauset's contributions to *The Crisis* were valuable and diverse, and included biographical sketches, essays on drama, articles, reviews, poems, short stories, essays, and translations of French West Indian poems. In addition, her innovative editorial work changed the face of *The Crisis* and fostered the **New Negro** Renaissance. In 1920 and 1921, Fauset was a writer and an editor for ***Brownies' Book***, a short-lived monthly magazine, created by Du Bois, for African American children. She and her sister made the apartment they shared in **Harlem, New York**, into a gathering place for the African American intellectuals and their friends to gather and discuss art and politics.

Fauset left *The Crisis* in 1926 to find a job that would allow her more time for writing. During this time, she traveled, lectured, and wrote poems. In 1927, she married Herbert E. Harris; they had no children. Fauset could not make a living from writing, however, and discrimination prevented her from working in a New York publishing house. She therefore turned to teaching and continued writing.

Between 1924 and 1933, Fauset produced four full-length novels exploring issues of identity and **race**, class and **gender** differences. These novels focus on the careers, courtships, and marriages of the Black professional class and offer sentimental resolutions to the complex problems they raise. *There Is Confusion* (1924) was the first published novel by a Black woman to explore the theme of "color"; arguably her best novel, *Plum Bun*, was published in 1929; and her third, *The Chinaberry Tree*, appeared in 1931. Her final work, *Comedy, American Style* (1933), became her best-known novel; it traces the Black female protagonist, Olivia Carey, who hates being Black while her son and her husband are proud of their African American cultural heritage. Fauset's best-known essay, "The Gift of Laughter" (1925), analyzes the Black comic character in American drama. Among her best-known poems are "La Vie C'est la Vie," "Noblesse Oblige," "Christmas Eve in France," and "Rondeau." **William Stanley Braithwaite**, in *Opportunity* (January 1934), called Fauset "the potential Jane Austen of Negro Literature." (*See* **Passing**.)

During the 1960s and 1970s, some critics charged that Fauset's work did not deal with the broader African American community, but critics today admire her portraits of African Americans and her literary influence. After her husband's death, in 1958, she left New Jersey for Philadelphia and lived with her stepbrother, Earl Huff, until her death from heart disease in 1961.

Resources: Paula C. Barnes, *The African American Encyclopedia*, vol. 3, 2nd ed., ed. R. Kent Rasmussen (New York: Marshall Cavendish, 2001), 892–893; Jessie Redmon Fauset: *The Chinaberry Tree: A Novel of American Life* (1931; repr. New York: G. K. Hall, 1995); *Comedy: American Style* (1933; repr. New York: G. K. Hall, 1994); *The Gift of Laughter* (1925; repr. New York: Atheneum, 1992); *Plum Bun: A Novel Without a Moral* (1929; repr. Boston: Beacon Press, 1990); *There Is Confusion* (1924; repr. Boston: Northeastern University Press, 1989); Shari Dorantes Hatch, "Jessie Redmon Fauset," in *African American Writers: A Dictionary*, ed. Shari Dorantes Hatch and Michael R. Strickland (Santa Barbara, CA: ABC-CLIO, 2000), 114; Langston Hughes, *The Big Sea: An Autobiography* (New York: Knopf, 1940); Rachel Kranz, "Jessie Redmon Fauset," in *The Biographical Dictionary of African Americans*, ed. Rachel Kranz and Philip J. Koslow (New York: Facts on File, 1999), 79–80; Dreiser Ledwidge, "Jessie Redmon Fauset," in *World Authors: 1900–1950*, vol. 2, ed. Martin Seymour-Smith and Andrew C. Kimmens (New York: H. W. Wilson, 1996), 834; Erin A. Smith, "Jessie Redmon Fauset," in *African American Lives*, ed. Henry Louis Gates, Jr., and Evelyn Brooks Higginbotham (New York: Oxford University Press, 2004), 293–294; Cheryl A. Wall, "Jessie Redmon Fauset," in *Encyclopedia of African-American Culture and History*, vol. 2, ed. Jack Salzman, David Lionel Smith, and Cornel West (New York: Macmillan Library Reference, 1996), 939–940.

Truong Le

Federal Writers' Project (c. 1936–1941). The Federal Writers' Project (FWP) was one of numerous smaller projects sponsored by the Works Progress Administration (WPA), which itself was part of the larger New Deal initiative advanced by President Franklin Roosevelt's administration during the **Great Depression**. As with other elements of the WPA, one goal of the FWP was to employ the unemployed, in this case unemployed writers. More specifically, Harold Ickes, director of the WPA, sought to develop a series of books and pamphlets under the general title *Guide to America*, one aim of which was to present historical and biographical material from and about different regions of the United States (Schindler-Carter). African American participation in the FWP was not widespread, and one writer even refers to it as having been "token" (White, 270) (*see* **Tokenism**). Nonetheless, many African American writers participated in what came to be known as **Negro units** of the FWP and of the parallel Federal Theatre Project. Through their participation in the FWP, they found employment, were given time to work on their own writing, and helped produce important works in the *Guide to America* series. Because the effects of the Great Depression had blunted much of the literary progress created by the **Harlem Renaissance** and other cultural activity during the 1920s, participation in the FWP is seen as having provided employment to some African American writers at a crucial point (Penkower). Among the writers who worked for the FWP in a variety of capacities were

Arna Bontemps, Sterling A. Brown, Zora Neale Hurston, Claude McKay, Willard Motley, Margaret Walker, and Richard Wright. Brown served as director of Negro affairs for the FWP. Like Wright, the dancer and choreographer Katherine Dunham worked for the FWP in Chicago. The Library of Congress in Washington, D.C., now contains nearly 3,000 documents related to the "life histories" part of the FWP, for which employees of the FWP interviewed ordinary citizens, wrote case histories, and drafted life histories of these individuals. The Library of Congress indicates that the life histories represent "the work of over 300 writers from 24 states" between 1936 and 1940 (American Life Histories Web page). Much of this material is now accessible electronically from the Library of Congress. One book to emerge from this fieldwork is *Drums and Shadows: Survival Studies Among the Georgia Coastal Negroes* (1940). Another was *The Negro in Virginia* (1940), an important compendium of African American **folklore**. The historian Harvard Sitkoff has observed that the Federal Writers' Project "collected hundreds of interviews with ex-slaves and first published such Negro authors as Ralph Ellison and Richard Wright. For these reasons many Negro spokesmen acknowledged their gratitude to the WPA and the Roosevelt Administration" (72).

Resources: American Life Histories (a collection of documents), Library of Congress, Washington, DC, http://lcweb2.loc.gov/ammem/wpaintro/wpahome.html; Jeutonne Brewer, *The Federal Writers' Project: A Bibliography* (Metuchen, NJ: Scarecrow Press, 1994); Georgia Writers' Project, *Drums and Shadows: Survival Studies Among the Georgia Coastal Negroes,* [compiled by the] *Savannah Unit, Georgia Writers' Project, Works Projects Administration* (Athens: University of Georgia Press, 1940); *The Negro in Virginia: Compiled by the Workers of the Writers' Program of the Works Progress Administration in the State of Virginia* (1940; Winston-Salem, NC: J. F. Blair, 1994); Monty Noam Penkower, *The Federal Writers' Project: A Study in Government Patronage of the Arts* (Urbana: University of Illinois Press, 1977); Petra Schindler-Carter, *Vintage Snapshots: The Fabrication of a Nation in the W.P.A. American Guide Series* (New York: Peter Lang, 1999); Harvard Sitkoff, *A New Deal for Blacks: The Emergence of Civil Rights as a National Issue,* vol. 1, *The Depression Decade* (New York: Oxford University Press, 1978); Craig Howard White, "Federal Writers' Project," in *The Oxford Companion to African American Literature,* ed. William L. Andrews, Frances Smith Foster, and Trudier Harris (New York: Oxford University Press, 1997), 270–271.

Hans Ostrom

Feminism/Black Feminism. Liberation movement focused on Black women. Black feminism is a political, artistic, and social movement that recognizes and resists the oppression experienced in the lives of Black women, an oppression involving racism and sexism as well as issues of social class. Elements of feminism have coexisted intimately with African American literature from the origins of that literature. Beginning with the oral tradition during American **slavery** and the work of one of the earliest published Black writers in the United States—**Phillis Wheatley**, a slave who published *Poems on*

Various Subjects, Religious and Moral in 1773, Black women have consistently produced culture and art that critiques sexism and racism in American life. In recent years, due to the rapid growth of scholarship by and about Black women, some scholars make a distinction between "Black feminism," which for many now encompasses research on Black women across the world, and "womanism," a term coined by the American feminist writer **Alice Walker**. (*See* **Theology, Black and Womanist**.)

While acknowledging the significant contributions to Black life and arts and to feminism by African American women in the nineteenth century and earlier, most scholars date the development of contemporary Black feminism to the early 1970s and to frustrations experienced by African American women in the **Civil Rights Movement** and Women's Liberation movement. In stressing that Black feminism has been in effect in the United States as long as African and African American women have been here, historians are recognizing a fundamental tenet of Black feminism: that Black women have created a long-standing and unique tradition of struggle, in art, politics, and other cultural venues, for survival and empowerment. These are the many named and un-named "foremothers" of the contemporary Black feminist movement that emerged in the 1970s in the United States and has subsequently evolved into a global movement for rights of women of color and for an end to all racial, class, and **gender** oppression.

A significant figure in the origins of Black feminism, known as much through legend as through fact, is **Sojourner Truth**, whose renowned "Ain't I a Woman?" speech, delivered at an 1851 Akron, Ohio, women's suffrage convention, was a defiant rebuttal to the prominent definitions of women as the "weaker sex" and of slaves as "less than human." Truth traveled as a preacher and lecturer for abolition and women's rights and published *The Narrative of Sojourner Truth* in 1850 ("Sojourner Truth"). Her famous speech serves as a touchstone of Black feminism, and it is the title phrase for the first of many works by contemporary the Black feminist cultural critic **bell hooks**, *Ain't I a Woman: Black Women and Feminism* (1981).

Many other women, especially in the nineteenth century, made contributions to Black feminism by recognizing that **race** and sex interact in the lives of Black women in such a way that speaking from one perspective or the other does not recognize the total picture of Black female existence in the United States, another idea central to Black feminism. According to the critic **Hazel V. Carby, Ida B. Wells-Barnett, Anna Julia Haywood Cooper**, and **Pauline E. Hopkins** all wrote and spoke about the "double jeopardy" of the social position of the Black female. Working in African American churches and in the **women's clubs** movement, Wells, Cooper, Hopkins, and many others encouraged and empowered Black women to work for racial uplift, as well as for their rightful place at the table of American politics. Cooper, who was born a slave in 1858, wrote *A Voice from the South, by a Black Woman of the South* in 1892, which is considered by many to be the "wellspring of modern Black feminist thought" ("Anna Julia Cooper").

Other significant contributors to Black feminism are **Frances Ellen Watkins Harper**, **Alice Moore Dunbar-Nelson**, and **Zora Neale Hurston**, to name just a few. While all three were creative writers, Harper and Dunbar-Nelson were also active in the suffrage and temperance movements, and Hurston was a leading talent of the **Harlem Renaissance** who also did important anthropological work preserving Afro-Caribbean and African American cultural heritage and folk traditions. She wrote many creative and scholarly works, including *Their Eyes Were Watching God* (1937). Contemporary African American feminists, particularly **Alice Walker**, in her collection *In Search of Our Mothers' Gardens* (1983), have reclaimed Hurston's work and significance as a foremother. These brief descriptions only imply the breadth and scope of African American women's contributions to struggles for the liberation of women and people of color in the United States prior to the feminist movements of the 1970s. The novels of **Jessie Redmon Fauset**, also a Harlem Renaissance writer, explore convergences between conflicts of race and those of gender. Her novels include *There Is Confusion* (1924) and *Plum Bun* (1929).

Contemporary Black feminism/womanism emerged in the United States in the late 1970s from Black women's experiences in the Civil Rights and Women's Liberation movements, specifically from frustrations with White feminists and male Black activists. Many Black feminists, among them bell hooks, Beverly Guy-Sheftall, **Audre Lorde**, Patricia Hill Collins, and **Angela Y. Davis**, add critiques of classism and sometimes heterosexism, voicing another tenet of black feminism: that race, class, gender, and other categories of identity exist in a complex web of power that is manifested in the lived experiences of black women. This principle has led to serious and extended critiques in contemporary Black feminist writing of the cultural institutions that carry out the social control of Black women.

In their groundbreaking history, analysis, and resource guide to Black Women's Studies, *All the Women Are White, All the Blacks Are Men, But Some of Us Are Brave: Black Women's Studies*, **Gloria T. Hull**, Patricia Bell Scott, and **Barbara Smith** provide accounts of key moments in the progression of Black feminist thought. In the spring of 1973, a group of politically active Black women gathered to discuss the relationship of Black women to the women's movement, resulting in the formation of the short-lived, but significant, National Black Feminist Organization. Michele Wallace noted in "A Black Feminist's Search for Sisterhood" that during that period she started a black feminist consciousness-raising group. Wallace's sense of the Black man's hostility to empowered Black women and her concerns about racism in parts of the feminist movement led her to conclude in 1974 that, despite the presence of Black feminists such as Eleanor Holmes Norton, Florynce Kennedy, **Faith Ringgold**, **Shirley Chisholm**, and **Alice Walker**, there was no separate Black women's movement. Wallace voiced her hopes for a "multicultural women's movement" (Hull et al., 2), which some consider a foreshadowing of the current global Black feminist movement.

Two essays written in the 1970s placed Black women's literary culture at the center of Black feminist inquiry. Alice Walker's 1974 essay, "In Search of Our Mothers' Gardens," asked, "What did it mean for a black woman to be an artist in our grandmothers' time? In our great-grandmothers' day?" Her answer—"It is a question with an answer cruel enough to stop the blood" (*In Search*, 233)—laid bare the agonizing reality of living in a culture that not only devalued the art of Black women but actually punished learning. Walker has continued to produce creative and critical writing about Black women from a feminist perspective, including the Pulitzer Prize–winning novel *The Color Purple* (1982) and recent writing about female genital mutilation, including *Possessing the Secret of Joy* (1992). Barbara Smith's groundbreaking essay, "Toward a Black Feminist Criticism," published in July 1977, claimed she was "attempting something unprecedented, something dangerous" in writing about "Black women writers from a feminist perspective and about Black lesbian writers from any perspective at all. These things have not been done" (Hull et al., 157). In her discussion, Smith calls for "a viable, autonomous Black feminist movement in this country" (158). Smith claims that the problem in the **Black Arts Movement** and feminist movement was that they did not focus clearly on Black women; their theories did not have the experience, perceptions, and ideas of Black women at their centers. Smith called for a Black feminist criticism that would begin with a "primary commitment to exploring how both sexual and racial politics and Black and female identity are inextricable elements in Black women's writings," and that would acknowledge Black women's writing as an "identifiable literary tradition" (163). Smith's call for Black feminist critics to be consistently vigilant in connecting their work to the "political situation of all Black women" (164) closely followed the growing imperative that Black feminist thought focus on the realities of life for Black women.

Another significant moment in the early public life of Black feminism was in April 1977, when the **Combahee River Collective**, a group of Black feminists in **Boston, Massachusetts**, who had been meeting since 1974, released a statement that addressed the issues and practices of contemporary Black feminism and provided a narrative of the herstory of their organization. Significantly, like many Black feminists, this group placed high emphasis on both the history of African American women and their day-to-day struggles.

Based on their experiences up to the 1970s, probably neither Walker nor Smith would have predicted the renaissance of Black women's literary productions of the 1970s and 1980s or the volume of subsequent critical attention the literature generated. The explosion of fiction by black women writers, many of whom identified as feminists, began around 1970 with the publication of **Toni Morrison**'s and Alice Walker's first novels, *The Bluest Eye* and *The Third Life of Grange Copeland*, respectively, and includes **Maya Angelou**'s *I Know Why the Caged Bird Sings* and **Toni Cade Bambara**'s collection *The Black Woman: An Anthology*. Other watershed works include three extremely influential collections of fiction and poetry: **Mary Helen Washington**'s *Black-Eyed*

Susans (1975); Cherríe Moraga's and Gloria Anzaldúa's *This Bridge Called My Back: Writings by Radical Women of Color* (1981); and Barbara Smith's *Home Girls: A Black Feminist Anthology* (1983). This short list excludes a great number of individual works and lesser-known anthologies produced during this period. By 1985 the critic **Hortense J. Spillers** wrote in *Conjuring: Black Women, Fiction, and Literary Tradition* (1985) that "the community of black women writing in the United States now can be regarded as a vivid new fact of national life" (245). The growth of fiction by Black women created a significant enough stir in academic and literary circles that the well-known African-American critic **Henry Louis Gates, Jr.**, said in 1990:

> The black women's literary movement, it seems safe to say, already has taken its place as a distinct period in Afro-American literary history, and could very well prove to be one of the most productive and sustained. Certainly it has features that make it anomalous in black literary history. (3)

From the 1980s on, there has been an enormous proliferation not just of literary criticism about the creative writing of Black women, but of Black feminist academic writing in general, as Black feminists have been researching and writing in nearly every academic discipline, producing a body of information, analysis, and interpretation spanning the experiences of Black women not just in contemporary and historical America, but around the globe.

A significant development in Black feminism in the 1990s was the growth of the "third wave" of the American feminist movement, which had a concurrent and connected Black/multicultural/global component. The third wave includes creative and critical writing that focuses on young women of color, including works by **Rebecca Walker**, and **Joan Morgan**, and the anthology *Colonize This!* (2002). While the impact of "third wave" and "hip-hop" feminism on Black culture and the feminist movement remains to be seen, the creative and critical writing that has emerged from young Black feminists is marked by a continuing commitment to Black women's historical struggles and an acknowledgment of the complexity of definitions of identity in twenty-first-century multicultural America and beyond. As young feminists influence literary and popular culture, their contributions will certainly draw on the tenets that have sustained Black feminism throughout the years. (*See also* **Feminist/Black Feminist Literary Criticism; Kitchen Table: Women of Color Press; Lotus Press.**)

Resources: "Anna Julia Cooper," in *Contemporary Black Biography*, vol. 20, ed. Ashyia N. Henderson (Detroit: Gale, 1998), repro. in *Biography Resource Center* (Farmington Hills, MI: Gale, 2004), http://galenet.galegroup.com/servlet/BioRC? locID=ohlnk130; Joanne Braxton and Andrée Nicola McLaughlin, eds., *Wild Women in the Whirlwind: Afra-American Culture and the Contemporary Literary Renaissance* (New Brunswick, NJ: Rutgers University Press, 1990); Hazel V. Carby, *Reconstructing Womanhood: The Emergence of the Afro-American Novelist* (New York: Oxford University Press, 1987); Barbara Christian, *Black Feminist Criticism: Perspectives on Black*

Women Writers (New York: Pergamon, 1985); Patricia Hill Collins, *Black Feminist Thought: Knowledge, Consciousness, and the Politics of Empowerment* (Boston: Unwin Hyman, 1990), 230; Angela Davis, *Women, Race, and Class* (New York: Random House, 1981); Mari Evans, ed., *Black Women Writers (1950–1980): A Critical Evaluation* (Garden City, NY: Anchor/Doubleday, 1984); Henry Louis Gates, Jr., "Introduction," in *Reading Black Reading Feminist: A Critical Anthology*, ed. Henry Louis Gates, Jr. (New York: Meridian, 1990), 1–17; Beverly Guy-Sheftall, ed., *Words of Fire: An Anthology of African American Feminist Thought* (New York: New Press, 1995); Daisy Hernández and Bushra Rehman, eds., *Colonize This! Young Women of Color on Today's Feminism* (New York: Seal, 2002); bell hooks: *Ain't I a Woman: Black Women and Feminism* (Boston: South End Press, 1981); *Feminist Theory from Margin to Center* (Boston: South End Press, 1984); *Talking Back: Thinking Feminist, Thinking Black* (Boston: South End Press, 1989); Gloria T. Hull, Patricia Bell Scott, and Barbara Smith, eds., *All the Women Are White, All the Blacks Are Men, But Some of Us Are Brave: Black Women's Studies* (Old Westbury, NY: Feminist Press, 1982); Audre Lorde, *Sister Outsider* (Trumansburg, NY: Crossing Press, 1984); Cherríe Moraga and Gloria Anzaldúa, eds., *This Bridge Called My Back: Writings by Radical Women of Color*, 3rd ed. (Berkeley, CA: Third Woman Press, 2001); "Pauline Hopkins," in *Notable Black American Women*, vol. 1, ed. Jessie Carney Smith (Detroit: Gale, 1992), repro. in *Biography Resource Center* (Farmington Hills, MI: Gale, 2004), http://galenet.galegroup.com/servlet/BioRC?locID=ohlnk130; Marjorie Pryse and Hortense J. Spillers, eds., *Conjuring: Black Women, Fiction, and Literary Tradition* (Bloomington: Indiana University Press, 1985); Barbara Smith, ed., *Home Girls: A Black Feminist Anthology* (New York: Kitchen Table: Women of Color Press, 1983); "Sojourner Truth," in *Feminist Writers*, ed. Pamela Kester-Shelton (Detroit: St. James Press, 1996), repro. in *Biography Resource Center* (Farmington Hills, MI: Gale, 2004), http://galenet.galegroup.com/servlet/BioRC?locID=ohlnk130; Alice Walker, *In Search of Our Mothers' Gardens: Womanist Prose* (San Diego, CA: Harcourt Brace Jovanovich, 1983); Michele Wallace, *Black Macho and the Myth of the Superwoman* (New York: Dial, 1979); Mary Helen Washington, ed., *Black-Eyed Susans and Midnight Birds: Stories by and About Black Women* (New York: Anchor, 1975; repr. 1990).

Sharon L. Barnes

Feminist/Black Feminist Literary Criticism. Black feminist literary criticism is a relatively recent development in the discipline of literary scholarship. In part, this newness is due to a lack of consensus among the literary establishment on an acknowledged body of writings by Black women, a tradition characterized by distinctive qualities that conforms to the normative ideology defined by White male and female critics. It is also in part due to a lack of agreement upon evaluative principles of literary criticism, whether the criticism is exercised by White critics upon the writings of Black women, or whether it is exercised by Black women writers themselves on their own writings or the writings of others.

As **Deborah E. McDowell** observes in her essay "Reading Family Matters," "It is not late-breaking news that literary criticism is another form of storytelling, of mythmaking" (Wall, 75). She emphasizes that "literary texts take shape in the minds of readers and critics who form disparate interpretive communities" (75).

Literary criticism, in general, both validates a body of received texts and evaluates that body of texts with the available tools of literary analysis to proclaim those texts as significant examples of the vitality of a particular culture. Until the 1970s, literary texts were, for the most part, evaluated by White males using western European philosophical models, a kind of literary analysis that, while valuable, excluded considerations of **gender**, **race**, and class.

Barbara Smith, in a 1977 essay that exposed this bias, writes, "Black women's existence, experience and culture, and the brutally complex system of oppressions which shape these, are in the 'real world' of white and/or male consciousness beneath consideration, invisible, unknown" (Mitchell, 410).

She confesses in her introduction that writing her essay, "Toward a Black Feminist Criticism," provoked in her a sense of danger, a conviction that she was writing something unprecedented because writing about Black women writers from a feminist perspective had not been done by White male writers, by "white women critics who think of themselves as feminists," or by "black women critics who, although they pay the most attention to black women writers as a group, seldom use a consistent feminist analysis or write about black lesbian literature" (Mitchell, 410).

She states plainly, "All segments of the literary world—whether establishment, progressive, black, female, or lesbian—do not know, or at least act as if they do not know, that black women writers and black lesbian writers exist" (410). Smith argues that racism allows "ostensible feminists" to be blind to the presence and power of Black women writers. At the time of her writing, she says, politics as much as "the practice of literature" is to blame for this blindness: "Any discussion of Afro-American writers can rightfully begin with the fact that for most of the time we have been denied not only literacy, but the most minimal possibility of a 'decent human life'" (411).

Smith calls for a Black feminist movement that will "open up the space needed for the exploration of black women's lives and the creation of consciously black woman-identified art" (411). In addition, she says, a redefinition of feminism that does not slight the racial oppression of Black women would broaden the scope of women's culture.

Recognizing that this proposal for a Black feminist movement must include literary criticism, she says, "For books to be read and remembered they have to be talked about. For the books to be understood they must be examined in such a way that the basic intentions of the writers are at least considered" (412). A part of the reason why such a Black feminist movement has not been promoted is that there is no political movement supporting it: "There is no political presence that demands a level of consciousness and respect from those who write or talk about our lives" (412). Discussions of Black literature usually do not include sexual politics. Smith says flatly that realizing "The politics of sex as well as the politics of race and class are crucially interlocking factors in the works of black women writers is an absolute necessity. Until a black feminist criticism exists we will not even know what these writers mean" (412). She quotes a perspective from **Alice Walker** to suggest a reason why Black women writers have been ignored in America: they are women, and they are the "least willing worshippers of male supremacy" (412).

Walker, writing in 1967, had anticipated many of Smith's concerns, and in the process of trying to find a literary tradition from which she descended, she redefined art, particularly as it is practiced by women. Her collection of essays, entitled *In Search of Our Mothers' Gardens*, attempts, among other objectives, to define a tradition of Black feminist creativity. A part of this redefinition includes a new word for "feminist." Walker uses "womanist" because this term includes Black feminists and other feminists of color. It also broadens the scope of feminism, so that "womanist" moves beyond White female literary criticism, which often involved a reaction against sexism in male discussions of literature.

White female literary criticism often finds its meaning in a primarily academic tradition and in theoretical definitions framed by male pronouncements about literary theory. Walker chooses instead to see "womanist" as a descriptive term that values and affirms female creativity, a spirituality often repressed or manifested in nonwritten ways. This redefinition was inspired by her reading of the Black male poet **Jean Toomer**, who, walking through **the South** in the early twentieth century, discovered in Black women prostitutes a spirituality that was "so intense, so deep, so unconscious, that they were themselves unaware of the riches they held" (Walker, 231, 232).

Toomer perceived beyond their broken bodies, made to serve the needs of White men, the remnants of a spirituality that defined them more truly than did their bodies. Walker, in a similar vein, asks, "What did it mean for a black woman to be an artist in our grandmother's time? How was the creativity of the black woman kept alive?" Her answer is that the descendants of these women recognize in their own art the remnants of this spiritual tradition, and this spiritual tradition is infinitely more important than money and a room of one's own, those necessary possessions that Virginia Woolf, lamenting the lack of a literary tradition for women, had prescribed in 1925 in *A Room of One's Own*. Walker contends that even without money or a room of one's own, these despised Black women had achieved the height of creativity.

Walker says, "Therefore we must fearlessly pull out of ourselves and look at and identify with our lives the living creativity some of our great-grandmothers were not allowed to know" (Walker, 237). She cites the example of her own mother, whose creativity was expressed in her gardens. Her mother handed on to her the seed of a creativity that she could not herself acknowledge or express in words. Her mother told her stories, which Walker discovered hidden in her own writing, and, like the flowers of her mother's garden, these stories constituted a vital tradition of creativity passed on from generation to generation.

Zora Neale Hurston was the literary foremother whom Walker discovered in the course of her search for a literary tradition to call her own. Walker was chiefly responsible for bringing Hurston back to the center of critical attention in the 1960s. She initially discovered Hurston in a class on Black American women writers taught by the black poet **Margaret Walker**. In 1973, Alice Walker went in search of Hurston's grave in Florida. After many harrowing experiences in her attempt to find the grave, she finally succeeded and placed a headstone on the grave with the inscription "Zora Neale Hurston, 'A Genius of the South,' Novelist, Folklorist, Anthropologist, 1901–1960."

Hurston deserves consideration as the first feminist Black literary critic for many reasons. She was a serious writer from an early age, at a time when recognition was hard to come by for Black writers in America. She had a strong sense of destiny as a writer and worked assiduously to establish a reputation as a writer. Precocious and powerful in personality, she was afforded many opportunities, which she used to good advantage. Her self-fashioning and her persistent self-definition revealed an ability to take her own subjectivity seriously, but not so seriously that she could not abstract herself from it and review it with a conscious determination.

Hurston dealt with two formidable challenges to the writing of Black women, challenges that prefigured the conflicts many Black women writers after her would experience. These were the forces of sexism in Black men's responses to her writings and racism in White women's responses. Hurston dealt with racism by creating characters of great depth and passion. She decried the apparent invisibility of the emotional lives of Black people to White Americans. In "What White Publishers Won't Print," an essay that first appeared in **Negro Digest**, she says, "I have been amazed by the Anglo-Saxon's lack of curiosity about the internal lives and emotions of the Negroes, and for that matter, any non-Anglo-Saxon peoples within our borders, above the class of skilled labor" (Mitchell, 117). To explain this phenomenon, she says, "The answer lies in what we may call *The American Museum of Unnatural History*. This is an intangible built on folk belief. It is assumed that all non-Anglo-Saxons are uncomplicated stereotypes" (Mitchell, 117).

In this regard, Hurston anticipated many of the works of Black women writers since the mid-1980s. In *Killing Rage*, **bell hooks** observes that in White supremacist society, White people often do not fully "see" Black people, and even imagine that they are not seen by Black people: "One mark of oppression was that black folks were compelled to assume the mantle of invisibility, to erase all traces of their subjectivity during slavery and the long years of racial apartheid, so that they could be better, less threatening servants" (hooks, 35).

Hurston felt the sexism of Black male writers, which she experienced in a very painful way. **Richard Wright** and **Langston Hughes**, struggling to prove their masculinity as well as their writing prowess in a predominantly White literary establishment, reacted negatively to Hurston's work, and perhaps more negatively to her than to her writing. In so doing, they doomed her to relative obscurity for the first half of the twentieth century. Hurston and Hughes collaborated on the play *Mule Bone*, but in the process, they had a falling out. **Mary Helen Washington**, in "A Woman Half in Shadow," suggests that Black male writers were offended by her powerful personality: "Few male critics have been able to resist sly innuendoes and outright attacks on Hurston's personal life, even when the work in question was not affected by her disposition or her private affairs. But these controversies have loomed so large in the reviews of her work that once again the task of confronting them must precede any reappraisal or reevaluation of her highly neglected work" (Bloom, 124).

In literary critical essays by prominent Black men in the **Harlem Renaissance**, Hurston is never mentioned as a writer embodying the values of Negro culture. **Alain Locke**, in the "The New Negro" (1925); **William Stanley Braithwaite**, in "The Negro in American Literature" (1925); and Langston Hughes, in "The Negro Artist and the Racial Mountain" (1926), make no comment on Hurston's writings. **W.E.B. Du Bois**, in the essay "Criteria of Negro Art," makes the case before an assembly of the **NAACP** that Negro art must be respected even as the art of White people is respected, but he concentrates mainly on the art of Negro men. Conspicuously absent is any reference to Hurston, the most prolific writer in the first thirty years of the twentieth century.

In 1966, in the midst of the **Black Arts Movement**, when black writers called for a kind of "art for art's sake" in Negro art, **Amiri Baraka** (LeRoi Jones) announced that until this point, there was no outstanding Black artist: "The mediocrity of what has been called 'Negro Literature' is one of the most loosely held secrets of American culture" (Mitchell, 165). Other Black male writers during this period included few Black women writers in their discussions of Black literature. The writings of **Ralph Ellison** and **Richard Wright** portrayed Black men struggling to become heroic figures in a racist America, and behind the depictions of their heroes is the implicit message that these heroes are capable of competing with White male American heroes.

Barbara Smith's 1977 essay, alluded to earlier, called for a Black feminist movement as the result of a keenly felt conviction that Black women writers were not being taken seriously, either by the mainly White literary establishment or by Black male writers who should have understood their concerns. White women writers, who were experiencing the support of a newly found feminism in the 1970s, addressed the disparity in the public and private domains that a bourgeois culture had imposed upon them as a form of male domination, and they addressed the burdens of rearing children by themselves and the widespread discrimination that existed in the marketplace. White women writers heralded the dawn of a new age of equal treatment for women, and they demanded respect in academic arenas. White feminist critics unearthed writings that had been buried and forgotten, and they began to redefine the canon of literature with the inclusion of forgotten female writings.

The feminists of the 1960s and 1970s, then, sought to balance the scales with White men. They called for an equal footing with White men. In their concern for this kind of equality, many of them neglected or overlooked the Black women's need for the same opportunities. At the same time, the **Civil Rights Movement**, while calling for equality of Black and White, implied an equality of Black men with White men. Although Black women played very active roles in the struggle for racial equality, the results of civil rights victories often overlooked the personal needs of Black women.

Smith proposes a Black feminist criticism that, first, recognizes that "black women writers constitute an identifiable literary tradition" and use common kinds of language and cultural expressions, and she urges that "they try to write out of their own identities and not try to graft the ideas of methodology of white/male literary thought upon the precious materials of black women's art" (Mitchell, 416). Above all, Smith argues, the Black feminist critic must be aware at all times of the political implications of literary criticism, of the ways in which Black women's lives are powerfully affected by the intersections of the oppressions of sex, class, and race.

Commenting on Smith's project in 1994, **Barbara T. Christian** said, "By 1977, Smith knew that the sexism of Afro-American literary/intellectual circles and the racism of white feminist literary journals resulted in a kind of homelessness for critical works on black women or other third world writers" (Wall, 62). Most feminist journals were White publications and dealt with White women writers. Christian knew, however, that in addition to the racism and sexism of these literary circles, White male, Black male, and White female literary critics did not know *how* to respond to the works of Black women.

Christian cites her own frustration in the attempt to define an "identifiable literary tradition" for Black women. Even more scarce were books on the history of Black women. Christian, who was working on a book, *Black Women Novelists*, revealed that she had little help from academia in conducting her research. The analyses of the novels of Black women writers on which Christian relied in writing her book came from ordinary Black women readers, not scholars: "women in the churches, private reading groups, women like my hairdresser and her clients, secondary school teachers, typists, my women friends, many of whom were single mothers, who discussed *The Bluest Eye* (1970) or *In Love and Trouble* (1973) with an intensity unheard of in the academic world" (Wall, 64).

From the 1980s to the present, Smith's program has largely been actualized. The profusion of novels written by Black women has become a formidable presence among the reading public. The fiction of Alice Walker, **Toni Morrison, Gloria Naylor, Ntozake Shange, Paule Marshall, Jamaica Kincaid, Michelle Cliff, Michele Wallace, J. California Cooper**, and many others have memorialized the lives of unforgettable, strong Black women characters. Toni Morrison's status as a Nobel laureate has given her an authority that few other Black women writers have enjoyed.

Black feminist literary criticism is arguably more pervasive and influential than ever before. Black women writers such as **Audre Lorde** and Gloria Naylor have explored the Black lesbian experience. Paule Marshall, Jamaica Kincaid, and Michelle Cliff have explored the detrimental effects of colonization in the Caribbean, which constituted, as the stopping place for African slaves before they were transported elsewhere, a missing link in many mainland American women's experiences of the **Middle Passage**.

Black feminist critics in academia have continued to explore the widening gap between Black male and female writers, and, most recently, Black feminist critics have used the tools of contemporary literary criticism. In the 1980s and 1990s, Black feminist critics confronted the need to consider recent trends in literary criticism: Jacques Derrida's theories of deconstruction; Jacques Lacan's psychoanalytic and literary theories, which fall under the rubrics of **postmodernism** and **poststructuralism**; the dialogics of Mikhail Bahktin; and the French feminist theories of such writers as Hélène Cixous, Luce Irigaray, and Julia Kristeva.

Barbara Christian discusses the challenges of these new forms of criticism in her 1987 essay "The Race for Theory." In that essay she says, "I have become convinced that there has been a takeover in the literary world by Western philosophies from the old literary elite, the neutral humanists" (Mitchell, 348). Christian states with conviction, "They have changed literary critical language to suit their own purposes as philosophers, and they have reinvented the meaning of theory" (348). Pondering the function of the critic in the last two decades of the twentieth century, she reflects upon the fact that, in previous years, critics were usually also creative writers, but critics of this new theoretical school are mainly philosophers. Christian emphasizes that "people of color have always theorized but in forms quite different from the Western form of abstract logic. And I am inclined to say that our theorizing . . . is often in narrative forms, in the stories we create, in riddles and proverbs, in the play with language, since dynamic rather than fixed ideas seem more to our liking." Black women, she says, "continually speculate on the nature of life through pithy language" (Mitchell, 349). Christian perceives in the race for theory a desire on the part of White male literary critics to maintain an elite academic hegemony. Christian feels that even the insistence within the academy that Black women define a Black feminist literary criticism is reductive. Academics' insistence that literature is political overlooks the fact that literature has always been political for Black writers. Further, Christian views the efforts by White male critics to hold onto a specialized Eurocentric literary tradition as an attempt to ignore the swelling production of writings by minority writers: "Variety, multiplicity, eroticism are difficult to control. And it may very well be that these are the reasons why writers are often seen as *persona non grata* by political states, whatever form they take, since writers/artists have a tendency to refuse to give up their way of seeing the world and of playing with possibilities; in fact, their very expression relies on that insistence" (355). Literary criticism, Christian insists, exists to preserve life, not to be monolithic.

Other Black feminist literary critics during these years have utilized the tools of the new literary criticism to insist upon a rearrangement of the literary canon. Toni Morrison, in "Unspeakable Things Unspoken: The Afro-American Presence in America Literature," and in "Black Matter(s)," suggests that an African presence has always existed in American literature, even when White writers have repressed it. The theoretical basis for Morrison's comments is the unnoticed impact that the shift from scholasticism to humanism made on the self-understanding of Western culture. That shift, she says, occurring within a few short years in the sixteenth century, obscured the impact of Egyptian culture on the whole Western tradition of literature and culture. To speak of Western culture, from that time forward, has meant a narrow concentration on Eurocentric culture, and the effect has been to conceal or elide the impact of an Afrocentric culture on the Western world.

Morrison concentrates on three areas that are important for a rearrangement of the Western canon of literature: "One is the development of a theory of literature that truly accommodates Afro-American literature: one that is based on its culture, its history, and the artistic strategies the works employ to negotiate the world it inhabits. Another is the examination and reinterpretation of the American canon, the founding nineteen-century works, for the 'unspeakable things unspoken'; for the ways in which the presence of Afro-Americans has shaped the choices, the language, the structure—the meaning of so much American literature. A search, in other words, for the ghost in the machine" (Mitchell, 377). A third objective, says Morrison, is the examination of contemporary literature for this presence.

Other recent black feminist literary critics have used the tools of contemporary criticism for in-depth studies of the writings of Black women. Mae Gwendolyn Henderson, in "Speaking in Tongues: Dialogics, Dialectics, and the Black Woman Writer's Literary Tradition," uses Mikhail Bahktin's theory of dialogics to examine the multiple discourses of Black women in literature. Specifically, Henderson discusses the construction of subjectivity in Black women's writings and its intersection with the "other," the selves that interact with that subjectivity.

Deborah McDowell, in her essay "Reading Family Matters," uses feminist theory and psychoanalytic theory to explore the possible reasons for the hostility of Black male critics to the writings of Alice Walker, Ntozake Shange, and Toni Morrison. McDowell cites Robert Staples, who suggests, in "The Myth of Black Macho: A Response to Angry Black Feminists," that Walker and Shange were rewarded for their "diatribes against black men" and that they had a "collective appetite for black male abuse" (78). Staples sympathizes, McDowell says, "with the black male need for power in the only two institutions left to black control: the church and the family (78). McDowell analyzes these responses and others like them from a psychological perspective and suggests that Black male critics are attempting "to rewrite origins, to replace the unsatisfactory fragments of a ... past by a totalizing fiction that recuperates loss and fulfills desire" (Wall, 78). She quotes Christine Froula, who argues that this kind of confrontation is between "the daughter's story and the father's law" (78). Froula suggests that "the relations of literary daughters and fathers resemble ... the model ... describing the family situation of incest victims: a dominating, authoritarian father, an absent, ill or compliant mother; and a daughter prohibited by her father from speaking about abuse" (78).

Claudia Tate, in "Allegories of Black Female Desire; or, Rereading Nineteenth-Century Sentimental Narratives of Black Female Authority," uses the critical tools of new historicism to analyze nineteenth-century romances by Black women writers, suggesting that these romances have been slighted by critics because they accept and encode a view of marriage to which Black nineteenth-century women, but not Black nineteenth-century men, adhered. Tate argues that marriage was of tremendous importance to newly freed Blacks, as important as achieving citizenship, but Black women inscribed in marriage the spiritual and social conduct needed for further societal enhancement. Black men, on the other hand, affirmed their personal integrity not by marriage but by direct confrontation of civil injustice. Marriage for Black men was often a sign of imprisonment, not liberty, whereas for women, marriage was a sign of personal and social freedom. Sentimental novels by Black women in the nineteenth century, both before and after emancipation, Tate argues, were narratives of liberation.

Hortense J. Spillers, in "'The Permanent Obliquity of an In(pha)llibly Straight': In the Time of the Daughters and the Fathers," explores the problem of incest in Black families and what that means for daughters. It means an indistinguishability or a kind of annihilation of what is ordinarily conceived as "family": "In this movement outward from a nuclear centrality, 'family' becomes an extension and inclusion—anyone who preserves life and its callings becomes a member of the family, whose patterns of kinship and resemblance fall into disguise" (Wall, 148). It means, essentially, that the Freudian model, so important for bourgeois culture, does not apply to the Black notion of family.

Patricia Hill Collins's book *Black Feminist Thought* is perhaps the most important sociological and philosophical study of Black women to date. Her discussions of the relations of Black women to their families, to American culture, and to more general philosophical concerns are grounded in Black women's writings. Collins's book attempts to articulate a fully developed Afrocentric feminist viewpoint. (*See* **Afrocentricity**.) In so doing, she relies on Black women intellectuals to be the medium through which this viewpoint is understood. The relationship of the Black woman intellectual draws upon two interrelated fields of knowledge: the everyday informal knowledge gained from the daily interaction of Black women, and the knowledge of specialists trained in academic disciplines. Black women's history of activism, she says, has always depended on these two traditions. Specifically, she says, "Black women's history and Black feminist literary criticism constitute two focal points of this renaissance in Black women's intellectual work" (Collins, 31). Further, she writes, "This Black feminist thought aims to develop a theory that is emancipatory and reflects ways which can aid in African-American women's struggles against oppression" (32). The primary guiding principle, says Collins, "is a recurring humanist vision" (37). The work of Black women is "the reclaiming of a black feminist intellectual tradition" (13).

Central to Collins's thought is her account of the Black mother in Afrocentric culture, including both blood mothers and those women in the Black community whom she calls "othermothers" and who assist in the rearing of children. (*See* **Afrocentricity**.) Collins notes that in American culture, even in the days of slavery, Black women were the repository of Afrocentric traditions. Particularly in slave households, Black women reiterated the aspects of West African culture likely to be lost in an alien existence such as slavery. Those stories and traditions were passed down by the women, and this custom helps to explain the pervasive influence of stories written by Black women: "The centrality of women in African-American extended families reflects both a continuation of West African cultural values and functional adaptations to race and gender oppression" (119). She continues, "Although the political economy of slavery brought profound changes to enslaved Africans, cultural values concerning the importance of motherhood and the value of cooperative approaches to child care continued" (121). Black women's fiction, she says, "can be read as texts revealing the multiple ways that African-American mothers aim to shield their daughters from the demands of being Black women in oppressive conditions" (126).

Collins also articulates a distinctive epistemology of Black women, describing their way of discerning truth and communicating that truth to their children. That epistemology, she says, is sustained in many ways through a network of Black women. It is forced to distinguish itself from White male ways of discerning truth: "The experiences of African-American women scholars illustrate how individuals who wish to rearticulate a Black women's standpoint through Black feminist thought can be suppressed by a white-male controlled knowledge validation process. Exclusion from basic literacy, quality educational experiences, and faculty and administrative positions has limited Black women's access to influential academic positions" (204). Collins includes in a Black feminist epistemology a valuing of experience as a criterion of meaning, the use of dialogue in assessing knowledge claims, an ethic of caring, and an ethic of personal responsibility (210ff.).

Resources: Catherine Belsey and Jane Moore, eds., *The Feminist Reader*, 2nd ed. (Malden, MA: Blackwell, 1997); Harold Bloom, ed., *Zora Neale Hurston* (New York: Chelsea House, 1986); Valerie Boyd, *Wrapped in Rainbows: The Life of Zora Neale Hurston* (New York: Scribner's, 2003); Gwendolyn Brooks, *Blacks* (1945; repr. Chicago: Third World Press, 1992); William Stanley Braithwaite, "The Negro in American Literature," in *Within the Circle: An Anthology of African American Literary Criticism*, ed. Angelyn Mitchell (Durham, NC: Duke University Press, 1994); Abena P. Busia, "What Is Your Nation? Reconnecting Africa and Her Diaspora Through Paule Marshall's *Praisesong for the Widow*," in *Changing Our Own Words*, ed. Cheryl Wall (New Brunswick, NJ: Rutgers University Press, 1989); Hélène Cixous, "The Laugh of the Medusa," in *The Longman Anthology of Women's Literature*, ed. Mary Kay DeShazer (New York: Longman, 2000); Michelle Cliff, "If I Could Write This in Fire, I Would Write This in Fire," in *The Longman Anthology of Women's Literature*, ed. Mary Kay DeShazer (New York: Longman, 2000); Patricia Hill Collins, *Black Feminist Thought: Knowledge, Consciousness and the Politics of Empowerment* (New York: Routledge, 1990); Barbara Christian: "But What Do We Think We're Doing Anyway? The State of Black Feminist Criticism(s) or My Version of a Little Bit of History," in *Changing Our Own Words*, ed. Cheryl Wall (New Brunswick, NJ: Rutgers University

Press, 1989); "The Race for Theory," in *Within the Circle: An Anthology of African American Literary Criticism*, ed. Angelyn Mitchell (Durham, NC: Duke University Press, 1994); Eugenia C. DeLamotte, *Places of Silence, Journeys of Freedom: The Fiction of Paule Marshall* (Philadelphia: University of Pennsylvania Press, 1998); Mary K. DeShazer, ed., *The Longman Anthology of Women's Literature* (New York: Longman, 2000); Mari Evans, ed., *Black Women Writers (1950–1980): A Critical Evaluation* (Garden City, NY: Anchor Books, 1984); Carolyn Finney, "Can't See the Black Folks for the Trees," in *Voices of a New Generation: A Feminist Anthology*, ed. Sara Weir and Constance Faulkner (New York: Longman, 2004); Mae Gwendolyn Henderson, "Speaking in Tongues: Dialogics, Dialectics, and The Black Woman Writer's Literary Tradition," in *Changing Our Own Words*, ed. Cheryl Wall (New Brunswick, NJ: Rutgers University Press, 1994); bell hooks, *Killing Rage: Ending Racism* (New York: Henry Holt, 1995); Zora Neale Hurston: *Dust Tracks on a Road: An Autobiography*, 2nd ed. (Urbana: University of Illinois Press, 1984); *Folklore, Memoirs, and Other Writings* (New York: Library of America, 1995); *Their Eyes Were Watching God* (1937; New York: Perennial Library, 1990); "What White Publishers Won't Print," in *Within the Circle: An Anthology of African American Literary Criticism*, ed. Angelyn Mitchell (Durham, NC: Duke University Press, 1994); LeRoi Jones (Amiri Baraka), "The Myth of a 'Negro Literature,'" in *Within the Circle: An Anthology of African American Literary Criticism*, ed. Angelyn Mitchell (Durham, NC: Duke University Press, 1994); Alain Locke, "The New Negro," in *Within the Circle: An Anthology of African American Literary Criticism*, ed. Angelyn Mitchell (Durham, NC: Duke University Press, 1994); Audre Lorde, "Use of the Erotic," in *The Longman Anthology of Women's Literature*, ed. Mary Kay DeShazer (New York: Longman, 2001); Deborah McDowell, "Reading Family Matters," in *Changing Our Own Words*, ed. Cheryl Wall (New Brunswick, NJ: Rutgers University Press, 1994); Angelyn Mitchell, ed., *Within the Circle: An Anthology of African American Literary Criticism* (Durham, NC: Duke University Press, 1994); Toni Morrison: *Beloved* (New York: Plume, 1988); "Black Matter(s)," in *Falling into Theory*, comp. David H. Richter (Boston: Bedford, 1994); *The Bluest Eye* (New York: Plume, 1970); *Playing in the Dark* (Cambridge, MA: Harvard University Press, 1992); *Sula* (New York: Plume, 1973); "Unspeakable Things Unspoken: The Afro-American Presence in American Literature," in *Within the Circle: An Anthology of African American Literary Criticism*, ed. Angelyn Mitchell (Durham, NC: Duke University Press, 1994); Bill Mullen, ed., *Revolutionary Tales: African American Women's Short Stories from the First Story to the Present* (New York: Laurel, 1995); David H. Richter, ed., *Falling into Theory* (Boston: Bedford, 1994); Barbara Smith, "Toward a Black Feminist Criticism," in *Within the Circle: An Anthology of African American Literary Criticism*, ed. Angelyn Mitchell (Durham, NC: Duke University Press, 1994); Valerie Smith, "Black Feminist Theory and the Representation of the 'Other,'" in *Changing Our Own Words*, ed. Cheryl Wall (New Brunswick, NJ: Rutgers University Press, 1994); Hortense Spillers, "'The Permanent Obliquity of an In(pha)llibly Straight': In the Time of the Daughters and the Fathers," in *Changing Our Own Words*, ed. Cheryl Wall (New Brunswick, NJ: Rutgers University Press, 1994); Claudia Tate, "Allegories of Black Female Desire; or, Rereading Nineteenth-Century Sentimental Narratives of Black Female Authority," in

Changing Our Own Words, ed. Cheryl Wall (New Brunswick, NJ: Rutgers University Press, 1994); Alice Walker, *In Search of Our Mothers' Gardens: Womanist Prose* (New York: Harcourt, 1983); Cheryl Wall, ed., *Changing Our Own Words* (New Brunswick, NJ: Rutgers University Press, 1994); Robyn Warhol and Diane Price Herndl, *Feminisms* (New Brunswick, NJ: Rutgers University Press, 1997); Mary Helen Washington, " 'The Darkened Eye Restored': Notes Toward a Literary History of Black Women," in *Within the Circle: An Anthology of African American Literary Criticism*, ed. Angelyn Mitchell (Durham, NC: Duke University Press, 1994).

Sandra Mayfield

Ferrell, Carolyn (born 1962). Short fiction writer. Ferrell's stories feature the voices and inner lives of complex characters who "usually don't see themselves reflected in teen magazines or mainstream U.S. culture" (Dobosz, 90). Ferrell was born to an African American father and a German mother in **Brooklyn, New York**, and raised on Long Island. She studied creative writing at Sarah Lawrence College, graduating with a B.A. in 1984. Ferrell then moved to Germany, where she taught high school with the support of a Fulbright scholarship while playing violin in several local orchestras. Returning to New York City in 1988, she taught adult literacy and received an M.A. in creative writing at the City College of New York. In 1994, her story "Proper Library" was selected for *The Best Short Stories of 1994* and was later reprinted in *The Best American Short Stories of the Century*. Her first book, *Don't Erase Me*, a collection of eight short stories, received the 1997 *Los Angeles Times* Art Seidenbaum Award, the *Ploughshares* Zacharis Award, and the 1998 *Quality Paperbacks* New Voices Award. Ferrell, Katharine Whitemore notes, "deftly drops her readers into another world—allowing us to eavesdrop on the inner life of the inner-city child" (26). **Michelle Cliff** characterizes the texture of Ferrell's work as a "chorus of voices, each story with its own, unique soloist" (65). Her stories have appeared in **Callaloo**, *The Literary Review, Ploughshares*, and *Fiction*, and *Children of the Night: The Best Stories by African American Writers, 1967 to the Present* (1995). In 2004, she received a National Endowment for the Arts grant for prose fiction. Currently pursuing a Ph.D. in English at the City University of New York, Ferrell teaches creative writing at Sarah Lawrence College and is at work on a novel set on Long Island.

Resources: Michelle Cliff, "Urban Renewal," review of *Don't Erase Me*, *The Village Voice*, Sept. 23, 1997, p. 65; Ann Marie Dobosz, "Review of *Don't Erase Me*, Ms., July–Aug. 1997, 90; Carolyn Ferrell, *Don't Erase Me* (Boston: Houghton Mifflin, 1997); Don Lee, "Carolyn Ferrell, Zacharis Award," *Ploughshares*, Winter 1997–1998, 222–224; Katharine Whitemore, "Phrasemaker in the City," review of *Don't Erase Me*, *New York Times Book Review*, Sept. 14, 1997, p. 26.

Alex Feerst

Fiction. *See* **Coming-of-Age Fiction; Crime and Mystery Fiction; Epistolary Novel; Graphic Novels; Historical Fiction; Horror Fiction; Novel; Romance Novel; Science Fiction; Short Fiction.**

Finney, Nikky (born 1957). Poet and journalist. At once both fierce and gentle, Nikky Finney's poetry celebrates the private familial nuances of her own Southern heritage and culture while redefining geopolitical boundaries to embrace the elemental and the spiritual. Born in the deeply racist South Carolina of the 1950s and 1960s and raised during the tension-fraught changes of the civil rights years, Finney developed an activist's awareness of the need for social justice along with her naturally reflective, meditative temperament. Her father was a civil rights attorney; her mother, a teacher who imbued their children with a sense of pride and purpose. Finney's early recognition of her relationship to the concentric circles of family, community, region, and race was coupled with her reverence for the sustaining, vitalizing power of poetic language.

An original member of the **Affrilachian poets**, whose members include Gurney Norman, Kelly Ellis, Bernard Clay, and Daundra Scis-Givvens, Finney's Southern identity reaches outside her coastal South Carolina roots to the Alabama and Georgia of her college years, to the Lexington, Kentucky, where she currently makes her home. Coined by writer Frank Walker in the late 1980s, the term "Affrilachian" was used to pointedly distinguish African Americans of the Appalachian region from their White counterparts, since reference to "Appalachian" folkways and culture invariably implied only White experience. "Affrilachian" has since been applied to writers, such as **Nikki Giovanni**, who have special ties and allegiance to the region.

Encouraged by influential supporters such as the actor Ruby Dee and writers such as Giovanni and **Toni Cade Bambara**, Finney published her first book of poems, *On Wings Made of Gauze*, in 1985, while she was a writer, editor, and photographer for *Vital Signs*, the magazine of Atlanta's National Black Women's Health Project. *Rice* (1995), which combines poetry with photographs of Finney's forebears and explores the intimate intermingling of Southern and African soils, was followed by *Heartwood* (1997), a collection of stories, and *The World Is Round* (2003). Finney also wrote the script for Heather Lyons's documentary, "For Posterity's Sake: The Morgan and Marvin Smith Story" (1995), about the 1930s photographers. She has received the 1999 PEN American Open Book Award as well as fellowships from the Kentucky Foundation for Women and the Kentucky Arts Council. She is an associate professor of creative writing at the University of Kentucky, where she has taught since 1991.

Resources: Kwame Dawes, "Reading *Rice*: A Local Habitation and a Name," *African American Review* 31, no. 2 (Summer 1997), 269–280; Nikky Finney: *Heartwood* (Lexington: University of Kentucky Press, 1997); *On Wings Made of Gauze* (New York: Quill, 1985); *Rice* (Toronto: Sister Vision Press, 1995); *The World Is Round* (Atlanta: InnerLight, 2003); Jeraldine Kraver, "'Mobile Images': Myth and Resistance in Nikky Finney's *Rice*," *Southern Literary Journal* 34, no. 2 (Sept. 2002), 134–148; Kyle Thompson, "*The World Is Round*: A Conversation with Nikky Finney," *Obsidian III* 4, no. 2 (2002), p. 10.

Kate Falvey

Fire!! **(1926).** Literary magazine. Published at the peak of the **Harlem Renaissance** in November 1926, the periodical *Fire!!* represents a concerted effort of the young and rebellious group of writers and artists who referred ironically to themselves the "Niggeratti," partly as a way to deflate what they regarded as the pretentiousness of some Harlem Renaissance attitudes. Edited by **Wallace Thurman, Langston Hughes,** and **Zora Neale Hurston,** with **Richard Bruce Nugent** in charge of distribution, John Preston Davis as business manager, and **Gwendolyn Bennett** and painter Aaron Douglas as assistants, *Fire!!* brought together the protagonists of the younger Renaissance set. **Countee Cullen, Arna Bontemps, Helene Johnson,** and other contributors added to the impressive lineup.

Striving for independence from White publishers and freedom from the limited space offered by **Opportunity** and **The Crisis,** magazines published by organizations with political and social rather than artistic objectives, the group of young writers and artists decided to produce a journal of their own. *Fire!!* became symbolic of their rejection of the burden of representation that the older Harlem Renaissance leaders had placed upon their shoulders and an embodiment of Hughes's literary credo: "We Negro artists who create now intend to express our individual dark-skinned selves without fear or shame."

Representing a fusion of transgressive sexuality, **Modernism,** and racial self-expression, most contributions to *Fire!!* were highly provocative. Outstanding were Nugent's and Thurman's stories "Smoke, Lilies and Jade" and "Cordelia the Crude," the first representing the first overtly homoerotic piece published by an African American and the other focusing on a young Black girl who becomes a prostitute. As Nugent recalled, sexual taboos were broken on purpose: He and Thurman "flipped a coin to see who wrote bannable material. The only two things we could think of . . . were a story about prostitution or about homosexuality." They decided on provocation on the highest scale and included both tales.

But the "Niggeratti's" high hopes failed: Neither was the journal, as they had planned, banned, nor did it, costing a steep $1 a copy, sell well or provoke the critical outcry they had desired. Contrary to some contributors' recollections, critics predominantly refused to respond to the Niggeratti's provocation. In the end there were more positive than negative reviews. Ironically, most copies of the journal that was to "burn up the old ideas" were destroyed in a storage room fire. A second edition never materialized, and Thurman, who had signed as responsible for debts, was left bankrupt. Despite the magazine's failure to meet the Niggeratti's expectations, *Fire!!* represents a highlight of Harlem Renaissance creativity and is central to an understanding of the movement. A facsimile reprint of the magazine appeared in 1981.

Resources: Michael L. Cobb, "Insolent Racing, Rough Narrative: The Harlem Renaissance's Impolite Queers," *Callaloo* 23 (2000), 328–351; Langston Hughes: *The Big Sea: An Autobiography* (1940; repr. New York: Hill and Wang, 1993); "The Negro Artist and the Racial Mountain," *The Nation,* June 23, 1926, pp. 692–694; Abby

Front cover of *Fire!!*, 1926. Yale Collection of American Literature, Beinecke Rare Book and Manuscript Library.

Arthur Johnson and Ronald Maberry Johnson, *Propaganda and Aesthetics: The Literary Politics of Afro-American Magazines in the Twentieth Century* (1979; repr. Amherst: University of Massachusetts Press, 1991); David Levering Lewis, *When Harlem Was in Vogue* (New York: Knopf, 1981); Alain Locke, "Fire: A Negro Magazine," *Survey* 58 (1927), 563; Richard Bruce Nugent [pseud. Bruce Nugent], "Lighting FIRE!!," insert to *Fire!!* (1926; repr. Metuchen, NJ: Fire!!, 1981), n.p.; Charles Michael Smith,

"Bruce Nugent: Bohemian of the Harlem Renaissance," in *In the Life: A Black Gay Anthology*, ed. Joseph Beam (Boston: Alyson, 1986), 209–220; Eleonore van Notten-Krepel, *Wallace Thurman's Harlem Renaissance* (Amsterdam: Rodopi, 1994); Cary D. Wintz, *Black Culture and the Harlem Renaissance* (Houston, TX: Rice University Press, 1988); Thomas H. Wirth, "FIRE!! in Retrospect," insert to *Fire!!* (1926; repr. Metuchen, NJ: Fire!!, 1981), n.p.

A. B. Christa Schwarz

Fisher, Rudolph John Chauncey (1897–1934). Novelist, short story writer, and medical doctor. Fisher is known chiefly as a novelist now, but also was one of the most multitalented intellectuals of his generation. Born on May 9, 1897, in **Washington, D.C.**, and reared mainly in Providence, Rhode Island, he arrived in **Harlem, New York**, in the mid-1920s—just in time to become a major protagonist of the **Harlem Renaissance**. Fisher's versatility—he became known as the "writer–doctor"—set him apart from the rest of the Renaissance crowd. After graduating with a B.A., an M.A., and numerous awards from Brown University, where he excelled in both biology and English, Fisher studied at Howard University Medical School. By then, he had already displayed his artistic talent, touring the eastern seaboard with the singer **Paul Robeson**, whom he accompanied on the piano. Only toward the end of his studies did Fisher achieve his artistic breakthrough: his first short story, "The City of Refuge," was published in *Atlantic Monthly* in 1925. From then on, Fisher blended a literary and a medical career, establishing a practice as a radiologist and gaining recognition as one of the Harlem Renaissance's most popular writers.

"The City of Refuge" caught the attention of **Walter White**, a leading Harlem Renaissance figure, who urged Fisher to move to New York because he believed he "[had] very real ability as a writer." **Carl Van Vechten**, a major **White** literary figure and sponsor of the Harlem Renaissance, also counted Fisher among "the most promising" of the younger Renaissance writers—a judgment shared by the leading Harlem Renaissance intellectual **Alain Locke**, as is evident in his inclusion of two stories by Fisher in his definitive Harlem Renaissance volume, *The New Negro* (1925). A first prize for Fisher's tale of intraracial color discrimination, "High Yaller," in *Opportunity*'s literary contest followed in 1926. While the older Renaissance establishment's literary taste rarely matched that of the majority of younger Renaissance members, they agreed at least initially in their assessment of Fisher and his work: **Wallace Thurman** deemed Fisher's "The City of Refuge" to be "one of the best short stories of Negro life ever written," and **Langston Hughes** in retrospect described Fisher as the "wittiest of these New Negroes of Harlem."

Fisher's early stories already display the trademarks of his fiction: a witty, predominantly humorous style, a mastery of African American dialect, and a focus on the "Negro metropolis," Harlem. Throughout his literary career, Fisher proved to be a keen observer of the Harlem scene who steered clear of propagandist efforts and fashionable exoticist trends. Instead, as is evident in his essay "The Caucasian Storms Harlem" (1927), he was highly critical of the faddish excesses of Harlem's development into New York's entertainment center. In his fictional work, Fisher focused on the daily experiences of African Americans in their new and complex urban environment, particularly highlighting intraracial color and class conflicts, and depicting Harlem and its inhabitants critically yet affectionately.

Migrants were among Fisher's favorite protagonists. In stories such as "The City of Refuge," "The Promised Land" (1927), and "Miss Cynthie" (1933), Fisher dramatizes the effects of the movement of thousands of African Americans from the South to the North, the ensuing disruption of social ties, and the clashes between newly arrived Southerners and Northern inhabitants. In "The City of Refuge," for instance, readers are introduced to the protagonist King Solomon Gillis, who fled the South for fear of being lynched and who is overwhelmed when he reaches Harlem. Here, he observes a miraculous reversal of prevalent racial power relations: in Harlem, African Americans form the majority while Whites are outsiders. The harsh reality of life in Harlem quickly catches up with Gillis, yet although in the end he has to submit to the force of law and is arrested, he is satisfied because the police officer in charge is Black, proving his first impression of Harlem: Blacks are in power.

Undated portrait of Rudolph Fisher. Yale Collection of American Literature, Beinecke Rare Book and Manuscript Library.

The Harlem life Fisher portrays is tough, violent, and ruled by capitalism. A recurrent theme is the lack of harmony and compassion—in Fisher's fiction a result of African Americans' adaptation to urban life. This grim effect is evident in "The Promised Land," which depicts the estrangement between two brothers who migrated to Harlem. In the "Negro capital," they are forced to submit to the survival of the fittest, a system distinguishing between those who quickly adapt to strenuous city life and prosper and those who lag behind. In the end, the weaker man is defeated: he is killed by his brother. But in Fisher's tales not all hope is lost. In "Miss Cynthie" (1933), the transition from tradition to modernity is depicted as a difficult yet manageable process demanding sensitivity and understanding from old and young, Southerners and Northerners. When Miss Cynthie, a Southern grandmother, visits her grandson, a successful Harlem entertainer, for the first time, a clash of values and traditions ensues. Yet music proves the binding link between old and young. Black cultural heritage is thus shown to be a valuable good—not only for White spectators but also within the Black community that it can reunite.

Fisher's success extended beyond the African American community with its major publishing outlets **The Crisis** and *Opportunity*. Many of his works were printed in journals such as *Atlantic Monthly* and *McClure's Magazine*. Fisher's awareness of the demands of his White readership is reflected in his writing: "The Promised Land," for instance, contains an explanation of the term "rent party," which would have required no further elaboration for a Black audience. Reminiscent of Van Vechten's provocative novel *Nigger Heaven* (1926), Fisher's novel *The Walls of Jericho* (1928) contained "An Introduction to Contemporary Harlemese," a glossary that made his work more accessible to White readers unfamiliar with Harlem slang expressions.

Fisher's stories were highly popular and earned him positive reviews from Black and White critics alike. It may have been exactly this appeal to White audiences that provoked **W.E.B. Du Bois**'s criticism of *The Walls of Jericho*, a novel that satirically contrasts working-class life in Harlem with that of the higher classes. Du Bois claimed that Fisher did not write "of Negroes like his mother, his sister and his wife. . . . The glimpses of better-class Negroes which he gives us are poor, ineffective make-believes." Viewing the Harlem Renaissance as an opportunity to replace stereotypical images of African Americans, Du Bois and other Black intellectuals were highly sensitive concerning the subject material chosen by Renaissance artists, favoring "moral" and middle-class Black characters. But Fisher opted for a bottom-up approach, focusing on the fundamental transformations occurring particularly among working-class Harlemites and on Harlem's vibrant entertainment world.

Unsurprisingly, Thurman, the leader of the "Niggeratti" group that rebelled against their elders' more conservative views, gladly defended Fisher. Yet Fisher refused to join the Niggeratti's ranks and resisted being claimed or co-opted by any Renaissance faction. While he was a prolific contributor to the Harlem Renaissance, Fisher at the same time stood somewhat apart. In contrast to most Renaissance protagonists, the well-liked and handsome Fisher was happily married and had a son, leading a lifestyle that differed decisively from the chaos characterizing many of his literary colleagues' lives. Following his parallel medical and literary ambitions, Fisher retained a measure of independence from the Harlem Renaissance.

Befitting this special status, Fisher dared to explore a literary genre heretofore left almost untouched by African American writers: detective fiction. There had been some earlier ventures—for instance, a serialized tale by **Pauline E. Hopkins** (1901–1902)—but Fisher's *The Conjure-Man Dies* (1932) was the first classic detective story published in book form that featured Black protagonists in an urban environment. By creating a tale revolving around the mysterious death of a voodoo priest in Harlem, Fisher took a literary risk. Detective fiction, "invented" by Edgar Allan Poe in the 1840s, was generally not regarded as a serious genre and was predominantly confined to pulp magazines or newspapers. Fisher's courage was rewarded with mainly positive reviews.

His mystery tale experienced a revival as a comic stage adaptation in Harlem's Lafayette Theatre in 1936. With *The Conjure-Man Dies* and his last published story "John Archer's Nose" (1935), Fisher helped establish a tradition of Black detection that was taken up by writers such as **Chester Himes** and **Ishmael Reed**, and later by **Barbara Neely** and **Walter Mosley**. His detective fiction is, however, frequently excluded from scholarly discussions—a fact that seems to indicate the unease with which the genre of crime fiction was and still is treated by some scholars.

It seems that Fisher's medical ambitions eventually proved fatal. On December 26, 1934, he died of intestinal cancer that may have been caused by overexposure to radiation. Fisher left a number of unpublished works and outlines for ambitious future projects. In Harlem Renaissance scholarship, he has not received much attention because many scholars assess his writings as light entertainment, lacking the seriousness necessary to describe African Americans' existence. Fisher's popularity during the Harlem Renaissance, however, indicates his works' relevance for White and Black audiences who appreciated his vivid capturing of life in 1920s Harlem. (*See* **Crime and Mystery Fiction**.)

Resources: Primary Sources: Rudolph Fisher: "The Caucasian Storms Harlem," *American Mercury* 11 (1927), 393–398; *The City of Refuge: The Collected Stories of Rudolph Fisher*, ed. John McCluskey, Jr. (Columbia: University of Missouri Press, 1987); *The Conjure-Man Dies* (New York: Covicie, Friede, 1932); *The Walls of Jericho* (New York: Knopf, 1928); Pauline E. Hopkins (pseud. Sarah A. Allen), "Hagar's Daughter: A Story of Southern Caste Prejudice," serialized in *Colored American Magazine*, Mar. 1901–Mar. 1902; Langston Hughes, *The Big Sea: An Autobiography* (1940; repr. New York: Hill and Wang, 1993); Wallace Thurman, "High, Low, Past and Present," *Harlem* 1 (1928), 31–35; Carl Van Vechten, *"Keep A-Inchin' Along": Selected Writings of Carl Van Vechten About Black Art and Letters*, ed. Bruce Kellner (Westport, CT: Greenwood Press, 1979); Walter White, letter to Rudolph Fisher, Feb. 14, 1925, Walter White Papers, NAACP Collection, Library of Congress, Washington, DC. **Secondary Sources:** Jervis Anderson, *Harlem: The Great Black Way, 1900–1950* (London: Orbis, 1982); Harish Chander, "Rudolph Fisher (1897–1934)," in *African American Authors, 1745–1945: A Bio-Bibliographical Critical Sourcebook*, ed. Emmanuel S. Nelson (Westport, CT: Greenwood Press, 2000), 161–169; Leonard J. Deutsch, "Rudolph Fisher's Unpublished Manuscripts: Description and Commentary," *Obsidian* 6 (1980), 82–98; Oliver Louis Henry, "Rudolph Fisher: An Evaluation," *The Crisis*, July 1971, 149–154; Nathan Irvin Huggins, *Voices from the Harlem Renaissance* (London: Oxford University Press, 1971); David Levering Lewis, *When Harlem Was in Vogue* (New York: Knopf, 1981); John McCluskey, Jr., "Introduction," in *The City of Refuge: The Collected Stories of Rudolph Fisher*, ed. McCluskey (Columbia: University of Missouri Press, 1987), xi–xxxix; Vincent McHugh, "The Left Hand of Rudolph Fisher," *Providence Journal*, Mar. 5, 1930, p. 13; Margaret Perry, "The Brief Life and Art of Rudolph Fisher," in *The Short Fiction of Rudolph Fisher*, ed. Perry (Westport, CT: Greenwood Press, 1987), 1–20; Calvin H. Sinnette, "Rudolph Fisher: Harlem Renaissance Physician–Writer," *Pharos* 53 (1990), 27–30; Stephen F. Soitos, *The Blues Detective: A Study of African American Detective*

Fiction (Amherst: University of Massachusetts Press, 1996); Eleanor Q. Tignor, "The Short Fiction of Rudolph Fisher," *Langston Hughes Review* 1 (1982), 18–24.

A. B. Christa Schwarz

Fleming, Sarah Lee Brown (1876–1963). Novelist, poet, and educator. Fleming, as the first Black teacher in the **Brooklyn, New York**, educational system, showed the great determination and strength that is evident in her work as a poet and novelist. Overcoming the difficulties of her youth, she devoted her life to helping minorities, especially women. She was honored with several awards, and in 1955, she was cited before Congress for her many community achievements.

Fleming's *Hope's Highway* (1918) is a novel of racial uplift, tracing the lives of two Black men. The novel has been characterized as a melodramatic historical romance, but Fleming's inclusion of atypical characters distinguishes it from other novels in this genre. Her integrationist and feminist views are clear in the novel's use of both Black and White and male and female characters as heroes.

Clouds and Sunshine, Fleming's 1920 volume of poetry, also expresses the political views that appeared in *Hope's Highway*. *Clouds and Sunshine* is divided into three sections; and the first, filled with poems of love, patriotism, and religion; the second, devoted to **dialect** poems; and the third, treating race issues. The poems are mostly rhymed and devoted to lofty subjects (with the exception of the dialect section, which was perhaps written in homage to **Paul Laurence Dunbar**'s work). Many of Fleming's poems explore the physical and spiritual damage of **slavery**, and the realities of life after emancipation. Some of her poetry has been criticized for its employment of negative racial stereotypes, and for an overall lack of skill, but she has also been praised for her sincerity.

In addition to her fiction and poetry, Fleming contributed biographies on Eliza A. Gardner and Josephine St. P. Ruffin to *Homespun Heroines and Other Women of Distinction* (1926), a volume that honored African American women.

Fleming strove to improve life for her fellow African Americans, and her books show the strength that she saw as innate in all good people who were willing to help her race.

Resources: Hallie Q. Brown, ed., *Homespun Heroines* (Xenia, OH: Aldine, 1926); Sarah Lee Brown Fleming: *Clouds and Sunshine* (Boston: Cornhill, 1920); *Hope's Highway* (New York: Neale, 1918); Jacquelyn Y. McLendon, "Introduction," in Sarah Lee Brown Fleming, *Hope's Highway/Clouds and Sunshine* (New York: G. K. Hall, 1995); Ann Allen Shockley, *Afro-American Women Writers, 1746–1933: An Anthology and Critical Guide* (Boston: G. K. Hall, 1988).

Patricia Kennedy Bostian

Flowers, Arthur Rickydoc (born 1950). Novelist, blues singer, performance poet, and activist. A native of **Memphis, Tennessee**, Flowers served in the army during the **Vietnam War** in 1968–1969, an experience that initiated an exploration of Black culture that would affect his literary style (Bennett). Following his return to the United States, he developed an interest in the **blues** as a cultural expression of Black history. Flowers moved to New York in 1973 to participate in a writing workshop at Columbia led by **John Oliver Killens** and became interested in hoodoo, a spiritual blend of Catholicism and traditional African religions that emerged among African slaves in America (*see* **Voodoo**). He cofounded the New Renaissance Writers' Guild, a derivative of the Harlem Writers' Guild, in New York City and led a writers' workshop called the "Griot Shop" in Memphis in the early 1990s. The workshop focused on Flowers's personal literary style, and celebrated myths and oral traditions of African heritage. His works include two novels, *De Mojo Blues* (1986) and *Another Good Loving Blues* (1993); a children's book, *Cleveland Lee's Beale Street Band* (1995), and a spiritual and philosophical memoir, *Mojo Rising: Confessions of a 21st Century Conjureman* (2002). (*See* **Conjuring**.)

Flowers considers himself "heir to two literary traditions, the western written tradition and the African (American) oral tradition" (Bennett). He believes literature is a form of decolonizing propagandistic power, and a spiritual shamanistic spell with the power to "reshape the soul" (Costello). Flowers has taught at Medgar Evers and Columbia universities, and is currently an assistant professor of creative writing at Syracuse University. He is also a performance artist of blues, African dance, and stories; the director of the New Renaissance Writers' Guild; and a political activist. Flowers contributes regularly to Rootworks, a Web site devoted to current affairs, and is writing his next novel, *Rest for the Weary*, based on theories of hypertext.

Resources: Allison Bennett, electronic mail interview with Arthur Flowers, Nov. 8, 2004; Margaret Costello, "Arthur Flowers: Literary Bluesman," *Syracuse University Magazine* 20, no. 2 (Spring 2003), 15–16; E. E., "Honors Program Distinguished Speaker Series," *Inside Dominguez Hills* (Carson: California State University–Dominguez Hills), Dec. 2000–Jan. 2001, 7; Arthur Flowers: *Another Good Loving Blues* (New York: Ballantine Books, 1993); *Auditory Perception, Speech, Language, and Learning* (Dearborn, MI: Perceptual Learning Systems, 1983); *Cleveland Lee's Beale Street Band* (Mahwah, NJ: Bridge Water Books, 1995); *De Mojo Blues: De Quest of HighJohn De Conqueror* (New York: Dutton, 1986); *Mojo Rising: Confessions of a 21st Century Conjureman* (New York: Wanganegresse Press, 2002); Arthur Flowers and Anthony Curtis, *The Art of Gambling Through the Ages* (Las Vegas, NV: Huntington Press, 2000).

Allison Bennett

Folklore. Folklore has been a vital force in African American literature. Abrams defines "folklore" as a "collective name applied to sayings, verbal compositions, and social rituals that have been handed down solely, or at least primarily, by word of mouth and by example rather than in written form" (70). From the first writings to the most recent ones, images, terms, concepts, and narrative forms have been transferred from folk culture to African

American literature. Among the earliest links between oral and written culture are folklore and **folktales** that found their way into print by various means and that now appear in widely available collections and anthologies (e.g., Abrahams; Courlander; Dance; Young). African American poets, including **Langston Hughes, Countee Cullen,** and **Paul Laurence Dunbar,** have used folklore extensively; with **Arna Bontemps,** Hughes edited a collection of folklore. Playwrights, too, have drawn on the folklore reservoir, including **Randolph S. Edmonds, Lorraine Hansberry,** and **Ntozake Shange.** Essayists, including **Audre Lorde, Cornel West,** and **bell hooks,** make frequent allusions to folk idioms and icons. Arguably, however, one sees the most extensive and sustained use of folklore in African American literature in the social worlds represented in fiction.

Many accomplished fiction writers—including **James Baldwin, Toni Cade Bambara, Charles Waddell Chesnutt, Alice Childress, Ernest J. Gaines, Ralph Ellison, Zora Neale Hurston, James Weldon Johnson, Toni Morrison, Ishmael Reed, Alice Walker, Margaret Walker,** and **Richard Wright**—incorporate folkloric elements in substantive ways within their literary works (Thomas). As Ted Olson points out, black magic, the "badman" figure (Bryant), the **blues, conjuring, sermons, trickster** figures, legendary heroes (such as John Henry), superstitions, and lore surrounding **voodoo/vodoun** are among the elements of folklore that these and other writers have used (Olson, 286).

As Abrams' definition suggests, folklore includes songs, stories, proverbs, parables, riddles, and sayings. African American folklore also includes ancestral understandings culturally transmitted through traditional beliefs, myths, tales, and language practices of African American people, whether that transmission takes place orally, observationally, or through writing about such lore. Much of this transmission has taken place in legends, tales, and stories, as well as in rituals that include narrative elements.

Recent analysts of African American folktales have interpreted the form's functions variously (Dundes; Gates; Levine). Some see tales as vehicles for self-affirmation, social protest, and/or psychological release. Others see folktales as reiterating, inculcating, and complementing cultural values, although many would warn against interpreting tales too literally. For instance, many scholars believe that animal tales and the paradigms those tales provide had their origin in substitutions of animal names for specific people's names. A literal approach, then, could mask important subtextual meanings of such texts (Gates).

Many present-day readers' notions about African American storytelling traditions have been filtered through the work of Joel Chandler Harris, whose *Uncle Remus: His Songs and His Sayings* (1880), came to represent—and in many instances misrepresent—African-American storytelling traditions. Harris claimed he was recording these stories in their original and unadulterated form. His language proves revealing, though, for when he refers to other people and their cultures as "simple" or "picturesque," he trivializes them and exposes a condescending attitude. While he may not consciously have set out to impose his own attitudes about African Americans on the folktales, he was not self-conscious about the implications of a White observer presenting African American culture to a White audience.

In terms of assessing the influence of folklore on African American literature, the works of Zora Neale Hurston, and in particular her tales collected in *Mules and Men*, offer one illuminating, representative case study and an important contrast to *Uncle Remus*. Although Hurston may be best known for her fiction, including such book-length fiction as *Their Eyes Were Watching God*, she was also a formally trained and published collector of African American folklore. Hurston's education took her to Columbia University and Barnard College, where she found a mentor in the noted anthropologist Franz Boas. In the preface to *Mules and Men*, Boas suggests that in the past, White interest in African American folklore, including Harris's interest, had been both halfhearted and biased.

It is difficult to appreciate fully the social world Hurston depicts so richly in the folklore she collected unless one is familiar with the traditions of boasting, the dozens (a practice of ritualized, playful insult), and storytelling to which it corresponds and pays tribute. To take one example, Hurston uses dialect extensively in both her folklore and her fiction, and readers new to her work may wonder why she "misspells" words so extensively. She misspells words chiefly to represent the sound of spoken language and, figuratively, to let African Americans speak for themselves and to recapture the flavor of such oral traditions as boasting and storytelling.

Toni Cade Bambara also stresses the power of folklore, pointing out how fables and parables (short, instructive tales) enabled storytellers, both in Africa and in American **slavery**, to encode meanings even within conventional narrative forms (Bambara). She discusses how this folkloristic technique of "talking back" to a cultural narrative is called **signifying**. The retold, revised, and sometimes reversed stories she then presents, including "The Three Little Panthers," show characters and storytellers signifying on familiar tales, in this case the traditional children's tale "The Three Little Pigs." In this retelling, three panthers move into a neighborhood where residents, responding to the differences they discern in the newcomers, seek to eradicate those distinctions. The story concludes with the panthers affirming rather than erasing their differences, and thus deflecting the host culture's normative expectations and intrusive need for conformity. The tale demonstrates how the panthers regard folk practices from attire to literature as integral to their communal and historical identity, and therefore decline to assume the practices of their new neighbors. Like Zora Neale Hurston and Alice Walker, Toni Cade Bambara recognized the importance of revisiting and interrogating the tales that surround and precede one's cultural position.

Elements derived from folklore also find expression within the domains of recent African American literary theory and criticism. In *The Signifying Monkey: A Theory of Afro-American Literary Criticism* (1988), for example, critic **Henry Louis Gates, Jr.**, uses the practice of signifying to characterize the way that African American literature contests the master narratives of American culture. Just as **W.E.B. Du Bois** argued that African American thought is characterized by "double consciousness," Gates suggests that African American literature is double-voiced, because it speaks both to and beyond existing cultural scripts. In much the same way that Bambara's three panthers dare to talk back to the insistent voices that threaten their traditions, so signifying texts in African American literature challenge the assumptions behind traditional literary and cultural narratives that would silence or slight the ancestral knowledge of historically disenfranchised populations.

The history of African American literature and criticism is rich in works that refer to African American folklore, whether in terms of style, content, or message. In his life narrative, abolitionist and former slave **Frederick Douglass** wrote about an experience in which he was given a piece of root to carry in his pocket, a practice suggestive of a lucky charm that also makes specific reference to one's literal and figurative roots, as applied within cultural practices such as conjuring. While Douglass conveys skepticism about the root's magical qualities, that bit of root, tucked away in his pocket, makes the journey to freedom with Douglass. Like this root tucked away in a pocket, folklore (in the form of the language and lessons of a shared cultural past) has accompanied African American writers ever since. From **Charles Waddell Chesnutt**'s *The Conjure Woman* and Ralph Ellison's *Invisible Man* to Toni Morrison's *Tar Baby* and Toni Cade Bambara's *The Salt Eaters*, tales and their tellers ground themselves in the soil of folk traditions. Whether reading **Jean Toomer**'s *Cane* or **Paule Marshall**'s *The Chosen Place, the Timeless People*, one has a clear sense that the collective past does not, and ought not to, pass away, but rather plays an important role in efforts to fight for and shape the future, on the page and in the lived world. (*See* **Vernacular.**)

Resources: Roger D. Abrahams, ed., *African American Folktales: Stories from Black Traditions in the New World* (New York: Pantheon, 1999); M. H. Abrams, *A Glossary of Literary Terms*, 6th ed. (Fort Worth, TX: Harcourt Brace Jovanovich, 1993); Toni Cade Bambara, *Deep Sightings and Rescue Missions: Fiction, Essays, and Conversations*, ed. Toni Morrison (New York: Pantheon, 1996); Jerry H. Bryant, *Born in a Mighty Bad Land: The Violent Man in African American Folklore and Fiction* (Bloomington: Indiana University Press, 2003); Keith Byerman, *Fingering the Jagged Grain: Tradition and Form in Recent Black Fiction* (Athens: University of Georgia Press, 1985); Harold Courlander, *A Treasury of Afro-American Folklore: The Oral Literature, Traditions, Recollections, Legends, Tales, Songs, Religious Beliefs, Customs, Sayings and Humor of Peoples of African American Descent in the Americas* (New York: Marlowe, 2002); Daryl Cumber Dance, ed., *From My People: 400 Years of African American Folklore* (New York: Norton, 2002); Alan Dundes, ed., *Mother Wit from the Laughing Barrel: Readings in the Interpretation of Afro-American Folklore* (Jackson: University Press of Mississippi, 1973); Henry Louis Gates, *The Signifying Monkey: A Theory of Afro-American Literary Criticism* (New York: Oxford University Press, 1988); Joel Chandler Harris, *Told by Uncle Remus: New Stories of the Old Plantation* (New York: Grosset and Dunlap, 1903); Langston Hughes and Arna Bontemps, eds., *The Book of Negro Folklore* (New York: Dodd, Mead, 1958); Lawrence W. Levine, *Black Culture and Black Consciousness:*

Afro-American Folk Thought from Slavery to Freedom (New York: Oxford University Press, 1977); Ted Olson, "Folkore," in *The Oxford Companion to African American Literature*, ed. William L. Andrews, Frances Smith Foster, and Trudier Harris (New York: Oxford University Press, 1997), 286–290; Marjorie Pryse and Hortense J. Spillers, eds., *Conjuring: Black Women, Fiction, and Literary Tradition* (Bloomington: Indiana University Press, 1985); H. Nigel Thomas, *From Folklore to Fiction: A Study of Folk Heroes and Rituals in the Black American Novel* (Westport, CT: Greenwood Press, 1988); Richard Alan Young and Judy Dockrey Young, eds., *African-American Folktales for Young Readers: Including Favorite Stories from African and African-American Storytellers* (Little Rock, AR: August House, 1993).

Linda S. Watts

Folktales. African American folktales are traditional oral narratives told across the United States in black dialects of English (or, in sections of south Louisiana, in black dialects of French). Many of these tales have been recorded and anthologized (Abrahams). Other traditions of Black folktales in the New World have proliferated historically in the Caribbean and in Central and South American (told, depending upon the nation, in English, French, Spanish, and Portuguese). Generally speaking, a folktale can be distinguished from a **ballad**, another major genre of orally transmitted narrative, in that the former is spoken while the latter is sung. Another type of traditional oral narrative in African American culture was the toast, which fell halfway between the folktale and the ballad. A lyrical form of expression like the ballad, the toast bore similarity to the folktale in the toast's emphasis on an improvised and spoken (as opposed to sung) presentation.

The African American folktale tradition emerged during colonial times, when slaves from numerous African groups recently transported in bondage to the New World were forced to live and work together on plantations. There was no commonly shared African language by which all those enslaved Africans from different groups could understand each other, and the slaves were prohibited from communicating with each other through the traditional African method of beating on drums. Indeed, the plantation system was structured to ensure the widespread adoption of English as the sole language spoken among the slave population. Further marginalizing the slaves was the fact that they were legally prohibited from learning to read and write in this new language. In an effort to avoid the suppression of their voices, the slaves created a repertoire of narratives told in some dialect of their adopted language. Circulated from person to person via the oral tradition, those stories blended blacks' own African cultural perspectives (especially their unique metaphysical attitudes) with Anglo-Celtic narrative forms and thematic elements (including certain motifs probably borrowed from White storytelling tradition).

While the African American folktale tradition emerged primarily in rural areas of **the South** during **slavery** days, folktales from that repertoire were transported across the nation after emancipation as blacks sought work in the

Slaves share stories during a social gathering at a Louisiana plantation. Courtesy of North Wind Picture Archives.

urban North and in the West. Transmitted from one generation to the next through word of mouth and through the interpretations by both Black and White authors, those folktales embodied the cultural values of a people who possessed a shared history; such folktales thus helped African Americans gain psychological empowerment for enduring the discrimination forced upon them by a racist society.

Historically, the repertoire of African American folktales—incorporating local variants of well-known and widely disseminated master narratives, as well as stories told exclusively within specific communities—included animal tales (most involving **"trickster"** figures and dating from the time of slavery); stories of famous or infamous people and events, real as well as imagined; narratives elaborating upon passages from the Bible; didactic stories told by parents, grandparents, and other elders to children regarding social behavior (concerning such rites of passage as getting married and becoming parents); tales of the supernatural (concerning human encounters with ghosts, witches, or the devil); humorous (and sometimes bawdy) anecdotes and stories; and narratives from more contemporary sources (including traditional stories overtly influenced by literary or musical works that were created by known African Americans).

Literary appropriations of African American folktales—whether by Black or White authors—tend to overlook or to downplay the importance of the audience within traditional Black culture. Indeed, the storyteller and his or her listeners—as part of a vital oral tradition—have always been equal participants in the telling of folktales, and each performance of a given traditional African

American narrative has always been highly improvisatory, reflecting upon and responding to the unique circumstances of that particular performance (*see* **Signifying**). Before emancipation, African Americans on plantations frequently shared stories at night with fellow slaves, and their narratives, told in Black dialects of English, invariably contained encoded references to their ongoing plight as a marginalized, controlled race. The protagonists of the slaves' stories—whether animal trickster figures or romanticized human heroes—generally symbolized the slaves' idealized views of themselves as ultimately more virtuous and intelligent than their oppressors. Nevertheless, despite their serious subtexts, African American folktales were often infused with exaggeration, indirection (resulting from the need of slaves to conceal or disguise their attitudes), wordplay (such as "signifying," a strategy of utilizing self-contradictory words or phrases in a narrative to call attention to the multiple ironies embedded in that narrative), or other types of humor; indeed, Black storytellers have frequently referred to their narratives as "lies" or "nonsense." The emphasis on wit, deception, and mistrust in traditional African American storytelling suggests the need of Blacks to learn and practice skills necessary for their survival in a society in which they were the recipients of extreme discrimination.

Perhaps to solidify their precarious position within Southern society, slaves on plantations would tell folktales to Whites utilizing more formal English speech (Blacks often referred to their efforts toward speaking like Whites as "talking sweet"). The ability of a slave to mimic White speech usually elevated that person's standing within plantation society, though such a storyteller was necessarily constrained when choosing repertoire and performance style. Slaves also gained social prestige within their African American communities by telling other slaves stories in which they mimicked White speech while impersonating Whites through nonverbal gestures.

The trickster has long held a crucial if ambivalent position in Black culture, which borrowed that folkloric figure from African belief systems. Trickster characters in Africa took on human, divine, or animal form, yet African Americans particularly valued tales involving animal tricksters. Fearing reprisal if they freely conveyed their own grievances on plantations, slaves told tales that employed animal characters as substitutes for human protagonists; serving as symbols for specific human actions and for generalized patterns of human behavior, the animal characters were usually depicted as formerly powerless creatures that had achieved success through patience and cunning. The ultimate goal of the trickster in African American folktales was to subvert the corrupt and divisive moral conventions of that narrative's antagonist character, who of course symbolized the established social order that ruled the Southern plantations. The best-known trickster figure in the canon of African American folktales was Br'er Rabbit, who represented the idealized human qualities valued by slaves. With didactic as well as narrative components, the Br'er Rabbit tales offered slaves both positive and negative examples of human behavior, which helped them better understand the society in which they lived. A set of related trickster tales, told in the post–**Civil War** era, concerned the ambivalent relationship of a fictional slave named John and his "ol' Marster." In these tales, John overcame his subservient position in racist society by subverting (usually covertly, but sometimes overtly) the stereotypes that he had previously been forced to endure from his white "marster" (*see* **John the Conqueror**).

The influential folklore scholar Richard Dorson, in his 1967 book *American Negro Folktales*, maintained that the African influence on African American folktales was relatively minor and that particular folktale tradition was primarily influenced by European sources. Subsequent scholars, however, have identified the fallaciousness of that argument. The scholar Christine Goldberg, for example, observed that Dorson had utilized Stith Thompson's folktale motif index—which was focused primarily on European oral narrative traditions—when speculating about the origin of the majority of African American folktales; Goldberg also speculated that Dorson had thus overemphasized the European influence on the African American folktale tradition. Indeed, recent research by such scholars as Alan Dundes and Florence Baer has advanced the probability that the African influence on the African American folktale tradition was historically far greater than had been previously discussed.

Numerous Black and White authors have infused their works written in various genres with elements borrowed from the African American folktale tradition. Acclaimed works by Black authors that incorporate aspects of the African American folktale include **Ernest J. Gaines**'s 1971 novel *The Autobiography of Miss Jane Pittman*, **Toni Morrison**'s 1987 novel *Beloved*, **Langston Hughes**'s 1926 poem "Aunt Sue's Stories," **Zora Neale Hurston**'s 1935 nonfiction work *Mules and Men*, and **August Wilson**'s 1987 dramatic work *The Piano Lesson*. Recent black comedians—from **Dick Gregory, William (Bill) Cosby**, and Richard Pryor to Chris Rock—have incorporated into their modern-themed monologues the themes, form, and style of traditional African American folktales, as have such contemporary Black performing storytellers as Jackie Torrence and Sparky Rucker.

Several major White authors, including **Mark Twain**, William Faulkner, and Flannery O'Connor, have similarly been influenced by the African American folktale tradition. Most closely associated with that tradition was the Eatonton, Georgia, native Joel Chandler Harris, whose "Uncle Remus" stories were freely adapted from African American folktales that Harris had been told when a youth by two elderly slaves he had befriended. While Harris endeavored to achieve "authenticity" by conveying his narratives in a literary approximation of Black dialectical speech, he nevertheless projected a stereotyped representation of African American culture. Originally published in late nineteenth-century periodicals and thereafter collected into popular book compilations, Harris's retellings of African American folktales focused on the exploits of such characters from Black folklore as the aforementioned trickster figure Brer Rabbit and the Tar-Baby (a doll covered with tar or another sticky substance and meant to entrap curious antagonists). A more recent literary work written by a White author in celebration of the African American penchant for storytelling is Emily Mann's 1995 play *Having Our Say: The Delaney Sisters' First 100 Years*. (*See* **Folklore**; **Vernacular**.)

Resources: Roger D. Abrahams, ed., *Afro-American Folktales: Stories from Black Traditions in the New World* (New York: Pantheon, 1985); Florence E. Baer, *Sources and Analogues of the Uncle Remus Tales* (Helsinki: Suomalainen Tiedeakatemic, 1980); Richard M. Dorson, *American Negro Folktales* (Greenwich, CT: Fawcett Publications, 1967); Alan Dundes, "African and Afro-American Tales," *Research in African Literatures* 7 (1976), 181–199; Christine Goldberg, "African-American Folktales: Where Do They Come from? Why Does It Matter?," *Folklore Fellows Network* no. 26 (May 2004), 6–9; Stith Thompson, *Motif-Index of Folk-Literature*, 6 vols. (Bloomington: University of Indiana Press, 1932–1936).

Ted Olson

Food. *See* **Cooking**.

Foote, Julia (1823–1900). Preacher and autobiographer. Foote wrote *A Brand Plucked from the Fire, an Autobiographical Sketch* (1879, 1886), which was later reprinted in an anthology (Andrews). Born in Schenectady, New York, to former slaves deeply committed to education and Methodism, Foote studied formally for only two years, but dedicated herself to reading the Bible. Her conversion at fifteen was accompanied by a highly sensual vision that authorized her to preach. In the vision, an angel led her to a tree surrounded by the members of the Trinity. She was taken to a body of water, where she was stripped naked and washed clean by Christ, who told her to preach His word. She resisted, but Christ wrote with a golden pen and ink upon golden paper a note, saying "Put this in your bosom, and wherever you go, show it, and they will know that I have sent you to proclaim salvation to all." According to her autobiographical sketch, she spent many years resisting her vocation as she tried to be a strong, quiet Christian woman.

In 1841 she married a sailor, George Foote, with whom she moved to **Boston, Massachusetts**, where she dedicated her time to informal evangelical work for the African Methodist Episcopal (AME) Zion Church. As she became more firmly convinced that she should preach, her husband sought to dissuade her, and eventually they separated. Despite resistance from her minister and congregation, Foote stood firm against church dictates that did not allow women to preach. She traveled extensively throughout New York and Ohio preaching, journeys detailed in her spiritual **autobiography**. The autobiography begins with her parents' story of enslavement, thereby underscoring the connection between "racial uplift" and Christianity. She declares, "The Spirit of Truth can never be mistaken, nor can he inspire anything unholy" (Andrews, 11). The first chapter functions as a personal recommendation from God that fully ordains Foote's right to speak on religious and social issues.

Despite her writing, the AME Zion Church refused to let Foote preach. Consequently, she became an itinerant minister, preaching wherever she could. During the 1890s, the AME Zion Church finally ordained Foote as a deacon and an elder, the first female deacon and second female elder in church history.

Resources: William Andrews, ed., *Sisters of the Spirit: Three Black Women's Autobiographies of the Nineteenth Century* (Bloomington: Indiana University Press, 1986); Sue E. Houchins, ed., *Spiritual Narratives* (New York: Oxford University Press, 1988).

Pamela Ralston

Forbes, Calvin (born 1945). Poet and professor. In his poetry, Forbes addresses individual human identity and the need to give voice to people who do not have a voice within the social contexts that define America. His books of poetry include *Blue Monday* (1974), *From the Book of Shine* (1979), and *The Shine Poems* (2001). Forbes also has contributed to more than eleven anthologies. Adopting the literary persona of an African American folk figure named Shine, Forbes comments on Black history and American society. Poets who have influenced him include John Donne, **Gwendolyn Brooks**, Philip Larkin, **Langston Hughes**, and Elizabeth Bishop.

Born on May 6, 1945, in Newark, New Jersey, the son of Jacob and Mary (Short) Forbes, Calvin Forbes attended the New School for Social Research and Rutgers University, then completed his M.F.A. at Brown University in 1978. Currently serving as chair of writing programs at the Art Institute in **Chicago, Illinois**, Forbes's teaching career has spanned several institutions: Emerson College in **Boston, Massachusetts** (1969–1973), assistant professor of English; Tufts University, Medford, Massachusetts (1973–1974), assistant professor of English; Howard University, **Washington, D.C.** (1975–1977), writer-in-residence; Washington College, Chestertown, Maryland (1988–1989), associate professor of creative writing; Art Institute of Chicago (1991–2005). Forbes was a Fulbright lecturer in Denmark, France, and England in 1974–1975 and a guest lecturer at the University of the West Indies in 1982–1983. Forbes has been awarded a Breadloaf Writers' Conference summer fellowship (1973), summer residency at the Yaddo writers' retreat (1976), and a National Endowment for the Arts fellowship (1982).

Resources: Ann Burns and Emily Joy Jones, "Review of *The Shine Poems*," *Library Journal*, Nov. 1, 2000, p. 103; Robert A. Coles, "Calvin Forbes," in *Dictionary of Literary Biography*, vol. 41, *Afro-American Poets Since 1955* (Detroit: Gale, 1985); William Doreski, "Review of *The Shine Poems*," *African American Review* 36, no. 2 (Summer 2002), 349; Rita Dove, "Many Years Ago, When I Was Still a College Student," *Washington Post*, June 17, 2001, p. T12; Calvin Forbes: *Blue Monday* (Middletown, CT: Wesleyan University Press, 1974); *From the Book of Shine* (Providence, RI: Burning Deck Press, 1979); *The Shine Poems* (Baton Rouge: Louisiana State University Press, 2001); Matthias Regan, "Review of *The Shine Poems*," *Chicago Review* 47, no. 3 (Fall 2001), 151–153.

Carol Elizabeth Dietrich

Ford, Nick Aaron (1904–1982). Literary critic, poet, anthologist, autobiographer, and educator. A founding father of African American literary criticism, Nick Aaron Ford was born in Ridgeway, South Carolina. He received a B.A. degree from Benedict College (1926) and an M.A. (1934) and a Ph.D. (1945) from the State University of Iowa. Ford held educational positions in South Carolina, Florida, Texas, and Oklahoma before he was appointed a professor of English at Morgan State College (now Morgan State University) in **Baltimore, Maryland**, in 1945. He was elected chairperson of the English Department three years after his arrival at the Baltimore campus and spent twenty-eight of his fifty-six years as an educator at Morgan. After his resignation in 1973, he was a visiting professor at the University of Massachusetts and coordinator of and professor in the Ph.D. program of the Center for Minority Studies at Union College.

Ford's landmark publication, *The Contemporary Negro Novel: A Study in Race Relations* (1936), preceded such other early studies of African American literary criticism as **Sterling A. Brown**'s *The Negro in American Fiction* (1937), **J. Saunders Redding**'s *To Make a Poet Black* (1939), and Hugh M. Gloster's *Negro Voices in American Fiction* (1948). Ford's other publications include *Songs from the Dark: Original Poems* (1940); *Best Short Stories by Afro-American Writers, 1925–1950* (edited with Harry L. Faggett, 1950); *Basic Skills for Better Writing* (with Waters Turpin, 1959); *American Culture in Literature* (1967); *Language in Uniform: A Reader on Propaganda* (1967); *Extending Horizons: Selected Readings for Cultural Enrichment* (edited with Waters Turpin, 1969); *Black Insights: Significant Literature by Black Americans, 1760 to the Present* (1971); *Black Studies: Threat-or-Challenge?* (1973); and *Seeking a Newer World: Memoirs of a Black American Teacher* (1983). Recognition of Ford's career achievements include a 1964 honorary doctorate in literature from Benedict College and the 1982 Middle-Atlantic Writers Association's Distinguished Literary Critic Award.

Resources: Margaret Walker Alexander, "Dr. Nick Aaron Ford: A Man in the Classic Tradition," in *Swords upon This Hill: Preserving the Literary Tradition of Black Colleges and Universities*, ed. Burney J. Hollis (Baltimore: Morgan State University Press, 1984), 116–124; Eugenia W. Collier, "Nick Aaron Ford and Afro-American Literary Criticism," in *Swords upon This Hill*, ed. Burney J. Hollis (Baltimore: Morgan State University Press, 1984), 104–115; Nick Aaron Ford: *Black Studies: Threat-or-Challenge?* (Port Washington, NY: Kennikat, 1973); *The Contemporary Negro Novel: A Study in Race Relations* (Boston: Meador, 1936); *Language in Uniform: A Reader on Propaganda* (New York: Odyssey, 1967); *Seeking a Newer World: Memoirs of a Black American Teacher* (Great Neck, NY: Todd & Honeywell, 1983); Nick Aaron Ford, ed., *Black Insights: Significant Literature by Black Americans, 1760 to the Present* (Waltham, MA: Ginn, 1971); Nick Aaron Ford and Harry L. Faggett, eds., *Best Short Stories by Afro-American Writers* (Boston: Meador, 1950); Nick Aaron Ford and Waters Turpin, *Basic Skills for Better Writing: A Guide and Practice Book for Those Who Intend to Master the Essentials of Good English* (New York: Putnam, 1959); Nick Aaron Ford and Waters Turpin, eds., *Extending Horizons: Selected Readings for Cultural Enrichment* (New York: Random House, 1969); Lucia S. Hawthorne, "In Memoriam: A Tribute to Nick Aaron Ford, 1904–1982," *CLA Journal* 25, no. 2 (1981), 263–264; Linda Metzger, ed., *Black*

Writers: A Selection of Sketches from Contemporary Authors (Detroit: Gale, 1989), 202; Ruthe T. Sheffey, "Nick Aaron Ford: Poet and Mentor," in her *Trajectory: Fueling the Future and Preserving the African-American Literary Past* (Baltimore: Morgan State University Press, 1989), 40–44.

Linda M. Carter

Formal Verse. Formal verse can be defined as poetry that closely follows European literary conventions in its line count and line structure or in its regular use of rhyme and meter. Formal verse thus includes at least three main groupings: (1) patterns between lines or within stanzas, such as the heroic couplet, terza rima, and quatrain; (2) general types of poems, such as the **ballad** and dramatic monologue; and (3) rigidly defined and complete poetic forms, such as the **villanelle**, sestina, and **sonnet**. The earliest African American poets wrote in traditional European verse forms. In the early twentieth century, however, Black poets and critics began to question the relevance and possible limitations of these traditional forms for Black poetic expression. By the middle of that century, many African American poets had moved away from formal verse toward **free verse**, an open form of poetry that enjoys widespread popularity to this day.

Early African American poetry demonstrates a strict adherence to the traditional meters, lines, and stanzaic patterns of European poetry or song. The earliest known literary work by a black author, **Lucy Terry**'s poem "Bars Fight" (1755), chronicles the fate of eight individuals during an Indian attack on August 25, 1746, and is written in iambic tetrameter with rhyming couplets. A second example is **Jupiter Hammon**'s earliest known published poem, "An Evening Thought" (1760), which adopts the highly regular meter and alternating rhyme of the Protestant hymn. Like the hymn, Hammon's poem is written in four-line units (quatrains), with the first and third lines in iambic tetrameter and the second and fourth lines in iambic trimeter. Finally, much of **Phillis Wheatley**'s poetry, including her most famous piece "On Being Brought from Africa to America" (1773), is written in heroic couplets (rhyming two-line units in iambic pentameter), a form that had been popularized by the early eighteenth-century English poet Alexander Pope.

Fewer in number are the **slavery** era works by Black poets that have overtly political content. Some poems parody the form and content of popular songs or hymns. **James Monroe Whitfield**'s "America" (1853) mockingly echoes "America the Beautiful" and points out the country's failure to realize the ideals presented in that popular and patriotic hymn. Similarly, the appendix to **Frederick Douglass**'s *Narrative of the Life of Frederick Douglass* (1845) contains a parody of the hymn "Heavenly Union" and indicts the hypocrisy of Christianity as practiced in **the South**. The formal but original verse of **Frances E. W. Harper**, such as "The Slave Mother" (1854) and "Bury Me in a Free Land" (1864), is often heralded as the origin of African American protest poetry. In comparison with these and later writers producing overtly political poems, the earliest African American poets have often been dismissed as purely derivative, echoing the forms and voices of their masters. In the final decades of the twentieth century, however, critics have reconsidered the use and value of conventional forms in early African American poetry. In particular, Hammon, Wheatley, and others—including **George Moses Horton**—are now more highly esteemed for using conventional forms, to varying degrees, to present subtle expressions of protest and to bolster claims of racial equality.

From the era of **Reconstruction** through the end of the twentieth century, many African American poets continued to work in a wide range of traditional Western poetic forms. **James Weldon Johnson**'s "O Black and Unknown Bards" (1908) is an ode, a song of praise written in a lofty style and usually addressed to a particular person or important abstract idea; Johnson's poem is addressed to the anonymous African American creators and performers of the **spirituals** that comforted and converted the slaves who listened to them. Similarly, **Paul Laurence Dunbar**'s "The Colored Soldiers" (1895) follows the conventions of the **epic**, a chronicle of events (usually in war) presented in verse form; Dunbar's poem begins with an invocation to the muse, a convention of epic poetry since antiquity, and recounts the sacrifices and achievements of black soldiers in the **Civil War**. (*See* **Epic Poetry/The Long Poem**.)

A wide range of formal poetry is represented in the works of African Americans collected in *The Poetry of the Negro 1746–1970*, an anthology edited by **Langston Hughes** and **Arna Bontemps** (1949; reprinted in expanded format in 1970). This anthology includes, especially among the later poets, examples of all three types of formal poetry: poems using regular patterns between lines or within stanzas, such as terza rima and the cinquain; general types of poems, such as the epigram and the ballad; and rigidly defined and complete poetic forms, such as the sonnet and villanelle.

Terza rima is a series of tercets, or three-line stanzas, in which the rhyme of one stanza is continued in the next stanza, with the outer lines of each following stanza rhyming with the middle line of the preceding stanza: *aba bcb cdc*, and so on. Terza rima is used famously in Dante's *Divine Comedy* but makes occasional appearance in African American poetry, as is the case in G. C. Oden's "A Private Letter to Brazil." **George Marion McClellan**'s "The Feet of Judas," also included in the anthology, follows the equally rare model of the cinquain (or quintain), a five-line stanza with a regular rhyme scheme.

Among the many general types of poems represented in the anthology are the epigram, dramatic monologue, and ballad. The epigram, a cleverly condensed observation or turn of thought, was developed into a literary form in ancient Greece and Rome, and was cultivated in Europe by Voltaire, Schiller and others during the seventeenth and eighteenth centuries. It is represented by **Countee Cullen**'s "For a Lady I Know," which pokes fun at a privileged White woman who assumes that in heaven, too, she will be waited on by Black servants. Dramatic poetry (including the dramatic monologue) uses the direct speech of the characters involved to tell a story or portray a situation, and is represented by Langston Hughes's "Mother to Son." The ballad, by contrast, is a far longer poem that has its origins in folk songs and presents an account of some past event, usually heroic or romantic but almost always catastrophic. The story is related in the third person and emphasizes dialogue and action over description and character development. The ballad form usually consists of alternating four- and three-stress lines, with simple and regular rhymes, and often includes a refrain. An example is what James Smethurst calls **Margaret Walker**'s "folk poems" in *For My People* (1942), such as "Molly Means," a ballad included in the 1970 anthology that is traditional in its depiction of young lovers and supernatural forces, yet emphatically African American in its use of Black **vernacular** and black folk magic, or "root work." Langston Hughes published numerous ballads, including twenty-five in which "ballad" was explicitly part of the poem's title (Ostrom).

Finally, the 1970 anthology includes a number of complete poetic forms, among them the sonnet and villanelle. The sonnet, a fourteen-line poem following one of several predetermined rhyme schemes, is particularly well represented. The anthology includes some of the most famous sonnets by **Claude McKay** ("If We Must Die"), **Countee Cullen** ("Yet Do I Marvel"), and **Helene Johnson** ("Sonnet to a Negro in Harlem"), as well as more recent and more experimental versions by **Robert Hayden**, Margaret Walker, and **Gwendolyn Brooks**. A far less common form in Black poetry is the villanelle, a nineteen-line poetic form that consists of five tercets, rhymed *aba*, and a concluding quatrain, rhymed *abaa*, and reuses the first and third lines of the opening stanzas at predetermined points throughout the poem. Walter Adolphe Roberts's poem "Villanelle of Washington Square" exemplifies this form in the 1970 anthology.

African American poets have long had a contested relation to European literary conventions and forms. As early as the 1920s one finds clearly formulated and partisan statements on both sides of the question of the relations between traditional European poetic forms and new African American poetry. In the foreword to his anthology *Caroling Dusk: An Anthology of Verse by Negro Poets* (1927), as in **William Stanley Braithwaite**'s arguments from two decades earlier, Countee Cullen maintains that there should be no forced distinction between Black and White poets in America, since the obligation of both is to maintain and further the British poetic traditions. Cullen's emulation of John Keats earned him praise among many White readers but criticism among some Black intellectuals. Without calling out Cullen by name, Langston Hughes criticizes him in the essay "The Negro Artist and the Racial Mountain" (1926) for wanting "to write like a white poet" or, on a subconscious level, "to be a white poet" or "to be white." Similarly, in his essay "Propaganda—or Poetry?" (1928), **Alain Locke** rejects a strict adherence to White European literary conventions; he develops a critical characterization of the average Black poet after **World War I** as "something of a traditionalist with regard to art, style and philosophy, with a little salient of racial radicalism jutting out front" and points to Claude McKay's sonnet "If We Must Die" as a case in point, finding (perhaps without justification) that the poem's strongly voiced opposition to racial oppression remains trapped within a form prescribed by the dominant White culture. Similar rejections of strict adherence to European poetic conventions can be found in **Richard Wright**'s "Blueprint for Negro Writing" (1937) and in **Hoyt Fuller**'s "Toward a Black Aesthetic" (1968), a manifesto of the **Black Arts Movement**. Wright argues that African American poetry up through the **Harlem Renaissance** was often formally sophisticated but rarely addressed Black readers, and Fuller characterizes the emerging poetry of the **Black Arts** era as one that rejects "the literary assumption that the style and language and the concerns of Shakespeare establish the appropriate limits and 'frame of reference' for black poetry and people" (1857).

Not all Black critics have dismissed the production of formal poetry by Black poets. In his study *Modernism and the Harlem Renaissance* (1987), **Houston A. Baker, Jr.**, has pointed to the strategic "mastery" and "deformation" of European forms within the African American literary tradition, and in "The Unreadable Black Body: 'Conventional' Poetic Form in the Harlem Renaissance" (1990), Amitai F. Avi-Ram has demonstrated that Black formal verse is not inherently more politically or socially conservative than free verse. Much of the recent criticism on African American poetry, however, has continued to move away from a discussion of traditional poetic forms. The essays in the collection *The Furious Flowering of African American Poetry* (1999) are a case in point; many of them focus on some aspect of the "vernacular matrix" of African American poetry. As a whole, this collection and other critical statements emphasize the central importance of African American oral traditions and maintain that these have always accompanied and informed the written word in works by Black poets.

Although free verse has displaced much of formal verse in African American poetry since the mid-1900s and much critical attention has shifted away from European forms toward Black vernacular forms, a number of significant contemporary African American poets insist on an attention to form. In the interviews recorded in D. H. Melhem's *Heroism in the New Black Poetry* (1990), for example, **Dudley Randall** discusses his systematic study of versification, and **Sonia Sanchez** explains how she has her poetry students write in fixed forms to develop both discipline and an attention to word choice so that their free verse, too, will be well crafted rather than "just go and sprawl" (Melham, 169).

Resources: Amitai F. Avi-Ram, "The Unreadable Black Body: 'Conventional' Poetic Form in the Harlem Renaissance," *Genders* 7 (Spring 1990), 32–46; Houston A. Baker, Jr., *Modernism and the Harlem Renaissance* (Chicago: University of Chicago Press, 1987); Countee Cullen, ed., *Caroling Dusk: An Anthology of Verse by Negro Poets* (1927; repr. New York: Harper & Row, 1955); Hoyt Fuller, "Toward a Black Aesthetic" (1968), in *The Norton Anthology of African American Literature*, ed. Henry Louis Gates, Jr., and Nellie Y. McKay, 2nd ed. (New York: Norton, 2004), 1853–1859; Langston Hughes and Arna Bontemps, eds., *The Poetry of the Negro, 1746–1970* (Garden City, NY: Doubleday, 1970); Alain Locke, "Propaganda—or Poetry," in *The Critical Temper of Alain Locke: A Selection of His Essays on Art and Culture*, ed. Jeffrey C. Stewart (New York: Garland, 1983); D. H. Melhem, *Heroism in the New Black Poetry:*

Introductions and Interviews (Lexington: University Press of Kentucky, 1990); Hans Ostrom, *A Langston Hughes Encyclopedia* (Westport, CT: Greenwood Press, 2002), esp. "Ballad," 19–20, and "Poetics, Hughes's," 306–308; James Edward Smethurst, *The New Red Negro: The Literary Left and African American Poetry, 1930–1946* (New York: Oxford University Press, 1999); Margaret Walker, *For My People* (New Haven, CT: Yale University Press, 1942); Richard Wright, "Blueprint for Negro Writing" (1937), in *The Norton Anthology of African American Literature*, ed. Henry Louis Gates, Jr., and Nellie Y. McKay, 2nd ed. (New York: Norton, 2004), 1403–1410.

James B. Kelley

Forman, Ruth (born 1968). Poet, novelist, and filmmaker. Born on Cape Cod, Massachusetts, and raised in Rochester, New York, Forman is the author of two books of poetry: *We Are the Young Magicians* (1993), which won the 1992 Barnard New Women Poets Prize, and *Renaissance* (1997), winner of the 1999 PEN Oakland Josephine Miles Award for Poetry. In addition to these two books, Forman is a well-known performance poet, and she often holds poetry workshops for aspiring poets. She has read her work at the United Nations and the National Black Arts Festival, on National Public Radio, and on PBS's *The United States of Poetry*. Her work has also been published in the first digital poetry anthology, *The World of Poetry* (1998). In 2001, she received a Durfee Artist Fellowship to finish her first novel, *Mama John*, which at this writing has not yet been published. In addition to poetry, she creates films and received a graduate degree in filmmaking from the University of Southern California.

Forman's work deals largely with issues of **race**, **gender**, love and sexuality. In *We Are the Young Magicians*, she tackles issues such as war, oppression, class, and poverty. Her poems are very often political and express a strong sense of urgency. She writes, "Poetry is always for the people/and it is always a time of war" (21). Her influences include **Audre Lorde**, **Alice Walker**, **Ntozake Shange**, and **Sonia Sanchez**. She studied at the University of California, Berkeley, with **Ishmael Reed**, **June Jordan**, and **Yusef Komunyakaa**. On the dust jacket of her first book, Komunyakaa writes the following: "A street-wise lyricism fuels these poems—a **blues** dialectic. Forman . . . refuses to let passion become an abstraction. *Young Magicians* is a collection that has a tough grace and rhythm balanced by a pragmatic compassion."

One of the most significant and defining characteristics of Forman's poetry is her use of Black **dialect** and the language of urban, African American **slang**. Her work reveals that she is keenly interested in the day-to-day life of African Americans—their language, their concerns, and their passions. As a result, her language is deeply imagistic and attempts to capture the mood, tempo, and local color of the Black community. Her poems are often autobiographical and lyrical, and much of her subject matter emerges from personal experience. She also writes about poetry itself and the extent to which it shapes and inspires our perceptions and thoughts about human experience. She states, "I write to keep magic in my life" (Powell, 430).

Resources: Ruth Forman: *Renaissance* (Boston: Beacon Press, 1997); *We Are the Young Magicians* (Boston: Beacon Press, 1993); Kevin Powell, ed., *Step into a World: A Global Anthology of the New Black Literature* (New York: John Wiley, 2000).

Mark Tursi

Forrest, Leon (1937–1997). Novelist, essayist, and teacher. Forrest's work represents a modernist and postmodernist strain in African American literature. For example, Forrest opens *Meteor in the Madhouse* (2001) with a poem from **Jean Toomer**'s *Cane* and a line from Gabriel García Márquez's "Bitterness for Three Sleepwalkers." Toomer, a Modernist and critically acclaimed **Harlem Renaissance** author, and García Márquez, the exemplar of South American magical realism, represent for Forrest two strains of consciousness. **Modernism** critiques the historical and cultural chaos of the modern era, and magical realism is a kind of **surrealism** that seamlessly fuses fantasy and reality to create a more authentic representation of our world.

Forrest's body of fiction "disrupts the narrative flow and structure of the conventional Western novel by introducing incoherent utterances, random punctuations, complete songs, and Christian sermons. He writes episodes rather than chapters, disorders time and space, and depicts history as myth and myth as truth. He imagines ghosts speaking back to humans and humans having the ability to fly" (Seretha Williams, 88). Forrest, a native of **Chicago, Illinois**, invents a world, Forest County, a mythic Chicago that is fragmented by **race**, religion, culture, and history.

Educated at Wilson Junior College, Roosevelt University, and the University of Chicago, Forrest was also a journalist, serving as a public information specialist in the military and editing and writing for *Muhammad Speaks*, the newspaper of the **Nation of Islam** (Black Muslims). He worked for the latter from 1969 to 1973. In 1973, Forrest joined the faculty at Northwestern University. He was a professor of English and served as chair of the African American Studies Department until his death in 1997. During his lifetime, Forrest's novels circulated primarily in academic circles; he was highly regarded as an innovator of literary styles and techniques. **Ralph Ellison**, the author of *Invisible Man*, wrote the introduction to Forrest's first novel, *There Is a Tree More Ancient Than Eden* (1973). **Toni Morrison**, Nobel Laureate and Pulitzer Prize winner, was his editor while she was at Random House; she also wrote the introduction to Forrest's third novel, *Two Wings to Veil My Face* (1983). In 1994, Forrest published a collection of essays, *Relocations of the Spirit* (reissued as *The Furious Voice for Freedom* in 1995), in which he assessed the social and political implications of historical literary figures such as William Faulkner and contemporary public figures such as the basketball player **Michael Jordan**. For his epic novel *Divine Days* (1993), Forrest received the *Chicago Sun-Times* Book of the Year Award for Fiction. The massive *Divine Days* focuses on seven days in 1966 and is set in the predominantly African American South Side of Chicago.

The aesthetic vision of Forrest's fiction is founded on his assertion that "re-invention" is a defining characteristic of African American culture and experience. In an interview with Kenneth Warren, Forrest observes: "Reinvention seems to me so much a part of the black ethos, of taking something that is available or maybe conversely, denied blacks and making it into something else for survival and then adding a kind of stamp and style and elegance" (81–82).

Moreover, Forrest draws upon another trope, the language of reversal, to challenge conventional modes of knowing. The metanarrative of Forrest's texts suggests that, for African Americans, things are not always what they seem. In *Meteor in the Madhouse* (2001), for example, Forrest writes a story about a White lesbian boxer who is trained by her Black lover. In the same collection, he tells a story about a funeral home, Fountain House of the Dead, that serves, ironically, as a brothel by night. For Forrest, the **trickster** figure in African American literature exemplifies this trope of reversal because the trickster is a master manipulator of language. Forrest's recurrent trickster figure, the mythical W.A.D. Ford, is the embodiment of several legendary tricksters: W. D. Fard, the angelic messenger who brings the Word of Allah to Elijah Muhammad; Ellison's trickster figure, the hustler Rinehart; and Tiresias, the blind seer of Greek mythology.

Finally, Forrest proposes that the most profound statement of African American culture is its redemptive power—its legacy of seeking a "way out of no way." In *Two Wings to Veil My Face* (1983), Sweetie Reed, storyteller, preacher, missionary, and blueswoman, is a symbol of what Forrest sees as the human spirit's ability to transcend suffering, and the transformation of that pain into art. Thus, Forrest attempts to do with prose what the Negro **spirituals**, **blues**, **gospel music**, **jazz**, and **soul** music have always done: to find some meaning in meaningless suffering.

Resources: Primary Sources: Leon Forrest: *The Bloodworth Orphans* (New York: Random House, 1977); *Divine Days* (New York: Norton, 1993); *The Furious Voice for Freedom: Essays on Life* (Wakefield, RI: Asphodel Press, 1995, originally published as *Relocations of the Spirit*); *Meteor in the Madhouse* (Evanston, IL: TriQuarterly Books, 2001); *There Is a Tree More Ancient Than Eden* (New York: Random House, 1973); *Two Wings to Veil My Face* (New York: Random House, 1983). **Secondary Sources:** John G. Cawelti, ed., *Leon Forrest: Introductions and Interpretations* (Bowling Green, OH: Bowling Green State University Popular Press, 1997); Michael George Davros, "Speak for Yourself: Style and Spirit in Leon Forrest's *Divine Days*," Ph.D. dissertation, University of Illinois at Chicago, 2002 (Ann Arbor, MI: UMI, 2003), AAT 3074135; M. Dubey, "The Mythos of Gumbo, Leon Forrest Talks about *Divine Days*," *Callaloo* 19, no. 3 (Summer 1996), 588–602; Peter Erickson, " 'Yet You Can Quote Shakespeare, at the Drop of a Pin': The Function of Shakespearean Riffs in Leon Forrest's *Divine Days*," *Upstart Crow* 22 (2002), 41–49; Robert Elliot Fox, "Righteous Rites and Royal Ramblings: Leon Forrest's *Divine Days*," *MELUS* 20, no. 4 (Winter 1995), 103–111; Bruce A. Rosenberg, "Forrest Spirits: Oral Echoes in Leon Forrest's Prose," *Oral Tradition* 9, no. 2 (October 1994), 315–327; Danille Taylor-Guthrie, "Sermons, Testifying, and Prayers: Looking Beneath the Wings in Leon Forrest's *Two Wings to Veil My Face*," *Callaloo* 16, no. 2

(Spring 1993), 419–430; Kenneth Warren, "The Mythic City: An Interview with Leon Forrest," in *Leon Forrest: Introductions and Interpretations*. ed. John G. Cawelti (Bowling Green, OH: Bowling Green State University Popular Press, 1997), 81–82; Dana Williams: "History, Memory, Narrative, and Culture: Figuring Ancestry in Leon Forrest's Bloodworth Trilogy," Ph.D. dissertation, Howard University, 1998 (Ann Arbor, MI: UMI, 1999), AAT 9911356; "Preachin' and Singin' Just to Make It Over: The Gospel Impulse as Survival Strategy in Leon Forrest's Bloodworth Trilogy," *African American Review* 36, no. 3 (Fall 2000), 475; Seretha Williams, "Modes of Telling: Reinvention in Leon Forrest's *Two Wings to Veil My Face*," Ph.D. dissertation, University of Georgia, 1998 (Ann Arbor, MI: UMI, 1999), AAT 9920109.

Seretha D. Williams

Forster, Gwynne (born c. 1966). Novelist, journalist, and educator. A native of North Carolina and a graduate of Howard University in **Washington, D.C.**, Gwynne Foster holds bachelor's and master's degrees in sociology, as well as a master's degree in economics and demography from Columbia University. Forster has had a successful career as a demographer, most notably with the United Nations as chief of the Fertility Studies Section, where she was responsible for research and analysis of the social, cultural, economic, and demographic factors influencing fertility levels throughout the world. While traveling across continents, Forster formulated stories that eventually turned into **romance novels**. She had published widely in the field of demography but made a smooth transition from academic to romance writing. Her first novel, *Sealed with a Kiss*, was published in 1995. The majority of Forster's female protagonists are highly educated women from the African American upper middle class. Forster writes about women like herself and other women she knows. She has published a number of titles, including *Against All Odds* (1996) and *Ecstasy* (1997), with the African American imprint Arabesque. In all, she has published sixteen novels and five novellas. Forster broke into the mainstream women's fiction market with *When Twilight Comes* (2001), which she followed with *Blues from Down Deep* (2003); both were published by Kensington. Forster has lectured about the writing process in various venues, including the New York Public Library system, at romance writing conferences, and at a seminar at Howard University. She has received numerous nominations and awards for her novels, including *Romance in Color*'s Award of Excellence and 1999 Author of the Year award. She also is a multiple-time recipient of the Affaire de Coeur Readers Award and the 2001 Black Writers Alliance Gold Pen Award.

Resources: Gwynne Forster: *Against All Odds* (New York: Pinnacle, 1996); *Against the Wind* (Columbus, MS: Love Spectrum, 1999); *Blues from Down Deep* (New York: Kensington, 2003); *Ecstasy* (New York: Pinnacle/Arabesque, 1997); *Last Chance at Love* (New York: Arabesque, 2004); *Sealed with a Kiss* (New York: Pinnacle, 1995); *When Twilight Comes* (New York: Kensington, 2001); Web site, www.gwynneforster .com; interview/information supplied by Forster, Oct. 2003.

Dera R. Williams

Fortune, T[imothy] Thomas (1856–1928). Journalist and political activist. Fortune was born into slavery in Marianna, Florida, and was freed by Lincoln's Emancipation Proclamation. Fortune's father was a prominent Republican politician during **Reconstruction**, which afforded Fortune certain advantages other former slaves did not have, including an education at the Freedmen's Bureau after the **Civil War**. Fortune's interest in journalism began when he learned the basics of the printer's trade at the *Marianna Courier*. His family was forced to flee Marianna, however, because of Ku Klux Klan terrorism and settled in Jacksonville, Florida. Fortune left Florida and traveled to **Washington, D.C.**, in 1874 to enroll at Howard University. After graduating, he moved to New York City, where he began his career as a journalist at the *Weekly Witness* in the late 1870s; he went to work at the *New York Globe* in 1881, and later he founded the *New York Age* (originally the *New York Freeman*) in 1887. He served as editor of the *New York Age* for twenty years, during which time it became one of the most influential African American papers in the United States because it protested discrimination, **lynching**, mob violence, and segregation.

Book illustration of Timothy Thomas Fortune, editor and publisher of *The New York Freeman*, 1891. Photographs and Prints Division, Schomburg Center for Research in Black Culture, The New York Public Library, Astor, Lenox and Tilden Foundations.

Fortune was one of the few African Americans who contributed to White newspapers such as the *New York Sun* and the *Boston Transcript*. In 1884 he wrote *Black and White: Land, Labor, and Politics in the South* (republished in 1970), in which he attacked the plight of Southern freedmen and focused on the unification of poor Whites and Blacks. In 1890 Fortune cofounded the National Afro-American League, a precursor of the Niagara Falls Movement and the National Association for the Advancement of Colored People (**NAACP**). During his tenure at the National Afro-American League, Fortune fought against the political and civil suppression of African American rights. He used his editorial columns to further the African American cause by citing examples of injustice in both the North and **the South**. In 1885 Fortune wrote *The Negro in Politics* because of what he regarded as the Republican Party's exploitation of African American voters. He continued his political activism in 1895 by speaking at the National Federation of Afro-American Women meeting. He also helped female African American activist **Ida B. Wells-Bennett** in her campaign against lynching. Fortune also befriended such other African American leaders as **Booker T. Washington**, who helped fund the *New York Age*. Fortune and Washington also created the National Negro Business League, an organization of African American businessmen. In his many speeches and editorial columns, Fortune advocated using the term "Afro-American."

In 1905 Fortune published *Dreams of Life: Miscellaneous Poems*, his private collection of poetry, republished in 1975. He then became editor of the *Colored American Review*. From 1923 until his death, Fortune was editor of **Marcus Garvey's** *Negro World*. In a tribute published in the *Amsterdam News* on the occasion of Fortune's death, Howard University dean Kelly Miller wrote that Fortune "represented the best developed journalist that the Negro race has produced" (Thornbrough, 368). (*See* **Newspapers**.)

Resources: William L. Andrews, Frances Smith Foster, and Trudier Harris, eds., *Oxford Companion to African American Literature* (New York: Oxford University Press, 1997); Perry J. Ashley, ed., *Dictionary of Literary Biography*, vol. 23, *American Newspaper Journalists, 1873–1900* (Detroit: Gale Research, 1983); Timothy Thomas Fortune: *Black and White: Land, Labor, and Politics in the South* (Chicago: Johnson Publishing, 1970); *Dreams of Life: Miscellaneous Poems* (New York: AMS Press, 1975); James A. Page, *Selected Black American Authors* (Boston: G. K. Hall, 1977); Emma Lou Thornbrough, *T. Thomas Fortune: Militant Journalist* (Chicago: University of Chicago Press, 1972).

Mary J. Sloat

Foster, Frances Smith (born 1944). Literary critic and professor. At this writing, Foster is Charles Howard Candler Professor of English and Women's Studies, and associate faculty in African American Studies and in American Studies, at Emory University in **Atlanta, Georgia**. Born in Dayton, Ohio, she received her Ph.D. from the University of California, San Diego, and has taught at San Diego State University and the University of California, San Diego. Foster's work has centered on nineteenth-century African American literature and women's literature. Her rediscovery of three novels by the nineteenth-century African American author **Frances Ellen Watkins Harper**, published in *Minnie's Sacrifice, Sowing and Reaping, Trial and Triumph: Three Rediscovered Novels by Frances Ellen Watkins Harper* (1994), contributed enormously to the field of African American literature. She has written numerous books and articles and is a coeditor of a critical edition of *Incidents in the Life of a Slave Girl* (by **Harriet Jacobs**) and of *The Oxford Companion to African American Literature* (1997).

Resources: Frances Smith Foster: "African Americans, Literature, and the Nineteenth Century Afro-Protestant Press," in *Reciprocal Influences: Literary Production, Distribution, and Consumption in America*, ed. Steven Fink and Susan Williams (Columbus: Ohio State University Press, 1999), 24–35; "Continuities with the Past/ Blueprints for the Future: Scholarly, Professional, and Activist Strategies for the New Century," *Legacy: A Journal of American Women Writers* 19, no. 1 (2002), 10–13; "Early African American Women Writers," in *The History of Southern Women's Literature*, ed.

Carolyn Perry and Mary Louise Weaks (Baton Rouge: Louisiana State University Press, 2002), 87–96; *Minnie's Sacrifice, Sowing and Reaping, Trial and Triumph: Three Rediscovered Novels by Frances E. W. Harper* (Boston: Beacon Press, 1994); *Written by Herself: Literary Production by African American Women, 1746–1892* (Bloomington: Indiana University Press, 1993); Frances Smith Foster, ed., *A Brighter Coming Day: A Frances Ellen Harper Watkins Reader* (New York: Feminist Press, 1990); Frances S. Foster and Nellie Y. McKay, eds., *Incidents in the Life of a Slave Girl* [by Harriet Jacobs]: *Contexts, Criticisms* (New York: Norton, 2001); Frances S. Foster, William L. Andrews, and Trudier Harris, eds., *Oxford Companion to African American Literature* (New York: Oxford University Press, 1997); Henry Louis Gates, Jr., and Nellie Y. McKay, eds., *The Norton Anthology of African American Literature* (New York: Norton, 1996).

Saundra K. Liggins

Foster, Sharon Ewell (born 1957). Christian novelist and devotional writer. Foster publishes in the category of religious and inspirational writing. She writes novels that feature African American characters who pray and who talk openly about their faith as they try to manage interpersonal relationships. Born in **Texas**, Foster grew up in Illinois and, at this writing, resides in Maryland. She has worked in professional and administrative capacities for the Department of Defense as an instructor, writer/editor, and logistician. She holds a B.A. degree in radio–TV–film from the University of Maryland. Early influences on her writing include Ernest Hemingway, John Steinbeck, **James Baldwin**, and Edgar Allan Poe (Delgado).

Her first novel, *Passing by Samaria* (2000), debuted on the Christian Book Association best-seller list in the first month of its release and received the Christy Award for best debut Christian novel. Set in 1919 in rural Mississippi, the novel, addressing racism and love, centers on an African American teenage girl, Alena Walker. After witnessing the **lynching** of her childhood friend J.C., Walker heads north to **Chicago, Illinois**, and thus must figuratively "pass through Samaria," struggling with tragedy and her faith in God in order to be at peace with her past and the uncertainty of her future.

Foster's second novel, *Ain't No River* (2001), is about a young black attorney in **Washington, D.C.**, Garvin Daniels, and Meemaw, her grandmother. The grandmother is dating a much younger man, an ex-pro football player named GoGo Walker, in rural North Carolina. While trying to find answers to her personal and professional dilemmas, Garvin returns to God, reflecting Foster's emphasis on a modern Black woman's struggle with faith and the issues of virtue and purity, loss and restoration.

Foster's third book, *Riding Through Shadows* (2001) is a **coming-of-age** story told through the eyes of eight-year-old Shirley Ferris, who experiences the challenges of living in a newly integrated neighborhood during the escalation of the **Vietnam War** and **Civil Rights Movement**, and then is rescued by Mother Johnson, a distant relative and spiritual healer. Mother Johnson takes Shirley to a small Texas town and prepares her for spiritual warfare. *Passing into Light* (2002) is a sequel about Shirley Ferris-Mills, newly widowed, and her two children who migrate from Alabama to California in search of a new life. During their journey, they assist a pregnant White teenage shoplifter, visit Mother Johnson, and encounter Tony Taylor, who had been Shirley's prom date, all the while coping with racial realities of **the South** in the 1960s. In her fiction, including *Ain't No Mountain* (2004), Foster offers glimpses of African American life, faith, and romance, infusing each novel with an evangelical Christian vision. She also writes devotionals for the periodical *Daily Guideposts* and the *Women of Color Devotional Bible* (2003).

Resources: Berta Delgado, "Author Sharon Ewell Foster Says Calling Was Clear," *Dallas Morning News*, Feb. 12, 2000, p. 12; Sharon Ewell Foster: *Ain't No Mountain* (Minneapolis, MN: Bethany House, 2004); *Ain't No River* (Sisters, OR: Multnomah, 2001); *Passing into Light* (Sisters, OR: Multnomah, 2002); *Passing by Samaria* (Sisters, OR: Alabaster Books, 2000); *Riding Through Shadows* (Sisters, OR: Multnomah, 2001); Monica Harris, "Fiction Reviews," *Black Issues Book Review* 4, no. 1 (Jan./Feb. 2003), 58; Sharita Hunt, "God's Reading Rainbow," *Black Issues Book Review* 3, no. 3 (May/June 2001), 35; Arlene McKanic, "*Passing by Samaria* by Sharon Ewell Foster," *Quarterly Book Review* 7, no. 1 (2000), 6; Jeff Zaleski, "Review of *Passing into Light*," *Publishers Weekly*, Feb. 14, 2003, p. 53.

Carol Elizabeth Dietrich

Franklin, C. L. (1915–1984). Preacher, sermon writer, and gospel singer. Clarence LeVaughn Franklin, whose recorded sermons sold millions of copies, is considered one of the most influential preachers in American history. Rev. **Jesse Jackson** called him "a prophet" and "the most imitated soul preacher in history" (Franklin 1989, vii). Born near Indianola, in Sunflower County, Mississippi, Franklin was raised by his mother, Rachel, and stepfather, Henry, a sharecropper. A precocious boy, Franklin was a soloist in his Baptist church choir, preached his first sermon at fourteen, and by sixteen was nominated for ordination at St. Peter's Rock Baptist Church in Cleveland, Mississippi. He studied religion at Greenville Industrial College and later at LeMoyne College (now Lemoyne-Owen College) in **Memphis, Tennessee**, while ministering to area churches. It was in Memphis that Franklin began delivering sermons on the radio. He left LeMoyne to become pastor of Friendship Baptist Church in Buffalo, New York, and to continue his studies at the State University of New York at Buffalo.

In 1946 Franklin moved to **Detroit, Michigan**, to become minister to the New Bethel Baptist Church. He remained for thirty-three years. Upon his arrival, the small congregation was meeting in an old bowling alley. In 1952, Franklin began preaching on WJLB radio and gained a large audience; recordings of his sermons were soon being sold nationwide by the Chess Recording Company. The income generated by these records, as well as by Franklin's tours with **gospel** groups such as the Ward Singers, allowed him to build his growing congregation a new church and erase their debts. In all, Franklin released at least seventy-six recordings of his sermons and gospel singing, selling millions of copies.

Franklin married Barbara Siggers, a church pianist. They had five children, including the famous **soul** singer Aretha Franklin, who got her start as a soloist on her father's gospel tours. Despite his growing church and family, Franklin continued his preaching tours through the 1960s. He was a member of the Southern Christian Leadership Conference and active in the **Civil Rights Movement**. In 1963 he helped organize and lead the "Walk Toward Freedom March" in Detroit with Dr. **Martin Luther King**. Dr. King's speech in Detroit, which he began by thanking his good friend C. L. Franklin, was his first delivery of the "I Have a Dream" speech, which he made famous two months later at the "March on Washington" (August 28, 1963).

Franklin was shot in his home by burglars in June 1979 and remained in a coma until his death in 1984. His recordings are still widely available, and posthumous transcriptions of his sermons are available in *Give Me This Mountain: Life History and Selected Sermons* (1989). One of Franklin's most famous sermons, "The Eagle Stirreth Her Nest," is often anthologized. Based on Deuteronomy 32:11–12, this piece displays many of the stylistic elements that make Franklin's work a bridge from the oral tradition of folk sermons and soul preaching to the larger audience formats of gospel performance and civil rights rallies. Using simple words for a general audience, Franklin constructs a direct emotional appeal which serves to deliver a more complex structure of logical narrative. Divided into the traditional four parts of introduction, statement, discussion, and conclusion, "Eagle" proceeds in the standard "calm to storm" method of African American folk preaching and shifts its central eagle symbol to represent first God, then the congregants, and finally the soul "caged" in the human body. This final image is reached halfway through the "discussion" part of the sermon, at which point Franklin's delivery shifts to "whooping" or intoned chanting. On the page, this whooping appears as poetry, and allows Franklin to build characteristically to his climax and conclusion.

Resources: Clayborne Carson and Kris Shepherd, eds., *A Call to Conscience: The Landmark Speeches of Martin Luther King, Jr.* (New York: IPM/Warner Books, 2001); C. L. Franklin: *Give Me This Mountain: Life History and Selected Sermons*, ed. Jeff Todd Titon (Urbana: University of Illinois Press, 1989); *Legendary Sermons*, audio CD (MCA Special Products, 1999); W. H. Pipes, *Say Amen, Brother! Old-time Negro Preaching: A Study in American Frustration* (New York: William-Frederick, 1951).

Robert Strong

Franklin, J. E. (born 1937). Playwright. A native of Houston, **Texas**, Franklin is best known for her play *Blackgirl*, which was made into a film of the same name (1972), directed by **Ossie Davis** and starring Ruby Dee and Brock Peters. In the play and movie, the main character, Billie Jean, struggles to continue her education as a dancer despite opposition from family. The play was produced by the New Federal Theater, directed by Shauneille Perry, and enjoyed an off-Broadway run of more than 800 performances. Franklin received the Drama Desk Award for 1971–1972 as one of the nation's most promising playwrights. She is the author of *Black Girl: From Genesis to Revelations*, a book that chronicles her experience as a writer through the video, stage, and filming process of *Black Girl*. Other plays include a musical, *The Prodigal Sister; Throw Thunder at This House, Wonder Child, Will the Real Black Racism Please Die?*, and *Christchild*. Her plays have been produced at Rites & Reason Theatre at Brown University, the University of Iowa, the Theater of the Open Eye, and at the Second Stage of New York, among others.

Founder of the Blackgirl Ensemble Theater in New York City, a theater troupe dedicated to performing her and other playwright's works, Franklin serves as its artistic director. She often writes in the ten-minute play genre and has produced a number of thematically related works in a group of ten ten-minute plays including *Coming to the Mercy Seat, Precious Memories*, and *The Daughters of Ham*. Franklin has received fellowships from the Rockefeller Foundation, the New York Foundation for the Arts, the National Endowment for the Humanities, and the John F. Kennedy Center for Performing Arts. She has taught playwriting at the Harlem School of the Arts and the New Federal Theater, and was a playwriting fellow at the Eugene O'Neill Center. Franklin was also a resident scholar at the Schomburg Center for Research and Black Culture. She is a graduate of the University of Texas.

Resources: J. E. Franklin: *Black Girl* (New York: Dramatists Play Service, 1971); *Black Girl: From Genesis to Revelations* (Washington, DC: Howard University Press, 1977).

Joan F. McCarty

Franklin, John Hope (born 1915). Historian and educator. Franklin is considered a preeminent scholar of African American history. He was born on January 2, 1915, in Rentiesville, **Oklahoma**, a segregated town sixty-five miles south of Tulsa, where his mother, Mollie Lee Franklin, taught school and he had his early schooling. His father, B. C. Franklin, practiced law in Tulsa. When a thirty-five-block section of the relatively prosperous African American community in Tulsa was burned in the **race riots** of 1921, B. C. Franklin's law offices also were destroyed. By 1926 the family had moved to Tulsa, the father having reestablished his practice. After graduating from Tulsa's Booker T. Washington High School, Franklin attended Fisk University in **Nashville, Tennessee**, his mind set on a career in law. The profound influence of his history professor and mentor at Fisk, Theodore S. Currier, a White man, convinced him to follow a career in history instead. Currier urged him to go to Harvard, an unthinkable dream for an African American scholar of modest means in the **Great Depression** era. Vowing that lack of money would not keep Franklin out of Harvard, Currier borrowed $500 and sent Franklin on his way to Harvard in 1935. In nine months he had earned his master's degree, and his Ph.D. by 1941. The African American presence at Harvard was sparse, one or two in each school—like the creatures taken into Noah's ark, he recalls.

Dedicated to academic life, Franklin taught at a number of colleges and universities, Howard University, Brooklyn College of New York, the

University of Chicago, and Duke University among them. His 1956 appointment as chair of the History Department at Brooklyn College, which had fifty-two white historians, was a front-page picture story in the *New York Times*. In 1964 Franklin joined the University of Chicago, where he had an eighteen-year tenure of distinguished teaching and three years of chairmanship. In 1982 Franklin joined Duke University as the James B. Duke professor of history; after his retirement he transferred to the Duke Law School as professor of legal history. In 2000, Duke University created the John Hope Franklin Center for Interdisciplinary and International Studies in his honor.

Franklin is the author of nearly two dozen books and hundreds of scholarly articles. As "a fledgling historian," he decided that for the sake of an effective learning process, he must write different kinds of history while still remaining in the field. Accordingly, he created a writing plan consisting of a monograph, a general work, a biography, a period piece, and an edited primary source, all of which can be found among his works, several of each.

Franklin's global reputation has been secured by his early and best-known work, *From Slavery to Freedom* (1947), written after a Knopf representative had given him "a philosophical charge and a $500 advance" to write a book on African American history. Tracing the genesis of the European slave trade to the medieval African ancestral cultures in Ghana, Mali, and Songhay, the book covers the thousand-year history of the African people who had been transported forcibly to the West. Currently in its eighth edition (2000), the book has positioned itself as the definitive source of the history of Western **slavery**, as well as of African Americans. It has been translated into Hindi, Japanese, Chinese, and a number of European languages. Alfred A. Moss, Jr., has been joint author with Franklin since the fifth edition.

Race and History: Selected Essays 1938–1988 (1989) is a thematic collection of twenty-seven essays, representing half a century of Franklin's scholarly agenda. Other titles of similar content include *The Militant South, 1800–1861* (1956); *Reconstruction After the Civil War* (1961); *The Emancipation Proclamation* (1963); and *The Color Line: Legacy for the Twenty-first Century* (1993).

Franklin's treatment of history involves historiography in equal measure, perhaps the reason it has been described as "revisionist." In his essay "History as Propaganda," for example, Franklin unearths **Reconstruction** history to show how D. W. Griffith's film *The Birth of a Nation* (1915) set the tone for the rebirth of the Ku Klux Klan. Likewise, *Runaway Slaves: Rebels on the Plantation* (1999), a monograph written with Loren Schweninger, refutes the traditional assumption that the antebellum plantation slaves easily yielded to authority, as claimed by Ulrich Phillip's *Life and Labor in the Old South* (1929). Franklin proves that slaves were often aggressive in self-defense, unafraid to resist or rebel against or run away from oppressive ownership, not hesitating even to murder if necessary. *Racial Equality in America* (1976), Franklin's Jefferson Lecture of 1976, argues that the Negro's emancipation came without equality. Franklin questions Jefferson's well-known antipathy to slavery as suspect in that he failed to prevail on the Continental Congress to affirm equality for the

Negro with other human beings. The craftsman of the Declaration of Independence, he argues, missed a model opportunity to show himself different from other slaveholders by releasing his own slaves. Franklin regrets that Jefferson's views on the physical attributes and the mental capabilities of the Negro helped the old order ignore the fact that equality was indivisible, a burden that fell upon the twentieth-century America. This book received the Clarence L. Holte Literary Prize in 1985.

Franklin believed that "biography was a legitimate area of inquiry for the historian." As a graduate student he had written an article on Edward Bellamy, which pleased his widow enough to give Franklin access to Bellamy's papers and records, and even to invite him to write Bellamy's biography, should Arthur Morgan, the would-be author, not find the time to do it. Morgan did find the time, which Franklin regretted. However, Franklin already had a series of biographical projects for many years hence. In 1947 he published *The Diary of James T. Ayers: Civil War Recruiter* (1947), the biography of a White Kentuckian Methodist preacher of the 1860s, an abolitionist who encouraged slaves and freedmen to join the U.S. Colored Troops. Ayer's *Diary* realistically documents the Northern attitude on the war, slavery, and the Confederacy. The next work, *Reminiscences of an Active Life: The Autobiography of John Roy Lynch* (1970), was already a published work, but Franklin saw the need to fill its many gaps, which "the Republican Stalwart from Mississippi" had overlooked. The work on Lynch "fulfilled my ambition to do serious editorial work of this sort," Franklin says, and further output followed. *George Washington Williams: A Biography* (1985) took forty years to finish, at times an unending quest for "elusive, fugitive materials." Franklin's service as general editor (since 1969) of the University of Chicago Press series Negro Biographies and Autobiographies shows his enduring interest in this genre of historical studies.

In *My Life and an Era: The Autobiography of Buck Colbert Franklin* (1997), Franklin reworks his deceased father's manuscript, by then forty years old, the editing done jointly with his own son John Whittington Franklin (B. C. Franklin's grandson). A good portion of Buck Colbert's story would later be part of a PBS documentary, *First Person Singular: John Hope Franklin* (2001). Franklin's own autobiography, *The Vintage Years*, is due for publication in 2006. He has given readings of portions of it on his lecture circuit.

In keeping with his conviction that a historian has the resources and the responsibility to serve his society with his skills, Franklin has been active in shaping public policy wherever he can. He appeared as an expert witness in the 1949 integration case of the University of Kentucky's graduate program. In 1953, he joined the nonlegal research staff of the **NAACP** Legal Defense Fund to prepare a brief for *Brown v. Board of Education*. This landmark case resulted in the Supreme Court ruling against segregation in public schools. Franklin and his colleagues prepared a similar document for the 1988 Supreme Court argument on *Brenda Patterson v. McLean Credit Union*, demonstrating how the Civil Rights Act of 1866 was intended to bar racial discrimination in the private as well as the public sector. Franklin also testified in the Robert Bork (1987) and the Clarence Thomas (1991) hearings, arguing that both of these men, if confirmed to the Supreme Court, could potentially hurt African American interests. Franklin's speech at the Harvard Law School, "The Scholar as Activist: The Appointment of Robert Bork and Clarence Thomas to the Supreme Court" (2003), offers the rationale for his testimonies.

The recipient of 135 honorary doctorates, Franklin has been president of national professional organizations such as the American Studies Association, the Southern Historical Association, the United Chapters of Phi Beta Kappa, the Organization of American Historians, and the American Historical Association. He has delivered the U.S. State Department and U.S. Information Service lectures in more than fifty countries. Himself once a Fulbright Professor in Australia, Franklin served on the Fulbright board from 1962 to 1969, the last three years as its chair. His other international assignments have included a stint at Cambridge University as Pitt Professor of American History; service as a consultant on American education in the Soviet Union; as a lecturer in American history in the People's Republic of China; and as U.S. delegate to the 1980 UNESCO General Conference, held in Belgrade. Franklin also served the Clinton White House on the Commission on Public Diplomacy, the Advisory Commission on Ambassadorial Appointments, and the 1997 Initiative on Race (as its chair).

Franklin was awarded the Presidential Medal of Freedom in 1995. Widely in demand for his expertise, he still travels the world on speaking engagements.

Resources: Primary Sources: John Hope Franklin: *The Color Line: Legacy for the Twenty-first Century* (Columbia: University of Missouri Press, 1993); *The Diary of James T. Ayers, Civil War Recruiter* (Springfield: Illinois Historical Society, 1947; repr. Baton Rouge: Louisiana State University Press, 1999); *The Emancipation Proclamation* (Garden City, NY: Doubleday, 1963); *The Free Negro in North Carolina, 1790–1860* (Chapel Hill: University of North Carolina Press, 1943); *From Slavery to Freedom: A History of African Americans*, 8th ed. (New York: Knopf, 2000) (with Alfred A. Moss, Jr.); *George Washington Williams: A Biography* (Chicago: University of Chicago Press, 1985); *The Militant South, 1800–1861* (Cambridge, MA: Belknap Press, 1956; Urbana: University of Illinois Press, 2002); *Race and History: Selected Essays 1938–1988* (Baton Rouge: Louisiana State University Press, 1989); *Racial Equality in America* (Chicago: University of Chicago Press, 1976); *Reconstruction After the Civil War* (Chicago: University of Chicago Press, 1961); John Hope Franklin and John W. Franklin, eds., *My Life and an Era* (Baton Rouge: Louisiana State University Press, 1997); John Hope Franklin and Loren Schweninger, *Runaway Slaves: Rebels on the Plantation* (New York: Oxford University Press, 1999). **Secondary Sources:** Eric Anderson and Alfred A. Moss, Jr., eds., *The Facts of Reconstruction: Essays in Honor of John Hope Franklin* (Baton Rouge: Louisiana State University Press, 1991); Peter Applebome: *First Person Singular: John Hope Franklin*, documentary motion picture (Lives and Legacies Films, 1997); "The Genius of John Hope Franklin," *Black Issues in Higher Education* 10 (Jan. 13, 1994), 16–32; "Keeping Tabs on Jim Crow: John Hope Franklin," *New York Times*

Magazine, Apr. 23, 1994, 34–37; James L. Podesta, "John Hope Franklin, 1915–: Historian, Educator, Writer," in *Contemporary Black Biography*, ed. Barbara C. Bigelow, vol. 5 (Detroit: Gale, 1994), 96–101.

Varghese Mathai

Frazier, Edward Franklin (1894–1962). Sociologist and activist. Frazier was born and raised in **Baltimore, Maryland**. As an adult he was committed to the Socialist Party, women's suffrage, and racial equality. He was educated at Howard University in **Washington, D.C.**, where he was influenced by **W.E.B. Du Bois**, who often lectured on feminism, socialism, and the importance of professional careers for African Americans. Frazier became actively involved in the Social Science, German, and Political Science clubs, was vice president of the **NAACP**'s Howard University chapter, and was president of his class in 1915. He began his teaching career at Tuskegee Institute (1916), where he met **Claude McKay**. In 1917 Frazier was drafted to serve in **World War I**, but he was exempted from active duty because he was his mother's sole financial support. Frazier developed strong antiwar views and expressed resentment at "being drafted in a war which...was essentially a conflict between imperialistic powers"; he noted that "in view of the treatment of the Negro in the United States, the avowed aim, to make the world safe for democracy, presented hypocrisy on the part of America" (Odum, 234). In late 1917 Frazier wrote a fifteen-page antiwar pamphlet titled *God and War*, which argued against the devastation of war and called for a new society in which human life of all races would be equally valued.

Frazier received an M.A. in sociology in 1919 from Clark University in Worcester, Massachusetts. His thesis, "New Currents of Thought Among the Colored People of America," studied the logic behind race equality by surveying the programs and literature of African American organizations, specifically the ideals presented by Du Bois, **Marcus Garvey**'s journal *The Messenger*, and the Tuskegee Institute. Frazier began his thesis with Claude McKay's militant poem "If We Must Die," and ended it by writing, "The new spirit which has produced the **New Negro** bids fair to transform the whole race. America faces a new race that has awakened, and in the realization of its strength has girt its loins to run the race with other men." Frazier trained under Frank Hankins, who became president of the American Sociological Association. He followed in Hankins's footsteps and become the ASA's first African American president. He conducted research in sociology at the New York School of Social Work (1920–1921) and the University of Copenhagen (1921–1922) before returning to the United States to teach at Morehouse College in **Atlanta, Georgia**, where he gained funding from many sources and built up the Sociology Department's academic reputation. His publication of "The Pathology of Race Prejudice" in *Forum* (June 1927), however, forced his resignation because many felt he was too outspoken about African American civil rights. Frazier returned to graduate school and earned his Ph.D. in sociology at the University of Chicago. He went on to become a research professor of sociology at Fisk University (1927–1934) and published *The Negro Family in Chicago* (1932) and *The Free Negro Family* (1932).

Frazier returned to the North in 1934 to head the Sociology Department at Howard University. Enrollment in the sociology program increased from 200 to 2,000 in fourteen years under his supervision. At Howard he earned the name "Forceful Frazier" because of his demanding yet invigorating teaching style. He practiced what he preached by involving himself in social work with the Harlem Commission (1935), the American Youth Commission (1939), the Guggenheim Foundation (1940), the Carnegie Corporation (1942), and the United Nations Educational, Scientific, and Cultural Organization, UNESCO (1951). He published a textbook titled *The Negro Family in the United States* (1939), which analyzed the history of the African American family in relation to **slavery**, segregation, racial discrimination, and migration. He wrote *Negro Youth at the Crossways* (1940) for the American Youth Commission, focusing on African American youth in different regions of the United States. *Race and Culture Contacts in the Modern World* (1957) emerged from Frazier's experiences with and travels for UNESCO in France, Africa, and the Middle East. His book *Black Bourgeoisie* was first published in French in 1955 because American publishers felt it was too controversial; it was published in English in 1957. In this book, Frazier argued that middle-class African Americans were trying to imitate White people and their lifestyles. He said African Americans were living in a make-believe world and needed to focus on their own issues and problems rather than imitating White people. Frazier died of cancer May 17, 1962, in Washington, D.C. A memorial published in the *American Sociological Review* observes, "There was on Frazier's part a dedication to academic life, and his contributions lie mainly in his teaching and research activities. In both of these areas he had rich and manifold experiences."

Resources: "E. Franklin Frazier," *Encyclopaedia Britannica*, www.britannica.com; Edward Franklin Frazier: *Black Bourgeoisie* (Glencoe, IL: Free Press, 1959); *The Free Negro Family* (Nashville: Fisk University Press, 1932); *Howard Year Book I* [College Year-book] (Washington, DC: Howard University, 1916), 20; *The Negro Family in the United States* (Chicago: University of Chicago Press, 1939); *The Negro in the United States*, rev. ed. (New York: Macmillan, 1957); *Negro Youth at the Crossroads* (Washington, DC: American Council of Education, 1940); *NIKH Year Book* (Washington, DC: College of Arts and Sciences, Howard University, 1914), 86; *Race and Culture Contacts in the Modern World* (New York: Knopf, 1957); "Edward Franklin Frazier," *American Sociological Review* 27 (1963), 890–892; Howard Odum, *American Sociology: The Story of Sociology in the United States Through 1950* (New York: Longmans, Green, 1951); Anthony M. Platt, *E. Franklin Frazier Reconsidered* (New Brunswick, NJ: Rutgers University Press, 1991); Michael R. Winston, "Through the Back Door: Academic Racism and the Negro Scholar in Historical Perspective," *Daedalus* 100 (Summer 1971), 689–694.

Mary J. Sloat

Free Southern Theater (1963–1979). Of the many experimental theater collectives that appeared during the 1960s, the Free Southern Theater (FST) stands with the Bread and Puppet Theatre, the San Francisco Mime Troupe, and El Teatro Campesino as one of the most important. The company took a genuinely grassroots approach to Black theater in **the South**. Though it was constantly plagued by financial difficulties and eventually closed, the commitment of its officers to social justice and community-centered performance established the FST as a significant African American cultural experiment.

Doris Derby, Gilbert Moses, and John O'Neal discussed the need for a theater in the Deep South while Moses was writing for the *Mississippi Free Press* and the others were field directors for the Student Nonviolent Coordinating Committee. They established the Free Southern Theater to fill a gap in the information and educational systems in Jackson, Mississippi, specifically, but also throughout Black southern communities in general. As conceived, this theater would cultivate a Black style of performance and be run with racially integrated administrative structures. With the help of a Tulane drama professor and experimental theater notable, Richard Schechner, as well as the New Yorkers Carol Feinman and Joy Manhoff, the company began an intense New York fund-raising campaign. Satisfactory financial backing allowed the Jackson pilot project to open in 1964 with Martin Duberman's *In White America*. The first FST tour was restricted mainly to Mississippi cities, but did have one performance in Tennessee and another in Louisiana.

In November 1964, the theater moved to **New Orleans, Louisiana**, where a strong middle-class Black population promised more reliable funding for the group's activities. The founders made the move with some regret, feeling they were abandoning communities more in need of the company's efforts (Dent, et al., 33). The new location proved to have its own challenges. The group needed to organize an audience that united middle-class **Creole** Blacks, who were not particularly concerned with Black empowerment, with impoverished, poorly educated, rural Blacks. Developing a dramatic repertoire was also a problem; their early offerings were mainly by such White authors as Samuel Beckett, Bertolt Brecht, and Sean O'Casey. Productions of **Ossie Davis**'s *Purlie Victorious* and **Langston Hughes**'s *Don't You Want to Be Free?* (written and first produced in 1938) enriched the fare, but it soon became clear that the company would have to cultivate dramas more directly relevant to Southern Blacks.

With the help of New York exhibitions that drew interest from a strong core of actors, directors, and writers, the FST became a composite professional touring company by 1966. Ironically, as the organization solidified, some members became ambivalent toward their integrated company, complaining that the White members did not fully understand the vision of a Black theater. In the words of the poet and associate director **Thomas Covington Dent**: "We were probing not only the role of FST but far larger territory, the unpleasant realities of race in America...attitudes about race which had never been talked out between us" (Dent et al., 98). By mid-1966, legal and personal issues led to the exodus of all three original founders, and the organization was destitute.

An anonymous $10,000 gift and a sizable Rockefeller grant saved it in the eleventh hour. Work began on *Ghetto of Desire*, Dent's controversial prose work that exposed the danger and alienation of life in New Orleans's Desire Project, an impoverished Black housing district to which the company had recently relocated. Despite the efforts of the Housing Authority, which began a furious letter-writing campaign against it, the program aired as planned on CBS's *Look Up and Live*. As a consequence of *Ghetto*'s popularity, coming tour performances throughout Mississippi, Alabama, Georgia, and Louisiana, of (among other works) Moses's *Roots* and the South African William Plomer's *I Speak of Africa* were followed by revitalized discussion of community and racial consciousness. Their 1967 season was also productive, despite administrative problems, and featured **Douglas Turner Ward**'s *Happy Ending* and a poetry reading titled *Uncle Tom's Second Line Funeral*.

The FST made considerable strides in cultivating Black drama in the South. John O'Neal devised a workshop program that concentrated on a form of documentary theater. The projects integrated factual information and original ideas in dramas with self-consciously pan-cultural African American influences. They meant to unite history, street rap, and religion in a new theatrical language that would both forward political goals and reflect the everyday experience of agrarian African Americans (Fabre, 58). In one of the workshop pieces, *Where Is the Blood of Your Fathers?* (1972), **slave narratives** and the autobiographies of **Frederick Douglass** and **William Wells Brown** collide in a montage with nineteenth-century newspaper clippings, travelers' notes, and songs to dramatize slave resistance before the **Civil War**. Dance and music, a white-masked actor playing all White roles, and a stage manager who speaks directly to the audience add to the nonlinearity and nonrealism of the event.

FST plays operated as part of an interactive performance/audience event rather than as conventional dramatic productions. Curtain speeches would urge the audience to consider themselves actors in the performance. Debates were held after each showing, and sometimes individuals would ascend to the stage and participate directly in the action during a production (Fabre, 55). Dent's description of a production of Brecht's *Carrar* at Dillard University suggests that it was FST's community connection that made the strongest impression on spectators. In his words: "The play was not impressive.... The production was not smooth or polished...[but] there was something in the energy, the seriousness, the lack of arty phoniness...a kind of idealism, that made me believe that the project had both social and artistic value" (Dent et al., 231). In describing a forum where play analysis blossomed into discussion of current police abuses in the French Quarter, Dent reaffirms the need for a Black theater that builds on the cultural forms of the African American community and rejects the detractions of jaded White critics (Dent et al., 231–233).

Over the twelve years between the 1967 and 1979 seasons, the FST continued to struggle financially, but also enjoyed a number of successes. It published an arts journal titled **Nkombo** and presented *Nation Time* on PBS in New Orleans (1972–1976). In 1979, it finally succumbed to external and internal pressures. After the FST dissolved, groups arose to take its place, many of which would join the Black Southern Cultural Alliance. During its sixteen-year history, the Free Southern Theater produced at least 200 original scripts and included such notable artists and authors as Arthur Ashe, Harry Belafonte, **Julian Bond**, **William (Bill) Cosby**, **Ossie Davis**, Fannie Lou Hamer, and Brock Peters in its ranks.

Resources: Annemarie Bean, ed., *A Sourcebook of African American Performance: People, Plays, Movements* (New York: Routledge, 1999); "Black Theatres," in *The Cambridge History of American Theatre*, ed. Don B. Wilmeth and Christopher Bigsby, vol. 1 (New York: Cambridge University Press, 1998); Bogdana Carpenter, "The Free Southern Theater Conference—A Valediction Without Mourning," *Southern Quarterly* 25, no. 4 (1987), 85–97; Thomas C. Dent, Richard Schechner, and Gilbert Moses, eds., *The Free Southern Theater by the Free Southern Theater: A Documentary of the South's Radical Black Theater, with Journals, Letters, Poetry, Essays, and a Play Written by Those Who Built It* (Indianapolis, IN: Bobbs-Merrill, 1969); Genevieve Fabre, "The Free Southern Theater, 1963–1979," *Black American Literature Forum* 17 (1983), 55–59.

Ben Fisler

Free Verse. In *Understanding the New Black Poetry* (1972), Stephen Henderson argues that African American poetry from its **slavery** era beginnings to the 1960s had been permeated by the theme of liberation. Particularly in the latter half of the twentieth century, this theme of liberation in poetry has often been coupled with a liberation in form, a move away from the fetters of rhyme and meter toward *vers libre*, free verse modeled on authentic and living speech.

"Free verse," writes Ron Padgett, "is just that—lines of poetry that are written without rules: no regular beat and no rhyme. The *vers libre* (French for 'free verse') movement began in late nineteenth century Europe, especially in France. But unrhymed poetry without a regular rhythm had appeared in translations of the Bible, and one of the first great poets to use the form was Walt Whitman, an American" (85). Free verse is unquestionably the most widely used form in modern poetry and is characterized by the absence of fixed metrical patterns, regular line lengths, or predictable rhyme schemes (*see* **Formal Verse**). The basic unit of free verse is the line or even the stanza, not the metric foot on which Western poetic conventions have been built. In the absence of traditional unifying devices, such as meter and rhyme, poems in free verse frequently repeat words, short phrases, or grammatical structures in order to reinforce the poem's unity. **Nikki Giovanni** is one of many twentieth-century African American poets to reject the constraints of conventional poetic forms and to write instead in free verse. Her poem "For Saundra" (1968), for example, begins with the speaker stating she will abstain from writing a poem that uses rhyme because "revolution doesn't lend/itself to be-bopping."

Arnold Rampersad (1979) credits **W.E.B. Du Bois** with being "the first black poet publicly to break with rhyme and blank verse in his most anthologized poem 'A Litany of Atlanta'" (53), published in 1906. Rampersad is correct in identifying Du Bois's poem as a very early instance of free verse in African American poetry. However, some of the most prominent African American poets writing in free verse in the twentieth century—including **Langston Hughes, Margaret Walker, Amiri Baraka**, and **June Jordan**—have identified not Du Bois but late-nineteenth- and early-twentieth-century White poets as their models, particularly Walt Whitman, Carl Sandburg, and William Carlos Williams. One of Hughes's earliest and best-known poems, "The Negro Speaks of Rivers," reflects the tone of Whitman and Sandburg especially. Regardless of its origins, free verse has come to be the dominant medium of modern African American poetry. In the course of its development, African American free verse has also drawn heavily from Black **vernacular** traditions, particularly of the religious **sermon** and of various types of African American music, including **spirituals, blues**, and **jazz**.

Fenton Johnson's poetry from the opening decades of the twentieth century draws on the forms of the spirituals, and **James Weldon Johnson**'s poems collected in *God's Trombones* (1927) use the sermon as a model. Other poets found flexible models for their poetry in more secular musical traditions. **Sterling A. Brown** includes the blues and work songs alongside the spirituals and at least one conventional poetic form, the **ballad**, in his first volume of poetry, *Southern Road* (1932). As the title of another first volume of poetry, *The Weary Blues* (1926), suggests, Langston Hughes likewise employed the three-line structure of the blues in some of his poetry, elsewhere using longer lines reminiscent of Walt Whitman or shorter lines recalling improvisational jazz pieces. **Michelle Cliff**'s "Within the Veil" (1985) is a third and more recent example of the use of the blues stanza as an organizing element that does not prescribe line length or number of stresses per line. Tony Bolden argues that such blues-based poetry is "resistance poetry," revising the Black vernacular musical form in order to describe and respond to black experiences "in styles that challenge conventional definitions of poetry" (37).

Particularly in the **Black Arts Movement**, free verse poetry became the primary artistic means of conveying a sense of directness, immediacy, and relevance to audiences. Perhaps all of the major poets active in that period who are frequently read and anthologized today—including Amiri Baraka, **Lucille Clifton**, Nikki Giovanni, June Jordan, **Audre Lorde, Michael S. Harper, Etheridge Knight**, and **Sonia Sanchez**—have written substantial works in free verse, as have many later poets. At its best, free verse as a form is limitless in its possibilities. **Alice Walker**'s "a woman is not a potted plant" (1991) demonstrates some of the strengths of the free verse form. The poem is held together only by sets of parallel grammatical constructions, none of which extends beyond a few lines, and this loose and changing form reflects and reinforces the liberating theme of the poem: a woman is not to be confined to the home and to live only to be caring and to be cared for by another. **Rita Dove** and

Colleen McElroy also have written free verse that is distinctive, original, and compelling. At its worst, however, free verse can, and often does, lack distinctiveness. Written quickly and easily, it can be just as quickly and easily forgotten.

Resources: Tony Bolden, *Afro-Blue: Improvisations in African American Poetry and Culture* (Urbana: University of Illinois Press, 2004); Stephen Henderson, *Understanding the New Black Poetry: Black Speech and Black Music as Poetic References* (New York: Morrow, 1973); Ron Padgett, ed., *The Teachers & Writers Handbook of Poetic Forms* (New York: Teachers & Writers Collaborative, 1987), 85–86; Arnold Rampersad, "W.E.B. Du Bois as a Man of Literature," *American Literature* 51, no. 1 (Mar. 1979), 50–68.

James B. Kelley

Fuller, Charles H., Jr. (born 1939). Playwright. In 1982, Charles Fuller won the Pulitzer Prize for *A Soldier's Play* (1982). He was the second African American playwright to win this prestigious award. Born in Pennsylvania, Fuller was not aware of racism until his teens, when he discovered that books he encountered reeked of racism toward Blacks. He decided to become a writer to "make a dent in the preponderance of antiblack material" ("Charles Fuller").

Fuller attended Villanova University, where he faced more racism. He remembers "a professor called his literary ambitions foolish," and "the editors laughed at him" when he submitted stories to the university magazine ("Charles Fuller"). Fuller left Villanova before graduating and, in 1959, joined the U.S. Army. In his off time, he continued to pursue his literary aspirations. Upon his discharge, he took several jobs and, with several others, started the Afro-American Theatre in **Philadelphia, Pennsylvania**.

Fuller got his first major theatrical opportunity when the McCarter Theater in Princeton, New Jersey, commissioned him to write *The Village: A Party in 1968* (1968). *The Village* is a play about an interracial community that collapses when the leader falls in love with a woman of his own race. This play was followed by others, such as *The Candidate* (1974), *In the Deepest Part of Sleep* (1974), and *Zooman and the Sign* (1980). Fuller received numerous awards and recognition for his work.

A Soldier's Play is about the murder of a Black sergeant on an army base during **World War II**. It is assumed that members of the Ku Klux Klan may be at fault. A Black officer, assigned to the case, reveals that the sergeant's own Black soldiers are to blame. Fuller also wrote the script for the movie version, *A Soldier's Story* (1984).

A Soldier's Play is representative of most of Fuller's work, in which he continually strives to expose racism. His focus is Black life, and his aim is to "yank us away from the idea that black people are stereotypical in any way, shape or form. By attacking the stereotype at the point of origin, you overthrow it" ("Charles Fuller").

Resources: Charles Fuller: *The Brownsville Raid* (perf. Negro Ensemble Company, Theater de Lys, New York City, 1976); *The Candidate* (perf. Negro Ensemble

Company, Henry Street Settlement, New York City, 1974); *In the Deepest Part of Sleep* (perf. Negro Ensemble Company, St. Marks Playhouse, New York City, 1976); *A Soldier's Play* (perf. Negro Ensemble Company, Theater Four, New York City, 1981; pub. New York: Hill and Wang, 1982); *The Village: A Party* (perf. McCarter Theater, Princeton, NJ, 1968); *Zooman and the Sign* (perf. Negro Ensemble Company, Theater de Lys, New York City, 1980); "Charles Fuller," in *Contemporary Black Biography*, vol. 8 (Detroit: Gale, 1994), also *Biography Resource Center*, Info2go, Tacoma Public Library, Tacoma, WA, http://galenet.galegroup.com/servlet/BioRC.com; Esther Harriott, *American Voices: Five Contemporary Playwrights in Essays and Interviews* (Jefferson, NC: McFarland, 1988); Paul Carter Harrison, ed., *Totem Voices: Plays from the Black World Repertory* (New York: Grove Press, 1989); Norman Jewison, director, *A Soldier's Story* (Columbia/TriStar Studios, 1984).

Gladys L. Knight

Fuller, Hoyt (1923–1981). Critic, editor, and professor. Born in **Atlanta, Georgia,** Fuller attended Wayne State University in **Detroit, Michigan,** and received a degree in literature and journalism. He is recognized as a significant participant in the **Black Arts Movement** of the 1960s and 1970s.

Fuller is perhaps most widely known for his 1968 essay "Towards a Black Aesthetic." This essay lays out the aims of revolutionary Black writers to define a Black aesthetic, one Fuller envisages as "a system of isolating and evaluating the artistic works of black people which reflect the special character and imperatives of black experience" (Gates and McKay, 1812). Fuller argues that such an aesthetic is necessary to combat the inevitable racism of White critics who, in either their rejection of or their pitying praise of the work of Black writers, continue the process of racist oppression. He argues persuasively that Black writers must define their own work according to their own standards. The essay is included in *The Norton Anthology of African American Literature*, edited by Gates and McKay, as well as other anthologies (1810–1816).

Fuller is also known as an editor. Most notably, he was the editor of **Negro Digest** in the late 1960s. *Negro Digest* was a national magazine that reported the social, political, and cultural activities of Black America. Fuller changed the name to *Black World* in 1970 and supported reporting that upheld the aims of the Black Arts Movement. In 1976, the publisher of *Black World* discontinued the magazine, despite protests, because of its increasing radicalism. Fuller then founded *First World*, a magazine and collective that he supported while teaching at Cornell University. He was instrumental in the establishment of the Organization of Black American Culture (**OBAC**). He also taught at Columbia College and Northwestern University. In 1971, Fuller published a set of autobiographical essays titled *Journey to Africa*, in which he detailed his experiences traveling in Africa as a young man. He died suddenly of a heart attack in 1981.

Fuller's influence as a mentor to other African American writers is arguably his most significant contribution to African American and American literature, even though the effect of such mentoring is difficult to document. He is often mentioned in conjunction with **Larry Neal** and George E. Kent as elder statesmen of the Black Arts Movement. The 1984 collection titled *Black Women Writers (1950–1980): A Critical Evaluation*, edited by **Mari Evans**, opens with this dedication:

> For Hoyt W. Fuller Jr., who planned to be a part of this book; for Larry P. Neal, who did not have the chance to respond; and for George E. Kent, who provided a revision for his article two weeks prior to his death. Their names are here in figure and in fact: earned space. They were our clear voices, our "long-distance runners." They bless our efforts.

Among the historical and contemporary writers Fuller is known to have championed or mentored are **Nella Larsen**, **Paule Marshall**, **Carolyn M. Rodgers**, and **Mary Helen Washington**. **Houston A. Baker, Jr.**, in his 1988 essay "An Editor from Chicago: Reflections on the Work of Hoyt Fuller," writes, "His legacy, finally, is the dramatic motion forward of the black expressive spirit that he resolutely championed during the past two decades of our collective cultural life in America" (168). A collection of Fuller's papers, letters, publications, and photographs from the years 1940–1981 is kept at the Woodruff Library of the Atlanta University Center. (*See* **Baraka, Amiri**; **Gayle, Addison, Jr.**)

Resources: Houston A. Baker, Jr., *Afro-American Poetics: Revisions of Harlem and the Black Aesthetic* (Madison: University of Wisconsin Press, 1988); Mari Evans, ed., *Black Women Writers (1950–1980): A Critical Evaluation* (Garden City, NY: Anchor Books, 1984); Hoyt Fuller, *Journey to Africa* (Chicago: Third World Press, 1971); Henry Louis Gates, Jr., and Nellie Y. McKay, eds., *The Norton Anthology of African American Literature* (New York: Norton, 1996).

Rachael Barnett

Fullilove, Eric James (born 1954). Novelist. The author of three genre novels, Fullilove was born in Elizabeth, New Jersey. His father was the first African American president of the Essex County Medical Society, and his mother was the first African American, and first female, president of the Newark Board of Education.

Fullilove completed a B.S. in urban studies, with a minor in economics, at the Massachusetts Institute of Technology and then enrolled in MIT's Sloan School of Management in finance and statistics, where he received an M.S. in finance. He next attended Northwestern University's Kellogg Graduate School of Management and obtained a professional accounting certificate. He subsequently completed the requirements to become a certified public accountant.

After holding positions with several corporations and philanthropic organizations, including Arthur Young (now Ernst and Young), CBS, Housing Works, and Teach for America, Fullilove became a regional vice president of internal audit with Young and Rubicam, an international firm specializing in communications and advertising. In 2002, he joined Scholastic Books as a vice president and head of their internal audit department. He was promoted to chief financial officer of the company.

Fullilove's first two novels have been typically classified as **science fiction**. *Circle of One* (1996) was named by *Locus* magazine as one of the year's best first novels, and it was included on *Starlog* magazine's list of the best science fiction titles of the year. A cyberpunk thriller set in the near future, the novel focuses on Jenny Sixa, a telepathic detective with the Homicide Division of the **Los Angeles, California**, Police Department. She is able to recover the final thoughts of murder victims, and she tracks a serial killer who has devised a way to leave tantalizing clues to his identity for her to recover in this manner. *The Stranger* (1997) is another novel featuring Jenny Sixa. In this instance, she is investigating two sets of serial killings, one involving the murders of teenage boys whose identities are difficult to trace and the other involving the murders of randomly selected young women; she is unsettled by her intuition that the cases may somehow be related.

Fullilove's most recent novel, *Blowback* (2003), is a technothriller set in the present. It focuses on Richard Whelan, the national security adviser to the president. A relatively young African American with impressive credentials and a winning personality, Whelan seems destined for a long and distinguished political career. But his personal life and his political ambitions are completely disrupted when he is implicated in a brutal murder. As he becomes a fugitive from the law and tries to prove his innocence, he uncovers evidence that his personal troubles may be connected to an international conspiracy involving the renegade use of nuclear weapons along the volatile frontier between India and Pakistan.

Resources: Jonathan Bing, "Review of *The Stranger*," *Publishers Weekly*, Oct. 6, 1997, p. 81; Connie Fletcher, "Review of *Blowback*," *Booklist*, Aug. 2003, 2096; Eric James Fullilove: *Blowback* (New York: Amistad, 2001); *Circle of One* (New York: Bantam Spectra, 1996); *The Stranger* (New York: Bantam Spectra, 1997); Jeff Zaleski, "Review of *Blowback*, *Publishers Weekly*, July 9, 2003, pp. 39–40.

Martin Kich

Fulton, David Bryant (1863–1941). Librarian, polemicist, and nonfiction writer. Fulton's best-known work, *Hanover; or, The Persecution of the Lowly. A Story of the Wilmington Massacre (Hanover)* was published in 1899. Fulton was born in Fayetteville, North Carolina, to Lavinia Robinson Fulton and Benjamin Fulton, both ex-slaves from North Carolina. In 1867 he and his family moved to Wilmington, North Carolina, where Fulton attended the Williston School and the Gregory Normal Institute. He moved to **Brooklyn, New York**, in 1887 and began working for the Pullman Palace Car Company in 1888. His first book-length publication, *Recollections of a Sleeping Car Porter* (1892), which bears the pseudonym he employed throughout his literary career, Jack Thorne, chronicles his experience as a Black porter. Fulton left the Pullman Company after nine years of service and worked at Sears Roebuck, a music publishing house, and the Central Branch of the YMCA in

Brooklyn before becoming librarian of the Negro Society for Historical Research in 1911.

Part exposé and part fiction, *Hanover* illustrates Fulton's efforts to present a truthful account of the White supremacist insurgency that took place in Wilmington in 1898. Fulton wrote primarily short stories and newspaper articles that brought him fame in Brooklyn around 1903–1906. *Eagle Clippings* (1907), a selection of Fulton's newspaper articles and Pullman Porter stories, is a good, if spare, representation of his oeuvre. "Race Unification: How It May Be Accomplished," published in *African Times and Orient Review* in 1913, shows Fulton's race pride as rooted in his belief in Black solidarity. He was also notable for his active interest in the welfare of African American women, best exemplified in his essay *A Plea for Social Justice for the Negro Woman*, issued by the Negro Society for Historical Research in 1912. His poem "Mother of Mine: Ode to the Negro Woman," appeared in 1923. Fulton married twice: Virginia Moore in 1884, and Katie Gummer in 1917. He died on November 14, 1941, in Brooklyn.

Resources: Jack Thorne [David Bryant Fulton]: *Eagle Clippings* (Brooklyn: D. B. Fulton, 1907); *Hanover; or, The Persecution of the Lowly* (1899; [place unknown]: M. C. L. Hill, 1901; repr. New York: Arno Press, 1969); *Mother of Mine: Ode to the Negro Woman* (New York: A. V. Bernier, 1923); *A Plea for Social Justice for the Negro Woman* (Yonkers, NY: Lincoln Press Association, 1912); *Poem, Abraham Lincoln . . . Written at the Request of the Colored Citizens' Lincoln Centenary Committee . . . and Read Before Two Thousand Five Hundred People at the Baptist Temple, Brooklyn, N.Y., February 12th, 1909* (Brooklyn, 1909); *Recollections of a Sleeping Car Porter* (Jersey City, NJ: Doan & Pilson, 1892).

Jeehyun Lim

Furious Flower Conference (1994, 2004). The first Furious Flower Conference was organized in 1994 by professor Joanne V. Gabbin of James Madison University. The purpose of this conference was to convene what Gabbin has described as "the largest gathering of poets, critics, and scholars in more than two decades" to discuss and celebrate African American poetry from 1960 to the present (Thomas, par. 1). The conference was dedicated to those poets who spoke out against various forms of racial oppression, including racism, sexism, economic exploitation, and violence.

The conference was dedicated to the Pulitzer Prize–winning poet **Gwendolyn Brooks**, the keynote speaker at the gathering, which drew approximately thirty-five Black activist poets, most of whom rose to prominence in the 1960s or 1970s, as well as approximately 200 scholars. The poets who attended were politically active in the **Civil Rights Movement, Black Nationalism**, and the **Black Arts Movement**. Rather than focus on the militant stands of that period, as had previously been done, the focus of this conference instead was to analyze the poetics of the poetry (Hawkins). Among the members of the conference were **Sonia Sanchez, Amiri Baraka, Nikki Giovanni**, Gwendolyn Brooks, **Haki R. Madhubuti, Lucille Clifton**, and Bernice

Johnson Reagon. The conference was necessary, according to Gabbin, because "Many of the poets who . . . gather here, like Amiri Baraka and Sonia Sanchez, were so busy fighting for justice, fighting for liberation and equality, that there wasn't the emphasis on trying to document the movement. And only now are historians going back and trying to assess the movement beyond seeing these poets as agents of social change" (Hawkins). This claim is reflected in the conference title, "Furious Flower," taken from Gwendolyn Brooks's poem "The Second Sermon on the Warplan."

Gabbin, who gave the conference its title, has said that the "furious" of the title reflects the anger, struggle, and frequent militancy in the poetry, and the "flower" refers to the beauty of the verse, and ways that these poets often broke with traditional verse and experimented with **jazz** and other traditionally Black music forms (Hindley).

Movements such as Black nationalism in 1960s altered the shape of African American art, since at that time art was so closely linked with political activism. This, in itself, brought the art to the masses, and widened the appeal of Black writing to both Black and White audiences. Many who study this period are not aware of the kinds of global as well as local scopes these writers came from, as is evident in this quotation from Gwendolyn Brooks: "They need to know that I am interested in Winnie Mandela, not just in **Harriet Tubman** and **Sojourner Truth**. They need to know that I am interested in what goes on in the streets" ("Furious Flower").

Out of this 1994 conference Gabbin edited a collection of essays and interviews with practicing poets titled *The Furious Flowering of African American Poetry* (1999). With this text readers come into a dialogue with the "leading poets and critics of African American literature and culture" through the essays that assess the work of the Black literary framework the poets arise from. Gabbin is a professor of English at James Madison University and is the author of *Sterling A. Brown: Building the Black Aesthetic Tradition* (1994). In 1994 she created the Furious Flower Poetry Center, a historic resource for the legacy of African American poetry. From this first conference Gabbin also compiled a video series, *Furious Flower: An Anthology of African American Poetry 1960– 1995*. The video series is taken from taped performances of the 1994 conference, and is divided into four volumes: *Elders, Warriors, Seers,* and *Initiates*. Among the *Elders* are **Jerry Ward, Jr.**, and **Mari Evans**; *Warriors* include Amiri Baraka, Haki Madhubuti, Sonia Sanchez, and Nikki Giovanni; *Seers* features **Rita Dove** and **Sherley Anne Williams**, among others; and *Initiates* features the "Dark Room Collective," which includes **Kevin Young** and **Sharan Strange**.

In September 2004 the Furious Flower II Conference was held in Harrisonburg, Virginia. It included readings and discussions by alumni of the first conference, among them Amiri Baraka, Rita Dove, Nikki Giovanni, Lucille Clifton, Haki Madhubuti, and Sonia Sanchez (" 'Furious Flower II'). Like the previous conference, this one celebrated past and future Black poetic expression with forty-six poets and a multitude of scholars. Gabbin believes this new conference "set the agenda in African American poetry for the 21st century" ("'Furious Flower II'"). For this reason, the conference included new award-winning African American poets and **hip-hop** writers, as well as presentations of critical papers and roundtable discussions on both the 1960 radical art and the future of African American poetry. The keynote speaker was literary critic **Houston A. Baker, Jr.**

In anticipation of the second conference, Gabbin edited *Furious Flower: African American Poetry from the Black Arts Movement to the Present*, a collection of poetry, biographies, and performance photographs of many of the "Furious Flower" participants of the 1994 conference. This text has been praised as providing "a fascinating collective portrayal of African American poetry at the close of the twentieth century—as well as an indication of where it may be headed as we enter the twenty-first" ("Furious Flower").

Resources: Gwendolyn Brooks: "Furious Flower: African American Poetry from the Black Arts Movement to the Present," *Furious Flower*, University Press of Virginia, www.upress.virginia.edu/books/gabbin2.html; "'Furious Flower II' to Draw Black Poets to JMU," *James Madison University News Bureau*, http://www.reviews.aalbc.com/furious_flower.htm; "The Furious Flowering of African American Poetry," *The Furious Flowering*, University Press of Virginia, www.upress.virginia.edu/books/gabbin.html; *Selected Poems* (New York: Harper & Row, 1963); Joanne V. Gabbin, ed.: *Furious Flower: African American Poetry from the Black Arts Movement to the Present* (Charlottesville: University of Virginia Press, 2004); *The Furious Flowering of American Poetry* (Charlottesville: University of Virginia Press, 1999); Meredith Hindley, "The Furious Flower: Black Poets Discuss Their Craft," *Humanities* 15, no. 5 (Sept./Oct. 1994), 28–29; Lorenzo Thomas, "The Furious Flowering of African American Poetry," *African American Review*, Spring 2001, also *African American Review*, www.findarticles.com/p/articles.

Lin Knutson

G

Gaines, Ernest James (born 1933). Novelist and short story writer. Gaines is noted for his poignant portrayals of the rural Southern African American experience. The settings of his published works (six novels and one collection of short stories) collectively span a period of 110 years and vividly pay homage to the place where he spent the first fifteen years of his life: River Lake Plantation in Oscar, Louisiana.

Born on January 15, 1933, to Manuel and Adrienne Gaines, Ernest James ("E.J.") Gaines, along with his six younger siblings, was cared for by his great-aunt Augusteen Jefferson while his parents worked in the fields. After his parents separated and his mother moved—first to **New Orleans, Louisiana**, to seek work and then to Vallejo, California (1947), to join her second husband, a merchant marine—Gaines was placed under the full-time guardianship of Aunt Augusteen ("Aunt Teen").

Unshaken by her lifelong disability or the wheelchair given to her by a social service agency, Aunt Augusteen performed daily chores by propelling herself across the floor with her hands; she also cultivated a small garden by sliding down the steps leading to her home. Of his aunt, Gaines would later comment, "she had the *greatest* impact on my life, not only as a writer but as a man" (Lowe, 121). Miss Augusteen Jefferson would eventually become one of the inspirations for the many strong maternal figures celebrated by Gaines as well as one of the persons to whom *The Autobiography of Miss Jane Pittman* (1971) would be dedicated.

It was during his early years on the sugarcane plantation that Gaines developed a keen sense of the language patterns that distinguish his fiction, for he was often called upon to read and write letters for the elderly; also, because of his aunt's confinement, people from the community would frequent her home, unwittingly supplying Gaines with a rich reservoir of material. He recalls "a place where people sat around and chewed sugar cane and roasted sweet potatoes and peanuts in the ashes and sat on ditch banks and told tales and sat on porches and went into the swamps and went into the fields—that's what [he] came from" (Gaudet and Wooten, 231), a heritage firmly rooted in the African American folk tradition.

At the age of eight, Gaines began working in the fields for 50 cents a day and performing other chores that would assist the family. Laboring in the fields, and eventually the swamps, provided him with an abiding love for the land and an understanding of the Black peasantry of this country—an understanding that has made him one of few African American writers to intimately explore the plight of such rural inhabitants (Lowe, 17). Years later, Gaines would additionally credit Russian writers such as Leo Tolstoy, Anton Chekhov, and Ivan Turgenev as early influences on his writing due to their ability to portray peasants in a manner that was more realistic than any of the American "caricatures" of Black and poor people he had read (Lowe, 20).

Between planting and harvesting seasons, Gaines attended rural schools until 1945, when he began three years of formal training at St. Augustine's Catholic School for African American Children. The school was located in New Roads, Louisiana, a neighboring city that is often identified as the "Bayonne" of Gaines's fiction.

When he was fifteen (1948), Gaines joined his mother and stepfather, Ralph Colar, Sr., to continue his education; there were no secondary schools in the parish that his family could send him to. This move to California, according to Gaines, was the "best thing that ever happened to [him]" (Lowe, 176), for its timing enabled him to hold on to a knowledgeable yet unembittered past: "Had I left five years earlier, I would not have had enough experiences. Had I stayed five years longer, I would have been broken—in prison, dead, insane" (Lowe, 279).

Unlike the racially segmented Louisiana parish from which he came, the integrated housing project in Vallejo offered Gaines an ethnically diverse environment. Filled with poor Whites, Japanese, Chinese, Filipinos, Latinos, and Blacks, the small suburb, located approximately thirty miles from **San Francisco, California**, assisted Gaines in gaining a broader view of the human experience, one that would result in the compassionate portrayal of all of his characters, both Black and White.

In 1948, Gaines's family relocated to a downtown area of Vallejo, and the impressionable youngster fell under the negative influence of a group of teenage boys. However, his stepfather, the individual around whom many of Gaines's strong male characters are built, sternly directed him away from the streets; consequently, Gaines, an avid reader who missed his native Louisiana, found solace in the downtown library.

In an account of his early reading experiences, Gaines admits that he was drawn to authors who wrote about **the South**. He concentrated on their descriptions of the natural surroundings, such as "the odor of grass and trees after a summer rain." After exhausting the library's supply of Southern writers, he "began to read any writer who wrote about nature or about the people who worked the land" ("Miss Jane and I," 27). William Faulkner, Ernest Hemingway, and the aforementioned Russians would figure prominently on this list; still, Gaines's inability to find his own people in the library's selections prompted him in 1949 to write his own novel, an early sketch of *Catherine Carmier* (1964). It would take years of training and fine-tuning his craft, however, before the novel would be realized, for the initial manuscript—typed on both sides of paper that was cut in half to resemble a book—was returned by a New York publisher in its original packaging, and consequently incinerated by the dejected writer (Lowe, 279–280).

The next ten years saw several milestones in Gaines's experiential development. After graduating from high school in 1951 and Vallejo Junior College in 1953, Gaines took a break from school and served in Guam in the U.S. Army (1953–1955). He then went on to receive a bachelor's degree from San Francisco State College (1957). In 1956 and 1957, the budding writer published his first short stories, "The Turtles" and "The Boy in the Double-Breasted Suit," in San Francisco State's literary journal, *Transfer*; he also received a Wallace Stegner Creative Writing Fellowship to Stanford University (1958–1959).

Ernest Gaines, 1996. © Bassouls Sophie/Corbis Sygma.

For Ernest Gaines, college successes signaled the beginning of a career that would be filled with an array of prestigious awards, including a Joseph Henry Jackson Award for Best Novel-in-Progress (1959), a Rockefeller Grant-in-Aid (1970), two Pulitzer Prize nominations (1971, 1993), a Guggenheim Fellowship (1972), a National Book Critics Circle Award (1993), a $355,000 MacArthur Fellowship (1993), which is often called a "Genius Grant," an Oprah Winfrey Book Club distinction (1997), and a National Humanities Medal (2000), which was awarded by President Clinton (Doyle, 24).

Furthermore, the film adaptations of four works—*The Autobiography of Miss Jane Pittman* on CBS (1974), "The Sky Is Gray" on PBS (1980), *A Gathering of Old Men* on CBS (1987), and *A Lesson Before Dying* on HBO (1999)—as well as a PBS documentary of his life (1993) brought Gaines additional exposure and recognition.

Since 1983, Gaines has held the tenured position of Writer-in-Residence at the University of Louisiana at Lafayette (Doyle, 24). In 1993, he married Dianne Saulney, a Miami, Florida, attorney and Louisiana native. Currently, he divides his time between the two states.

Gaines's first novel, *Catherine Carmier*, began as his attempt to "write a simple little novel about people at home" ("Miss Jane and I," 28). Generally classified by scholars as a love story, the novel is set in Louisiana in the early 1960s and focuses on the life of Jackson Bradley. Having recently graduated from college in California, Jackson returns to the woman who raised him (Aunt Charlotte) and to the place where he was raised (Grover Plantation), intending to visit for only one month. However, his plans are complicated when he finds himself smitten with the title character, a beautiful **Creole** whose loyalty to keeping her family together dictates that she remain in the South.

The possibility of a relationship between Jackson and Catherine sets in motion a story that addresses much more than love, for in addition to exploring their feelings for one another, Jackson and Catherine must confront long-standing cultural issues that pervade this community—primarily the tensions between the Creoles (epitomized by Raoul Carmier) and the darker-skinned Blacks, especially Jackson, who wants to take Raoul's daughter away. Gaines also explores the impact of the Cajun farmers' encroachment on land historically that has been cultivated by Black tenant farmers. Standing alone against the Cajuns' machinery, Raoul refuses to give in to this changing way of life.

Gaines's second novel, *Of Love and Dust* (1967), set in 1948, reveals the communal impact of interracial relationships in the South. The novel's protagonist is Marcus Payne, an impetuous Black man who has been bailed out of jail in exchange for five years of labor on Marshall Hebert's plantation. From the moment of his arrival, however, Marcus declares to James Kelly, the first plantation worker he encounters (and the novel's narrator), that he has no plan to repay his debt. Throughout the novel, he also makes it clear that he will not conform to the expectations of his environment, and even sets himself apart from the other field workers by wearing short-sleeved silk shirts and dress shoes to work. However, his final message of rebellion comes forth when, after failing to win the affections of the Cajun overseer's Black mistress, he dares to pursue a relationship with Louise Bonbon, the overseer's White wife.

Gaines's next book-length publication, *Bloodline* (1968), is a collection of five short stories that explores many of the central character types, plots, and themes of his longer works. In the first story, "A Long Day in November" (initially published in 1964), a young child (Sonny) describes the day's events when his mother leaves home because of his father's obsession with his car. In 1971, Gaines also published this story as a children's book. The second story, "The Sky Is Gray" (previously published in 1963), records the journey of a young boy (James) to town on a cold day to have his tooth pulled and the lesson in manhood that he learns through his mother's tenacity and love. The third story, "Three Men," tells of Proctor Lewis, a hormone-driven nineteen-year-old who turns himself in to the police after killing another Black man. In the collection's title story, "Bloodline," Copper, the illegitimate **mulatto** son of Walter Laurent, returns to Louisiana to claim his birthright: a share of the Laurent plantation. The final story of the collection, "Just like a Tree," uses shifting narration to describe the evening before the community's matriarch, Aunt Fe, is to be moved north by family members trying to protect her from racially motivated bombings in the area. The story was originally published in 1963. Its central figure, Aunt Fe, is often seen as the prototype for Gaines's most memorable character, Jane Pittman—the protagonist of his fourth, and perhaps, most critically acclaimed, work.

Beginning during the **Civil War** and ending during the initial stages of the **Civil Rights Movement**, *The Autobiography of Miss Jane Pittman* (1971) recounts the life of a 110-year-old Black woman. Readers are introduced to a ten-year-old slave (Ticey) as she hauls water for soldiers who are passing through. A significant event in the young girl's life occurs when a Yankee officer gives her a new name, Jane Brown, which she thinks is the prettiest name she has ever heard. She keeps the name until adulthood, when she falls in love and agrees to cohabit with Joe Pittman, a widower and horse breaker.

Although Jane's barrenness prevents her from biologically giving birth, during the course of her life she becomes a maternal figure to a number of characters, most significantly Ned, a five-year-old who is left in her charge after emancipation when his mother is killed by a group of raiding patrollers. Mirroring the same spirit with which his mother fought back, Ned devotes his life to the fight for civil rights.

Believing as a young girl that "Luzana must be the whole wide world" (33), and as an adult that she is "married to this place" (75), Jane Pittman remains in Louisiana her entire life. Her credible recollections of significant historical events (such as **Reconstruction** and the floods of 1912 and 1927), historical figures (such as Huey Long and **Jackie Robinson**), and tragic events (such as the massacre of northward-bound former slaves, and the murders of civil rights activists Ned and Jimmy) reveal why critics, scholars, and students alike find it hard to believe Miss Jane is not a real person but a "creation of [Gaines's] imagination" ("Miss Jane and I," 23).

Gaines's fifth publication, *In My Father's House* (1978), deviates from his established rural setting by venturing into the city of St. Adrienne, Louisiana. Reverend Phillip Martin, a prominent religious and civil rights leader, is haunted by his past when a stranger, Robert X, arrives in town, seeking revenge against his father, after twenty years, for not taking responsibility for his illegitimate children. The novel experienced a cold reception from reviewers.

In his sixth work, *A Gathering of Old Men* (1983), Gaines returns to the more receptive and familiar rural environment. Set in Louisiana in the 1970s, the novel utilizes shifting narration to depict the unexpected events that occur one hot day on the Marshall plantation. Cajun farmer Beau Boutan lies dead in Mathu's yard. Therefore, in an effort to protect Mathu (the person whom everyone believes is guilty) and to take a stand for once in their lives, eighteen old men assert their manhood when they gather at Mathu's house with twelve-gauge shotguns that have fired number 5 shells—the same gauge and shell as the murder weapon. As the White sheriff questions the men one by one, he discovers that all of them claim to have killed Beau, for somewhere in each man's history lies a motive that has festered for years.

A Lesson Before Dying (1993) is Gaines's most recent publication. Like *Of Love and Dust*, this novel is also set in the 1940s. However, while the protagonist of the earlier novel is released after killing a Black man, the later work's protagonist, Jefferson, is sent to the electric chair after being wrongfully convicted of killing a White man. In response to the defense attorney's attempt to prove Jefferson's innocence by likening him to a hog, Jefferson's godmother and her friend commission Grant Wiggins, the plantation schoolteacher, to teach Jefferson how to walk to the chair like a man.

Collectively, the works of Ernest Gaines reveal one man's love and understanding of the place of his youth. The remarkable skill with which he reconstructs the rural settings, events, and characters gives credence to his assertion that "[t]he early impressions on the artist are the most lasting" (Rowell, 40).

Resources: Primary Sources: Ernest J. Gaines: "Auntie and the Black Experience in Louisiana," in *Louisiana Tapestry: The Ethnic Weave of St. Landry Parish*, ed. Vaughan B. Baker and Jean T. Kreamer (Lafayette: Center for Louisiana Studies, University of Southwest Louisiana, 1983), 20–29; *The Autobiography of Miss Jane Pittman* (New York: Bantam, 1971); *Bloodline* (1968; repr. New York: Norton, 1976); "Bloodline in Ink," *CEA Critic* 51, no. 2 (1989), 2–12; *Catherine Carmier* (New York: Atheneum, 1964); *A Gathering of Old Men* (New York: Knopf, 1983); "Home: A Photo Essay," *Callaloo* 1, no. 3 (May 1978), 52–67; *In My Father's House* (New York: Knopf, 1978); *A Lesson Before Dying* (New York: Knopf, 1993); "Miss Jane Pittman's Background," *New York Times Book Review*, Aug. 10, 1975, p. 23; "Miss Jane and I," *Callaloo* 1, no. 3 (May 1978), 23–38; *Of Love and Dust* (New York: Dial Press, 1967); "A Very Big Order: Reconstructing Identity," *The Southern Review* 26 (1990), 245–253. **Secondary Sources:** Valerie Babb, *Ernest Gaines* (Boston: Twayne, 1991); Karen Carmean, *Ernest J. Gaines: A Critical Companion* (Westport, CT: Greenwood Press, 1998); Mary Ellen Doyle, *Voices from the Quarters: The Fiction of Ernest J. Gaines* (Baton Rouge: Louisiana State University Press, 2002); David C. Estes, ed., *Critical Reflections on the Fiction of Ernest J. Gaines* (Athens: University of Georgia Press, 1994); Marcia Gaudet, "Folklore in the Writing of Ernest J. Gaines," *The Griot* 3, no. 1 (1984), 9–16; Marcia Gaudet and Carl Wooten: *Porch Talk with Ernest Gaines: Conversations on the Writer's Craft* (Baton Rouge: Louisiana State University Press, 1990); "Talking with Ernest J. Gaines," *Callaloo* 11, no. 2 (1988), 229–243; John Lowe, ed., *Conversations with Ernest Gaines* (Jackson: University Press of Mississippi, 1995); Charles H. Rowell, "This Louisiana Thing That Drives Me: An Interview with Ernest J. Gaines," *Callaloo* 1, no. 3 (1978): 39–51.

Veronica Adams Yon

Gaines, Patrice (born 1949). Nonfiction writer and journalist. Gaines grew up in a military family and spent part of her youth on the U.S. Marine Corps base in Quantico, Virginia. Later her life became extremely difficult as she suffered from racism, abusive relationships with men, and addiction to heroin. At age twenty-one, she was arrested for selling narcotics, spent time in jail, but reached a plea agreement that enabled her to avoid going to prison. Gaines changed the direction of her life and ultimately joined the staff of the *Washington Post* as a newswriter. She chronicles her journey in *Laughing In the Dark: From Colored Girl to Woman of Color—A Journey from Prison to Power* (1994). The book includes poignant writing about a friend and coworker at the *Post* who was among the first Americans to die of complications from AIDS. She received an award for her journalistic commentary from the National Association of Black Journalists, and she was part of a team at the *Washington Post* that was nominated for a Pulitzer Prize in journalism. She is also the author of *Moments of Grace: Meeting the Challenge to Change* (1998).

Resources: Patrice Gaines: *Laughing in the Dark* (New York: Crown, 1994); *Moments of Grace: Meeting the Challenge to Change* (New York: Crown, 1997).

Hans Ostrom

Garnet, Henry Highland (1815–1882). Activist and minister. Now best known for his radical "Address to the Slaves of the United States of America," Garnet was a lifelong political activist.

Born into **slavery** in Kent County, Maryland, Garnet escaped with his family in 1824. Eventually, they settled in New York City, where Garnet attended the African Free School (which counted **Samuel Cornish** among its agents). Garnet became a sailor, but because of a leg injury that later resulted in amputation, he decided, in 1831, to return to New York and attend the High School for Colored Youth. He later attended Noyes Academy in New Hampshire and the Oneida Institute in Whitesboro, New York, and married Julia Williams.

After he was ordained as a Presbyterian minister in 1841 and accepted a charge at the Liberty Street Church in Troy, New York, Garnet quickly became an important voice in the American and Foreign Anti-Slavery Society and the Black convention movement. It was in this latter role that he delivered his infamous "Address to the Slaves of the United States of America" (1843). The stirring call to arms, which carried echoes of **David Walker**'s *Appeal* and considered slave revolution, was rejected as too militant by the delegates (**Frederick Douglass** chief among them) after heated debate. In 1848, Garnet published it in a new edition of Walker's *Appeal*; that same year, he also published his lecture *The Past and Present Condition, and the Destiny, of the Colored Race*.

Garnet traveled in England and the West Indies between 1850 and 1855, then returned to the United States to take charge of New York City's Shiloh Presbyterian Church. After another trip abroad in 1861, he moved to **Washington, D.C.**'s Fifteenth Street Presbyterian Church in 1864. In the following year, he became the first African American to preach at the White House. He served for two years as the president of Avery College in **Pittsburgh, Pennsylvania**, and returned to Shiloh in 1870. By now a widower, he married Sarah Smith Tompkins in 1879. Garnet traveled to Liberia in 1881 as the U.S. minister, and died there in 1882. (*See* **Abolitionist Movement**.)

Resources: Henry Highland Garnet, *The Past and Present Condition, and the Destiny, of the Colored Race: A Discourse Delivered at the Fiftieth Anniversary of the Female Benevolent Society of Troy, New York, Feb. 14, 1848* (Troy, NY: J. C. Kneeland, 1848); Joel Schor, *Henry Highland Garnet* (Westport, CT: Greenwood Press, 1977); Sterling Stuckey, "Henry Highland Garnet," in *Black Leaders of the Nineteenth Century*, ed. Leon Litwack and August Meier (Urbana: University of Illinois Press, 1988), 128–147; David E. Swift, *Black Prophets of Justice* (Baton Rouge: Louisiana State University Press, 1989); David Walker and Henry Highland Garnet, *Walker's Appeal, With a Brief Sketch of His Life* (New York: J. H. Tobitt, 1848).

Eric Gardner

Garvey, Marcus (1887–1940). Pamphleteer, publisher, political leader, and poet. This prolific writer for the Pan-African cause, who instigated the first worldwide movement devoted to the universal improvement of people of African descent, was born in St. Ann's Bay, Jamaica. He moved to Kingston and worked in a print shop, and later established a newspaper, *The Watchman*. In 1908 he led Jamaica's first printers' strike. He wrote *The Struggling Mass* (1910) and traveled throughout Central and South America to learn about the conditions of Blacks. Upon his return to Jamaica in 1911, he was determined to alleviate the appalling conditions of West Indian laborers, and appealed for government assistance. Seeking further support, he went to England, where he wrote for Dusé Mohammed Ali's *African Times and Oriental Review* (1912).

While in London he was enormously influenced by **Booker T. Washington's** *Up from Slavery*. Garvey returned to Jamaica with the goal of "uniting all the Negro peoples of the world into one great body to establish a country and Government absolutely their own" (A. Garvey, 126). He founded the Universal Negro Improvement Association (UNIA) and published *The Negro Race and Its Problems* (1914). Realizing he had to raise money to fund his ambitious program, he contacted Washington, who subsequently invited him to visit Tuskegee Institute. But Garvey soon found the road to solidarity was blocked by apathy among Black day laborers and hostility from lighter-skinned middle-class African Americans who did not want to be identified as "negroes." (*See* **Negro; New Negro, The; Talented Tenth**.)

After Washington died (1915), Garvey went directly New York City. Despite an inauspicious first public lecture, he pushed on with a thirty-eight-state speaking tour. In 1918, beginning with just thirteen members, the New York City branch of UNIA was founded and its "constitution" was written, and the **Negro World** began publication. All of these activities stemmed from Garvey's dream of Blacks running their own businesses, catering to their needs. This ran the gamut from the manufacturing of Black-skinned dolls to the incorporation of a steamship line by and for Blacks, the Black Star Line (BSL). At the height of the movement there were 1,200 UNIA branches, and so, in 1919, Garvey's activities came under the intense scrutiny of J. Edgar Hoover, head of a new division of the Department of Justice (which became the Federal Bureau of Investigation in 1935). Since his responsibilities included arresting and deporting suspected Communists and radicals, Hoover had his operatives infiltrate Garvey's ranks, which resulted, ironically, in the hiring of the first Black agents.

Negro World (UNIA's weekly publication from 1918 through the early 1930s) was banned in parts of the Caribbean at about the same time that the BSL raised enough capital to purchase its first, if ill-fated, ship, the S.S. *Yarmouth*, unofficially rechristened the S.S. *Frederick Douglass*. Its send-off was a stirring symbol for investors and well-wishers worldwide, but, unbeknownst to Garvey, this thirty-year-old cargo ship needed extensive repairs. A second voyage, launched in January 1920, just before Prohibition, carried whisky to Cuba; two days later, after listing badly, it was rescued by the U.S. Coast Guard and brought back to port; its multimillion-dollar cargo was seized, so none of the profit was realized. After several other unfortunate episodes, it was at last dry-docked and the BSL was forced to defer all payments. Although two other ships had been purchased, Garvey looked toward other avenues of investment and, in 1920, formed the Negro Factory Corporation.

Also in 1920, the First UNIA International Convention was held at Madison Square Garden in New York City with delegates from twenty-five countries. Garvey was elected "Provisional President of Africa" and a "Declaration of Rights" was adopted, in which serious grievances were aired. Toward the end of the document, it was specified that red, black, and green were to be the official colors "of the Negro race" (colors still in use today, as can be seen, for example, in the flags of Kenya and the African National Congress). One of the principal aims of UNIA, featured prominently on its handbills, was "To establish a government for Negroes in Africa where they will be given the opportunity to develop themselves." Garvey's doctrine of immigration, separatism, and racial purity, however, was not met with universal acclaim. It offended, among others, **W.E.B. Du Bois**, who in "Back to Africa" objected to Garvey's "West Indian conception of the color line" (*see* **Back-to-Africa Movement**). This criticism is echoed in Charles S. Johnson's 1923 sociological essay "Opportunity." That same year "The Madness of Marcus Garvey," by the NAACP's

Marcus Garvey, 1924. Courtesy of the Library of Congress.

Robert Bagnall, was published. And Kelly Miller reported that Garvey could not be taken seriously because his displays of pomp and costume were grotesque and bizarre. And yet, in the special issue of **Survey Graphic** (March 1925) on **Harlem, New York**, Miller did admit that Garvey had succeeded in showing the world "the possibility of focusing the racial mind, and of mobilizing racial resources about a formulated ideal."

Garvey's writings reiterate that people of African descent must see beauty in themselves, write their own history, criticize their own literature, and build and lead their own organizations. During the early 1920s, though, he was under attack from all sides: black intellectuals, BSL creditors, members of his inner circle, and the U.S. government. In 1920 he was arrested on charges of mail fraud and indicted by a federal grand jury. Once out on bail, he toured the country to raise funds. At this time he also obtained a divorce from Amy Ashwood (a founding member of the UNIA, and later general secretary) and married Amy Jacques, who later collected and published his writings as *Philosophy and Opinions of Marcus Garvey* (1923–1925).

Garvey then surprised Blacks and Whites alike when he held an amicable meeting with the imperial wizard of the Klu Klux Klan; both of them shared a similar dream, if for different reasons, of Black Americans relocating to Africa. The mail fraud trial concluded in 1923 with Garvey receiving a five-year sentence; he served three months and then was released on bail while his case was being appealed. The UNIA, still under his control, sent a delegation to Monrovia that led to the Liberian government's signing a pact with the Firestone Rubber Company. In 1924 the UNIA's Universal Negro Political Union endorsed the presidential candidacy of Calvin Coolidge, who in 1927 commuted Garvey's prison sentence (which had been upheld by the U.S. Court of Appeals), and then had him deported. Garvey traveled to Europe, most notably to Geneva, Switzerland, where he renewed the petition to the League of Nations that the UNIA receive African colonies taken from Germany after **World War I**.

Once back in Jamaica, Garvey set up new headquarters and a printing company that published a daily newspaper, *Blackman* (1929–1931). In 1935, after many financial and political disappointments, Garvey moved to London and published a new edition of *The Tragedy of White Injustice*. This poem was substantially longer than his quickly drafted rhymes penned for *Negro World* (1918–1933), *Daily Negro Times* (1922), and *New Jamaican* (1933). Although his poetic skill often seems more fully developed in his prose, there are times when Garvey's epic mission and message are communicated most faithfully through high-sounding verse. This long poem spans the globe and human history, apostrophizing Black oppression. His wholesale indictment of Whites is curiously paralleled in his anti-Semitism (notwithstanding that many Jewish businessmen contributed funds to his various schemes for African colonization). This remains one of the great contradictions of Marcus Garvey, for while he frequently called on Blacks to emulate the successes and homeland ambition of Jews, he also preached that Blacks should never trust them. Likewise, although he admired the aggressive nationalism of totalitarian leaders of the day, including Hitler and Stalin, he condemned Mussolini's invasion of Ethiopia in 1935, which went against his "Africa for Africans" policy.

Notwithstanding his personal convictions though, the Pan-African vision that crystallized under the banner of Garveyism, with its call to mobilize the world's scattered Blacks in Africa, remains his powerful legacy. Indeed, many African leaders in the decades since Garvey's death in 1940 have acknowledged their debt, most notably Kwame Nkrumah of Ghana and Jomo Kenyatta of Kenya. And, in America, Elijah Muhammad was a member of the UNIA in **Detroit, Michigan**, and his **Nation of Islam** bears many similarities to Garvey's movement in style and ideology. The parents of **Malcolm X** both were local UNIA leaders; and the entire **Black Power** movement of the 1970s is filled with the symbols and ideas that Marcus Garvey presented.

Resources: E. David Cronon, *Black Moses: The Story of Marcus Garvey and the Universal Negro Improvement Association* (1955; repr. Madison: University of Wisconsin Press, 1969); Amy Jacques Garvey, *The Philosophy and Opinions of Marcus Garvey: or Africa for the Africans* (Dover, MA: Majority Press, 1986); Marcus Garvey: *Life and Lessons*, ed. Robert A. Hill (Berkeley: University of California Press, 1987); *The Negro Race and Its Problems* [pamphlet] (Kingston, Jamaica: Marcus Garvey [privately published], 1914); *The Struggling Mass* [pamphlet] (Kingston, Jamaica: Marcus Garvey [privately published], 1910); *The Tragedy of White Injustice* (1935; repr. Baltimore: Black Classic Press, 1980); Rupert Lewis and Patrick Bryan, *Garvey: His Work and Impact* (1991; repr. Trenton, NJ: Africa World Press, 1994).

Bill Engel

Gates, Henry Louis, Jr. (born 1950). Professor, editor, literary theorist and historian, and public intellectual. One of the most influential literary scholars of his time, Gates has successfully highlighted **race** and ethnicity not only in an American setting but also in a global one. Not only has he put forth compelling theoretical paradigms for the analysis of race and ethnicity in literature, but he has also advanced his arguments in contemporary social and political settings, published his views in both scholarly and nonacademic settings, and helped to expand institutional settings for the study of African American literature and culture.

Gates was born and grew up in Keyser, West Virginia. After attending a small community college, he transferred to Yale University, where he received his B.A. in history in 1973. While he was an undergraduate, Gates traveled through fifteen countries in Africa, absorbing the diversity of African cultures that would later inform his work on both literature and history. With the assistance of fellowships from the Ford and Mellon foundations, Gates pursued graduate work at Cambridge University, under the guidance of the Nigerian writer Wole Soyinka, who convinced him to study literature. He received his M.A. in 1974 and his Ph.D. in 1979, both from Cambridge. After returning to teach at Yale (1979), he joined the faculty at Cornell (1985–1990) and Duke (1991) universities before arriving at Harvard University in 1992. He is currently the W.E.B. Du Bois Professor of the Humanities, chair of the Department of African and African American Studies, and the director of the W.E.B. Du Bois Institute for African and African American Research. From such a position of prominence, Gates has been able to acquire considerable resources to study African American literature and culture both within and beyond the academic setting.

In the 1980s, Gates began to develop an argument that has shaped the bulk of his scholarly writing and **multicultural theory**. His contention was that African American literature, like texts that were regarded then as more "canonical" or mainstream, should be studied through a critical analysis of its particular textuality, utilizing terms not simply "provided by the master" (Gates, *"Race," Writing, and Difference*). In other words, African American literature should be studied on its own terms, in Gates's view. Instead of agreeing that African American literature merely serves to describe the experience of Blackness to a White readership, Gates argues that readers should utilize a range of critical tools—many rooted in African American traditions—to analyze the specific complex texture of African American works. (Joining Gates in the effort to change modes of criticism was literary theorist **Houston A. Baker, Jr.**, among others.)

Gates calls his particular theoretical concept "signifyin(g)," a term developed in his seminal theoretical texts *Figures in Black* (1987) and *The Signifying Monkey* (1988). **Signifyin(g)** is a concept that synthesizes the deconstructive literary theories at the vanguard of postmodern American scholarship with the indigenous African tradition of literary interpretation that Soyinka had taught Gates. His poststructuralist training leads him to see race as a category not simply forged by biology, but rather as a text that can be *"read* with painstaking care and suspicion" (*see* **Poststructuralism**). Gates's work with Soyinka informs this practice of reading race. The mythical trickster figure in the Yoruba culture of West Africa told stories about the present through the refashioning of stories from the past in often ironic, critical, humorous, and provocative ways. Gates calls this kind of improvisation and ironic refashioning "signifyin(g)," and he sees it at work in much African American literature. The spoken nature of this mode of storytelling traveled with African slaves to the Americas. African American texts for Gates are thus double-voiced, telling a familiar story and a radically new one at the same time, voicing both an invitation and an implicit critique. This **vernacular** tradition, Gates argues, is thus inflected in African American writing across history. He uses this framework to read the **slave narratives** of the eighteenth and nineteenth centuries, the poetry of **Phillis Wheatley, Zora Neale Hurston**'s novel *Their Eyes Were Watching God* (1937), **Ishmael Reed**'s novel *Mumbo Jumbo* (1972), and **Alice Walker**'s novel *The Color Purple* (1982).

Gates's way of interpreting race and ethnic literature merges Euro-American practices of scholarship with the uniqueness of the African American experience. For many literary scholars, cultural theorists, and a wider public audience, this merging made Gates's ideas not just credible but useful.

Loose Canons: Notes on the Culture Wars (1992) put Gates at the center of the controversy concerning education and multiculturalism. In Gates's view, one task for teachers involved in teaching African American literature is to be aware of the political implications of teaching. Gates, therefore, was connecting ways of interpreting race and ethnicity with politically alert ways of teaching and learning. Those believing in the possibility and desirability of politically neutral teaching opposed Gates's ideas, as did those who did not agree with his ethnic-based mode of criticism.

Gates has not only helped to reconceptualize the existing American literary canon, but he has also added to American literature by collecting and publishing manuscripts written by African Americans in the eighteenth and nineteenth centuries. One of his first pieces of scholarship was to establish **Harriet O. Wilson**'s *Our Nig, or Sketches from the Life of a Free Black* (1859) as the first novel by an African American to be published in the United States. He has also clarified the life experience of the eighteenth-century poet Phillis Wheatley (*The Trials of Phillis Wheatley: America's First Black Poet and Encounters with the Founding Fathers*). In 2002 he published a manuscript by **Hannah Crafts**, dated about 1855 (*The Bondwoman's Narrative*).

Gates's position as an American public intellectual has allowed him to produce numerous other works with nonacademic audiences in mind. For example, in 2003, Gates and the Public Broadcasting Services produced an award-winning television miniseries investigating the wonders of the African world, from the ancient kingdoms of the Nile to the Swahili Coast. And in 1999, Gates and his colleague Kwame Anthony Appiah published *Africana*, an encyclopedic compendium of African and African American culture and history, a project an earlier African American public intellectual, **W.E.B. Du Bois**, spent much of his life conceptualizing. In 2004 Gates produced another television miniseries, *America Beyond the Color Line*. (*See* **Black Arts Movement; Folklore; Folktales**.)

Resources: **Primary Sources:** Henry Louis Gates, Jr.: *Colored People: A Memoir* (New York: Knopf, 1994); *Figures in Black: Words, Signs and the "Racial" Self* (New York: Oxford University Press, 1987); *Loose Canons: Notes on the Culture Wars* (New York: Oxford University Press, 1992); *The Signifying Monkey: A Theory of Afro-American Literary Criticism* (New York: Oxford University Press, 1988); *Thirteen Ways of Looking at a Black Man* (New York: Random House, 1997); *The Trials of Phillis Wheatley: America's First Black Poet and Encounters with the Founding Fathers* (New York: BasicCivitas, 2003); Henry Louis Gates, Jr., ed.: *The Bondwoman's Narrative*, by Hannah Crafts (New York: Warner Books, 2002); *"Race," Writing and Difference* (Chicago: University of Chicago Press, 1987); Henry Louis Gates, Jr., and Cornel West, *The African-American Century: How Black Americans Have Shaped Our Country* (New York: Free Press, 2002); Henry Louis Gates, Jr., and Kwame Anthony Appiah, eds., *Africana: The Encyclopedia of the African and African American Experience* (New York: BasicCivitas, 1999); Henry Louis Gates, Jr., and Nellie Y. McKay, eds., *The Norton Anthology of African American Literature* (New York: Norton, 1996). **Secondary Sources:** Diana Fuss, "'Race' Under Erasure? Poststructuralist Afro-American Literary Theory," in her *Essentially Speaking: Feminism, Nature and*

Difference (London: Routledge, 1989), 73–96; Theodore O. Mason, Jr., "Between the Populist and the Scientist: Ideology and Power in Recent Afro-American Literary Criticism; or, 'The Dozens' as Scholarship," *Callaloo* 11 (Summer 1988), 605–615; Miele Steele, "Metatheory and the Subject of Democracy in the Work of Ralph Ellison," *New Literary History* 27 (Summer 1996), 473–502; Robert M. Young, "The Linguistic Turn, Materialism, and Race: Toward an Aesthetic of Crisis," *Callaloo* 24, no. 4 (Winter 2001), 334–345.

Keith Feldman

Gay Literature. Gay literature, as envisioned and written by African Americans, speaks to the desire to represent the self in its totality. Most of this literature addresses the complex, multivalent intersection between the Black identity and the gay identity. The majority of Black authors who write gay literature choose to do so because they know it is disingenuous, if not impossible, to disentangle one's "Blackness" from one's "gayness." Both identities live within the individual and inform that individual's outlook and life choices. Gay literature by African Americans is notable because it illuminates the unique experiences of the Black gay subject, and there is no foregrounding of one identity—Black or gay—over the other in this literature. The two coalesce, resulting in a more accurate, multifaceted representation of the Black gay individual.

Gay literature by African Americans differs from the better-known, canonical works of gay literature by White authors because Black gay literature seeks to peel away the additional layers of cultural marginalization and silencing experienced by Black gay individuals but not by White gay individuals or Black heterosexuals. Generally, African American gay individuals are discouraged, if not excluded, from contributing to—and are often misrepresented in—both Black and gay literatures. These exclusions, however, create an irrepressible impetus to write and to share the realities of the Black gay experience.

Traces of Black gay experience have been embedded in African American literature since African Americans began putting pen to paper centuries ago. Some critics have discovered gay threads in some of the earliest texts written by African Americans, for instance, in **slave narratives**. Charles Clifton, for example, in *The Greatest Taboo* identifies and examines gay underpinnings in **Olaudah Equiano**'s eighteenth-century autobiography. Other critics locate the beginnings of an African American gay literary tradition in the **Harlem Renaissance**—particularly in works by **Langston Hughes, Countee Cullen, Richard Bruce Nugent**, and **Wallace Thurman**. Such conceptions are easily contested, because most authors of slave narratives, as well as most Harlem Renaissance writers, neither considered nor positioned themselves as gay. Although self-identifying as gay is not a prerequisite for writing gay literature, the absence of this self-identification may reinforce the cultural silence and marginalization that precluded Black gay individuals from sharing their experiences in the first place. Much of what might be considered an early Black gay literary tradition is written in a coded fashion designed to draw attention to Black gay characters without shedding any light on the author's own sexuality, gay or not.

James Baldwin was, arguably, the first Black author to claim a gay identity. In addition to claiming this identity, Baldwin infused gay sensibilities into several of his better-known texts, such as *Giovanni's Room* (1956) and *Just Above My Head* (1979), his last novel. One reason Baldwin may have been able to address Black gay sexuality is the cultural cachet he possessed as an author and a critic. Although individuals writing gay literature always run the risk of incensing the masses, resulting in the further demonization of gay literature and those who write it, Baldwin enjoyed a measure of success as a writer that allowed him to avoid the aspersions that might have been cast on lesser-known and less-esteemed authors who addressed gay sexuality in their writings.

Samuel R. Delany, who began writing around the same time as Baldwin, also incorporates gay issues into his texts. Delany writes in the **science fiction** genre, locating his gay subjects elsewhere in space and time, away from "here." The fact that Delany fashions so many of his subjects as gay bears witness to his sustained engagement with issues of gay subjectivity. As an openly gay Black author, Delany continues to include gay subjects in his texts. One of his more recent works, *Times Square Red, Times Square Blue* (1999), received a Lambda Literary Award for Gay Men's Studies.

Authors such as Baldwin and Delany helped to pave the way for other writers to address Black gay experience. The texts that followed Baldwin's *Just Above My Head* and Delany's earlier works were written largely in response to the AIDS crisis. Indeed, Black gay literature includes some of the most harrowing and provocative critical responses to AIDS. Writers such as **Melvin Dixon**, **Essex Hemphill**, and **Joseph Beam** offered valuable commentary on the experience of Black gay individuals during the first decade of the AIDS pandemic. This emphasis is all the more valuable given the fact that mainstream culture, in the early years of the pandemic, generally envisioned individuals living with AIDS exclusively as White gay men. It is important, therefore, to consider the seminal Black gay anthologies *In the Life* (1986) and *Brother to Brother* (1991) in order to gauge how Black authors situated themselves within the culture of AIDS. Many of these authors were writing about the disease from which they would ultimately die, a trend that continues virtually unabated; almost a quarter of the contributors to the most recently published anthology of black gay authors, *Freedom in This Village* (2005), died from AIDS.

AIDS inspired a legion of Black gay writers, as it also inspired White gay collectives such as the Violet Quill and individual authors such as Larry Kramer and Paul Monette. Previously, Black gay writers had been concerned primarily with shedding light on their efforts to survive cultural stigma and marginalization based on their homosexuality. AIDS changed the focus from surviving oppression to survival in general. These authors, and by extension their readers, resolved to combat what Melvin Dixon has termed the "chilling threat of erasure" (201), by which individuals are removed not only from the physical space but from the cultural narrative and history as well.

Although efforts to represent the Black gay response to AIDS continue intermittently, Black gay literature shifted focus in the early-to-mid-1990s with the rise of best-selling authors such as **E. Lynn Harris** and **James Earl Hardy**. Harris struck a nerve with his depictions of Black gay and bisexual subjectivity in mainstream (i.e., heterosexual) Black communities. Perhaps more than any other Black gay author, including James Baldwin, Harris has achieved a popular acclaim that shows no sign of tapering off. Although not as commercially successful as Harris, James Earl Hardy has experienced a string of successes with his *B-Boy Blues* series of novels. Both Harris and Hardy indicate the future of gay literature by Black gay authors, particularly in the ways they introduce new considerations to the literature. Harris, for example, imbricates a class consciousness in his novels that does not appear as often in other Black gay texts, while Hardy includes numerous instances of socio-linguistic code-shifting in his texts in order to lend verisimilitude to his characters. (*See* **Glave, Thomas; Lesbian Literature.**)

Resources: James Baldwin: *Giovanni's Room* (1956; New York: Delta, 2000); *Just Above My Head* (1979; New York: Delta, 2000); Joseph Beam, ed., *In the Life: A Black Gay Anthology* (Boston: Alyson, 1986); Devin W. Carbado et al., eds., *Black like Us: A Century of Lesbian, Gay, and Bisexual African American Fiction* (San Francisco: Cleis Press, 2002); Delroy Constantine-Simms, *The Greatest Taboo: Homosexuality in Black Communities* (Los Angeles: Alyson, 2001); Samuel R. Delany, *Times Square Red, Times Square Blue* (1999; New York: New York University Press, 2001); Melvin Dixon, "I'll Be Somewhere Listening for My Name," in *Sojourner: Black Gay Voices in the Age of AIDS*, ed. B. Michael Hunter (New York: Other Countries, 1993), 199–203; Olaudah Equiano, *The Interesting Narrative of the Life of Olaudah Equiano, or Gustavus Vassa the African*, ed. Henry Louis Gates, Jr. (New York: Signet, 2002); E. Lynn Harris, ed., *Freedom in This Village: Black Gay Men's Writing, 1969 to the Present* (New York: Carroll and Graf, 2005); Essex Hemphill, ed., *Brother to Brother: New Writings by Black Gay Men* (Boston: Alyson, 1991); Bruce Morrow and Charles H. Rowell, eds., *Shade: An Anthology of Fiction by Gay Men of African Descent* (New York: Avon, 1996); Robert Reid-Pharr, *Black Gay Man: Essays* (New York: New York University Press, 2001).

Chris Bell

Gayle, Addison, Jr. (1932–1991). Editor, essayist, and critic. Born in Newport News, Virginia, and a graduate of the City College of New York, Addison Gayle, Jr., personified the spirit of the **Black Arts Movement** and dedicated himself to the study of the culture and literature of African Americans. As a graduate student at the University of California, Los Angeles, he explored the boundaries within which African American literary discourse operated within a literary canon dominated by Anglo-European texts and assumptions. Gayle sought to advance the study of Black literature, gathering significant documentation about the African American experience while still a graduate student. In 1969, he published *Black Expression*, a collection of essays by and about Black literary pioneers on culture, poetry, drama, and fiction.

However, it was his exemplary collection of selected works, *The Black Aesthetic* (1971), that gained notoriety as an implicit manifesto for the Black Arts Movement, expressing an idealized concept of Blackness and its intrinsic beauty. (*See* **Afrocentricity**.) *The Black Aesthetic* was a cultural blueprint of collected essays that ranged from music to literature and were written by adherents of the movement. In his essay "The Black Arts Movement," **Larry Neal** defines the movement as being "radically opposed to any concept of the artist that alienates him from his community; Black art is the aesthetic and spiritual sister of the Black Power concept" (273). The Black Arts Movement envisioned "an art that speaks directly to the needs and aspirations of Black America" (273). With a unique vision of his own, Gayle explored "the dimensions of the black artist's war against society" (xxiv). It was his position that "due to his historical position in America at the present time, [the Black artist] is engaged in a war with this nation that will determine the future of black art" (xxiv). Ideas of human as well as social progression through Black art translated into a universal experience. Gayle believed that black writers should create positive images of African American life based on the lives of Black people, and in order to ensure constant credibility and viable art, he also believed that Black art should be analyzed by Black critics. "Negro literature has never been considered an integral part of American literature" (vii). It "is the consensus among Americans, black and white, that whites are more capable of rendering objective, unbiased opinions about Negro literature than Negroes" (vii).

Gayle is one of the most important members of the Black Arts Movement and is considered to have been as influential as Larry Neal, **Hoyt Fuller**, **Dudley Randall**, **Sonia Sanchez**, and **Amiri Baraka**, for example. With passion and excellence he helped to establish the formula for Black literary art in the 1970s. Gayle spent the last twenty-five years of his life as professor and critic. He taught English at Baruch College of the City University of New York until his death in 1991.

Resources: Henry Louis Gates and Nellie Y. McKay, eds., *The Norton Anthology of African American Literature* (New York: Norton, 1996); Addison Gayle, Jr., *Wayward Child: A personal Odyssey* (Garden City, NY: Anchor, 1977); Addison Gayle, Jr., ed.: *The Black Aesthetic* (Garden City, NY: Doubleday, 1971); *Black Expression* (New York: Weybright and Talley, 1969); *Bondage, Freedom, and Beyond: The Prose of Black Americans* (Garden City, NY: Zenith, 1971); *The Way of the New World: The Black Novel in America* (Garden City, NY: Anchor, 1975).

Earnest M. Wallace

Gayle, Roberta (born 1963). Romance novelist and short story writer. Gayle is among a small group of contemporary writers of African American historical romances that includes **Beverly Hunter Jenkins**, Shirley Hailstock, and Francine Craft. A native of New York, Roberta Gayle (the pseudonym for Roberta Cohen) is the daughter of an African American mother and a Jewish father, Ida and Melvin Cohen. Her interracial background contributes to her interest in writing about multiethnic topics. She attended Friends Academy, a prep school on Long Island, where she wrote for *Voices*, the student newspaper. While attending Union College in Schenectady, New York, she wrote for *Concordia*, the college's student newspaper (Dandridge).

Gayle launched her career as a romance writer with the publication of *Sunshine and Shadows* (1995) and *Moonrise* (1996), two historical romances. *Sunshine and Shadows* details the experiences of Roses Jordan, daughter of a Black couple who fled to the Ute reservation during the 1870's; *Moonrise* relates the experiences of Pascale de Ravenault, daughter of a French artist and granddaughter of an African princess who fled to Paris and reared four children alone. Unlike her contemporary **Anita Richmond Bunkley**, who bases her novels on actual people, Gayle invents characters. When her publisher, BET Publications, thought the market for historical romances had dried up, Gayle turned to contemporary romances that include *Worth Waiting For* (1998), *Something Old, Something New* (1999), *Mad about You* (2000), *Nothing But the Truth* (2001), *Coming Home* (2002), and *The Holiday Wife* (2003). She has published two short stories—"The Gamble," in *Bouquet* (1998), and "Just in Time," in *Season's Greetings* (1998). At this writing, Gayle is working on a mystery-romance novel titled *Sweetness and Lies*, scheduled for publication in 2004. She owns the Cohen Agency, a literary agency for writers of women's romances and mysteries. Her future interest is to write and publish her mother's biography (Dandridge).

Resources: Rita B. Dandridge, telephone interview with Roberta Gayle, Nov. 2, 2003; Roberta Gayle: *Coming Home* (Washington, DC: BET Publications, 2002); "The Gamble," in *Bouquet*, ed. Roberta Gayle, Anna Larence, and Gail McFarland (New York: Arabesque, 1998); *The Holiday Wife* (Washington, DC: BET Publications, 2003); "Just in Time," in *Season's Greetings*, ed. Margie Walker, Roberta Gayle, and Courtni Wright (Washington, DC: BET Publications, 1998); *Mad about You* (Washington, DC: BET Publications, 2000); *Moonrise* (1996; repr. New York: Kensington, 2002); *Nothing But the Truth* (Washington, DC: BET Publications, 2001); *Something Old, Something New* (Washington, DC: Arabesque/BET, 1999); *Sunshine and Shadows* (New York: Kensington, 1995); *Sweetness and Lies* (New York: BET Books, 2005); *Worth Waiting For* (Washington, DC: Arabesque, 1998).

Rita B. Dandridge

Gender. The association of certain traits and characteristics with individuals based on their biological sex has played a significant role in the history and development of African American literature and African American literary theory. From the earliest eras of African American authors to the present, gender has shaped the literature produced by individuals, influenced how audiences have read that literature, and affected our means for understanding and critiquing that work.

Most scholars and critics recognize gender as a category distinct from sexuality, one that is historically contingent and shaped by social forces rather than by biology or genetics. Sexuality consists of physical and biological characteristics that differentiate between men and women. These categories are fixed at birth and virtually unchangeable. Gender, on the other hand, consists of the traits and characteristics—both positive and negative—that are typically associated with persons of either sex, such as the belief that boys are made of "snips and snails and puppy dog tails" and girls of "sugar and spice and everything nice." More persuasive and damaging, and a testament to the rhetorical and sociological power of gendered assumptions, are the affiliation of specific traits solely with men or women: men are stoic, brave, strong, and ruled by thought, while women are sensitive, moved by feeling, and less physically capable. Most scholars recognize the aforementioned characteristics that one might view as "masculine" or "feminine" as socially constructed; that is, the characteristics are regarded not as biological or scientific fact, but instead as being the result of social conditioning. Importantly, these socially constructed, historically contingent characterizations of gender are subject to constant revision. What constitutes "manliness," for instance, Gail Bederman notes in *Manliness and Civilization*, might at one point in history mean possessing attributes of gentility and courtesy, while at another it might be associated with virility and strength.

These shifting notions of gender have made it an important and constantly changing thematic for African American authors to identify themselves. To provide a more complete accounting of the roles played by gender in African American literature, two trajectories may be traced: the first addresses the manner in which African American authors of fiction, nonfiction, poetry, and **drama** have been shaped and have shaped their literary productions in response to concerns about gender; the second explores the ways in which African American literary theory has been simultaneously shaped by and strived to shape discussions of gender in African American literature and culture.

From the earliest of African American letters—the poetry of **Phillis Wheatley**, the autobiographies of **Olaudah Equiano, William Wells Brown, Harriet Jacobs,** and others—gender has played a crucial role as a means for African Americans to claim and assert their humanity by asserting possession of a distinct gender. Since one of the many rationales given to support the institution of **slavery** was that African Americans were a different species or "lesser" humans only fit for manual labor, one crucial means by which African Americans could assert their humanity and mark themselves as autonomous individuals was through the claiming of a gender. While gender was not the only means by which African Americans could counter the dehumanizing effects and rationales for slavery, it was perhaps just as effective as other humanizing endeavors, such as professed adherence to Christian beliefs, outpourings of feelings of love and loss, and rapacious desire for education and self-improvement. Numerous examples exist among antebellum African American texts of authors cognizant of the power of claiming gender for themselves as an important first step to having their greater humanity recognized.

For example, **David Walker**, in his *Appeal in Four Articles; Together with a Preamble, to the Coloured Citizens of the World* (1829), includes the following admonition to his audience: "Are we MEN!!—I ask you, O my brethren! are we

MEN?" to make the claim that as men, Walker's readers have the innate rights to freedom and equality bequeathed to all men. **Frederick Douglass**, in his *Narrative of the Life of Frederick Douglass, an American Slave, Written by Himself* (1845), similarly marks the importance of identifying oneself as a man as a necessary step on the path to freedom and equality. Douglass's transformation begins with the recognition that during the time he was loaned out to the notorious slave breaker Edward Covey, when Douglass was subject to his most brutal treatment, including inadequate food and frequent beatings, that we "behold a man transformed into a brute!" Later, prefacing his successful fight with Covey, Douglass notes that we "have seen how a man was made a slave; you shall see how a slave was made a man." Following the fight, he notes that his success was "a turning-point in [his] career as a slave" that revived in him a "sense of [his] own manhood." Douglass's transformation by the institution of slavery into a brute and his later resurrection into a man marks the close association between gender—in this instance, manhood—and claims to humanity for African American authors. Gender also required claiming by African American women who were similarly denied their humanity and seen as existing outside of traditional femininity. One need only look to the title of **Sojourner Truth**'s address to the Women's Rights Convention in Akron, Ohio (1851), for confirmation: "Ar'n't I a Woman?" **bell hooks** used this question as the title for her 1981 examination of sexism and racism in African American literature, modified to *Ain't I a Woman*. Truth, hooks, and others recognized the importance for African American women writers of associating themselves with traditional femininity—love, sentiment, and domesticity— just as Douglass, Walker, and others recognized the need to claim traditional masculine attributes such as rationality and physical strength for themselves.

Throughout the antebellum period, through the **Civil War** and **Reconstruction**, and into the twentieth century, gender continued to play a significant role in African American literature. While, following emancipation, less emphasis was placed on the simple necessity of claiming a gender for African Americans, gender nevertheless played a powerful role in shaping ideas about African Americans, most often in the form of gendered stereotypes that came to be closely associated specifically with African American men or African American women. African American authors, as a result, had to respond to these mischaracterizations. A few telling examples, all readily apparent in the D. W. Griffith film *The Birth of a Nation* (1915), illustrate some of the ways that gender became a tool for disseminating racist stereotypes in the early twentieth century. (The film was a runaway success, despite its racist depictions of African Americans and its revisionist historical account of the Ku Klux Klan as agents for peace and stability. The film still manages to garner praise as the first major motion picture despite decades of protest against it. The film's use as a recruiting tool for the Ku Klux Klan and its historical significance as the first motion picture screened at the White House mark the pervasiveness of gendered stereotypes of African Americans and their general acceptance.) The film introduces stereotypes through characters such as Gus (the black male sexual predator), Lydia Brown (the duplicitous and seductive **mulatto**), and Mammy (the docile and benevolent maternal figure) while also including other traditional African American stereotypes from minstrelsy: **Sambo** (immature, lazy, and incompetent), Zip Coon (inept imitator of White culture), and Uncle Tom (docile and happy with slavery). Important in these examples is their lack of coherence: African American men were either docile and inept or sexually threatening, African American women were either motherly and benevolent or untrustworthy seductresses. Nevertheless, all of these stereotypes gained and maintained currency through much of the twentieth century, thus necessitating the creation of complex, multidimensional, and realistic African American men and women in fiction and poetry as realistic counters. Sadly, these gendered stereotypes persist today, emerging in figures from Aunt Jemima to the plucky African American sidekick of films such as *Lethal Weapon* and *Rush Hour* (for a thorough discussion of the **race** and gender associations inherent in the interracial buddy film, see Robyn Wiegman's *American Anatomies*).

Because of these complications inherent in the role played by gender in African American literature, African American literary criticism has frequently strived to make manifest these concerns and articulate versions of African American identity and authorship free from negative gender stereotypes. This endeavor, however, has been fraught with complications, and is still very much an issue today. Thus, a brief overview of gender's role in African American literary criticism will probably suffice. One place to locate the ways in which gender has shaped African American literary criticism is to begin with a specific period, such as the **Harlem Renaissance**. While the Renaissance enjoyed relatively equal participation by men and women as authors and editors, it was for a time remembered as the domain almost exclusively of male authors—**Jean Toomer**, **Claude McKay**, **Langston Hughes**, and **Alain Locke**, among others. Cheryl Wall's *Women of the Harlem Renaissance* addressed this imbalance by demonstrating the ways in which **Jessie Redmon Fauset**, **Nella Larsen**, and **Zora Neale Hurston** were important contributors to and participants in the outpouring of African American literary production of the 1920s and 1930s. Previously, critics had relegated female authors to the "rear guard" of the Harlem Renaissance; Wall's work shows their centrality.

Even the ways in which critics and scholars have categorized African American literature demonstrate how gender concerns influence literary criticism. The title of the collection by **Gloria T. Hull**, Patricia Bell Scott, and **Barbara Smith**, *All the Women Are White, All the Blacks Are Men, But Some of Us Are Brave: Black Women's Studies* (1982), sums up how African American literary studies has been gendered such that "African American" is taken to apply only to men, and "women" or "feminism" is perceived to apply exclusively to White women, thus marking the double erasure of African American women from critical discourse. For example, literature produced by African Americans between 1940 and 1960 has been loosely categorized as **protest literature**; thus, authors such as **Ralph Ellison, Richard Wright**, and **James Baldwin** receive attention while contemporary African American female novelists are left with no literary tradition prior to the 1970s. **Alice Walker**'s essay "In Search of Our Mothers' Gardens" (1974) rectified this lack of coherence by tracing connections between herself and her contemporaries—**Audre Lorde, Paule Marshall, Toni Morrison, Gloria Naylor**, and others—and their literary antecedents in the Harlem Renaissance. For Walker, this meant rediscovering Zora Neale Hurston and tracing a literary tradition from Hurston, to **Dorothy West** and **Ann Lane Petry**, to the present.

Following the **Black Arts Movement** of the 1960s, which was in part motivated and supported by developments in the women's rights movement and **Civil Rights Movement**, greater effort has been paid to discovering, recognizing, and celebrating the contributions of African American women to the African American literary tradition. This has included the development of distinct models of African American feminism, such as "womanist theory," promulgated by critics including Barbara Smith, **Deborah E. McDowell, Hortense J. Spillers, Barbara Christian, Joyce Anne Joyce**, and others (*see* **Theology, Black and Womanist**). One consequence of the recent attention to African American female expression has been a critical reassessment of Black masculinity by critics including George Cunningham, **Hazel V. Carby**, and Maurice Wallace. The result of all of this recent attention to the interplays of gender and race has been a broader understanding of African American literature, an enlargement of the canon to include women and men more equally, and the creation of a critical vocabulary by which we can better understand the significance of gender to African American literary studies. (*See* **Feminism/Black Feminism; Feminist/Black Feminist Literary Criticism; Gay Literature; Lesbian Literature; Queer Theory; Sexual Revolution**.)

Resources: Gail Bederman, *Manliness and Civilization: A Cultural History of Gender and Race in the United States, 1880–1917* (Chicago: University of Chicago Press, 1995); Hazel V. Carby, *Reconstructing Womanhood: The Emergence of the Afro-American Woman Novelist* (New York: Oxford University Press, 1987); Barbara Christian, *Black Feminist Criticism: Perspectives on Black Women Writers* (New York: Pergamon Press, 1985); Patricia Hill Collins, *Black Sexual Politics: African Americans, Gender, and the New Racism* (New York: Routledge, 2004); bell hooks, *Ain't I a Woman: Black Women and Feminism* (Boston: South End Press, 1981); Gloria T. Hull, Patricia Bell Scott, and Barbara Smith, eds., *All the Women Are White, All the Blacks Are Men, But Some of Us Are Brave: Black Women's Studies* (Old Westbury, NY: Feminist Press, 1982); Audre Lorde, *Sister Outsider: Essays and Speeches* (Trumansburg, NY: Crossing Press, 1984); Cheryl A. Wall, *Women of the Harlem Renaissance* (Bloomington: Indiana University Press, 1995); Robyn Wiegman, *American Anatomies: Theorizing Race and Gender* (Durham, NC: Duke University Press, 1995).

Matthew R. Davis

Genesis Press (1993–present). Genesis Press is one of the largest and most accomplished African American-owned publishers in America. Wilbur and

Dorothy Colom created Genesis Press in 1993. Since its inception, the company has opened the door to numerous writers of color historically denied access by white publishers, and has made African American books available to a significant African American and growing non-African American audience.

Located in Columbus, Mississippi, Genesis Press had its start in romance fiction, and is still largely romance-based. Currently, Genesis features a mix of young and veteran authors that includes **Charlene A. Berry**, Steve Cannon, Sinclair LeBeau, **Rochelle Alers**, Natalie Dunbar, and Robert Dalby.

Genesis Press offers several genres to suit its readers' literary tastes, each with its own imprint. The Indigo imprint includes stories that focus on African American characters and traditional romance plots, such as *Vows of Passion* (2004), *A Heart's Awakening* (2004), and *Crossing Paths, Tempting Memories* (2004). Indigo Love Spectrum breaks ground with interracial love stories, such as *Fate* (1999) and *A Happy Life* (2004). Indigo After Dark features erotica, such as *Brown Sugar Diaries* (2003) and *Stories to Excite You* (2004). The Sage Inspirational imprint includes nonfiction titles, such as *Lasting Valor* (1997), an autobiography of Vernon J. Baker, a lieutenant in the all-black 92nd Infantry during **World War II**. Other titles from Genesis include *How to Write a Romance for the New Markets and Get Published* (1999), as well as books for children and teens, thrillers/mysteries, and self-help and inspirational literature. Recently, Genesis Press expanded to include Hispanic and Asian novels.

Genesis Press thrives in a time when many other African American book presses have failed in the face of the powerful White-owned publishers that dominate the market. Its presence ensures a voice for people of color.

Resources: Byron Anderson, "African American Press," in *St. James Encyclopedia of Popular Culture*, ed. Tom Pendergast and Sara Pendergast (Detroit: St. James Press, 2000); Vernon J. Baker and Ken Olson, *Lasting Valor* (Columbus, MS: Genesis Press, 1997); Delores Bundy, *Brown Sugar Diaries* (Columbus, MS: Indigo After Dark, 2003); Kathryn Falk, ed., *How to Write a Romance for the New Markets and Get Published* (Columbus, MS: Genesis Press, 1999); Devine Forrest, *Stories to Excite You* (Columbus, MS: Indigo After Dark, 2004); Genesis Press home page, http://www.genesispress.com; Charlotte Harris, *A Happy Life* (Columbus, MS: Love Spectrum, 2004); Dorothy Elizabeth Love, *Crossing Paths, Tempting Memories* (Columbus, MS: Indigo, 2004); Bella McFarland, *Vows of Passion* (Columbus, MS: Indigo, 2004); Brenda Mitchell-Powell, "The Trouble with Success," *Publishers Weekly*, Dec. 12, 1994, pp. 33–34; Veronica Parker, *A Heart's Awakening* (Columbus, MS: Indigo, 2004); Pamela Leigh Starr, *Fate* (Columbus, MS: Love Spectrum, 1999).

Gladys L. Knight

George, Nelson (born 1957). Journalist and critic. George is an influential commentator on African American urban culture, particularly music and film. Born in **Brooklyn, New York**, he began writing for the *Amsterdam News* and *Billboard* while completing a B.S. in communication at St. John's

University. He served as *Billboard*'s music editor from 1982 to 1989, and wrote several books on popular music, including *Where Did Our Love Go? The Rise and Fall of the Motown Sound* (1986) and *The Death of Rhythm and Blues* (1988), which won the ASCAP Deems Taylor Award and a National Book Critics Circle nomination. George's involvement with film and television includes coproducing *The Chris Rock Show* on HBO and cowriting screenplays for *Strictly Business* and the **rap** "mockumentary" *CB4*. From 1988 to 1992 he wrote a column in *The Village Voice* titled "Native Son." George's work has also appeared in *Record World*, *The New York Times Magazine*, *Rolling Stone*, *Musician*, and *Essence*.

George's nonfiction includes a collection of wide-ranging essays from three decades, *Buppies, B-boys, Baps, and Bohos: Notes on Post-Soul Culture* (1992); a sweeping account of the participation of African Americans in shaping basketball, *Elevating the Game: Black Men and Basketball* (1992); a cultural history, *Hip Hop America* (1998), which was a finalist for the National Book Critics Circle Award for criticism; an autobiographical reflection on black cinema since the 1970's, *Blackface: Reflections on African-Americans and the Movies* (1994); and a biography of **Russell Simmons**, written with Simmons: *Life and Def: Sex, Drugs, Money, and God* (2001). George's fiction has focused on the professional lives and personal relationships of urban African American characters while conveying an insider's perspective on the "political climate, styles, club-scene and rap-music culture of New York" (O'Connell, 18). His novels include *Urban Romance: A Novel of New York in the 80's* (1993), *Seduced: The Life and Times of a One-Hit Wonder* (1996), *One Woman Short: A Novel* (2000), *Show and Tell* (2001), and *Night Work* (2003). George is currently at work on a biography of Edgecombe Lenox, titled *King Heroin*, and a play, *Treat My Brother as I Treat Myself*.

Resources: Primary Sources: Nelson George: *Blackface: Reflections on African-Americans and the Movies* (New York: HarperCollins, 1994); *Buppies, B-boys, Baps, and Bohos: Notes on Post-Soul Culture* (New York: HarperCollins, 1992); *The Death of Rhythm and Blues* (New York: Pantheon, 1988); *Elevating the Game: Black Men and Basketball* (New York: HarperCollins, 1992); *Hip Hop America* (New York: Viking, 1998); *Night Work* (New York: Touchstone, 2003); *One Woman Short: A Novel* (New York: Touchstone, 2000); *Post-Soul Nation: The Explosive, Contradictory, Triumphant and Tragic 1980s as Experienced by African Americans (Previously Known as Blacks and Before That Negroes)* (New York: Viking, 2004); *Seduced: The Life and Times of a One-Hit Wonder* (New York: Putnam, 1996); *Show and Tell* (New York: Touchstone, 2001); *Urban Romance: A Novel of New York in the '80s* (New York: Putnam, 1993); *Where Did Our Love Go? The Rise & Fall of the Motown Sound* (New York: St. Martin's Press, 1986); Web site, http://www.nelsongeorge.com; Nelson George and Russell Simmons, *Life and Def: Sex, Drugs, Money, and God* (New York: Crown, 2001). **Secondary Sources:** Debra J. Dickerson, "After the Revolution: A Renowned Critic Tries to Define a Nameless Generation," review of *Post-Soul Nation*, *Washington Post*, Jan. 11, 2004, sec. T, p. 4; Michiko Kakutani, "From Underground Music to Fashion Statement," review of *Hip-Hop America*, *New York Times*, Dec. 4, 1998, sec. E2, p. 45; "Nelson George," *Contemporary*

Authors Online (Detroit: Gale, 2001), http://galenet.galegroup.com; Patricia O'Connell, "Review of *Urban Romance*," *New York Times Book Review*, Feb. 13, 1994, p. 18.

Alex Feerst

Gibson, Patricia Joann (born 1952). Playwright, poet, and fiction writer. Born in **Pittsburgh, Pennsylvania**, Gibson was raised primarily in Trenton, New Jersey. She completed a B.A. at Keuka College in New York and an M.F.A. at Brandeis University, where she was a Schubert Fellow. She has subsequently served as creative director or playwright-in-residence at a number of arts centers and regional and university theaters. She has also taught at Boston College, Brown University, the College of New Rochelle, Rutgers University, the University of California at Berkeley, and the John Jay College of Criminal Justice, where she has won an award for distinguished teaching.

Although Gibson has published some fiction and poetry, she is known primarily as a playwright. Mentored by some of the leading teachers of playwriting, she has nonetheless acknowledged that her work has been most pointedly influenced by her exposure the plays of **Lorraine Hansberry**. A prolific playwright, Gibson has sometimes been accused of a certain stridency. An ardent feminist with progressive political views, she has focused on the ways in which indomitable African American women have confronted the oppressive effects of **gender** bias and racism. She has also explored the distorted passions that often define relations between men and women, the deep bonds between women connected by blood or friendship, and the demoralizing effects of social, economic, and political marginalization.

Gibson's best-known plays have included *Brown Silk and Magenta Sunsets* and *Long Time Since Yesterday*. *Brown Silk and Magenta Sunsets* is a fierce melodrama that centers on a woman who, in trying to realize her passionate obsessions, so ruins the lives of everyone close to her that she ultimately commits suicide. *Long Time Since Yesterday* has been compared to the film *The Big Chill* because it concerns the reunion of a group of college friends following the suicide of one of their number.

Resources: Primary Sources: (All dates are of first production.) *Ain't Love Grand?* (1980); *The Androgyny* (1979); *Angel* (1981); *The Black Woman* (one-act) (1972); *Brown Silk and Magenta Sunsets* (1981), published in *9 Plays by Black Women*, ed. Margaret B. Wilkerson (New York: New American Library, 1986); *"But I Feed the Pigeons"/"Well, I Watch the Sun"* (1981); *Can You Tell Me Who They Is?* (1981); *Clean Sheets Can't Soil* (1983); *Doing It to Death* (1977); *Konvergence* (one-act) (1973), published in *New Plays for the Black Theatre*, ed. Woodie King, Jr. (Chicago: Third World Press, 1989); *Long Time Since Yesterday* (1985), published (New York: Samuel French, 1986); *Miss Ann Don't Cry No More* (1980); *My Mark, My Name* (1981); *The Ninth Story Window* (one-act) (1974); *Shameful in Your Eyes* (1971); *The Unveiling of Abigail* (1981); *Void Passage* (one-act) (1973); *You Must Die Before My Eyes as I Have Before Yours* (1981); *The Zappers and the Shopping Bag Lady* (one-act) (1979). **Secondary Sources:** Terry Doran, "A Long Day of Family Soul-Searching,"

Buffalo News, Mar. 10, 1998, p. C5; Ronald Ehmke, "Supporting Cast Shores Up *Brown Silk*," *Buffalo News*, Sept. 27, 1995, p. B5; Marianne Evett, "Capable Cast Delivers Strong Performances," *Cleveland Plain Dealer*, Jan. 21, 1998, p. B7; Mel Gussow, "The Stage: *Long Time*," *New York Times*, Feb. 10, 1985, sec. 1, p. 63; Julia M. Klein, "Blackness, Lightness, and Absurdity," *Philadelphia Inquirer*, Mar. 6, 1998, WKD, p. 31; Clifford A. Ridley, "Sophocles Proves Out of Place in Trenton," *Philadelphia Inquirer*, Apr. 12, 1996, WKD, p. 35.

Martin Kich

Gilbert, Mercedes (1889–1952). Songwriter, actress, playwright, poet, and novelist. A talented but neglected performer and writer, Mercedes Gilbert should be remembered for her literary and artistic contributions to the **Harlem Renaissance**.

Born to middle-class parents in Decatur, Georgia, Gilbert migrated in 1916 to New York, where acting and writing became her vocation after a nursing career did not materialize. Blending her Southern roots with an urban cultural renaissance, she collaborated with Chris Smith, a songwriter, who helped her to set her poetry to such tunes as "The Decatur Street Blues" and "Got the World in a Jug." In 1922, she married Arthur J. Stevenson and began performing in Black films, such as *The Call of His People* (1922) and *Secret Sorrow* (1922). She is best remembered, however, for her role as Cora, a young Georgia woman who exposes **gender** exploitation in **Oscar Micheaux**'s silent film *Body and Soul* (1924).

In 1927, Gilbert made her stage debut in *The Lace Petticoat* (1927). She performed in *Bomboola* (1929) and portrayed Zipporah, the wife of Moses, in *The Green Pastures* (1930) and Cora, the mistress-servant, in Langston Hughes's *Mulatto* (1936). To counter the stereotypic maid role she was offered in others' plays, she wrote a one-act satire called *In Greener Pastures* (1938).

During her acting career, Gilbert penned *Selected Gems of Poetry, Comedy and Drama* (1938), a literary collection that manifests her continuing effort to expand the portrayal of rural Southern Black women. The poems "How Liza Saved the Deacon" and "My Dear John's Place" illuminate Southern churchgoing women trying to snare a husband. "Why Adam Ate the Apple," a comedy, is a Black womanist rendition of the biblical story of the Garden of Eden; "I'm Glad I Ain't No Hand to Talk" lampoons churchgoing gossipers. *Environment*, a three-act drama, highlights a popular Harlem Renaissance theme, the inhospitable North, as Mary Lou Williams, a Southern-bred Christian woman, tries to hold her disintegrating family together in the basement of a Northern tenement.

Gilbert's only novel, *Aunt Sarah's Wooden God* (1938), details a mother's faith in her prodigal son. Like Harlem Renaissance novelists **Zora Neale Hurston, Jessie Redmon Fauset**, and **Nella Larsen**, Gilbert explores sensitive issues relating to Black women's vulnerability, faith as a survival tool, and the pitfalls in the North.

Gilbert spent her last years performing in various dramas and in her own off-Broadway dramatic skits. In 1946, she toured the United States and Canada in her one-woman show.

Resources: Mercedes Gilbert: *Aunt Sarah's Wooden God* (1938; repr. New York: AMS Press, 1974); *Selected Gems of Poetry, Comedy and Drama* (1938; repr. New York: G. K. Hall, 1997); Lorraine Elena Roses and Ruth Elizabeth Randolph, *Harlem's Glory: Black Women Writing, 1900–1950* (Cambridge, MA: Harvard University Press, 1996).

Rita B. Dandridge

Gillespie, Dizzy (1917–1993), Charlie Parker (1920–1955), and Thelonius Monk (1917–1982). Musicians and composers. Dizzy Gillespie, Charlie Parker, and Thelonious Monk were three of the most pivotal musicians and composers in the history of **jazz**. Effectively inventing bebop as a recognizable subgenre of jazz in the 1940s, these three key innovators extracted jazz from the highly popularized and potentially hackneyed **swing** style of the 1930s, moving it into the dramatically more intellectual and technically complex forms of bebop.

Jazz has played a central but widely varied role in the history of African American aesthetics and literature. Sometimes it influences the form of or is the subject of works of literature, as in the writings of **Langston Hughes, Ralph Ellison, Xam Wilson Cartiér, Amiri Baraka,** and **Jayne Cortez,** for example. Sometimes jazz is more of an implicit undercurrent in a text, as in works by **James Baldwin, Ishmael Reed,** and **Toni Morrison.**

Bebop is a style of jazz that the now familiar jam session developed as a central creative structure. It is a style sometimes associated with drug or alcohol abuse as the means to enhance a musical genius, as in the case of Charlie Parker. The bebop musician has, in turn, been romanticized and dramatized in literature. Baldwin's "Sonny's Blues" (1957) and Rafi Zabor's *The Bear Comes Home* (1997) are two examples wherein the protagonist is the solitary jazz musician who exists on the margins of society and is in the process of realizing his creative impulse.

More specific references to each of the three musicians are found in the many literary and musical biographies of each. Dizzy Gillespie (John Birks) was a trumpet player, a composer, and a bandleader. Raised primarily in **Philadelphia, Pennsylvania,** Gillespie moved to New York City at the age of twenty and went on to be a leading figure in jazz, exploring numerous alternative musical influences as well as formalizing many of the innovations of bebop. Furthermore, he played an important role in the introduction of Latin American and Afro-Cuban rhythms in jazz. Renowned for his outgoing personality, Gillespie posed a stark contrast to the more somber and introspective Parker, with whom he developed a remarkable musical partnership. There are only a few biographical studies of Gillespie. Two central examples are his autobiographical *To Be, or Not…to BOP: Memoirs* and Alyn Shipton's *Groovin' High.*

Charlie Parker, also known as "Bird," is by far the most written about of the three. He was a Kansas-born alto saxophone player who, despite unstable mental health and an addiction to heroin and alcohol, became one of the most influential soloists in jazz, exploring innovative approaches through creative harmonic improvisations and breakneck speeds. In addition to interviews, articles, and chapters, numerous full-length biographies of the musician have been written, including Robert Reisner, *Bird: The Legend of Charlie Parker*; Ross Russell, *Bird Lives!*; and Carl Woideck, *Charlie Parker: His Music and Life*.

Thelonious Monk, a composer and piano player, initially achieved more recognition for his influential compositions than for his striking style of piano playing. Living in New York for most of his life, Monk was for many years the house pianist alongside Gillespie at the renowned Minton's Playhouse in **Harlem, New York**, playing a crucial part in the development of bebop. Regarded as eccentric and stylistically controversial, Monk suffered from bouts of depression, receiving significant acclaim only from the late 1950s. In addition to Robin D. G. Kelley's *Thelonious: A Life*, works about Monk include Chris Sheridan's comprehensive discography, *Brilliant Corners*; Leslie Gourse's *Straight, No Chaser*, and Thomas Fitterling's *Thelonious Monk: His Life and Music*.

In addition to these biographies, the works of these musicians have been explored in a diverse array of musicological and literary texts. Ralph Ellison and LeRoi Jones (Amiri Baraka) have written seminal jazz essays investigating the musical, aesthetic, and cultural implications of bebop in general, and of these musicians in particular. Ross Russell's *The Sound* and Julio Cortazar's "The Pursuer" offer fictionalizations of Parker's life, concentrating on the musician's creative genius and excessive appetites. While contemporary African American literature continues to explore a jazz aesthetic, there are few explicit inclusions of these figures in recent texts. An important exception is **Percival Everett**'s *Erasure* (2001), whose protagonist is tellingly named Thelonious Ellison, and referred to generally as Monk. While not a jazz novel, as such, the deliberate reference is indicative of the lasting influence these musicians have had on African American culture.

Resources: Primary Sources: *Fiction:* James Baldwin, "Sonny's Blues," in *James Baldwin: Early Novels and Stories* (New York: Library of America, 1998); Xam Wilson Cartiér, *Be-bop, Re-bop* (New York: Available Press, 1987); Julio Cortazar, *"The Pursuer,"* *Blow-Up and Other Stories* (New York: Pantheon, 1985); Jayne Cortez, *Coagulations: New and Selected Poems* (New York: Thunder's Mouth Press, 1984); Percival Everett, *Erasure* (Hanover, NH: University Press of New England, 2001); Langston Hughes, *Selected Poems of Langston Hughes* (New York: Vintage Classics, 1959); Ishmael Reed, *Mumbo Jumbo* (Garden City, NY: Doubleday, 1972); Ross Russell, *The Sound* (New York: Dutton, 1961); Rafi Zabor, *The Bear Comes Home* (New York: Norton, 1997). *Biography:* Thomas Fitterling, *Thelonious Monk: His Life and Music*, trans. Robert Dobbin (1987; Berkelely, CA: Berkeley Hills Books, 1997); Dizzy Gillespie and Al Fraser, *To Be, or Not...to BOP: Memoirs* (Garden City, NY: Doubleday, 1979); Leslie Gourse, *Straight, No Chaser* (New York: Schirmer Books, 1997); Robin D. G. Kelley, *Thelonious: A Life* (New York: Free Press, 2005); Robert Reisner, *Bird: The Legend of Charlie Parker* (New York: Citadel Press, 1962); Ross Russell, *Bird Lives!* (New York: Charterhouse, 1973); Chris Sheridan, *Brilliant Corners*

(Westport, CT: Greenwood Press, 2001); Alyn Shipton, *Groovin' High* (New York: Oxford University Press, 2001); Carl Woideck, *Charlie Parker: His Music and Life* (Ann Arbor: University of Michigan Press, 1996). **Secondary Sources:** Scott DeVeaux, *The Birth of Bebop: A Social and Musical History* (New York: Picador, 1999); Ralph Ellison, *Shadow and Act* (New York: Vintage International, 1953); LeRoi Jones: *Black Music* (New York: Morrow, 1967); *Blues People* (New York: Payback Press, 1965); Robert O'Meally, ed., *Jazz Cadence of American Culture* (New York: Columbia University Press, 1998); Peter Townsend, *Jazz in American Culture* (Edinburgh: Edinburgh University Press, 2000).

Keren Omry

Gilmore, Brian (born 1962). Poet. Born in **Washington, D.C.**, Brian Gilmore grew up in a household in which his parents prohibited most television watching and in a number of direct and indirect ways fostered a love of reading—in particular, an appreciation of African American literature.

Trained as a lawyer, Gilmore worked for seven years at a free legal clinic serving the poor neighborhoods of southeastern Washington. He is currently legislative counsel at the City Council for the District of Columbia.

Gilmore has taught poetry at the Catholic University of America and at Lorton Prison. He has contributed reviews of poetry collections and African American fiction to the *Washington Post* and other regional publications, and he has contributed articles to *Africana.com*, *Emerge*, the *Christian Science Monitor*, and *The Nation*. His commentaries on current issues have appeared regularly in **The Crisis** and *The Progressive*, and he has written a feature column for the *Progressive Media Project*.

Gilmore's collections of poems have include *Elvis Presley Is Alive and Well and Living in Harlem* (1993) and *Jungle Nights and Soda Fountain Rags: Poem for Duke Ellington* (2000). The titles of the collections suggest the degree to which popular music and popular culture have captured Gilmore's interest as a poet. In *Elvis Presley Is Alive and Well and Living in Harlem*, Gilmore exploits salient aspects of the folklore surrounding Elvis Presley and the history of his development into an icon of American popular culture. Within a satiric poetic frame, he cleverly links the rash of postmortem Elvis sightings with the discussions of Elvis's great debt to African American musical influences.

As several reviewers have noted, *Jungle Nights and Soda Fountain Rags* can be read as a single poem with thirty sections or as thirty poems arranged in a purposeful sequence to emphasize their interconnections. In part a biography of **Edward Kennedy "Duke" Ellington**, in part a study of Ellington's musical development, in part a survey of African American culture, and in part a history of race relations in the United States, the collection is as accessible to the reader only passingly familiar with Ellington's life and career as it is a bonanza of insights and details for **jazz** aficionados.

A selection of Gilmore's work has been chosen for inclusion in **Kevin Powell**'s *Step into a World: A Global Anthology of the New Black Literature*

(2000). His poems have appeared in such literary magazines as *Bum Rush the Page, Eyeball, Gargoyle,* and *Obsidian II.* He has edited and published the intermittent literary magazine *The Bridge.*

Resources: Brian Gilmore: *Elvis Presley Is Alive and Well and Living in Harlem* (Chicago: Third World Press, 1993); *Jungle Nights and Soda Fountain Rags: Poem for Duke Ellington* (Hyattsville, MD: Karibu, 2000); Tyehimba Jess, "Review of *Jungle Nights and Soda Fountain Rags,*" *Black Issues Book Review,* May/June 2001, 36.

Martin Kich

Gilmore-Scott, Monique (born c. 1967). Romance novelist. Born and raised in New Jersey, Gilmore-Scott was working at ordinary jobs when her enjoyment of **Terry McMillan**'s novels and the great critical and commercial success of those novels inspired her to try her own hand at writing novels. Before her marriage to Kenneth Scott, she wrote four **romance novels** for Kensington as Monique Gilmore. More recently, she has shifted her focus to writing Christian fiction. In 1997, having moved with her husband to Charlotte, North Carolina, she founded the small publishing house Writing Minds primarily to self-market her own work in both traditional and e-book formats. She and her husband have also begun another entrepreneurial venture, Small Office Home Office Professionals (www.sohop.com), a firm that supports small business owners, entrepreneurs, artists, entertainers, and professionals with their telecommunications needs.

Gilmore-Scott's novels are fairly conventional romances. *No Ordinary Love* (1994) centers on a reporter who enjoys her job and is contentedly engaged to a successful businessman. Then, on a ski trip, she meets a firefighter who makes her want more than just contentment. In *Hearts Afire* (1995), the young female protagonist moves from an unhappy relationship with a computer geek who becomes involved in cybercrime to a more satisfying but in some ways still deficient relationship with a basketball coach. In *Grass Ain't Greener* (1996), a young woman named Ramona returns to her hometown of **Detroit, Michigan**, to recharge herself physically and emotionally, and unexpectedly finds herself involved in a serious romance. *Arabesque: Soul Deep* (1997) has an element of mystery-suspense. When Yvonne Taylor's fiancé breaks her heart, she decides to get a fresh start in **Los Angeles, California**. On the flight from **Atlanta, Georgia**, to Los Angeles, she meets a fighter pilot with whom she makes an almost immediate romantic connection. But, as their relationship is just developing, they are stalked by someone who seems to have a very intimate knowledge of their lives.

In *Ties That Bind: Way Down Deep* (1998), Gilmore-Scott explores the ways in which the accidental romance between Kaj Richards, a construction worker, and Dana Alexander, a veterinarian, is very much defined by their inability to come completely to terms with their pasts. Kaj seems permanently embittered about the knee injury that wrecked any chance he had at a professional football career, and Dana is haunted by her memories of her alcoholic and promiscuous mother.

Resources: Monique Gilmore-Scott: *Grass Ain't Greener* (New York: Kensington, 1996); *Hearts Afire* (New York: Kensington, 1995); *No Ordinary Love* (New York: Kensington, 1994); *A Simple Guide to Football* (Pleasanton, CA: Writing Minds, 1999); *Soul Deep* (New York: Kensington, 1997); *Ties That Bind: Way Down Deep* (Pleasanton, CA: Panache, 1998); Michele Slung, "Book Report: Black Is the Color...," *Washington Post Book World*, Jan. 28, 1996, p. 15.

Martin Kich

Gilpin Players. American theater troupe. Based at the Karamu House in Cleveland, Ohio, the Gilpins rose to prominence during the **Harlem Renaissance**. A settlement playhouse founded in 1922 by Rowena and Russell Jelliffe, they were the nation's oldest amateur, primarily Black, theatrical society. Originally the Dumas Dramatic Club, the players adopted the name of the actor Charles S. Gilpin, an artistic benefactor and recipient of the 1921 **NAACP** Spingarn Medal for his performance in Eugene O'Neill's *The Emperor Jones* (1920). In 1931, what Gates terms the "most notorious literary quarrel in African American cultural history" (5) erupted between **Langston Hughes** and **Zora Neale Hurston** over the authorship of *Mule Bone: A Comedy of Negro Life*. Written a year earlier in a **vernacular** style now reminiscent of comic segments from Hurston's *Mules and Men* (1935) and *Their Eyes Were Watching God* (1937), the play details how a romantic duel over the resident beauty provokes the spirited (and spiritual) involvement of Eatonville, an all-Black Florida community. The Gilpins, having first received the rollicking piece from the Samuel French agency, planned a February opening and envisioned the play's eventual Broadway success. They became embroiled in the acrimonious exchanges between the two writers, the Jelliffes, and a host of other prominent Renaissance figures: **Carl Van Vechten** (a mutual friend of the feuding pair), Louise Thompson (who collaborated as secretary and observer), Charlotte Osgood Mason (the writers' patron, with whom Hughes had quarreled in 1930), and even **Alain Locke** (also supported by Mason, and a Howard University professor). Persistent bickering, personal inconsistencies (Hurston missed an important planning meeting with the troupe), and the inherently unstable nature of the project caused the Gilpins to suspend *Mule Bone* despite having invested time, money, and enthusiasm in its production. Hughes acknowledges the company's participation and subsequent disappointment in his autobiography *The Big Sea* (1940). With attempts at reconciliation failing, the play was never performed during either Hughes's or Hurston's lifetime. Neither published in full nor performed until 1991, *Mule Bone* nevertheless showcased the Gilpins' active involvement in the attempt to create new dramatic modes for African American expressive culture during those fruitful decades.

Consistently dedicated to increasing the visibility of Blacks in popular theater, the Gilpins lived up to their playhouse's Swahili name: "Karamu" generally translates as "a central meeting place for entertainment in the community." In particular, they performed many of Hughes's plays, among them *Mulatto* (1935), *Little Ham* (1936), and *When the Jack Hollers* (1936). The company's commitment to Hughes was not without detractors, however; as Rampersad notes, certain segments of the Black bourgeoisie in Cleveland scoffed at "Those-Awful-Gilpins-That-Do-Those-Awful-Langston-Hughes-Plays" (38–39). Their creative energy, in concert with the sometimes comedic but often tragic flair that characterized the Karamu House players, merits consideration alongside the endeavors of the New York-based Krigwa troupe, the Harlem Suitcase Theater, and the string of prominent Black Broadway musicals whose prototype was *Shuffle Along* (1921), composed and arranged by Eubie Blake, Noble Sissle, Flournoy Miller, and Aubrey Lyles.

Resources: Henry Louis Gates, Jr., "Introduction, 'A Tragedy of Negro Life,'" in *Mule Bone: A Comedy of Negro Life*, by Langston Hughes and Zora Neale Hurston, ed. George Houston Bass and Henry Louis Gates, Jr. (New York: HarperPerennial, 1991), 5–24; Robert Hemenway, *Zora Neale Hurston: A Literary Biography* (Urbana: University of Illinois Press, 1977); Langston Hughes, *The Big Sea* (New York: Hill and Wang, 1940); Hans Ostrom, *A Langston Hughes Encyclopedia* (Westport, CT: Greenwood Press, 2002); Arnold Rampersad, *The Life of Langston Hughes*, 2 vols. (New York: Oxford University Press, 1986–1988).

Nancy Kang

Gilroy, Paul (born 1956). Sociologist and cultural theorist. Paul Gilroy is a provocative social and cultural theorist whose work has extended the methodological and pedagogical parameters of African American literary study to include the literatures and cultures of the African **diaspora**.

Gilroy is Professor of Sociology and Chair of African American Studies at Yale University. A British citizen, he was born in London in 1956 and received his Ph.D. from the Centre for Contemporary Cultural Studies (CCCS), University of Birmingham, in 1986. From 1982 to 1985, Gilroy was employed as a research officer for the Greater London Council, which allowed him to combine intellectual and policy concerns. Since becoming a full-time academic, Gilroy has taught at the University of Essex; Goldsmiths' College, University of London; and the University of California at Santa Cruz. His articles, essays, and book, movie, and music reviews have appeared in a wide range of periodicals, from *Sight and Sound* and the *Times Literary Supplement* to *New Statesman* and *Marxism Today*.

In 1982 Gilroy coauhored, with other race-minded members of the CCCS, *The Empire Strikes Back*, a groundbreaking collection of essays that is widely credited for constituting Black British cultural studies as a coherent academic and political project. The discursive field of cultural studies had promised a reorientation of the concept of culture toward materialist, working-class, and counterhegemonic analysis; Gilroy and his colleagues qualified this theoretical move with a structural account of capitalist critique's occasional but no less pernicious investments in racism and nationalism. His first monograph, *"There Ain't No Black in the Union Jack,"* further works against the ethnocentric bias of British cultural studies by offering readings of how racist political culture in

England is discursively challenged by the circulation of expressive musical forms—ska and funk, **reggae** and **soul**—in the African diaspora, particularly in the United States and former British colonies. Key to these readings is the notion that Black diasporic musical forms at once materially and politically transcend the determinate bounds of the nation-state, which, according to Gilroy, is "modernity's most impressive achievement." In both of these books, Gilroy is indebted to the theoretical contributions of former CCCS director Stuart Hall, whose essays on **race**, class, and the state paved the way for the emergence of Black British cultural studies.

Of all Gilroy's studies, *The Black Atlantic* (1993) has had the most striking impact on African American literary study for its continued theorization of *There Ain't No Black*'s thesis about the racial valences of postnational politics. Here Gilroy proposes the concept of the **Black Atlantic**, which in its hybrid fusion of African, American, Caribbean, and British cultures is a veritable "counterculture of modernity." The archive from which Gilroy draws has a distinctly literary-critical or literary-historical edge: the internationalist careers and oeuvres of the most famous men in "African American" letters, from **Martin R. Delany** and **Frederick Douglass** to **W.E.B. Du Bois** and **Richard Wright**. Though many have taken issue with the masculinist leanings of this archive, it has also granted Gilroy an audience among Americanists and African Americanists interested in reconceptualizing their objects of study to include diasporic, postcolonial, and indeed Black Atlanticist writings and cultures. Published in Britain the same year as *Black Atlantic*, *Small Acts* engages a similarly diasporic but more contemporary archive: art and criticism by David A. Bailey, Isaac Julien, **Spike Lee**, and **bell hooks**.

In his most recent work, Gilroy has controversially called for an abandonment of race-based thinking to the extent that "raciology" is crucially linked with fascism in the way both are wielded by our globalized consumer society as modes of insidious, identitarian domination. *Against Race* (2000) has garnered about as much praise as it has enmity; it could be read as Gilroy's coming to terms with the inextricable relationship between race and the nation-state in the age of global capitalism. His alternate political vision, a cosmopolitics of "strategic universalism," is recast in *Postcolonial Melancholia* (2005) as a defense of the "multiculture," which he claims is all the more important to take up in the wake of the post-9/11 "politics of security."

Resources: Joan Dayan, "Paul Gilroy's Slaves, Ships, and Routes: The Middle Passage as Metaphor," *Research in African Literatures* 27, no. 4 (1996), 7–14; Simon Gikandi, "Race and Cosmopolitanism," *American Literary History* 14, no. 3 (2002), 593–615; Paul Gilroy: *Against Race: Imagining Political Culture beyond the Color Line* (Cambridge, MA: Harvard University Press, 2000); *The Black Atlantic: Modernity and Double Consciousness* (Cambridge, MA: Harvard University Press, 1993); *Postcolonial Melancholia* (New York: Columbia University Press, 2005); *Small Acts: Thoughts on the Politics of Black Cultures* (London: Serpent's Tail, 1993); *"There Ain't No Black in the Union Jack": The Cultural Politics of Race and Nation* (London: Hutchinson, 1987); Paul Gilroy with the Centre for Contemporary Cultural Studies, *The Empire Strikes Back:*

Race and Racism in '70s Britain (London: Hutchinson, 1982); Paul Gilroy, Lawrence Grossberg, and Angela McRobbie, eds., *Without Guarantees: Essays in Honour of Stuart Hall* (London: Verso, 2000); Charles D. Piot, "Atlantic Aporias: Africa and Gilroy's Black Atlantic," *South Atlantic Quarterly* 100, no. 1 (2001), 155–170.

Kinohi Nishikawa

Giovanni, Nikki (born 1943). Poet and essayist. Nikki Giovanni is one of the most prolific and widely read poets to spring from the **Black Arts Movement** of the 1960s. Her work exemplifies the ethnic pride and social engagement found in other expressions of **Black Power** at the end of the **Civil Rights Movement**. Her continued success as a poet, however, owes itself to an adaptive style that is both conversational and musical. A poet of the people, Giovanni has always had great popular appeal, if not close critical attention. Critics have alternately praised her work as warm and unaffected or castigated it as trivial, sentimental, and bitter. Few have attempted to understand the relationship between the overtly political and the deeply personal within her work.

Born Yolande Cornelia Giovanni, Jr., on June 7, 1943, in Knoxville, Tennessee, to Jones and Yolande Giovanni, Nikki grew up in Cincinnati, Ohio, but frequently returned to Knoxville to spend time with her maternal grandparents. She graduated from high school there in 1960. Her grandmother, Emma Louvenia Watson, was a powerful influence on Giovanni's attitudes and figures prominently in many of her poems and essays.

Giovanni entered Fisk University in **Nashville, Tennessee**, at the age of seventeen, but her attitudes were often in conflict with the strict university administration. She was dismissed from school at the end of her first semester, in part because of an unauthorized visit to her grandparents in Knoxville during the Thanksgiving holiday. She spent the years 1961–1963 living with her parents in Cincinnati, working odd jobs, and taking courses at the University of Cincinnati. In 1964, she returned to Fisk and became engaged in campus literary and political activities. She abandoned her earlier conservative politics and took up more progressive views. She edited the student literary magazine, *Élan*, and helped reestablish a chapter of the Student Nonviolent Coordinating Committee. Giovanni completed a B.A. degree in history at Fisk in 1967. She then moved back to Cincinnati to be near her parents. There, she immersed herself in reading and writing poetry.

Nikki Giovanni, 1973. © Bettmann/Corbis.

In Cincinnati, Giovanni met H. Rap Brown and other leaders of the Black Arts Movement and then organized a Black Arts Festival for the city. Later that year, with assistance from the Ford Foundation, she moved to Delaware and enrolled in the University of Pennsylvania School of Social Work. In 1968, she privately published *Black Feeling, Black Talk* and dropped out of graduate school to pursue a career in writing. With a National Endowment for the Arts grant, she moved to New York City. Her second book of poetry, *Black Judgment*, was published later the same year. In 1969, she gave birth to a son, Thomas Watson Giovanni. A year after the birth of her son she formed her own publishing company, NikTom Limited, to publish the works of Black female poets.

Throughout the 1970s, Giovanni published a prodigious volume of poetry and became one of the most recognized artists in the country. She gave frequent public readings and lectures, appeared on television and radio, and released several sound recordings, which further served to make her a poet of the people. The spoken word album she released in 1971, *Truth Is on Its Way*, became a best-seller. In 1971 Giovanni also published a book of poems for children dedicated to her son, *Spin a Soft Black Song*. She would return to **children's literature** repeatedly in the future, primarily as a means of giving positive images and a sense of pride to African American children.

Giovanni held instructor and professorial positions at several universities: Queens College (1968), Rutgers University (1968–1972), Ohio State University (1984–1985), Mount St. Joseph's College (1985–1987). In 1987, Giovanni accepted a position as visiting professor of English at Virginia Tech in Blacksburg. She was given permanent, tenured status at Virginia Tech in 1989.

Giovanni's earliest works *Black Feeling, Black Talk*, and *Black Judgement* (published together in a single volume in 1970) are often seen as expressions of an angry and militant Black consciousness. "The True Import of Present Dialogue, Black vs. Negro" (from *Black Feeling, Black Talk*), says of African Americans,

> We ain't got to prove we can die
> We got to prove we can kill

Her subsequent works are usually considered to be a retreat from this early revolutionary stance toward a more private poeticism. But even in her earliest work, the revolutionary and the private live side by side. "The Great Pax Whitie" (*Black Judgement*), considered one of Giovanni's most militant expressions of Black pride, asks in a recurring refrain whether White America has any shame, and answers itself, "nah, they ain't got no shame." The very birth of America, in this poem, is a genesis of genocide. Yet this expression appears immediately after "Nikki-Rosa," a poem of intense personal sentiment and well-crafted childhood nostalgia. Within "Nikki-Rosa," anger and joy form two sides of one coin. The narrator of the poem (Giovanni) hopes that no White person will ever write about her. The happiness alluded to in "Nikki-Rosa" is poignantly described a few pages later in "Knoxville, Tennessee," with a remembered childhood of picnicking, **gospel music** in church, and familial warmth.

Giovanni's works in the early 1970s, *Re:creation* (1970), *Gemini*, an autobiography (1971), and *My House* (1972) continue to address questions about equality and justice, but they also embrace a more personal aesthetic, one that takes precedence over political action. In "Revolutionary Dreams" the narrator talks about former dreams of militancy, but comes to embrace the revolutionary personally. Many of the poems in *Re:creation* abandon angry invective for biting humor and irony. "No Reservations" plays off a double or perhaps triple meaning for the word "reservation." The narrator leads the reader to realize that one cannot make "reservations" to attend the revolution at one's convenience. Neither can one *have* reservations about taking part. Finally, she warns, "there will be reservations only if we fail."

My House (1972) again exhibits moments of personal introspection, coupled with comments about public events. The book is divided into sections titled "The Rooms Inside" and "The Rooms Outside," the sections forming an exchange between the poet's personal and public selves. The "inside" poems make observations about relationships, family members, and childhood memories. The "outside" poems comment with quiet rage on events such as the use of napalm in Vietnam, the actions of Richard Nixon, and the dealings of the FBI.

Cotton Candy on a Rainy Day (1978) deals poignantly with the failures of the revolution. As in many of Giovanni's collections from the later 1970s, there is a great emphasis on the music of the poetry. Many critics, however, complain that the structure of Giovanni's poetry never quite reaches a level of distinction to equal the content of her work, or that the sense and meaning are sacrificed to musicality. In *Those Who Ride the Night Winds* (1983) Giovanni seems to give up poetic form altogether in favor of startling bits of phrase linked together by ellipses in a staccato manner that is neither prose nor **prose poem**.

In addition to poetry, Giovanni has published several notable volumes of nonfiction. These are primarily collections of magazine articles, reviews, and occasional pieces. Of these, *Gemini* (1971) gives the most insightful look into Giovanni's psyche, development as a writer, and political engagement. It includes a number of nostalgic essays on her relationship with her grandparents and the sadness she felt when their social order was disturbed by urban development in Knoxville. *Sacred Cows . . . and Other Edibles* (1988) employs a much more biting sense of humor and irony. *Racism 101* (1994) contains remembrances of Giovanni's experiences growing up in Cincinnati and attending Fisk University. It also comments at length on such important Black leaders as **Malcolm X** and **W.E.B. Du Bois**. The state of higher education in America comes under severe scrutiny in several essays.

Giovanni continues to produce poetry with a unique and enduring style, wedding intimacy and activism into a single musical voice. Our understanding of her work was enhanced by the publication of *The Selected Poems of Nikki Giovanni* (1996) and *The Collected Poetry of Nikki Giovanni* (2003). The latter, unfortunately, excludes her children's poetry and the new work published in

Love Poems (1997), *Blues: For All the Changes. New Poems* (1999), and *Quilting the Black-eyed Pea: Poems and Not Quite Poems* (2002). *The Prosaic Soul of Nikki Giovanni* (2003) brings together most of her published nonfiction. The reading public recognizes Giovanni as a distinctive poetic persona, a lively consciousness and conscience for Americans of all ethnicities. In time, Nikki Giovanni may receive critical attention that is the equal of her popular readership.

Resources: **Primary Sources:** Nikki Govanni: *Black Feeling, Black Talk* (1968; repr. Detroit: Broadside Press, 1970); *Black Feeling, Black Talk, Black Judgement* (New York: Morrow, 1970); *Black Judgement* (Detroit: Broadside Press, 1968); *Blues: For All the Changes. New Poems* (New York: Morrow, 1999); *The Collected Poetry of Nikki Giovanni, 1968–1998* (New York: Morrow, 2003); *Cotton Candy on a Rainy Day* (New York: Morrow, 1978); *A Dialogue: James Baldwin and Nikki Giovanni* (Philadelphia: Lippincott, 1973); *Ego-Tripping and Other Poems for Young People* (New York: Lawrence Hill, 1973); *Gemini: An Extended Autobiographical Statement on My First Twenty-Five Years of Being a Black Poet* (Indianapolis, IN: Bobbs-Merrill, 1971); *The Genie in the Jar* (New York: Henry Holt, 1998); *Knoxville, Tennessee* (New York: Scholastic, 1994); *Love Poems* (New York: Morrow, 1997); *My House: Poems* (New York: Morrow, 1972); *A Poetic Equation: Conversations Between Nikki Giovanni and Margaret Walker* (Washington, DC: Howard University Press, 1974); *The Prosaic Soul of Nikki Giovanni* (New York: Perennial, 2003); *Quilting the Black-eyed Pea: Poems and Not Quite Poems* (New York: Morrow, 2002); *Racism 101* (New York: Morrow, 1994); *Re:creation* (Detroit: Broadside Press, 1970); *Sacred Cows...and Other Edibles* (New York: Morrow, 1988); *The Selected Poems of Nikki Giovanni* (New York: Morrow, 1996); *Shimmy Shimmy Shimmy Like My Sister Kate: Looking at the Harlem Renaissance Through Poems* (New York: Henry Holt, 1996); *Spin a Soft Black Song: Poems for Children* (New York: Hill & Wang, 1971); *The Sun Is So Quiet* (New York: Henry Holt, 1996); *Those Who Ride the Night Winds* (New York: Morrow, 1983); *Vacation Time: Poems for Children* (New York: Morrow, 1980); *The Women and the Men* (New York: Morrow, 1975); Nikki Giovanni, ed.: *Grand Fathers: Reminiscences, Poems, Recipes and Photos of the Keepers of Our Traditions* (New York: Henry Holt, 1999); *Grand Mothers: Poems, Reminiscences, and Short Stories about the Keepers of Our Traditions* (New York: Henry Holt, 1994). **Secondary Sources:** Virginia C. Fowler, *Nikki Giovanni* (New York: Twayne, 1992); Judith Virginia C. Fowler, ed., *Conversations with Nikki Giovanni* (Jackson: University Press of Mississippi, 1992); Pinkerton Josephson, *Nikki Giovanni, Poet of the People* (Berkeley Heights, NJ: Enslow, 2000).

Steven R. Harris

Glave, Thomas (born 1964). Short story writer, essayist, poet, activist, and teacher. Glave, born in New York City on November 10, 1964, has become one of the best-known Black gay writers of the late twentieth and early twenty-first centuries. Following in the footsteps of writer-activists such as **James Baldwin**, **Audre Lorde**, and **Essex Hemphill**, Glave in his short stories has created characters whose needs, desires, and fears until fairly recently were not represented truthfully or fully in either U.S. or Caribbean literatures.

Having grown up both in the Bronx and in Kingston, Jamaica, Glave is intimately familiar with languages and ideas from both locales, and he uses this knowledge as material for his stories. As a young man in New York City, Glave danced for Dance Theater of Harlem and went to college, graduating with a major in English and a minor Latin American Studies from Bowdoin College. After college, according to Gene Jarrett, Glave became a James Michener Scholar at the Caribbean Writers' Institute at the University of Miami and won an Academy of American Poets Prize (1227). His activism on behalf of oppressed peoples has been constant; he has participated in HIV/AIDS educational outreach for the Gay Men's Health Crisis and has worked at an AIDS Hospice in Kingston. Glave has received fellowships from the Bronx Council on the Arts, a travel grant from the National Endowment for the Arts and, in the later 1990s, fellowships from the New York Foundation for the Arts and from the Fine Arts Center in Provincetown, Massachusetts (Jarrett, 1227) His most prestigious honor so far came in 1997 when he received an O. Henry Award for his short story "The Final Inning." According to Jarrett, Glave is the first gay Black writer since James Baldwin, in 1959, to win this prize (1228).

Glave earned an M.F.A. from Brown University in 1998, and in the same year won a Fulbright fellowship to study in Jamaica. While in Jamaica he cofounded the Jamaica Forum of Lesbians, All-Sexuals, and Gays, known as J-FLAG. In 2000, his debut collection, *Whose Song? and Other Stories*, which contains stories previously published in important literary journals such as **Callaloo** and *The Kenyon Review*, was published to wide acclaim. The book jacket displays the admiration of such important writers as Nadine Gordimer, **Clarence Major**, and **Gloria Naylor**, with Naylor making a comparison between Glave and important earlier writers such as **Richard Wright** and Baldwin. The stories in *Whose Song?* use a variety of narrative techniques to center the experiences of people, particularly Black men and women in both the United States and the Caribbean, whose sexuality is fluid and not well defined by reductive labels and stereotypes. Glave continues to write and is currently an assistant professor at Binghamton University.

Resources: Thomas Glave, *Whose Song? and Other Stories* (San Francisco: City Lights Press, 2000); Gene Jarett, "A Song to Pass On: An Interview with Thomas Glave," *Callaloo* 23, no. 4 (2000), 1227–1240.

Bill Clem

Goines, Donald (1937–1974). Novelist. Born December 15, 1937, the prolific novelist Donald Goines spent his writing career examining the criminal realm of Black urban life. Born and raised in **Detroit, Michigan**, he experienced a childhood that was tame compared with the violent world he treats in his novels. However, during high school, he decided to drop out, and, lying about his age, he joined the U.S. Air Force. While serving in Japan during the Korean War, Goines became addicted to heroin and remained addicted throughout his life. Arrested numerous times for various crimes linked to his addiction, he spent six and a half years in prison. During a term in Jackson State Prison in 1965, he wrote his first novels, which were Westerns, but found this genre unsuitable (*see* **Prison Literature**). After reading some of the works of Robert **"Iceberg Slim"** Beck, Goines turned to writing about criminals and drug addicts in the ghetto of Detroit. In 1969, back in Jackson State Prison, Goines produced the first of his ghetto novels. *Whoreson: The Story of a Ghetto Pimp* (1972), his most autobiographical work, is the story of the son of a prostitute who grows up to become a pimp. However, the first of his novels to be published was *Dopefiend: The Story of a Black Junkie* (1971), a tale of how devastating the drug dealer's influence over drug users can be.

Released from prison in 1970, Goines resumed his life as a heroin addict. In 1972 he wrote *Black Gangster*, the tale of a gang leader named Prince who uses his organization, the Freedom Now Liberation Movement, as a front for illegal activity. In this book, Goines wanted to demonstrate how American society makes it difficult for African Americans to succeed in legitimate business and how tempting it is for them to turn to illegal activities. He went on to write *Street Players* (1973) and *White Man's Justice, Black Man's Grief* (1973), stories about the injustices of the bail bond system. *Black Girl Lost* (1973) is Goines's only book written from a woman's point of view. Some of his books published in 1974 are *Eldorado Red*, *Swamp Man*, *Never Die Alone*, and *Daddy Cool*.

In 1974, Goines' publisher, Holloway House, requested he use a pseudonym, which he did, choosing a friend's name, Al C. Clark. Under that name he wrote *Cry Revenge!* (1974) and a four-book series—*Crime Partners* (1974), *Death List* (1974), *Kenyatta's Escape* (1974), and *Kenyatta's Last Hit* (1975), featuring Kenyatta, a militant leader, and his army of rebels as they mount a campaign to kill **White** policemen and eliminate crime from the black ghetto. Goines's life was cut short when he and his common-law wife, Shirley Sailor, were shot and killed in Detroit on October 21, 1974. His last book, *Inner City Hoodlum*, was published posthumously in 1975. Goines' books have never gone out of print. All of his works were reprinted as mass-market paperbacks in the late 1990s and 2000.

Resources: Donald Goines: *Black Girl Lost* (1973; repr. New York: Holloway House, 1999); *Cry Revenge* (New York: Holloway House, 1995); *Daddy Cool: A Father Out to Revenge His Daughter's Shame* (1974; repr. New York: Holloway House, 2000); *Dopefiend* (1971; repr. New York: Holloway House, 2000); *Eldorado Red* (1974; repr. New York: Holloway House, 2000); *Inner City Hoodlum* (New York: Holloway House, 1975); *Kenyatta's Last Hit* (1975; repr. New York: Holloway House, 1998); *Street Players* (1973; repr. New York: Holloway House, 2000); *White Man's Justice, Black Man's Grief* (1973; repr. New York: Holloway House, 2000); *Whoreson: The Story of a Ghetto Pimp* (1972; repr. New York: Holloway House, 2000); Greg Goode, "Donald Goines," in *Dictionary of Literary Biography*, vol. 33, *Afro-American Fiction Writers After 1995*, ed. Thadious M. Davis and Trudier Harris (Detroit: Gale Press, 1984), 96–100; Eddie Stone, *Donald Writes No More: A Biography of Donald Goines* (Los Angeles: Holloway House, 1974).

Craig Loomis

Goldberg, Whoopi (born 1955). Comedienne, actress, political activist, autobiographer, and children's writer. Born Caryn Johnson in New York City, Goldberg and her brother were raised by a single mother on the Lower West Side of Manhattan. Frustrated with school, she dropped out at the age of thirteen. Many years later, Goldberg discovered that she was dyslexic, which undoubtedly contributed to her academic frustration. She floundered; she had two miscarriages and fell into drug addiction. She kicked her habit, married and divorced her drug counselor, and had a baby girl, all before she was twenty years old. Goldberg's love of theater and performing led her to California, where she developed a one-woman show. That show was seen by Broadway producer Mike Nichols, who subsequently arranged for Goldberg to appear on the Great White Way. She was an instant success. Soon after, Goldberg struck movie pay dirt in *The Color Purple*, based on **Alice Walker**'s novel. Goldberg's cinematic debut as Celie in *The Color Purple* earned her an Oscar nomination. More movie roles followed, including successful turns in *Sister Act* and *Ghost*, but some of her most memorable projects, such as her portrayal of the ill-fated friend in the screen of adaptation of **Terry McMillan**'s novel *How Stella Got Her Groove Back*; her homage to Black suburbia as the matriarch in the movie *Good Fences*, based on **Erika Ellis**'s satirical novel; and her lead role in **August Wilson**'s play *Ma Rainey's Black Bottom*, began with the written word. Goldberg remains one of the few artists to win an Oscar, an Emmy, a Grammy, a Tony, and a Golden Globe. Off-screen, Goldberg (an original investor in Planet Hollywood) has become well known for her support of humanitarian efforts on behalf of children, the homeless, human rights, substance abuse and the battle against AIDS; between 1994 and 1996 alone, for instance, she supported over sixty charitable causes.

Whoopi Goldberg in the 1985 film *The Color Purple*. Courtesy of Photofest.

In February 2004, Goldberg entered into a multibook deal with Hyperion to write children's books. Twelve years earlier, she had authored her first children's book, *Alice*, an urban takeoff on *Alice In Wonderland*. In 1997, Goldberg published her autobiography, *Book*. In it, she sums up her life's philosophy this way: "I believe I belong wherever I want to be, in whatever situation or context I place myself. I believed a little girl could rise from a single parent household in the Manhattan projects, start a single-parent household of her own, struggle through seven years of welfare and odd jobs, and still wind up making movies. You can go from anonymity to Planet Hollywood and never lose sight of where you've been" (231).

Resources: Mary Agnes Adams, *Whoopi Goldberg: From Street to Stardom* (New York: Dillon, 1993); William Caper, *Whoopi Goldberg: Comedian and Movie Star* (Springfield, NJ: Enslow, 1999); Ann Graham Gaines, *Whoopi Goldberg* (Philadelphia: Chelsea House,1999); Whoopi Goldberg: *Alice* (New York: Bantam, 1992); *Book* (New York: R. Weisbach, 1997); Sandor Katz, *Whoopi Goldberg: Performer with a Heart* (Philadelphia: Chelsea House, 1997).

Joy Duckett Cain

Golden, Marita (born 1950). Novelist and autobiographer. Golden is best known for her **autobiography**, which deals with her experiences as an African American living in Nigeria. She was born April 28, 1950, in **Washington, D.C.** Her parents, Francis Sherman Golden and Beatrice Reid Golden, worked as a taxi driver and rooming house manager, respectively. She earned a bachelor's degree in journalism from American University and also holds a master's degree in that field from Columbia University (Woodard, 177). Before marrying and moving to Nigeria, she briefly worked in television. She met her husband while they were students in New York and returned to Nigeria with him. During her four years in Nigeria, she taught at the Lagos Comprehensive Girls' School and at the University of Lagos (Woodard, 177). Upon her return to the United States, she taught English and writing at several colleges and universities before devoting her career to her own writing. She currently holds a position in George Mason University's creative writing program. In 1990, she established the Hurston/Wright Foundation, which sponsors workshops and awards for African American writers and students (www.hurston-wright.org).

Golden's first book is an autobiography that she began writing at age twenty-nine ("Marita Golden," 157). Golden notes that her mother predicted she would write a book when Golden was fourteen (Golden, "Marita," 127). Golden's early experiences of dealing with **race**, being educated during the **Black Power** movement, and living in Africa all shaped her identity as an African American. Golden says that she writes "to make sense of a very disorderly world" and that "as long as the world continues to make no sense," she will continue to write (Farley, 58). She notes that "the beginning of her real storytelling" came with her return from Nigeria, and she recognizes the irony that her writing career began with something other than a **novel** (Golden, "Marita," 131).

That first work, her autobiography *Migrations of the Heart*, covers her childhood, education, and relationship with her parents; her marriage to a Nigerian; her life in Africa; and the breakup of her marriage and eventual return to the United States. She has also written several novels that explore themes of family, women's roles, marriage, and culture. For her, fiction is a means of wish fulfillment, and she often lives vicariously through her characters (Farley, 58). Her first novel, *A Woman's Place* (1986), traces the lives of three women who become friends during college in the 1960s. One woman marries and converts to Islam, another moves to Africa and works as an activist, while the third marries a White man (Woodard, 179). *Long Distance Life* (1989) traces a woman and her family from her migration to the city in the 1920s to the present day, and was inspired by her mother's migration from **the South** to the northeastern U.S. (Farley, 58). *And Do Remember Me* (1992) deals with an incest survivor rebuilding her life during the Civil Rights era, while *The Edge of Heaven* (1998) portrays a family coming together again after their mother's release from prison. (*See* **Civil Rights Movement.**)

In addition, Golden has published several works of nonfiction, including a book about raising her son in a violent, uncertain world and one about being a successful single mother. Her most recent book deals with her experiences with racial politics, from childhood through adulthood. She also has served as editor or coeditor for a number of anthologies, including *Wild Women Don't Wear No Blues* (1993), *Skin Deep: Black Women and White Women Write about Race* (1995), and an anthology that served as a literary "rent party" to benefit the Hurston/Wright Foundation, *Gumbo: A Celebration of African American Writing* (2002).

Resources: Christopher John Farley, "Marita Golden: Wishful Writing," *Essence*, Sept. 1992, 58; Marita Golden: *And Do Remember Me* (New York: Doubleday, 1992); *Don't Play in the Sun: One Woman's Journey through the Color Complex* (New York: Doubleday, 2004); *The Edge of Heaven* (New York: Doubleday, 1998); *Long Distance Life* (New York: Doubleday, 1989); "Marita Golden," in *I Know What the Red Clay Looks Like: The Voice and Vision of Black Women Writers*, ed. Rebecca Carroll (New York: Crown, 1994), 126–133; *Migrations of the Heart* (Garden City, NY: Anchor, 1983); *A Miracle Every Day: Triumph and Transformation in the Lives of Single Mothers* (New York: Anchor, 1999); *Saving Our Sons: Raising Black Children in a Turbulent World* (New York: Doubleday, 1995); *A Woman's Place* (New York: Doubleday, 1986); "Marita Golden," in *Contemporary Authors*, new rev., vol. 82 (Detroit: Gale, 2000), 156–159; Loretta G. Woodard, "Marita Golden," in *Contemporary African American Novelists*, ed. Emmanuel S. Nelson (Westport, CT: Greenwood Press, 1999), 177–184.

Elizabeth Blakesley Lindsay

Gomez, Jewelle (born 1948). Novelist, short story writer, poet, essayist, and political activist. Born in **Boston, Massachusetts**, Jewelle Gomez skirts the fringes of contemporary American letters. As an African American, a feminist, and a lesbian, she is primarily known for her speculative **novel** *The Gilda Stories* (1991), which won two Lambda Literary awards in 1991. Gomez's work has been widely anthologized not only in gay and lesbian publications but also in more mainstream publications. Although she has been influenced by such diverse writers as **Toni Morrison, Audre Lorde**, and **James Baldwin**, Gomez's literary career really began after she read **Ntozake Shange**'s play *for colored girls who have considered suicide/when the rainbow is enuf* (1975). Gomez also states that "Joanna Russ' novel *The Female Man* (1975) confirm[ed] my belief that art and politics are intertwined" (Jay, 13). In 1985, Gomez became a founding board member of the Gay and Lesbian Alliance against Defamation (GLAAD), and continues to be active in political and social issues that affect not only gay, lesbian, bisexual and transgendered people but all oppressed people. Her first two collections of poetry, *The Lipstick Papers* (1980) and *Flamingoes and Bears* (1986), were published to great critical success.

The Gilda Stories, a postapocalyptic tale that begins in the southern United States in 1850s Louisiana and ends in 2050 in the ruins of Machu Picchu in Southern Peru, can be read as a **slave narrative** and is about a group of African American, Native American, and White lesbian and gay vampires who differ from vampires portrayed in previous speculative fiction because they are in many ways more human than their human counterparts. One of Gomez's most famous essays, "Recasting the Mythology: Writing Vampire Fiction," published in Joan Gordon and Veronica Hollinger's *Blood Read: The Vampire as Metaphor in Contemporary Culture* (1997), is about the creation of *The Gilda Stories*. Following the success of *The Gilda Stories*, Gomez published *Forty-three Septembers* (1993), a kind of autobiographical collection of essays about life and literature, and *Don't Explain* (1998), a collection of short stories.

Resources: Jewelle Gomez: *Don't Explain: Short Fiction* (Ithaca, NY: Firebrand Books, 1998); *Flamingoes and Bears* (Jersey City, NJ: Grace Publications, 1986); *Forty-three Septembers: Essays* (Ithaca, NY: Firebrand Books, 1993); *The Gilda Stories: A Novel* (Ithaca, NY: Firebrand Books, 1991); *The Lipstick Papers* (Jersey City, NJ: Grace Publications, 1980); *Oral Tradition: Selected Poems Old & New* (Ithaca, NY: Firebrand Books, 1995); Jewelle Gomez and Eric Garber, eds., *Swords of the Rainbow* (Los Angeles: Alyson, 1996); Jewelle Gomez, Dale Peck, Mab Segrest, and David Deitcher, eds., *Over the Rainbow: Lesbian and Gay Politics since Stonewall* (Los Angeles: Alyson, 1996); Jewelle Gomez and Tristan Taormino, eds.: *Best Lesbian Erotica 1997* (San Francisco: Cleis Press, 1997); *Best Lesbian Erotica 2000* (Los Angeles: Cleis Press, 2000); *Conversemos! Let's Talk!* (Dubuque, IA: Kendall/Hunt, 1988); Karla Jay, "Books That Shaped Us: Women's Writes," *Lambda Book Report* 10, no. 6 (Jan. 2002), 13.

Keith B. Mitchell

Gordone, Charles (1925–1995). Playwright, poet, and scholar. Gordone was the first African American playwright to win the Pulitzer Prize in drama, for *No Place to Be Somebody* (1970). His biographer Paul Christensen claims this early success made Gordone fear he was a one-hit wonder (255). Nonetheless, Gordone's subsequent contributions to **drama** were ample. He also authored dozens of poems and essays on Black culture and contributed to film and audio productions.

The New York Public Theater originally produced *No Place to Be Somebody*, Gordone's multilayered exploration of racial relations and crime in a New York City bar. Though an unusual collaboration between Gordone, "barefoot, barechested and pigtailed," and Ted Cornell, "a blue-eyed...Yale Drama School student," the production was an immediate success (Papp, ix). Walter Kerr called Gordone the finest playwright since Edward Albee (Costa, 1). The play expands on the **Black Arts Movement**, incorporating references to contemporary racial tensions, poetry, and multiple varieties of ethnic English in a work that, according to Harry Elam, "foreground[s] the power of the black

Charles Gordon, winner of the 1970 Pulitzer Prize for Drama, was the first Black man to receive the award. AP/Wide World Photos.

performer to renegotiate meanings of blackness" (Elam and Krasner, 288). With its brutal themes and complex characters, it advances Black revolutionary drama, confronting Black as well as **White** Americans (Papp, x). Despite the importance of his play to African American theater, Gordone, in a variety of writings, resisted the label "Black playwright," preferring that audiences regard his work in a broader, more transcendent, context.

Gordone received a National Institute of Arts and Letters grant (1971) and a D. H. Lawrence fellowship (1987). He served on the faculty of Texas A&M University from 1986 until his death. Although several of his plays have been widely produced, they are, at this writing, unpublished. These include *A Little More Light Around the Place* (1964), *Baba Chops* (1974), *The Last Chord* (1976), and *A Qualification for Anabiosis* (1978).

Resources: Primary Sources: Charles Gordone: assorted writings, *Black Drama* (Alexandria, VA: Alexander Street Press, 2002), http://www.alexanderstreet2.com/bldrlive; *Breakout*, in *Black Drama Anthology*, ed. Woodie King and Ron Milner (New York: Columbia University Press, 1972); *Charles Gordone*, sound recording (Kansas City, MO: New Letters, 1978); *Coonskin*, directed by Ralph Bakshi, Barry White, Charles Gordone, Scat Man Crothers, and Philip Michael Thomas, video recording (Los Angeles: Badcat Entertainment, 1974); *Cures*, sound recording (Kansas City, MO: New Letters, 1978); *Five Plays* (New York: Charles F. Gardon, 1969); "Gordone Is a Mutha," in *Best Short Plays of 1973*, ed. Stanley Richards (Radnor, PA: Chilton, 1973); *His First Step*, in *The New Lafayette Theater Presents*, ed. Ed Bullins (Garden City, NY: Anchor Press, 1974); *I am a Man=Powa ta da Peepas* (New York: Applause Books, 1995); *No Place to Be Somebody: A Black Black Comedy in Three Acts* (Indianapolis, IN: Bobbs-Merrill, 1969); *The Resurrection of Lady Lester: A Poetic Mood Song Based on the Legend of Lester Young* (New York: Theatre Communications Group, 1981). **Secondary Sources:** Joseph Anthony, director, *Walter Kerr on Theater*, video recording (New York: Coronet/MTI Films & Video, 1979); Lilla Browstone, director, *The Black Experience in the Arts*, video recording (Pleasantville, NY: Warren Schloat Productions, 1971); Lilla Browstone, ed., *Charles Gordone, Playwright*, slides/sound recording (New York: Warren Schloat Productions, 1971); Corey Everette Carter, *Charles Gordone's "No Place to Be Somebody": An Analysis* (Petersburg, VA: Virginia State University, 1999); Paul Christensen, *West of the American Dream: An Encounter with Texas* (College Station: Texas A&M University Press, 2001); Richard H. Costa, "The Short Happy Afterlife of

Charles Gordone," *The Touchstone*, Feb./Mar. 1996, http://www.rtis.com/reg/bcs/pol/touchstone/February96/costa.htm (May 14, 2004); Harry Justin Elam and David Krasner, eds., *African-American Performance and Theater History: A Critical Reader* (New York: Oxford University Press, 2001); Oliver F. Hubbard, *A Critical Analysis of Selected American Dramas (1950–1975) in Light of a Christian View of Man* (Kent, OH: Kent State University, 1981); Joseph Papp, "Introduction," in *No Place to Be Somebody: A Black Black Comedy in Three Acts* (Indianapolis, IN: Bobbs-Merrill, 1969); Jean W. Ross, "Charles Gordone," in *Twentieth-Century American Dramatists*, ed. John MacNicholas, vol. 1 (Detroit: Gale Research, 1981); Susan Harris Smith, "Charles Gordone," in *Speaking on Stage: Interviews with Contemporary American Playwrights*, ed. Phillip C. Kolin and Colby H. Kullman (Tuscaloosa: University of Alabama Press, 1996); Sanford V. Sternlicht, *A Reader's Guide to Modern American Drama* (Syracuse, NY: Syracuse University Press, 2002).

Ben Fisler

Gospel Music. The word "gospel" dates back at least as far as 1000 C.E., according to the *Oxford Dictionary of the English Language*, and it denoted "glad tidings" or "good news" related to the Kingdom of God and delivered by Jesus Christ (*OED* online). With regard to African American literature and culture, "gospel" is often used as a shortened form of the term "gospel music," and as one might guess, gospel music refers to music that is intimately related to Christian faith and that is often performed in churches by church singers and musicians. Gospel music, which includes songs known as **spirituals**, has been part of the African American culture since the 1700s and may be traced back to the time of **slavery**. Most of the Africans who were kidnapped and forced into slavery came from West African societies where the most characteristic music was the communal song, which was played/sung for all occasions including war, birth, marriage, death, and worship. In his *Life*, a **slave narrative**, **Olaudah Equiano** speaks of this communal African music: "We are almost a nation of dances, musicians, and poets. Thus every great event ... is celebrated in public dances which are accompanied with songs and music" (14). Musical instruments such as drums, rattles, and bells sometimes accompanied singing, but occasionally the instruments were played alone.

During the African **diaspora**, and especially in the American **South** during the period of slavery, this communal music, once it was connected to African American versions of Christianity, produced gospel music. Some of the best known traditional American gospel songs are of African American origin. They include "Swing Low, Sweet Chariot," "Go Tell It on the Mountain," "Sometimes I Feel Like a Motherless Child," "Nobody Knows the Trouble I've Seen," and "Somebody's Knockin' on My Door." (Such traditional songs, whose originators are not known, are widely available now in individual sheet music, countless songbooks, and numerous recordings.) As with work songs and the **blues**, gospel music was at first transmitted orally through numerous generations before it was written down and/or recorded electronically.

Signifying was a prevalent form of singing the spirituals in the **Negro** slave culture. In this context, signifying refers to linguistic improvisation, which may include a kind of "coding" whereby words are used in a deliberately deceptive way so that some listeners are bound to misinterpret them. In spirituals, African American slaves used signifying in this way. To the ears of the masters and other Whites, the lyrics used by the slaves may have seemed innocent and God-fearing, yet to the slaves themselves, the words often created additional layers of meaning (Lawrence-McIntyre). For example, a reference to Jesus might be understood by the slaves as establishing a link between Jesus' suffering and the slaves' plight. In the same vein, mention of Satan in a song might be understood as a reference to slave owners and slave masters, "Heaven" might be equated with the North and/or escape from slavery, "home" might be equated with Africa, and "Israelites" might be equated with enslaved Blacks. Such double meaning in spirituals could even be used to transmit secrets about a planned escape (Lawrence-McIntyre). These double meanings of the lyrics sung by the slaves permeated the Negro slave spirituals, providing a secret language the slaves knew and could use, but to which the slave masters and other Whites were generally oblivious.

The practice of call-and-response was also important to early African American gospel music. The lyrical phrases used in the call-and-response spirituals are short, but often varied. The structure of the call-and-response spiritual is based on repetition of the short lyrical phrases with the "call" person singing a phrase first and the "response" people either repeating the same lyrical phrase or answering the phrase with another lyrical phrase. In the song "Somebody's Knockin' on My Door," for example, the "call" of "Somebody's knockin' on my door," which might be sung by one person, is followed by the "response" of "Must be Jesus," which might be sung by the choir. The rhythm of the call-and-response can be quite complex, with syncopation being very common. The term "spiritual" also encompasses other religious song types such as Protestant hymns and the "shout" or "ring shout" (Nettl, 93–94).

Olaudah Equiano also makes reference to the **spirituals** in his *Life*. For instance, he mentions the following lines from a traditional spiritual: "Though rocks and quicksands deep thro' all my passage lie/Yet Christ shall safely keep and guide me with his eye/How can I sink with such a prop/That bears the world and all things up" (150). In this manner, Equiano used the spirituals as a means of emotional and physical survival during his enslavement.

African American gospel music, including spirituals, has influenced works of fiction by African American authors. These works include **Zora Neale Hurston**'s *Moses, Man of the Mountain* (1939), in which she identifies Blacks with the enslaved Hebrews, using theme and structure, and **Margaret Walker**'s *Jubilee* (1966). **James Baldwin**'s first novel, *Go Tell It On the Mountain* (1953), the title of which is identical to that of a renowned African American gospel song, was significantly influenced by the African American fundamentalist Christian church, gospel music, and spirituals, as were many of his subsequent works. As a young man, Baldwin was a preacher in a **Harlem, New York**, church for a short time, something he discusses in his nonfiction book *The Fire Next Time*, the title of which is taken from the Old Testament.

Ralph Ellison's *Invisible Man* (1952) exhibits the influence of gospel music and spirituals, and the call-and-response method of singing spirituals plays an important role in **Toni Morrison**'s *Song of Solomon* (1977).

African American gospel music has also influenced African American **drama**, including works by **Langston Hughes**. In his play *Don't You Want to Be Free?* Hughes incorporates spirituals as the voice for the suffering slaves. In *The Sun Do Move* (1942), Hughes attempts to define both the religious and the secular meanings of the spirituals. Other plays written by Hughes that exhibit the influence of the Negro spirituals include *The Prodigal Son* (1965), *Gospel Glory* (1963), *Tambourines to Glory: A Play with Spirituals, Jubilees, and Gospel Songs* (1958), and *Black Nativity* (1961), which at this writing is still often produced, including an annual run at Seattle, Washington's, Intiman Theatre. The chapter "Salvation" in Hughes's first autobiography, *The Big Sea*, points to Hughes's own complex, uncertain attitude toward Christianity, an attitude that by no means prevented him from drawing on and exploring religion, gospel music, and spirituals in his work.

African American poetry has also been influenced by African American gospel music and spiritual songs. **Robert Hayden** incorporated lyrics from the spiritual "Trinity Hymnal #497" in his poem "Middle Passage" (1962), in which he graphically depicts the passage of the captured Africans from Africa to the New World. **Paul Laurence Dunbar** referred to the signifying aspects of the Negro spirituals when he wrote his poem "We Wear the Mask" (1895). In his book of poetry *Majors and Minors* (1895), the influence of spirituals is also evident. Other African American poets who were influenced by the Negro spirituals include **James Weldon Johnson**, author of *God's Trombones* (1927) and *Lift Ev'ry Voice and Sing* (1961), and Langston Hughes (*see* "Religion" in Ostrom).

Although African American gospel music in general and the spirituals in particular to some extent sprang from the physical and emotional pain, torment, and abuse suffered by African and African American slaves, the influence of the music and songs on African American literature has been enormously rich and varied.

Resources: James Baldwin: *The Fire Next Time* (1953; repr. New York: Dial Press, 1963); *Go Tell It on the Mountain* (New York: Grossett and Dunlap, 1953); Viv Broughton, *Black Gospel: An Illustrated History of the Gospel Sound* (London: Blandford Press, 1985); Robert Darden, *A New History of Gospel Music* (New York: Continuum, 2004); Frederick Douglass, *Narrative of the Life of Frederick Douglass* (1845), in *The Classic Slave Narratives*, ed. Henry Louis Gates, Jr. (New York: Mentor, 1987), 243–331; Paul Laurence Dunbar, *Majors and Minors: Poems* (1895; repr. Miami, FL: Mnemosyne Publishing Co., 1969); Ralph Ellison, *Invisible Man* (New York: Random House, 1952); Dena J. Epstein, *Sinful Tunes and Spirituals: Black Folk Music to the Civil War* (Urbana: University of Illinois Press, 1977); Olaudah Equiano, *The Life of*

Olaudah Equiano (1789), in *The Classic Slave Narratives*, ed. Henry Louis Gates, Jr. (New York: Mentor, 1987), 1–182; Miles Mark Fisher, *Negro Slave Songs in the United States* (New York: Citadel Press, 1953), 176–191; Samuel A. Floyd, Jr., *The Power of Black Music* (Oxford: Oxford University Press, 1995); Henry Louis Gates, Jr., and Nellie Y. McKay, eds., *The Norton Anthology of African American Literature* (New York: Norton, 1997); Robert Hayden, *Collected Poems*, ed. Frederick Glaysher (New York: Liveright, 1985); Anthony Heilbut, *The Gospel Sound: Good News and Bad Times*, 25th anniversary issue (New York: Limelight, 1997); Langston Hughes: *The Big Sea: An Autobiography* (New York: Knopf, 1940); *The Collected Works of Langston Hughes*, 16 vols., ed. Arnold Rampersad, et al. (Columbia: University of Missouri Press, 2001–2004); Zora Neale Hurston, *Moses, Man of the Mountain* (1939; repr. New York: HarperPerennial, 1991); James Weldon Johnson: *God's Trombones: Seven Negro Sermons in Verse* (1927; repr. New York: Viking, 1938); *Lift Ev'ry Voice and Sing* (1961; repr. New York: Scholastic, 1995); Charshee Charlotte Lawrence-McIntyre, "The Double Meanings of the Spirituals," *Journal of Black Studies* 17, no. 4 (June 1987), 379–401; Toni Morrison, *Song of Solomon* (New York: Knopf, 1977); Bruno Nettl, *Folk Music in the United States* (Detroit: Wayne State University Press, 1976); see especially pp. 88–102; Hans Ostrom, "Religion," in his *A Langston Hughes Encyclopedia* (Westport, CT: Greenwood Press, 2002), 323–326; Leslie Catherine Sanders, "'I've Wrestled with Them all My Life:' Langston Hughes's *Tambourines to Glory*," *Black American Literature Forum* 25, no. 1 (Spring 1991), 63–72; *Oxford Dictionary of the English Language* [online], http://dictionary.oed.com/; Margaret Walker, *Jubilee* (Boston: Houghton Mifflin, 1966).

DaNean Pound

Gossett, Hattie (born 1942). Poet, nonfiction writer, **jazz** poetry performer, short story writer, editor, and teacher. Gossett is best known for the book of poems *Presenting... Sister No Blues* (1988), an exuberant yet sharp-edged satiric book that often celebrates women, especially African American women, but also critiques aspects of society that have made life difficult for working-class women. Gossett uses wide-open poetic forms full of improvised language, acerbic wit, and mercurial changes of mood and tone, and she is a popular performer of her poetry by herself and with jazz accompaniment. For many years Gossett was a staff editor for the magazines *True Story*, *Redbook*, *McCall's*, and *Black Theater*; she also was the first managing editor of *Essence* magazine but was fired for, in her words, "being too black" (*Writers' Register*). Before pursuing a career in magazine editing, she worked, in her words, as "office girl, cleaning person, retired barfly, florist's assistant, telephone solicitor, and waitress" (*Writers' Register*). She earned an M.F.A. in creative writing from New York University in 1993, and she cowrote books (which were accompanied by compact disc recordings of the artists) about jazz performers Ella Fitzgerald, Nat King Cole, **Billie Holiday**, and Louis Armstrong. Gossett has given numerous performances of her work, led many writing workshops nationwide, and produced a compact disc recording of her poetry performance. One of the most highly regarded selections from *Presenting... Sister No Blues* is "21st century black warrior wimmins chant for strengthening the nerves & getting yourself together," which serves as a kind of unifying anthem for working-class and politically active African American women.

Resources: Hattie Gossett: "Biography," in *Writers' Register*, http://www.writers register.com/artists/NY6; *Presenting . . . Sister No Blues* (Ithaca, NY: Firebrand Books, 1988); Andrew Hagan, Hattie Gossett, and Fred Karl, Jr., *Ella Fitzgerald; Nat King Cole; Billie Holiday; Louis Armstrong* (New Providence, NJ: Black Dog & Leventhal Publishers, 1997).

Hans Ostrom

Gothic Literature. The word "Gothic" can apply to a variety of subjects, from cathedrals to clothing. Entering the English language in the early 17th century, it originally referred to the Goths, a Teutonic people. Later the word took on a remarkably wide variety of connotations, some connected to styles of architecture, others related to medieval times, and still others related to uncouth behavior. With regard to literature, it refers to a subgenre of the novel that is often foreboding and "dark" in tone and explores extreme psychological conflict.

While the historic parameters of the Gothic novel in England are 1764 and 1820, the Gothic reached the height of its popularity during the French Revolutionary era of the 1790s, when it was politically revitalized. It was then that Charles Brockden Brown, a writer based in **Philadelphia, Pennsylvania**, influenced by the political philosophy and fiction of William Godwin, adapted British Gothic conventions to address distinctly American concerns. He thus became the father of American Gothic fiction, setting the stage for the three classic Gothicists of the American Renaissance—Edgar Allan Poe, Nathaniel Hawthorne, and Herman Melville. Various manifestations of the "return of the repressed" furnish the primary dynamic in Gothic fiction. Such authors indirectly fulfilled the commandment enunciated in the preface to a classic Gothic work, *The Castle of Otranto* (1764), by Horace Walpole—that "the sins of the fathers are visited on their children to the third and fourth generations." Gothic works chronicle the invasion of pasts upon presents and raise the joint specters of individual and social regression. Haunted houses abound, with such invasions generally taking place in a manor house or other dwelling, more modest but direct descendants of the classic Gothic's haunted, contested castle. The related fixation with the return of repressed aspects of the psyche is often represented by way of a "double" or "shadow self"—that is, another personality, one that often represents or acts out transgressions. (One of the most famous narratives concerning this kind of "double" is Robert Louis Stevenson's *Strange Case of Dr. Jekyll and Mr. Hyde*, from the late Victorian period, but in fact the convention of the Gothic "double" developed much earlier.)

Especially in the form known as the Female Gothic, the repression is usually revealed to be socially sanctioned by way of the increasingly influential nineteenth-century ideology of the "separate spheres" that promoted a strict

gender division between public/professional/masculine and private/domestic/feminine selves. In his seminal work *Love and Death in the American Novel* (1960), Leslie Fiedler describes American literature as "bewilderingly and embarrassingly, a gothic fiction" (9) that wrestles with moral and psychological questions and exposes the hidden "blackness" of the American soul. Attentive to the dark side of the concept of sociopolitical legacy and "the sins of the fathers," American Gothic especially engages, according to Fiedler, with that nation's two "special guilts"—"the slaughter of the Indians" and "the abominations of the slave trade" (130). In more recent criticism, Kari J. Winter has identified the beginning of a Gothic tradition in African American literature in the genre of the female **slave narrative** as epitomized by **Harriet Jacobs**'s *Incidents in the Life of a Slave Girl* (1861). Such works draw on the Female Gothic popularized by Britain's Ann Radcliffe and forge parallels between African American female slaves and women confined to the British domestic sphere. Gothic conventions are also prevalent in the recently discovered *The Bondwoman's Narrative* by **Hannah Crafts**, a fictionalized slave narrative dating from the 1850s, which is perhaps the first novel written by an African American woman. The conventions in this novel include an original crime, a series of haunted houses, the theme of confinement, and a figurative vampire persecutor in the form of a lawyer named Mr. Trappe.

In his prefacing essay to *Native Son* (1940), **Richard Wright** comments that African American reality is so rife with horrors that they need no Hawthorne or Poe to invent new ones. In the light of Wright's sobering observations, a more judicious theorization of the relationship between symbolic and actual violence, and between figurative and literal **slavery**, is probably necessary with regard to American and African American Gothic literature. While Kari J. Winter notes that the Female Gothic and the female slave narrative expose the terror, the sexual politics, and the "repressed, noctural, secret, and unconscious" truths about patriarchy, "substantial differences" also exist between these two categories of American literature. Given the slave narrative tradition, the African American Gothic was not only, as Jerrold Hogle has argued, "established and deeply rooted by the twentieth century but... [already] deliberately articulating profound social horrors" (218).

W.E.B. Du Bois's *The Souls of Black Folk* (1903), a provocative and poetic sociological commentary on African American reality in **the South** after **Reconstruction**, brings the Gothic to bear on race relations. As such, it follows in the tradition of such antebellum literary classics as Edgar Allan Poe's *The Narrative of Arthur Gordon Pym* (1838), Nathaniel Hawthorne's *The House of the Seven Gables* (1851), and Herman Melville's *Moby Dick; or, The Whale* (1851). According to Du Bois, forty years after the Emancipation Proclamation of 1863, the "Nation has not yet found peace from its sins": "the swarthy spectre [of slavery] sits in its accustomed seat at the Nation's feast." The sins of the fathers persist in the form of economic slavery as "the shadow-hand of the master's grand-nephew or cousin or creditor stretches out of the gray distance to collect the rack-rent remorselessly." Du Bois's portrait of a purgatorial, benighted region handcuffed to history is strikingly familiar to the Gothicist, as are the book's echoes of biblical apocalypse and revelation.

In the twentieth century, American Gothic was most recognizable as a regional form (Goddu, 3). As works by such masters as William Faulkner and Flannery O'Connor illustrate, the South often functions as the repository for America's irrational impulses. Twentieth-century African American Gothic literature continues to adhere to the established American Gothic recipe of disrupting "the dream world of national myth with the nightmares of history" (Goddu, 10). In the words of Richard Wright, "in the oppression of the Negro a shadow [lies] athwart our national life dense and heavy" (*Native Son*, xxxiv). Recent examples of the Gothic have ranged from more traditional narratives (e.g., **Toni Morrison**'s *Beloved*) to parodies of the subgenre (e.g., **Ishmael Reed**'s *Flight to Canada*, 1976). African American women writers seem particularly adept with this form, often successfully combining the Female Gothic with the political Gothic, which exposes and exorcises crimes and repressions fostered by the nation's institutions. **Gloria Naylor**'s *Linden Hills* (1985) is a sinister, politically loaded novel set in a Dantesque Black suburban community. In this compelling yet disturbing tale of a mortician with a deadly secret, a truly Gothic figure who blurs the traditional Female Gothic boundary between husband and prison master, Naylor indicts the repressive, self-loathing propensities of middle-class African American society. While many of Toni Morrison's works possess a significant Gothic component, *Beloved* (1987) has been singled out as her Gothic masterpiece. In its chilling declaration that "Not a house in the country ain't packed to its rafters with some dead Negro's grief" (5), *Beloved* offers up a singular revision of the haunted house tradition in American Gothic. The house known as 123 becomes the site where both a horrifying act of a slave mother and the crimes of a nation's fathers who sanctioned the "peculiar institution" and the Fugitive Slave Act are jointly explored and laid to rest. (*See* **Romance Novel**.)

Resources: Wesley Britton, "The Puritan Past and Black Gothic: The Haunting of Toni Morrison's *Beloved* in Light of Hawthorne's *The House of the Seven Gables*," *Nathaniel Hawthorne Review* 21 (1995), 7–23; David Dudley, "Toni Morrison," in *Gothic Writers: A Critical and Bibliographical Guide*, ed. Douglass H. Thomson, Jack G. Voller, and Frederick S. Frank (Westport, CT: Greenwood Press, 2002), 295–302; Leslie A. Fiedler, *Love and Death in the American Novel* (1960; rev. ed., New York: Dell, 1966); Teresa A. Goddu, *Gothic America: Narrative, History, and Nation* (New York: Columbia University Press, 1997); Jerrold E. Hogle, "Teaching the African American Gothic: From Its Multiple Sources to *Linden Hills* and *Beloved*," in *Gothic Fiction: The British and American Traditions*, ed. Diane Long Hoeveler and Tamar Heller (New York: Modern Language Association, 2003), 215–222; Kari J. Winter, *Subjects of Slavery, Agents of Change: Women and Power in Gothic Novels and Slave Narratives, 1790–1865* (Athens: University of Georgia Press, 1992).

Carol Margaret Davison

Gould, Sandra Lee (born 1949). Fiction writer and visual artist. Gould is best known for her work of fiction, *Faraday's Popcorn Factory* (1998). In this book, an African American woman living in the town of Good Sky, Ohio, meets her new neighbor and finds her heart opening for the first time since a long-ago relationship ended. Willow, the protagonist, who works in a popcorn factory, accepts her new neighbor, Clement, despite his oddness, and through their connection she is able to love again. The reader discovers that Clement has the ability to assume different forms, and his supernatural parents have the ability to control the weather and bring on storms. *Faraday's Popcorn Factory* is within the magical-realism tradition, as supernatural elements drive the book's plot.

Gould worked in a **Pittsburgh, Pennsylvania**, steel mill while raising two children and earning a college degree. She received her M.F.A. in creative writing from the University of Pittsburgh in 1990. She now works as a writer, quilt artist, and photo-essayist. Two of her latest fiction projects are *The Magnolia*, a multinovel series about betrayal, healing, and redemptive love, with some surreal elements, and *In Search of Purdy Loy*, a novel about seven saucy sisters. At this writing, both projects are unpublished. In 1994, while a fellow at the Alden B. Dow Creativity Center, Gould worked on a book-length collection of essays, entitled *The Works*, which explores Pittsburgh's last working steel mill through writing and photographs. Now retitled *Hot Metal*, the book explores the history, traditions, and wisdom of the mill where she once worked (the Jones & Laughlin steel mill on the Monongahela River in western pennsylvania's Steel Valley) through photography and words. At this writing, this book is unpublished.

Resource: Sandra Lee Gould, *Faraday's Popcorn Factory* (New York: St. Martin's Press, 1998; Griffin Press, 2000).

Elline Lipkin

Graham, Lorenz [Bell] (1902–1989). Fiction writer. Known for his books for young adults, Lorenz Graham was born in **New Orleans, Louisiana**. He attended the University of Washington at Seattle in 1921 and the University of California at **Los Angeles, California**, in 1923 and 1924, but he did not complete a baccalaureate degree until 1936, when he graduated from Virginia Union University. Eighteen years later, in 1954, he would complete a Masters of Social Work at Columbia University.

From 1924 to 1928, Graham lived in Liberia, where he taught school as a missionary. After he returned to the United States, he worked as a fund-raiser for the National Baptist Convention's Foreign Mission Board. Then he served for seven years as an administrator with the Civilian Conservation Corps and for three years as a manager of a public housing project. In the years immediately following **World War II**, he worked in retail and in construction. Then, from 1950 to 1966, he was employed for roughly equal periods as a social worker and as a probation officer. From 1970 to 1977, he taught at California State Polytechnic College at Pomona.

Graham will be most remembered for two significant contributions to the literature for young adults: his stories featuring a young Liberian boy named

Momolu and his novels in the "Town" series. The Momolu stories include retellings in West African dialect of biblical stories and reworkings of elements of West African folk tales into contemporary maturation stories set in Liberia. *How God Fix Jonah* and *Tales of Momolu* were originally published privately in 1946 and received relatively limited notice. But when the first few books in the "Town" series proved popular, Crowell divided the Liberian books into seven titles that were published for the most part in the early-to-mid-1970s. This time, their value was acknowledged much more widely.

But Graham's most enduring work may be the "Town" series. Focusing on the experiences of an African American boy named David Williams, the series chronicles the ways in which he gradually overcomes the obstacles of impoverishment, racial prejudice, and very limited precedents to realize his ambition of becoming a physician. With the success of this series and of the Liberian books, Graham was inspired to write a number of new non-series books on contemporary themes, as well as on biblical and historical subjects.

Resources: Primary Sources: Lorenz Graham: *Carolina Cracker* (Boston: Houghton Mifflin, 1972); *David He No Fear* (New York: Crowell, 1971), originally published in *How God Fix Jonah*; *Detention Center* (Boston: Houghton Mifflin, 1972); *Every Man Heart Lay Down* (New York: Crowell, 1970), originally published in *How God Fix Jonah*; *God Wash the World and Start Again* (New York: Crowell, 1971), originally published in *How God Fix Jonah*; *Hongry Catch the Foolish Boy* (New York: Crowell, 1973), originally published in *How God Fix Jonah*; *I, Momolu* (New York: Crowell, 1966); *John Brown: A Cry for Freedom* (New York: Crowell, 1980); *John Brown's Raid: A Picture History of the Attack on Harpers Ferry, Virginia* (New York: Scholastic, 1972); *North Town* (New York: Crowell, 1965); *Return to South Town* (New York: Crowell, 1976); *A Road Down in the Sea* (New York: Crowell, 1970), originally published in *How God Fix Jonah*; *Runaway* (Boston: Houghton Mifflin, 1972); *Song of the Boat* (New York: Crowell, 1975), originally published in *How God Fix Jonah*; *South Town* (Chicago: Follett, 1958); *Stolen Car* (Boston: Houghton Mifflin, 1972); *Whose Town?* (New York: Crowell, 1969). **Secondary Sources:** Ilene Cooper, "Top 10 Religion Books for Youth," *Booklist*, Oct. 1, 2001, p. 333; Charles C. Irby, "A Writer Speaks: An Interview with Lorenz Bell Graham (2 June 1983)," *Explorations in Ethnic Studies* 6 (July 1983), 1–7; Elizabeth Schafer, "'I'm Gonna Glory in Learnin': Academic Aspirations of African American Characters in Children's Literature," *African American Review* 32 (Spring 1998), 57–66.

Martin Kich

Graham, Ottie B. (1900–1982). Playwright, short story writer, and choreographer. Ottie B. (Lottie Beatrice) Graham wrote one-act plays under the guidance of the educator, dramatist, and historian Thomas Montgomery Gregory, and she is considered a relatively minor but nonetheless important figure of the **Harlem Renaissance**. Gregory, a leading figure in the National Negro Theatre Movement, ran a drama program in New York through which Graham encountered the social philosophy and political activism that underpins her short fiction, most famously "Slackened Caprice" (1924).

As Gregory's student in 1921, Graham wrote two of her most celebrated plays, *The King's Carpenters*, which appeared in *The Stylus* in May 1926, and *Holiday*, published in **W.E.B. Du Bois**'s magazine *The Crisis* in May 1923. Indeed, beyond Gregory's writing classes, one important forum for Graham was the regular playwriting contests sponsored by Casper Hostein in *The Crisis*, as well as similar contests sponsored by Amy Springarn in **Charles Spurgeon Johnson**'s magazine *Opportunity*.

As Gregory's disciple, and with attention to Du Bois's Krigwa Little Theatre movement from 1926 on, Graham tried to define her drama against an eighty-year-old tradition of **minstrelsy**. Her plays belong with the serious melodrama of the mid-1920s, alongside works such as G. D. Lipscomb's *Francis* (1925) and **John F. Matheus**'s *Cruiter* (1926). Critics, including Crystal Lucky, also group her drama with **Zora Neale Hurston**'s *Color Struck* (1926), **Angelina Grimké**'s *Rachel* (1921), and **Georgia Douglas Johnson**'s *A Sunday Morning in the South* (1925) because she foregrounded topical issues in the lives of African American women and engaged with the period's lively debate on propaganda versus art.

But few Harlem Renaissance artists turned their attention to serious drama while Graham was writing, and the Washington-based artist **Willis Richardson**, with his Broadway play *The Chip Woman's Fortune* (1923), was the only Black playwright to emerge fully onto the national stage. The popular revue *Shuffle Along* of 1921, a mélange of slapstick, dance, and song, had produced a relentless spate of imitations, and Black-themed plays by White writers such as Eugene O'Neill and Paul Green were also dominant. (*See* **Drama**.)

Resources: Crystal J. Lucky, "Black Women Writers of the Harlem Renaissance," in *Challenging Boundaries: Gender and Periodization*, ed. Joyce W. Warren and Margaret Dickie (Athens: University of Georgia Press, 2000), 91–106.

Zoe Trodd

Graham, Shirley (1896–1977). Activist, essayist, biographer, novelist, composer, and playwright. One of the great African American artist–activists of the twentieth century, Shirley Graham led a politically charged and enormously varied life, only a fraction of which she spent married to her second husband, **W.E.B. Du Bois**. The outspoken Graham began her career as a composer and music director but turned to biography in the 1940s, penning several popular books that at once reflected her radical Communist beliefs and were accessible to younger readers.

Born in Indianapolis, Indiana, in 1896, Graham spent the early years of her life studying music and participating in the fine arts. Between stints at the Sorbonne and Oberlin College, she oversaw the production of her opera *Tom-Tom* in Cleveland in 1932. The opera, with approximately 500 Black cast members, was the first by an African American woman to be produced professionally. Graham spent most of the 1930s working with the New Deal's Federal Theater Project, directing, designing sets, composing musical scores, and writing and producing her own plays. (*See* **Federal Writers' Project**.)

With the onset of **World War II** and increasing indifference to her stage projects, Graham abandoned the theater, spent some time working with Black soldiers at Fort Huachuca in Arizona, and finally moved to Manhattan to become more involved with national politics. She was an active and visible member of the **NAACP**, organizing alongside Ella Baker and serving as a special confidante to Du Bois, one of the organization's senior figureheads. During this period, Graham combined her emergent political consciousness with a commitment to the literary arts. She wrote critically acclaimed biographies of towering male personalities in African American history, stressing the political valences of their lifelong work: *Dr. George Washington Carver* (1944); *Paul Robeson* (1946), in which she praised Moscow alongside the Communist actor; *There Once Was a Slave* (1947), a biography of **Frederick Douglass** that won the Julian Messner Award for the Best Book Combating Intolerance; and *Your Most Humble Servant* (1949), a biography of **Benjamin Banneker**.

Graham married Du Bois in 1951, and after they had endured a tumultuous decade of government harassment and NAACP falling-outs, in large part a result of the Red Scare, they moved to Ghana, where Du Bois died in 1963. Graham embraced Pan-Africanism upon her expatriation, becoming the director of television in Ghana and an influential adviser to its leader, Kwame Nkrumah. However, the political turmoil in that country eventually forced Graham to move to Gamal Adbel Nasser's Egypt and then to Mao Zedong's China, where she died in 1977. Her later years left a literary legacy that includes her only published novel, *Zulu Heart* (1974), set during South Africa's apartheid regime, as well as *His Day Is Marching On* (1971), a memoir of Du Bois that stands as the most intimate biography of the paradigmatic African American intellectual, a title which she justifiably could have claimed for herself.

Resources: Shirley Graham: *Booker T. Washington, Educator of Hand, Head, and Heart* (New York: Messner, 1955); *His Day Is Marching On: A Memoir of W.E.B. Du Bois* (Philadelphia: Lippincott, 1971); *Paul Robeson, Citizen of the World* (New York: Messner, 1946); *The Story of Phillis Wheatley* (New York: Messner, 1949); *The Story of Pocahontas* (New York: Grosset & Dunlap, 1953); *There Once Was a Slave: The Heroic Story of Frederick Douglass* (New York: Messner, 1947); *Your Most Humble Servant* (New York: Messner, 1949); *Zulu Heart: A Novel* (New York: Third Press, 1974); Shirley Graham, with George D. Lipscomb, *Dr. George Washington Carver, Scientist* (New York: Messner, 1944); Gerald Horne, *Race Woman: The Lives of Shirley Graham Du Bois* (New York: New York University Press, 2000); David Levering Lewis, *W.E.B. Du Bois: The Fight for Equality and the American Century, 1919–1963* (New York: Henry Holt, 2000).

Kinohi Nishikawa

Graphic Novels. These publications grew out of the comic-book movement in the 1960s, and came into being at the hands of writers who sought to use the comic book format to address more mainstream topics. There is some debate about who coined the term "graphic novel," but one of the first graphic novels, if not the first, was Will Eisner's *Contract with God*, published in 1978 (Arnold, Nov. 14, 2003, par. 2; Weiner, 17). Eisner, who began working in comics in 1936, has stated that he devised the term as a marketing technique to increase the chances that his comic book about working-class Jewish families during the **Great Depression** might be published (Arnold, Nov. 14, 2003, par. 2; Weiner, 17).

The graphic novel has gained popularity since 1980 in a variety of geographic and topical areas. A Japanese form called *manga* is exceptionally popular. Art Spiegelman's *Maus* (1986), a Holocaust memoir that casts the Germans and Jews as cats and mice, respectively, is one of the best-known examples of a graphic novel. Graphic novels have embraced a wide array of subjects, including superhero stories, **historical fiction**, nonfiction topics, and memoirs. Several graphic novels have been adapted into feature films, including Daniel Clowes's *Ghost World*, Max Allan Collins and Richard Piers Raynner's *Road to Perdition*, and Harvey Pekar's *American Splendor*. Other highly regarded graphic novelists include Lynda Barry, Gilbert Hernandez, Chris Ware, and Neil Gaiman.

African American history is one of the topics tackled by graphic novelists. *Still I Rise*, by Roland Owen Laird and Elihu Bey, tells the history of African Americans in the United States, beginning in 1619. The book includes extensive historical information and chronicles the accomplishments and struggles of African Americans. The novelist **Charles R. Johnson** contributed the introduction, which includes information about African Americans' little-known contributions to the field of cartoons and comics. Ho Che Anderson has written a three-volume series of graphic novels about **Martin Luther King, Jr.** The first volume tells of King's life through 1960, while the second and third volumes cover the rest of his life and the **Civil Rights Movement** in great detail. Cartoonist Aaron McGruder ("The Boondocks") and writer/director Reginald Hudlin recently teamed up to write *Birth of a Nation*, which portrays a secession movement in East St. Louis. The African American writer Jimmie L. Westley, Jr., has begun a series of online graphic novels under the general title *Tribal Science*.

Resources: Primary Sources: Ho Che Anderson: *King* (Seattle, WA: Fantagraphics, 1993); *King 2* (Seattle, WA: Fantagraphics, 2002); *King 3* (Seattle, WA: Fantagraphics, 2003); Roland Owen Laird and Elihu Bey, *Still I Rise: A Cartoon History of African Americans* (New York: Norton, 1997); Aaron McGruder and Reginald Hudlin, *Birth of a Nation* (New York: Crown, 2004); Jimmie L. Westley, Jr., *Tribal Science*, online graphic novels in progress, http://www.geocities.com/~tribalscience/01page.html. **Secondary Sources:** Andrew D. Arnold: "A Graphic Literature Library," *Time*, Nov. 21, 2003, http://www.time.com/time/columnist/arnold/article/0,9565,547796,00.html; "The Graphic Novel Silver Anniversary," *Time*, Nov. 14, 2003, http://www.time.com/time/columnist/arnold/article/0,9565,542579,00.html; Jan Baetens, ed., *The Graphic Novel* (Louvain, Belgium: Leuven University Press, 2001); Scott McCloud, *Understanding Comics* (New York: HarperPerennial, 2004); Roger Sabin, *Comics, Comix & Graphic Novels: A History* *of Comic Art* (London: Phaidon, 1996); Stephen Weiner, *Faster Than a Speeding Bullet: The Rise of the Graphic Novel* (New York: NBM, 2003).

Elizabeth Blakesley Lindsay

Great Depression (1929–1939). Owing to a collapse of the financial markets, droughts that crippled farming, and other factors, the decade of the 1930s was beset with overwhelmingly difficult economic and social conditions, to the extent that the era is known as the Great Depression. During this period, which immediately followed the **Harlem Renaissance**, the focus of African American literature shifted from the romanticized and exotic to a more realistic portrayal of economic, cultural, and social problems.

As the Roaring Twenties drew to a close, the cataclysmic decline of the economy and the accompanying deterioration of both lifestyles and hope brought an end to the exhilaration of the Harlem Renaissance. **Arna Bontemps**, poet and novelist, stated that "The Depression put an end to the dream world of renaissance Harlem" ("Famous WPA Authors," 46), but brought about a new awareness of the realities of African American life in the United States. During the Great Depression millions struggled against the worst economic downturn in the history of the United States; African Americans faced a situation exacerbated by both lack of education and racial discrimination in many parts of the country. The number of jobless African Americans was almost universally higher than that of corresponding White laborers, while job potential and earnings steadily declined. In New York, for example, the situation was dire; a government study showed that many African Americans in **Harlem, New York**, were near starvation by the time President Franklin Delano Roosevelt instituted the sweeping New Deal Programs (Bell, 152–154).

One of these programs, the **Federal Writers' Project** (FWP), had a massive impact on the African American community throughout the country. The Project employed scholars, writers, journalists, and myriad administrative staff to study and teach the African American community. The more than 6,000 employees of the FWP included both established and young writers such as **Claude McKay**, **Zora Neale Hurston**, **Richard Wright**, **Chester Himes**, **Ellen Tarry**, Arna Bontemps, **Margaret Abigail Walker**, and **Ralph Ellison**, while **Sterling A. Brown** was appointed the editor for Negro affairs (Bell, 154). While the most famous and far-reaching contribution of the FWP is the extensive American Guide Series, which delved into the history, culture, and **folklore** of the numerous states, cities, towns, and communities, some publications focused exclusively on the African American community. For example, *The Negro in Virginia* (Roscoe E. Lewis and the FWP, 1940) uses oral histories and anecdotes to paint a vivid picture of the African American experience in the state of Virginia, and is praised as one of the finest pieces to emerge from the FWP (Brown et al., 847–862). The FWP also interviewed more than 2,000 ex-slaves in seventeen states to document slave narratives (Hillegas et al., ix). In addition to the opportunities available to authors on the FWP, African American playwrights such as **Theodore Ward, Hughes Allison, Frank Wilson,** and **Langston Hughes** found both a creative outlet and financial benefits from an association with the Federal Theatre Project (1935–1939), another New Deal program (Fraden, 98, 108, 116). In conjunction with the many other agencies of the Works Progress Administration, these projects allowed African American writers the chance to hone their craft, study their culture and people, and reach a wide audience of mixed races while receiving a steady paycheck (Greenberg, 66).

While Roosevelt's New Deal put many writers back to work in their field, an ideological shift was forever altering the ways in which African Americans perceived themselves in American culture and society. As the precursor to the Depression, the Harlem Renaissance created an environment in which, according to Langston Hughes, the "Negro was in vogue" (*The Big Sea*, 22). African American literature written during this period was often praised for its pride in African heritage and an exotic, primitive flavor that appealed to many White critics and helped these authors to reach a wider audience. The **"New Negro"** (a term popularized by **Alain Locke**'s *The New Negro* in 1925) also tended to focus on "low life," a feature that several of the more genteel writers criticized as indecorous. In contrast, many writers in the 1930s rejected these methods on the grounds that they attempted to humanize African Americans by emulating those traits valued by White society. The generation of writers that came of age during the Depression discarded the romanticized characterizations of African Americans prevalent during the 1920s, using economic and social inequities—not race—to interpret the lives of African Americans with unabashed realism that would expose the ugliness of their existence and demonstrate the universality of human experience (Young, x–xi).

Initially, the frustrations of young African American writers emerged in the form of satire tinged with social realism. **Countee Cullen,** the poet whom the critic **Gerald Early** has dubbed the "boy wonder" of the Harlem Renaissance, wrote *One Way to Heaven* (1932), a novel satirizing the golden days of the 1920s. Likewise, **Wallace Thurman**'s biting obituary of the period and the "New Negro," *Infants of the Spring* (1932), focused on disabusing his readers of the "exaggerations of the New Negro movement" (Brown, *The Negro in American Fiction*, 143). **George W. Schuyler**'s *Black No More* (1931) describes a new scientific procedure by which Black people become White, mercilessly skewering those who received personal gain from racial agitation. This unforgiving perspective was characteristic of society's ideological shift during the Great Depression as America struggled to cope with the economic and social despair that distinguished the era.

While certainly not characteristic of all African American literature during the Great Depression, this documentary perspective, coupled with an emphasis on social and economic problems for the working class, is apparent in much of the influential fiction, essays, poetry, and drama of the period. Writers such as Arna Bontemps and George Schuyler, for example, used historical events to comment on the social situation for African Americans. Bontemps's *Black Thunder* (1936), the novel many critics dub his most successful, uses Gabriel Prosser's failed slave revolt of 1800 as a parallel to contemporary race struggles, while *Drums at Dusk* (1939) portrays the infamous Haitian insurrection led by Toussaint L'Ouverture (Bell, 103–104). Similarly, Schuyler's *Slaves Today: A Story of Liberia* (1931) uses the backdrop of the stories of **slavery** in Liberia for contemporary commentary. In these ways, the romanticized, amusing stories so popular in the Roaring Twenties were replaced by writing that endeavored to alter the place of the race in society.

Carter G. Woodson, known as the "Father of Negro History," likewise set about to alter the place of African Americans in history through writing. He founded both the Association for the Study of Negro Life and History (1915) and the *Journal of Negro History* (1916), instituted Black History Week (now Black History Month, 1926) and wrote numerous articles and books in an attempt to bring the historical contributions of African Americans to light for a wide public audience. In addition to his many articles, Woodson's book *The Miseducation of the Negro* (1933) pointed to widespread ignorance of African American contributions to history and argued that the American school system must rethink the curriculum to right this wrong. Attention to history is also seen in the numerous autobiographies written by African American writers during the Great Depression (*see* **Autobiography**). Pieces such as **James Weldon Johnson**'s *Along This Way* (1933), **W.E.B. Du Bois**'s *Dusk of Dawn: An Essay Toward an Autobiography of a Race Concept* (1940), and Claude McKay's *A Long Way from Home* (1937) paint a picture of the African American fight for dignity, respect, and the ability to support one's family.

The attention to history was soon married with fiction as Social Realism began widespread domination of African American literature during the Great Depression. Langston Hughes's novel *Not Without Laughter* (1930) was one of the first to deal with the lives of common African Americans in a realistic manner; in it, Hughes created complex relationships and characters from the Black community in a way that would be seen in the work of many African American authors of the period. Hughes's next publication, *The Ways of White Folks* (1934), discussed the myriad ways in which White people attempted to shape African Americans into roles that fit societal expectations. **Waters E. Turpin** addresses similar themes in *These Low Grounds* (1937) and *O Canaan!* (1939), tracing the survival of black families through slavery, the northern migration, and continued prejudice. One of the most popular pieces of African American literature published during the Great Depression was **Richard Wright**'s *Native Son* (1940). A gripping example of Social Realism documenting the corrupting effect of a racist society, *Native Son* sold more than 200,000 copies in the first three weeks (Nelson, 490), outselling John Steinbeck's incredibly popular *The Grapes of Wrath* (1939). Wright's first published work, *Uncle Tom's Children: Four Novellas* (1938), rejects the famous title character created in Harriet Beecher Stowe's *Uncle Tom's Cabin* through a violent defense of African American rights (Bell, 156–158).

African American writing of the Great Depression also explored Southern life. George Lee's *River George* (1937), for example, delves into discrimination in Southern sharecropping. Zora Neale Hurston, a leading African American novelist and dramatist in the 1930s and one of the most prolific female African American writers in history, also used **the South** in her writing. During the 1930s Hurston conducted her own study of African American and Caribbean folklore, an action that reflected both the trend toward Social Realism and Hurston's own dual interests in anthropology and folklore. The resulting works, *Mules and Men* (1935) and *Tell My Horse* (1938), were some of the first anthropological studies that recorded the folklore, ceremony, and ritual of her people; her study also set the stage for novels such as *Their Eyes Were Watching God* (1937), a celebration of African American heritage, the rural folk tradition, and community (Nelson, 260). Like Hurston, Sterling Brown also followed his interest in Black culture, storytelling, and folklore to small rural communities in the South. The volume titled *Southern Road* (1932) illustrates Brown's Southern encounters, using extensive knowledge of Black folklore and culture to denote the African American experience (Brawley, 260). In addition to his poetry, Brown wrote several vital critical studies during the Depression, including *The Negro in American Fiction* (1937) and *Negro Poetry and Drama* (1937), in which he critiques the diverse writings of African American poets, dramatists, and novelists.

While many African American authors wrote in the style of Social Realism during the Great Depression, others wrote poetry, drama, and fiction that avoided the literary trend. Margaret Abigail Walker, for example, published her well-known poem "For My People" (1937), while dramatists such as **Theodore Browne** (*The Natural Man*, 1936), **Abram Hill** (*Stealing Lighting*, 1937; *Hell's Half Acre*, 1938; *So Shall You Reap*, 1938), and Augustus J. Smith (*Louisiana*, 1933; *Turpentine*, 1936) saw their works published and produced by local theaters. Langston Hughes wrote numerous dramas, including the Broadway hit *Mulatto* (1931); the serious dramas *Scottsboro Limited* (1932) and *Harvest* (1935), and the satires *Little Eva's End* (1938) and *Uncle Tommy's Cabin* (c. 1938). **Willis Richardson**, one of the most successful African American playwrights of the era, and **May Miller** collaborated on *Negro History in Thirteen Plays* (1935), an anthology that focused on the long history of African American heroes and heroines. Playwright **S. Randolph Edmonds** focused on "worthwhile themes, sharply drawn conflict, positive characters, and a melodramatic plot" in historical dramas such as *Nat Turner* (1934) and *Breeders* (1934) (Edmonds, 7–8). In addition to these successes in the theater, **Rudolph John Chauncey Fisher**'s *The Conjure-Man Dies* (1932) is considered by many to be the first African American detective novel, and was the first to place the detective story genre in a completely African American environment (Soitos, 93). Finally, a number of **newspapers** and journals were founded and edited by African Americans during the 1930s, including the *Los Angeles Sentinel* (Leon H. Washington, founder, 1933), *The Michigan Chronicle* (Louis E. Martin, founder, 1936), and the magazine dedicated to stimulating interest in the African American cultural heritage, *Challenge* (**Dorothy West**, editor, 1934). Reflecting the Social Realist movement of the period, Richard Wright assumed the position of editor for *Challenge* in 1937, changed the name to *New Challenge*, and immediately issued a request for articles and fiction in the style of Social Realism. (*See* **Labor**; **Marxism**.)

Resources: Bernard W. Bell, *The Afro-American Novel and Its Tradition* (Amherst: University of Massachusetts Press, 1987); Harold Bloom, ed., *Black American Poets and Dramatists of the Harlem Renaissance* (New York: Chelsea House, 1995); Arna Bontemps, "Famous WPA Authors," *Negro Digest* 7 (June 1950), 43–47; Benjamin Brawley, *The Negro Genius: A New Appraisal of the Achievement of the American Negro in Literature and the Fine Arts* (New York: Biblo and Tannen, 1966); Sterling A. Brown: *The Negro in American Fiction* (1937; repr. Port Washington, NY: Kennikat Press, 1968); *Negro Poetry and Drama* (1937; repr. New York: Arno Press, 1969); Sterling A. Brown, Arthur P. Davis, and Ulysses Lee, eds., *Negro Caravan* (New York: Dryden Press, 1943); Donald C. Dickinson, *A Bio-Bibliography of Langston Hughes, 1902–1967* (Hamden, CT: Archon Books, 1967); S. Randolph Edmonds, "Preface," in *Six Plays for a Negro Theatre* (Boston: Walter H. Baker, 1934); Rena Fraden, *Blueprints for a Black Federal Theatre, 1935–1939* (New York: Cambridge University Press, 1994); Cheryl Lynn Greenberg, *Or Does It Explode?: Black Harlem in the Great Depression* (New York: Oxford University Press, 1997); Robert E. Hemenway, *Zora Neale Hurston* (Urbana: University of Illinois Press, 1977); Jan Hillegas, Ken Lawrence, and George P. Rawick, eds., *The American Slave: A Composite Autobiography*, vol. 1 (Westport, CT: Greenwood Press, 1977); Langston Hughes: *The Big Sea: An Autobiography* (New York: Knopf, 1940); *Not Without Laughter* (New York: Knopf, 1930); Deirdre Mullane, ed., *Crossing the Danger Water: Three Hundred Years of African-American Writing* (New York: Anchor Books, 1993); Emmanuel S. Nelson, ed., *African American Authors, 1745–1945: A Bio-Bibliographical Critical Sourcebook* (Westport, CT: Greenwood Press, 2000); James Edward Smethurst, *The New Red Negro: The Literary Left and African American Poetry, 1930–1946* (New York: Oxford University Press, 1999); Stephen F. Soitos, *The Blues Detective: A Study of African American Detective Fiction* (Amherst: University of Massachusetts Press, 1996); Carter G. Woodson, *The African Background Outlined; or, Handbook for the Study of the Negro* (Washington, DC: Association for the Study of Negro Life and History, 1936); Richard Wright: *Native Son* (New York: Harper & Bros., 1940); *Uncle Tom's Children* (New York: Harper & Bros., 1938); James O. Young, *Black Writers of the Thirties* (Baton Rouge: Louisiana State University Press, 1973).

Elizabeth A. Osborne

Great Migration. The Great Migration refers to the mass exodus of African Americans from the rural **South** to the urban North during **World War I** and **World War II**, although extensive relocation also had occurred following the collapse of **Reconstruction** after the **Civil War**. This migration fueled the evolution of African American art, literature, music, and literary movements. Other significant but smaller-scale migrations include **back-to-Africa movements** that occurred in the 1700s through the 1900s; slaves who escaped to the North, sometimes by means of the **Underground Railroad**, in search of freedom; Blacks who scurried west in search of gold in the mid-1800s; and discontented individuals, such as **W.E.B. DuBois, Josephine Baker, Richard Wright**, and others, who moved to foreign countries (*see* **Expatriate Writers; Paris, France**). Recently, some middle-class African Americans have been migrating from the North to the South.

The westward migration of African Americans during Reconstruction preceded the major movement known as the Great Migration. Freed slaves, desiring to build a life for themselves, created towns in Kansas, **Oklahoma,** Arizona, Nevada, California, and New Mexico. Like Whites, some went to settle the frontier as trappers and guides. Others went for adventure and opportunity. Some well-known Blacks who moved west included George Washington, who founded Centralia, Washington; Mifflin W. Gibbs, the founder of California's first Black newspaper, *Mirror of the Times*; and **Nat Love**, also known as "Deadwood Dick," a cowboy and autobiographer. Others, such as **Thomas P. Detter**, helped prepare the way for more African American settlers. Detter advocated voting rights, public education, and African American representation on juries.

African Americans started their great migration into the North in the 1880s, through World War I (1914–1918) and World War II (1939–1945). As the economic and industrial power of America's cities grew, so did the lure to go north. Many African Americans were dissatisfied with rural life: the Jim Crow laws, the slow economy, poor crops, and the threat of racist groups, such as the Ku Klux Klan. The release of "D.W. Griffith's immensely popular and artistically acclaimed *The Birth of a Nation* in 1915—an epic Civil War film that portrayed the Klan as heroic, and particularly after World War—surely had to intensify the miasma of fear, loathing, and impending violence that permeated the South, and gave blacks more reason to leave" (Early). **Ida B. Wells-Barnett**, part owner of the newspaper *Free Speech*, wrote an article in 1892 that denounced **lynching** and encouraged Blacks to leave the South. As a result of her article, hundreds of African Americans relocated North. Robert S. Abbott, founder of the **Chicago Defender** newspaper, also "urged African Americans living in the southern United States to migrate north, where he believed that more opportunities for employment and social advancement existed" (Ostrom, 72). The *Chicago Defender* was a popular paper among African Americans, and its influence "may have induced as many as 50,000 African Americans to migrate north in 1915 alone" (Ostrom, 72). The *Defender* also published "letters from newly transplanted blacks saying that life was better in the North, and by writing editorials that praised the North and condemned the South" (Early).

Both world wars brought "new booming shipyards, munitions factories, and aircraft plants" and an enormous demand for laborers (Divine et al., 730). Many African Americans willingly journeyed north to fill this need. **Gerald Early**, professor of English and Afro-American Studies at Washington University in **St. Louis, Missouri**, writes in "Black Migration" that "recruiting agents representing various northern industrial concerns went south to lure African-Americans north." Historians state that "between 1916 and 1918, over 450,000 African Americans left the Old South for the booming industrial cities of Saint Louis, **Chicago**, **Detroit**, and Cleveland" (Divine et al., 730). African American men "found jobs in factories, railroad yards, steel mills, packing houses and coal mines; black women worked in textile factories, department stores, and restaurants" (730). A Chicago migrant from Mississippi writes the following ("The World They Came To"):

> Old boy, I was promoted on the first of the month. I was made first assistant to the head carpenter. When he is out of the place I take everything in charge and was raised to $95 a month. You know I know my stuff...I should have been here 20 years ago. I just begin to feel like a man. It's a great deal of pleasure in knowing that you have some privilege.

The North represented better wages, better education, more freedom and opportunities, and in many cases, a better lifestyle. However, the transition was not always easy. An online site about the African American migration quotes Richard Wright's novel *American Hunger* (1977) ("The World They Came To"):

> My first glimpse of the flat black stretches of Chicago depressed and dismayed me, mocked all my fantasies.... What would happen to me here?... There were no curves here, no trees; only angles, lines, squares, bricks and copper wires.

African Americans experienced racism in the workplace. African Americans were often forced to live in segregated and impoverished neighborhoods. Racial tensions and limited housing triggered a series of **race riots**. Beginning in 1917, "white gangs went on violent rampages from **Washington, D.C.**, to Omaha, Nebraska, and other cities where African-American presence had grown" ("Conflict"). Nine whites and forty blacks were killed in a "race war" in Illinois; six people died in Washington, D.C., and thirty-eight died in Chicago riots (Divine et al., 731). A group of Whites stoned an African American teenager swimming in a "White area" of Lake Michigan ("Conflict"). (*See* **Race Riots**.)

Many African Americans, "despite these problems, [built] new lives and new institutions, drawing on the strong sense of family and mutual support that had marked their lives 'down home'" ("The World They Came To"). Furthermore, African Americans utilized these trials and tribulations of their life in the North to create artistic and literary works. The theme of migration became "one of the most persistent themes in all of black literature" (Early). **Jacob Lawrence** produced sixty panels illustrating the African American migration from the South to the North. The migration North was also responsible for the development of **jazz**. The North provided "access to machine-made instruments, some network of organization for musical instruction, and places where people could go and hear this music" (Early). Also, "the increase in black income as blacks became more urban meant that blacks could afford to buy records and phonographs" (Early). The presence of jazz in Northern cities also increased its exposure to an enthusiastic White audience.

The Great Migration helped produce the **Harlem Renaissance**, the **Chicago Renaissance**, and numerous "migration narratives," such as *Cane* (1923) by **Jean Toomer**, *Invisible Man* (1952) by **Ralph Ellison**, *Go Tell It on the Mountain* (1953) by **James Baldwin**, and *The Women of Brewster Place* (1982) by **Gloria Naylor** (Griffin, 198). Lawrence Rodgers also "identifies the Afro-American Great Migration Novel," which "generally [focuses] on how to come to terms with the spatial, communal, and psychological differences between South and North, Rural and urban, industrial and rural, down home and downtown" (198). These novels include *The Autobiography of an Ex-Colored Man* (1912) by **James Weldon Johnson**, *O Canaan!* (1939) by **Waters Turpin**, and *The Living Is Easy* (1948) by **Dorothy West**. Langston Hughes's first **autobiography**, *The Big Sea* (1940), describes his journey from the Midwest to New York City and **Harlem, New York**, in the early 1920s; his poem "Migration" (1923) explicitly concerns the Great Migration, as does his poem "Bound No'th Blues" (1926). **Wallace Thurman**'s short story "Cordelia the Crude" is a kind of cautionary tale about rural African American women moving to "the big city"; it was published in the magazine *Fire!!* during the Harlem Renaissance.

Resources: Malaika Adero, ed., *Up South: Stories, Studies, and Letters of This Century's Black Migrations* (New York: New Press, 1993); James Baldwin, *Go Tell It on the Mountain* (New York: Knopf, 1953); "Conflict & Change in the North," *American Social History Project,* http://www.ashp.cuny.edu/video/up5.html; Robert A. Divine, T. H. Breen, George M. Fredrickson, and R. Hal Williams, *America: Past and Present*, 3rd ed., vol. 2 (New York: HarperCollins, 1991); Gerald Early, "Black Migration: African Americans Journey North Searching for Prosperity and Freedom," *Places, Spaces & Changing Faces,* PBS Online, http://www.pbs.org/jazz/places/faces_migration.htm; Ralph Ellison, *Invisible Man* (New York: Random House, 1952); John Hope Franklin and Alfred A. Moss, Jr., *From Slavery to Freedom: A History of Negro Americans*, 8th ed. (Boston: McGraw-Hill, 2000); Farah Jasmine Griffin, "Migration," in *The Oxford Companion to African American Literature*, ed. William L. Andrews, Frances Smith Foster, and Trudier Harris (New York: Oxford University Press, 1997), 497–498; James A. Henretta, David Brody, and Lynn Dumenil, *America: A Concise History*, vol. 1 (Boston: Bedford Books, 1999); Langston Hughes: *The Big Sea* (New York: Knopf, 1940); "Bound No'th Blues" and "Migration," in *The Collected Poems of Langston Hughes*, ed. Arnold Rampersad (New York: Vintage Classics, 1995)—regarding these poems, also see Ostrom (below); James Weldon Johnson, *The Autobiography of an Ex-Colored Man* (Boston: Sherman, French, 1912); William Loren Katz, *The Black West*, 3rd ed., rev. and enl. (Seattle, WA: Open Hand, 1987); Gloria Naylor, *The Women of Brewster Place* (New York: Viking Press, 1982); *Northwest Black Pioneers: A Centennial Tribute* (Seattle, WA: BON, 1987).

Hans Ostrom, *A Langston Hughes Encyclopedia* (Westport, CT: Greenwood Press, 2002), 57, 72, 246–247; Lawrence Rodgers, *Canaan Bound: The African American Great*

Migration Novel (Chicago: University of Illinois Press, 1997); Amritjit Singh, "Harlem Renaissance," in *The Oxford Companion to African American Literature*, ed. William L. Andrews, Frances Smith Foster, and Trudier Harris (New York: Oxford University Press, 1997), 340–342; Wallace Thurman, "Cordelia the Crude," in *Fire!!* (facs. repr. New York: Fire Press, 1988), 5–7; Jean Toomer, *Cane* (New York: Boni and Liveright, 1923); Waters Turpin, *O Canaan!* (New York: Doubleday, Doran, 1939); Andrea Ades Vasquez, Pennee Bender, and Joshua Brown, dirs., *Up South*, narr. Robert Horton and Clara Robinson, videocassette (1996); Craig H. Werner, "Chicago Renaissance," in *The Oxford Companion to African American Literature*, ed. William L. Andrews, Frances Smith Foster, and Trudier Harris (New York: Oxford University Press, 1997), 132–133; Dorothy West, *The Living Is Easy* (Boston: Houghton, Mifflin, 1948); Richard Wright, *American Hunger* (New York: Harper & Row, 1977); "The World They Came To," *American Social History Project*, http://www.ashp.cuny.edu/video/up4.html.

Gladys L. Knight

Green, Carmen (born 1963). Romance novelist. Born in Buffalo, New York, Green is a graduate of Fredonia State University, from which she later received a Distinguished Alumna Award (1997). After graduation, she worked for nine years in the insurance industry and moved with her husband to **Atlanta, Georgia**. When they started a family, she became a stay-at-home mom and found time to pursue her interest in writing. Since her first novel was published in 1996, Green has written eight full-length novels and six novellas in the **romance** genre. This output would be remarkable under any circumstances, but it is even more extraordinary given that Green has at the same time raised three children and that, despite chronic difficulties with rheumatoid arthritis, she has recently resumed full-time employment outside the home as a health information manager at a physician's office. She has served as president of the Georgia Chapter of the Romance Writers of America, one of the largest chapters in the country, with over 200 members.

Green's novels feature predominantly African American characters, and although they adhere to many of the conventions of the romance genre, they are somewhat unusual for the range in their settings and in the backgrounds and occupations of their female protagonists. In *Now or Never* (1996), a successful physician named Mia Jacobs relocates from **Chicago, Illinois**, to Atlanta in order to reconstruct her personal life. *Commitments* (1998) is set in North Carolina and focuses on the vacation adventures of a New York economist named Fox Giovanni. In *Keeping Secrets* (1999), the main character is a bounty hunter named Jade Houston. *Wine and Roses* (1999) chronicles the unlikely romance between an ordinary employee of candy company named Neesie Claiborne and an ambitious young executive with the company. *Endless Love* (2000) centers on an M.B.A. candidate named Teri O'Shaughnessy, who manages an apartment building. In *Island Bliss* (2002), a successful entrepreneur named Toni Kingsley vacations in St. Croix.

Green's "Crawford" novels include *Silken Love* (1997) and *Doctor, Doctor* (2002). In *Silken Love*, Lauren Michaels, a financial adviser and an aspiring singer, and her adopted daughter Shayla must adjust to the sudden involvement in their lives of Shayla's biological father, Eric Crawford. *Doctor, Doctor* is set in Atlanta and describes Shayla's experiences as a young female physician.

Among Green's novels, *Kissed* (2004) is unusual because it is told from the point of view of a male main character, a career-obsessed ambassador named Justin Crawford. In some of Green's novels, the focus is on a group of friends. In *Atlanta Live* (2003), the three main characters, two female and one male, work on a talk-radio show. In *Date Night* (2004), three young women from diverse backgrounds are not only friends but also partners in a successful investment club.

Green has received several awards and other recognitions for her novels. For *Doctor, Doctor*, she received a Desert Rose Golden Quill Award. *Keeping Secrets* was included on *Emerge* magazine's annual best-sellers list. *Atlanta Live* was voted #4 in the Romance Writer's of America Favorite Book of the Year contest, and *Commitments* was adapted in a made-for-television film starring Allen Payne, Victoria Dillard, and Virginia Capers, which aired on BET.

Green's novellas have been published with those by one or two other authors in the thematic collections *Silver Bells* (1996), *Midnight Clear: A Holiday Anthology* (2000), *A Kwanzaa Keepsake* (2001), *Sister, Sister* (2001), and *Midnight Clear: An Indigo Holiday Collection* (2000). Green also contributed a chapter to *Reunion at Mossy Creek* (2002), a romance novel written by a group of authors.

Resources: Carl Allen, "Carmen Green—On Life, Love, and Romance," *Buffalo News*, Nov. 13, 1996, p. D1; Monica Harris, "Passion Picks," *Black Issues Book Review* 6 (July/Aug. 2004), 46; Don O'Briant, "Romantic Encounters: Suspense Reigns as Publishers Reach out to Changing Readership," *Atlanta Journal-Constitution*, Feb. 26, 2004, NW, p. 10; Barb Twardowski, "An Interview with Carmen Green," *Points North*, Feb. 2005, 78, 82; Carmen Green: *Atlanta Live* (Washington, DC: Sepia, 2003); *Commitments* (New York: Kensington, 1998); *Date Night* (New York: Kensington, 2004); *Doctor, Doctor* (Washington, DC: BET, 2002); *Endless Love* (Washington, DC: Arabesque, 2000); *Island Bliss* (New York: St. Martin's, 2002); *Keeping Secrets* (New York: Kensington, 1999); *Kissed* (New York: Dafina, 2004); *A Kwanzaa Keepsake* (Washington, DC: BET, 2001); *Midnight Clear* (Columbus, MS: Genesis, 2000); *Now or Never* (New York: Kensington, 1996); *Reunion at Mossy Creek* (Smyrna, GA: Bellebooks, 2002); *Silken Love* (New York: Arabesque, 1997); *Silver Bells* (New York: Kensington, 1996); *Sister, Sister* (New York: St. Martin's, 2001); *Wine and Roses* (New York: Kensington, 1999).

Martin Kich

Green, John Patterson (1845–1940). Attorney, politician, civil servant, autobiographer, and nonfiction writer. Green is known for having written a book about the Ku Klux Kan and for his autobiographical writing. He was born in New Bern, North Carolina, to free, mixed-race parents, John Rice Green and Temperance Durden Green. Growing up in poverty, Green was in and out of school due to the family's financial difficulties. While working at various odd jobs, he published, at his own expense, *Essays on Miscellaneous Subjects by a Self-Educated Colored Youth* in 1866, a booklet which he sold in several states to pay for his education. Green attended Cleveland High School (1866–1869) and the Union Law School in Cleveland (1869–1870). From 1870 to 1872, he lived in South Carolina, where he passed the bar in 1870 and embarked on a legal career. He returned to Cleveland in 1872 and was elected justice of peace there in 1873. He was the second African American to serve in the Ohio House of Representatives (1881) and became Ohio's first African American state senator in 1892. In return for his service to William McKinley's presidential campaign as a traveling speaker in Ohio, Green was appointed U.S. postage stamp agent in **Washington, D.C.,** to supervise the printing and distribution of postage stamps for the entire nation. Green returned to Cleveland in 1906 and resumed his law practice. He was a Republican and was frequently sent as delegate, or alternate delegate, to national conventions of the Republican Party, including those in 1882 and 1896.

In 1880 Green wrote *Recollections of the Inhabitants, Localities, Superstitions and Ku Klux Klan Outrages of the Carolinas*, with the purpose of serving the Republican cause in James Garfield's presidential campaign. Later in his life he published an autobiography, *Fact Stranger Than Fiction* (1920), which to date offers the most detailed account of his life. Green married Annie Walker after graduating from high school, and some time after her death in 1911, married a widow, Lottie Mitchell Richardson. He died following a car accident on August 30, 1940.

Resources: William L. Andrews, "Green, John Patterson," in *The Oxford Companion to African American Literature*, ed. William L. Andrews, Frances Smith Foster, and Trudier Harris (New York: Oxford University Press, 1997), 326; John Patterson Green: *Essays on Miscellaneous Subjects by a Self-Educated Colored Youth* (Cleveland, OH: John Patterson Green, 1866); *Fact Stranger Than Fiction* (Cleveland, OH: John Patterson Green, 1920); Papers of John Patterson Green, 1869–1910, 7,000 items, microfilm 17,820-6P (Washington, DC: Library of Congress); *Recollections of the Inhabitants, Localities, Superstitions, and Ku Klux Klan Outrages of the Carolinas* (Cleveland, OH: John Patterson Green, 1880).

Jeehyun Lim

Greenfield, Eloise (born 1929). Children's writer of poetry, fiction, and nonfiction. Greenfield's work exemplifies her firm commitment to providing African American children with quality literature that empowers them and affirms their existence. In this regard her work is similar to that of **Sharon Bell Mathis** and **Walter Dean Myers**. Greenfield was born in Parmele, North Carolina, at the beginning of the **Great Depression**. Later, her family moved to **Washington, D.C.,** where Greenfield grew up. She began her writing career with the publication of several stories for adults; however, she is best known for her fiction and poetry for children. *Bubbles* (reissued in 1977 as *Good News*), her first book for children, was published in 1972.

Sharon Bell Mathis, who was the director of the children's division of the Black Writers' Workshop in Washington, D.C., in 1969, encouraged Greenfield to contribute to eliminating the dearth of quality literature for young people that featured African American characters. Some of Greenfield's earlier works include biographies for young readers: *Rosa Parks* (1973), *Paul Robeson* (1975), and *Mary McLeod Bethune* (1977). Since the 1970s, she has written a number of books for babies, beginning readers, and middle grade children. In 1997, Greenfield published *For the Love of the Game: Michael Jordan and Me*, a book that furthers her dedication to empowering young people. Some of Greenfield's fiction includes difficult themes, such as divorce, poverty, and death, while other pieces embrace love, family relationships, and community bonding.

Though her body of work includes award-winning picture books, fiction, poetry, and biographies, critics consider Greenfield's verse to be her strongest contribution to children's literature. Her first book of poetry, *Honey, I Love, and Other Poems*, published in 1978, is still a favorite among elementary school children and their teachers. *Nathaniel Talking* (1988) earned Greenfield acknowledgment for being one of the first to introduce **rap** poetry to children's literature. She has received a number of awards. In fact, Greenfield received the first **Carter G. Woodson** Prize, in 1974, for *Rosa Parks* (1973) and the Jane Addams Children's Book Award in 1976 for *Paul Robeson* (1975). With three Coretta Scott King Awards to her credit for individual titles—*Africa Dream* (1977), *Nathaniel Talking* (1990), and *Night on Neighborhood Street* (1991)—and honors for her entire body of work, Greenfield's fiction and nonfiction have left an indelible impression on fans and critics.

Resources: Eloise Greenfield: *Africa Dream* (1977; repr. New York: HarperCollins, 1992); *For the Love of the Game: Michael Jordan and Me* (New York: Harper Trophy, 1999); *Grandpa's Face* (New York: Putnam, 1996); *Honey, I Love, and Other Love Poems* (1978; repr. New York: Harper Trophy, 1986); *In the Land of Words: New and Selected Poems* (New York: Amistad, 2003); *Mary McCloud Bethune* (1977; repr. New York: Harper Trophy, 1994); *Nathaniel Talking* (1988; repr. New York: Writer & Readers Press, 1993); *Night on Neighborhood Street* (1991; repr. New York: Turtleback Books, 1996); *Paul Robeson: The Life and Times of a Free Black Man* (1975; repr. New York: HarperCollins, 1996); *Rosa Parks* (1973; repr. New York: HarperCollins, 1996); "Eloise Greenfield," in *Children's Literature Review*, ed. Alan Hedblad, vol. 38 (Detroit: Gale Research, 1998), 76–96; "Eloise Greenfield," in *Something About the Author: Facts and Pictures about Authors and Illustrators of Books for Young People*, ed. Alan Hedblad, vol. 105 (Detroit: Gale Research, 1999), 85–93.

KaaVonia Hinton-Johnson

Greenlee, Sam (born 1930). Poet, novelist, and screenwriter. Greenlee is best known for having written *The Spook Who Sat by the Door* (1969), a controversial, influential novel published during the **Black Arts Movement**. At this writing, Greenlee continues to tour, speaking on college campuses and at events such as the Milwaukee Black Film Festival and the Annual Visions

Blu Film Symposium. *The Spook Who Sat by the Door* concerns a Black U.S. government operative. The book is now considered an African American literary classic and was made into a movie in 1973. Greenlee was born in **Chicago, Illinois**, in 1930. His family had migrated from **the South**, and he was educated in the inner city schools of Chicago. He studied at the University of Wisconsin, the University of Chicago, and the University of Salonica in Greece. The characters in *The Spook Who Sat by the Door* are believed to have been created from Greenlee's experience with the United States Information Service. He served in Iraq, Pakistan, Indonesia, and Greece, and received honors for his service in the 1958 Kassem revolution in Iraq. His book about those experiences is *Baghdad Blues* (1991).

The Spook Who Sat by the Door captured the fervor of **Black Nationalism** during the late 1960s and 1970s. Dan Freedman, the main protagonist, who was taught his espionage skills by the Central Intelligence Agency, was characterized as a black James Bond. In the novel Freedman turn out not to be a U.S. agent but a Black revolutionary who organizes groups of gangs within inner cities to liberate African Americans "by any means necessary," in the words of **Malcolm X**. *The Spook* was so realistic in its portrayal of the climate within the Black community that it frightened many White readers, who believed that Black groups such as the **Black Panther Party** for Self-Defense and the **Nation of Islam** would use the same tactics depicted in the novel. The film version (1973) of the novel starred J. A. Preston and was directed by Ivan Dixon. Greenlee wrote the screenplay. The film was suppressed by the Federal Bureau of Investigation, which confiscated copies of it (Wickham). It was given a special screening for the Black Congressional Caucus in 2003.

Greenlee's works of poetry include *Ammunition! Poetry and Other Raps* (1975) and *Blues for an African Princess* (1971). (*See* **Censorship**.)

Resources: Ivan Dixon, dir., *The Spook Who Sat by the Door* (1973; repr. Los Angeles: Monarch Video, 2004), DVD format; Sam Greenlee: *Ammunition! Poetry and Other Raps* (London: Bogle–L'Overture, 1975); *Baghdad Blues: The Revolution That Brought Saddam Hussein to Power* (Chicago: Kayode Press, 1991); *Blues for an African Princess* (Chicago: Third World Press, 1971); *The Spook Who Sat by the Door* (1969; repr. Detroit: Wayne State University Press, 1990); DeWayne Wickham, "Sam Greenlee's Book Is Still Making a Statement," *Chicken Bones: A Journal for Literary and Artistic African American Themes*, Sept. 25, 2003, http://www.nathanielturner.com/spookbythedoor2.htm.

Imelda Hunt

Gregory, Dick [Richard] (born 1932). Comedian, writer, and political and humanitarian activist. Dick Gregory is known for his social and political commentary in both his comedy and his writing. Born in 1932 in a **St. Louis, Missouri**, ghetto, Gregory attended Southern Illinois University for three years on a track scholarship. Before finishing, he was drafted into the Army and served two years. In the mid-1950s, Gregory pursued his interest in stand-up comedy and struggled to make a living as a master of ceremonies in Black clubs. In 1959 he opened his own club, the Apex, in a Black suburb of **Chicago, Illinois**, but the club soon failed. Finally, in 1960, while working at a carwash, Gregory was offered a stand-in appearance at the Playboy Club in Chicago. His performance marked a major turning point for Black entertainers; not only was Gregory one of the first Black men invited to perform at a White club, but he won over the White audience with his composed manner. After Hugh Hefner caught Gregory's second act, he asked him to sign a three-year contract. Gregory's appearance at the Playboy Club led to national recognition and an appearance on Jack Paar's *Tonight* show.

Gregory's most ardent admirers, of whom **William (Bill) Cosby** is one, believe that Gregory's success as a comic in the early 1960s stemmed from his ability to confidently mix one-liners with political commentary in a way that captivated both Black and White audiences. Initially, Gregory avoided direct politics in his comedy. The result, as Nachman puts it, is that "he made racism, in a strangely ironic way, manageable" (487). In his **autobiography**, *Nigger* (1964), Gregory states that his color was incidental to his comic talent. Yet, Gregory's comic style was also criticized by other Black comics for its appeal to a White audience and its "mechanical quality" (Nachman, 489).

In 1962, Gregory began speaking out about civil rights, keeping his commentary separate from his comic routine. Around the time he wrote his first autobiography, he risked his career and bankrupted himself for civil rights, putting it before his family. In 1963, Gregory was arrested for civil disorder during a civil rights demonstration in Birmingham, Alabama. He did benefits for the Congress of Racial Equality and the **NAACP**, and participated in demonstrations. In 1965, he ran for mayor of Chicago, and later for president. By 1968, Gregory had become a radical, and in 1973 he decided he would not work in clubs that sold alcohol. In the 1970s, he became well known for his fasting for political and social causes.

Gregory's other autobiographies are *Up from Nigger* (1976), the title of which is a play on **Booker T. Washington**'s *Up from Slavery*, and, most recently, *Callus on My Soul: A Memoir* (2000). During his run for the presidency, Gregory wrote *Write Me In!* (1968), *The Shadow That Scares Me* (1968), *No More Lies* (1971), and *Dick Gregory's Political Primer* (1972), which express Gregory's social and political beliefs. Gregory's conspiracy theory about the murder of **Martin Luther King, Jr.**, resulted in the books *Murder in Memphis: The FBI and the Assassination of Martin Luther King* (1993) and *Code Name "Zorro": The Murder of Martin Luther King, Jr.* (1977). He also became an expert on nutrition and wrote a book on the subject, as well as one about the Bible.

While Gregory's comedy is well known for its subtly sociopolitical satire, his life beyond comedy, especially his controversially titled autobiography, approaches racism head-on. In his foreword to *Nigger*, Gregory suggests that his title appropriates the word that had once been meant to destroy. Recently, he has become well known for his commitment to healthy living, yet even this pursuit demonstrates his ability to offer audiences unique and entertaining perspectives on the status quo.

Resources: Leila B. Gemme, *New Breed of Performer* (New York: Washington Square Press, 1976); Dick Gregory: *Dick Gregory's Bible Tales, with Commentary*, ed. James R. McGraw (New York: Stein and Day, 1974); *Dick Gregory's Political Primer*, ed. James McGraw (New York: Harper & Row, 1972); *Nigger: An Autobiography* (New York: Dutton, 1964); *No More Lies* (1971; repr. New York: Buccaneer Books, 1993); Dick Gregory and Mark Lane: *Code Name "Zorro": The Murder of Martin Luther King, Jr.* (1977; repr. New York: Pocket Books, 1978); *Murder in Memphis: The FBI and the Assassination of Martin Luther King* (New York: Thunder's Mouth Press, 1993); Dick Gregory and Shelia Moses, *Callus on My Soul: A Memoir* (Atlanta: Longstreet, 2000); Gerald Nachman, *Seriously Funny: The Rebel Comedians of the 1950s and 1960s* (New York: Pantheon Books, 2003).

J'Lyn Simonson

Griggs, Sutton E. (1872–1933). Novelist, biographer, and social theorist. Born in Chatfield, **Texas**, on June 19, 1872, Sutton Elbert Griggs graduated from Bishop College in Marshall, Texas, and from the Virginia Union Theological Seminary in Richmond in 1893. From 1893 to 1906 he held pastorates in Berkeley, Virginia, and in **Nashville, Tennessee**. During these years, he wrote most of his novels and established himself as a committed religious leader as well as a community activist. In 1897, he married Emma Williams, a public school teacher.

While in the Nashville area, Griggs spearheaded the National Baptist Convention's Educational Committee and established the Nashville School, a religious institution dedicated to educating young African Americans entering into the ministry. Committed to elevating African Americans through education and political rights, Griggs also enlisted as a founding member of the Niagara Movement, the civil rights organization that was the forerunner to the **NAACP**.

Griggs published some thirty-three texts, including social addresses, biographies, and five novels. In 1899, he self-published his first novel, *Imperium in Imperio* (nation within a nation). The novel as a whole is a deliberation about the internal claims of nation. It culminates in a detailed revelation about a Black countergovernment headquartered in Waco, Texas, and intent upon taking over a section of the southern United States, should a set of clearly defined racial grievances not be redressed.

Griggs established the Orion Publishing Company in 1901 to better circulate his work to a Black readership and, in the same year, published *Overshadowed*, a text more pessimistic than revolutionary. The novel examines the internal conflicts within the Black middle class and the frustrations and obstacles that overshadow Black development in America. Griggs's third novel, *Unfettered* (1902), promoted Black cooperation with the federal government as a viable solution for overthrowing Jim Crow. In order to work among African Americans at home, its hero, Dorlan Warthell, rejects the opportunity to be incorporated back into Africa as a royal prince's descendant. Griggs wrote *Hindered Hand* (1905), commissioned by the National Baptist

Convention as a response to Thomas Dixon's racist characterizations of Blacks in *The Leopard's Spots*. *The Hindered Hand* largely treats the Du Boisian conflicts of doubleness in Black life as well as the location of **race** and African emigration. *Pointing the Way* (1908) presents a detailed adjudication of law, resulting in a Black-initiated Supreme Court case for voting rights. (*See* **Du Bois, W.E.B.**)

In 1912 Griggs and his wife moved on to **Memphis, Tennessee**, where for nineteen years he was pastor at the Tabernacle Baptist Church. From this position, he organized the National Public Welfare League to promote greater self-sufficiency and opportunities for African Americans in 1914. Griggs was also committed to preserving his family's legacy, as *Paths of Progress* (1925) attests. Here he memorializes his father, Rev. A. R. Griggs, a former slave said to have founded the first Black newspaper and the first Black school in **Texas**. At the end of his life Griggs moved to Denison, Texas, where he assumed his father's former pastorate. In 1932, he attempted to launch the National Religious and Civic Institute in Houston, but the project remained unrealized due to his death.

Resources: Bernard Bell, *The Afro-American Novel and Its Tradition* (Amherst: University of Massachusetts Press, 1987); Sutton E. Griggs: *Hindered Hand: Or, the Reign of the Repressionist* (Nashville, TN: Orion, 1905); *Imperium in Imperio* (1899; New York: Modern Library, 2003); *The Story of My Struggle* (Memphis, TN: National Public Welfare League, 1914); James Kinney, *Amalgamation! Race, Sex, and Rhetoric in the Nineteenth-Century American Novel* (Westport, CT: Greenwood Press, 1985); Wilson J. Moses, "Literary Garveyism: The Novels of Reverend Sutton E. Griggs," *Phylon* 40, no. 3 (Fall 1979), 203–216; Jon Christian Suggs, *Whispered Consolations: Law and Narrative in African American Life* (Ann Arbor: University of Michigan Press, 2000).

Judith Mulcahy

Grimes, Terris McMahan (born 1952). Novelist. Born in Tucker, Arkansas, a small community near Pinebluff, Terris McMahan Grimes grew up in Oakland, California. She received her B.A. from California State University at Chico and also attended Coe College in Iowa. For several decades, she has worked for the Department of Water Resources of the State of California.

Grimes is the author of a series of mystery novels featuring Theresa Galloway, who, like Grimes, works for the state of California (but in the Department of Environmental Equity), is married with two children, and is caring for her aging but still indomitable mother. Despite the obvious autobiographical elements, Galloway's personality is distinct from Grimes's own because Galloway is attracted to and capable of handling the sort of dangerous predicaments that Grimes has drawn largely from her imagination. In addition, although Grimes knowingly emphasizes how complicated ordinary life can be for a professional woman with family responsibilities, Galloway's personal relationships are much more tumultuous than the author's have been.

For the initial novel in the series, *Somebody Else's Child* (1996), Grimes has received the **Chester Himes** Award for best mystery by an African-American novelist, a nomination for an Agatha Award for best first mystery, and Anthony Awards for best first mystery and best paperback original. In the novel, Galloway investigates the drive-by shooting of one of her mother's elderly neighbors. In *Blood Will Tell* (1997), Galloway's mother invites a young man to move in with her, believing his claim that he is the illegitimate son of Galloway's deceased father. Galloway herself is much more skeptical, and her curiosity about his identity funnels into the investigation of a crime when he is murdered. The third novel in the series has been tentatively titled *Other Duties as Required*.

Resources: Terris McMahan Grimes: *Blood Will Tell* (New York: Signet, 1997); *Somebody Else's Child* (New York: Onyx, 1996); Carolyn Tillery, "The Fiction of Black Crime: It's No Mystery," *American Visions*, Apr.–May 1997, 18–21.

Martin Kich

Grimké, Angelina Emily (1805–1879). Nonfiction writer, abolitionist, and feminist. Angelina was the youngest child of John and Mary Grimké, White aristocratic Southern planters and slaveholders in Charleston, South Carolina. Angelina and her overprotective sister **Sarah Moore Grimké** eventually fled **the South** to escape the abuses of **slavery** they witnessed firsthand (Lerner). Neither sister believed in the inferiority of blacks nor wanted to abide by the slave codes, such as those preventing slave literacy. In effect, the sisters became political exiles. Angelina was the first of the two to protest openly against the injustices of slavery when she wrote a letter to William Lloyd Garrison in support of the **abolitionist movement**. Garrison published the letter in *The Liberator*, the leading antislavery periodical of the time. From then on, writing and speaking became Angelina's main activities as an abolitionist. She and Sarah became the first female agents fully supported by a national antislavery organization. Angelina was bold and assertive in her political views. Her best-known publications included *An Appeal to the Christian Women of the South* (1836) and *An Appeal to the Women of the Nominally Free States* (1837). In both works, Angelina recognizes the importance of women acting as equals to men and engaging in moral, social, and political reform on the basis of this assumed equality. Like her sister Sarah, Angelina relied on biblical support for her arguments to show how important women were to the development of civilization in ancient times. These principles remained true for Angelina even after her marriage to Theodore D. Weld, another radical abolitionist. The couple bristled at Victorian domestic standards and insisted on being equal partners in their marriage (Lerner; Lumpkin). Therefore, Angelina continued her public service outside the home with the support of her husband. Together, along with Sarah, the couple completed a compilation of documentary materials, *American Slavery as It Is* (1839), providing a factual account of the system.

Angelina once declared " 'I want to be identified with the negro; until he gets his rights, we [women] shall never have ours' " (Lerner, 353). This statement testifies to Angelina's solemn commitment to the fair and equal treatment of African Americans and women alike. She promoted her beliefs throughout her political career and even in "retirement," when she openly acknowledged the familial ties with her illegitimate black nephews—**Archibald Henry Grimké**, **Francis James Grimké**, and John Grimké. Archibald, the eldest, named his only daughter, the lesbian writer of the **Harlem Renaissance, Angelina Weld Grimké**, after her great-aunt. The elder Angelina once proclaimed to Archibald, "I am glad you have taken the name of Grimké—it was *once*, one of the noblest names of Carolina" (Lerner, 361). Angelina's pride and shame in her heritage were due to her slaveholding past combined with the exceptional ability of a few family members to transcend it. She hoped that her nephews would "lift *this name* out of the dust, . . . and set it once more among the princes of our land" (Lerner, 361), if they devoted their lives to humanitarian efforts just as she and her sister Sarah had done. Archibald's and Francis's public service as a politician and a minister, respectively, was a prophecy fulfilled.

Resources: Angelina Grimke: *Appeal to the Christian Women of the South* (1836; repr. New York: Arno Press, 1969); *An Appeal to the Women of the Nominally Free States* (1837; repr. Freeport, NY: Books for Libraries, 1971); Gerda Lerner, *The Grimké Sisters from South Carolina: Pioneers for Woman's Rights and Abolition* (New York: Schocken Books, 1971); Katharine Du Pre Lumpkin, *The Emancipation of Angelina Grimké* (Chapel Hill: University of North Carolina Press, 1974); Mark Perry, *Lift Up Thy Voice: The Grimké Family's Journey from Slaveholders to Civil Rights Leaders* (New York: Viking, 2001).

Sherita L. Johnson

Grimké, Angelina Weld (1880–1958). Playwright, poet, and short story writer. Grimké is most noted as the author of the first significant play by a Black female and, more recently, as the author of early poems with lesbian themes. Her play *Rachel* (1916) stands out as a classic among numerous antilynching dramas that found popularity during the **Harlem Renaissance**.

Angelina Weld Grimké was a member of the famous biracial Grimké family of South Carolina. She was born in **Boston, Massachusetts**, on February 27, 1880 to **Archibald Henry Grimké**, a Harvard-trained lawyer, and Sarah Stanley, a White woman. Archibald Grimké was the grandson of Henry Grimké, a South Carolina plantation owner, and a slave woman, Nancy Weston. His aunts were the famous abolitionists **Sarah Moore Grimké** and **Angelina Emily Grimké** Weld, after whom Angelina Weld Grimké was named. Angelina was raised principally by her father after he and her mother separated in 1883. She was educated in some of the best schools in the country, including the Fairmount School in Hyde Park, Massachusetts, the Carleton Academy in Minnesota, the Cushing Academy in Massachusetts, and the Boston Normal School of Gymnastics. Beginning shortly after her graduation in 1902, Grimké taught school in **Washington, D.C.**; from 1916 until 1926, she was on the faculty of the famous Dunbar High School in Washington. In 1930, after the death of her father, whom she nursed during an extended illness, she moved to New York City where she lived in relative obscurity until her death in 1958.

Grimké's play *Rachel* (1920) was a highly popular drama that had successful runs in Washington, **Harlem, New York**, and Cambridge, Massachusetts. As a work of drama, it shows the far-reaching and implacable negative effects of race prejudice as much as it foregrounds the heinousness of **lynching**. The Loving family has left **the South** for a new life of safety and progress in the North after the lynching of Mr. Loving and his stepson, George. Regardless of how much distance they try to put between themselves and the despicable, cowardly act, the Lovings—Rachel, her mother, and her brother Tom—continue to suffer from the effects of the color prejudice manifested in education, employment, and social standing. Rachel is the most severely affected, vowing never to marry or to bring into the world a Black child who must live in fear for his life at the hands of would-be lynchers. Grimké's play is a damning indictment of lynching and the ever-present White prejudice that promotes it.

Grimké wrote a second antilynching play, *Mara*, that remains unpublished and unproduced. In addition, much of her fiction focused on lynching. Notable in this genre is the short story "Goldie," which was based substantially on an actual lynching that occurred in Georgia in 1918. Although less successful, these works are no less searing in their denunciation of lynching.

Although Grimké's poems date back to her girlhood, many of them were never published. Others, however, appeared in a number of anthologies of the period, including **Countee Cullen**'s *Caroling Dusk* (1927). A number of her poems were published in *Opportunity*; although she collected her poems later in life, they were never published together. Recent biographers such as **Gloria Hull** have noted that many of Grimké's poems were love poems written to women, while others were lyrical poems that focused on nature. Although Grimké produced high-quality work, she could not sustain her writing thematically or in tone beyond the Harlem Renaissance. Her work is available now in an anthology edited by Patton and Honey.

Resources: Gloria Hull, *Color, Sex, and Poetry: Three Women Writers of the Harlem Renaissance* (Bloomington: Indiana University Press, 1987); Venetria K. Patton and Maureen Honey, eds., *Double-Take: A Revisionist Harlem Renaissance Anthology* (New Brunswick, NJ: Rutgers University Press, 2001); Lorraine Roses and Ruth Randolph, eds., *Harlem's Glory: Black Women Writing, 1900–1950* (Cambridge, MA: Harvard University Press, 1996).

Warren J. Carson

Grimké, Archibald Henry (1849–1930). Journalist, essayist, lawyer, and civil rights activist. Grimké was born a slave near Charleston, South Carolina, to a White plantation owner and one of his slaves. After emancipation, he and his brother **Francis James Grimké** attended Lincoln University in Pennsylvania, and with the support of their White aunts—the prominent abolitionists **Sarah Moore Grimké** and **Angelina Emily Grimké**—he earned a law degree from Harvard in 1874. Setting up his law practice in **Boston, Massachusetts**, Grimké became editor of *The Hub*, a local Republican-sponsored newspaper, in 1883, and through the platform that the paper provided him, began to play a leading role in Black politics in Massachusetts.

Grimké left the newspaper and the Republicans in 1886 because of the party's failure to address the needs of African Americans, but he continued to use the press as a tool for political advocacy and to argue for civil rights and women's suffrage. His essays ran in all of the major Black newspapers of the era and in a number of White-edited publications, including *The Atlantic* and *Arena*. Beginning in 1905, he wrote a column for the *New York Age*, perhaps the most important Black newspaper of the day. Grimké also made significant contributions to scholarship, publishing biographies of the abolitionists William Lloyd Garrison (1891) and Charles Sumner (1892).

After serving for four years as U.S. consul to the Dominican Republic, Grimké divided his time between Boston and **Washington, D.C.**, before permanently moving to the capital in 1905. At the turn of the century, Washington was the center of Black intellectual and political life in the United States, and Grimké quickly became an important community figure. He was invited to join the Bethel Literary and Historical Association, the country's most prestigious Black literary society, and the American Negro Academy, an organization of the nation's Black intellectual elite. Serving as president of the academy from 1903 to 1919, Grimké presented some of his most compelling essays before the group, including a groundbreaking study of Denmark Vesey's slave revolt. He also joined the National Association for the Advancement of Colored People (**NAACP**) and served as president of the Washington chapter from 1913 to 1923.

Beyond his own literary career, Grimké encouraged his daughter **Angelina Weld Grimké** to be a writer, and with his support, her play *Rachel* was the first drama by an African American woman to be professionally staged.

Resources: Archibald Henry Grimké Papers, Manuscript Division, Moorland-Spingarn Research Center, Howard University, Washington, DC; Dickson D. Bruce, Jr., *Archibald Grimké: Portrait of a Black Independent* (Baton Rouge: Louisiana State University Press, 1993); Robert L. Johns, "Archibald Henry Grimké," in *Notable Black American Men*, ed. Jessica Carney Smith (Detroit: Gale, 1998), 487–490.

Brett Beemyn

Grimké, Charlotte Forten (1837–1914). American diarist, essayist, poet, translator, and activist. A fourth-generation free Black woman, Charlotte L. Forten was born in **Philadelphia, Pennsylvania**, to Robert Bridges Forten and Mary Virginia (Woods) Forten on August 17, 1837. As a member of a socially prominent family in abolitionist, intellectual, and business circles, the young Charlotte grew up influenced by relatives and friends who instilled in her a desire to work in public service, especially on behalf of enslaved peoples and, later, in church and religious duties. Though moving often after her mother's early death and enduring ill health that would plague her all her life, the future writer achieved an exemplary education, equal to that of any educated women in nineteenth-century U.S. culture. Her father sent her to Salem,

Massachusetts, when she was an adolescent to spare her the segregated schools of Philadelphia and to prepare her for a life in a stable and respectable profession, teaching. In Salem, Forten began her journals, for which she is now best known. In these journals, which she named *ami inconnu* (unknown friend), Forten writes of matters significant to her personally and to African American history and letters. Written intermittently over more than thirty years, the journals contain entries devoted to her reading interests, reactions to plights of fugitive slaves, romance, the "Port Royal Experiment," and marriage and work.

While in Port Royal, on St. Helena, an island off the coast of South Carolina, Forten met for the first time and taught former slaves; from this experience she was able to understand firsthand the oppression of **slavery** and to record local customs. Her best-known essay, "Life on the Sea Islands," which appeared in *Atlantic Monthly* in 1864, details this experience. The year 1869 saw the publication of Forten's translation of the French novel *Madame Therese; or the Volunteers of '92*. In 1878 Forten married **Francis James Grimké**, a former slave who had studied law and theology and had become a minister. They had one daughter, Theodora Cornelia. Charlotte Grimké spent the remainder of her life writing and working with her husband to combat injustice. She died in her home, in **Washington, D.C.**, on July 23, 1914.

Charlotte L. Forten Grimké, c. 1873. Photographs and Prints Division, Schomburg Center for Research in Black Culture, The New York Public Library, Astor, Lenox and Tilden Foundations.

Resources: Emile Erckman and Alexandre Chatrian, *Madame Therese; or, The Volunteers of '92*, trans. Charlotte Forten Grimké (New York: Scribner's, 1869); Charlotte Forten Grimké: "Life on the Sea Islands," *Atlantic Monthly*, May 1864, 587–596; June 1864, 666–676; Katharine Rodier, "Charlotte L. Forten," in *Dictionary of Literary Biography*, vol. 239, ed. Amy Hudock and Katharine Rodier (Detroit: Gale, 2001); Brenda Stevenson, ed., *The Journals of Charlotte Forten Grimké* (Oxford: Oxford University Press, 1988).

Bill Clem

Grimké, Francis James (1850–1937). Minister, orator, and civil rights activist. Francis Grimké was born a slave near Charleston, South Carolina, to a White plantation owner and one of his slaves. Like his brother **Archibald**

Henry Grimké, Francis attended Lincoln University in Pennsylvania, where he graduated as valedictorian of his class in 1870, and studied law, first at Lincoln and then at Howard University. But, deciding to enter the ministry, he transferred to Princeton Theological Seminary in 1875.

After graduating in 1878, Grimké became pastor of the Fifteenth Street Presbyterian Church in **Washington, D.C.**, one of the country's most prominent Black churches, and married writer and educator Charlotte Forten (*see* **Grimké, Charlotte Forten**), the daughter of a leading Black **Philadelphia, Pennsylvania**, family. Except for four years he spent as a minister in Jacksonville, Florida, in order to improve his health, Grimké remained associated with the Fifteen Street Church until his death in 1937.

Grimké's role in the church gave him a public platform for his views, but it was his eloquence and ability to speak to the concerns of African Americans that enabled him to become a leader in Washington's Black community. His sermons were so popular that many were published as pamphlets. He also regularly contributed essays to the *New York Independent* and the *New York Evangelist*.

In his sermons and articles, Grimké spoke out against **lynching** and other racial injustices and criticized the predominantly White Presbyterian church for its acquiescence to racism. He also argued that African Americans needed to adhere to conservative Christian moral standards in order for the Black community to make significant social progress, which led him to be known as the Black Puritan. The sermons and speeches in the four-volume collection *The Works of Francis J. Grimké* (1942) reflect his concern for both White racial prejudice and Black personal improvement. Among the topics addressed are race relations and racial problems, the lives of prominent African Americans, the training of children, and the qualities of a "worthy woman."

Although Grimké's advocacy was primarily from the pulpit, he was also active in the political and educational life of the Black community. Initially a strong backer of **Booker T. Washington**'s self-help approach, he later joined with **W.E.B. Du Bois** and other Black leaders who favored a liberal education rather than industrial training for African Americans and became a supporter of the **NAACP**. He also helped found the American Negro Academy, an organization of the nation's Black intellectual elite, in 1905 and served on the board of trustees of Howard University from 1880 to 1925.

Resources: Daniel Ross Chandler, "Francis James Grimké," in *African-American Orators: A Bio-Critical Sourcebook*, ed. Richard W. Leeman (Westport, CT: Greenwood Press, 1996), 163–170; Francis James Grimké papers, Manuscript Division, Moorland-Spingarn Research Center, Howard University, Washington, DC; Robert L. Johns, "Francis J. Grimké," in *Notable Black American Men*, ed. Jessica Carney Smith (Detroit: Gale, 1998), 490–492; Darryl M. Trimiew, "Francis J. Grimké: Responsiblist as Puritan Critic," in *Voices of the Silenced: The Responsible Self in a Marginalized Community* (Cleveland, OH: Pilgrim Press, 1993), 49–62; Louis B. Weeks III, "Racism, World War I and the Christian Life: Francis J. Grimké in the Nation's Capital," in *Black Apostles: Afro-American Clergy Confront the Twentieth Century*, ed.

Randall K. Burkett and Richard Newman (Boston: G. K. Hall, 1978), 57–75; Carter G. Woodson, ed., *The Works of Francis J. Grimké*, 4 vols. (Washington, DC: Associated Publishers, 1942).

Brett Beemyn

Grimké, Sarah Moore (1792–1873). Abolitionist and feminist. As the older of the pioneering Grimké sisters from South Carolina, Sarah rebelled against her aristocratic slaveholding heritage to become a leader in the **Abolitionist Movement** and an advocate of women's rights. As a young girl, she yearned for the same type of formal education her brothers received and aspired to become a lawyer, an unorthodox career choice for any woman during the nineteenth century and especially one of her social status. Sarah's domestic training, on the other hand, would prove beneficial when she was nurturing her younger sister, Angelina, but it did not provide the intellectual stimulation she craved (Lerner, *The Grimké Sisters*). Sarah was further agitated by the treatment of slaves she witnessed firsthand. As she grew to adulthood, the religious argument that justified **slavery** failed to convince Sarah, and only alienated her more from her family and high society in Charleston. She detested the immorality of slavery and sought solace in her discovery of Quakerism. Her moral stance was an insult to the community and a public embarrassment for her family (Lerner, *The Grimké Sisters*). She moved to **Philadelphia, Pennsylvania**, in 1821 to freely practice her new religion there. The Quakers' liberalism initially supported Sarah's interest in gender equality and racial sympathy. This liberalism would later be attractive to Angelina as well. The sisters broke with the Quakers once they became active in the antislavery movement. Under the guidance of the revolutionary abolitionist William Lloyd Garrison, they became the first female agents of the American Anti-Slavery Society. They led an extensive lecture tour throughout New England that inspired the development of hundreds of antislavery societies and increased membership twofold. The successful tour was a first of its kind with women speakers as headliners.

As Garrisonians, the sisters were radical abolitionists advocating immediate slave emancipation and promoting racial tolerance and social equality in their speeches and publications. Sarah, less assertive than her younger sister, focused more on moral and theological concerns, as evidenced by her *Epistle to the Clergy of Southern States* (1836). This early antislavery pamphlet attacked the religious argument for slavery, which was the source of Sarah's earliest internal struggles with religious dogma in **the South**. From her point of view, the tenets of pure Christianity contradicted the practice of slavery. The political activism of Sarah and Angelina Grimké, who were seen as former "Southern belles," was vital to the development of a women's rights campaign. The Grimké sisters' feminist approach to abolition was distinctive, if not unique, among their peers. Sarah believed "whatsoever it is morally right for a man to do, it is morally right for a woman to do" (Lerner, *Grimke Sisters*, 193). Sarah's *Letters on the Equality of the Sexes and the Condition of Women* (1838) is her best-known work. She never married and lived until her death with Angelina and her husband, Theodore Weld, another celebrated abolitionist. Together, the trio continued to work on the behalf of slaves and freedmen alike. The genuine love, "parental" guidance, and financial support they provided for their illegitimate Black nephews—**Archibald Henry Grimké**, **Francis James Grimké**, and John Grimké—are practical evidence of Sarah and Angelina Grimké's humanitarianism.

Resources: Gerda Lerner, *The Grimké Sisters from South Carolina: Pioneers for Woman's Rights and Abolition* (New York: Schocken Books, 1971); Gerda Lerner, ed., *The Feminist Thought of Sarah Grimké* (New York: Oxford University Press, 1998); Mark Perry, *Lift Up Thy Voice: The Grimké Family's Journey from Slaveholders to Civil Rights Leaders* (New York: Viking, 2001).

Sherita L. Johnson

Gronniosaw, James Albert Ukawsaw (c. 1710–?). Memoirist. Sometime before 1772, Gronniosaw dictated the story of his life. The result, *A Narrative of the Most Remarkable Particulars in the Life of James Albert Ukawsaw Gronniosaw, an African Prince, as Related by Himself*, is part **slave narrative**, part conversion narrative, and part autobiographical account of one man's passage from freedom in Africa to enslavement in the Americas and finally to provisional freedom at sea and in England. It is also a document of his desire to learn: it is here that the trope of the "Talking Book," as identified by **Henry Louis Gates, Jr.**, first appears in print. Gronniosaw recounts seeing his first owner read aloud, and feels betrayed that the book will not speak to him. This trope, with its emphasis upon literacy and the desire to acquire it, is considered the most influential aspect of Gronniosaw's narrative, and recurs in slave narratives by **John Marrant**, Ottobah Cugoano, **Olaudah Equiano**, and John Jea.

Gronniosaw's tale opens in Africa. He was born in Borno (Nigeria) to the daughter of the king. This placed him firmly within the inner circle of a literate and worldly Islamic family. However, from the beginning of his narrative Gronniosaw foregrounds his desire to explore. He therefore travels to the Gold Coast with a merchant, only to be sold into slavery. Bought by a Dutch sea captain, Gronniosaw is treated well and provided with religious instruction.

After arriving in Barbados, Gronniosaw is sold to a Dutch Reformed minister, Theodorus Frelinghuysen of New Jersey, who ignited America's Great Awakening. For twenty years, then, Gronniosaw lived under **slavery** in the era's greatest spiritual revival. His account of his "awakening" has been cited as potential inspiration for William Blake's poem "Little Black Boy."

Freed by Frelinghuysen's will, around 1759 Gronniosaw signed on with a privateer. He then enlisted with the British during the Seven Years' War (1756–1763), which took him to Barbados, Martinique, Cuba, Spain, and finally England. While in London he visited Frelinghuysen's friend, the minister George Whitefield. Still curious about the world, Gronniosaw once again satisfied his wanderlust by visiting Holland. After a year there, Gronniosaw returned to England to be baptized by the theologian Andrew Gifford, and to marry a widow he had met previously.

Gronniosaw's life as a husband and father was characterized by much hardship, and yet his attachment to his religious faith was unwavering. This faith grounds the narrative, though we cannot be sure whether this is the result of the intervention of the amanuensis. But it is clear that the tale does not conform to the slave narrative as it is often understood: it does not cite the injustices of slavery, and it includes no antislavery arguments. Instead, the narrative is presented as a quest, first for adventure, then for spiritual enlightenment, and finally for domestic security. It is on this final quest that the narrative closes, as the expanding family finds itself in Kidderminster, hoping to establish an economically viable household. Nothing else is known of their fate.

Resources: Henry Louis Gates, Jr., *The Signifying Monkey: A Theory of African-American Literary Criticism* (New York: Oxford University Press, 1998); James Albert Ukawsaw Gronniosaw, *A Narrative of the Most Remarkable Particulars in the Life of James Albert Ukawsaw Gronniosaw, an African Prince, as Related by Himself*, in *Pioneers of the Black Atlantic: Five Slave Narratives from the Enlightenment, 1772–1815*, ed. Henry Louis Gates, Jr., and William L. Andrews (Washington, DC: Civitas, 1998), 31–59; Lauren Henry, "Sunshine and Shady Groves: What Blake's 'Little Black Boy' Learned from African Writers," *Blake: An Illustrated Quarterly* 29 (1995), 4–11; Adam Potkay and Sandra Burr, eds., *Black Atlantic Writers of the Eighteenth Century: Living the New Exodus in England and the Americas* (New York: St. Martin's Press, 1995); Helen Thomas, *Romanticism and Slave Narratives: Transatlantic Testimonies* (Cambridge: Cambridge University Press, 2000).

Jennifer Harris

Grooms, Anthony (born 1955). Novelist, short story writer, and poet. Two-time winner of the Lillian Smith Award for his fictional explorations of Southern race relations, Anthony Grooms is interested in how ordinary people respond to the challenges of extraordinary historical events. In particular, he has written extensively about young men and women caught up in the turmoil of the **Civil Rights Movement**. For many of his characters, that movement initially represents a wasted effort against an intractable force, and thus they are tempted to withdraw from the conflict in favor of personal safety. Against this, however, Grooms explores how the pull of commitment operates on these same characters, how historical forces offer them opportunities for personal and social change if they will embrace hope and take risks. In the story "Negro Progress," for instance, the narrator begins by refusing to march against Bull Connor. As a young businessman with a bright future, "he had nothing to lose if he played it smart" (41). However, at the end of the story he takes a "clumsy step" (50) toward hope and engagement, facing down the fire hoses and risking his future for the woman he loves.

Born in rural Louisa County, Virginia, Grooms was among the first group of African American students whose parents petitioned for integration. He graduated from the College of William and Mary in 1978, where he studied theater and speech, and in 1985 he received his M.F.A. from George Mason University. He published *Ice Poems* in 1988, but it was with his second book, *Trouble No More: Stories* (1995), that he received his first critical acclaim. A nuanced exploration of Black middle-class family life in the 1960s **South**, *Trouble No More* earned Grooms his first Lillian Smith Award. He followed with *Bombingham* (2001), the story of Walter Burke, an American soldier in Vietnam who responds to the death of a fellow serviceman by remembering the murder of his own best friend in the aftermath of the Birmingham church bombing. Searching for understanding, Walter confronts a problem that all Grooms's characters must face if they are to act in meaningful ways. "Having faith," Walter surmises, "wasn't the problem; the problem was what to have faith in" (220). *Bombingham* also received a Lillian Smith Award and was selected as a *Washington Post* Notable Book in 2001. (*See* **Vietnam War**.)

Grooms is currently professor of creative writing at Kennesaw State University in Georgia.

Resources: Jabari Asim, "Homegrown Terrorism," *Washington Post*, Oct. 9, 2001, p. C11; Alida Becker, "Review of *Trouble No More*," *New York Times Book Review*, Sept. 24, 1995, p. 26; Anthony Grooms: *Accidents* (play) (William and Mary Premier Theatre, 1975); *Bombingham* (New York: Free Press, 2001); *Dr. Madlove* (play) (William and Mary Premier Theatre, 1975); *Ice Poems* (Atlanta: Poetry Atlanta, 1988); *Trouble No More: Stories* (Palo Alto, CA: La Questa, 1995); Don O'Briant, "People in the Arts: The Practice of Writing for Anthony Grooms, Putting Words on Paper Is Daily Habit," *Atlanta Journal Constitution*, July 19, 1992, p. N2; Ishmael Reed, "In the Line of Fire," *Village Voice*, Dec. 4, 2001, p. 74; Diane Roberts, "Books: Atlanta Author Mines the Eras of Vietnam and Civil Rights," *Atlanta Journal Constitution*, Oct. 28, 2001, p. B6.

Christopher Metress

Gulf War (1991) (also known as the Persian Gulf War or the First Gulf War). These names have been given to the liberation of Kuwait by a U.S.-led coalition of U.N. forces in early 1991. On August 2, 1990, 140,000 Iraqi air, ground, and naval forces under the leadership of longtime dictator Saddam Hussein invaded the small, oil-rich sovereign nation of Kuwait on Iraq's southeastern border. Saddam apparently miscalculated the strong negative world response his actions would draw. Just five days after the invasion, U.S. rapid-deployment forces began to arrive in Saudi Arabia at the request of King Fahd to assist in the defense of the Saudi kingdom should Iraq continue the attack to the south. The defense of Saudi Arabia, dubbed Operation Desert Shield, was the first phase of the Persian Gulf War and successfully deterred further Iraqi aggression with what President George H. W. Bush called the United States' "line in the sand." When Iraq failed to withdraw its forces from Kuwait by a January 15, 1991, deadline imposed by a U.N. Security Council resolution, the United Nations authorized the coalition to use "all necessary means" to enforce previous resolutions calling for Iraqi withdrawal. During the night of January 16, allied air forces began an offensive campaign against Iraqi military targets in Kuwait and Iraq.

Thus began the war's second phase, Operation Desert Storm, designed to liberate Kuwait. Following five weeks of intensive attack from the air, allied forces began the ground phase of Operation Desert Storm on February 24. Coalition ground forces attacked north out of Saudi Arabia on a broad front that stretched from the Persian Gulf, along the eastern border of Kuwait, well to the west along the Saudi–Iraq border. The Iraqi military had been so decimated by the air campaign that it did not realize how far west the coalition had deployed. Forces on the western flank moved swiftly north into Iraq, then turned east, forming a hook-shaped deployment deep into the Tigris–Euphrates area north of Kuwait. Coalition forces commander Gen. Norman Schwarzkopf would call this the "Hail Mary play," alluding to a long, deep pass pattern in football. Meanwhile, allied forces attacking directly into Kuwait, some from the Gulf itself, quickly pushed the Iraqis back into Iraq. Iraqi units fleeing Kuwait City on Highway 8, which became known as the "highway of death," were decimated by coalition air and ground forces. This, along with the fact that the conditions of the U.N. mandate had been achieved, caused President Bush, Chairman of the Joint Chiefs of Staff Colin Powell, and General Schwarzkopf to halt the war and the pursuit of the Iraqi army after only 100 hours of ground combat. This decision would be the subject of repeated debate because it left Saddam in power and, as some argue, set the stage for the U.S.-led invasion of Iraq in 2003.

The Persian Gulf War has, at this writing, produced a relatively small amount of literature. Most of what is published is history, **autobiography**, and memoir, along with the expected military and political analysis. This paucity of literature, especially fiction and poetry, is not surprising, given the very short duration of the war and the fact that although reserve and National Guard units were activated and deployed to the Gulf, there was not a prolonged, extensive mobilization in the United States. At its peak, there was a grand total of about 539,000 U.S. service members in the entire Persian Gulf region. This was a war fought by career professionals and trained volunteers, not draftees from the population at large.

Particularly notable about African Americans and the Persian Gulf War was the fact that U.S. forces had been so fully integrated for so long that Black Americans served at all levels of the chain of command. Indeed, during the 1980s the presence of Black, Hispanic, Asian, Polynesian, and other minorities throughout the armed services had become such a normal state of affairs as to be taken for granted among service members. The group whose integration into new roles throughout the military drew the greatest public scrutiny and comment during the war was women, who were now filling more combat and combat support roles than ever. Many of the racial tensions present within the services as late as the war in Vietnam had more or less disappeared, partly because of a long, concerted effort to integrate the armed forces thoroughly.

General Colin Powell, an African American born in **Harlem, New York**, and raised in the Bronx, was national security advisor to President Ronald Reagan and chairman of the Joint Chiefs of Staff during the war, and went on to become secretary of state under President George W. Bush. Powell's compelling autobiography, *My American Journey*, contains a very authoritative account of the Gulf War from the level of the national command authority. Moreover, his story reflects the determination of Army leadership to pull itself up from widespread low standards prevailing at the end of the **Vietnam War**. William Jerome Simmons, for example, in his memoir, *Operation Desert Shield/ Storm Through the Eyes of a Black Lieutenant* (1995), alleges that racial discrimination existed in his South Carolina National Guard hospital.

Ruth Forman's 1993 poetry collection *We Are the Young Magicians* skillfully and wryly captures life in the speaker's **Philadelphia, Pennsylvania**, neighborhood during the late 1980s and early 1990s. A section of the volume titled "Cesarean Section" contains several poems dealing with the speaker's reaction to the war and with soldiers leaving for or returning from the conflict.

Resources: Peter Forbes, "A Hundred Harms: Poetry and the Gulf War," *Poetry Review*, Summer 1992, 3–26; Ruth Forman, *We Are the Young Magicians* (Boston: Beacon Press, 1993); Colin Powell, *My American Journey* (New York: Random House, 1995); Al Santoli, *Leading the Way: How Vietnam Veterans Rebuilt the U.S. Military. An Oral History* (New York: Random House, 1993); William Jerome Simmons, Sr., *Operation Desert Shield/Storm Through the Eyes of a Black Lieutenant* (Pittsburgh, PA: Dorrance, 1995); Harry G. Summers, Jr., *On Strategy II: A Critical Analysis of the Gulf War* (New York: Dell, 1992); Joel Turnipseed, *Baghdad Express: A Gulf War Memoir* (New York: Penguin, 2003);Tom Willard, *Sword of Valor* (New York: Tom Doherty Associates, 2003).

David M. Owens

Gumby, Levi-Sandy Alexander (1885–1961). Collector and author. Gumby was not only an enthusiastic collector of African Americana and a prominent host, but also was among the most remarkable personalities of the **Harlem Renaissance**. Not much is known about the years before Gumby, who was born in Maryland in 1885, reached New York around 1906. In New York, he started working as a bellhop, saved his wages, sought out artistic circles, and managed to become a leading society figure.

Gumby was openly gay (although the term, as referring to homosexuality, was not current then) and highly flamboyant. Supported by his intimate friend Charles Newman, a White stockbroker, he rented a large studio at 2144 Fifth Avenue that—given his penchant for collecting rare books and scrapbooks filled with clippings, photographs, letters, and manuscripts—became known as "Gumby's Bookstore." The studio opened in 1926 and developed into a popular gathering place for **Harlem, New York**'s cultural elite. Here, writers—ranging from **Claude McKay** to **Dorothy West**—celebrated, artists presented their paintings, and musicians, among them **Paul Robeson**, gave recitals. Gumby was a generous host and sometimes entertained by reciting his own unpublished sexually explicit sonnets. His ambitious magazine project—the *Gumby Book Studio Quarterly* (1930/1931)—failed: only one issue was printed and presumably was never distributed.

In 1931, Gumby contracted tuberculosis and was forced to spend five years in hospital. During this time, parts of his collection disappeared, but after his return from hospital Gumby immediately began to update his collection and in 1950 presented it to Columbia University as the L. S. Alexander Gumby Collection of Negroiana, to which he added further material until his death in 1961.

Resources: L. S. Alexander Gumby, "The Adventures of My Scrapbooks," *Columbia Library Columns* 2 (1952), 19–23; L. S. Alexander Gumby Collection of Negroiana, Rare Book and Manuscript Library, Columbia University; Richard Bruce Nugent, "On Alexander Gumby," in *Gay Rebel of the Harlem Renaissance: Selections from the Work of Richard Bruce Nugent*, ed. Thomas H. Wirth (Durham, NC: Duke University Press, 2002), 223–226; Thomas H. Wirth, "Introduction," in *Gay Rebel of the Harlem Renaissance: Selections from the Work of Richard Bruce Nugent*, ed. Thomas H. Wirth (Durham, NC: Duke University Press, 2002), 1–61.

A. B. Christa Schwarz

Gunn, Bill (1934–1989). Film director, screenwriter, actor, and novelist. Born in **Philadelphia, Pennsylvania**, Bill (William Harrison) Gunn published two novels, *Rhinetone Sharecropping* (1981) and *Black Picture Show* (1975). (For a list of his other literary works, including plays, see Williams.) As a television actor, he appeared in episodes of the series *The Fugitive* and *The Outer Limits*. He developed the original story and wrote the screenplay for the motion picture *The Landlord* (1970), directed by Hal Ashby and produced by Norman Jewison. It concerns a young, wealthy White man purchasing and renovating a building in Harlem. In 1973 he directed the vampire film *Ganja and Hess*, and in 1981 he directed, with **Ishmael Reed**, the film *Personal Problems*, which is set in a **Harlem, New York**, hospital. Gunn died in Nyack, New York, in 1989.

Resources: Bill Gunn: *Black Picture Show* (New York: Reed Cannon & Johnson, 1981); *Rhinestone Sharecropping* (New York: Reed Cannon & Johnson, 1975); P. Jane Splawn, "Bill Gunn (1934–1989)," in *Contemporary African American Novelists: A Bio-Bibliographical Critical Sourcebook*, ed. Emmanuel S. Nelson (Westport, CT: Greenwood Press, 1999), 192–197; John Williams, "Bill Gunn: Black Independent Filmmaker, Scenarist, Playwright, Novelist: A Critical Index of the Collected Film, Dramatic, and Literary Works," *Obsidian II: Black Literature in Review* 5, no. 2 (Summer 1990), 115–147.

Hans Ostrom

Gunn, Gay G. (born 1947). Newspaper columnist and romance novelist. A **Washington, D.C.**, native, a Howard University graduate (B.A. 1969, M.S.W. 1971), and a social worker by profession, Gay G. Gunn distinguishes her writings by infusing popular tunes in an African American cultural setting. Her love of music is evident in the column she wrote, "Personal Reflections," from 1982 to 1987 in the *Washington Living* magazine, while employed as a social worker in the District of Columbia Supreme Court (1971–1985). In the column "If You Are Blessed with a Living Mother," Gunn captures the title of a Negro spiritual and gives thanks to her mother on Mother's Day. The column "First Love" invokes the lyrics of Mary Wells's then popular tune, "You Lost Your Sweetest Boy," to recall Gunn's first beau, a generous but macho Puerto Rican. Excerpts from her unpublished collection of essays *Taffeta, Dotted Swiss and Gingham* (1983), retitled *Dotted Swiss and Gingham* (1986), also appeared in *Washington Living*.

Gunn's first published romance novel, *Everlastin' Love* (1996), takes its title from Raw Cilk's "Everlastin' Love." Set during the **Vietnam War**, the novel records the undying love between Jasmine (Jaz) Culhane and her husband, Quinton (Qwayz) Chandler IV, who has been recorded as killed in action. Music sets the tone of despondency and anxiety, especially since Qwayz's body has not been found, and it typifies Jaz's feelings about America's war effort announced in the Temptations' "Ball of Confusion," Edwin Starr's "War," Freda Payne's "Bring the Boys Home," and Stevie Wonder's "Heaven Help Us All."

Nowhere to Run (1997), a historical novel, acquired its title from Martha and the Vandellas' 1960s tune "Nowhere to Run," which was adapted from the old Negro spiritual "You Better Run." The novel details the daring flight of Cassie Lee from a Georgia slave plantation to the Sierra Nevada Mountains with a stranger named Solomon Hawk, whom Cassie Lee falls in love with and names her "forever man," an endearment that calls up the title of a lyric by Eric Clapton, a popular **blues** guitarist.

Marvin Gaye's 1963 hit tune "Pride and Joy," composed to show his enduring love for Anna Gordy Gaye, his wife, became the inspiration for Gunn's third novel, *Pride and Joi* (1998), which documents the love between Joe Pride and Joi Martin. In this novel, Gunn reverses the trend of the independent, professional woman and the equally independent but sexist male found in most romance novels by **Beverly Hunter Jenkins** and **Shirley Hailstock**. A down-at-the-heels waitress who looks for a man to take care of her, Joi Martin spurns a middle-class snob and falls in love with Pride, a high school dropout and factory worker who can cook, clean, and sew.

The mother of two grown sons, Gunn currently resides in Silver Spring, Maryland. (*See* **Historical Fiction**.)

Resources: Rita B. Dandridge, *Black Women's Activism: Reading African American Women's Historical Romances* (New York: Peter Lang, 2004); Gay G. Gunn: "Destination Paradise" (unpublished novel, 1991); *Dotted Swiss and Gingham* (Silver Spring, MD: TreMar Productions, 1986); *Everlastin' Love* (New York: Ballantine Books, 1996); "First Love," *Washington Living* 2 (Feb. 1984), 55–57; "If You Are Blessed with a Living Mother," *Washington Living* 2 (May 1983), 55–56; "The Message in Our Music," *Washington Living* 2 (Sept. 1983), 53–54; *Nowhere to Run* (Columbus, MS: Genesis Press, 1997); *Pride and Joi* (Columbus, MS: Genesis Press, 1998).

Rita B. Dandridge

Guy, Rosa (born 1925). Fiction writer for adults and young adults, playwright, and organizer. Guy is known for writing that appeals to a broad spectrum of readers and for cofounding the Harlem Writers Guild. She was born in Diego Marti, Trinidad. When she was seven, Guy and her sister, Ameze, joined their parents, Henry and Audrey Cuthbert, in the United States. The family settled in **Harlem, New York**, the setting of a number of her stories. The rich dialogue in her novels is a combination of West Indian dialect and the language spoken by Blacks in large urban areas in the United States. In 1951, Guy founded the Harlem Writers Guild with **John Oliver Killens**. A number of well-known contemporary Black writers, including **Maya Angelou**, **Audre Lorde**, and **Paule Marshall**, were members of this workshop. Guy told one critic that members of the guild "wanted . . . to have a group that really projected the life, the style, the dialogue, the type of writing, [the] expression that could only come from the black experience in the United States, and in my situation . . . the U.S. and the West Indies" (Norris, 12).

Her one-act play, *Venetian Blind* (1954), produced at the Topical Theatre in New York, marked Guy's first professional literary work as well as her acting debut. In 1960, two short stories published in Trinidad in C.L.R. James's newspaper served as her first published works, though no surviving copies exist. Six years later, her first book, *Bird at My Window* (1966), a novel for adults, was published. The turmoil that erupted during the 1960s after the deaths of several internationally known figures, including **Malcolm X** and **Dr. Martin Luther King, Jr.**, prompted Guy to embark upon a project that would bring her closer to the experiences of young people. She traveled around the United States to talk to youth about their perceptions and feelings as a result of the assassinations of such prominent heroes.

Guy made her research available to the public via *Children of Longing*, a book that featured the voices and perspectives of Black youth around the United States, including those of **Eleanora Elaine Tate** and **Nikki Giovanni**. Norris asserts that the data Guy obtained became "raw material for her later works" for young people (22). Perhaps Guy's personal experiences further contributed to her keen insight into young adulthood. Her mother died in 1934, a few years after the family emigrated to the United States, and her father died in 1937, while she was an adolescent. Orphaned, Guy and her sister lived in foster and orphans' homes. At sixteen, Rosa married Warner Guy and later gave birth to a son, Warner, Jr. While working at a factory, Guy decided to try acting, and soon became affiliated with the American Negro Theatre (ANT).

Guy has written in a number of genres for different audiences, including very young children: *Mother Crocodile/Maman-Caiman* (1981) won the 1982 Coretta Scott King Award. She is, however, best known nationally for her literature for young adults. Critics credit her with being one of the first writers to include themes related to homosexuality in young-adult literature. Guy's work confronts other issues as well: death, sexuality, abuse, poverty, prejudice, racism, and crime. Despite the bleak messages that her novels sometimes convey, her work also suggests, as noted in *Children's Literature Review*, "that young people can learn to cope with, and ultimately survive, their circumstances and problems" (74). Her critically acclaimed trilogy—*The Friends* (1973), *Ruby* (1976), and *Edith Jackson* (1978)—continues to be on required reading lists in the United States and abroad. The trilogy depicts the struggles of two families: the Cathys, West Indian natives, and the Jacksons. The novels focus specifically on the concerns of Phylissia, Edith, and Ruby. Norris says, Guy's "treatment of the growth to womanhood of the three young black women in these novels has marked the trilogy as among Guy's finest work. Internationally praised, the trilogy has been translated into many languages" (27). Her second trilogy—*The Disappearance* (1979), *New Guys Around the Block* (1983) and *And I Heard a Bird Sing* (1987)—offers one of the first African American-centered mystery trilogies in young-adult literature. This trilogy focuses on her first male protagonist, Imamu Jones, as he solves mysteries in the inner city. Guy's other books include her first novel for children, *Paris, Peewee and Big Dog* (1984); *My Love, My Love, or the Peasant Girl* (1985); *Measure of Time* (1983); *The Ups and Downs of Carl Davis III* (1989); *Billy the Great* (1991); and *The Music of Summer* (1992). According to *Children's Literature Review*, Guy stated, "If I have proven to be popular with young people, it is because when they have finished one of my books, they not only have a satisfying experience—they have also had an education" (75).

Resources: Rosa Guy: *And I Heard a Bird Sing* (New York: Delacorte, 1987); *Billy the Great* (New York: Orion, 1991); *Bird at My Window* (Philadelphia: Lippincott, 1966); *The Disappearance* (New York: Delacorte, 1979); *Edith Jackson* (New York: Viking, 1978); *The Friends* (New York: Holt, Rinehart and Winston, 1973); *Measure of Time* (New York: Holt, Rinehart and Winston, 1983); *The Music of Summer* (New York: Delacorte, 1992); *My Love, My Love, or the Peasant Girl* (New York: Holt, Rinehart and Winston, 1985); *New Guys Around the Block* (New York: Delacorte, 1983); *Paris, Peewee and Big Dog* (New York: Delacorte, 1984); *Ruby* (New York: Viking, 1976); *The Ups and Downs of Carl Davis III* (New York: Delacorte, 1989); *Venetian Blind* (produced in New York: Topical Theatre, 1954); Rosa Guy, ed., *Children of Longing* (New York: Holt, Rinehart, 1970); Rosa Guy, trans., *Mother Crocodile/Maman-Caiman*, by Birago Diop (New York: Delacorte, 1981); "Rosa (Cuthbert) Guy," *Children's Literature Review* 13 (1987), 74–89; Jerrie Norris, *Presenting Rosa Guy* (Boston: Twayne, 1988).

KaaVonia Hinton-Johnson

H

Haiku. A compressed form of contemplative poetry, originating in Japan. It traditionally consists of seventeen *jion* (Japanese sound symbols), arranged in three unrhymed lines of five-seven-five and creating a sense of unity between the human and natural worlds. Additional features common to the form include reference to particular seasons, direct treatment of the subject without the use of simile or metaphor, and sudden shift in the focus of the poem that usually occurs at the end of the first or second line. Because haiku traditionally addresses subjects remote to the modern (especially urban) experience and seems detached from concerns of social justice, it is perhaps surprising to find a number of twentieth-century African American poets writing in this poetic tradition. When Black poets have chosen to write haiku, they have often transformed the conventions in subtle ways.

Haiku translated from the Japanese were featured in at least one issue of the **NAACP** journal *The Crisis* in the early decades of the twentieth century, but haiku by African Americans is difficult to find prior to the late 1950s. **Richard Wright**'s posthumously published *Haiku: This Other World* (1998) presents some 800 poems and is the largest published collection of haiku by an African American poet, although it includes only a selection of the more than 4,000 haiku Wright reportedly wrote in the eighteen months before his death in 1960. Wright's interest in the form grew out of conversations with a South African friend and his reading of R. H. Blythe's four-volume work *Haiku* (1950). Poem 455 in Wright's collection focuses on the harmony between nature (represented by "green cockleburs") and an African American youth, and poem 31 presents a laughing boy whose hands are turned white by falling snow, but overall only a few of the haiku address racial identity or difference.

Wright's haiku closely follow the traditional syllable count of five-seven-five and almost always include a seasonal reference.

Robert Hayden included several haiku in his *Selected Poems* (1966) that were reprinted in his collection *Angle of Ascent: New and Selected Poems* (1975); these haiku demonstrate a degree of formal experimentation not found in Wright's work. For example, Hayden often varies the syllable count or enjambs the lines, placing one or more breaks in surprising places in the poem. One such haiku begins "Not sunflowers, not/roses, but rocks" (83). In an anthology he edited, *Kaleidoscope: Poems by American Negro Poets* (1967), Hayden included poems by **Julius Lester** that he characterized as being "close in spirit...to the three-line Japanese haiku." Lester's poems also show experimentation, particularly in syllable count and the use of enjambment.

Sonia Sanchez adheres much more closely to the structural conventions of haiku than Hayden or Lester, yet she also modifies the tradition in her free use of simile and metaphor and her incorporation of specifically Black themes. In one of her best-known haiku, for example, she reports seeing an African sunset in her father's eyes, and in others she offers up praise for **John Brown**, **Gwendolyn Brooks**, and **Paul Robeson**, among others. She describes Robeson's voice, for example, as "unwrapping/itself from the Congo" (Sanchez, 86).

According to one explanation of the form's origins, haiku were at first not written to stand alone but served as units in longer, linked chains of poetry known as *renga*. **Etheridge Knight**'s short chain of nine such poems, called "Haiku" and published in his collection *Poems from Prison* (1968), presents modern themes (including violence, **blues**, and **jazz**) and modern settings (including the city and the prison) even as it sometimes conforms to the traditional forms. For example, "Haiku" begins with a poem that adheres to the five-seven-five syllable count and that establishes a connection between humans and nature; convicts are described here as sunning themselves like lizards in the prison courtyard. Knight's "Haiku" ends in a piece that again follows the traditional syllable count, yet also calls attention to the difficulties of writing compelling poetry in this particular form: "Making jazz swing" in a poem that requires a fixed syllable count, he writes, "AIN'T/No square poet's job" (19).

Haiku is a minor but interesting feature in modern Black poetry. It continues to appear in writing by contemporary African American poets such as **Lenard Moore, Kalamu Ya Salaam,** and **James A. Emanuel.**

Resources: Robert Hayden, *Angle of Ascent: New and Selected Poems* (New York: Liveright, 1975); Robert Hayden, ed., *Kaleidoscope: Poems by American Negro Poets* (New York: Harcourt, Brace, and World, 1967); William J. Higginson, "African-American Haiku," in *A Haiku Path: The Haiku Society of America 1968–1988*, ed. Haiku Society of America (New York: Japan Society, 1994); Etheridge Knight, *Poems from Prison* (Detroit: Broadside Press, 1968); Sonia Sanchez, *I'VE BEEN A WOMAN* (Sausalito, CA: Black Scholar Press, 1978); Richard Wright, *Haiku: This Other World*, ed. Yoshinobu Hakutani and Robert L. Tener (New York: Arcade, 1998).

James B. Kelley

Hailstock, Shirley (born 1948). Romance novelist and short story writer. Hailstock is a best-selling, award-winning writer of **romance novels**. A native of Newberry, South Carolina, who currently lives in New Jersey, Hailstock had planned to become the first female astronaut, but she became a writer instead. After graduating from Howard University with a B.S. in chemistry and from Fairleigh Dickinson University with an M.B.A. in chemical marketing, she wrote her first novel, *Ice Maiden* (1986), on a dare from a school friend who was an avid romance reader (Williams). *Whispers of Love* (1994), reprinted four times, won the Holt Medallion from a group called the Virginia Romance Writers. It was the first of many awards in fiction Hailstock has won. *Clara's Promise* (1995), Hailstock's only historical romance, won the Utah Romance Writers Heart of the West Award; *White Diamonds* (1996) earned the Kiss of Death Award for mystery and suspense; *Legacy* (1997) won an Award of Excellence from Colorado Writers and the Waldenbooks Award for Bestselling Multicultural Romance; *More Than Gold* (2000) captured the Barclay Award; and *Mirror Image* (1998) won the Artemis Award. In addition, *Opposites Attract* (1999), *His 1-800 Wife* (2001) and *Family Affair* (2002) have been nominated for awards.

Hailstock collaborated with Francis Ray and Donna Hill in publishing *Winter Nights* (1998), an anthology of Christmas and Kwanzaa stories, in which Hailstock's novella "Kwanzaa Angel" appears. The same year, Hailstock's "Engagement" appeared as the feature story in the Valentine's Day anthology *I Do!* (1998), which she edited with **Gwynne Forster** and **Robyn Amos**.

Despite her busy writing career, Hailstock has taught accounting at Rutgers University and novel writing at Middlesex County College. She was the first African American board member of Romance Writers of America and served as president of the organization's New Jersey chapter (2002–2003).

Resources: Rita B. Dandridge, "The Race, Gender, Romance Connection: A Black Feminist Reading of African American Women's Historical Romances," in *Doubled Plots*, ed. Susan Strehle and Mary Carden (Jackson: University Press of Mississippi, 2003), 185–201; Shirley Hailstock: *Clara's Promise* (New York: Pinnacle, 1995); *A Father's Fortune* (New York: Harlequin, 2003); *His 1-800 Wife* (Washington, DC: Arabesque, 2001); *Legacy* (New York: Pinnacle, 1997); *Mirror Image* (New York: Pinnacle, 1998); *More Than Gold* (Washington, DC: Arabesque, 2000); *Opposites Attract* (New York: Pinnacle, 1999); *Whispers of Love* (New York: Pinnacle, 1994); *White Diamonds* (New York: Pinnacle, 1996); Shirley Hailstock, Rochelle Alers, and Angela Benson, eds., *Holiday Cheer* (New York: Pinnacle, 1995); Shirley Hailstock, Gwynne Forster, and Robyn Amos, eds., *I Do!* (New York: Pinnacle, 1998); Shirley Hailstock, Francis Ray, and Donna Hill, eds., *Winter Nights* (New York: Kensington, 1998); Web page, http://www.geocities.com/Paris/Bistro/6812; Karen Williams, "Interview with Shirley Hailstock," *Romance Communications: The Romance Magazine for the 21st Century*, Oct. 22, 1998, http://www.romcom.com/11Nov/11Shailstock.htm.

Rita B. Dandridge

Hair. African American hair has long been a symbol of difference and dissonance in literature. It has often been described, characterized, and discussed against a background of preconceived notions about "good" hair (straight or manageably curly), "bad" hair (nappy, woolly), and White Americans' standards of beauty, standards that often have celebrated hair that is straight. Once it was thought that "woolly" hair was among the physical attributes that somehow affirmed the inferiority of African Americans (Byrd and Tharps). **Harriet Beecher Stowe** makes use of hair in *Uncle Tom's Cabin* (1852), marking differences of character through White persons' "curls" versus Black persons' "wool," thereby showing how a popular and representative White author such as Stowe implicitly judged African American hair. **Wallace Thurman**'s novel *The Blacker the Berry* (1929) details the life of Emma Lou, a dark-skinned woman whose best trait is her "good" hair. Having straight hair or straightening curly hair is often a consideration in narratives about **passing**, including **Jessie Redmon Fauset**'s novel *Plum Bun* (1928). Ironically, one of the most socially influential participants in the **Harlem Renaissance** was arts patron and socialite A'Lelia Walker, daughter of Madame C. J. Walker, who had acquired considerable wealth from sales of a hair-straightening product for African Americans.

Maya Angelou has written of her past frustrations with her hair's inability to meet the White standard of beauty in *I Know Why the Caged Bird Sings* (1970). In the 1960s and early 1970s, the "afro" hair style was seen by some observers might "cool" or "hip," but others interpreted it as radical or rebellious. As represented by the enormously popular *Hair: The American Tribal Love-Rock Musical* (1967), which includes African American characters, this was a time when men with long hair and beards, women who did not shave their legs or armpits, and African Americans with "afro" hairstyles were often automatically associated with antiestablishment politics and protest.

A recent anthology of writings about hair includes an essay by **Angela Y. Davis** concerning the extent to which her "afro" became an icon in the popular media of the 1960s (Harris and Johnson). **John Oliver Killens** explores Black hair as a marker of political and social pride in *The Cotillion* (1971). The critic Monica Coleman discusses "doing hair" (including braiding) as a form of "religious language" in the novel *Mama Day* (1988) by **Gloria Naylor**. Bertram D. Ashe notes that hair and the standard of beauty are important in **Zora Neale Hurston**'s *Their Eyes Were Watching God* (1937) and **Toni Morrison**'s *Song of Solomon* (1977). **Carolivia Herron**'s *Nappy Hair* (1997) and **bell hooks**'s *Happy to be Nappy* (2001) are examples of recent **children's literature** which reflect pride in natural African American hair and disavow former negative views.

Resources: Bertram D. Ashe, "Why Don't He Like My Hair?" Constructing African American Standards of Beauty in Toni Morrison's *Song of Solomon* and Zora Neale Hurtson's *Their Eyes Were Watching God*," *African American Review* 29, no. 4 (1995), 579–592; Ayana D. Byrd and Lori L. Tharps, *Hair Story: Untangling the Roots of Black Hair in America* (New York: St. Martin's Griffin, 2001); Monica A. Coleman, " 'The Work of Your Own Hands': Doing Black Women's Hair as Religious Language in Gloria Naylor's *Mama Day*," *Soundings: An Interdisciplinary Journal* 85, no. 1–2 (Spring–Summer 2002), 121–139; Adaeze Enekwechi and Opal Moore, "Children's

Literature and the Politics of Hair in Books for African American Children," *Children's Literature Association Quarterly* 24, no. 4 (Winter 1999–2000), 195–200; Juliette Harris and Pamela Johnson, eds., *Tenderheaded: A Comb-Bending Collection of Hair Stories* (New York: Washington Square Press, 2001); Carolivia Herron, *Nappy Hair* (New York: Knopf, 1997); Gerome Ragni and James Rado, *Hair: The American Tribal Love-Rock Musical* (New York: Pocket Books, 2001).

James Bucky Carter

Haiti. The place of the Caribbean nation of Haiti in African American literature has been solidified by African American writers. In the twentieth and twenty-first centuries, the African **diaspora** has included Haiti as a point on its literary map. Writing from different physical and mental spaces, **Langston Hughes** and **Zora Neale Hurston** depict the nature of Haiti's complexity as a colonized island with a bloody, rebellious past that Hughes describes as "a free country of dark-skinned peoples" a full half century before American emancipation.

Hughes, who went to Haiti in 1931, there considered the effect of American occupation and Haitian class difference (*The Big Sea*). At Cap-Haitien, he was able to experience what Maurice A. Lubin calls " 'va-nu-peds'. . .people without shoes who carried the weight of the country's economic problems." He published articles about Haiti in *New Masses* and *The Crisis*, as well as a children's book titled **Popo and Fifina** (1932; republished 1993), written with **Arna Bontemps**. Popo is also a character in the play *Troubled Island* (1936), which was first performed in Cleveland, Ohio, in 1936. Retitled *Drums of Haiti*, it was performed in **Detroit, Michigan**, in 1937, and, retitled as *Emperor of Haiti*, it was performed in New York City in 1937 (Ostrom). Hughes also drew on this play for his three-act opera *Troubled Island*, created with **William Grant Still**. The two began working on the opera in 1938, but it did not premiere until 1949, when it was performed at the New York City Center, choreographed by George Balanchine and Jean Leon Destine. Robert Weede sang the title role of the Black Haitian revolutionary and former slave, Jean-Jacques Dessalines, on whom the opera and play are based.

In this play and opera, Hughes comments on the nature of Dessalines's reign as liberator of Haiti. Drawing from an American Christian perspective, and notably using an American **vernacular** as part of the of the dialogue between characters, Hughes regards Dessalines as both a slave and a freedman. Set in 1791, the play focuses on the nature of slave rebellion and unrest as they are played out in the Haiti Dessalines rules, one with what C.L.R. James calls "psychological, racial, and social scars." Furthermore, Hughes's Dessalines calls for a Eurocentric majesty that renders Black and **mulatto** alike inadequate—in spite of real physical scars these same people faced for real freedom.

Hughes wrote a brief protest note in *New Masses* in July 1931, regarding " a world of black people without shoes—who catch hell," and the Haitian fortress known as the Citadel, which he describes as "futile ruin now . . . while the planes of the U.S. Marines hum daily overhead." In the same publication, he openly criticized the "American Occupation" with its seemingly bourgeois living as symptomatic of Haiti's deep class striations. In *The Crisis* of May 1932 he published "White Shadows in a Black Land," in which he commented on this same sort of military stranglehold on the Haitian people, supported by American troops. Castigating America's role in supporting an economy and a government that condoned graft and corruption, Hughes highlighted these "white shadows" in a land that had established a complex Black Republic. In Hughes's view, slowly, this Republic became its colonizers' "cultural...careless...conceited" cousin.

Hughes also, because of his friendship with the Haitian writer Jacques Roumain, worked with Mercer Cook to translate Roumain's *Masters of the Dew* in 1947 for Americans and English-speakers worldwide. He exchanged letters and ideas with this important "conspiratorial writer," bringing to the attention of the world his having been unjustly jailed for his writing (Kelley).

Zora Neale Hurston, in her part ethnography, part travelogue *Tell My Horse* (1938; republished 1990), engages in what critics called a "reflexive and reactionary" political perspective. Influenced by an eleven-month stay in Haiti, Hurston's writing partially records her investigation of **voodoo** in Haiti.

Given her perspective as an ethnographer for the Works Progress Administration (*see* **Federal Writers' Project**), Hurston's shift from the transformative possibilities for cultural and folkloric study to commentary on political and power relations between the United States and Haiti has been criticized as "superficial" and, at the same time, a serious study of voodoo in Haiti. Since voodoo was taboo among the Haitian elite, Hurston notes class and race distinctions and considers Haitian cultural self-awareness. *Tell My Horse*, or "Parlay Cheval Ou," is, as Hurston says, " in daily, hourly use in Haiti and no doubt is used as a blind for self-expression"; those genuinely "mounted" are capable of social criticism. In the voodoo tradition, one's "mount" is a spirit taking over the senses, which in some cases, Hurston notes, becomes "feigning possession in order to express...resentment general and particular." Using the protective cloak of voodoo spiritual ritual, Haitians thus proclaim their own critiques and legends regarding cultural mores, political stances, and expository or revealing narrative. Hurston notes this with examples of various Haitians who use "Parlay Cheval Ou" in this way for everything from social consciousness and justice to "burlesque and slapstick." In this way she signifies their complicity in the Haitian narrative tradition and places herself within that tradition. (*See* **Voodoo/Voudoun**.)

The politics and personalities that drive Haitian culture are also a part of Hurston's narrative. Part II of her ethnography focuses on Haitian public reaction to national leadership and controversy. Noting public scrutiny of rebellious and vigilante behavior, she observes that peace is no nearer, and describes with gory detail the "bloody blades" of both military personnel and civilians. Noting mulattoes' achievement of freedom as happening a generation before Blacks, Hurston further shows the Haitian body politic fighting for itself at a time when American slaves could not build a movement. She notes this advancement in an American essentialist way, while also acknowledging Haitian individualism and nationalism. Her experience with the upper class and the peasant class with regard to these cultural ideals of government and revolution contrasted the practicality of lives in ruin.

Hurston describes the Garde d'Haiti, "trained and established under the American military officers of the Occupation," as a part of this battle between mulattoes and blacks, alluding to President (Vincent) and Colonel (Calixe) in their desire to "clean" Haiti of any "obstacles to national unity," including rebels and beggars alike. Alluding as well to Rafael Trujillo, the dictator whose presence is felt from the neighboring Dominican Republic, Hurston chronicles the Haitian sense of this man as an enforcer and leader who "threatened in a veiled manner to clean up the Haitian end of the island." In her language Hurston alludes to the mythmaking surrounding the dictator that becomes a part of the national storytelling psyche, the body politic in motion and in contrast with "young Haitian intellectuals [who] feel that Santo Domingo's great advancement should spur Haiti out of her fog of self-deception, internal strife and general backwardness." Hurston's sense of Haiti, then, comes colored with these intellectuals' views of education and common language, but stays mindful of common people's contrasting participation in cultural formation, something not exclusive to Haiti's intellectual microcosm of the diaspora.

For her role in the late twentieth and early twenty-first centuries, **Edwidge Danticat** brings the Haitian and American diasporas together via her perspective as a Haitian national transplanted to America. Today's version of Haiti moves beyond voodoo to some extent and considers the insidious nature of oppression. Considering Haiti from the space of New York and Florida, Danticat steps away from what Hughes and Hurston threw themselves into. She chooses to relate the opposite of travelogue while maintaining an exploration of social injustice via the performance of pain as the nature of storytelling. In the early twentieth century, Hughes and Hurston made groundbreaking efforts to consider the African diaspora for a wide American audience; Danticat takes her national perspective and reflects on it from a distance, physically widening the diaspora to a part of what has now become African American literature.

Resources: Langston Hughes: *The Big Sea* (New York: Knopf, 1940); "A Letter from Haiti," *New Masses* 12, no. 7 (July 1931), 9; "People Without Shoes," *New Masses* 12, no. 10 (Oct. 1931), 12; *Troubled Island* (also known as *Drums of Haiti* and *Emperor of Haiti*), in *The Collected Works of Langston Hughes*, ed. Arnold Rampersad et al. (Columbia: University of Missouri Press, 2001), vol. 5; Langston Hughes and Arna Bontemps, *Popo and Fifina: Children of Haiti* (New York: Macmillan, 1932; repr. New York: Oxford University Press, 1993); Langston Hughes and William Grant Still, *Troubled Island*, in *The Collected Works of Langston Hughes*, ed. Arnold Rampersad et al. (Columbia: University of Missouri Press, 2001), vol. 6; Zora Neale Hurston: *Tell My Horse* (Philadelphia: Lippincott, 1938); *Tell My Horse: Voodoo and Life in Haiti and Jamaica* (New York: Perennial Library, 1990); Diane Duffrin Kelley, "*Masters of the Dew*," in *A Langston Hughes Encyclopedia*, ed. Hans Ostrom (Westport, CT: Greenwood Press, 2002), 235–238; Hans Ostrom, *A Langston Hughes Encyclopedia*

(Westport, CT: Greenwood Press, 2002), 377–378; 401–402 (concerning the play and the opera *Troubled Island*).

Elizabete Vasconcelos

Haley, Alex (1921–1992). Journalist and novelist. Haley is the author of two of the most widely read works in all of American literature: *The Autobiography of Malcolm X* and *Roots: The Saga of an American Family*. A worldwide audience continues to embrace these books (and their film and television adaptations), but questions about Haley's honesty and integrity have placed a cloud over his professional reputation and made him something of an invisible man among African American writers. His impact as an international cultural icon, however, is unquestioned.

Alexander Murray Palmer Haley was born on August 11, 1921, in Ithaca, New York, the first of three sons of Simon Alexander Haley and Bertha George Palmer. Haley's parents were both pursuing graduate degrees when he was born. The family returned to Henning, Tennessee, Bertha's hometown, soon after the birth of Alex. In Henning, Haley grew up surrounded by an extended family of grandparents, aunts, and cousins. It was here that he began to hear the stories and family **folklore** that would become the basis for *Roots*. Haley excelled in his studies and graduated from high school at age fifteen. After completing two years of college, however, he began to feel indifferent about his education and enlisted in the U.S. Coast Guard. He served for twenty years, working first in the ship's mess, then, after he began to write and publish stories in magazines, as a Coast Guard journalist. Haley retired from the service in 1959 and began to pursue a freelance writing career.

His first major break came when he was commissioned by *Reader's Digest* to write an article about the **Nation of Islam** and its controversial minister, **Malcolm X**. His success with *Reader's Digest* led to a series of interviews with celebrities, entertainers, and political leaders for *Playboy* magazine. The *Playboy* interviews featured cutting-edge figures, including **Muhammad Ali, Dr. Martin Luther King, Jr.**, the American Nazi leader George Lincoln Rockwell, Miles Davis, and Malcolm X, and were known for their frankness and depth in dealing with important topics.

Haley interviewed many prominent African Americans for *Playboy*, but his relationship with Malcolm X became one of the most important in his career. Initially Malcolm X did not trust Haley, but as Haley demonstrated his sincerity and intelligence, Malcolm began to open up. Their discussions became the basis for *The Autobiography of Malcolm X*, in which Haley was initially uncredited, though later printings included "with the assistance of Alex Haley" or "as told to Alex Haley" on the cover and title page.

Historians question many of the factual details of *The Autobiography of Malcolm X*, but it was an instant success with the public, including White readers, because of the power of Malcolm's personality. Although the conversations that form the basis of the book were freewheeling and disjointed—psychoanalysis sessions, as one critic said (Bloom, 40–41)—through his extensive notes, Haley was able to piece together a narrative that is a classic of African American biography and representative of all American **coming-of-age** stories as well. It methodically describes the protagonist's transformation from criminal and angry Malcolm Little to the spiritually focused Malcolm X, the X replacing the name of the slave master, Little, and standing for an unknown ancestral African name. Malcolm X never saw the impact of his story on the American public; he was assassinated shortly before its release in 1965. His story, however, became an important touchstone in the nascent **Black Power** movement. *The Autobiography* continues to sell well, even forty years after its initial publication, due in part to **Spike Lee**'s 1992 film adaptation, *Malcolm X*, which Lee dedicated to Alex Haley.

After completing *The Autobiography*, Haley began to think about his own unknown African ancestors. He hoped to work some of the family stories he had heard from grandparents and aunts into a saga about African American perseverance and determination. He began to do library and genealogical research to tie the family stories together with documented facts. The project led him on more than "half a million miles" of travel to archives on three continents, as he describes in the final chapters of the book. Through this research, Haley claimed to find documentary evidence for a personal genealogy extending all the way back to Kunta Kinte, a young Mandinka warrior abducted into the slave trade in Gambia, deposited in America at Annapolis, and sold as chattel in Virginia. After twelve years of work, *Roots* was finally published in 1976 to instant and overwhelming popular acclaim.

Although marketed as nonfiction, *Roots* tells an imagined personal history of Kinte and each successive generation in the Haley family, based on the oral tradition Alex heard in childhood and the evidence of his research. Haley claimed that all of the statements about lineage in the book were verified by some existing document. As America celebrated its bicentennial and reveled in the strength and dignity of the Founding Fathers, African Americans embraced the feeling of history that *Roots* gave them, seeing in Kunta Kinte an ancestor worthy of veneration alongside the White national heroes. But White Americans also read and admired *Roots* in great numbers. The joy and wonder that Haley expressed upon uncovering documentation of his ancestors translated into a worldwide boom in genealogical research. The television miniseries adapted from the book in 1977 was no less a national phenomenon. By many accounts, something approaching half of the country sat down to watch the broadcast of the eighth and final episode. The cast of the program included a veritable who's who of African American performers, from Cicely Tyson and Leslie Uggams to **Maya Angelou**, Louis Gossett, Jr., and Ben Vereen. The relatively unknown **LeVar Burton** parlayed the role of Kunta Kinte into an outstanding film and television career.

On the eve of this television success, however, Haley was dealing with questions about his integrity. In 1977, **Margaret Abigail Walker** brought suit against Haley for copying plot elements from her novel *Jubilee*. This case was dismissed, but a year later another author, Harold Courlander, sued Haley for plagiarism

Roots author Alex Haley, 1988. AP/Wide World Photos.

over several passages he said were lifted from his novel *The African*. During the trial it seemed clear that Haley had, indeed, borrowed the phrases without permission. Although his lawyers counseled against it, Haley agreed to a settlement before the judged handed down a decision, paying Courlander $650,000. Haley claimed in court and afterward that the passages were notes that people at various speaking engagements had given him, which were mistakenly included in the manuscript of the book. It seemed to many critics and journalists a rather implausible explanation, but the settlement kept the case out of the public consciousness. Sales of the book and, more important, Haley's reputation were unaffected. The fame Haley achieved, however, made it difficult for him to continue writing. He produced little more in his career. *Roots: The Next Generations*, a television sequel based on the later part of the book, was produced in 1979. Two unfinished novels, *Queen* and *Mama Flora's Family*, were edited and completed by David Stevens and published in 1993 and 1998, respectively.

After Haley died in 1992, and his brother George was forced to auction off many of his papers to help pay $1.5 million in debts accumulated by Alex, more questions about his honesty began to arise. Philip Nobile, working for the *Village Voice*, examined the Haley archival material held at the University of Tennessee in Knoxville. His inspection of notebooks and manuscripts there led him to believe that, in addition to copying large passages of *Roots* from other sources, the whole story about discovering a family link to Kunta Kinte in Gambia was a fiction. Nobile also claimed that Haley was a writer of modest skills whose work required a great deal of rewriting by his editor, Murray Fisher. None of this controversy has had much effect on Haley's popularity with the reading public. The African American scholarly and literary communities, however, have expressed little interest in Haley and his legacy. A thorough and sensitive examination of Haley's continuing cultural impact, set against the questions about his personal integrity and literary significance, has yet to be written.

Resources: Harold Bloom, ed., *Alex Haley & Malcolm X's The Autobiography of Malcolm X* (New York: Chelsea House, 1996); Doreen Gonzales, *Alex Haley: Author of "Roots"* (Hillside, NJ: Enslow, 1994); Alex Haley: *The Autobiography of Malcolm X*

(New York: Grove, 1965); *A Different Kind of Christmas* (New York: Doubleday, 1988); *The Playboy Interviews*, ed. Murray Fisher (New York: Ballantine, 1993); *Roots: The Saga of an American Family* (Garden City, NY: Doubleday, 1976); Alex Haley and David Stevens: *Alex Haley's "Queen": The Story of an American Family* (New York: Morrow, 1993); *Mama Flora's Family: A Novel* (New York: Scribner's, 1998); Marilyn Kern-Foxworth, "Alex Haley," in *Dictionary of Literary Biography*, vol. 38, *Afro-American Writers After 1955: Dramatists and Prose Writers* (Detroit: Gale, 1985); Philip Nobile, "Uncovering *Roots*," *Village Voice*, Feb. 23, 1993, pp. 32–38; David Shirley, *Alex Haley* (New York: Chelsea House, 1994).

Steven R. Harris

Hall, Prince (c. 1735–1807). Abolitionist, orator, and Freemason. Hall founded African Lodge No. 459 of the Black Masonic Grand Lodges, thereby establishing what was later known as Prince Hall Freemasonry. Hall was of mixed-race, West Indian descent. He was born in a place unknown sometime between 1735 and 1738. Records indicate that Hall was either a slave or an indentured servant in the **Boston, Massachusetts**, home of leather dresser William Hall from 1749 to 1770, when he was emancipated (Crawford; Grimshaw). Hall then was a pastor at a Methodist church in Cambridge, Massachusetts, and a free artisan. In 1775 he entered a British encampment of soldiers stationed near Bunker Hill, where he and fourteen others were inducted by the members of Army Lodge No. 441 (for the price of 25 guineas each) into the Ancient and Accepted Order of Freemasons (Grimshaw). In 1776, African Lodge No. 1 was formed, with Hall elected as the lodge's first grand master. Continuing to meet in secret in the years following, Hall and his compatriots continually sought recognition from the Massachusetts Grand Lodge of Freemasons by requesting a warrant that would allow them to practice all of the Masonic rites and privileges, including the induction of new members and the establishment of additional affiliated lodges. The Masons of Massachusetts continually refused Hall's application for a warrant, effectively sending him to seek validation in England, where, in 1784, he received a permanent charter from the Grand Lodge of England.

The warrant issued to Prince Hall and his fourteen associates in Boston created African Lodge No. 459 of Free and Accepted Masons. It was not until 1787, however, when the fee for the warrant was received in England, that the warrant delivered to Hall and the lodge's name was entered on the roll of lodges holding obedience to the Grand Lodge of England that Prince Hall Freemasonry could claim legitimacy. Since that time, Prince Hall Freemasonry has operated in the United States as a Masonic body independent from White American traditions of Freemasonry—establishing lodges, initiating members, electing officials, and holding national conventions. This situation continues despite the fact that White Masons have perceived Prince Hall Freemasonry as an inauthentic, unauthorized, and imitative fraternal order with no true ties to the larger traditions of Masonry.

Twenty-nine members of the Prince Hall no. 47 in Brooklyn, New York, 1905. Photographs and Prints Division, Schomburg Center for Research in Black Culture, The New York Public Library, Astor, Lenox and Tilden Foundations.

Hall's literary production consists largely of letters and speeches dedicated to improving the status of African Americans. Many of these writings—letters to Boston newspapers, Masonic officials, and others—seek recognition for the legitimacy of African American Freemasonry. Additionally, Hall petitioned for the abolition of **slavery** in Massachusetts and helped recruit African Americans to military service to aid in putting down Shays's Rebellion in western Massachusetts in 1786. Hall also sought financial support for the recolonization of African Americans to Africa and for the public education of African American children in Boston. Hall's greatest significance springs from the establishment of the African American tradition of Freemasonry that still bears his name. He was also, however, an important early advocate for African American social equality. Hall's influence can be seen in the nationalistic writings of subsequent African Americans affiliated with the traditions of Prince Hall Freemasonry, including **David Walker**, **Martin R. Delany**, and **Sutton E. Griggs**. (*See* **Back-to-Africa Movement**; **Black Nationalism**.)

Resources: George W. Crawford, *Prince Hall and His Followers: Being a Monograph on the Legitimacy of Negro Masonry* (New York: AMS, 1971); William H. Grimshaw, *Official History of Freemasonry Among the Colored People in North America* (New York:

Negro Universities Press, 1969); Sidney Kaplan, *The Black Presence in the Era of the American Revolution, 1770–1800* (Greenwich, CT: New York Graphic Society, 1973); William A. Muraskin, *Middle-Class Blacks in a White Society: Prince Hall Freemasonry in America* (Berkeley: University of California Press, 1975).

Matthew R. Davis

Hambone (1974–present). Magazine of poetry and poetics. The title of the magazine alludes to a figure in an African American **vernacular** rhyme, "Hambone, Hambone, where you been?" *Hambone* features work that attempts to retrieve the poetics lost in the African **diaspora** and through the avant-garde innovations of contemporary poetry (Mackey 2000, 665). First published in 1974, *Hambone* was sponsored by Stanford University's Committee on Black Performing Arts. Though it resisted preconceived ideas about how representations of racial politics or the work of African American artists should "look" and "sound," *Hambone* emerged concurrently with African American journals and little magazines such as *Yardbird Reader*, *Umbra*, *Soulbook*, **Callaloo**, and **Journal of Black Poetry** (Clay and Phillips, 157). The first issue included work by African American artists such as **Michael S. Harper**, **Al Young**, Gloria Watkins, **Ishmael Reed**, and **Nathaniel Mackey**. After this inaugural issue, *Hambone* did not appear again until 1982, when the poet and scholar Mackey (who was on the editorial board as a graduate student) saw to its revival. Mackey has edited *Hambone* ever since, and it is a reflective extension of his own dedication to tracing the spiritual and historical depths of music, dreams, and prayer. Mackey has given *Hambone* its signature characteristic—an expanding but focused eclecticism.

While *Hambone* 1 featured work by African American artists only, beginning with *Hambone* 2, Mackey decided to "include work from a variety of racial and ethnic backgrounds, albeit continuing to present work by African-American writers and artists" (Mackey 2000, 665–666). As a result, *Hambone* has come to be known as "the main meeting-place for Third World, American minority and white avant-gardists" (Weinberger, 232). *Hambone* consistently publishes literature by African, African American, and Caribbean artists such as Wilson Harris, **Amiri Baraka**, Edward Kamau Braithwaite, Will Alexander, **Clarence Major**, Ed Roberson, **Harryette Mullen**, George Lamming, and Mackey himself, but it also has productively cut across the assumed racial and national identities of literary schools, and therefore undermined what Mackey describes in his critical study *Discrepant Engagement: Dissonance, Cross-Culturality, and Experimental Writing* (1993) as "the current institutionalization of an African-American canon and the frequent assumption . . . that black writers are to be discussed only in relation to other black writers" (Mackey 1993, 3). A poem appearing in *Hambone* might engage with the African pantheon through forms and themes associated with the San Francisco Renaissance. Translations of African genesis myths are as likely to appear in *Hambone* as the work of Barbara Guest, a poet associated with the New York School. The idea guiding *Hambone* 2, Mackey explains, "was to make a particular mix available that one would not normally find—for instance, **Sun Ra** and Robert Duncan in the same publication" (Funkhouser, 333).

In *Discrepant Engagement*, Mackey argues that "[c]reative kinship and the lines of affinity it effects are much more complex, jagged, and indissociable than the totalizing pretensions of canon formation tend to acknowledge," a formulation that applies to both Mackey's work and the work he publishes in *Hambone* (Mackey 1993, 3).

Hambone resists the forms of fixed literary genres and focuses on the imaginative "poesis" (making), which of course includes but is not exclusive to poetry. Mackey's description of Guyanese novelist Wilson Harris's work also serves to describe one of *Hambone*'s most consistent themes: a "simultaneity of integrative and disintegrative tendencies attendant upon the pursuit of a wholeness admitted to be out of reach" (Mackey 1993, 4).

In Mackey's work, music is a crucial inspiration in the pursuit of an ever elusive wholeness, and the work of *Hambone* often works within the figurative relations between poetry and music to bring a sensuous plasticity to language, and to reimagine political dissent. Since the mid-1980s, Mackey's epistolary sequence *From a Broken Bottle Traces of Perfume Still Emanate* (1986–2001) has appeared in *Hambone*, a series of letters written by a composer named N, who is "a founding member of a band known as Mystic Horn Society" (Mackey 1985, 54). Many of the letters are addressed to "Angel of Dust," and testify to the descriptive and metaphorical repertoires within music's forms and themes. Similar to much twentieth- and twenty-first-century experimental poetry, the texts published in *Hambone* foreground the fact that they are partial and ambiguous constructions, open to interpretation. However, since the artists of *Hambone* often summon a diasporic muse, and the African diaspora's traumatic scattering of people, culture, and language is one of the journal's most important historical contexts, texts in *Hambone* share the value and necessity of "laying claim to one's authority," as Mackey explains (Funkhouser, 329).

Resources: Kamau Braithwaite, *Conversations with Nathaniel Mackey* (Staten Island, NY: We Press, 1999); Stephen Clay and Rodney Phillips, *A Secret Location on the Lower East Side: Adventures in Writing, 1960–1980* (New York: New York Public Library, 1998); Christopher Funkhouser, "An Interview with Nathaniel Mackey," http:// wings.buffalo.edu/epc/authors/funkhouser/mackey.html; Nathaniel Mackey: "Editing *Hambone*," *Callaloo* 23, no. 2 (2000), 665–668; "*From a Broken Bottle Traces of Perfume Still Emanate*," *Hambone* 5 (Fall 1986); *Discrepant Engagement: Dissonance, Cross-Culturality, and Experimental Writing* (New York: Cambridge University Press, 1993); Eliot Weinberger, "News in Briefs," *Sulfur* 31 (Fall 1992).

Kimberly Lamm

Hamilton, Virginia (1936–2002). Children's author. Since the publication of her first book, *Zeely* (1967), Hamilton has been recognized for her work in **children's literature** and young-adult literature. The recipient of every major award in the field, Hamilton published more than thirty-five books before her death in 2002. Her writing consistently addressed issues of racial identity and

feminism as she explored relationships between races, **gender**s, and children and adults.

Hamilton's writing was greatly influenced by her childhood. She was raised just outside of Yellow Springs, Ohio, on land that her family lived on for five generations. The area was steeped in a sense of history; it had been at the center of activity for the **Underground Railroad**. In part due to an environment that was fertile with mysterious stories and intriguing history, Hamilton, from an early age, was keenly aware of issues of **race** and African American history.

Both of Hamilton's parents delighted in storytelling. Her father, Kenneth James, a college graduate and musician, favored tales about influential African Americans. Hamilton was particularly taken with the story he told about **Paul Robeson**. After hearing about Robeson's remarkable accomplishments, Hamilton vowed not only to be the best at what she would do, but to be original in her work.

Hamilton's love of storytelling was also shaped by the female voices in her life. Her mother, Etta Belle (Perry), and her aunts, who lived on the surrounding farms, shared tales of history and family. As an adult, Hamilton remembered her childhood as being full of music, tales, reading, and spending time with relatives.

After high school, Hamilton attended nearby Antioch College, but after a couple of years at Antioch, and on the advice of a trusted professor, she moved to New York City. Later she attended Ohio State University and the New School for Social Research—and later still she returned to live in Yellow Springs. There she thrived on the lively African American culture and music. She also met **Arnold Adoff**, a poet and anthologist of African American literature. The pair married and had two children, Leigh and Jaime Levi.

After a novel Hamilton wrote for adults was rejected by publishers, a friend recommended that she submit Zeely, a story she had written while a student at Antioch. The publication of that title marked the start of Hamilton's career in children's literature. The story of a curious girl named Elizabeth who, while visiting an uncle's farm with her brother, befriends a six-foot-tall African American woman named Zeely, the novel was a refreshing change from earlier, stereotypical books about African Americans. Hamilton's work was about a normal Black family and included none of the problems that would face such a family in a typical children's book, such as poverty, powerlessness, or hopelessness. For this novel, Hamilton won her first award, the Nancy Block Memorial Award from the Downtown (NY) Community School Awards Committee (1967). It was the first of many awards Hamilton would win over the course of her long and prolific career.

In her writing, Hamilton revisits many themes. Her characters are typically survivors—strong, vivid people who go about their lives and overcome the challenges they face. She often addresses issues of identity, one's place in their family, tradition, music, traveling, and personal issues. She has written across a variety of genres, including nonfiction, fiction, fantasy, mystery, and contemporary stories. Her books include *A White Romance* (1987), *M.C. Higgins the Great* (1974), *The Planet of Junior Brown* (1971), *The Magical Adventures of Pretty Pearl* (1983), *Anthony Burns: The Defeat and Triumph of a Fugitive Slave* (1988), *The Time-Ago Tales of Jahdu* (1969), and *The House of Dies Drear* (1968). In addition to her full-length works, Hamilton has published several collections of stories based on African American history and tradition. These include *The People Could Fly: American Black Folktales* (1985), *Her Stories: African-American Folktales, Fairy Tales and True Tales* (1995), *When Birds Could Talk and Bats Could Sing* (1996), and *A Ring of Tricksters* (1997).

Among her many awards, Hamilton received the Newbery Medal (for *M.C. Higgins the Great*), and three of her works were Newbery Honor books. She was also awarded the National Book Award for Young People's Literature (1975) and the NAACP Image Award (1996). She was a three-time winner of the Coretta Scott King Award (for *Her Stories*, 1996; *The People Could Fly*, 1986; and *Sweet Whispers, Brother Rush*, 1983), and six of her books were Coretta Scott King honor books. In 1992, Hamilton was recognized with the prestigious international Hans Christian Andersen award for her body of work. Three years later, she received the Laura Ingalls Wilder Award from the American Library Association for her "substantial and lasting contribution to children's literature." In addition, Hamilton was the first writer of children's and young-adult literature to receive a MacArthur fellowship (1995).

Resources: Yolanda Robinson Coles, "Talking with Virginia Hamilton," *American Visions*, Dec. 1994–Jan. 1995, 31; Virginia Hamilton: *Anthony Burns: The Defeat and Triumph of a Fugitive Slave* (New York: Knopf, 1988); *Bruh Rabbit and the Tar Baby Girl* (New York: Blue Sky, 2003); *Cousins* (New York: Putnam, 1990); *Her Stories: African-American Folktales, Fairy Tales, and True Tales* (New York: Scholastic, 1995); *The House of Dies Drear* (New York: Macmillan, 1968); *In the Beginning: Creation Stories from Around the World* (San Diego: Harcourt Brace Jovanovich, 1988); *Jahdu* (New York: Greenwillow, 1980); *Justice and Her Brothers* (New York: Greenwillow, 1978); *The Magical Adventures of Pretty Pearl* (New York: Harper & Row, 1983); *Many Thousand Gone: African Americans from Slavery to Freedom* (New York: Knopf, 1993); *M. C. Higgins the Great* (New York: Macmillan, 1974); "The Mind of a Novel: The Heart of the Book," *Children's Literature Quarterly*, Winter 1983, 10–13; *Paul Robeson: The Life and Times of a Free Black Man* (New York: Harper & Row, 1974); *The People Could Fly: American Black Folktales* (New York: Knopf, 1985); *The Planet of Junior Brown* (New York: Macmillan, 1971); *A Ring of Tricksters: Animal Tales from America, the West Indies, and Africa* (New York: Blue Sky, 1997); *Sweet Whispers, Brother Rush* (New York: Philomel, 1982); *The Time-Ago Tales of Jahdu* (New York: Macmillan, 1969); *W.E.B. Du Bois: A Biography* (New York: Crowell, 1972); *When Birds Could Talk and Bats Could Sing: The Adventures of Bruh Sparrow, Sis Wren, and Their Friends* (New York: Blue Sky, 1996); *A White Romance* (New York: Philomel, 1987); *Zeely* (New York: Macmillan, 1967); Nina Mikkelsen, *Virginia Hamilton* (New York: Twayne, 1994); "Virginia Hamilton," in *Contemporary Black Biographies*, vol. 10

(Detroit: Gale, 1995); "Virginia Hamilton," in *Notable Black American Women*, ed. Jessie Carney Smith (Detroit: Gale, 1992).

Heidi Hauser Green

Hammon, Briton (flourished 1760). Captivity narrative writer. What is known about the life of Briton Hammon is recorded in his 1760 *Narrative of the Uncommon Sufferings, and Surprizing Deliverance of Briton Hammon, a Negro Man*. The brief narrative is currently regarded as the first African American prose text published in British North America (Mulford, in Hammon, 2000). The account begins in late 1747 when, "with the leave of [his] Master" (864), Hammon departs Massachusetts on a British ship bound for the Caribbean. The enterprise goes awry at "Cape Florida," and during the next thirteen-year span Hammon is buffeted from one "Mount of Difficulty" (865) to another. In 1760, he is reunited with his master en route to New England.

Hammon's protracted journey constitutes the majority of the *Narrative*. Misfortune comes six months into the venture when the captain prefers to save his cargo rather than his crew, and Hammon is captured by Florida Indians. Later, he escapes and seeks refuge on a Spanish schooner, but his refusal to serve the Spanish against the English lands him in prison for almost five years. Hammon's release begins a long period of servitude to a Spanish governor and a Catholic bishop, authorities from whom he finally escapes after three attempts. A British man-of-war takes him to battle and then to London, where he earns wages, takes sick, and becomes impoverished. He begs for release from work on a slave ship bound for Guinea when he learns about a ship set for New England. During the transatlantic voyage, the Black cook is restored to his "good master" (866). This "Surprizing Deliverance" he gratefully receives: "I am freed from a long and dreadful Captivity" (867).

Scholars generally agree that reading Hammon's captivity narrative bears on crucial points of historical and cultural import. For one, Hammon's **race** is downplayed and his nationality is emphasized (Weyler, 42, 45). Additionally, his social status as a slave or servant in colonial **Boston, Massachusetts**, remains uncertain, as does his role in composing the narrative. The voice of an amanuensis is most pronounced in the providential discourse and instructive tone of the prefatory and concluding sections, a frame that serves slaveholder, Protestant, and English interests during the Seven Years' War (1756–1763). Some scholars have explored ways in which Hammon's experiences within different cultures and socioeconomic structures sometimes constrain him and at other times allow him to negotiate varying degrees of agency and liberty (Desrochers, 154, 159–160).

Resources: Robert Desrochers, Jr., "'Surprizing Deliverance'? Slavery and Freedom, Language and Identity in the *Narrative of Briton Hammon, 'A Negro Man*'," in *Genius in Bondage: Literature of the Early Black Atlantic*, ed. Vincent Carretta and Philip Gould (Lexington: University Press of Kentucky, 2001), 153–174; Briton Hammon, *Narrative of the Uncommon Sufferings, and Surprizing Deliverance of Briton*

Hammon, a Negro Man (1760), in *Early American Writings*, ed. Carla Mulford (New York: Oxford University Press, 2002), 864–867; Karen A. Weyler, "Race, Redemption, and Captivity in the Narratives of Briton Hammon and John Marrant," in *Genius in Bondage: Literature of the Early Black Atlantic*, ed. Vincent Carretta and Philip Gould (Lexington: University Press of Kentucky, 2001), 39–53.

Keat E. Murray

Hammon, Jupiter (1711–c. 1806). Poet and essayist. Jupiter Hammon, the "gentleman slave" of colonial New York, was the first known African American to publish literary verse in what would become the United States. His work represents the first bridge between African American folk narratives, oral verses, and songs, and formal, composed literary verse. The theme of his work was almost invariably religious, although he also used the lens of religion to examine the social realities of **slavery** and race relations.

An Evening Thought. Salvation by Christ, with Penitential Cries (1760) was Hammon's first published work. It concentrates on the importance of surrendering to Christ in order to gain salvation, and describes the Lord as the "captive slave" of the devoted Christian. In "An Address to Miss Phillis Wheatly" (1778), his poetic contemporary, Hammon again emphasizes the importance of embracing Christianity in order to gain spiritual liberation. In *A Dialogue Intitled* [sic] *The Kind Master and the Dutiful Servant* (n.d.), Hammon presents a theological exchange between master and slave, with parallels drawn between earthly servitude and spiritual devotion to Christ.

Hammon's emphasis on religion is unsurprising given his strong Methodist background and the religious mores of the period in which he wrote. Although he was certainly educated in part in the home of his master, Henry Lloyd, he probably also received some education from Christian missionary movements such as the Society for the Propagation of the Gospel in Foreign Parts. Such movements aimed to educate and convert enslaved African Americans both in order to save them spiritually and to challenge the institution of slavery, since the morality of enslaving fellow Christians was considered to be dubious.

Hammon's relationships with Christianity and **race** continue to provoke discussion among critics. *A Dialogue Intitled the Kind Master and the Dutiful Servant* has been criticized by some readers as subservient and conciliatory toward the narrator's White master. Other readers have interpreted the poem as a subversive, ironic exchange in which the dutiful servant (revealed eventually to be Hammon himself) rhetorically undermines the master's authority (Johnson; O'Neale).

In his prose works, Hammon counsels slaves to be patient and masters to be mild, and he reminds both that in Heaven there will be no distinction between them. While Hammon himself was never emancipated, he argues in *An Address to the Negroes of the State of New York* (1787) for the emancipation of others, particularly the young.

Stylistically, Hammon's work never achieved greatness, but it is remarkable as a bellwether for African American writing. His poems use simple rhythmic and rhyme patterns reminiscent of hymn forms, from which he certainly gained much inspiration. Unlike traditional African American genres such as the **spiritual**, work song, folk narrative, and toast, Hammon's works were original, independently authored, and published in print. His work made the way clear for other African American authors to publish their works, and implicitly contradicted the pro-slavery argument that Black people were incapable of higher intellectual labor.

Resources: "Hammon, Jupiter," *African-American Writers: A Dictionary*, ed. Shari Dorantes Hatch and Michael R. Strickland (Santa Barbara, CA: ABC-CLIO, 2000); Jupiter Hammon, *America's First Negro Poet: The Complete Works of Jupiter Hammon of Long Island*, ed. Stanley Austin Ransom, Jr. (Port Washington, NY: Associated Faculty Press, 1983); Lonnell E. Johnson, "Dilemma of the Dutiful Servant: The Poetry of Jupiter Hammon," in *Language and Literature in the African American Imagination*, ed. Carol Aisha Blackshire-Belay (Westport, CT: Greenwood Press, 1992), 105–117; "Jupiter Hammon," in *African American Authors, 1745–1945*, ed. Emmanuel S. Nelson (Westport, CT: Greenwood Press, 2000); Sondra A. O'Neale, *Jupiter Hammon and the Biblical Beginnings of African-American Literature* (Metuchen, NJ: Scarecrow Press, 1993); Oscar Wegelin, *Jupiter Hammon: American Negro Poet* (1915; repr. Miami, FL: Mnemosyne, 1969).

Karen Munro

Hansberry, Lorraine (1930–1965). Playwright, screenwriter, journalist, essayist, and short story writer. With her classic play *A Raisin in the Sun* (*Raisin*), Hansberry became the first African American woman to have a play on Broadway and the first African American playwright to enjoy a successful run in **New York City**'s central theater district. Though most noted for her prize-winning *Raisin* (New York Drama Critics Circle Award 1959), she was a prolific author in several fields and part of a new generation of African American playwrights whose literary activities contributed to the struggle for civil rights.

Born in **Chicago, Illinois**, to Carl Augustus and Nannie Perry Hansberry, Lorraine grew up wealthy, her father having made a considerable fortune in real estate. Still, the family's economic status did not protect it from the institutionalized racial segregation of the times. In 1938, they were threatened, terrorized, and finally forced to vacate by court order when they attempted to occupy a home in an officially White neighborhood. Despite a successful appeal to the Supreme Court, her father sought to relocate the family to Mexico, having become bitter toward race relations in the United States. This effort was cut short by his death in 1945.

Hansberry studied at the University of Wisconsin at Madison (UWM) in 1948. Though a predominantly White institution, UWM had a number of racially progressive educators. In 1950, she withdrew without graduating. Her brief college career provided a foundation for Hansberry's activism. She was the first Black student in her dormitory, served in the presidential campaign of Progressive Party candidate Henry Wallace (the 1948 counter to Strom

Thurmond's pro-segregation States' Rights bid), and was the 1949 campus president of the Young Progressives of America. After college, she moved to **Harlem, New York**.

As a consequence of her 1952 appointment as associate editor of the Black newspaper *Freedom*, Hansberry interacted with such major political and artistic figures as the newpaper's founder, **Paul Robeson**; its editor, Louis Burnham; and **Langston Hughes** and **W.E.B. Du Bois**. Her first theatrical production was a spectacle celebrating the newspaper's anniversary. Her time at *Freedom* helped shaped many of the themes of her major dramas. Hansberry's ex-husband, in his introduction to Hansberry's "last plays," mentions books such as Du Bois's *Black Folk: Then and Now* and Jomo Kenyatta's *Facing Mount Kenya* among her readings (37). This interest in the broad scope of the African **diaspora** resulted in a number of articles on both African American and African national politics and society. Others, in their focus on reconciling Black America to Africa, discern a "call [on] Africans and diasporic blacks to develop the sense of belonging to a single cohesive family" (Effiong, 35) in *A Raisin in the Sun*.

While reporting on a protest at New York University, Hansberry met Robert Barron Nemiroff, a White student, whom she married the following year. Though they eventually divorced, Nemiroff proved a significant promoter of Hansberry's work, both before and after her untimely death. She left *Freedom*

Lorraine Hansberry, 1964. Courtesy of the Library of Congress.

shortly thereafter, intending to focus on her writing. The couple struggled in various jobs during the early years of their marriage, and Hansberry's literary efforts were slowed. Fortunately, in 1956, her husband and a colleague, Burt D'Lugoff, wrote a popular song titled "Cindy, Oh Cindy," which provided adequate regular income for Hansberry to cease gainful employment. She spent the next three years writing and seeking production for the play that would make her famous.

A number of Hansberry's and her husband's friends and colleagues reviewed *Raisin* with interest. Among them was the music publisher Phil Rose, who later became its producer with David J. Cogan. But Broadway investors were generally disinclined to risk money on a "Negro play," and the only interested individual made demands for changes in the production team to which Hansberry was unwilling to submit. The producers opted to finance a series of out-of-town tryouts (in New Haven, Connecticut, Chicago, and **Philadelphia, Pennsylvania**). Strong audience responses and a sold-out run in Philadelphia encouraged their endeavors, and the show finally opened at New York's Ethel Barrymore Theatre on March 11, 1959. Lloyd

Richards, the director, was the first Black director of a Broadway show since the 1920s. The original cast included such future notables as Ruby Dee, Lou Gosset, Claudia McNeil, Sydney Poitier, Diana Sands, and Glynn Turman. The play was an immediate success, running 538 performances and leading to a 1961 Columbia Pictures release starring nearly all of the original cast members, as well as a Tony Award-winning musical, *Raisin* (1973).

Hansberry cited witnessing a production of Irish playwright Sean O'Casey's *Juno and the Paycock* as a transfiguring moment in her artistic development. Both *Raisin* and *Juno* share a quality of cultural specificity, a lens into the particular experiences of a social group. Yet both derive universal humanist themes from the local struggles of their communities. Consequently, the plot of *Raisin* marries Hansberry's early experiences with American economic injustice to a global African consciousness she had cultivated as a journalist, and weaves those themes through the public and private conflicts of a middle-class Black family, the Youngers. Hansberry borrowed the final title (originally *The Crystal Stair*) from a verse in the Langston Hughes poem "Harlem."

In its most elementary summary, *A Raisin in the Sun* depicts a conflict within a middle-class African American family over how they will spend a $10,000 inheritance, left by the family father. The matriarch, Lena Younger, intends to purchase a home in a White suburban neighborhood. Her son, Walter, wants to invest in a liquor store. After Lena makes the down payment on their new home, she gives the rest of the money to Walter with instructions to deposit it in the bank. Walter defies his mother, and gives the remaining inheritance to his business partner, Willie Harris. The partner is revealed a grifter, and he disappears with the remainder of the family fortune. A representative of the Youngers' new neighborhood visits them; the White households have made an offer to buy the house from the Youngers in order to keep them out. Walter, lamenting his foolishness and concerned for the family's financial future, nearly accepts the offer. In the end, the Youngers decide to move into their new home. In the official refusal, Walter invokes his father's life of service, the family's many vocations, and their "pride," promising not to "join any protests" or cause any grief for their new neighbors, but affirming their right to live in whatever home they can afford.

The assertion of individual economic rights, the emphasis on personal responsibility, and the avowal of the work ethic connect *Raisin* thematically to earlier important African American folk dramas and White problem plays. *Raisin* became a watershed event in theatrical representation, bringing to the mainstream Broadway theater a project begun in the 1920s with the Little Negro Theatre Movement and the **Harlem Renaissance**. At the same time, the play marries domestic values to an ideological conflict over Pan-Africanism through the relationship between Beneatha Younger, Walter's sister, and Asagai, a Nigerian intellectual. His pro-Africa platitudes collide with the anti-Africa Western assimilationism of George Murchison. Caught between them is Beneatha, who performs a traditional Yoruba welcome dance and contradicts George's cynicism with romantic claims about the Ashanti knowing surgery in antiquity, but later is hesitant to accept Asagai's invitation to wed and live in Nigeria (Effiong, 39–42).

Hansberry's original screenplay for the film version of the play sharpened its attack on segregation and called for more combative resistance to racism. Such changes were rejected; Asagai's substantive comparisons between African revolutions and African American struggles for civil rights were also deleted from the final script. In the end, the motion picture, though a critical success, was an enervated version of the stage play. The more aggressive side of Hansberry's work would not be silenced, however. Her last six years of life were characterized by increasingly radical advocacy in her dramatic, political, and journalistic efforts.

Hansberry delivered "The Negro Writer and His Roots" to the American Society of African Culture in New York, a speech in which she demanded that African American writers participate in intellectual and social progress for all humankind, vilifying exclusive attempts to reach only the middle classes or American citizens. Later, she publicly advocated violent defense against White attacks. Her 1960 television play, *The Drinking Gourd*, commissioned by NBC as the opening for a **Civil War** series, represented **slavery** as a system that victimized both Blacks and poor Whites. Deemed too controversial, NBC eventually abandoned the project. Her film adaptation of the Haitian novel *Masters of the Dew* by Jacques Roumain was also discontinued, this time for contract problems. She completed three other stage plays before her premature death in 1965 (though only one was produced in her lifetime): *The Sign in Sydney Brustein's Window*, *Les Blancs*, and *What Use Are Flowers?*

Less than three months before her death, Hansberry showcased her second major play, *The Sign in Sydney Brustein's Window*. It tells of a Jewish intellectual who, though previously detached from politics, becomes involved in a city reform candidate's election by hanging a sign in his window. In this comprehensive critique of the political spectrum, Brustein's politician proves to be connected to crime, a Black character proves to be a racist, and friends and family prove to be disloyal. Critical response was mixed and, despite the efforts of friends and several sympathetic fellow artists, the play closed the night of Hansberry's death (January 12, 1965). Many found it overwritten and depressing; others praised it as an honest and astute depiction of life's moral complexities.

Hansberry remained a diligent writer throughout a losing battle with cancer. She managed to drag herself from the hospital to deliver two crucial speeches in 1964, one for the United Negro College Fund's writing contest and another for a public debate titled "The Black Revolution and the White Backlash." In the latter, she admonished White liberal criticism of militant civil rights action. After her death, her ex-husband brought much of her work to the public, including a collection of her writings titled *To Be Young, Gifted, and Black* (after a comment in her speech to the UNCF), a number of posthumous stage productions, and *Les Blancs: The Collected Last Plays of Lorraine Hansberry* (1972).

Les Blancs stands as the first recorded play by an African American author to deal with armed resistance to African colonial rule. With its combination of realism and thematic expressionist techniques, Hansberry achieved in *Les Blancs* what would be a primary objective of the rising **Black Arts Movement**, a Black American aesthetic informed by native African ethics. A 1970 staging produced by Nemiroff at the Longacre Theatre in New York received mixed reviews. Many audiences were uncomfortable with its seeming defense of combative revolution when democratic evolution fails. *What Use Are Flowers?*, a study of the aftermath of a nuclear holocaust, has never had a Broadway production.

In the early 1980s, two fiction stories by Hansberry appeared in prominent magazines. In 1978, **Woodie King, Jr.**, released *The Black Theatre Movement: "A Raisin in the Sun" to the Present*, a documentary film based on over sixty interviews with artists and writers. More than two-thirds of those interviewed noted their debt to Hansberry's pioneering accomplishments. Her early death robbed America of innumerable contributions to literature, journalism, and the burgeoning **Civil Rights Movement**. But a 1988 television production of *Raisin*, starring Danny Glover and Esther Rolle, included the more radical, previously unused, scenes from Hansberry's film script, had the largest Black audience in public television history, and proved the enduring social relevance of her work. (*See* **Drama**.)

Resources: Primary Sources: Lorraine Hansberry: "All the Dark and Beautiful Warriors," *Village Voice*, Aug. 16, 1983, pp. 1+; "The Black Revolution and the White Backlash," *National Guardian*, July 4, 1964, pp. 5–9; "The Buck Williams Tennessee Memorial Association," *Southern Exposure*, Sept.–Oct. 1984, 28–30; *Les Blancs: The Collected Last Plays of Lorraine Hansberry*, ed. Robert Nemiroff (New York: Random House, 1972); *Lorraine Hansberry Speaks Out: Art and the Black Revolution*, ed. Robert Nemiroff (audiocassette) (Caedmon Records, 1972); *The Movement: Documentary of a Struggle for Equality* (New York: Simon and Schuster, 1964); "On Summer," *Playbill*, June 27, 1960, pp. 3+; *Raisin* (New York: Samuel French, 1978); *A Raisin in the Sun*, dir. Bill Duke (American Playhouse, 1988); *A Raisin in the Sun*, dir. Daniel Petrie (Columbia Pictures, 1961); *A Raisin in the Sun: A Drama in Three Acts* (New York: Random House, 1959); *The Sign in Sydney Brustein's Window: A Drama in Three Acts* (New York: Samuel French, 1965); *To Be Young, Gifted, and Black: Lorraine Hansberry in Her Own Words*, ed. Robert Nemiroff (Englewood Cliffs, NJ: Prentice-Hall, 1969); *To Be Young, Gifted, and Black: Lorraine Hansberry in Her Own Words*, dir. Michael A. Schultz (Educational Broadcasting Corp., 1972); "Willy Loman, Walter Lee Younger, and He Who Must Live," *Village Voice*, Aug. 12, 1959, pp. 7–8. **Secondary Sources:** Doris E. Abramson, *Negro Playwrights in the American Theatre, 1925–1959* (New York: Columbia University Press, 1969); *The Black Theatre Movement: "A Raisin in the Sun" to the Present*, dir. Woodie King, Jr. (AM Video, 1978); Elizabeth Brown-Guillory, *Their Place on the Stage: Black Women Playwrights in America* (Westport, CT: Greenwood Press, 1988); Steven R. Carter, *Hansberry's Drama: Commitment amid Complexity* (Urbana: University of Illinois Press, 1991); Anne Cheney, *Lorraine Hansberry* (Boston: Twayne, 1984); Lynn Domina, *Understanding*

"A Raisin in the Sun": A Student Casebook to Issues, Sources, and Historical Documents (Westport, CT: Greenwood Press, 1998); Philip Uko Effiong, *In Search of a Model for African American Drama: A Study of Selected Plays by Lorraine Hansberry, Amiri Baraka, and Ntozake Shange* (Lanham, MD: University Press of America, 2000); Christy Gavin, ed., *African American Women Playwrights: A Research Guide* (New York: Garland, 1999); John Cullen Gruesser, *Black on Black: Twentieth-Century African American Writing About Africa* (Lexington: University Press of Kentucky, 2000); James Haskins, *Black Theater in America* (New York: Thomas Y. Crowell, 1982); *Lorraine Hansberry: The Black Experience in the Creation of Drama*, dir. Ralph J. Tangney (Films for the Humanities, 1975); Elizabeth C. Phillips, *The Works of Lorraine Hansberry: A Critical Commentary* (New York: Monarch Press, 1973); Jacques Roumain, *Masters of the Dew*, trans. Langston Hughes and Mercer Cook (New York: Reynal and Hitchcock, 1947); Catherine Scheader, *They Found a Way: Lorraine Hansberry* (Chicago: Children's Press, 1978); Sanford V. Sternlicht, *A Reader's Guide to Modern American Drama* (Syracuse, NY: Syracuse University Press, 2002); Margaret B. Wilkerson, "Lorraine Hansberry," *African American Writers* (New York: Scribner's, 1991), 147–158.

Ben Fisler

Hansen, Joyce (born 1942). Teacher, young-adult author, and historical novelist. Born and raised in New York City, Hansen grew up in a household where stories were valued. Her father was a photographer who loved to tell stories about growing up in the West Indies and what **Harlem, New York**, was like in the 1920s and 1930s. Hansen's mother had wanted to be a journalist, but because she had to work during the **Great Depression**, she quit high school and never got the chance to become one. Instead, she passed her love of writing and books on to her daughter. Hansen had dreamed of becoming a writer since high school. After graduating from Pace University (she also holds a master's degree in English education from New York University), she taught English and reading in New York City public schools for twenty-two years. Teaching helped Hansen's writing because through it, she learned firsthand what teenagers cared about, thought about, wanted to read about. She also learned that in order to hold a reader's attention, books could not be corny—characters had to have real voices and experience real-life problems. In 1980 Hansen's first book, *The Gift-Giver*, was published. Seven years later, her fourth book, *Which Way Freedom?* earned a Coretta Scott King Award honorable mention.

Many of the characters and situations in Hansen's books are based upon childhood experiences or people she knew—including her students. Hansen also enjoys the challenge of writing historical nonfiction, as many of her later works reveal. Retired from teaching since 1995, she currently lives in South Carolina with her husband, Matthew Nelson.

Resources: Joyce Hansen: *African Princess: The Amazing Lives of Africa's Royal Women* (New York: Jump at the Sun, 2004); *Between Two Fires: Black Soldiers in the Civil War* (New York: F. Watts, 1993); *Bury Me Not in a Land of Slaves: African-Americans in the Time of Reconstruction* (Danbury, CT: F. Watts, 2000); *The Captive*

(New York: Scholastic, 1994); *The Gift-Giver* (New York: Houghton Mifflin/Clarion, 1980); *The Heart Calls Home* (Madison, WI: Turtleback, 2002); *Home Boy* (New York: Clarion, 1982); *I Thought My Soul Would Rise and Fly: The Diary of Patsy, a Freed Girl* (New York: Scholastic, 1997); *One True Friend* (Boston: Houghton Mifflin, 2001); *Out from This Place* (New York: Walker, 1988); *Which Way Freedom?* (New York: Walker, 1986), also published as *Which Way to Freedom* (1991); *Women of Hope: African Americans Who Made a Difference* (New York: Scholastic, 1998); *Yellow Bird and Me* (New York: Clarion, 1986); Joyce Hansen and Gary McGowan, *Breaking Ground, Breaking Silence: The Story of New York's African Burial Ground* (New York: Henry Holt, 1998); Joyce Hansen, Gary McGowan, and James Ransome, *Freedom Roads: Searching for the Underground Railroad* (Chicago: Cricket, 2003).

Joy Duckett Cain

Hardy, James Earl (born c. 1972). Novelist and nonfiction writer. James Earl Hardy burst onto the literary scene in 1994 with *B-Boy Blues*, a novel that unabashedly depicts a sexual and romantic relationship between its two Black male protagonists. To date, *B-Boy Blues* has spawned four sequels, thus solidifying Hardy's status as one of the most successful Black gay writers of the late twentieth and early twenty-first centuries. The *B-Boy Blues* series examines the joys and travails of Mitchell "Little Bit" Crawford and Raheim "Pooquie" Rivers's relationship once Crawford, a straitlaced journalist, falls head over heels for Rivers, a bike messenger-cum-eventual male model. The series explores the different backgrounds from which the two hail and shows how they are able to reconcile their differences for the sake of their attraction.

The world Hardy depicts is reminiscent of that of **Harlem Renaissance** writer **Claude McKay**'s novel *Home to Harlem* (1928). Just as McKay deployed slang discourse to depict dialogue between his characters, Hardy invokes sociolinguistic devices to make his characters sound more "authentic." Perhaps the best example of this practice is Hardy's tendency to have his characters identify as "same gender loving," an identifier claimed by many young Black men in contrast to the more White-oriented "gay." Additionally, in McKay's text, the characters engage in sexual activity with some frequency. Hardy has unapologetically designed the *B-Boy Blues* series in a similar vein, often regaling his readers with page-long sequences of frank, explicit sexual imagery. As a whole, the *B-Boy Blues* series is notable for representing two young Black men striving to build a life for and with one another in a world that is not designed to allow that to happen easily. A native of New York City, Hardy graduated from the Columbia School of Journalism. He has also written biographies of the recording group Boyz II Men (1997) and filmmaker **Spike Lee** (1996), although he remains best known as the author of the *B-Boy Blues* series. (*See* **Erotica**; **Gay Literature**.)

Resources: James Earl Hardy: *B-Boy Blues: A Seriously Sexy, Fiercely Funny, Black-on-Black Love Story* (Boston: Alyson, 1994); *Boyz II Men* (Philadelphia: Chelsea House, 1997); *The Day Eazy-E Died* (Los Angeles: Alyson, 2001); *If Only for One Nite* (Los Angeles: Alyson, 1997); *Love the One You're with* (New York: Amistad, 2002);

2nd Time Around (Los Angeles: Alyson, 1996); *Spike Lee: Filmmaker* (New York: Chelsea House, 1996).

Chris Bell

Harland-Watts, Joette [Kupenda Auset] (born 1967). Poet. While a student at Spelman College, Kupenda Auset (as she prefers to be known) used to make believe that she was a writer like **Zora Neale Hurston** during the **Harlem Renaissance** (Abernathy). Currently, she is one of many new talents who have contributed to the New Black Renaissance (1990s).

Auset's interest in literature has its roots in her childhood. Born Joette Harland on June 21, 1967, in **Atlanta, Georgia**, Kupenda inherited her creativity and passion for music, the arts, reading, and writing from her parents, who were both teachers (Janich, M10). She received her degree in English at Spelman College, where she was named "Kupenda Auset" during an initiation ceremony into a black sisterhood. She is currently a candidate for a Master of Arts degree in Africana Women's Studies at Clark Atlanta University. Her work has been published in *Honey* magazine, *Rolling Out UrbanStyle Weekly*, and *Upscale* magazine. *In the Tradition: An Anthology of Young Black Writers* (1992), edited by **Kevin Powell** and **Ras Baraka**, and *Catch the Fire!!! A Cross-Generational Anthology on Contemporary African-American Poetry* (1998), edited by Derrick I. M. Gilbert, feature her poetry. She has also published *Life Poems: For Yesterday, Today and Tomorrow* (1994) and *Time Change: New "Life" Poems* (1998). Auset was a contributor to *African-American Stories: A Treasury of Tradition* (2003). Her poetry deals with diverse themes: self-reflection, love, social change, creativity, relationships, identity, and womanhood (Abernathy, 11). Her mentors include such esteemed women writers of color as **Pearl Cleage**, Judy Gebre-Hiwet, **Mari Evans**, **Sonia Sanchez**, and **Gloria Wade-Gayles** (Abernathy, 11).

Auset presently works for the National Black Arts Festival (NBAF), and is founder and executive producer of the Harlem Renaissance-inspired House of Life Dinner Theatre & Supper Club in Atlanta. House of Life features performances that present various aspects of contemporary and traditional Black culture. It also includes "fine dining, author readings, community outreach, educational programs, lectures and book signings" ("Kevin Powell's State of Black Men").

Resources: Eloise Abernathy, "Good Reading," review of *Time Change: New "Life" Poems* by Kupenda Auset, *Spelman Messenger* 114, no.1 (2000), 11; Kupenda Auset: *Life Poems: For Yesterday, Today and Tomorrow* (Self-published, 1994); *Time Change: New "Life" Poems* (Self-published, 1998); Vincent Golphin, Cathy Johnson, and John Patterson, eds., *African-American Stories: A Treasury of Tradition* (Lincolnwood, IL: Publications International, 2003); Kathy Janich, "Faces to Watch: A Culture of Caring About Issues," *Atlanta Journal-Constitution*, Oct. 12, 2003, p. M10; "Kevin Powell's State of Black Men in America Tour," http://www.atlantahapps.com/kevin%20powell.html.

Gladys L. Knight

Harlem, New York. Harlem, a section of New York City, lies between 110th Street and 155th Street, bounded by the East River and by the Hudson River on its western side. While Spanish Harlem and Italian Harlem also lie within those boundaries, Black Harlem, with such landmarks as the Abyssinian Baptist Church, the Apollo Theater, and the Schomburg Center for Research in Black Culture, remains a vital center of African American art and business. Harlem served as an incubator of 20th-century African American culture, and it is now home to over 250,000 people.

Holland acquired Manhattan Island from indigenous people in 1626. Dutch governor Peter Stuyvesant named the area Nieuw Haarlem, after the Dutch city of Haarlem. Taking control of the colony in 1664, the English shortened the name to Harlem. Blacks had populated Manhattan since 1626, when eleven African slaves built the first road. For the next 200 years, slaves worked on Dutch and English farms there. However, the colony had free Blacks as early as 1630; in 1644, some slaves who had been given conditional freedom settled in lower Manhattan, now Greenwich Village, which would remain a Black neighborhood for nearly two centuries. On September 16, 1776, west Harlem was the site of a clash between British and Continental forces, called the Battle of Harlem Heights. After the Revolutionary War, Manhattan's Black population numbered nearly 10 percent of the total.

By 1820, many Blacks lived in the infamous Five Points slum (now City Hall), where they shared an uneasy existence with the Irish. The neighborhood known as Stagg Town or Negro Plantation was dominated by freed slaves. Despite the poverty and violence, the area also included civic organizations: the African Society of Mutual Relief, founded in 1808; the theater African Grove; the African Free School Number 2; and many churches, among them Abyssinian Baptist Church, Bethel African Methodist Episcopal Church, and African Methodist Episcopal Zion Church. A large cemetery for African Americans lay nearby. Five Points was also close to the site of the 1741 Great Negro Plot, as a result of which the English burned thirteen Blacks at the stake for allegedly planning to secure their freedom and to seek revenge on their masters. Four Whites, two men and two women, were hanged as accomplices, and seventy-one Africans were returned to Africa. When New York abolished slavery in 1827, Manhattan's Black population was nearly 14,000. The Anti-Slavery Society of New York was founded in 1833.

Prominent citizens, including Alexander Hamilton, once inhabited Harlem, which was a beautiful rural area in the eighteenth and nineteenth centuries. His landmark 1802 country home, Hamilton Grange (near Amsterdam Avenue), now serves as a branch of the New York Public Library. In 1831, the New York and Harlem Rail Road linked lower Manhattan to the north, which remained primarily open farmland until 1870. New York annexed the area in 1873 and built wide boulevards and elegant apartment buildings. The architect Stanford White designed row houses on West 138th and 139th Streets. In 1879, completion of the Third Avenue El transformed the area into an urban community. Between 1870 and 1920, Harlem's population consisted predominantly of Jewish, Italian, German, and Irish immigrants and their families; however, the relocation of city dwellers from lower Manhattan and African Americans migrating from **the South** turned the suburb into the largest Black community in the country (*see* **Great Migration**).

By the end of the nineteenth century, most Blacks in the city lived in the midtown Tenderloin and San Juan Hill areas. The Tenderloin area lay along West 53rd Street between Sixth and Seventh Avenues; many churches, civic organizations, and cabarets were located within its boundaries. Known for a time as Black Bohemia, the area attracted artists, writers, and actors, including **James Weldon Johnson**, who lived on West 53rd Street. Jelly Roll Morton and Scott Joplin played in Tenderloin clubs. The area was the site of a **race riot** in 1900 in the midst of an August heat wave. Fights occurred between Blacks and police officers, and White mobs targeted Black citizens in the streets. San Juan Hill, west of Columbus Circle, was one of the most congested parts of the city; 3,500 people inhabited a single block. Open railroad tracks, a deadly site for neighborhood children, constituted its western boundary at Eleventh Avenue. Named for the black veterans of the Spanish-American War, San Juan Hill became known for its many ethnic street battles.

In the real estate speculation of 1904 and 1905, housing values in Harlem collapsed. Anticipation of an economic boom when the Lenox Avenue subway line was to be completed in 1904 had created a land and housing boom above 125th Street; however, too many houses were built for too few people. The transition from a White community to a black one was engineered by Philip Payton's Afro-American Realty Company, which leased White apartment buildings and encouraged Black families and recent Southern and Caribbean immigrants to move into them. Payton's efforts opened up buildings that had never before had Black tenants. The shift intensified when the prestigious St. Philip's Protestant Episcopal Church moved from midtown Manhattan to West 133rd Street in 1910. In 1914, the area's population was estimated at nearly 50,000. By 1920, two-thirds of New York's Blacks lived in Harlem. Many prominent Black citizens relocated to the area, among them Rev. Dr. Adam Clayton Powell and Madame C. J. Walker, the first Black woman millionaire. Other dominant churches moved to Harlem: Abyssinian Baptist, Bethel African Methodist Episcopal, and African Methodist Episcopal Zion ("Mother Zion"). In addition, civic organizations such as the African Society of Mutual Relief, the YMCA, the Urban League, and the **NAACP** relocated to Harlem. Two **newspapers** were established, the *New York News* and the *Amsterdam News*; the latter is a weekly still in existence.

The Black American cultural renaissance centered in Harlem was prefaced in February 1919 by the 369th Infantry's march up Fifth Avenue to Harlem. The National Guard unit of 1,300 Black men, along with their officers, had made a reputation for itself, serving 191 days in European trenches during **World War I**. Named the "Hell Fighters," the regiment was awarded France's Croix de Guerre; one of its members, coal dealer Sergeant Henry Johnson, killed four enemies with a knife, and captured twenty-two. Among the cheering crowds were William Randolph Hearst, John Wanamaker, Henry Clay Frick, and NAACP official James Weldon Johnson, who reported the march for a Black newspaper, *The Age* (Lewis).

Harlem in the 1920s proved a mecca for Black artistic and intellectual life. **W.E.B. Du Bois, Zora Neal Hurston, Jean Toomer, Claude McKay, Countee Cullen,** and **Langston Hughes** were among the writers living or working in Harlem during this decade. In 1923, the National Urban League published its first issue of ***Opportunity***, a literary magazine of **Harlem Renaissance** authors. Music venues such as the Apollo Theater, the Cotton Club, and the Savoy Ballroom embraced **Bessie Smith**, "Fats" Waller, **Edward Kennedy "Duke" Ellington**, and Eubie Blake. The dancer Florence Mills was one of the most popular entertainers of the era, and Bill "Bojangles" Robinson was nicknamed "Mayor of Harlem." The Cotton Club became an enormously famous **jazz** venue, one at which Duke Ellington and his orchestra played, but also one that, aside from performers and workers, was open only to Whites, ironically (Lewis). One well-to-do neighborhood occupied by upper-middle-class African Americans was known as Striver's Row; it is featured in the **historical novel** *Harlem Redux* (2002) by **Persia Walker**. Harlem actor **Paul Robeson**, who caused a sensation with his role in Eugene O'Neill's *Emperor Jones*, also starred as Joe in *Show Boat*; his rendition of the song "Ol' Man River" is still the standard against which other performances are measured.

The era saw scholar **Arthur A. Schomburg**'s preeminent collection of Black letters added to the Harlem branch of the New York Public Library. Located on **Malcolm X** Boulevard at 135th Street, the 5-million-item collection remains the most substantive site for research in Black culture. During the 1920s, intellectuals such as Franz Boaz, James Weldon Johnson, W.E.B. Du Bois, and Carl Van Doren gave lectures in Harlem. The area's wealth of artistic expression seemed to fulfill aspirations outlined in **Alain Locke**'s special issue of ***Survey Graphic*** magazine (1925), which had called for a **"New Negro"** cultural renaissance after the horrors of World War I and a decade of urban race riots.

One influential patron of African American art and culture was A'Lelia Walker, the wealthy daughter of Madame C. J. Walker, founder of a black cosmetics line. At her two expensively furnished Harlem homes, she hosted salons for writers, journalists, artists, musicians, and actors. The Dark Tower Tea Club and the Walker Studio provided meeting places for Harlem's artistic community. Her death in 1931 was one of several symbolic events signaling the end of the Harlem Renaissance, the major event being the stock market crash in 1929. Langston Hughes wrote a poem for Walker's funeral ("To A'Lelia"). Hughes maintained different residences in Harlem over the years, eventually purchasing a town house at 20 East 127th Street in 1948 (Ostrom). One of Hughes's most famous poems is "Harlem," which asks the question, "What happens to a dream deferred?" Hughes wrote many poems about Harlem, and many of his tales featuring Jesse B. Simple are set there as well (Rampersad).

One of the most influential, yet controversial, political figures in early twentieth-century Black politics was **Marcus Garvey**, founder of the Universal Negro Improvement Association (UNIA). The organization, which relocated to Harlem in 1916, advocated **Black Nationalism**, self-reliance, and a return to Africa (*see* **Back-to-Africa Movement**). In 1920, UNIA held its first convention at Madison Square Garden; the convention, nearly a month long, had delegates from all over the world in attendance. Claiming a membership of 4 million to 6 million, the organization was the dominant Black rights' movement in the early part of the century. Many argue that Garvey, convicted of mail fraud in 1925, was unfairly hounded by the young J. Edgar Hoover. UNIA is now headed by Garvey's son.

While Blacks gained some political clout in Harlem, they still held less than 20 percent of its business in 1929, and the **Great Depression** threw thousands of people onto relief. Harlem had become economically impoverished: in the 1920s, rents skyrocketed, fueled by the increasing immigration from the South and Caribbean nations. Harlem's Black population increased 600 percent between 1910 and 1935. Because the average citizen of Harlem held a menial position, salaries were poor, so people in Harlem paid nearly 40 percent of their salary in rent. In an effort to force hiring of African Americans, Black leaders in 1937 formed the Greater New York City Coordinating Committee for the Employment of Negroes, an organization utilizing boycotts of White businesses. Economic conditions were slow to improve; however, a record shop on 125th Street became the first Black-owned business in the area. In addition, in the 1920s and 1930s Harlem was plagued with tuberculosis, which, ironically, increased access to health care: Harlem Hospital, founded in 1887, admitted five Black doctors to its staff in 1925 and established a school for Black nurses. By 1932, the hospital counted 75 African American physicians and interns among its staff. Today, the hospital boasts a comprehensive sickle cell anemia center and an award-winning tuberculosis clinic.

Adam Clayton Powell, Jr., a Harlem minister and activist, came to prominence during the Depression. During the 1930s, he initiated boycotts of White-owned stores, calling the protests "Don't Buy Where You Can't Work." One store in particular was his focus: Blumsteins, founded by German Jewish immigrants, refused to hire Black workers for anything other than menial positions. The store later became the first in the area with a Black Santa and Black mannequins. In addition, Powell organized protests to demand reforms at Harlem Hospital and organized an extensive relief program to aid the area's homeless and unemployed. Powell was elected to Congress in 1944 for the first of twelve terms; once in Washington, he challenged the "Whites only" Capitol Hill dining policies and attached antidiscrimination clauses to much of the legislation. Defeated for renomination by Charles Rangel in 1970, Powell resigned as minister of the Abyssinian Baptist Church in 1971 and died in 1972.

During the Great Depression and afterward, Harlem was plagued by a series of riots, stemming from a combination of alleged police brutality and

Street scene in Harlem, New York, 1943. Courtesy of the Library of Congress.

economic resentment. In 1935, Harlem was the site of a major riot, triggered by rumors of police brutality when a young Black man was arrested for shoplifting at a White-owned store. The riot killed three, left thirty injured and 200 jailed, and destroyed $2 million worth of property. An even more serious riot in 1943 left six blacks dead, 700 hundred injured (including forty police), and left $5 million worth of property damage. The 1964 riot, stemming from clashes between police and Congress of Racial Equality (CORE) protesters after a police shooting of a fifteen-year-old boy, saw one death and more than 100 injured in two nights of mayhem. The infamous 1977 twenty-six-hour electrical blackout in New York led to 4,000 arrests and $60 million in damage.

Harlem regained strength as a literary and political center for African Americans beginning in the 1950s. Founded in 1950, the Harlem Writers Guild served as a workshop for the luminaries **Maya Angelou, Ossie Davis, Audre Lorde, Terry McMillan,** and **Paule Marshall.** Its mission remains the encouragement and preservation of African American art and culture. The influential member John Henrik Clarke, a prolific historical and literary author, edited works on Malcolm X, Marcus Garvey, Africa, and Harlem itself. Harlem has also provided a home to the writers **Ralph Ellison, James Baldwin, Lorraine Hansberry,** and **Amiri Bakara.** On the political side, Harlem had its first Black borough leader, Hulan Jack, in 1953. Malcolm X, taking up where Marcus Garvey left off, promoted Black Nationalism and the **Nation of**

Islam as sources of spiritual, physical, and economic independence from White racism and violence. Assassinated in 1965 in Harlem's landmark Audubon Theatre and Ballroom (built in 1912), Malcolm X is recognized for his 1964 Cleveland speech "The Ballot or the Bullet," a condemnation of White hypocrisy. In 1989, Harlem resident David N. Dinkins became mayor of New York City.

At the end of the twentieth century, Harlem's economic situation had improved. Congressman Charles Rangel, serving his district since 1970, helped create "empowerment Zones" for poor urban areas in order to improve conditions. The 1992 legislation created the Upper Manhattan Empowerment Zone, which allotted $550 million for capital investment. The Abyssinian Baptist Church, along with many other area churches, has developed local businesses. Rangel was instrumental in persuading former president William Jefferson Clinton to establish his post-White House office on West 125th Street in Harlem. Clinton's Harlem Small Business Initiative program provides professional consultants to new and struggling businesses. Harlem's revitalization includes name-brand department stores, large supermarkets, restaurants, and renovated brownstone houses. In 2000, Geoffrey Canada established the Harlem Children's Zone, now a sixty-block area, that provides services to Harlem's children in order to encourage more to complete school and to attend college.

Famous natives of Harlem include Kareem Abdul-Jabbar, Maya Angelou, Roberta Flack, and **rap** artist DMX. The Apollo Theatre remains an important venue for African American entertainment, and tourists, many from Europe, visit Sugar Hill, Harlem's most exclusive community (former home to Supreme Court justice Thurgood Marshall and boxer **Joe Louis**). Other popular landmarks include Hamilton Grange, Strivers' Row, the National Black Theater, Sylvia's Soul Food, El Museo del Barrio, and Museum of the City of New York, all cultural sites important to Harlem's evolving history.

Resources: Michael Henry Adams and Paul Rocheleau, *Harlem Lost and Found: An Architectural and Social History, 1765–1915* (New York: Monacelli Press, 2002); Nat Brandt, *Harlem at War: The Black Experience in WWII* (Syracuse, NY: Syracuse University Press, 1996); Jeffrey S. Gurock, *When Harlem Was Jewish 1870–1930* (New York: Columbia University Press, 1979); David Levering Lewis, *When Harlem Was in Vogue* (New York: Penguin, 1979); Gilbert Osofsky, *Harlem: The Making of a Ghetto. Negro New York, 1890–1930* (New York: Elephant Paperbacks, 1971); Arnold Rampersad, *The Life of Langston Hughes*, 2 vols. (New York: Oxford University Press, 1986–1988).

Cheryl D. Bohde

Harlem Renaissance (c. 1920–1932). The Harlem Renaissance was the first cohesive literary and artistic movement in African American cultural history. Occasioned by the unprecedented numbers of Black people who moved to cities such as **Washington, D.C.**, **Philadelphia, Pennsylvania**, and New York (including **Harlem** and **Brooklyn**) during the **Great Migration**, the movement was then vitalized by Black and White visionaries such as **W.E.B. Du Bois**, **Jessie Redmon Fauset**, **Langston Hughes**, **Alain Locke**, and **Carl Van Vechten**, who believed that the arts would be an essential avenue for racial progress. While the Harlem Renaissance inspired, and was inspired by, African American arts generally, the following paragraphs will focus on its effects on African American literature, after a short discussion of the factors that gave rise to the movement.

In the 1890s, the years that commenced the era known as the Great Migration, African Americans found themselves grappling with a host of factors that were pushing them out of **the South** and pulling them toward the North. The "push" factors in the South included an increasing degree of racist repression and violence, natural disasters (both a boll weevil infestation and a drought), and a lack of viable job opportunities. The "pull" factors in the North—more freedom and better jobs, relatively speaking—made big cities look like places where Black people might have a fair chance at a future, particularly when the United States entered **World War I** in 1917, and scores of able-bodied White men joined the armed forces. By 1920, at least 300,000 African Americans had left the South and taken up residence in Northern industrial centers.

Life in the North came with its troubles. Some rural Black laborers discovered too late that they had been lured to urban centers in order to break strikes by White workers attempting to unionize. Meanwhile, Black people who had fled the escalating violence in the South saw the North erupt in flames as well. The summer of 1919 was known as the "Red Summer," and **race riots** broke out in Washington, D.C., **Chicago, Illinois**, Charleston, South Carolina, Longview, **Texas**, and elsewhere. But even these dismal events could not keep African Americans from migrating North, where the dream of self-determination seemed much more within reach.

Not only a year marked by violence, 1919 was also a period of triumph and optimism. "Here Comes My Daddy" was the song that accompanied 369th Infantry as it made its way through Harlem on February 17, 1919. This regiment of Black soldiers had been dubbed the "Hell Fighters," and the all-Black military band that preceded the Hell Fighters that day was led by Bill "Bojangles" Robinson. All of Harlem was celebrating not only the heroism and success of the World War I soldiers, which was formidable—they were the only American unit awarded the Croix de Guerre, after they spent 191 consecutive days in the trenches—but also the hope and sense of possibility embodied by the victorious men. The music, dignity, and sense of selfhood evoked by the parade of returning soldiers directly gave way to hopes that an equitable cultural victory could be won by the art and artists of the Harlem Renaissance.

Some scholars argue that the term "Harlem Renaissance" is misleading. They hold that what took place during this period was not actually a renaissance, or rebirth, but another stage in the evolution of African American art that had begun with the inception of African presence in America. In addition, they point out that the cultural activity that characterizes the Harlem Renaissance was by no means limited to the two square miles at the northern end of New York, where Harlem is located. African American music, art, literature, and politics also thrived during these years in Chicago, **Detroit, Michigan**, Philadelphia, and Washington, D.C., where Blacks settled in record numbers. Finally, it is important to recognize the creative interplay developing between African American, Caribbean and African writers. Not only were African American writers in the 1920s reading the work of blacks in other parts of the **diaspora**—and vice versa—but several Harlem Renaissance writers spent significant parts of their careers abroad, and otherwise far away from Harlem.

But even though African American arts of the 1920s flourished all over the country and the world, Harlem was still unique as a city that spoke to black hopes and dreams. "I'd rather be a lamppost in Harlem than Governor of Georgia," went a popular saying of the day. No city in the North captured the imagination of the Black migrant more fiercely than Harlem, which first was a Dutch settlement, then German, then Irish, then Jewish, and then Black, after a considerable real estate war and subsequent White flight out of Harlem neighborhoods. The neighborhoods that comprised Harlem, known as the "Black Mecca," were not only famously elegant, but they became home to some of the most diverse Black populations in the country. Laborers fresh from the South rubbed elbows with African Americans who had known wealth, independence, and social prestige in the North for generations. Immigrants from the West Indies and Africa encountered Black people with entirely different sensibilities and customs. Some of these subcultures blended harmoniously while others did so grudgingly, but all of this mixing provided excellent fodder for African American artists determined to translate the cultural upheaval they saw around them into their art. In 1928, Harlem claimed 200,000 Black residents.

Black migrants mingled with African American natives of New York across cultural and class lines both outdoors—along the elegant avenues and broad sidewalks that characterized Harlem—and indoors—inside cabarets, buffet flats, speakeasies, and ballrooms that dominated nightlife in the city. The Harlem Renaissance flourished alongside the Jazz Age, an era that recalls the institutions that made it famous, such as the Cotton Club, which catered to Whites and featured Black entertainment. Nightclubs such as the Cotton Club, Connie's Inn, and Small's Paradise, which featured performers including **Edward Kennedy "Duke" Ellington**, Louis Armstrong, and **Bessie Smith**, brought White people—and their money—to Harlem in droves. White financial support was essential to the success of the Harlem Renaissance, but it also forced restraints on Black creative expression. In the case of Harlem nightlife, for instance, while White interest meant increased revenue in Harlem neighborhoods, it also meant that Black patrons had to sit in segregated, "Jim Crow" sections in order to accommodate the downtown clientele, who wanted to watch Black people but not experience them as equals. "Rent parties," thrown ostensibly to raise rent money for the host, became important avenues for blacks to congregate privately, away from the curious gazes of White people. However successful these parties were at giving Blacks in Harlem sanctuary from inquiring White eyes, they could not resolve the larger conundrum of White influence on the Harlem Renaissance, a phenomenon to which this essay will return.

While Harlem called to many, its appeal for African American writers was very specific. For Black people with literary ambitions, New York City was important because it had recently replaced **Boston, Massachusetts**, as the center of American publishing. New York and Harlem were also home to the most important social and political institutions of the Harlem Renaissance period: the National Association for the Advancement of Colored People (**NAACP**), the National Urban League, and the Universal Negro Improvement Association (UNIA). Each of these institutions had a distinct personality embodied both by the individuals most closely associated with it and the magazines and newspapers it produced. The NAACP had its most visible spokesperson in the scholar and novelist W.E.B. Du Bois, who edited **The Crisis**, the house organ of the NAACP. The National Urban League had educator and writer **Charles Spurgeon Johnson**, who edited its magazine, **Opportunity**. The UNIA was founded and led by **Marcus Garvey**, who also edited the organization's weekly newspaper, **Negro World**. These organizations and magazines were among several that were crucial during the Harlem Renaissance because of their dedication to social and political progress for Black people. In addition, the two magazines, in particular, were critical because of their commitment to the identification and development of African American literature and art. For most African American writers, getting a book published was the ultimate goal, but newspapers and magazines reached the broadest audiences and, because of this, constituted significant vehicles for cultural expression during the Harlem Renaissance.

This entry identifies 1924 as the initial year of the Harlem Renaissance period because of a party given in March of this year by Charles S. Johnson, editor of *Opportunity*. Johnson originally intended to throw this party as a way of honoring Jessie Fauset, literary editor of *The Crisis*, on the publication of her first novel, *There Is Confusion* (1924). In the end, 110 members of the New York literati, Black and White, attended the dinner, which was held at the Civic Club, the only elite club in Manhattan that welcomed both Black people and White women. Black and White editors, writers, and publishers addressed the crowd and referred to their common belief that a new era had begun for Black creativity.

After the dinner, Paul Kellogg, editor of the sociological periodical **Survey Graphic**, suggested to Charles S. Johnson that his magazine devote an entire issue to African American culture, and that Johnson serve as editor of the volume. Johnson enlisted the philosopher Alain Locke to help him assemble the issue. In March 1925, a special edition of *Survey Graphic*, titled "Harlem:

Mecca of the New Negro," was released. It was the most widely read issue in the magazine's history, selling 42,000 copies—more than twice its regular circulation. Months later, Alain Locke expanded this special edition into an arts anthology, *The New Negro* (1925), widely recognized as the first manifesto produced by the Harlem Renaissance. *The New Negro*, which featured portrait drawings as well as essays, poetry, and fiction, includes the work of most of the key figures of this movement, with the notable exception of **Zora Neale Hurston**. (*See* **New Negro, The**.)

Inspired by the success of his 1924 dinner, Charles S. Johnson decided that *Opportunity* would host a literary contest; prizes would be awarded in May 1925. The first announcement for the contest appeared in the August 1924 issue of *Opportunity*. Johnson titillated his readers by adding new names of influential Whites who would serve as judges in each issue. Ultimately, twenty-four respected White and Black editors, publishers, and artists served as contest judges in five categories: essays, short stories, poetry, drama, and personal experiences. The wife of Henry Goddard Leach, editor of *Forum* magazine, contributed the prize money, which totaled $470.

The awards ceremony, held in May 1925, was a resounding success; 316 people attended to witness such future luminaries as **Sterling A. Brown**, Roland Hayes, **Edward Franklin Frazier**, Zora Neale Hurston, **Eric Walrond**, **Countee Cullen**, and Langston Hughes accept their awards. Cullen and Hughes, who would always be rivals for hearts of Harlem's poetry lovers, dominated the poetry category. One of Hughes' signature poems, "The Weary Blues" (1925), took the first prize. At the end of the evening, Johnson announced that Casper Holstein, king of the Harlem numbers racket, would fund the second annual *Opportunity* contest.

Charles S. Johnson and *Opportunity* provided an impetus for the literary flowering of the Harlem Renaissance, but no magazine and no single figure meant more to this period than *The Crisis* and its editor, W.E.B. Du Bois. *The Crisis* also held literary contests, and Du Bois presided over the first, which was held in November 1925. *The Crisis* had an enormous circulation—95,000 at its peak in 1919—so to be published there was a sign of success, at least among the Black middle class. Nothing was published in *The Crisis* that did not meet Du Bois's exacting standards. Between 1919 and 1924, when he became deeply involved in the Pan-African Congress movement, Du Bois relied upon his literary editor at *The Crisis*, Jessie Redmon Fauset. These years were rich for African American writing, and Jessie Fauset's understanding of the literary contours of the Harlem Renaissance was reflected in the foresight she demonstrated by publishing writers such as Langston Hughes and **Jean Toomer** before other gatekeepers had even heard of them. Fauset left *The Crisis* in 1926. By that time she had made a substantial impact on the magazine and, by extension, the Harlem Renaissance. She would go on to write four novels of her own.

Du Bois had seen the coming of a Negro renaissance as early as 1920, when he had announced in the pages of *The Crisis* his belief in the importance of

Black writers asserting authority over their own experience. For too long, he believed, Blacks had endured the ridicule of White artists who had risen to success by reducing African Americans to their most debased elements. Because art had the potential to liberate Black people from social bondage, Du Bois believed, it should be approached with gravity. In 1926, he wrote, famously, that he did not "care a damn" for any art that did not do the work of racial uplift. Because he was editor of *The Crisis*, his words carried weight.

The passion in Du Bois's words signals a larger tension that was at work in the Harlem Renaissance literary community by 1926. On one side were intellectuals such as Du Bois, who believed that Black art should serve as good propaganda for the **race**. On the other side were writers such as Langston Hughes and **Wallace Thurman**, who defended their right to represent the **Negro** as they pleased, in both positive and negative lights. Hughes wrote a 1926 essay for *The Nation*, "The Negro Artist and the Racial Mountain," which represented not only his personal philosophies about artistic freedom but also the philosophies of the "younger generation of Negro Artists," as Hughes christened them. Explicitly, "The Negro Artist" was a response to "The Negro Art-Hokum," a caustic essay by the satirist **George S. Schuyler**, also published in *The Nation* in 1926, who used his essay to lampoon the idea that an authentic Black art actually existed. In "The Negro Artist," Hughes staked his own position in the continuous debate about the meaning and purpose of Negro art. Both essays have been reprinted in the *Portable Harlem Renaissance Reader*.

These disparate aesthetic philosophies found concrete purpose in the scandal surrounding a single book, *Nigger Heaven*, and its singular author, Carl Van Vechten. When *Nigger Heaven* was published in 1926, Van Vechten, a novelist, cultural critic, and Negro arts enthusiast, had been a presence in the Harlem Renaissance since its inception. At the 1925 *Opportunity* awards dinner, he made a point of introducing himself to the evening's brightest star, Langston Hughes. Within three weeks of this meeting, Van Vechten had secured for Hughes a contract with **Alfred A. Knopf** for his first book of poetry, *The Weary Blues* (1926), and suggested the title for the volume, as well. Van Vechten would serve as a mentor to Hughes for the rest of his life. He would also come to serve as a champion of the work of **Nella Larsen**, whom he would also guide to publication at Knopf, as well as Zora Neale Hurston, who humorously deemed him a "Negrotarian." Van Vechten also rescued from obscurity the anonymously published *Autobiography of an Ex-Coloured Man* (1912), and reissued it in 1927 as a novel by **James Weldon Johnson**, the well-known African American political and cultural figure. Van Vechten was far from the only White person who championed the cause of Black arts during the Harlem Renaissance. Charlotte Mason, for instance, patron of Langston Hughes and Zora Neale Hurston, exercised power over the movement, albeit in her private, individual relationships with Hughes, Hurston, and Alain Locke, who introduced Mason to Hughes and Hurston, among others. There were other powerful White figures in the New Negro

Movement, but none outdistanced Carl Van Vechten in his commitment to and impact on Black arts and letters.

Van Vechten called *Nigger Heaven* his most serious novel, and it was the only novel he would publish about African American life and culture. When the book came out, he was already the author of four novels that had, collectively, made him a best-seller and celebrity. In addition, he had published numerous articles in mainstream publications, such as *Vanity Fair*, extolling the virtues of **spirituals** and the **blues**, arguing for their recognition as authentic American art forms. Still, Van Vechten had concerns about how African Americans, not his primary readership heretofore, would react to his representation of Harlem life. In order to address these concerns, he anonymously composed a questionnaire for *The Crisis*, "The Negro in Art: How Shall He Be Portrayed?" in 1926. Answers to this questionnaire were solicited from a racially diverse group of literary figures from all corners of the American literary world, and then published in *The Crisis* over a period of several months. Six months later, *Nigger Heaven* was published.

Du Bois hated the book, and published a scathing review in *The Crisis*, advising readers to dispose of it. Hughes defended the book in newspaper articles and even in his 1940 **autobiography**, *The Big Sea*. The opposing viewpoints held by these two were matched by reviews that were equally extreme. Both loved and hated, *Nigger Heaven* went through nine printings in its first four months, selling more copies than any other Harlem Renaissance novel.

In 1926, Van Vechten and his novel *Nigger Heaven* became handy symbolic means for some Black writers to announce their desire to break away from literary conventions that had, according to these writers, traditionally constrained the Black writer. The 1926 journal **Fire!!** became the clearest articulation of the aesthetic goals of this younger generation, which included Langston Hughes, Zora Neale Hurston, **Richard Bruce Nugent**, and Wallace Thurman. In *Fire!!*, conceived and edited by Wallace Thurman, these writers and their peers wrote about sex and Carl Van Vechten, among other topics, as a way of critiquing censorship and racial parochialism in literature. As much as the editors of *Fire!!* dreamed that their magazine would operate free of White support, such a goal proved unrealistic. An actual fire put an end to the journal, which published only one issue.

The Harlem Renaissance, a Black movement that was necessarily dependent on White support, was diminished by the Wall Street crash of 1929, and then effectively terminated by the **Great Depression**, even though significant numbers of its key figures continued to produce work well beyond these years. Some scholars believe the Harlem Renaissance was compromised by the degree to which it relied upon White influence for its existence. Still, the New Negro Movement is unmatched as the first collective attempt by Black writers and artists to grapple with the complexity of their identity in the modern world.

Resources: George Chauncey, *Gay New York: Gender, Urban Culture, and the Making of the Gay Male World, 1890–1940* (New York: Basic Books, 1994); Jessie

Redmon Fauset, *There Is Confusion* (New York: Boni & Liveright, 1924); Robert Hemenway, *Zora Neale Hurston: A Literary Biography* (Urbana: University of Illinois Press, 1977); Nathan Irvin Huggins, *Harlem Renaissance* (New York: Oxford University Press, 1971); Langston Hughes: *The Big Sea* (New York: Knopf, 1940); *The Weary Blues* (New York: Knopf, 1926); George Hutchinson, *The Harlem Renaissance in Black and White* (Cambridge, MA: Harvard University Press, 1995); James Weldon Johnson, *The Autobiography of an Ex-Coloured Man* (New York: Knopf, 1927); Bruce Kellner, ed., *The Harlem Renaissance: A Historical Dictionary for the Era* (New York: Methuen, 1987); David Levering Lewis, *The Portable Harlem Renaissance Reader* (New York: Viking, 1994); *When Harlem Was in Vogue* (New York: Knopf, 1981); Alain Locke, ed., *The New Negro* (New York: Atheneum, 1925); Carl Van Vechten, *Nigger Heaven* (New York: Knopf, 1926); Steven Watson, *The Harlem Renaissance: Hub of African-American Culture, 1920–1930* (New York: Pantheon, 1995).

Emily Bernard

Harper, Frances Ellen Watkins (1825–1911). Poet, essayist, novelist, short story writer, orator, and political activist. Born free in 1825 in **Baltimore, Maryland**, Frances Ellen Watkins Harper wrote ten poetry collections, four novels, the first published short story by an African American, and countless political essays that appeared in African American periodicals such as *Frederick Douglass's Paper*, the *New York Independent*, the *Weekly Anglo African*, *The Provincial Freeman*, and *The African Methodist Episcopal Church Review*. She also served on the editorial board of the *Anglo-African Magazine*, the first African American literary journal. Harper is considered an extremely important figure in nineteenth-century American and African American literature.

Orphaned at age three, Harper was raised by her aunt and uncle, Henrietta and William Watkins. William, an outspoken abolitionist orator, writer, educator, and church leader, influenced Frances, who became an educator, writer, activist, and reformer who worked with numerous organizations committed to social justice, including the National Council of Negro Women, the Women's Christian Temperance Union, and the American Equal Rights Association. Harper was friendly with individuals involved in the **Underground Railroad**, lived for a time in a station of the Railroad in **Philadelphia, Pennsylvania**, and therefore probably participated directly in ferrying fugitive slaves to freedom. Harper joined the State Anti-Slavery Society of Maine and began lecturing on the abolitionist circuit at age twenty-nine. She was well regarded as an orator, traveling the United States and Canada delivering speeches to audiences of women and men, Black and White. During the **Reconstruction** era, she advocated political enfranchisement for African Americans, an end to **lynching**, and education. In particular, Harper emphasized the importance of literacy for recently freed African Americans, and while her writing was read by Whites, her poetry, essays, and fiction were especially intended for Black readers. For example, she hoped her poems and fiction would be used as texts for freedmen's schools and Black Sunday schools. A feminist and radical Christian reformer, her activism included

Frances E. W. Harper, 1898. Courtesy of the Library of Congress.

suffrage and temperance efforts, and she emphasized the essential role of American women in political and moral reform, criticizing White women's groups for their racism when they failed to include women of color in their ranks or their analysis of patriarchal oppression.

Like many nineteenth-century American women writers, Harper employed her poetry and fiction as a tool for reform work and political argumentation. Harper's poetry directly analyzes the effects of racism, classism, and sexism in America, charting a path by which her readers can contribute to bringing about needed change. Her poetry collections are *Forest Leaves* (1845), *Poems on Miscellaneous Subjects* (1854; 2nd ed., 1857), *Moses: A Story of the Nile* (1869), *Poems* (1871; repr. 1895 as *Atlanta: Offering Poems*), *Sketches of Southern Life* (1872), *The Martyr of Alabama and Other Poems* (c. 1894), *The Sparrow's Fall* (no date), and *Light Beyond the Darkness* (no date). The collections represent Harper's wide variety of theme and form. *Poems on Miscellaneous Subjects* introduces many themes Harper would later explore in essays, speeches, and fiction, such as religion, **slavery**, **gender**, temperance, and poverty, while the title poem of *Moses: A Story of the Nile* is over 700 lines long, written in blank verse, and tells Moses' tale from the perspective of his two mothers. In *Sketches*, Harper further develops the incorporation of Black dialect in her poetry (Boyd, 14). While much of Harper's poetry had been out of print, the publication of *A Brighter Coming Day* (1990), which includes Harper's letters, prose, poetry, and speeches, and *The Complete Poems of Frances E. W. Harper* (1988) has made her work available to contemporary readers. Harper scholars continue to search for a surviving manuscript of *Forest Leaves*, which remains unrecovered.

Harper's fiction has also only recently been made available to today's readers. Her three serialized novels, *Minnie's Sacrifice* (1869), *Sowing and Reaping* (1876–1877), and *Trial and Triumph* (1888–1889), which appeared in *The Christian Recorder*, the journal of the African Methodist Episcopal Church, were recovered by Frances Smith Foster and republished in 1994. Harper's short story "The Two Offers" (1859) is believed the first short story published by an African American. A character in Harper's last and best-known novel, *Iola Leroy* (1892), argues that novels can "inspire men and women with a deeper sense of justice and humanity" (262). In all of her fiction, Harper sets out to achieve just that goal, creating characters whose decisions either warn readers of the risks of living an immoral life or inspire readers with the possibilities of a life lived true to justice and humanity. Within conventional constructs of women's sentimental fiction, such as courtship, marriage, and women's struggles, Harper's fiction engages political, social, and ideological issues of her day, including racial identity and ambiguity, **passing**, class struggles, Christian morality, equal rights for women, egalitarian marriages, racial uplift work, **lynching**, temperance, political corruption, education, and the psychological legacies of slavery.

In her treatment of Christian morality and the legacy of sexual oppression of Black women in America, Harper participates in a tradition influenced by **Harriet Jacobs's slave narrative**, *Incidents in the Life of a Slave Girl* (1846). Like Jacobs, Harper had to negotiate nineteenth-century rhetoric associating "true womanhood" with piety and purity in order to write of Black women's sexual violation during a time when it was not acceptable for women to speak openly about sex, yet to address such truths was a necessary risk by which Black women exposed the epidemic of White men's rape of Black women during and after slavery. Critic **Melba Boyd** also links Harper's "black abolitionist-feminist aesthetic" to the influence of the poet Sarah Forten (13). Reading Harper's work is crucial to a fuller understanding African American literature and the legacy of Black feminism in America. Her incorporation of political activism into art makes her a forerunner of the **Black Arts Movement**, and her combining of folk and formal language in poetry and fiction predicts **Zora Neale Hurston's** and **Langston Hughes's** writing. In her analysis of the intersections among racism, sexism, and classism, she lays the foundation for contemporary feminist theory by such women of color as **Audre Lorde**, **Barbara Smith**, Cherríe Moraga, and Gloria Anzaldúa. (*See* **Abolitionist Movement**; **Feminism**; **Women's Clubs**.)

Resources: Primary Sources: Frances Ellen Watkins Harper: *A Brighter Coming Day: A Frances Ellen Watkins Harper Reader*, ed. Frances Foster (New York: Feminist Press, 1990); *Complete Poems of Frances E.W. Harper*, ed. Maryemma Graham (New York: Oxford University Press, 1988); *Iola Leroy, or Shadows Uplifted* (1892; repr. New York: Oxford University Press, 1988); *Minnie's Sacrifice, Sowing and Reaping, Trial and Triumph: Three Rediscovered Novels by Frances E. W. Harper*, ed. Frances Smith Foster (Boston: Beacon Press, 1994); *Moses: A Story of the Nile*, 3rd ed. (Philadelphia: Frances Harper, 1889); *Poems on Miscellaneous Subjects* (1857; repr. Philadelphia: Rhistoric Publications, 1969); *Poems* (Philadelphia: G. S. Ferguson, 1895, 1896, 1898, 1900; repr. Freeport, NY: Books for Libraries, 1970); *Sketches of Southern Life* (Philadelphia: Merrihew and Son, 1872, 1873, 1887, 1888). **Secondary Sources:** Elizabeth Ammons, *Conflicting Stories: American Women Writers at the Turn into the Twentieth Century* (New York: Oxford University Press, 1991); Michael Bennett, "Frances Ellen Watkins Sings the Body Electric," in *Recovering the Black Female Body: Self-Representations by African American Women*, ed. Michael Bennett and Vanessa Dickerson (New Brunswick, NJ: Rutgers University Press, 2001), 19–40; Lauren Berlant, "The Queen of America Goes to Washington City: Harriet Jacobs, Frances

Harper, Anita Hill," *American Literature* 65, no. 3 (Sept. 1993), 549–574; Melba Joyce Boyd, *Discarded Legacy: Politics and Poetics in the Life of Frances E. W. Harper 1825–1911* (Detroit: Wayne State University Press, 1994); Hazel Carby, *Reconstructing Womanhood: The Emergence of the Afro-American Woman Novelist* (New York: Oxford University Press, 1987); James Christmann, "Raising Voices, Lifting Shadows: Competing Voice-Paradigms in Frances E. W. Harper's *Iola Leroy*," *African American Review* 34, no. 1 (Spring 2000), 5–18; Anne duCille, *The Coupling Convention: Sex, Text, and Tradition in Black Women's Fiction* (New York: Oxford University Press: 1993); John Ernest, "From Mysteries to Histories: Cultural Pedagogy in Frances E. W. Harper's *Iola Leroy*," *American Literature* 64, no. 3, 497–518. Frances Smith Foster, "Gender, Genre and Vulgar Secularism: The Case of Frances Ellen Watkins Harper and the AME Press," in *Recovered Writers/Recovered Texts*, ed. Dolan Hubbard (Knoxville: University of Tennessee Press, 1997), 46–59; Farah Jasmine Griffin, "*Minnie's Sacrifice:* Frances Ellen Watkins Harper's Narrative of Citizenship," in *The Cambridge Companion to Nineteenth-Century American Women's Writing*, ed. Dale M. Bauer and Philip Gould (Cambridge: Cambridge University Press, 2001), 308–319; Phillip Brian Harper, "Private Affairs: Race, Sex, Property, and Person," *GLQ: A Journal of Lesbian and Gay Studies* 1, no. 2 (1994), 111–133; Debra Rosenthal, "Deracialized Discourse: Temperance and Racial Ambiguity in Harper's 'The Two Offers' and *Sowing and Reaping*," in *The Serpent in the Cup: Temperance in American Literature*, ed. David S. Reynolds and Debra Rosenthal (Amherst: University of Massachusetts Press, 1997), 153–164; Claudia Tate, *Domestic Allegories of Political Desire: The Black Heroine's Text at the Turn of the Century* (New York: Oxford University Press, 1992); Michelle Campbell Toohey, "'A Deeper Purpose' in the Serialized Novels of Frances Ellen Watkins Harper," in *"The Only Efficient Instrument": American Women Writers and the Periodical, 1837–1916*, ed. Aleta Feinsod Cane and Susan Alves (Iowa City: University of Iowa Press, 2001), 202–215.

Vanessa Holford Diana

Harper, Michael S. (born 1938). Poet and editor. "Precision" is a word especially applicable to Harper's poetry. His poems achieve many effects and describe many situations, yet each always displays an attention to craft, particularly to prosody, the practice of musical, metrical techniques in verse. Rhythms come not just from the **jazz** and **blues** of which he is so fond but also from original phrasings built around the sounds of the words and the subject of each stanza or sentence. He has described himself as a "narrative poet with syntax for musical overtones" (Rowell, 786).

Born in **Brooklyn, New York**, Harper moved with his family to **Los Angeles, California**, in 1951. As a middle school student, he was discouraged from pursuing a career as a doctor by a zoology teacher who told him to "pick up a broom and forget the microscope" (Harper, "Poetic Technique," 30). He received an associate's degree from Los Angeles City College in 1959 and earned bachelor's and master's degrees from Los Angeles State College (now California State University–Los Angeles) in 1961 and 1963, respectively; for much of this time, he worked the graveyard shift at a local post office. In 1963 he received an M.F.A. from the University of Iowa Writers' Workshop, where he was the only Black student in the fiction and poetry programs.

A correspondence with **Gwendolyn Brooks** led to the publication of Harper's first book, *Dear John, Dear Coltrane*, in 1970 and its nomination for the National Book Award in 1971. Since then he has published ten volumes of poetry, including *History Is Your Heartbeat* (1971), winner of the poetry award from the Black Academy of Arts and Letters; *Nightmare Begins Responsibility* (1975); *Images of Kin* (1977), winner of the Melville-Cane Award from the Poetry Society of America and nominated for the National Book Award; *Healing Songs for the Inner Ear* (1985); and *Songlines in Michaeltree: New and Collected Poems* (2000). He received a Guggenheim fellowship in 1976 and a National Endowment for the Arts grant in 1977. From 1988 to 1993 he was poet laureate of Rhode Island, the first person to hold this position. A professor of English at Brown University since 1970, Harper numbers among his former students the novelist **Gayl Jones**, the poet **Kevin Young**, and the writer **Anthony Walton**, with whom Harper edited *The Vintage Book of African American Poetry* (2000) and the well-regarded anthology of postwar African American poetry *Every Shut Eye Ain't Asleep* (1994).

"Making, the mode of creation," Harper writes in "Notes on Making: The Heroic Pattern Updated: 1997" (2000), "is time-driven, and time-lost" (*Songlines*, 277). For Harper, history and art are as inextricably bound as a poem's form and content: an artist must represent the present moment in whatever medium—visual, aural, or written—best embodies her or his experience. This dictum is especially important for ethnic minorities, who have been literally and figuratively erased from the historical record, as he points out in "American History" (1970). There he links the 1963 bombing of a church in Alabama to the drowning of **Middle Passage** slaves in South Carolina during the nineteenth century and ends by asking, "Can't find what you can't see/can you?" (repr. in *Songlines*, 19). Creating art thus becomes a political act, since it announces, much like graffiti on the side of a building, a presence, which is then made permanent by art's inherent immortality. Arguably, as long as Harper's poem is read, someone will remember the deaths of the four girls and 500 slaves.

Throughout his work Harper praises and mourns those whose paintings, musical compositions, and writings serve as a permanent record, including **Romare Bearden**, Miles Davis, **Ernest James Gaines**, **Sterling A. Brown**, **Ralph Ellison**, and **Richard Wright**. "Alice" (1975), Harper's encomium, or poem of praise, for **Alice Walker**, depicts her discovery and marking of **Zora Neale Hurston**'s grave in Florida. "Double Elegy" (1985) acknowledges the literary debt he owes to **Robert Hayden** and James Wright. This concept of kinship extends beyond the confines of artistic creation to other key figures: **Joe Louis** wields "brute poetry" in "Homage to the Brown Bomber" (*Honorable Amendments*, 32–33). **Frederick Douglass**, **Paul Laurence Dunbar**, and

Harper's two sons who died in infancy are remembered elsewhere. "History as Apple Tree" (1972) stitches together fact (the founding of Rhode Island by Roger Williams, the settlement's short-lived tolerance of American Indians and African Americans), religious symbolism (in Western, Judeo-Christian beliefs, "apple" often signifies knowledge and temptation), cultural myth ("apple" also echoes the American fable told to illustrate George Washington's honesty), and metaphor (the poem suggests the interrelationship of history, individuals, imaginative representation, and geographic location in Harper's unique revisionist aesthetic in its ending: "black human photograph: apple tree") (repr. in *Songlines*, 80–81).

As he resees history through literature, Harper longs for unity on the microcosmic level of his individual poems and on the macrocosmic level of contemporary civilization. Although he criticizes White writers, such as John Berryman, in "Tongue-Tied in Black and White" (1977), who appropriate Black idioms in their work, he closely identifies with the White Modernists W. H. Auden and William Butler Yeats. His presence in the "black tower," as he terms it in "Psychophotos of Hampton" (1977), allows him to look out over art's "great rainbowed swamp" and read or reject at will (35). This willingness to collate themes and techniques from across the cultural spectrum has earned Harper critical accolades, but the obscure personal codes that sometimes result have garnered negative reviews. "For me literature is a study in comparative humanity," Harper claimed in a 1990 interview (789), and indeed the poems reveal the need for thoughtful compassion in any activity that similarly seeks to flatter and foment, scan and sing, riff and roam. (*See* **Modernism.**)

Resources: Primary Sources: Michael S. Harper: *Dear John, Dear Coltrane* (Pittsburgh, PA: University of Pittsburgh Press, 1970); *Debridement* (Garden City, NY: Doubleday, 1973); *Healing Song for the Inner Ear* (Urbana: University of Illinois Press, 1985); *History Is Your Own Heartbeat* (Urbana: University of Illinois Press, 1971); *Honorable Amendments* (Urbana: University of Illinois Press, 1995); *Images of Kin: New and Selected Poems* (Urbana: University of Illinois Press,1977); "My Poetic Technique," in *Black American Literature and Humanism*, ed. R. Baxter Miller (Lexington: University Press of Kentucky, 1981), 27–32; *Nightmare Begins Responsibility* (Urbana: University of Illinois Press, 1975); *Song: I Want a Witness* (Pittsburgh, PA: University of Pittsburgh Press, 1972); *Vintage Book of African American Poetry* (New York: Vintage Books, 2000). Michael Harper, ed., *Collected Poems of Sterling A. Brown* (Evanston, IL: TriQuarterly Books, 1996); Michael Harper and Anthony Walton, eds.: *Every Shut Eye Ain't Asleep: An Anthology of Poetry by African Americans Since 1945* (Boston: Little, Brown, 1994); *Songlines in Michaeltree: New and Collected Poems* (Urbana: University of Illinois Press, 2000); Michael S. Harper and Robert B. Stepto, eds., *Chant of Saints: A Gathering of Afro-American Literature, Art, and Scholarship* (Urbana: University of Illinois Press, 1979). **Secondary Sources:** Norris B. Clark, "Michael S. Harper," in *Dictionary of Literary Biography*, vol. 41; *Afro-American Poets Since 1955*, ed. Trudier Harris and Thadious M. Davis (Detroit: Gale, 1985), 152–166; Elizabeth Dodd, "The Great Rainbowed Swamp: History as Moral Ecology in the Poetry of

Michael S. Harper," in *Beyond Nature Writing: Expanding the Boundaries of Ecocriticism*, ed. Karla Armbruster and Kathleen R. Wallace (Charlottesville: University Press of Virginia, 2001), 177–194; "Michael S. Harper, American Poet: A Special Section," *Callaloo* 13, no. 4 (Autumn 1990), 749–829; Charles H. Rowell, "'Down Don't Worry Me': An Interview with Michael S. Harper," *Callaloo* 13, no. 4 (Autumn 1990), 780–800; Robert B. Stepto, "After Modernism, After Hibernation: Michael Harper, Robert Hayden, and Jay Wright," in *Chant of Saints*, ed. Michael S. Harper and Stepto (Urbana: University of Illinois Press, 1979), 470–487.

Jessica Allen

Harper, Phillip Brian (born 1961). Literary critic and cultural theorist. Working across academic disciplines and engaging with a range of theoretical models, Phillip Brian Harper is regarded as a leading practitioner of Black cultural studies and one of the most innovative theorists of the relay between the public and private spheres of contemporary American social life.

Harper is Professor of English and Director of American Studies at New York University, and serves on the editorial boards of the journals *Camera Obscura*, *Social Text*, and *GLQ*. In 1981 he received an A.B. in literature and creative writing from the University of Michigan. Harper pursued graduate study at Cornell University, where he received an M.F.A. in creative writing in 1985 and a Ph.D. in English in 1988. His dissertation, which examines the historically decentered subjectivities that constitute the "social logic" of **postmodernism**, was published as *Framing the Margins* in 1994. The monograph stands as a revisionary historicization of postmodern culture's emergence out of "socially marginalized and politically disenfranchised" groups, as one finds represented, for example, in novels by **Gwendolyn Brooks** and **Ralph Ellison**.

The publication of *Are We Not Men?* in 1996 signaled new ways of thinking the intersection of **race**, class, **gender**, and sexuality in the field of U.S. cultural production through the then-understudied subject of Black masculinity. Drawing from a vast repertoire of written texts, print and televisual images, and musical performances, Harper traces the modes by which Black manhood has come to embody discrete social fissures, tensions, and anxieties in American culture. His readings of the **rap** group Run-DMC and the O. J. Simpson trial highlight the commercialized appropriation of Black masculinity, but Harper is also careful to point out how both the mass media and the African American community have routinely held back frank acknowledgment of the growing AIDS epidemic among Black males. The complex motivations for this silence, ranging from homophobia to class politics, inform the subject of Harper's most recent book, *Private Affairs* (1999). The study deconstructs the public/private binary in social relations through a queer critique of American culture's rendering public spectacles out of "private" same-sex acts of intimacy. Here Harper's critical practice reflects the confounding of public and private boundaries in the way he uses **autobiography** to frame analysis of contemporary visual culture. Such scholarship reconfigures the relation between textual and social concerns, thereby extending its consequences for academic and political life. (*See* **Queer Theory**.)

Resources: *Are We Not Men? Masculine Anxiety and the Problem of African-American Identity* (New York: Oxford University Press, 1996); Brian Philip Harper: *Framing the Margins: The Social Logic of Postmodern Culture* (New York: Oxford University Press, 1994); *Private Affairs: Critical Ventures in the Culture of Social Relations* (New York: New York University Press, 1999).

Kinohi Nishikawa

Harrington, Oliver (Ollie) (1912–1995). Cartoonist. Harrington was an accomplished, highly regarded, and well-recognized cartoonist of the twentieth century. Combining trenchant visual imagery and provocative captions, he augmented the African American literary tradition through his large body of narrative efforts for several publications throughout his long career. Born in Valhalla, New York, on February 14, 1912, he was trained at the Yale School of Fine Art and began creating cartoons for various Black **newspapers**.

He socialized with many of the literary figures of the **Harlem Renaissance**, especially **Langston Hughes**, who remained a friend and supporter for life. By 1935, he developed his signature series, *Dark Laughter*, for the **Amsterdam News**, the era's major Black newspaper. This cartoon featured as its main character Bootsie, a bald, hefty African American male whose adventures shed humorous and critical light on American **race**, life, and culture. Bootsie's popularity made him a fictional celebrity in **Harlem, New York**, and led other Black papers, including the **Pittsburgh Courier** and the **Baltimore Afro-American**, to feature Harrington's cartoons.

During **World War II**, Harrington created cartoons addressing the scandal of **lynching** and government indifference toward the continuing murders of African Americans. He also produced many other works critiquing American racism and social injustice. Later, his leftist political views brought him official attention during the anticommunist hysteria of the early **Cold War**. In 1951, he left the United States and lived as an expatriate in Europe. In **Paris, France**, he joined the vibrant Black creative community that included **Richard Wright**, **James Baldwin**, Beauford Delaney, **Chester Himes**, and many others.

During his self-imposed exile, Harrington produced radical cartoons for various publications, including the American Communist *Daily World*. His themes included scathing attacks on domestic racism, South African apartheid, the Reagan administration, global capitalism, imperialism, nuclear proliferation, poverty, and homelessness. He died on November 2, 1995 in Berlin. (*See* **Expatriate Writers**.)

Resources: Michel Fabre, *From Harlem to Paris: Black American Writers in France, 1840–1980* (Urbana: University of Illinois Press, 1991); Oliver Harrington: *Bootsie and Others: A Selection of Cartoons by Ollie Harrington* (New York: Dodd, Mead, 1958); *Why I Left America and Other Essays*, ed. M. Thomas Inge (Jackson: University Press of Mississippi, 1993); Chester Himes, My *Life of Absurdity* (New York: Doubleday, 1976); M. Thomas Inge, ed., *The Satiric Art of Oliver W. Harrington* (Jackson: University Press of Mississippi, 1993).

Paul Von Blum

Harris, Bill (born 1941). Playwright, poet, and essayist. Formerly the production coordinator for Jazz Mobile and the New Federal Theatre in New York City, Bill Harris has also served as the chief curator at the Charles H. Wright Museum of African American History in **Detroit, Michigan**.

Harris's plays include *Stories About the Old Days* (1990) and *Riffs & Coda* (1998). Some of his plays and poetry have been published in anthologies such as *The National Black Drama Anthology: New Plays for the Black Theatre*, *Voices of Color*, edited by Woodie King, Jr., and *African American Literature*, edited by Al Young.

Harris's plays have been performed in many theaters across the country. For example, *Stories About the Old Days* starred Abbey Lincoln and has been performed at the North Coast Repertory Theatre in Solana Beach, California; the Karamu Playhouse in Cleveland, Ohio; the Freedom Theatre in **Philadelphia, Pennsylvania**; and the New Federal Theatre in New York City. *Every Goodbye Ain't Gone* starred Denzel Washington and S. Epatha Merkerson, and has been performed at the New Federal Theatre in New York City (2000); Carrie Production, Burbank (1997); Billie Holliday Theater (1989), and Southern Illinois University (1988).

Harris's two volumes of poetry are *Yardbird Suite: Side One* (1997), a collection about Charlie Parker, and *The Ring Master's Array* (1997), a collection of poetry honoring visual and musical artists.

An excerpt from Harris's *Coda* (1993), a full-length drama with music, was presented on Bravo, the Canadian cable network. His *Robert Johnson: Trick the Devil* aired on the Public Broadcasting System in a half-hour version.

As a playwright and poet, Harris has received many awards for his works. In 2001, he received the Charles H. Gershenson Distinguished Faculty Fellow Award at Wayne State University. He was awarded the Silver Medal for Drama (1997) by the International Radio Programming Festival. He received the Naomi Long Madgett Poetry Award (1996) for *Yardbird Suite: Side One*.

Harris's contributions to African American poetry and **drama** have established him as a leading literary artist. His work embodies a celebration of historical and contemporary African American culture. An active member of the community, he is currently working on several plays and two novels—one is set in 1954, during the era of **McCarthyism**, and the other is a mystery set on an Alabama plantation in 1854. He is also completing an epic poem on **minstrelsy**. (*See* **Epic Poetry/The Long Poem**.)

Resources: Bill Harris: "He Who Endures," in *American Literature: A Brief Introduction and Anthology* (New York: HarperCollins, 1996); *Riffs & Coda* (Detroit: Broadside Press, 1998); *The Ringmaster's Array* (Ferndale, MI: Past Tents Press, 1997); "Robert Johnson: Trick the Devil," in *The National Black Drama Anthology* (New

York: Applause Books, 1995); *Stories About the Old Days* (New York: Samuel French, 1990); "Up and Gone Again," in *Roots & Blossoms: African American Plays for Today*, ed. Daphne Williams Ntiri (Troy, MI: Bedford Publishing, 1991); *Yardbird Suite: Side One* (East Lansing: Michigan State University Press, 1977); Al Hunter, Jr. "Robert Johnson, a Bedeviling Challenge: Play Tries to Demystify the 30s Blues Legend," *Philadelphia Daily News*, Mar. 4, 2004, p. 35; Douglas J. Keating, "Blueman's Story Devilishly Well Told," *Inquirer Theater Critic*, Feb. 20, 2004, p. 40; Glen Manisto, "Books Unbound: A Festival of Artist–Poet Collaborations Invades the Scene," [Detroit] *Metro Times*, Mar. 26–Apr. 1, 2003, pp. 22–23; Judith Newmark, "African-American Folk Hero Comes to Life—in Song," *St. Louis Post Dispatch*, Oct. 12, 2001, p. E-1; Kimberly Roberts, "A Devil of a Delight, 'Trick the Devil' Swings with Jook-Joint Swagger in Latest Production at Freedom Theatre," *Philadelphia Sunday Tribune*, Feb. 22, 2004, sec. D, p. 1.

Ella Davis

Harris, E[verette] Lynn (born 1955). Novelist. Harris's several novels portray nonnormative, nonmainstream sexualities in African American communities. The fact that these novels have been embraced by a largely African American readership, both straight and gay, is testimony to his immense popularity in these communities.

Harris's rise to literary stardom began inauspiciously. His first novel, *Invisible Life* (1991), failed to find a major publisher. Harris resorted to selling the book out of his car trunk and in beauty shops patronized primarily by Blacks, among other unusual book vending venues. Favorable word-of-mouth brought Harris to the attention of the publishing powerhouse Anchor, which reissued *Invisible Life* in a trade paperback in 1994. That same year, *Just as I Am*, the sequel to *Invisible Life*, was published by Anchor. Since then, Harris has published six additional novels as well as a memoir, all by Doubleday. Each of Harris's novels has made best-seller lists, with the latter six appearing on the venerable *New York Times* list.

Harris's commercial success is notable primarily because of the content of his novels. He frequently discusses the intricacies of same-sex relationships in these texts, relationships that are presumed to be nonexistent in African American communities. For instance, one of Harris's several recurring characters is Raymond Tyler, Jr., a thirty-something attorney who falls in love with ex-professional football player Basil Henderson. Over the course of several novels, Tyler is wooed and disappointed by Henderson. During the process, Tyler becomes more comfortable with his (homo)sexuality, while Henderson grows more and more frustrated with his, most likely because Henderson feels restrained by the expectations the mainstream culture has foisted onto him, expectations which assume that heterosexuality is the norm. Another noteworthy gay character in Harris's novels is Raymond's best friend, Kyle. Conceived of and written as a flamboyant alternative to Raymond's more staid subjectivity, Kyle pays the ultimate price for his ostentatious ontology, dying from AIDS-related complications in *Just as I Am*. Kyle's spirit and untimely passing haunt Raymond and, in a failed bid at magic realism, Kyle reappears in a subsequent novel, although this reconjuring will strike some readers as unnecessarily contrived.

Prior to becoming a writer, Harris held highly paid corporate jobs at multinational corporations, including International Business Machines. He frequently infuses his knowledge of corporate America into his novels, providing a palpable tinge of authenticity. Although these positions brought him monetary satisfaction, it has, as his memoir suggests, been primarily through writing that Harris has achieved a more thorough sense of accomplishment and self-worth. In addition to making the best-seller list, Harris has turned one of his novels, *Not a Day Goes By* (2000), into a successful touring stage play. He was also attached to the film remake of *Sparkle*, which stopped preproduction when its star, Aaliyah, was killed in 2001. Harris is frequently invited to college campuses, where he is revered for his writing. Harris has received an **NAACP** Image Award nomination and has been included on *Ebony* magazine's "Most Intriguing Blacks" list. (*See* **Gay Literature**.)

Resources: E. Lynn Harris: *Abide with Me* (New York: Doubleday, 1999); *And This Too Shall Pass: A Novel* (New York: Doubleday, 1996); *Any Way the Wind Blows* (New York: Doubleday, 2001); *If the World Were Mine* (New York: Doubleday, 1997); *Invisible Life* (1991; repr. New York: Anchor, 1994); *Just as I Am* (New York: Anchor, 1995); *Not a Day Goes By* (New York: Doubleday, 2000); *What Becomes of the Brokenhearted: A Memoir* (New York: Doubleday, 2003).

Chris Bell

Harris, Eddy L. (born 1956). Journalist, travel writer, and memoirist. Reflecting on his travels around the world and within the United States has allowed Eddy L. Harris to become one of the most perceptive contemporary writers on questions of identity, racism, and cultural difference. His nonfiction prose achieves a certain elegance, even lyricism, that confounds distinctions between aesthetics and critique.

A native of Kirkwood, Missouri, Harris has called the Midwest his home for much of his life. After receiving his B.A. from Stanford University in 1977, he studied in London and wrote for an English-language newspaper in **Paris, France**, before returning to **St. Louis, Missouri**. Harris has taught and served as writer-in-residence at Washington University in St. Louis, and his articles and reviews have appeared in *Outside* magazine, the *Washington Post*, and the *New York Times Book Review*. In October 2004 Harris won the Missouri Governor's Humanities Award; he currently divides his time between Paris and Maryland.

Harris has published four critically acclaimed travelogues, which he might prefer to call memoirs, given the deeply personal and self-reflexive nature of his writing. *Mississippi Solo* (1988) recounts his canoeing the entire length of the Mississippi River alone from Lake Itaska in Minnesota to **New Orleans, Louisiana**. Here Harris embarks on a quest of extraordinary import to the national cultural imaginary, most notably fictionalized in **Mark Twain's**

Adventures of Huckleberry Finn (1885). Though Harris's quest is frequently met with acts of generosity and encouragement, he also survives a few harrowing episodes that recall nature's color-blind force as well as the legacy of racism in the United States: a pack of wild dogs corners him into a showdown, and two backwoods hunters threaten to make him their prey.

Harris's most engaging work is *Native Stranger* (1992), which documents his extensive travels across the African continent from Tunisia to South Africa. Enduring physical hardship, including a bout with malaria, and bearing witness to the atrocities of ethnic cleansing and the machinations of government corruption (he is jailed in Liberia for refusing to give up his belongings), Harris comes to the uncomfortable but necessary conclusion that Africa is not, and never was, his home. His "roots" are in the United States, and the fact of cultural difference renders false the African American's essential or natural relation to Africa. Harris closes this chapter of his life by saying, "My skin is black. My culture is not. After almost a year in Africa, I have no answers. Only this one question remains: *Who am I?* I have more in common, it sometimes seems, with the Dutch Afrikaner, the Boer" (311).

In *South of Haunted Dreams* (1993) and *Still Life in Harlem* (1996), Harris returns to the United States to demythologize both the White fantasy of the American South and the Black dream of Harlem life. His motorcycle tour of **the South** is met with White resistance to Black mobility, and his two-year stay in **Harlem, New York**, is characterized by Black middle-class flight from the once vibrant neighborhood. *Living with the Nez Perce* (2005) will continue troubling fixed notions of the Black experience in the United States by tracing its complex yet intimate interconnections to other lives, peoples, and experiences. (*See* **Travel Writing.**)

Resources: Ineke Bockting, "Travel Writing as Autobiography: The Case of Eddy L. Harris," in *Writing Lives: American Biography and Autobiography,* ed. Hans Bak and Hans Krabbendam (Amsterdam: VU University Press, 1998), 146–155; Eddy L. Harris: *Living with the Nez Perce* (New York: Lyons, 2005); *Mississippi Solo: A River Quest* (New York: Lyons, 1988); *Native Stranger: A Black American's Journey into the Heart of Africa* (New York: Simon and Schuster, 1992); *South of Haunted Dreams: A Ride Through Slavery's Old Backyard* (New York: Simon and Schuster, 1993); *Still Life in Harlem* (New York: Henry Holt, 1996).

Kinohi Nishikawa

Harris, Peter J. (born 1955). Poet and editor. Born, raised, and educated in **Washington, D.C.,** Harris graduated from Howard University with a degree in journalism (1977). A nationally published poet since the late 1970s, he also teaches writing and has conducted creative writing workshops in educational institutions ranging from elementary schools through colleges in Maryland, Washington, D.C., and California.

His early poetry was influenced by major figures in the **Black Arts Movement** in the 1960s and 1970s, including **Gwendolyn Brooks, Haki Madhubuti, Larry Neal,** and **Jayne Cortez,** to name a few. His interest in Black literature was also inspired by the writings of poets **Henry Dumas**, with his effort to critique the American political economy and its historical legacies, and the dense, ritualistic poetry of **Jay Wright**. The expression of Black life using urban **vernacular** and the ritualism of call-and-response, historical for its strong sense of community, continues to influence Harris's poetry.

Between 1982 and 1999, firmly grounded in the ideas of fatherhood and Black love as imperative topics, Harris published and edited numerous magazines. *Genetic Dancers: The Magazine for and About the Artistry Within African/American Fathers* (1984–1991) was a quarterly publication that provided a forum for addressing family issues. The first issue of *Genetic Dancers* featured poetry by **Ntozake Shange** and **Kalamu ya Salaam**. The magazine *The Drumming Between Us: Black Love & Erotic Poetry* (1994–1999) featured work that asserted the importance of Black love. Harris's close association with Kamau Da'ood, cofounder of the Los Angeles World Stage, and his active membership in the Anansi Writers Workshop provided the inspiration for *Drumming*.

Harris's book of poetry, *Hand Me My Griot Clothes: The Autobiography of Junior Baby*, won the 1993 PEN Oakland Josephine Miles Award for Multicultural Literature. From 1999 to 2003, Harris was the producer and host of the Public Radio show *Inspiration House: Voice Music for Whole Living*, on which poets were invited to read with musical accompaniment. His work has also appeared in anthologies edited by **Terry McMillan** and **Kalamu Ya Salaam**.

Resources: Peter Harris: *Hand Me My Griot Clothes: The Autobiography of Junior Baby* (Washington, DC: Black Classic Press, 1993); Sebastian Matthews, "Uncensored Voice: A Talk with Peter J. Harris," *North Carolina: Literary Arts Journal* 1, no. 1 (Winter 2002), 8–14; Terry McMillan, ed., *Breaking Ice: An Anthology of Contemporary African-American Fiction* (New York: Penguin, 1990); Kalamu ya Salaam and Kwame Alexander, *360°: A Revolution of Black Poets* (Alexandria, VA: BlackWords, 1998).

Nancy M. Padron

Harris, Trudier (born 1948). Literary critic, memoirist, and professor. Trudier Harris's contributions to criticism on African American literature have focused on depictions of Black women in African American literature and on the ways in which Black **folklore** informs African American literature. The body of Harris's insightful, accessibly written criticism approaches an encyclopedic treatment of women's depiction in African American literature.

Harris has often integrated her dual interests in Black folklore and depictions of Black women. For instance, in *From Mammies to Militants* she explores the possibility that Black women domestics, members of the Black folk community, might circulate folk narratives about Black domestics' lives that also occur in African American literature and thus shed light on Black folklore's influence on the literature. Her study argues that domestics in African American literature show an enduring connection to the folk communities from which they come, and it traces the arc of forms of resistance available to such women between the historical figures of the mammy and the militant. In *Fiction and Folklore* Harris examines the presence of folkloric elements in the work of **Toni Morrison**, which features women as central characters. *Black Women in the Fiction of James Baldwin* also focuses on the work of a single author, showing that Baldwin's women are limited by their notions of what is possible for them as women. Harris notes that *how* Baldwin's narratives are told reflects the women characters' limitations: "Most of the women are revealed through omniscient narration or through male narrators in a third-person, limited point of view" (10). Harris notes that the most memorable of Baldwin's women characters "are solidly within the tradition of the fundamentalist church as it exists in black communities," a fact that places narrow constraints on their abilities to develop as individuals (5).

Harris's memoir, *Summer Snow: Reflections from a Black Daughter of the South*, also pays particular attention to Black women's lives, tracing the ways in which women in midcentury Tuscaloosa, Alabama, shaped Harris's experiences growing up. *Summer Snow* demonstrates the author's double consciousness as an academic and as a daughter of Black folk culture through the many connections it draws between works of African American literature and the folkways in which Harris was raised. At the same time that Harris's advanced education gave her a depth of knowledge about Black literature that few can match, mastery of Standard English and its literature marked her as a "black nerd." She has been a Professor of English at the College of William and Mary and at the University of North Carolina at Chapel Hill. (*See* **Baldwin, James.**)

Resources: Trudier Harris: *Black Women in the Fiction of James Baldwin* (Knoxville: University of Tennessee Press, 1985); *Exorcising Blackness: Historical and Literary Lynching and Burning Rituals* (Bloomington: Indiana University Press, 1984); *Fiction and Folklore: The Novels of Toni Morrison* (Knoxville: University of Tennessee Press, 1993); *From Mammies to Militants: Domestics in Black American Literature* (Philadelphia: Temple University Press, 1982); *The Power of the Porch: The Storyteller's Craft in Zora Neale Hurston, Gloria Naylor, and Randall Kenan* (Athens: University of Georgia Press, 1996); *Saints, Sinners, Saviors: Strong Black Women in African American Literature* (New York: Palgrave, 2001); *Summer Snow: Reflections from a Black Daughter of the South* (Boston: Beacon Press, 2003); Trudier Harris-Lopez, *South of Tradition: Essays on African American Literature* (Athens: University of Georgia Press, 2002); Loverlie King and Trudier Harris, *A Student's Guide to the Study of African American Literature: 1760 to the Present* (New York: Peter Lang, 2003).

Douglas Steward

Harrison, Hubert Henry (1883–1927). Journalist, essayist, editor, and critic. Harrison, a self-educated working-class intellectual, wrote and lectured on history, politics, science, literature, and the theater from a race-conscious, class-conscious, internationalist, and mass-oriented perspective. He was the leading Black activist and theoretician in the Socialist Party (1911–1914);

founded *The Voice* and the Liberty League, the first newspaper and the first organization of the militant **New Negro** movement (1917); and he edited and reshaped **Marcus Garvey**'s *Negro World* into a powerful international political and literary force that, with the "Poetry for the People" and book review sections he initiated, fostered a mass interest in literature and the arts (1920–1922). Harrison served as the first regular African American book reviewer (1920–1922), was a featured lecturer for the New York City Board of Education's "Literary Lights of Yesterday and Today" series (1922–1926), and was a cofounder and builder of the Department of Negro Literature and History of the 135th Street Public Library (1925–1927), which subsequently grew into the internationally famous Schomburg Center for Research in Black Culture.

Born in St. Croix, Virgin Islands, Danish West Indies, Harrison immigrated to New York in 1900 and lived in **Harlem, New York**, from 1907 until his death. Beginning in his teens, many of his letters were published in the *New York Times*, and in 1907 his comments on literary criticism were featured in the *Times Saturday Review of Books*. In 1911 he served as an editor of *The Masses*, which soon grew into America's foremost left-literary publication. His influential paper, *The Voice*, was soon followed by other **New Negro** publications, including **A. Philip Randolph** and Chandler Owen's *Messenger* (1917), Garvey's *Negro World* (1918), Cyril Briggs's *Crusader* (1918), and Harrison's *New Negro* (1919). His writings appeared in the major Black newspapers and in prominent periodicals of the day, and his two books, *The Negro and the Nation* (1917) and *When Africa Awakes* (1920), are collections of some of his editorials, reviews, and articles.

Harrison's mass-oriented literary/political New Negro movement marked a major shift from the White patron-based leadership of **Booker T. Washington** and the **"Talented Tenth"** orientation advanced by **W.E.B. Du Bois**, and it preceded, and was qualitatively different from, the more middle-class, arts-based, and apolitical movement associated with the 1925 publication of **Alain Locke**'s *The New Negro*. Critically independent, Harrison challenged the genuineness of the Black "literary renaissance" of the 1920s because of what he saw as a tendency to take standards of value ready-made from White society and because there had been an uninterrupted, though much ignored, stream of literary and artistic products flowing from Black writers since the 1850s. The historian J. A. Rogers considered Harrison "perhaps the foremost Afro-American intellect of his time" (vol. 2, 432), and the activist A. Philip Randolph referred to him as the father of Harlem radicalism. Harrison was very popular among his contemporaries, and thousands attended his Harlem funeral.

Resources: Philip S. Foner, *American Socialism and Black Americans: From the Age of Jackson to World War II* (Westport, CT: Greenwood Press, 1977); Kevin K. Gaines, *Uplifting the Race: Black Leadership, Politics, and Culture in the Twentieth Century* (Chapel Hill: University of North Carolina Press, 1996); Hubert Harrison: *The Negro and the Nation* (New York: Cosmo-Advocate, 1917); *When Africa Awakes: The "Inside Story" of the Stirrings and Strivings of the New Negro in the Western World* (Baltimore: Black Classics Press, 1996); Portia James, "Hubert H. Harrison and the New Negro

Movement," *Western Journal of Black Studies* 13 (1989), 82–91; Winston James, *Holding Aloft the Banner of Ethiopia: Caribbean Radicalism in Early Twentieth-Century America* (New York: Verso, 1999); Jeffrey B. Perry, ed., *A Hubert Harrison Reader* (Middletown, CT: Wesleyan University Press, 2001); Joel A. Rogers, "Hubert Henry Harrison: Intellectual Giant and Free-Lance Educator," in Joel A. Rogers, *World's Great Men of Color*, vol. 2, ed. John Henrik Clarke (New York: Macmillan, 1972), 432–442.

Jeffrey B. Perry

Haskins, James S. (born 1941). Children's writer. Known for his nonfiction books for young readers, Haskins was born in Demopolis, Alabama. In 1960, when he was just nineteen years old, he completed a B.A. in psychology at Georgetown University, and two years later, he earned a B.S. in history at Alabama State University. After completing an M.A. in social psychology at the University of New Mexico in 1963, he worked for two years as a stock trader and as a reporter for the *New York Daily News*. Then he did further graduate study at the New School for Social Research from 1965 to 1967 and at Queens College of the City University of New York from 1968 to 1970. During this period, he was employed as a high school teacher. From 1970 to 1977, he was an associate professor at Staten Island Community College of the City University of New York and a visiting lecturer at Indiana University/Purdue University at Indianapolis and at the College of New Rochelle in New York. In 1977, he joined the faculty at the University of Florida, where he has subsequently taught as a full professor in the English Department. Throughout his career, he has been an active member of a long list of advisory boards.

An extraordinarily prolific author, Haskins has written, cowritten, or edited more than 160 books. His contributions to **children's literature** and young-adult literature have been acknowledged through a long list of citations, awards, and other honors. His books can be divided into six broad categories: nonfiction on topics of African American interest, including historical events, **folklore**, literature, social issues, and popular culture; biographies of prominent African Americans, including statesmen and politicians, social activists, performers, and athletes; cowritten celebrity autobiographies; general-interest nonfiction titles; guides and handbooks; and titles in the "Count Your Way" series, which introduce children to the geography, history, and culture of a long list of nations by way of the numbers one through ten, expressed in the languages of those nations.

Resources: Primary Sources: James Haskins: *African American Entrepreneurs* (New York: Wiley, 1998); *Against All Opposition: Black Explorers in America* (New York: Walker, 1992); *Black Dance in America: A History through Its People* (New York: Crowell, 1990); *Black Music in America: A History through Its People* (New York: Crowell, 1987); *Black Theatre in America* (New York: Crowell, 1982); *Blacks in Colonial America* (New York: Lothrop, Lee & Shepard, 1999); *Colin Powell: A Biography* (New York: Scholastic, 1992); *Deep Like the Rivers: A Biography of Langston Hughes, 1902–1967* (New York: Holt, 1973); *Diary of a Harlem School Teacher* (New York: Grove, 1969); *The Geography of Hope: Black Exodus from the South after Reconstruction* (Brookfield,

CT: Twenty-first Century Books, 1999); *The Harlem Renaissance* (Brookfield, CT: Millbrook, 1996); *The Life and Death of Martin Luther King, Jr.* (New York: Lothrop, Lee & Shepard, 1977); *The Long Struggle: The Story of American Labor* (Philadelphia: Westminster, 1976); *Louis Farrakhan and the Nation of Islam* (New York: Walker, 1996); *One Nation Under a Groove: Rap Music and Its Roots* (New York: Hyperion, 2000); *Resistance: Profiles in Nonviolence* (Garden City, NY: Doubleday, 1970); *The Scottsboro Boys* (New York: Holt, 1994); *Spike Lee: By Any Means Necessary* (New York: Walker, 1997); *Street Gangs: Yesterday and Today* (New York: Hastings House, 1974); *Thurgood Marshall: A Life for Justice* (New York: Holt, 1992); *Voodoo and Hoodoo: Their Tradition and Craft as Revealed by Actual Practitioners* (New York: Stein and Day, 1978); James Haskins and Kathleen Benson, *Bound for America: The Forced Migration of Africans to the New World* (New York: Lothrop, Lee & Shepard, 1999); James Haskins and Rosa Parks, *The Autobiography of Rosa Parks* (New York: Dial, 1990). **Secondary Sources:** Beth Dunlop, "Books on African-American History Transcend Race," *Miami Herald*, Feb. 3, 1995, p. F5; John S. Wilson, "Review of *Mabel Mercer: A Life*" (with comments on Haskins's other biographies), *New York Times Book Review*, Feb. 28, 1988, p. 21.

Martin Kich

Hassan, Umar Bin (born 1948). Poet. Hassan has been a member of the various incarnations of the spoken-word group **The Last Poets**.

Born in Akron, Ohio, as Jerome Huling, Hassan moved to New York City and joined The Last Poets for their first recording, *The Last Poets*, in 1970. Two more albums followed: *This Is Madness* (1971) and *At Last* (1974).

Hassan's association with The Last Poets has been a tumultuous one, and he has left and rejoined the group many times. In the 1980s he became addicted to powder and crack cocaine. In the early 1990s, while waiting to perform, Hassan was stabbed by a former Last Poets member, Jalal Nuridden, but he made a comeback with a new recording, *Be Bop or Be Dead* (1993).

With **Abiodun Oyewole**, he still performs under the name of The Last Poets. They have made two recordings: *Holy Terror* (1995) and *Time Has Come* (1997).

Resources: Eric Arnold, "What It Means to Be a Last Poet," http://archive. blackvoices.com/articles/daily/index_20010302.asp (Mar. 2001); Abiodun Oyewole, Umar Bin Hassan, and Kim Green, *The Last Poets on a Mission: Selected Poems and a History of the Last Poets* (New York: Henry Holt, 1996).

Patricia Kennedy Bostian

Hawkins, Walter Everette (1883–?). Poet. Hawkins, often called a transitional figure, moved away from the conservative, sentimental verse of traditional late nineteenth-century African American poetry to embrace social and political radicalism.

Born in Warrenton, North Carolina, Hawkins followed his brother in attending Kittrell College, graduating in 1901. He later moved to **Brooklyn, New York**, where he settled into life as a poet.

In his first published volume of poems, *Chords and Discords* (1909), Patterson wrote on both the racial concerns commonly addressed by Black writers at the time and the more sentimental topics of nature and love. In the book, he attacks the hypocrisy and materialism he sees in the Black community. He condemns **Booker T. Washington**'s accommodation views in a fierce attack presaging the more militant African American poetry to come.

Hawkins achieved prominence through his publications in the **Harlem, New York**, magazine *The Messenger*. "The Mob Victim," an antilynching poem published in *The Messenger*, drew the attention of the U.S. Department of Justice for its radical political views. The poem was one of the few race poems that appeared in the revised 1920 edition of *Chords and Discords*. This edition of the books was more radical in its socialist themes, yet it also showcased many poems of a sentimental nature.

The poetry of sentiment formed the bulk Hawkins's *Petals and Poppies* (1936). Although his leftist sympathies are seen in such poems as "My Heart Is a Poppy," Hawkins defended the inclusion of his sentimental poems. Following the precedent set in his early published works, he remained a transitional figure looking both forward in his radicalism and backward in his sentimentalism.

Resources: Dickson D. Bruce, "Walter Everette Hawkins," in *Dictionary of Literary Biography*, vol. 50, *Afro-American Writers Before the Harlem Renaissance* (Detroit: Thomson-Gale, 1986), 174–181; Walter Everette Hawkins: *Chords and Discords* (Washington, DC: Murray Brothers, 1909); *Petals and Poppies* (1936); Robert T. Kerlin, *Negro Poets and Their Poems*, 2nd ed., rev. and enl. (Washington, DC: Associated Publishers, 1935).

Patricia Kennedy Bostian

Hayden, Robert (1913–1980). Poet, professor, and Consultant in Poetry to the Library of Congress. Robert Hayden was born in **Detroit, Michigan**, in 1913 to Ruth Sheffey. His birth mother soon gave him up for adoption, although she would continue to be a presence in his childhood. Hayden's adoptive parents, William and Sue Hayden, were strict Baptists. William Hayden's religious beliefs and work ethic would play an important role in Robert's poetry. Hayden showed interest in writing at an early age, preferring books to sports. His early influences include **Countee Cullen**, Carl Sandburg, Edna St. Vincent, and **Langston Hughes**.

Hayden's poem "Africa" was published in 1931 in *Abbott's Monthly*, and a year later he enrolled at Detroit City College (now Wayne State University), where he majored in Spanish. During this time, he published poems in the *Detroit Collegian*, researched the **Underground Railroad** for the **Federal Writers' Project**, and twice received the Hopwood Award for poetry. In 1940, he published his first book of poems, *Heart-Shape in the Dust*. He began working on his M.A. at the University of Michigan in 1941. At Michigan, Hayden met W. H. Auden, whom he credited as a major influence on his work.

After graduating from the University of Michigan, Hayden taught at Fisk University in **Nashville, Tennessee,** from 1946 to 1969. Two important events during Hayden's tenure at Fisk solidified his place as a major American poet, bringing him the attention he desired and deserved, but in a way he could not have expected. On April 7, 1966, his *Ballad of Remembrance* received the Grand Prix de la Poésie at the World Festival of Negro Arts in Dakar, Senegal. The volume had been submitted by Dr. Rosey Pool, and the award validated Hayden's work. At the same time, however, Hayden was losing credibility on campus. The Black Writers' Conference at Fisk in April 1966 came during a period when students and writers wanted to see Black art take a decisively political stand. Hayden had not shied away from discussing his experiences as an African American in his work. Such poems as "Night, Death, Mississippi," "Homage to the Empress of the Blues," and "Middle Passage" are a few of those in *Ballad of Remembrance* that comment on the history, culture, and struggle of African Americans. Still, Hayden refused to be viewed or classified as a "Black poet." This placed him at a distance from his peers. Fisk placed its new writer-in-residence, **John Oliver Killens,** in charge of the conference. Hayden tried to defend his position but quickly become the target of criticism by other attendees, including the poet **Melvin B. Tolson.** The critic John Hatcher describes Hayden's view of his own work:

> Poetry to him was an art and he was a consummate poet. He dedicated himself to his art, and dedicated his art to mankind. Every spare minute of his life he devoted to the cause of becoming the best poet he was capable of becoming, and this is how he saw his usefulness as an individual, whether as a Black American, as a Baha'i, or simply as a human being. He cherished civil rights, abhorred the war in Vietnam, detested injustice and small-mindedness wherever it occurred, yet his standards for his art were inviolable. (*From the Auroral Darkness*, 39–40)

Hayden maintained this stance as a poet for the rest of his life, whether it was popular or not. In 1970, he returned to the University of Michigan as the first African American member of the English faculty. In 1976 was named Consultant in Poetry to the Library of Congress, a position that eventually became the nation's poet laureateship.

Hayden published several books of poetry while teaching: *The Lion and the Archer* (1948), *A Ballad of Remembrance* (1962), *Selected Poems* (1966), *Words in the Mourning Time* (1970), and *Angle of Ascent: New and Selected Poems* (1975). Race, religion, and childhood are central themes in Hayden's work. He joined the Baha'i faith in 1943, and later edited the Baha'i journal, *World Order*. His poem "Electrical Storm" deals with the issues of faith and education and the reconciliation of the two. The first stanza of the poem describes the strict religious views of his youth. The pious formerly "huddled under Jehovah's oldtime wrath" when the storms came (line 9), but the poem's narrator grows up and discovers the scientific explanation for thunderstorms:

"pressure systems/colliding massive energies." At the end of the poem, his neighbors must keep the narrator from crossing dangerous electrical lines that have fallen in his yard during a rainstorm. The value of faith even in the face of a rational, scientific explanations is questioned, and the poet recognizes that his higher learning cannot explain some things.

One of Hayden's best-known poems, "Those Winter Sundays," also reflects on his strict Baptist upbringing. Instead of science versus faith, however, this poem focuses on Hayden's relationship with his adoptive father. He comes to terms with his father's hard and sometimes cruel work ethic, learning that love can be "austere and lonely." As often is the case, Hayden's reflections on his childhood lead him away from easy definitions of right and wrong. He chooses to examine his subjects as real people and attempts to understand how their flaws make them human.

Hayden died in 1980. He never defined himself as exclusively or even primarily an African American poet, and he never understood the need for the distinction:

> There's a tendency today—more than a tendency, it's almost a conspiracy—to delimit poets, to restrict them to the political and the socially or racially conscious. To me, this indicates gross ignorance of the poet's true function as well as of the function and value of poetry as art. (King, 68)

Hayden wanted his work placed beside the rest of modern poetry, where it stands out as among the best.

Resources: Laurence Goldstein and Robert Chrisman, eds., *Robert Hayden: Essays on the Poetry* (Ann Arbor: University of Michigan Press, 2001); Michael S. Harper and Anthony Walton, eds., *The Vintage Book of African American Poetry* (New York: Vintage Books, 2000); John Hatcher, *From the Auroral Darkness: The Life and Poetry of Robert Hayden* (Oxford: G. Ronald, 1984); Robert Hayden: *Angle of Ascent: New and Selected Poems* (New York: Liveright, 1975); *A Ballad of Remembrance* (London: Paul Breman, 1962); *Collected Poems*, ed. Frederick Glaysher (New York: Liveright, 1985); *Heart-Shape in the Dust* (Detroit: Falcon Press, 1940); *The Night-Blooming Cereus*, 2nd ed. (London: Paul Breman, 1972); *Words in the Mourning Time* (New York: October House, 1970); Woodie King, Jr., *The Forerunners: Black Poets in America* (Washington, DC: Howard University Press, 1981); Pontheolla T. Williams, *Robert Hayden: A Critical Analysis of His Poetry* (Champaign: University of Illinois Press, 1987).

Jeff Cleek

Hayes, Terrance (born 1971). Poet and painter. Hayes's work ranges freely from references to pop culture icons such as Mr. T, Shaft, Fat Albert, and Big Bird to important literary and cultural figures, including **Paul Robeson, Billie Holliday, Audre Lorde**, and Betty Shabazz. His work also alludes to classical poets, including Homer, and mythic figures, including Orpheus. Hayes veers through time and poetic tradition to explore the multiple dimensions of Black male identity. His moods range from the sardonic to the sentimental; his modes of expression, from the lyric ardor of a poem such as "Autumn" (from the 2002 collection, *Hip Logic*) to the charged evocation of street rap in "Ballad of Bullethead" (from *Muscular Music*, 1999). He both claims and transcends a poetic past, paying wry and earnest tribute to literary ancestors as he plays artfully with traditional structures, bringing forth **prose poems**, dramatic monologues, **sonnets**, an invented eleven-line anagram, and revamped, revitalized sestinas and **villanelle**s.

Born in Columbia, South Carolina, Hayes was a talented athlete and a serious painter before turning his attention full-time to poetry. At Coker College, where he studied both painting and English, he played basketball and was an Academic All-American. Though he had written poems since adolescence, he was prompted to choose poetry as his profession after being deeply affected by two achingly rare poems about parenting and loss, **Gwendolyn Brooks**'s "The Mother" and **Robert Hayden**'s "Those Winter Sundays." He began a formal study of poetry and received his M.F.A from the University of Pittsburgh in 1997.

Hayes finds the emotional and intellectual challenge of making poems more gratifyingly difficult than the intuitive ease with which he composes his paintings. He continues to paint, though poetry is his primary focus; his art appears on the covers of his two award-winning collections. *Muscular Music* received a Whiting Writers Award and the Kate Tufts Discovery Award. *Hip Logic* was chosen by the poet **Cornelius Eady** for the National Poetry Series and was a finalist for the *Los Angeles Times* Book Award and the Academy of American Poets' James Laughlin Award.

A committed educator, Hayes has taught in Japan and has served as author-in-residence at the James Monroe Campus School's Family Literacy program in the Bronx. He lives with his wife, the poet Yona Harvey, and their children, Ua and Aaron, in Pittsburgh, where he is an associate professor of creative writing at Carnegie Mellon University.

Resources: Duriel E. Harris, "*Muscular Music* by Terrance Hayes," *Black Issues Book Review* 2, no. 6 (Nov./Dec. 2000), 53; Terrance Hayes: *Hip Logic* (New York: Penuin, 2002); *Muscular Music* (Chicago: Tia Chucha Press, 1999); Tonya Maria Matthews, "*Hip Logic* by Terrance Hayes," *Black Issues Book Review* 4, no. 5 (Sept./Oct. 2002), 49–50.

Kate Falvey

Haynes, David (born 1955). Novelist. In his novels both for adults and for young adults, David Haynes has focused on the experiences of African Americans in middle America—that is, middle-class families in the Midwest. A novelist in the realist mode, Haynes has seldom focused pointedly on issues of **race** in the manner of naturalistic or protest **literature**. Thus, his ostensibly conventional approach to depicting an often ignored segment of African American life has been quite unconventional and very distinctive. In 1996, *Granta* included Haynes on its list of the best young American novelists.

Haynes's first novel, *Right by My Side* (1993), treats the experiences of a fifteen-year-old boy named Marshall Field Finney, who attempts to come to terms with his parents' separation while trying to develop a mature sense of his own identity. The novel received a citation from the American Library Association as one of the best books for young adults of 1993. Haynes, however, had never conceived of it as a book written specifically for young adults.

Somebody Else's Mama (1995) may be Haynes's best-known and highly regarded novel. A domestic novel, it focuses on the Johnson family at a point when two decisions dramatically affect daily life in the household. Al Johnson decides to run for mayor of their Missouri town, and his wife Paula decides that her elderly mother-in-law should come to live with them. Haynes's portrayal of Paul's mother, called Miss Kezee, is fully engaging and transcends most of the clichés about feisty and eccentric old women.

Heathens (1996) is a collection of interrelated stories focusing on the Gabriel family. The father is a teacher who has gotten romantically involved with a real estate broker sentenced to jail for fraud. His wife does everything she can to sabotage the affair, while their twelve-year-old son tries to figure out adolescence as well as what his parents are doing to one another.

In *Live at Five* (1996), Haynes demonstrates that he can tackle racial issues head-on. In a ratings stunt, a television newsman named Brandon Wilson decides to move into a poor neighborhood, and unexpectedly discovers that the people who live there transcend stereotypes as much as or more than people of greater means.

All American Dream Dolls (1997) may be Haynes's most wryly comic and most pointedly satiric novel. It focuses on the two Wilkerson sisters. Deneen, a successful advertising executive, retreats to her family home in a self-indulgent funk after her boyfriend breaks off their relationship at the beginning of what was supposed to be a romantic getaway. For the first time, she gets to know her precocious twelve-year-old stepsister, who is so determined to become a beauty queen that she is in danger of developing an eating disorder.

In 1997, Haynes also published two novels clearly aimed at young-adult readers. The beginning of a series, the novels relate the daily activities, adventures, and misadventures of a group of young boys, known collectively as the West 7th Wildcats, who are growing up in a multicultural, middle-class neighborhood.

Haynes' most recent novel, *The Full Matilda* (2004), centers on Matilda Housewright, the matriarch of an African American family in **Washington, D.C.** Most of the men of the family work as butlers, gardeners, and chauffeurs in the homes of the wealthiest and most influential families of the capital. Over several generations, Matilda manages to keep her extended family together, despite the missteps of many of the men and despite the increasingly disruptive effects of social changes. In the end, Matilda is honored for her longevity and genuinely appreciated for her many contributions to the family, but she has become something of a caricature to her family and even something of a self-caricature.

Haynes coedited the anthology *Welcome to Your Life: Writings for the Heart of Young America* (1998).

Resources: Ronald Barron, "David Haynes: Chronicler of the African American Middle Class," *English Journal* 86 (Dec. 1997), 45–49; Daylanne K. English, "Somebody Else's Foremother: David Haynes and Zora Neale Hurston," *African American Review* 33 (Summer 1999), 283–297; Brad Hooper, "Read-Alikes: Male African American Fiction," *Booklist*, Feb. 15, 2002, p. 1005; David Haynes: *All American Dream Dolls* (Minneapolis, MN: Milkweed, 1997); *Business as Usual* (West 7th Wildcats 1) (Minneapolis, MN: Milkweed, 1997); *The Everyday Magic of Walterlee Higgins* (Minneapolis, MN: Minnesota Center for Book Arts, 1998); *The Full Matilda* (New York: Harlem Moon/Broadway, 2004); *The Gumma Wars* (West 7th Wildcats 2) (Minneapolis, MN: Milkweed, 1997); *Heathens* (Minneapolis, MN: New Rivers Press, 1996); *Live at Five* (Minneapolis, MN: Milkweed, 1996); *Right by My Side* (Minneapolis, MN: New Rivers, 1993); *Somebody Else's Mama* (Minneapolis, MN: Milkweed, 1995); Jill McCorkle, "Home Again," review of *Somebody Else's Mama*, *New York Times Book Review*, June 18, 1995, p. 21; Nathalie Op de Beeck, "David Haynes: A Twin Cities Maverick," *Publishers Weekly* Apr. 22, 1996, pp. 48–49; Nancy Pearl, "Waiting for Terry: African American Novels," *Library Journal*, Jan. 1, 2001, p. 200.

Martin Kich

Haynes, Lemuel (1753–1833). Essayist, short story writer, patriot, abolitionist, and preacher. Lemuel Haynes, one of the first published African American essayists and short story writers, was born to an African American father and a white mother in West Hartford, Connecticut. Five months after his birth, Haynes was carried to Middle Granville, Massachusetts, where he was raised in the household of Deacon David Rose as an indentured servant until he turned twenty-one, in 1774. That same year, he joined the American Revolution as a minuteman. As early as 1775, Haynes condemned slavery in his poem "The Battle of Lexington." During his tenure as a soldier, he urged that the American Revolution liberate those in bondage. In 1776 Haynes volunteered in the expedition that captured Fort Ticonderoga from the British, and he wrote "Liberty Further Extended: Or Free Thoughts on the Illegality of Slave-keeping." "The Battle of Lexington" and "Liberty Further Extended" are among the earliest extant works by an African American, yet they remained unpublished until the 1980s.

After serving in the Continental Army, Haynes became a minister in 1780. During his fifty-three-year career, he served as pastor of at least five White churches in Massachusetts, Connecticut, Vermont, and New York. Haynes, who is recognized as the first African American minister with White congregations, gained national and international recognition. In 1804 he was the first African American to receive an honorary Master of Arts degree; the degree was awarded by Middlebury College. "Universal Salvation" (1805), a sermon that appeared in more than seventy editions, and "Mystery Developed" (1820), an early example of a short story by an African American writer, are among Haynes's manuscripts that were published during his lifetime. Lemuel Haynes's prose legacy confirms his threefold pursuit for America's independence, **slavery**'s abolition, and the Revolutionary Era's greater spirituality.

Resources: Linda M. Carter, "Lemuel Haynes," in *Notable Black American Men*, ed. Jessie Carney Smith (Detroit: Gale, 1998), 532–533; Timothy Mather Cooley, *Sketches of the Life and Character of the Rev. Lemuel Haynes, A.M.* (1837; repr. New York: Negro Universities Press, 1969); Sidney Kaplan and Emma Nogrady Kaplan, *The Black Presence in the Era of the American Revolution*, rev. ed. (Amherst: University of Massachusetts Press, 1989); Richard Newman, ed.: *Black Preacher to White America: The Collected Writings of Lemuel Haynes, 1774–1833* (Brooklyn, NY: Carlson, 1990); *Lemuel Haynes: A Bio-Bibliography* (New York: Lambeth, 1984); John Saillant: *Black Puritan, Black Republican: The Life and Thought of Lemuel Haynes, 1753–1833* (New York: Oxford University Press, 2003); "Lemuel Haynes," in *The Oxford Companion to African American Literature*, ed. William L. Andrews, Frances Smith Foster, and Trudier Harris (New York: Oxford University Press, 1997), 348–349.

Linda M. Carter

Haywood, Gar Anthony (born 1954). Novelist. Haywood was raised, and continues to live, in Baldwin Hills, a suburb of **Los Angeles, California**. From 1976 to 1988, when his first novel was published, he worked as a field engineer for Bell Atlantic. He has since worked as a computer repairman to supplement the income from his novels. A largely self-taught writer, he has acknowledged being influenced by the novels of **Chester Himes** and has described the Cleveland, Ohio, mystery writer Les Roberts, whom he met while Roberts was writing screenplays in Los Angeles, as a mentor and friend.

Writing under the pseudonym **Ray Shannon**, Haywood has published a series of novels featuring the African American private investigator Aaron Gunner. Based in South Central Los Angeles, Gunner is a fairly traditional detective working in an all too combustible contemporary setting. *Fear of the Dark* (1988), Haywood's first novel and the first featuring Gunner, earned Haywood a Shamus Award for Best First Private Eye Novel. As he investigates the murder of an African American activist in a barroom shooting, Gunner's contacts run the gamut from young street thugs to highly placed political operatives. Eventually, Gunner himself becomes a suspect in the murder of a White supremacist. Other novels in the series have included *Not Long for This World* (1990), in which Gunner helps to clear a gangbanger of murder; *You Can Die Trying* (1993), in which he helps to exonerate a racist cop who has committed suicide in the wake of a controversial shooting; *It's Not a Pretty Sight* (1996), in which he tries to determine who murdered a former lover who had been a victim of abuse; *When Last Seen Alive* (1997), in which he investigates the disappearance of a young man during the Million Man March; and *All the Lucky Ones Are Dead* (1999), in which he sets out to prove that a gangsta rapper's apparent suicide was actually murder.

Haywood has also written two mystery novels featuring the husband-and-wife team of Joe and Dottie Loudermilk. Joe, a retired police officer, and Dottie, a retired college professor, travel around the country in Lucille, their

Airstream motorhome. A further ironic gimmick in these novels is that the Loudermilks are attempting to put some distance between themselves and their problematic children. The Loudermilk novels, *Going Nowhere Fast* (1994) and *Bad News Travels Fast* (1995), have a more comic tone than the Gunner series, but they nonetheless confront many gritty realities.

Resources: Gar Anthony Haywood: *All the Lucky Ones Are Dead* (New York: Putnam, 1999); *Bad News Travels Fast* (New York: Putnam, 1995); *Fear of the Dark* (New York: St. Martin's, 1988); *Going Nowhere Fast* (New York: Putnam, 1994); *It's Not a Pretty Sight* (New York: Putnam, 1996); *Not Long for This World* (New York: St. Martin's, 1990); *When Last Seen Alive* (New York: Putnam, 1997); *You Can Die Trying* (New York: Penguin, 1993); William F. Miller, "Shortage of Black Peers Is a Mystery to Writer," *Plain Dealer* (Cleveland, OH), Aug. 28, 1993, p. B8.

Martin Kich

Hazzard, Alvira (1899–1953). Playwright, poet, and short story writer during the **Harlem Renaissance**. A lesser known writer in the movement to portray African Americans as sophisticated, educated citizens, Hazzard produced plays that were performed in small community theaters. Born in North Brookfield, Massachusetts, to John and Rosetta Curry Hazzard, she attended the Worcester Normal School. Little is known about her literary aspirations during childhood. She devoted her early adult years to teaching in the **Boston, Massachusetts**, public schools and working as a clerk in the Boston City Hospital. The latter would remain her lifelong occupation. She remained single and wrote for personal satisfaction. Her focus on interracial relationships and the rejection of folk dialect in her writing suggest familiarity with the work of the activist and poet **Anne Spencer**, also a comparatively minor Harlem Renaissance writer.

Hazzard became a member of the exclusive Saturday Evening Quill Club. Founded in 1925 by young intellectuals, the club welcomed all writers and annually published a member-financed journal, *The Saturday Evening Quill* (1928–1930). Her two widely read plays, *Mother Liked It* (1928) and *Little Heads* (1929), were published in *The Saturday Evening Quill*. During this time, Hazzard formed friendships with *Quill* writers **Dorothy West** (*Prologue to a Life*) and **Helene Johnson** (*I Am Not Proud*). Other members of the club included Joseph Mitchell (*Son-Boy*) and Edythe Mae Gordon (*If Wishes Were Horses*). The Quill Club literary topics ranged from **lynching** to interracial relationships. Although the club lasted a short time, the writers received exposure, recognition, and personal satisfaction. Hazzard, like many women writers of her time, refused to portray African Americans, especially women, in a derogatory manner. *Mother Liked It*, a lighthearted comedy, satirizes desire and racial mixing. *Little Heads*, a drama, exposes the fallacy of racial status. Hazzard continued to write occasionally during the 1930s while working as a hospital clerk. She died of leukemia on January 10, 1953.

Resources: Lorraine Elena Roses and Ruth Elizabeth Randolph, *Harlem Renaissance and Beyond* (Boston: G. K. Hall, 1990); Lorraine E. Roses and Ruth E. Randolph, eds.,

Harlem's Glory: Black Women Writing, 1900–1950 (Cambridge, MA: Harvard University Press, 1996); *Zora Neale Hurston, Eulalie Spence, Marita Bonner, and Others: The Prize Plays and Other One-Acts Published in Periodicals* (New York: G. K. Hall, 1996).

Janice E. Fowler

Heard, Nathan (1936–2004). Novelist. Heard was born in Newark, New Jersey. He was raised by his mother, a **blues** singer, and by his maternal grandmother. At fifteen, he dropped out of school and spent most of the next seventeen years behind bars, first in reform school and then at the New Jersey State Prison at Trenton, where he served eight years of a thirteen-year sentence for armed robbery. After a fellow inmate introduced him to the work of such writers as Jean Genet, Samuel Beckett, and **Langston Hughes**, Heard became an avid reader. After he had read a large number of pulp novels, he decided that he could write more effectively and more credibly about crime and the hard realities of life on the streets of urban America. He has identified **James Baldwin, Richard Wright,** and Norman Mailer as major influences on his novelistic style.

Eight months before Heard was released from prison, his first novel, *Howard Street* (1968), was published. Because of its matter-of-fact description of urban squalor and its unsparing depiction of predatory behaviors, the novel created something of a sensation. Heard's criminal record, of course, only enhanced the sense of the novel's authenticity. Heard had actually written his second novel, *To Reach a Dream* (1972), before he had written *Howard Street*, but he was unable to find a publisher for the novel until the critical and commercial success of *Howard Street*. The story of a grifter who unexpectedly falls in love, *To Reach a Dream* is not as fully conceived or as fully realized as *Howard Street* is. Heard's other novels include *A Cold Fire Burning* (1974), which treats a street hustler's infatuation with a White social worker; *When Shadows Fall* (1977), which explores the subculture that surrounds drug dealing; and *House of Slammers* (1983), in which Heard attempts to present prison life as a consequential part of, rather than a separate existence from, the broader social and cultural mix. (*See* **Prison Literature**.)

Resources: Eric Beaumont, "The Nathan Heard Interviews," *African American Review* 28 (Fall 1994), 395–410; Christopher Hawtree, "Nathan Heard: Tough Teller of Hard Tales" (obituary), *Guardian* (London), May 12, 2004, p. 27; Nathan Heard: *A Cold Fire Burning* (New York: Simon and Schuster, 1974); *House of Slammers* (New York: Macmillan, 1983); *Howard Street* (New York: Dial Press, 1968); *To Reach a Dream* (New York: Dial Press, 1972); *When Shadows Fall* (New York: Playboy, 1977).

Martin Kich

Hemans, Donna (born 1970). Novelist. Born in Brown's Town, Jamaica, Hemans completed a B.A. in English and journalism at Fordham University and then earned an M.F.A. at American University. She has subsequently worked as a writing instructor at the Writers Center in Bethesda, Maryland.

Inviting almost inevitable comparisons with the works of **Jamaica Kincaid** and **Edwidge Danticat**, Hemans's first novel, *River Woman* (2002), is a tautly told story of interconnected crises in the life of a teenage single mother named Kelithe. She lives in the Jamaican town of Steadfast, located along the Rio Minho. Kelithe's mother, Sonya, had emigrated to New York City when Kelithe was a small child but had repeatedly promised to send for her as soon as she got settled. Kelithe has never entirely given up on the dream of being reunited with her mother.

One day, while Kelithe and the other women of her neighborhood are doing laundry at the river, her son, Timothy, who is little more than a toddler, drowns. Kelithe seems not to have recognized what was happening and, then, withdraws strangely in her grief. Her neighbors begin to wonder whether she let Timothy drown in order to be free of the burden of caring for him. It turns out that Sonya had finally agreed to provide a home for Kelithe in New York, but only on the condition that she leave Timothy to be raised by relatives in Jamaica. So there is some real suspense about whether Kelithe is culpable in her son's drowning. When Sonya returns to Steadfast, mother and daughter discover that they do not really know one another—that they may be one another's salvation or they may no longer mean anything to one another.

As Jeff Zaleski has pointed out in his review in *Publishers Weekly*, the novel explores the theme of abandonment on multiple levels, for the broader backdrop to Kelithe's story is the political crisis that develops as the residents of Steadfast and other poor Jamaican communities begin to protest the government's seeming disregard for their long economic stagnation. The novel also frames Kelithe's experiences in a broader cultural tradition, incorporating the folk myth of a treacherous river goddess named Mumma.

Resources: Donna Hemans, *River Woman* (New York: Washington Square, 2002); Sadeqa M. Johnson, "Review of *River Woman*," *Black Issues Book Review* 4 (Jan./Feb. 2003), 56; James Polk, "Review of *River Woman*," *New York Times Book Review*, July 28, 2002, p. 17; Renee H. Shea, "The New Voice of a Graceful Lady: An Interview with Donna Hemans," *MaComere: Journal of the Association of Caribbean Women Writers and Scholars* 3 (2000), 12–18; Jeff Zaleski, "Review of *River Woman*," *Publishers Weekly*, Dec. 24, 2001, p. 43.

Martin Kich

Hemings, Sally (1773–1835). Literary and historical figure. The slave who, according to tradition, bore children to Thomas Jefferson, Sally Hemings embodies some of the gravest consequences of **slavery**: the sexual exploitation of African American women by their white masters, and the complex and even hidden genealogies that resulted from these unions. Although the various narratives that focus upon Sally Hemings point out the moral corruption and hypocrisy of the author of the Declaration of Independence, these fictions also argue that the nation is the literal birthright of African Americans.

Not much is truly known of Sally Hemings. She was most likely the daughter of John Wayles, Jefferson's father-in-law. At fifteen, she accompanied Jefferson's daughter to **Paris, France**, where she served as her maid. In 1802, after years of public gossip, the journalist James Callender, in an apparent act of political revenge, reported that the president had children through a slave named Sally, a story that proved to be a major scandal during the presidential campaign of 1804. Jefferson eventually freed all of Hemings's children, an act he performed for no other family group of slaves. In the years after the death of Sally Hemings, her two sons, Madison and Eston, publicly claimed Thomas Jefferson as their father, an account that has passed down through generations of Hemingses. In 1998, genetic detectives gave greater credence to the gossip and the oral tradition when they announced that DNA evidence links Eston Hemings to the male line of the Jefferson family. Although the DNA evidence strongly links the Hemings and Jefferson families biologically, some historians still deny any possibility of a relationship between the president and his slave as inconsistent with his public moral character.

To nineteenth-century abolitionists, the idea of Sally Hemings, the slave–mistress to a president, established a blood connection between African American slaves and the founders of the nation. In an 1851 speech before a "Convention of Colored Citizens" that he subsequently published in his abolitionist newspaper, *The North Star*, **Frederick Douglass** declared that "the best blood of Virginia" flowed through the veins of slaves, to argue for full rights of citizenship on behalf of all African Americans. Other abolitionists made more direct references to Sally Hemings in their claims for African American suffrage. **William Wells Brown** published the anonymous poem "Jefferson's Daughter" in his abolitionist songbook, *The Anti-Slavery Harp*. In addition to its claims for a truly American paternity for slaves, the poem charges Jefferson with tyranny and hypocrisy for owning slaves while preaching liberty to a new nation.

In literature, Sally Hemings is a figure of romance: fair-skinned and so beautiful that the powerful find her irresistible. Werner Sollors argues that by employing this romantic image of Hemings in his novel *Clotel; or, the President's Daughter*, William Wells Brown "makes an interracial romance in the world of slavery the story of American origins" (209). Jefferson abandons his slave–lover and his slave–children to serve the call of his country, then promptly forgets them. Corrupted morally by the relationship with a powerful white man, Currer—Sally Hemings under another name—grooms her daughters to become concubines for great men as the only means of survival for a woman in slavery. The daughters are likewise representations of Sally Hemings, beautiful near-White slaves worshiped by wealthy and powerful men. Clotel is purchased at auction by her young lover, a man who, like Jefferson, will abandon her to the degradation of slavery. The other daughter,

Althesa, fares much better when she marries a White physician who purchased her after being struck by her chaste beauty. This romantic image of the
love-struck master and the beautiful near-White slave influences the central
narratives of such early African American novels as **Frank J. Webb**'s *The
Garies and Their Friends* and **Frances E. W. Harper**'s *Iola Leroy*.

In her novel *Sally Hemings*, **Barbara Chase-Riboud** has helped shape the
image of Sally Hemings and her relationship with Jefferson by blending
the romantic tradition with a feminist message of self-determination. The love
story between master and slave becomes as much a metaphor for the suffering
of women in a patriarchal society as it does for the abuses of slavery. Hemings
uses her position as privileged mistress to determine her own fate and free her
children. *The President's Daughter*, the sequel to *Sally Hemings*, continues
Chase-Riboud's saga of feminine self-determination, the daughter Harriet
passing as White and venturing through major historical events of the
nineteenth century.

Since the enigmatic Hemings left no written record, recent writers have
tried to give her a voice by imagining her inner life through letters and diaries.
In his recent poem "Sally Hemings to Thomas Jefferson," **Cyrus Cassells**
imagines a love letter to explore the emotional contradictions of a slave in
love. In her libretto for composer William Bolcom's song cycle *From the Diary
of Sally Hemings*, Sandra Seaton renders the complex inner life of a privileged
slave in a series of impressionistic entries in a diary that reflect upon moments
of romantic intimacy as well as the **middle passage**.

In satiric works, writers treat the idea of Sally Hemings less as a figure of
romance and more as an image of racial and sexual exploitation. Early in
Ralph Ellison's *Invisible Man*, one of the mental patients at the Golden Day
addresses the beleaguered White donor Norton as Thomas Jefferson, adding,
"I'm his grandson—on the 'field-nigger' side," implying that the oppression of
slavery lives on in the descendants of masters and slaves. In *Yellow Back Radio
Broke-Down*, **Ishmael Reed** connects Hemings to an ongoing legacy of imperialism by arguing that Jefferson's womanizing among the slaves directly
affected the nation's policy on slavery and expansion into the western terri-
tories.

Sally Hemings remains a controversial figure. In her play *House Arrest*,
Anna Deveare Smith uses the testimony of historians, tour guides, doc-
umentarians, and Jefferson himself to explore the vexed nature of the current
debate over the relationship between Hemings and the president. Both sides
of the debate having become entrenched, the subject of Sally Hemings has
become a litmus test for attitudes on **race** and history (Gordon-Reed).

Resources: Fawn Brodie, *Thomas Jefferson: An Intimate History* (New York: Norton,
1974); Ann duCille, *The Coupling Convention: Sex, Text, and Tradition in Black
Women's Fiction* (New York: Oxford University Press, 1993); William Edward Farri-
son, "Clotel, Thomas Jefferson, and Sally Hemings," *CLA Journal* 17 (1973), 147–
174; Eugene A. Foster et al., "Jefferson Fathered Slave's Last Child," *Nature* (Nov. 5,
1998), 27–28; Annette Gordon-Reed, *Thomas Jefferson and Sally Hemings: An*

American Controversy (Charlottesville: University Press of Virginia, 1997); Elise Lemire, *Miscegenation* (Philadelphia: University of Pennsylvania Press, 2002); Jan Ellen Lewis and Peter S. Onuf, eds., *Sally Hemings and Thomas Jefferson: History, Memory, and Civic Culture* (Charlottesville: University Press of Virginia, 1999); John Chester Miller, *The Wolf by the Ears: Thomas Jefferson and Slavery* (Charlottesville: University Press of Virginia, 1991); Werner Sollors, *Neither Black nor White yet Both: Thematic Explorations of Interracial Literature* (New York: Oxford University Press, 1997).

Charles D. Martin

Hemphill, Essex (1957–1995). Poet essayist, activist, and editor. Born in **Chicago, Illinois**, and raised in **Washington, D.C.**, Essex Hemphill was the leading Black gay poet of his generation and is widely regarded as one of the most important poets of the late twentieth century. His writing, editing, and political activity focused on the dual identities of being both Black and gay in the United States. Clearly influenced by **Langston Hughes** and **James Baldwin**, Hemphill's work may be linked to that of the contemporary poet–writer–activists **Audre Lorde** and **Melvin Dixon** through his insistence on breaking silence by privileging the knowledge and experiences of oppressed peoples, specifically of Black gays and lesbians.

After graduating from high school, Hemphill studied English at the University of Maryland and the University of the District of Columbia. At this time he proclaimed his gay identity and eschewed **Black Nationalism**, to which he had been attracted in his early twenties, because of its open homophobia and rigid insistence on maintaining traditional gender and sexual roles. He began publishing poetry and essays in important literary journals and magazines, among them **Callaloo**, *Black Scholar*, and *Essence*, and emerged as an important voice among Black gay and lesbian writers. The mid-1980s saw a flurry of publication for Hemphill. Two chapbooks, *Earth Life* (1985) and *Conditions* (1986), were privately printed. He contributed poems to *In the Life* (1986), a groundbreaking anthology of Black gay writings edited by **Joseph Beam**; they included "Isn't It Funny," "Better Days," "Cordon Negro," "Serious Moonlight," and "For My Own Protection." Hemphill's inclusion in this anthology began an important personal and literary friendship with Beam.

When Beam died of complications from AIDS in 1988, Hemphill assumed Beam's duties of collecting and editing manuscripts for another Black gay anthology, *Brother to Brother: New Writings by Black Gay Men* (1991), which won the American Library Association's Gay and Lesbian Book Award. The book's title page indicates the collaborative nature of the project, listing Hemphill as editor, Beam as the man who conceived and began work on the collection, and Beam's mother, Dorothy, as the project's manager. To this anthology, a welcome expansion on the ideas of breaking silence and expressing Black gay men's desires, fears, needs, and joys showcased first in *In the Life*, Hemphill contributed numerous pieces. Among these are the poems "Commitments," "The tomb of sorrow," and "When my brother fell," a moving tribute to Beam; an essay, "Undressing Icons"; and "*Looking for Langston*: An

Interview with Isaac Julien." These last two pieces are concerned with Isaac Julien's film *Looking for Langston*, controversial because of its depiction of Langston Hughes as gay man. To this film, Hemphill contributed poetry. Continuing to work with filmmakers, he appeared in Marlon Riggs's *Tongues Untied* and narrated a documentary on AIDS, *Out of the Shadows*.

Cleis Press published Hemphill's only major collection, *Ceremonies*, which contained both poetry and essays, in 1992. Hemphill is best known for this collection, which includes some of his earlier work, including poems from his chapbooks, and the work for which he is best remembered. Opening with a biographical and critical introduction by Charles S. Nero, *Ceremonies* is divided into seven sections. Poetry and essays alternate to produce the effect of Hemphill's total engagement with his subjects: Black gay men's desires and positions in White supremacist and heterosexist U.S. culture as well as the necessary pain and excitement that come with speaking the truth. Among the poems are "American Hero," "Black Machismo," "To Some Supposed Brothers," the explicit and famous "American Wedding," and "Heavy Breathing," which A. Boxwell calls Hemphill's "longest, most complex and deliberately provocative poem." In these poems, Hemphill is at his technical best and acutely conveys the need for a coming-to-voice of Black gay men. "Black Machismo" shatters the racist myth of Black males and large penis size as it incorporates social and personal history to understand stereotype. "To Some Supposed Brothers" admonishes those men who treat women as inferior objects to be used by those who are also oppressed—Black men. And "American Wedding" asserts the need for both physical and emotional love between Black men and promises that with every kiss between Black gay men, a new world comes (184). The essays in the collection also mark Hemphill as an important thinker and writer. "Does Your Momma Know About Me?" tackles AIDS, Robert Mapplethorpe's racist images of Black men, and the need for family and community; "If Freud Had Been a Neurotic Colored Woman: Reading Dr. Frances Cress Welsing" challenges homophobic attitudes among Black heterosexuals and academics; and "Ceremonies," a painful personal essay, details the exile in which Hemphill found himself as a gay adolescent and the actions he took to feign normalcy in the midst of antigay rhetoric.

Throughout his career, Hemphill received many awards, including grants from the National Endowment for the Arts and the Washington, D.C., Commission for the Arts, and the Gregory Kolovakos Award for AIDS Writing. After Hemphill's death of complications from AIDS on November 4, 1995, many Black gay and lesbian writers and activists paid tribute to him as a visionary poet and leader who made possible contemporary Black gay and lesbian writing and consciousness. (*See* **Gay Literature**.)

Resources: A. Boxwell, "'Where the Absence of Doo Wop Is Frightening': The Body Politic in Essex Hemphill's 'Heavy Breathing,'" paper given at the Conference on Contemporary Poetry: Poetry and the Public Sphere, Apr. 24–27, 1997, http://english.rutgers.edu/boxwell/htm; "Essex Hemphill," http://www.africanpubs.com; Thomas Glave, "(Re-)Recalling Essex Hemphill: Words to Our Now," *Callaloo* 23, no. 1 (2000), 278–284; Essex Hemphill, *Ceremonies: Prose and Poetry* (New York: Plume, 1992); Essex Hemphill, ed., *Brother to Brother: New Writings by Black Gay Men*, conceived by Joseph Beam (Boston: Alyson, 1991); Charles S. Nero, "Fixing Ceremonies: An Introduction," in *Ceremonies: Poetry and Prose*, by Essex Hemphill (San Francisco: Cleis Press, 1992).

Bill Clem

Henderson, David (born 1942). Poet. Born in **Harlem, New York**, and raised in the Bronx, David Henderson attended several colleges, but **Calvin Coolidge Hernton** recalls him as a "teenaged poet . . . practically living on the Lower East Side," sleeping on friends' sofas (580). By 1964, however, Henderson was a founding member of **Umbra Workshop** and had coedited a few issues of *Umbra* magazine, and two of his poems had appeared in *New Negro Poets: USA*.

In 1967, Henderson published *Felix of the Silent Forest*, with an introduction by **Amiri Baraka**, who affirms the poems' "purity of description," disclosing the "beauty of the place." That "place" is the Bowery where, viscerally at one with "the low in the streets," the poet's "cells . . . have memory/of siren days/ . . . a high kind of poison" that he transmutes into "third eye" vision, "the astral base of the Third World," shared by the "low" in this case, by the "conk heads" in "Black Art at the Oakland Skills Center" (in *Neo-California*, 1998), and by the Indian woman selling "lottery like pottery" in "Mexico City Subway Inaugural." *De Mayor of Harlem* (1970) and *The Low East* (1980) are more grim: "Walk with De Mayor of Harlem" is not "dream stuff," but a "nightcoach . . . to Auschwitz," and in "C.C.'s Blues" (**signifying** on Yeats's "The Second Coming"), C.C. *"don't see no Christmas."* Yet, by *Neo-California*, "the deities correspond/the powers here with us."

By the early 1970s, having given more than 100 readings, Henderson moved to Berkeley, California, where he edited *Umbra* until 1975 and wrote a biography of Jimi Hendrix. Henderson currently lives in New York City, where he teaches at the **Brooklyn** campus of Long Island University.

Resources: David Henderson: *De Mayor of Harlem* (New York: Dutton, 1970); *Felix of the Silent Forest*, intro. LeRoi Jones (New York: Poets Press, 1967); *The Low East* (Richmond, CA: North Atlantic Books, 1980); *Neo-California* (Berkeley, CA: North Atlantic Books, 1998); *The Poetry of David Henderson* (Soul Syndicate, 1968); "The Poetry of Soul" (mimeographed, n.d.); Calvin Hernton, "Umbra: A Personal Recounting," *African American Review* 4 (1993), 579–584.

Chauncey Ridley

Henderson, George Wylie (1904–1965). Novelist. George Wylie Henderson's work marks the interval between the heightened literary movement during the **Harlem Renaissance** in the 1920s and the social protest movement during the 1940s. His writing portrays the hopefulness and the helplessness experienced by African Americans who fled **the South** in search of better living conditions in the North during the years of the **Great Depression**.

Born in Warrior's Stand, Alabama, Henderson moved as a young child to Tuskegee, where his father became pastor of a local church. Following in his father's footsteps, Henderson attended college at Tuskegee Institute (University), where he learned printing. After completing his education at Tuskegee, he moved to New York City during the early years of the Depression, and he worked as a printer with the *Daily News*. He wrote short stories for the *News* and several magazines, including *Redbook*. It was not until the 1935 publication of *Ollie Miss* that Henderson became recognized as an accomplished writer.

Like **Zora Neale Hurston**, Henderson wrote from his personal experiences in the rural South, infusing the folk customs of the rural Negroes in *Ollie Miss*. Its sequel, *Jule* (1946), follows the pattern of another voice from the Harlem Renaissance, **Carl Van Vechten**, by concentrating on the nightlife in **Harlem, New York**. Anticipating **Richard Wright**, Henderson begins *Jule* with a typical flight motif, in which Jule is forced to escape from Alabama after a fight with a White man. Jule discovers, however, that there are opportunities in New York that did not exist in Alabama.

Resources: Peter Christensen, "George Wylie Henderson," in *African American Authors, 1745–1945: A Bio-Bibliographical Critical Sourcebook*, ed. Emmanuel S. Nelson (Westport, CT: Greenwood Press, 2000), 224–230; George Wylie Henderson, *Ollie Miss* (New York: F.A. Stokes, 1935); Noel Schraufnagel, *From Apology to Protest: The Black American Novel* (Deland, FL: Everett/Edwards, 1973), 16, 58–59.

Ondra K. Thomas-Krouse

Henry, John (c. 1870–present). Legendary figure and folk hero. The African American folk hero and icon of American popular culture, John Henry has been memorialized in the traditional blues-ballad of the same name, which is among the best-known of American folk songs. The narrative of "John Henry" concerns the trials of a sledgehammer-wielding African American working alongside other laborers in the blasting of a railroad tunnel through a mountain. When the railroad company brings a new steam-powered drilling machine to the site of the tunnel to replace the less efficient human workers, this laborer proposes a contest to determine which is superior: man or machine. The laborer wins the contest, displaying seemingly superhuman strength in doing so; in some versions of the tale, he dies from exhaustion after his victory. The laborer is known as "John Henry" in approximately 100 collected versions of the blues-ballad.

During the final years of the nineteenth century, many African Americans regarded John Henry as a symbol of strength in the midst of adversity. John Henry may also have been infused with ritual power adapted from West African **folklore**. For instance, he bears resemblance to Ogun, a Yoruban deity associated with iron and steel and charged with the task of building roads into new territory. In any event, the blues-ballad was first sung by Blacks across **the South**.

In the early twentieth century, John Henry became an icon for many working-class Southern Whites, who viewed the folk hero as symbolizing the importance of economically marginal people resisting the dehumanizing forces of industrialization. In the late 1920s and early 1930s, two White West Virginia-based scholars, Guy Johnson and Louis Chappell, investigated the origins of this blues-ballad. Johnson wrote *John Henry: Tracking Down a Negro Legend* (1929), and Chappell authored *John Henry: A Folk-Lore Study* (1933). Johnson and Chappell asserted that "John Henry" had been based on an actual incident involving a real person whose exact identity the scholars could not determine. Local traditions variously maintained that John Henry the person was born in Alabama, Georgia, North Carolina, or Virginia. Johnson and Chappell speculated that the incident described in "John Henry" occurred between 1870 and 1872, during construction of the Chesapeake and Ohio Railroad's Big Bend Tunnel in southeastern West Virginia.

Johnson's and Chappell's research into the blues-ballad has recently been challenged by the scholar John Garst, whose scholarly article concludes that the situating of John Henry in West Virginia is not supportable by documented evidence. Garst asserts that Johnson and Chappell had favored unreliable testimony when placing the incident in West Virginia, and that they had ignored letters sent them by railroad workers who claimed to have witnessed John Henry's feat along railroad tracks owned by the Columbus & Western Railway Company (C&WR) between Oak Mountain and Coosa Mountain near Leeds, Alabama, in 1887. The C&WR was later incorporated into the Central of Georgia Railroad, which today is known as the Norfolk Southern Railroad.

According to Garst, those letters provided clues, overlooked by Johnson and Chappell, that help clarify John Henry's identity, including an acknowledgment in one letter that the folk hero was a former slave born in Mississippi named "John Henry Dabner." Through Internet searches, Garst found 1870 census records from Mississippi that listed a male ex-slave named Henry Dabney, then aged twenty; he also unearthed strong circumstantial evidence that this person, Henry Dabney, lived in northern Alabama during the 1880s and was working on railroad tunnel construction in that vicinity.

Throughout the twentieth century, "John Henry" was a favorite song of countless American traditional, popular, and classical musicians. Sometimes the blues-ballad has brought its arrangers and performers considerable commercial success. In 1922 the African American composer W. C. Handy published a sheet music arrangement of the song, titled "John Henry Blues." In 1924 the White musician Fiddlin' John Carson recorded for the OKeh Phonograph Company a more traditional rendition of the blues-ballad, also titled "John Henry Blues," which was the first of many commercial and documentary sound recordings of "John Henry." Subsequent musicians to record versions of "John Henry" include the African American musicians **Leadbelly**, Josh White, Odetta, and Harry Belafonte, and the white musicians Woody Guthrie, Pete Seeger, Merle Travis, and Johnny Cash. In 1940, the American composer Aaron Copland composed a short piece for chamber orchestra based on the blues-ballad.

Nonmusicians—railroad workers, union organizers, visual artists, and authors—have also been interested in John Henry as hero and icon. The legend of John Henry has inspired creative works by African American authors, including poems by **Margaret Abigail Walker, Sterling A. Brown,** and **Melvin B. Tolson. Colson Whitehead**'s novel *John Henry Days* (2001) concerns a middle-class African American journalist who reassesses the John Henry legend and African American identity in general. The journalist is assigned to cover the annual John Henry Days festival in Talcott, West Virginia. Other African American fiction writers have utilized John Henry as a prototype for their own characters. **James Alan McPherson**, in his short story "A Solo Song: For Doc," infused the character Doc Craft with John Henry's qualities. In *Catherine Carmier* (1964) and *The Autobiography of Miss Jane Pittman* (1971), **Ernest J. Gaines** draws on the John Henry legend in constructing the characters Raoul Carmier in the former novel and Joe Pittman in the latter.

The story of John Henry has been retold in several literary works intended for younger readers written by African American authors, including **John Oliver Killens**'s 1975 novel *A Man Ain't Nothin' but a Man: The Adventures of John Henry* (1975) and **Julius Lester**'s illustrated children's book *John Henry* (1994). Works by White authors have also reinterpreted the John Henry legend, including Roark Bradford's stereotype-laden novel *John Henry* (1931). A musical based on Bradford's novel and featuring **Paul Robeson** was produced on Broadway. **Ezra Jack Keats**'s illustrated book *John Henry: An American Legend* appeared in 1965, and Terry Small's *The Legend of John Henry* was published in 1994.

In recent years, a number of scholars—most notably Archie Green and Norm Cohen—have chronicled the folkloric history of the John Henry legend in books as well as in articles published in scholarly periodicals. Brett Williams's *John Henry: A Bio-Bibliography* (1983) traces the evolution of John Henry as an iconic figure within mainstream American popular culture. Mary Ann Fitzwilson's article surveys the changing scholarly reception of the John Henry legend. (*See* **Ballad; Blues; Folktales; Labor.**)

Resources: Norm Cohen, *Long Steel Rail: The Railroad in American Folksong* (Urbana: University of Illinois Press, 1981); Mary Ann Fitzwilson, "With Hammers of Their Own Design: Scholarly Treatment of the John Henry Tradition," *Missouri Folklore Society Journal* 17 (1995), 33–54; John Garst, "Chasing John Henry in Alabama and Mississippi," *Tributaries: Journal of the Alabama Folklife Association* no. 5 (2002), 92–129; Archie Green, "John Henry Revisited," *JEMF Quarterly* 19, no. 69 (Spring 1983), 12–31; Brett Williams, *John Henry: A Bio-Bibliography* (Westport, CT: Greenwood Press, 1983).

Ted Olson

Henson, Josiah (1789–1883). Slave, Methodist preacher, community leader, and **Underground Railroad** conductor. A native of Charles County, Maryland, Henson is less renowned for his narrative *The Life of Josiah Henson, Formerly a*

Undated illustration of Josiah Henson. Courtesy of the Library of Congress.

Slave, Now an Inhabitant of Canada, as Narrated by Himself (1849) and its subsequent versions than for his symbolic impact on American literature. Henson has been mythologized as the prime inspiration for the title character of **Harriet Beecher Stowe**'s antebellum novel *Uncle Tom's Cabin: Or, Life Among the Lowly* (1852). Subsequent inquiries by recent literary historians have placed the validity of this assumption in question.

Henson's *Life* begins by detailing the daily abuses that led to his father's psychological breakdown, his mother's humiliation, and the dissolution of his family. It concludes with plans for a vocational school that would concentrate on offering mechanical education for men and domestic science training for women. This experimental project sought to facilitate gradual intellectual and economic independence for ex-slaves and freedmen. Henson's idea eventually emerged as the British and American Institute, built in the town of Dawn in present-day Ontario, Canada. Ideological similarities between this plan and such enterprises as **William and Ellen Craft**'s industrial and farm schools in Georgia (1870, 1871) and **Booker T. Washington**'s Tuskegee Normal and Industrial Institute (founded in 1881 and explored in his 1901 autobiography *Up from Slavery*) offer rich possibilities for in-depth comparison and analysis.

Life describes the hazardous journey undertaken by the Henson family to achieve a more amenable lifestyle in Canada. En route encounters with racist residents, frightened but accommodating Native Americans, and extreme physical and mental hardships present a representative portrait of conditions for many fugitive slaves. Henson aided in the escape of more than 100 refugees via the Underground Railroad.

A notable aspect of Henson's **autobiography** is the sympathy he expresses for the condition of the female slave, "compelled to perform unfit labor, sick, suffering, and bearing the burdens of her own sex unpitied and unaided" (509). A veiled commentary on his mother's experiences, these observations foreshadowed the protofeminist concerns of such testimonials as **Sojourner Truth**'s *The Narrative of Sojourner Truth* (1850), **Harriet Ann Jacobs**'s *Incidents in the Life of a Slave Girl* (1861), and **Harriet E. Wilson**'s novel *Our Nig* (1859). Indeed, it was Henson's mother who first imparted to him a sense of muted but resilient spirituality. This early influence, combined with a chance meeting with a visiting preacher from Georgetown, led to Henson's rebirth as a member of the Methodist Episcopal Church. An unlettered but fervent preacher, Henson affirmed his religious calling numerous times over the course of his life and narrative. His introduction to literacy through his son's inquiries about the Bible provides a memorable instance of Henson's perceived proximity to God.

During his period in bondage, the demonstrated qualities of diligence, charismatic leadership, and a tenacious work ethic resulted in Henson's promotion to superintendent of farm work and, over time, his masters' personal assistant, temporary nurse, and even business confidant. These examples of ambition rewarded, along with other privileges attained despite his subordinate social position, illuminate the complexities and vicissitudes of the master–slave relationship. In particular, Henson's refusal to take advantage of an opportunity for freedom (also barring that of the eighteen fellow slaves under his command during a move to Kentucky) asks readers to consider the price of personal conviction, as well as the author's literary representation of such difficult moral choices. In terms of themes, Henson's narrative merits examination vis-à-vis the plantation tradition and its tendency to sentimentalize the relationship between a "benevolent" master and his "loyal" slave.

While lacking the rhetorical complexity that characterized the 1845 narrative of **Frederick Douglass**, Henson's work remains optimistic and matter-of-fact in tone. It is not without occasional lapses into self-congratulatory reflection. As an abolitionist document, it traces the subject's ascent from ignominy to favor, from servitude to freedom, and from American residency to Canadian citizenship. Such themes as the importance of religious faith, enterprising determination, and the collective imperative of racial uplift resonate as part of the larger generic tradition of the African American **slave narrative**. Henson consistently attributes his success to his "own strength of character, the feeling of integrity, [and] the sentiment of high honor" (516) in moments of crisis, not the obsequiousness often ascribed to Stowe's Uncle Tom persona. (The latter characterization is evident in the more contemporary cultural usage of "Uncle Tom" as a disparaging racial epithet.) Stowe's literary popularity boosted sales of subsequent editions of Henson's life story, including a version of his autobiography titled *Uncle Tom's Story of His Life* (1877), for which Stowe wrote a brief preface. Henson died in 1883.

Resources: *The Life of Josiah Henson, Formerly a Slave, Now an Inhabitant of Canada, as Narrated by Himself*, in *African American Slave Narratives: An Anthology*, ed. Sterling Lecater Bland, Jr., 3 vols. (Westport, CT: Greenwood Press, 2001), vol. 2, 505–539; Harriet Beecher Stowe, *Uncle Tom's Cabin: Or, Life Among the Lowly*, ed. Ann Douglas (New York: Penguin Books, 1986); Robin W. Winks, "The Making of a Fugitive Slave Narrative: Josiah Henson and Uncle Tom—A Case Study," in *The Slave's Narrative*, ed. Charles T. Davis and Henry Louis Gates, Jr. (New York: Oxford University Press, 1985), 112–146.

Nancy Kang

Hercules, Frank (1911–1996). Novelist and nonfiction writer. Frank Hercules is considered a minor writer of African American literature. The whole of his literary output consists of three novels and a few sociological works. Nevertheless, the important themes treated by Hercules establish his place in the African American **literary canon**.

Frank Hercules was born February 12, 1917, in Port-of-Spain, Trinidad, the son of an educator and activist father who was exiled from the island because of his political activism. Hercules studied law in London in the late 1930s and emigrated to America in the 1940s. He became a naturalized American citizen in 1959. He died in New York City on May 6, 1996.

Hercules began writing in the early 1940s; however, his first novel, *Where the Hummingbird Flies*, was not published until 1961. Set in Trinidad, it is a folk novel that deals with the complex effects of colonization on both the colonizer and the colonized. It was an artistic rather than a commercial success, earning several distinctions including the Fletcher Pratt Memorial fellowship to the prestigious Breadloaf Writers' Conference. In 1967, Hercules' second novel, *I Want a Black Doll*, appeared. Its reception in the United States was lukewarm; it was received more enthusiastically in England and Europe. The subject matter, interracial marriage, and its timing, during the explosive period of **Black Nationalism**, perhaps combined to prevent a more positive critical reception. *On Leaving Paradise*, published in 1980, is largely a picaresque novel in the comic tradition. The protagonist, Johnny de Paria, is a modern day Candide who is forced to leave his homeland of Trinidad and test his values against a world full of conflict and opposing values. Taken together with his first novel, *On Leaving Paradise* demonstrates Hercules' intimate knowledge of the West Indian setting and psyche, and shows his keen knowledge of and sensitivity to the West Indian colonization.

Hercules' essays about **Harlem, New York**, and his major nonfiction work, *American Society and Black Revolution* (1972), show the author's keen insight into societal matters. These works, which are critical of both White racism and the ineptitude of Black leadership, show Hercules as a powerful and complex writer and thinker. Hercules was not extraordinarily prolific, nor was he a popular writer, but he is remembered for an insight and a bravery that are matched by few others of his era.

Resources: Warren J. Carson, "Frank Hercules," in *The Oxford Companion to African American Literature*, ed. William Andrews, Frances Smith Foster, and Trudier Harris (New York: Oxford University Press, 1997), 353; Frank Hercules: *American Society and Black Revolution* (New York: Harcourt Brace Jovanovich, 1972); *I Want a Black Doll* (New York: Simon and Schuster, 1967); *On Leaving Paradise* (New York: Harcourt Brace Jovanovich, 1980); *Where the Hummingbird Flies* (New York: Harcourt, Brace, 1961); Carol P. Marsh, "Frank Hercules," in *Dictionary of Literary Biography*, vol. 33, ed. Trudier Harris and Thadious Davis (Detroit: Gale, 1984), 115–119.

Warren J. Carson

Hernton, Calvin Coolidge (1932–2001). Poet, novelist, teacher, literary and social critic. Calvin C. Hernton made a major contribution to African American literature and culture as a social commentator on the relationship between sex and racism; as cofounder of the Umbra Literary Society (1961), which is regarded as a precursor of the **Black Arts Movement**; and as a literary critic who showed early support for African American female writers and feminist objectives. Hernton was also an innovative teacher and theorist in the field of **Black Studies**, and he was a prolific writer of poetry, essays, scripts, plays, and fiction.

Born in Chattanooga, Tennessee, Hernton was raised primarily by his grandmother, Ella Estell. "Chattanooga Black Boy" (1966), an autobiographical essay, discusses Hernton's first encounters with racism and his growing awareness of the connections between racism and identity. Hernton earned a B.A. in sociology from Talladega College (1954). His professors at Talladega brought his poetry to the attention of **Langston Hughes**, who became an early mentor when Hernton began spending summers in New York City as a college student. One of his poems was published in a professional journal during his junior year. Throughout his life, Hernton thought of himself first and foremost as a poet.

Hernton received an M.A. in sociology from Fisk University (1956). His M.A. thesis, "A Thematic Analysis of Editorials and Letters to the Editors Regarding the Montgomery Bus Protest Movement," demonstrates his early interest in African American social and political conditions. He was married to Mildred Webster from 1958 until their divorce in 1975. They had one son, Antone. Hernton taught social science at four historically Black colleges and universities: Benedict College (1957–1958), Alabama A&M (1958–1959), Edward Waters College (1959–1960), and Southern University and A&M (1960–1961). He moved to New York to study sociology at Columbia University (1961), and he worked there for the Department of Welfare (1961–1962) and the National Opinion Research Center (1963–1964). Of greatest significance to his literary career was Hernton's move to the Lower East Side, which brought him into contact with other Black writers, including **Raymond Patterson, Thomas Covington Dent**, and **David Henderson**. Seeking to establish a group of artists, writers, and musicians to encourage each other's work, Hernton cofounded a collective called the Society of Umbra (1961), which is widely considered to have played a seminal role in the Black Arts Movement (*see* **Umbra Workshop**). Hernton discusses this period in the essay "Umbra: A Personal Recounting" (1993). Umbra participants included others who became important African American literary figures: Dent, Henderson, **Ishmael Reed, Lorenzo Thomas**, and **Askia M. Touré**. The group produced *Umbra*, an influential magazine edited by Hernton, Dent, and Henderson, which published well-known African American writers such as Hughes, Reed, and **Alice Walker**, as well as new writers.

Hernton received a fellowship (1965–1969) to study in London at the Institute of Phenomenological Studies, directed by R. D. Laing. From 1970 to

1972, he was writer-in-residence at Oberlin College. In 1972, when the college established **Black Studies** as a separate field, Hernton was appointed Associate Professor and became one of the program's most esteemed teachers and scholars. In 1980, he became Professor of African American Studies and Creative Writing, and served as Chair of African American Studies from 1997 until his retirement in 1999. Hernton's second marriage, to Mary O'Callaghan in 1998, lasted until his death.

Hernton's poetry and short stories were published in numerous anthologies and magazines, including *19 Necromancers from Now* (comp. Ishmael Reed), *You Better Believe It* (comp. Paul Breman), *I Am the Darker Brother* (ed. Arnold Adoff), *The Poetry of Black America* (comp. Adoff), *Essence*, and *Black Scholar*. He published three poetry collections: *The Coming of Chronos to the House of Nightsong* (1964), *Medicine Man* (1976), and *The Red Crab Gang and Black River Poems* (1999). Hernton's poetry is connected to the Black Arts Movement and later developments in **performance poetry** by its skillful use of oral traditions, as well as its references to African American culture and the African **diaspora**. His most famous poem is "The Distant Drum," which is often taught, quoted, and anthologized. His longer poems display the influence of modernists such as **Melvin B. Tolson**.

Hernton also wrote plays, and television scripts for "A Man Called Hawk," which starred his former student, Avery Brooks. Hernton published one novel, *Scarecrow* (1974), the main theme of which is found in much of Hernton's writing: namely, that sexual issues are generally hidden beneath racism. Hernton wrote a groundbreaking study of black women writers, *The Sexual Mountain and Black Women Writers* (1987). He boldly frames Alice Walker's novel *The Color Purple* (1982) as a **slave narrative**, and includes a chapter on **Ann Lane Petry**'s *The Street* (1946), which he calls a pivotal work by an African American woman. Another chapter focuses on African American women poets, including **Rita Dove**, **Thulani N. Davis**, **Jayne Cortez**, and **Sonia Sanchez**, and explains the oral–poetic–narrative tradition of African American women. The book's title alludes to Langston Hughes's famous essay, "The Negro Artist and the Racial Mountain" (1926), but it metaphorically refers to "the sexual mountain" as the obstacle faced by Black female writers. Hernton argues that writers such as **Ralph Ellison** and **Richard Wright** harmed the image of African American women by negative portrayals in their fiction, in contrast with more positive images in the writing of **James Baldwin** and Langston Hughes.

Hernton's most famous book is *Sex and Racism in America* (1965), a bestseller reprinted fourteen times by 1981 and translated into Japanese, French, Spanish, and Swedish. The book's central premise is contained in its epigraph from **James Weldon Johnson**'s **autobiography**, *Along This Way* (1933): "In the core of the heart of the American race problem the sex factor is rooted." Hernton's other major works of social commentary are *White Papers for White Americans* (1966) and *Coming Together: Black Power, White Hatred, and Sexual Hang-ups* (1971).

Hernton's career showed great consistency and progressive development in delving deeply into key issues that were paramount in his writing, lecturing, research, and teaching: race consciousness and prejudice, oppression of African American women, and the inextricability of sex from racism. By doing so, he made topics that had been partially hidden more accessible. His writing is still considered influential, brave, and thought-provoking.

Resources: Calvin C. Hernton: "Chattanooga Black Boy: Identity and Racism," in *Names We Call Home: Autobiography on Racial Identity*, ed. Becky Thompson and Sangeeta Tyagi (New York: Routledge, 1996); *The Coming of Chronos to the House of Nightsong: An Epical Narrative of the South* (New York: Interim Books, 1964); *Coming Together: Black Power, White Hatred, and Sexual Hang-ups* (New York: Random House, 1971); *Medicine Man: Collected Poems* (New York: Reed, Cannon & Johnson, 1976); *The Red Crab Gang and Black River Poems* (Berkeley, CA: Ishmael Reed Publishing Co., 1999); *Scarecrow* (Garden City, NY: Doubleday, 1974); *Sex and Racism in America* (Garden City, NY: Doubleday, 1965); *The Sexual Mountain and Black Women Writers: Adventures in Sex, Literature, and Real Life* (New York: Anchor Press, 1987); "Umbra: A Personal Recounting," *African American Review* 27, no. 4 (1993), 579–584; *White Papers for White Americans* (Garden City, NY: Doubleday, 1966).

Lauri Ramey

Herron, Carolivia (born 1947). Novelist, children's writer, and multimedia producer. Born in **Washington, D.C.**, Herron grew up and attended school in the Washington area and received her Ph.D. in comparative literature at the University of Pennsylvania. She has taught in many universities across the United States and was the head of Epicenter at Harvard University, where she also taught courses on epic literature. Herron's book for children, *Nappy Hair* (1997), became the center of controversy after its publication. In September 1998, Ruth Ann Sherman, a third-grade teacher in **Brooklyn, New York**, used the book in a class. She was severely criticized by members of the African American and Hispanic communities who were angered by content they perceived to be racist. Sherman and Herron later appeared together at California State University, Chico, to explain that *Nappy Hair* celebrates African American culture through delightful descriptions of the main character, Brenda, and her **hair** (CSU Chico online archive).

Herron's most remarkable contribution to African American literature, however, may be *Thereafter Johnnie* (1991). This novel chronicles the demise of a middle-class African American family in Washington, D.C., as the incestual relationship between the father, Christopher, and his youngest daughter, Patricia, tears the family apart. This complex novel develops the problematic theme of incest running through African American literature, as in **Ralph Ellison**'s *Invisible Man* (1952), **Toni Morrison**'s *The Bluest Eye* (1970), and **Alice Walker**'s *The Color Purple* (1982). The novel's theme of incest gains a mythic dimension, set against a history of systematic **slavery** and wrought with allusions to works from the literary epic traditions, including allusions to John Milton's *Paradise Lost*. In the book, Herron probes the origins of incest embedded in

American history and predicts an apocalyptic end to the United States as it faces defeat from Third World countries while African Americans flee to the mountains. Written in an acclaimed lyrical, poetic language, *Thereafter Johnnie* draws together several important strands in African American literary history to reach a new epic height. Herron's other important contributions include an edited volume, *Selected Works of Angelina Weld Grimké* (1991), and the short stories "That Place" and "The Old Lady." She is currently completing a memoir titled *Peacesong*. Aside from writing, Herron is engaged in multimedia projects intended to educate multicultural communities. She is also the originator of Epicenter Literary Software, a company founded in 1988.

Resources: "Controversy and Children's Literature: Author and Teacher Discuss Nappy Hair," California State University, Chico, March 1999, http://www.csuchico.edu/pub/inside/archive/99_04_08/nappy.html; Carolivia Herron: *Happy Hair* (New York: Element Books, 2000); *Nappy Hair* (New York: Knopf, 1997); *Thereafter Johnnie* (New York: Random House, 1991); Carolivia Herron, ed., *Selected Works of Angelina Weld Grimké* (New York: Oxford University Press, 1991).

Jee Hyun An

Heyward, [Edwin] DuBose (1885–1940) and Dorothy [Hartzell Kuhns] Heyward (1890–1961). DuBose Heyward was a playwright, novelist, and poet. Dorothy Heyward was chiefly a playwright. DuBose Heyward's novel *Porgy* (1925) is widely considered to be the first major **novel** written by a Southerner that characterized African Americans in a realistic rather than a stereotypical manner. The husband and wife team transformed the novel into a popular play titled *Porgy* (1927), which ultimately provided the story for the classic George and Ira Gershwin folk opera *Porgy and Bess* (1935). DuBose and Dorothy Heyward are known primarily for works on which they collaborated. However, playwright Dorothy Heyward's works were regularly seen in New York theaters, and the poetry, **drama**, and novels of DuBose Heyward created a newfound respect for Southern literature.

Born in Charleston, South Carolina, to a poor—though formerly aristocratic—family, DuBose Heyward quit school to join the workforce after his father's death (Durham). Eventually he found employment checking cotton on the waterfront, working alongside the local African Americans who would provide the dialect and real-life observations for the characters of Catfish Row; the resulting novel, *Porgy*, portrayed African Americans as passionate and sympathetic and established Heyward as a professional writer. Dorothy Kuhns, the young woman from Ohio who would author numerous plays with Heyward, began her career touring the country as an actress, then shifted her focus to playwrighting. She attended George Pierce Baker's infamous "47 Workshop" at Harvard University, where her play *Nancy Ann* won the Harvard Prize (1924). Kuhns and Heyward married during the early production stages of *Nancy Ann* on Broadway (1923).

DuBose Heyward went on to write a number of novels, including *Angel* (1926), *Mamba's Daughters* (1929), and *Peter Ashley* (1932), while Dorothy

Heyward began work on the play *Porgy*. Her husband joined her during the rewrites, and they agreed that the original New York cast must be composed of African American actors; the ensuing combination of African American actors (instead of white actors in blackface) playing realistic characters both revolutionized the American stage and helped to create a place for African American actors in serious drama (1927). *Porgy and Bess*, the Gershwin opera, recovered admirably from initially mixed reviews, and has become a mainstay of the American musical stage.

Themes of racial discrimination and Southern glory are frequent in the writings of the Heywards. A progressively more liberal social critic as his life went on, DuBose Heyward is credited with helping to bring about a cultural renaissance in **the South**. Heyward was elected to the National Institute of Arts and Letters and received a Rockefeller Foundation grant. (*See* **Minstrelsy**.)

Resources: Frank Durham, *DuBose Heyward: The Man Who Wrote Porgy* (Columbia: University of South Carolina Press, 1954); DuBose Heyward: *Angel* (New York: George H. Doran, 1926); *Brass Ankle, a Play in Three Acts* (New York: Farrar & Rinehart, 1931); *Lost Morning* (New York: Farrar & Rinehart, 1936); *Mamba's Daughters* (New York: Doubleday Doran, 1929); *Peter Ashley* (New York: Farrar & Rinehart, 1932); *Porgy* (New York: George H. Doran, 1925); *Star Spangled Virgin* (New York: Farrar & Rinehart, 1939); DuBose Heyward and Dorothy Hartzell Heyward: *Mamba's Daughters, a Play* (New York: Farrar & Rinehart, 1939); *Porgy: A Play in Four Acts* (Garden City, NY: Doubleday, Page, 1927); James M. Hutchisson, *DuBose Heyward: A Charleston Gentleman and the World of Porgy and Bess* (Jackson: University Press of Mississippi, 2000); James M. Hutchisson, ed., *A DuBose Heyward Reader* (Athens: University of Georgia Press, 2003); *Porgy and Bess*, libretto by DuBose Heyward; lyrics by DuBose Heyward and Ira Gershwin (New York: Gershwin Publishing, 1935); William H. Slavick, *DuBose Heyward* (Boston: Twayne, 1981).

Elizabeth A. Osborne

Hill, Abram (1910–1986). Playwright, teacher, and theater organizer. Hill was born in **Atlanta, Georgia,** and his original given name was Abraham Barrington Hill. He is best known for the play *On Strivers' Row*, which satirizes upper-middle-class African Americans in **Harlem, New York**, circa 1940. They live in an area of Harlem—sections of 138th and 139th Streets—that was sarcastically dubbed "Strivers' Row" during the **Harlem Renaissance**, hence the title of Hill's play ("Home to Harlem"; "Virtual Tour"). The play was first produced in Harlem in 1940 and has been revived as recently as 2003. Hill moved to New York City when he was still in his teens and worked for a photographer ("Hilarious and Biting"). Later he taught **drama** at several Harlem churches, took some premedical-school courses at the City College of New York, and then transferred to Lincoln University (Pennsylvania), where he graduated with a B.A. in English ("Hilarious and Biting"). He returned to the New York area in the 1930s and ultimately worked for the Federal Theatre (*see* **Federal Writers' Project**). Subsequently, he helped to establish the American Negro Theatre (Walker).

Resources: "Hilarious and Biting Social Satire Opens the 2003–2004 Season at Black Theatre Troupe," American Express Presents a Culture Without Borders, www .blacktheatretroupe.org/press/092903-strivers.php; "Strivers's Row, Home to Harlem," http://www.hometoharlem.com/Harlem/hthcult.nsf/weblandmarks/StriversRow (includes vintage photographs); "Virtual Tour of Harlem," http://www.nyc.gove/htmol/ mxb/mxmap139.html; Ethel Pitts Walker, "The American Negro Theatre," in *The Theatre of Black Americans*, vol. 2, *The Presenters: Companies of Players; The Participators: Audience and Critics*, ed. Errol Hill (Englewood Cliffs, NJ: Prentice-Hall, 1980), 49–62.

Hans Ostrom

Hill, Donna (born 1955). Novelist, educator, columnist, and public relations coordinator. A native of **Brooklyn, New York,** where she still resides, Hill began writing when she submitted a short story to *Black Romance Magazine* in 1987, and then became an advice columnist for *Jive* magazine. Hill was the first author to join Odyssey Publishers, the predecessor to Arabesque Books (BET Enterprises), which opened the door to the **romance novel** for writers of color. Her first novel was *Rooms of the Heart* (1990), and Hill has since turned out twenty novels. Well respected and recognized as a pioneer, Hill has thrilled her fans with stories of positive love between Black men and women in novels with titles such as *Temptation* (1994) and *Intimate Betrayal* (1997). Not one to follow conventional romance writing methods, Hill wrote a romance titled *A Private Affair* (1998) that does not have the requisite happy ending. Hill also has contributed to numerous anthologies and collections of novellas. In 2000 Kensington published her first mainstream novel, *If I Could,* which tells the story of a woman who rebuilds her life after she decides to leave her marriage. *Rhythms* (2001), Hill's first hardback, defined a new direction, as a work **historical fiction** that spans three generations. Hill established herself further with the best-selling novels *An Ordinary Woman* (2002) and *In My Bedroom* (2004). Her honors include the Career Achievement Award from *Romantic Times* (1998), and she was among *Shades of Romance* magazine's 2000 All-Time Favorite Romance Authors. Three of Hill's novels have been made into movies produced by Black Entertainment Television. Hill is a radio show hostess for Literally Yours for Book Crazy Radio, and she coordinates author events in her capacity as publication relations specialist. She continues to teach writing workshops and give lectures in New York City.

Resources: Donna Hill: *Divas, Inc.* (New York: St. Martin's, 2004); *If I Could* (New York: Kensington, 2000); *In My Bedroom* (New York: St. Martin's, 2004); *A Private Affair* (New York: Pinnacle, 1998); *Rhythms: A Novel* (New York: St. Martin's, 2001); *Rooms of the Heart* (Grass Valley, CA: Odyssey, 1990); *Scandalous* (New York: Pinnacle, 1995); *A Scandalous Affair* (New York: Kensington, 2000); Web site, www.donnahill.com; interview from *Nubian Chronicles* Web site, http://www .intothespolight-inc.com/tnc.html (2001); interview/information from Donna Hill (Oct. 2003).

Dera R. Williams

Hill, Ernest (born 1961). Novelist. Hill has published three critically acclaimed novels: *Cry Me a River* (2003), *A Life for a Life* (1998), and *Satisfied with Nothin'* (1992; 1996). Hill is a native of Oak Grove, Louisiana, and his fiction explores the lives of working-class African Americans in **the South** in the 1970s, 1980s, and 1990s (Bush). *A Life for a Life* is set in Brownville, Louisiana, as is *Cry Me a River*, which combines elements of **crime and mystery fiction** with the story of a father and son attempting to reconcile. *Satisfied with Nothin'* concerns the integration of a high school in rural Louisiana in the 1970s. Hill attended the University of Louisiana at Monroe from 1979 to 1981, playing football there (Bush). He went on to earn degrees from the University of California at Berkeley; Cornell University; and the University of California at Los Angeles. At this writing he lives in Louisiana.

Resources: Timothy Bush, "Ernest Hill to Speak at Freshman Seminar Class," *The PowWow* (student newspaper of the University of Louisiana at Monroe), May 7, 2004, p. 1; Ernest Hill: *Cry Me a River* (New York: Dafina, 2003); *A Life for a Life* (New York: Simon and Schuster, 1998); *Satisfied with Nothin'* (Los Angeles: Pickaninny Productions, 1992; New York: Simon and Schuster, 1996).

Hans Ostrom

Himes, Chester (1909–1984). Novelist, essayist, and short story writer. Chester Bomar Himes was born on July 29, 1909, in Jefferson City, Missouri, to Joseph Sandy Himes and Estelle Bomar Himes. He is recognized now chiefly for his popular fiction, especially the novel *A Rage in Harlem* (1957; published as *For Love of Imabelle*) and *Cotton Comes to Harlem* (1965), but he was a far more versatile, politically alert, and enormously prolific writer than is commonly known. He attended Ohio State University after high school but dropped out by the end of 1926, frustrated by the rigor of his studies and the segregationist policies of the college. Abandoning higher education altogether, Himes preferred the company of pimps, gamblers, and hustlers (*The Quality of Hurt*). For "Little Katzi," as he became known on the street, criminality became second nature. The seventeen-year-old smoked opium, pimped for his girlfriend (and future wife) Jean Johnson, and committed crime. Himes's unchecked behavior eventually led to his arrest for armed robbery. He was sentenced to twenty-five years in prison on December 27, 1928.

In the first volume of his autobiography, *The Quality of Hurt* (1972), Himes writes that he "grew to manhood in the Ohio State Penitentiary" (60). "Little Katzi's" isolation from the free world forced him to mature and consider his future. With nothing but time on his hands, writing provided him with an opportunity to channel his emotions. Himes began to study human behavior and draw upon his own experiences to construct vibrant narratives and quixotic characters. After publishing his first short stories in African American periodicals—the *Atlanta Daily World*, the **Pittsburgh Courier**, *Abbott's Monthly*, and the **Baltimore Afro-American**—he began to make his mark by publishing in *Esquire* magazine.

Paroled on April 1, 1936, Himes emerged from prison as a writer of considerable ability. His short stories increasingly focused on interracial conflict and the African American struggle for civil rights. And along with his penchant for naturalist plotting, by the late 1930s he had developed the Modernist effects of omission, moral confusion, and psychological uncertainty in his narratives. As he continued writing, he sought emotional and economic stability in his life: he married his longtime girlfriend, Jean Johnson, in August 1937, and for the next three years he served as a researcher for the federal Works Progress Administration program. During this period Himes also completed his first novel, *Cast the First Stone* (1953), a narrative focusing on prison life and social confinement. Although he had finished it in 1937, the negative response of editors to whom he sent the book kept it from being published for nearly fifteen years. The unexpurgated version, titled *Yesterday Will Make You Cry* (1998), is a homoerotic love story set in a penitentiary during the **Great Depression**. *Yesterday Will Make You Cry* is compelling in its frank investigation of masculinity, sexuality, and the violence inherent in the prison system. Based loosely on his own experiences behind bars, this is the only novel by Himes in which same-sex desire is treated with compassion. While the protagonist, James Monroe, is not African American, his homosexual experiences directly parallel Himes's own relationship with a fellow inmate, Prince Rico.

In 1941 Himes and his wife relocated to Southern California. In the 1940s, Himes's writing reflected the anger and frustration building up in the Black community. African Americans who had expected their service in **World War II** to result in improved civil rights legislation felt betrayed. Himes himself became discouraged as he encountered racial hostility while in the workforce. For the next fifteen years he was part of the literary period often known as the Protest Era (*see* **Protest Literature**). Himes's protest novels include *If He Hollers Let Him Go* (1945), *Lonely Crusade* (1947), and *The Primitive* (1955).

If He Hollers Let Him Go tells the story of Bob Jones, an African American shipyard foreman during World War II. After a heated confrontation with a White female coworker, Madge Perkins, Jones is summarily demoted and, after a series of flirtations between the two, he is falsely accused of rape. Although Jones is ultimately found innocent of the charges, during his hearing the judge decides he must be punished for expressing interracial desire: "Suppose I give you a break, boy. If I let you join the armed forces... will you give me your word you'll stay away from white women and keep out of trouble?" (203). The judge forces Jones to make a choice; he either accepts a rape conviction and goes to prison, or he volunteers to enter World War II.

The absurdity that often characterizes African Americans' experience with White supremacy is expertly rendered in *Lonely Crusade*, which also takes place during World War II. The protagonist, Lee Gordon, has been hired as a union organizer who, it is hoped, can lead cynical African American workers into the union. But the corporation, Comstock Aircraft Organization, hopes that it can use Gordon as a puppet in order to control and manipulate the employees. Similarly, the Communist organizers who pretend to support the workers have been corrupted by power and ideology. The upbeat conclusion notwithstanding, Himes paints a stark picture of African Americans' place in White America's power structure. This novel continues Himes's exploration of interracial conflict and desire that can be found in *If He Hollers Let Him Go*. One of the elements that differentiate *Lonely Crusade* from its predecessor is its attempt to articulate a sophisticated analysis of the African American working class. For many reviewers, however, the structure of the novel was uneven and the pacing was haphazard (Silet). While *If He Hollers* received mixed, if not strong, reviews, *Lonely Crusade* was panned. Black and White critics alike considered it outrageous and politically irresponsible (Silet).

Due to the controversial nature of his novels, critics at the time regarded Himes as a propagandist; writers of protest literature often face the charge of writing mere propaganda, as **Langston Hughes** (for example) did in the 1930s. Himes attempted to make his work more popular, and therefore lu-

Chester Himes, 1946. Courtesy of the Library of Congress.

crative, by writing a semiautobiographical work titled *The Third Generation* (1954). This novel fictionalized his parents' tumultuous marriage and his family history. Stephen Milliken has said of this novel that its characters "have a largeness of size" that is reminiscent of an "epic, of romance, of allegory—and of life itself" (140). The intraracial conflicts between matriarch Lillian Taylor and her husband are drawn vividly from Himes's own childhood experiences. And like that of the youngest son, the protagonist Charles Taylor, Himes's streak of independence contributed to his lawlessness and brazen attitude.

Unfortunately, *The Third Generation* did little to make Himes a more popular writer. He was separated from his wife, confounded by his inability to thrive in the American literary marketplace, and disgusted by American racism. Consequently, on April 3, 1953, he used his publisher's advance for the novel to leave the United States and go to Europe. Himes had already garnered a substantial readership in Europe with his first two novels, and, prompted by **Richard Wright**, he thought going to Europe was a good idea (*see* **Paris, France**). With the **Cold War** in full swing, Himes realized that a wave of conservatism had affected American tastes, and he pragmatically concluded that he needed to repackage himself if he was to be successful as an author.

Before abandoning overtly political fiction altogether, he wrote what some critics today consider his masterpiece, *The Primitive* (1955).

Himes had been at odds with the publishing industry, book reviewers, and even some of his readers since he began his career as a novelist. *If He Hollers Let Him Go*, for example, had its circulation mysteriously compromised by his publishing company, Doubleday (Silet; Sallis). And after *Lonely Crusade* appeared, promotional activities for the book were suddenly canceled. Following the debacle with *Cast the First Stone*, Himes decided to strike back. *The Primitive* fully exposes the animosity he had toward the publishing industry as well as his disappointment with the limits of didactic Black fiction.

Living in Europe seems to have provided Himes with the peace of mind to compose *The End of a Primitive*. The multilayered plot exposes White privilege, the presumptions readers have about Black art, and the American publishing industry's disloyalty to its African American authors. The book was released in Europe as *The End of a Primitive*. Himes boasted in the introduction to the book that he considered the novel an "affront to all white American editors" (11). The witty narrative is a complex hybrid of **satire**, protest, **autobiography**, tragedy, and absurdity. Even today, literary critics have great difficulty ascertaining the moments in which Himes is being coldly analytical and when he is being ironic (Silet). *The End of a Primitive* arguably captures the author at his artistic best, evincing his skills as both an aesthetician and a rhetorician.

The story concentrates on the experiences of Jesse Robinson, a protest author who believes that his personal and professional life is about to improve. Robinson travels to New York City after receiving a publisher's advance and, after his novel is abruptly rejected, the protagonist murders his White lover in a drunken stupor. Despite the liberating effect its publication had on his psyche, Himes explained in the introduction, "I paid for writing *The End of a Primitive*, I paid my dues as the brothers say" (12). The unexpurgated version of the novel was not published in the United States until 1990.

In the fall of 1954 Chester Himes met the director of the Gallimard detective series, Marcel Duhamel. Desperate for money, and uncertain about his prospects in the American market, Himes was convinced by Duhamel to begin writing detective novels. Between 1957 and 1969 he acquired international fame through a series of detective novels set in **Harlem, New York**. These "action stories," as Himes called them, focused on the detectives Grave Digger Jones and Coffin Ed Johnson and their bizarre exploits in Harlem. Unlike his earlier novels, these stories are purged of subversive political commentary and are written for a mass-market audience. Two of these novels were made into motion pictures: the blaxploitation films *Come Back Charleston Blue* (1974) and *Cotton Comes to Harlem* (1978). His crowning achievement came in 1957 when he won the French Grand Prix du Roman Policier for best detective novel. (*See* **Crime and Mystery Fiction**.)

Himes died on November 12, 1984, from Parkinson's disease. Arguably, Himes deserves to be remembered as one of the most articulate literary

observers of the human condition in the United States. His prolific contributions to African American literary history include essays, film scripts,
nearly twenty novels, and more than fifty short stories. His influence on
American fiction is so profound that **Calvin C. Hernton** has identified him as
one of the two "founding authors of the African-American short story" (ix).
While he is more readily acknowledged for his popular "action stories," Himes
is, at this writing, clearly underappreciated as a serious novelist. His literary
investigations into national identity and racial psychology augment American
literary history and help to enrich such fields of scholarship as cultural studies,
gender studies, Whiteness studies, and **queer theory**.

Resources: Primary Sources: *Political Fiction:* Chester Himes: *A Case of Rape* (1965;
repr. Washington, DC: Howard University Press, 1984); *The End of a Primitive* (New
York: Norton, 1997; first published as *The Primitive*, 1955); *If He Hollers Let Him Go*
(1945; repr. New York: Thunder's Mouth Press, 1986); *Lonely Crusade* (1947; repr.
New York: Thunder's Mouth Press, 1997); *The Third Generation*, ed. Michel Fabre
(1954; repr. New York: Thunder's Mouth Press, 1989); *Yesterday Will Make You Cry*
(New York: Norton, 1998; first published as *Cast the First Stone*, 1953). *Popular Fiction:*
Chester Himes: *All Shot Up* (1960; repr. New York: Thunder's Mouth Press, 1996); *The
Big Gold Dream* (1960; repr. New York: Thunder's Mouth Press, 1996); *Blind Man with
a Pistol* (1969; repr. New York: Knopf, 1989); *Cotton Comes to Harlem* (1965; repr. New
York: Knopf, 1988); *The Crazy Kill* (1959; repr. New York: Knopf, 1989); *The Heat's
On* (1961; repr. New York: Knopf, 1988); *Pinktoes* (1961; repr. Jackson, MS: Banner
Books, 1996); *Plan B* (1983; repr. Jackson: University Press of Mississippi, 1993); *A
Rage in Harlem* (New York: Knopf, 1989; first published as *For Love of Imabelle*, 1957);
The Real Cool Killers (1959; repr. New York: Knopf, 1988); *Run Man, Run* (1959; repr.
New York: Carroll & Graf, 1995). *Selected Additional Works:* Chester Himes: *Black on
Black: Baby Sister and Selected Writings* (Garden City, NY: Doubleday, 1973); *The
Collected Stories of Chester Himes*, ed. Calvin C. Hernton (New York: Thunder's Mouth
Press, 1990); "Dilemma of the Negro Novelist in the U.S.," in *Beyond the Angry Black*,
ed. John A. Williams (New York: Cooper Square Publishers, 1966); *My Life of
Absurdity*, vol. 2 of *The Autobiography of Chester Himes* (Garden City, NY: Doubleday,
1976); *The Quality of Hurt*, vol. 1 of *The Autobiography of Chester Himes* (Garden City,
NY: Doubleday, 1972). **Secondary Sources:** Michel Fabre and Robert Skinner, eds.,
Conversations with Chester Himes (Jackson: University Press of Mississippi, 1995); James
Lundquist, *Chester Himes* (New York: Frederick Ungar, 1976); Stephen F. Milliken,
Chester Himes: A Critical Appraisal (Columbia: University of Missouri Press, 1976);
Gilbert H. Muller, *Chester Himes* (Boston: Twayne, 1989); James Sallis, *Chester Himes:
A Life* (New York: Walker, 2001); Charles L. P. Silet, ed., *The Critical Response to
Chester Himes* (Westport, CT: Greenwood Press, 1999).

Lawrence A. Davis

Hip-Hop. Hip-hop is a subculture, chiefly urban and initially created and
defined by **rap** artists and their audience; the term can be used as either a noun
or an adjective. Hip-hop has developed over time to include not only music
but also new forms of literature and literary discourse, art, dance, and fashion.

Nonetheless, rap is the foundation of hip-hop's culture, and therefore hip-hop is a direct product of the ethnic, historical, sociological, musical, and philosophical circumstances that spawned rap music. All of the defining elements of hip-hop, despite their later international commercialization, remain expressions of urban experiences. These elements spring from ethnic and socioeconomic circumstances shared by African Americans and Latinos in the urban Northeast of the United States and, subsequently, in other urban centers, including **Los Angeles, California**; **Detroit, Michigan**; and **Atlanta, Georgia**.

Hip-hop culture began with the development of rap music in the South Bronx section of New York City in the mid-1970s. Rap often concerned itself (and continues to concern itself) with everyday life in the Bronx and other urban centers, with surviving in that environment, with violence and racism, and especially with how young African American men and women view their lives. Hip-hop was also associated early on with graffiti art, specific styles of dress, and break dancing. The term "hip-hop" seems first to have appeared in 1982 (*Oxford English Dictionary* online). Hip-hop culture has, however, constantly redefined itself, partly in response to the larger culture's views of it.

The Source: The Magazine of Hip-Hop Music, Culture, and Politics (*The Source*) was established in 1988 as a newsletter and later graduated to a full-color glossy publication, reflecting the expansion of the culture on which it reported. It was published originally for a hip-hop audience, but its readership became more diverse. Employing the language of both African American **vernacular** and Standard American English, the magazine communicates with and disseminates information to both a marginalized hip-hop community and mainstream readers. Other hip-hop magazines emerged in the late 1990s, including *XXL* and *Blaze*. These magazines do not simply cover the rap music industry but extend their coverage to include the culture and politics that surround the music, such as racism and discrimination, American politics and policy, African American literature, sports, and other items of specific interest to the hip-hop community. Additionally, hip-hop culture has turned rappers, such as **Gil Scott-Herron**, **Sister Souljah**, and KRS-One, and most recently, **the Last Poets** and DMX, into published writers, not just performers or recording artists.

Literature published in the **Black Arts Movement** has become popular among rappers and in hip-hop culture. One example is the work of **Donald Goines**. His work has reemerged, becoming popular among rappers and their audiences. Goines, one of the best examples of a literary resurgence spawned by hip-hop, used language adopted by rap lyricists, and his books have sold briskly since the 1980s, primarily because his name and titles are mentioned in rap lyrics by artists such as Grand Puba of Brand Nubian, **Tupac Shakur**, and Norega.

Because of its language, its subject matter, and its perspectives on sexuality, women, the police, and violence, hip-hop has, from the beginning, been controversial in mainstream society. However, its controversial nature has not prevented it from becoming popular. Because rap artists use the vernacular and because they work in the mass medium of recording, they have introduced the vernacular to a world audience, which in turn uses the language of the Black community in new ways, some of them commercial. One result of hip-hop's mass distribution is that the language of hip-hop appears in nonfiction works produced by scholars and journalists, including **Michael Eric Dyson**, Keith Gilyard, and **Nelson George**.

Dyson's *Open Mike: Reflections on Philosophy, Race, Sex, Culture, and Religion* (2002) is a compilation of his conversations with several interviewers on his ideas and thoughts concerning **race**, identity, and cultural studies. Dyson and some of his interviewers not only discuss hip-hop but also use its language in their verbal exchanges. In Dyson's attempt to bridge the gap between the academy and urban "street culture," his scholarship provides new avenues that potentially close gaps between academics and other members of mainstream culture (on the one hand) and members of the urban hip-hop community (on the other).

George's *Hip Hop America* (1998) examines not only rap music and hip-hop culture, which is now more than thirty years old, but also the politics and issues of commercialization connected to rap and hip-hop.

Gilyard uses the vernacular of hip-hop to address issues of pedagogy surrounding students' rights and language practices in American schools. In Gary Olson's *Rhetoric and Composition as Intellectual Work* (2002), Gilyard's article "Holdin' It Down: Students' Rights and Struggle over Language Diversity," discusses language, race, identity, and diversity in public schools.

With regard to another linguistic issue, hip-hop culture has generated new interest in the word "nigger," especially how and why it is prominent in the language of hip-hop, and the complications of its usage among non-African American hip-hoppers. A Tribe Called Quest's lyric "Sucka Nigga," from their 1994 CD *Midnight Marauders*, claimed that the "youth say [nigger] all over town" and that the term's negative connotations are removed by the new generation of African American hip-hoppers. Randall Kennedy's *Nigger: The Strange Career of a Troublesome Word* (2002) notes that there are different relationships to and understandings of the word among African Americans. Kennedy explains that, on the one hand, there are African Americans who believe the term "to be only and unalterably a debasing slur," while rappers, including Ice T, insist "upon being called a nigger," similarly to the way Kennedy's "father declared [himself] a 'stone nigger,'" which for the senior Kennedy "meant [to be] a black man without pretensions," standing "unafraid," "loud," and "proud" (Kennedy, xvii).

Mainstream perceptions of hip-hop culture sometimes serve as the sceneries, verbal expressions, and social relations presented in new fiction by African American novelists, such as **Eric Jerome Dickey, Zane, Omar Tyree**, and **E. Lynn Harris**, as they seem to express mainstream assumptions regarding the culture. However, other writers, including **Amiri Baraka, Sonya Sanchez, Nikki Giovanni**, and Ursula Rucker, often write against mainstream perceptions while absorbing hip-hop's expressions and ideas. Another complicating factor connected to hip-hop is that the main consumers of rap music are young White males. African Americans and Hispanics consume less of the commercial music and concerts, yet they are responsible for almost all of the creativity in hip-hop, including the art, music, dance, and literature.

Hip-hop's commercial refinement by an international audience ultimately creates a tension within the culture and the community out of which hip-hop emerges. Over time a large segment of American's mainstream White youth has been integrated into the culture, bridging gaps of racism and classism, with rebellion against authority being one symbolic unifying element.

Hip-hop culture's appeal to mass audiences creates an environment similar to that of the **blues**, **jazz**, and rhythm and blues (R&B). It introduces the culture to outsiders, and in so doing subjects the culture to mimicry. However, because outsiders come to the culture armed with more capital than hip-hop's originators, and also with genuine interest, there exists the opportunity for such global success as that of rap artist Eminem. His success is arguably determined by sales rather than by longevity, street credibility, or appeal within the community of hip-hop.

The complex issues of commercialism, language, ethnicity, and so on inform **Greg Tate**'s edited book, *Everything but the Burden: What White People Are Taking from Black Culture* (2003). From Robin D. G. Kelley's "Reds, Whites, and Blues Peoples" to Carl H. Rux's "Eminem: The New White Negro," Tate's book dedicates itself to examining the growth of hip-hop and the influence of White culture on hip-hop culture. Earlier, Del Jones had examined similar issues in *Culture Bandits II: Annihilation of Afrikan Images* (1993). The argument underlying Tate's and Jones's books is that hip-hop culture, like rap, blues, jazz, and R&B, was created out of a particular Black experience of racial and economic oppression. Although Whites can consume the culture, the argument goes on to claim, they are by no means the main producers of it and will therefore appropriate it in ways that will create anxiety within hip-hop culture. A counterargument is that hip-hop has always been a multiracial, multicultural enterprise that does not negate or define what Rap music represents. From this point of view, the "loss" of hip-hop culture to outsiders is unlikely.

In any event, as hip-hop has become more popular, even globally known, the gap between hip-hop culture and mainstream culture seems to shrink, even as responses to hip-hop culture become more complex and less easy to analyze.

The tags painted by graffiti artists constitute a fascinating form of literature or textual art. Just as Egyptian hieroglyphs inscribe a history transposed into texts, so graffiti art arguably inscribes the history of urban America, its politics and values, thoughts and notions. Historically used by activists to communicate political statements, urban graffiti reports events and can present local reactions to those events.

The 1992 case of Malice Green is one example. Green was a young African American man beaten to death by Detroit, Michigan, police officers Larry Nevers and Walter Budzyn. The mural of Green, painted by Bernie White with tag speed, inscribes the event on its actual site: 24th and West Warren in Detroit. The location of the work, White's muralist style, and his creative timetable (he completed the work soon after the murder) raised Green's killing to national prominence.

Former graffiti artists are now paid by cities. They produce well-crafted artwork covering large areas of space and reflecting Afrocentric and multicultural ideas. Some works stand several stories high. In **Philadelphia, Pennsylvania**, the Mural Arts Programs (PMAP) and the Philadelphia Anti-Graffiti Network (PAGN) are two of the oldest programs that encourage and employ graffiti artist to paint murals, offering them not only monetary reward but also autonomy over the many of messages they convey. In essence, graffiti artists have transcended being labeled criminal. Michael White and Andrew "Zephyr" Witten, in *Style Master General: The Life of Graffiti Artist Dondi White* (2001), offer readers the history of Dondi White, one of the first graffiti artists to move his work from New York's subways into the city's galleries. As part of Sam Esses's program of 1980, Dondi began painting on canvas and, with KEL 139, he produced his finest work, not only for the subway but also for the gallery.

Hip-hop's continuous evolution has made the culture into an international enterprise, defying conventional barriers of race, class, **gender**, and nationality. Like most grassroots movements, significant parts of it remain underground, and arguably the most important creative work in hip-hop culture remains outside the mainstream. Through evolutions of language, art, and music, hip-hop culture will continue to move beyond its own early conventions, but it remains rooted in African American experiences, language, sense of resistance, and sense of independence.

Resources: Jim Fricke and Charlie Ahearn, eds., *Yes, Yes, Y'All: The Experience Music Project Oral History of Hip-Hop's First Decade* (Cambridge, MA: Da Capo Press, 2002); Nelson George, *Hip-Hop America* (New York: Penguin, 1998); Yusef Ja and Chuck D., *Fight the Power: Rap, Race, and Reality* (New York: Delta Books, 1988); Del Jones, *Culture Bandits II: Annihilation of Afrikan Images* (Philadelphia: Hikeka Press, 1993); Randal Kennedy, *Nigger: The Strange Career of a Troublesome Word* (New York: Vintage Books, 2002); Alan Light, ed., *Vibe History of Hip Hop* (Los Angeles: Three Rivers Press, 1999); Glen Mannisto, "Detroit Renaissance Art," *Metro Times*, Nov. 16, 1992, late ed., pp. F1+; Richard J. Powell, *Black Art: A Cultural History*, 2nd ed. (London: Thames and Hudson, 2002); Tricia Rose, *Black Noise: Rap Music and Black Culture in Contemporary America* (Hanover, NH: Wesleyan University Press; published by University Press of New England, 1994); Greg Tate, ed., *Everything But the Burden: What White People Are Taking from Black Culture* (New York: Harlem Moon, 2003); A Tribe Called Quest, "Sucka Nigga," on *Midnight Marauders* (Jive, 1994).

Ellesia Ann Blaque

Historical Fiction. Historical fiction remains difficult to define because of the variety and nature of texts that may qualify as historical fiction. However, main elements of the genre include the following: (1) historical fiction tends to represent a time that is clearly distinct from the contemporary time of the author; (2) historical fiction tends to include many references to authentic places, events, things, and/or public figures that most readers will quickly see as "factual" elements woven into a fictional narrative; (3) historical fiction clearly aims for a representation of historical truth and, subsequently, for accuracy of historical information—but nonetheless within a fictional narrative, in which numerous persons, events, and places may be entirely invented. More basically, a work of literature qualifies as historical fiction if it is a narrative about a historical period, event, or figure. However, the specifics of determining what counts as historical fiction remain contested. For example, precisely how far removed in time must the author be from the historical event he or she writes about for the fiction to qualify as "historical"? Lynda Adamson contends that if a work is set in an earlier era than that with which the reader is familiar, it is historical fiction (vii). The Historical Novel Society offers the criterion that the author must not have been alive at the time of the event. A. T. Dickinson, Jr., gives a broad overview of academic stances on historical fiction, citing authors from the early 20th century, and asserts that the work should contain an *identifiable time or period*, an *identifiable place*, and a historical *agent* such as a recognizable person, event, or social, political, or economic phenomenon characteristic of a period (11–12).

Additional concerns with what constitutes historical fiction include the degree of historical accuracy within the text and the degree of liberty taken with actual history vis-à-vis fictionalized elements. This concern raises the question of the extent to which the truth of history is being conveyed. However, the meaning and understanding of historical truth is just as contested as the question of time and the definition of the genre. The trend in defining the genre seems to be moving away from the concerns with time and the position of author and audience in time to the concern of representation of an overall historical truth. If one of the major considerations for defining the genre broadly is the accuracy of historical information and ultimately the representation of historical truth, then African American authors sometimes complicate the traditional definitions of historical fiction further because they raise the additional question of the goal or purpose of historical fiction, and some African American authors implicitly call into question the nature of the traditional discourse and understanding of history. They question what modes of representation count as "official" and accurate history, and what is understood to be true in relation to that understanding of what constitutes history.

Two distinctive factors that set African American historical fiction apart from historical fiction generally are (1) the purpose of the literature and (2) a differing perspective on what counts as accurate history and, subsequently, truthful representations. The purpose of the literature frequently includes (1) the desire to present a larger social truth of the collective and (2) an effort to represent perspectives that were suppressed either intentionally, due to shame by a certain generation of the community, or unwittingly. For instance, African American writers might want to represent and emphasize episodes and details of American history that previous writers of historical fiction have overlooked or even suppressed, or they might want to represent parts of history that have not been included in mainstream histories of the United States or of African Americans.

African American historical fiction seeks to illuminate both the omissions of "official" accounts of history as well as those dictated by social circumstances wherein generations of African Americans chose to "forget" parts of history considered too painful or dangerous to relate. **Toni Morrison**, for example, suggests that this kind of "forgetting" occurs in **Harriet Ann Jacobs**'s *Incidents in the Life of a Slave Girl* (Christian, 329). This effort to revive and revise historical occurrences, figures, or events to some degree differentiates much African American historical fiction from other works in this genre, and may even cause concern among generalists seeking to develop definitive criteria for the genre as a whole, particularly with the question of the degree and kind of historical accuracy offered in the text and its subsequent credibility.

Many African American writers are sympathetic to relying on oral traditions and **folklore** as valid avenues to approach history, and they often respect the notion of a collective understanding of historical truth. In oral transmission, questions of historical accuracy sometimes take on folkloristic characteristics, mixing fact and fiction and sometimes blurring details in a manner that is troubling for traditional historians, though less so for folklorists. African American writers are all too familiar with the fallacy of assuming that "official documents" are always more accurate and factual than accounts preserved orally. Toni Morrison implicitly questions the mainstream view in her novel *Song of Solomon* (1977), in which she depicts ways in which illiterate African Americans were frequently at the mercy of inept or careless officials who would record names, dates of birth, and other factual information on official documents incorrectly. With such occurrences misrepresenting the truth of African American experiences, the importance of oral transmission through folkloric methods of storytelling is viewed as an important, if not a primary, means by which the truth of a social context is transmitted.

The idea of collective memory runs through a number of texts. One example of this idea of collective memory and its relation to the representation of a larger historical truth is **Ernest James Gaines**'s novel *The Autobiography of Miss Jane Pittman* (1971). Gaines uses a single narrator, the fictional Miss Jane Pittman, to relay the perspective of African Americans in a particular region over several major historical incidents significant to the African American community. At various times, other members of the society, young and old, help her remember and retell parts of the story (told so many times that it has become part of the collective's body of memory); also included in the narration is a critique of the role of traditional history as the narrator states "I knew that the history Miss Jane had to tell was not in the history books."

As noted earlier, historical fiction is a potentially broad category that encompasses a wide array of subgenres, including but not limited to biographical fiction, domestic fiction, epic literature, the love story, the family saga, the mystery, the picaresque, the political novel, and the western. Often, texts fit within multiple categories. For example, Toni Morrison's *Paradise* (1998) could be counted as a family saga, a western, and a domestic fiction. **Jewell Parker Rhodes**'s *Douglass' Women* (2002) could be counted as biographical fiction, love story, domestic fiction, and neo-**slave narrative**; it is based in part on the life of **Frederick Douglass**. **Persia Walker**'s *Harlem Redux* (2002) combines historical fiction with **crime and mystery fiction**.

Questions of historical accuracy and the effort to represent a larger historical truth about the African American experience are revealed in the subgenre of the family saga. Mody Boatright defines the family saga as lore generated around a venerable matriarch or patriarch of a family that is preserved and orally transmitted through generations, and is believed to be true (1). One of the best-known family sagas, **Alex Haley**'s *Roots* (1976), illustrates the tension between this notion of historical fact and a larger social truth. In telling his family story, he started with the family's lore, stories transmitted down through the generations about their ancestor directly from Africa. In order to write about that distant ancestor, however, he was required to conduct historical research to fill in the gaps and give a sense of the social/cultural context and truth of his family.

Caroline Rody suggests that some African American historical fiction contains, beyond the ideological roles of revising history and revealing new or suppressed persectives, a psychological project in the narrative revisiting of historical circumstances such as **slavery** (95). Good examples of fiction that revisits the historical circumstantces of slavery include **Arna Bontemps**'s historical novel *Black Thunder* (1936), which is based on an actual uprising by slaves, as well as **Charles R. Johnson**'s *Middle Passage* (1990) and Toni Morrison's *Beloved* (1987), both of which are also set in the era of slavery. **Margaret Abigail Walker**'s widely acclaimed novel *Jubilee* (1966) is set in both the antebellum and the post-**Reconstruction** eras in **the South**.

Other important historical novels by African Americans include **David Henry Bradley, Jr.**'s, *The Chaneysville Incident* (1981), **Sherley Anne Williams**'s *Dessa Rose* (1986), **Barbara Chase-Riboud**'s *Echo of Lions* (1989), **Thulani N. Davis**'s *1959: A Novel* (1992), **Alice Walker**'s *The Color Purple* (1982) and *The Third Life of Grange Copeland* (1970), Toni Morrison's *Jazz* (1992), Williams H. Armstrong's award-winning novel for young adults, *Sounder* (1969), **Edward P. Jones**'s *The Known World* (2003), which is set in the pre–**Civil War** era, and **James McBride**'s *Miracle at St. Anna* (2002), which is based on a true story concerning African American soldiers in Italy during World War II. (*See* **Holder, Laurence**.)

Resources: Primary Sources: William H. Armstrong, *Sounder* (New York: Harper & Row, 1969); Arna Bontemps, *Black Thunder* (1936; repr. New York: HarperCollins, 1971); David Bradley, *The Chaneysville Incident* (1981; repr. New York: Perennial, 1990); Barbara Chase-Riboud, *Echo of Lions* (New York: Morrow, 1989); Thulani Davis, *1959: A Novel* (San Francisco: Publishing Group West, 1992); Ernest J. Gaines, *The Autobiography of Miss Jane Pittman* (1971; repr. New York: Bantam Books, 1982); Alex Haley, *Roots* (1976; repr. New York: Dell, 1980); Edward P. Jones, *The Known World* (New York: Amistad, 2003); James McBride, *Miracle at St. Anna* (New York: Riverhead Books, 2002); Toni Morrison: *Beloved* (1987; repr. New York: Plume, 1994); *Paradise* (New York: Knopf, 1998); *Song of Solomon* (New York: Random House, 1977); Jewell Parker Rhodes, *Douglass' Women: A Novel* (New York: Atria, 2002); Alice Walker: *The Color Purple* (New York: Harcourt Brace Jovanovich, 1982); *The Third Life of Grange Copeland* (New York: Harcourt Brace Jovanovich, 1970); Persia Walker, *Harlem Redux* (New York: Simon and Schuster, 2002); Sherley Anne Williams, *Dessa Rose* (New York: Morrow, 1986). **Secondary Sources:** Lynda G. Adamson, *American Historical Fiction: An Annotated Guide for Adults and Young Adults* (Phoenix, AZ: Oryx Press, 1999); Mody C. Boatright, *The Family Saga and Other Phases of American Folklore* (Urbana: University of Illinois Press, 1958); Jane Campbell, *Mythic Black Fiction: The Transformation of History* (Knoxville: University of Tennessee Press, 1989); Barbara Christian, "Somebody Forgot to Tell Somebody Something: African-American Women's Historical Novels," in *Wild Women in the Whirlwind: Afra-American Culture and the Contemporary Literary Renaissance*, ed. Joanne M. Braxton and Andrée Nicola McLaughlin (New Brunswick, NJ: Rutgers University Press, 1990), 326–341; A. T. Dickinson, Jr., *American Historical Fiction* (New York: Scarecrow Press, 1958); Klaus Ensslen, "History and Fiction in Alice Walker's *The Third Life of Grange Copeland* and Ernest Gaines' *The Autobiography of Miss Jane Pittman*," in *History and Tradition in Afro-American Culture*, ed. Günter H. Lenz (New York: Campus Press, 1984), 147–163; Geneviève Fabre and Robert O'Meally, eds., *History and Memory in African-American Culture* (New York: Oxford University Press, 1994); George Lukács, *The Historical Novel*, trans. Hannah Mitchell and Stanley Mitchell (1962; London: Merlin, 1965); Deborah McDowell, "Negotiating Between Tenses: Witnessing Slavery After Freedom—*Dessa Rose*," in *Slavery and the Literary Imagination*, ed. Deborah McDowell and Arnold Rampersad (Baltimore: Johns Hopkins University Press, 1989); James Robert Payne, "Griggs and Corrothers: Historical Reality and Black Fiction," *Explorations in Ethnic Studies: The Journal of the National Association for Ethnic Studies* 6, no. 1 (1983), 1–15; Caroline Rody, "Toni Morrison's *Beloved*: History, 'Rememory,' and a 'Clamor for a Kiss,'" *American Literary History* 7, no. 1 (Spring 1995), 92–119; Maggie Sale, "Historical Novel," *The Oxford Companion to African American Literature*, ed. Williams L. Andrews, Frances Smith Foster, and Trudier Harris (New York: Oxford University Press, 1997), 358–359; Robert O. Stephens, *The Family Saga in the South: Generations and Destinies* (Baton Rouge: Louisiana State University Press, 1995).

Esther L. Jones

Hoagland, Everett H., III (born 1942). Poet and educator. Like many poets of the 1960s and 1970s, Hoagland was captivated by the creative and political fervor of the **Black Arts Movement**. He is a native of **Philadelphia, Pennsylvania**, where he grew up reading, on average, a book a day. He began his undergraduate studies at Lincoln University with plans of becoming a wildlife zoologist, but changed his major from biology to English at the end of his sophomore year. While at Lincoln, he was editor of the student newspaper, *The Lincolnian*, and president of the school's poetry society. Lincoln was also where he met the poet and Lincoln alumnus **Langston Hughes**, who took the time to critique some of his early poems. The meeting with Hughes inspired Hoagland to start writing on a daily basis. After graduating from Lincoln in 1964 (and having won one of the university's two creative writing awards), he continued to write poetry while pursuing a career in education. He taught junior high school English and adult night school literacy in Philadelphia from 1964 to 1967 and served as assistant director of admissions at Lincoln from 1967 to 1969.

Hoagland's first nationally published poem, "Night Interpreted," appeared in **Clarence Major**'s *The New Black Poetry* in 1969. Responding to what he perceived as a dearth of Black Arts love poems, he sent some he had written between 1965 and 1970 to **Broadside Press** founder **Dudley Randall** for publication. Randall's response was enthusiastic, and in 1970, Broadside published the poems under the title *Black Velvet*. A year later, Randall included excerpts from *Black Velvet* in his landmark anthology, *The Black Poets* (1971). Hoagland entered Brown University's graduate creative writing program in 1971 and completed his master's thesis under the guidance of the poet and professor, **Michael S. Harper**. He obtained his master's degree in 1973 and joined the faculty of the University of Massachusetts at Dartmouth that same year. During his thirty-year tenure at the university, Hoagland created five African American literature courses, taught poetry workshops, helped develop an African and African American Studies minor, and served as poet laureate of New Bedford, Massachusetts (1994–1998). His poetry, best represented in the collections *This City and Other Poems* (1997) and *...Here...* (2002), reflects his diverse literary influences, impressive command of history, and activist spirit. Hoagland's language is intense and often didactic, but rarely abstruse, underscoring his belief that "most poems should be accessible, even colloquial" (Walton, 40).

Resources: Everett H. Hoagland: *Black Velvet* (Detroit: Broadside Press, 1970); *...Here...* (Wellfleet, MA: Leapfrog Press, 2002); *This City and Other Poems* (New Bedford, MA: Spinner Publications, 1997); "Everett H. Hoagland," in *Contemporary Black Biography*, vol. 45 (Farmington Hills, MI: Gale Group, 2004), also in *Biography Resource Center*, http://galenet.galegroup.com/servlet/BioRC; Clarence Major, comp., *The New Black Poetry* (New York: International Publishers, 1969); Dudley Randall, ed., *The Black Poets* (New York: Bantam, 1971); Christopher Walton, "The Afterlife of Words," *UU World*, July/Aug. 2004, 34–40.

Stacy Torian

Holder, Laurence (born 1939). Playwright, novelist, poet, and professor. Holder, a native of New York City, is best known for writing plays based on the lives African American performers and activists. Among these are *When the Chickens Came Home to Roost*, which debuted in 1981 with Denzel Washington as the lead actor and concerned conflict within the **Nation of Islam** between the Honorable Elijah Muhammad and **Malcolm X**, and *Zora Neale Hurston*, which debuted in 1998 and starred Joseph Edwards and Elizabeth Van Dyke. His other plays in this vein include *Ethel Waters, Hot Snow* (based on the life of the trumpeter Valaida Snow), *They Were All Gardenias* (which concerns **jazz** performers **Billie Holiday**, Charlie Parker, Lester Young, and Coleman Hawkins), *Fagan* (a play about an African American "Buffalo Soldier"), *Scott Joplin*, and *Red Channels* (concerning **McCarthyism** and its effects on **Paul Robeson** and **W.E.B. Du Bois**, among others). At this writing, Holder is a member of the faculty at the John Jay College of Criminal Justice (City University of New York), where he has taught English for more than twenty-five years. He has won a **Garland Anderson** Award from the National Black Theatre Festival ("Laurence Holder").

Resources: Laurence Holder: *Renaissance Collection: Seven Plays*, ed. Richard Gaffield-Knight (Bloomington, IN: First Books, 2003); *Renaissance Men 1: Three Plays*, ed. Richard Gaffield-Knight (New York: Authorhouse, 2001); *Renaissance Men 2: Six Plays*, ed. Richard Gaffield-Knight (New York: Authorhouse, 2002); *Renaissance Solos: 12 Plays* (one-act plays) (New York: Authorhouse, 2001); *Renaissance Women: 5 Plays* (New York: Authorhouse, 2001); "Laurence Holder" (one-page biography), www.laurenceholder.com; Woodie King, Ossie Davis, and Woodie King, Jr., *The Impact of Race: Theatre & Culture* (New York: Applause Theatre & Cinema Books, 2004); Chris Nickson, *Denzel Washington* (New York: St. Martin's, 1996).

Hans Ostrom

Holiday, Billie (1915–1959). Singer. Holiday is considered one of the most renowned and beloved American **jazz** and **blues** singers. She has achieved a kind of secondary fame in various authors' portrayals of her as a siren and a woman scorned. Alice Adams's *Listening to Billie* (1975) and Elizabeth Hardwick's *Sleepless Nights* (1979) concern Holiday. In African American literature, **Maya Angelou**'s **autobiography** *Heart of a Woman* (1981), and **Ntozake Shange**'s *Sassafrass, Cypress and Indigo* (1982) are among the prose works in which Holiday makes an appearance. Her presence in these books lends an air of realism regarding the Black female lived experience through the eyes of an artist and performer. The subjectivity of both autobiographical and fictional versions of Billie Holiday in literature lends credibility to her mythology as renowned jazz singer and tragic African American female icon.

Leon Forrest, in "A Solo Long-Song: For Lady Day," alludes to this "artistic identity," proclaiming that Billie Holiday's music and persona were so charged with realism in the public eye because she knew how to "surrender to love." Holiday, in her autobiography *Lady Sings the Blues* (1956), proclaims that no one could put a label on her; in others' eyes, her "slow...lazy...drawl" was something beyond the blues. In her autobiography she also candidly considers her popularity and her own self-satisfaction with success in spite of her struggle as a Black female artist. The film based on this autobiography starred Diana Ross as Lady Day.

Alice Adams's *Listening to Billie* (1975) portrays Lady Day within the lives of the book's characters. Adams focuses on Holiday's sound, noting her "rich and lonely voice" colored by unsuccessful relationships. Billie thus becomes Eliza Hamilton's (Adams's main character) backdrop music, depicted as the soundtrack to her life filled with men who are self-important; Eliza is obsessed with these men as, seemingly, Holiday is in her stylistic musical rendition of them. Adams writes about Evans, one of these men present in the scene with Billie Holiday, making commentary on how bad Holiday looks as she steps onto the stage, saying, "She can't last long" as she sings *Georgia on My Mind*. Adams highlights Holiday's performance by noting that "She scans the crowd as though she could see everyone there," perhaps contrasting the male character's vision of her as an incapable, broken woman.

Elizabeth Hardwick's *Sleepless Nights* (1979) presents Holiday as both siren and scorned, subtly proclaiming her presence amid the characters of the novel as "bizarre deity." Holiday's description is both tangible and subtle in Hardwick's characterization. Considering the myth surrounding Holiday's self-destruction, Hardwick notes: "She died in misery. . . . Her whole life had taken place in the dark." Here she alludes both to Lady Day's jazz stage presence and her personal reaction to success, given her experience of substance abuse and bad relationships. Ultimately, Hardwick writes, Holiday "Somehow . . . had retrieved from darkness the miracle of pure style." Hardwick also spends time with "the sheer enormity of her vices," from heroin to Scotch and brandy, noting that she was never free of these "consumptions" and that "For the grand destruction one must be worthy," perhaps indicating that Holiday was worthy (even in her self-destruction) of greatness. She also alludes to Holiday's time in the Federal Women's Prison in West Virginia and how she walked away from this with equal regality, befitting her role as jazz "deity."

Maya Angelou, in her fourth installment of her autobiography, *The Heart of a Woman* (1981), focuses one of her first chapters on a visit with Billie Holiday arranged by friend and voice coach, Frederick "Wilkie" Wilkinson. The message of the chapter centers on the contrast of the popularized songstress Billie Holiday and the woman who appears on Angleou's doorstep, "bloated face . . . holding only a shadow of its former prettiness," meeting a "square" Angelou and her son, Guy, who blows Holiday's vision of Black female performers as harlots and children as troublemakers. Angelou portrays their similarities as performers and experiences they've shared, characterizing the nature of the business for Black women. Holiday's outspokenness, she says, "was a mixture of mockery and vulgarity that caught [her] without warning . . . in new arrangements, and spoken in that casual tone which seemed to drag itself, rapping across the ears." In the process of telling her own story as a performer, Angelou records her reactions to her colleague in her wiry bitterness, most revealing in Holiday's performance of " Strange Fruit" for Guy—which ends in a bitter dialogue regarding **lynching**.

In *Sassafrass, Cypress and Indigo* (1982), Ntozake Shange qualifies Holiday's siren side by focusing on her peformance mask. Personally addressing Shange's Sassafras, a writer gone astray from her writing, Holiday as character highlights the major female performers of color: Ma Rainey, Maimie Smith, Big Mama Thornton, Freddie Washington, **Josephine Baker**, and Carmen Miranda. Featuring these artists as examples, "The Lady," as written by Shange, becomes a shining example of unfettered female creative energy intended to inspire not only this down-and-out writer but, inevitably, an audience of women of color who aspire to be artists. Shange writes with the irony of the jazz and blues artist's life in mind, noting that Lady Day's presence is a magic that transforms women's lives—in keeping with the "magic" present in her book.

In *Blues Legacies and Black Feminism* (1998), **Angela Y. Davis** points out in her chapter " 'Strange Fruit': Music and Social Consciousness" that Holiday's biographers, including John Chilton (1975) and Donald Clarke (1994), "capture Holiday in a web of gendered, classed, and raced inferiority and present her as capable of producing great work only under the tutelage of her racial superiors." Davis points out with a womanist perspective on Holiday that popular music was forever changed by the social critique of "Strange Fruit" and gained the Black female voice as part of a tradition upheld by various Black female recording artists to the present day. Her view of Holiday as instigator and artist lifts Holiday from the dark mythology surrounding her addictions and abuses to the light of the jazz stage on which she stood, holding captive many audiences with her voiced rendition of oppression.

Resources: Maya Angelou, *The Heart of a Woman* (New York: Bantam, 1997); John Chilton, *Billie's Blues: Bille Holiday's Story 1933–1959* (New York: Stein & Day, 1975); Donald Clarke, *Wishing on the Moon: The Life and Times of Billie Holiday* (London: Viking, 1994); Angela Y. Davis, *Blues Legacy and Black Feminism: Gertrude "Ma" Rainey, Bessie Smith, and Billie Holiday* (New York: Vintage Books, 1998); Leon Forrest, "A Solo Long-Song: For Lady Day," *Callaloo* 16, no. 2 (Spring 1993), 332; Ntozake Shange, *Sassafrass, Cypress and Indigo* (New York: St. Martin's, 1982).

Elizabete Vasconcelos

Holton, Hugh (1946–2001). Novelist. Hugh Holton was born in **Chicago, Illinois**, and spent almost his entire life in the city. Immediately after his high school graduation, Holton was accepted into the police academy, but before he could join the force, he was drafted into the military. After a tour of duty in the **Vietnam War**, he returned to Chicago, and in 1969, he began a long career in the Chicago Police Department. In his off-hours, he earned a bachelor's degree and then a master's degree in journalism from Roosevelt University. His experiences as a police detective and his interest in writing eventually led him to write **crime and mystery fiction**.

Holton's novels feature Larry Cole, an African American detective with the Chicago Police Department. Some of the novels in the series are fairly conventional police procedurals, but in others, Holton integrates elements from **horror fiction**—in particular, occult materials—into the crimes and Cole's investigations of them. In the first novel in the series, *Presumed Dead* (1994), Cole uncovers "mad science" in the bowels of a prestigious museum. In *Windy City* (1995), Cole tracks a married pair of serial killers who are obsessed with very different types of victims. *Chicago Blues* (1996) delineates the consequences of the preemptive murder of a couple of hit men. *Violent Crimes* (1997) gathers an eccentric mix of characters, living and dead, into a plot involving secret weapons developed for the military. *Red Lightning* (1998) explores the world of personal security services, focusing on a particular specialist who is an imaginative sadist. In *The Left Hand of God* (1999), Cole investigates a secret society whose ultimate goal is to exterminate everyone but the elite. *Time of the Assassins* (2000) is a very traditional suspense tale, pitting Cole against an international assassin with an aristocratic pedigree. In *The Devil's Shadow* (2001), psychic insights help Cole to solve two very different types of cases involving theft, mob-organized bank heists, and high-end burglaries executed by a beautiful master thief. In the posthumously published *Criminal Element* (2002), Holton returns to the more conventional mystery-detective form, as Cole unravels the long-standing alliance between a crooked police officer and a corrupt politician.

Resources: Scott Fornek, "Cops Make Great Storytellers," *Chicago Sun-Times*, Apr. 1, 2001, p. 16; Hugh Holton: *Chicago Blues* (New York: St. Martin's, 1996); *Criminal Element* (New York: Forge, 2002); *The Devil's Shadow* (New York: Forge, 2001); *The Left Hand of God* (New York: St. Martin's, 1999); *Presumed Dead* (New York: St. Martin's, 1994); *Red Lightning* (New York: St. Martin's, 1998); *Time of the Assassins* (New York: Forge, 2000); *Violent Crimes* (New York: St. Martin's, 1997); *Windy City* (New York: St. Martin's, 1995); Dom Najolia, "Details Are No Mystery to Chicago Cop," *Chicago Sun-Times*, Mar. 30, 1997, p. 18.

Martin Kich

Holtzclaw, William Henry (1870–1943). Educator and autobiographer. The son of former slaves, William Henry Holtzclaw is considered a pioneer in African American education. He was born into extreme poverty near Roanoke, Alabama. He received a sporadic early education in rural schools that were in session for only a few months each year. In 1890, after seeing an ad for Tuskegee Institute in a local newspaper, he sent a letter to Tuskegee with "to Booker T. Washington" inscribed on the envelope. Somehow it reached Washington, and Holtzclaw began attending Tuskegee, experiencing the privations of many of its poor students. After the death of his father in 1893, Holtzclaw returned home to care for his mother and siblings, and to begin to pay off his father's debt. He began teaching in a small school in Whitesburg, Georgia, to help his family financially, but returned to Tuskegee in 1896. After impressing **Booker T. Washington** while at Tuskegee, Holtzclaw was offered the position of substitute teacher in the night school. Holtzclaw graduated in 1898, and then ran the print shop at Snow Hill Institute in Snow

Hill, Alabama, a school modeled after the Hampton–Tuskegee idea. While living in Snow Hill, Holtzclaw organized the Black Belt Improvement Company of Wilcox County, Alabama, and was influential in helping African American families improve their farms and farming techniques, and subsequently their economic situation. Holtzclaw rose to the positions of financial agent and treasurer of the Snow Hill Institute.

In 1902, after several attempts, Holtzclaw moved to Mississippi, motivated by his belief that it was the cradle of African American ignorance. In November of that year he became principal of a tiny, two-teacher school in Utica, Mississippi, and under his leadership, it grew into the Utica Normal and Industrial Institute. While a basic academic component of reading, writing, and math was present, the Institute emphasized the useful vocations of farming, stock and poultry raising, carpentry, and the domestic sciences, among other subjects. Because of Holtzclaw's untiring fund-raising, Utica Institute abandoned its original 100-acre campus and established itself on nearly 2,000 acres in 1910. Under Holtzclaw's direction, many of the original buildings were dismantled and reconstructed on the new campus.

At the urging of William Pickens, George Washington Carver, and Booker T. Washington, Holtzclaw wrote his **autobiography**, *The Black Man's Burden*, in 1915, in which he described his early education and experience at Utica. In 1916 he received an honorary Master of Arts degree from Alabama Agricultural and Mechanical Institute in Normal, Alabama, and in 1942 Tuskegee conferred on him a Master of Science degree for his exemplary work in improving the conditions of African Americans in **the South**. Holtzclaw remained principal of the Utica Institute his entire life. He died on August 27, 1943, at his home in Utica, Mississippi.

Resources: R. Fulton Holtzclaw, *William Henry Holtzclaw: Scholar in Ebony* (Cleveland, OH: Dillon/Liederbach, 1977); William H. Holtzclaw, *The Black Man's Burden* (New York: Neale, 1915).

Philip J. Kowalski

hooks, bell (born 1952). Social critic, cultural critic, essayist, teacher, children's writer, poet, and autobiographer. hooks (who spells her name without capitalization) is one of the most prolific African American writers and thinkers in contemporary American culture. Her analyses of **race**, **gender**, class, and sexual oppression have contributed enormously to how issues connected to **feminism**, racism, economic exploitation, and systems of domination are perceived. She is the author of more than twenty books and numerous articles and essays written over a period of less than twenty-five years. hooks has written on subjects ranging from art, film, and the act of writing, to self-esteem, teaching, and love. Her analyses have centered predominantly on feminist theory, representations of race and gender, class, and identity, but the forms and applications of her work are wide-ranging. Her diverse and accessible writing has crossed disciplinary boundaries and earned her a secure place among academic and public audiences nationwide. She is now regarded as one of America's leading public intellectuals and cultural critics.

hooks was born Gloria Watkins on September 25, 1952, in Hopkinsville, Kentucky. She has used the lower case pseudonym bell hooks throughout her writing career both to establish a voice and identity separate from the person Gloria Watson, and to honor her maternal great-grandmother Bell, whose name she now shares. In addition, the use of a pseudonym underscores hooks's desire to have her work and ideas receive more focus and attention than she as a person receives. She is also committed to writing in a style that is accessible and pertinent to the lives of her many readers, many of whom are not directly affiliated with academic institutions, but whom she considers part of a larger intellectual community.

hooks's working-class roots and experiences growing up in **the South** during segregation provided a foundation from which to later explore and expose the many vectors of oppression, and hooks often draws upon personal stories of her home life, upbringing, and community in her work. Her father, Veodis Watkins, was employed as a custodian by the Postal Service. Known as the patriarch of the family, his relationship with hooks was strained due to abuse and the emotional distance between them. Though hooks acknowledges that her father worked hard to provide for his growing family, he is also characterized as a man who often withheld his affection and who believed in strict definitions regarding gender roles and responsibilities, especially as they pertained to child rearing and household tasks. These definitions and assumptions surrounding appropriate gender roles are critiqued in much of hooks's writing, as is the patriarchal culture that supports them. Her mother, Rosa Bell Watkins, was the primary caretaker for bell and her six siblings—five sisters and one brother.

In literature, hooks found a sense of community in the midst of a childhood that was sometimes difficult. She was often filled with self-doubt as an adolescent and frequently battled low self-esteem. Although her writing makes clear that she did have many moments of joy in her young life and that her home served as a site of affirmation at times, she struggled with her identity and feared that she would not be perceived as normal by others. Literature and writing helped her develop her own voice and sense of place in the world. Her memoir, *Bone Black: Memories of Girlhood* (1996), for instance, recalls her first experience reading Louisa May Alcott's *Little Women*. hooks states that when reading about Jo, the serious sister who wanted to write and was often punished, she felt a "little less alone in the world" (77). Her newfound relationship with texts and characters continued to develop as she was exposed to ever more writers and genres of literature.

Later in her childhood, hooks was able to acquire several books written by such authors as Homer, Shakespeare, George Eliot, and Emily Dickinson from the collection of a retired schoolteacher. She writes in her memoir that "these books are a new world. I am even less alone" (78). This sense of connection to literature and to writing really flourished when she was introduced to the work of other African American women writers. She writes in the foreword to *Bone Black* that **Toni Morrison**'s *The Bluest Eye*, for example, shook her to the "very roots" of her being, changing her life forever (xii). hooks was able to find girls who not only were confronting similar issues of class, race, and identity in Morrison's portrayal of girlhood in the text, but who also acted as "critical thinkers, theorizing their lives, telling the story, and by so doing making themselves subjects of history" (xxi). These explorations of identity, oppression, and subjectivity informed hooks's own work as well, and helped shape her vision and voice as a writer.

Writing for hooks became a sanctuary, an activity she describes in *Remembered Rapture: The Writer at Work* (1999) as the place where she could "collect the bits pieces . . . and put them back together again" (7). She began writing diary entries as a child, and found that keeping a diary was both healing and threatening—healing because writing was a way for her to "talk back" and come to understand herself and the world around her better, but threatening because she considered the confessions written in her diary to be testimony that documented realities she was "not always able to face" (5). She writes in *Remembered Rapture* of her desire to destroy the diaries as a response to that threat, but also of how years of sustained diary writing were very important to her later development as a writer. It was this confessional writing, she maintains, that enabled her to "find a voice" (6). In writing she could express herself freely and openly, and later, she learned of its power to effect self-definition and self-transformation. Writing and the process of grappling with words became what she calls her "true home, a place of solace and comfort" (22).

hooks's first major publication was her groundbreaking text *Ain't I a Woman: Black Women and Feminism* (1981). She completed the first draft of the text when she was just nineteen years old. It was hooks's first book-length investigation of issues surrounding the lives of Black women and women of color at a time in which the field of Black Women's Studies was just establishing itself and drawing increasing attention from the academy and larger public. Along with her 1984 publication, *Feminist Theory: From Margin to Center*, the text helped to expose the reluctance of the women's movement to shift its focus from gender oppression to interlocking oppressions based on one's gender, race, and class. hooks insisted that feminist theory could not be truly revolutionary unless it worked to adequately address the impact of racism, sexism, and economic oppression on Black women's lives. Thus, she joined other African American women writers and thinkers, such as **Audre Lorde**, **Angela Davis**, and **Barbara Smith**, in challenging and clarifying the movement's overall focus, aims, and ultimate goals.

hooks has continued to examine gender, race, and class oppression. *Talking Back: Thinking Feminist, Thinking Black* (1989), *Yearning: Race, Gender and Cultural Politics* (1990), *Black Looks: Race and Representation* (1992), *Outlaw Culture: Resisting Representations* (1994), *Killing Rage: Ending Racism* (1995), and *Feminism Is for Everybody: Passionate Politics* (2000) all contribute to her ongoing investigations of racial representations, the dynamics of White supremacy, and the importance of revolutionary feminism, feminist theory, and feminist scholarship. She has also written specifically on processes of self-actualization in *Sisters of the Yam: Black Women and Self-Recovery* (1993) and *Rock My Soul: Black People and Self-Esteem* (2004), texts that situate self-esteem and healing within the contexts of patriarchy, class oppression, and racism.

More recently hooks has focused on African American men and constructions of masculinity in *We Real Cool: Black Men and Masculinity* (2004) and *The Will to Change: Men, Masculinity and Love* (2004). (The title of the former book is taken from a famous poem by **Gwendolyn Brooks**.) These texts explore such topics as stereotypes surrounding Black men, Black male violence, parenting, confronting oppressive systems of domination, and the need and practice of love. Always interested in new forms of writing and expression, hooks has recently completed three children's book that focus on similar themes explored in her critical work. She engages issues of female beauty, **hair**, and self-esteem in *Happy to be Nappy* (1999); home, family, and tenderness in *Homemade Love* (2002); and African American boyhood in *Be Boy Buzz* (2002).

hooks pursued a Bachelor of Arts degree in English at Stanford University, which she received in 1973. She went on to receive a Master of Arts in English from the University of Wisconsin in 1976 before earning her Ph.D. in English from the University of California at Santa Cruz in 1983. She has taught at Yale and Oberlin but has spent most of her time as an educator at the City University of New York, where in 1994 she was appointed Distinguished Lecturer of English Literature. Many of her experiences teaching are featured in her two books focused on pedagogy, *Teaching to Transgress: Education as the Practice of Freedom* (1994) and *Teaching Community: A Pedagogy of Hope* (2003). In both texts she offers her thoughts on how the classroom might be conceptualized as a site of affirmation, community, resistance, and growth.

Resources: bell hooks: *Ain't I a Woman: Black Women and Feminism* (Boston: South End, 1981); *All About Love: New Visions* (New York: HarperPerennial, 2001); *And There We Wept: Poems* (Los Angeles: Golemics, 1978); *Art on My Mind: Visual Politics* (New York: New Press, 1995); *Be Boy Buzz* (New York: Jump at the Sun, 2002); *Black Looks: Race and Representation* (Boston: South End, 1992); *Bone Black: Memories of Girlhood* (New York: Henry Holt, 1996); *Communion: The Female Search for Love* (New York: Morrow, 2002); *Feminism Is for Everybody* (Boston: South End, 2000); *Feminist Theory: From Margin to Center* (Boston: South End, 1984); *Happy to Be Nappy* (New York: Hyperion, 1999); *Homemade Love* (New York: Jump at the Sun, 2002); *Killing Rage: Ending Racism* (New York: Henry Holt, 1995); *Outlaw Culture: Resisting Representations* (New York: Routledge, 1994); *Reel to Real: Race, Sex, and Class at the Movies* (New York: Routledge, 1996); *Remembered Rapture: The Writer at Work* (New York: Henry Holt, 1999); *Rock My Soul: Black People and Self-Esteem* (New York: Washington Square Press, 2004); *Salvation: Black People and Love* (New

York: HarperPerennial, 2001); *Sisters of the Yam: Black Women and Self-Recovery* (Boston: South End, 1993); *Talking Back: Thinking Feminist, Thinking Black* (Boston: South End, 1989); *Teaching Community: A Pedagogy of Hope* (New York: Routledge, 2003); *Teaching to Transgress: Education as the Practice of Freedom* (New York: Routledge, 1994); *We Real Cool: Black Men and Masculinity* (New York: Routledge, 2004); *Where We Stand: Class Matters* (New York: Routledge, 2000); *The Will to Change: Men, Masculinity, and Love* (New York: Routledge, 2004); *A Woman's Mourning Song* (New York: Harlem River, 1993); *Wounds of Passion: A Writing Life* (New York: Henry Holt, 1997); *Yearning: Race, Gender, and Cultural Politics* (Boston: South End, 1990); bell hooks and Cornel West, *Breaking Bread: Insurgent Black Intellectual Life* (Boston: South End Press, 1991).

Amanda Davis

Hopkins, Pauline Elizabeth (1859–1930). Novelist, short story writer, editor, playwright, and actress. Hopkins is a crucial transitional link between the **slave narratives** and autobiographical novels of the nineteenth century and the groundbreaking novels of the **Harlem Renaissance**. A contemporary of **Frances Ellen Watkins Harper** and **Charles Waddell Chesnutt**, Hopkins and her contributions to the development of the African American novel have been underplayed. Hopkins was born in 1859 in Portland, Maine, but was raised and educated in **Boston, Massachusetts**. She first received recognition for her writing at age fifteen, when she won an award for a temperance essay in a contest sponsored by **William Wells Brown**. Brown influenced Hopkins's only published play, *Slaves' Escape: Or the Underground Railroad* (1879). With her mother and stepfather, Hopkins toured as an actress and singer with Hopkins' Colored Troubadours from 1880 to 1892. She returned to Massachusetts in the 1890s and worked at the Bureau of Statistics. She began her association with the *Colored American* magazine in 1900 with her story "The Mystery Within Us." Hopkins was hired as its editor for the Women's Department in late 1901 and became literary editor in 1903. In that capacity she foreshadowed the editorial career of **Jessie Redmon Fauset** at *The Crisis*. She left her editorial position in 1904 due to ill health.

In 1900 Hopkins's most famous novel, *Contending Forces: A Romance Illustrative of Negro Life North and South*, was published. This historical **romance novel** addresses most of the issues found in her later novels. Principal themes include sexual exploitation of women, the temptation of **passing**, violence against African Americans, educational opportunities, and cultural identity. Hopkins's later novels were serialized in the *Colored American: Hagar's Daughter, A Story of Southern Caste Prejudice* (1901–1902), *Winona: A Tale of Negro Life in the South and Southwest* (1902), and *Of One Blood: or, The Hidden Self* (1902–1903). These novels are a unique blend of domestic ideology and sensationalism (false identity, disguise, adventure). In addition to fiction, Hopkins contributed to the *Colored American* a series of biographical sketches on prominent African American men and women, including William Wells Brown, **Frederick Douglass**, **Sojourner Truth**, and Frances E. W. Harper.

Hopkins's last published work, the short story "Topsy Templeton," appeared in *New Era* in 1916. She died in 1930 as a result of a fire in her apartment. After decades of obscurity, Hopkins's work has started to receive significant critical attention with the reissue of *Contending Forces* in 1988 and the Oxford University Press collection of her three magazine novels in 1988.

Resources: Michael Bennett and Vanessa Dickerson, eds., *Recovering the Black Female Body: Self-Representations by African American Women* (New Brunswick, NJ: Rutgers University Press, 2001); Janet Gabler-Hover, *Dreaming Black/Writing White: The Hagar Myth in American Cultural History* (Lexington: University Press of Kentucky, 2000); John Cullen Gruesser, ed., *The Unruly Voice: Rediscovering Pauline Elizabeth Hopkins* (Urbana: University of Illinois Press, 1996); Pauline E. Hopkins: *The Magazine Novels of Pauline Hopkins*, intro. Hazel V. Carby (New York: Oxford University Press, 1988); *Of One Blood: or, The Hidden Self*, ed. Deborah E. McDowell (New York: Washington Square Press, 2004).

Ann Beebe

Hopkinson, Nalo (born 1960). Science fiction novelist and short story writer. Nalo Hopkinson draws broadly from Caribbean culture in creating her speculative fiction. She is the daughter of Freda and Muhammed Abdur-Rahman Slade Hopkinson, a librarian and a poet, respectively, of Kingston, Jamaica. Growing up, she lived in Jamaica, Trinidad, Guyana, and the United States, and read widely, discovering **science fiction** in the Kingston Public Library while a teenager. Her family moved to Toronto while she was a teenager, and she attended York University there from 1977 to 1982, studying French and Russian and graduating with honors. Inspired by the work of black science fiction writers such as **Stephen Emory Barnes**, **Octavia E. Butler**, and **Samuel R. Delany** (whom she profiled in the 27 October–9 November, 1994, issue of *WORD: Toronto's Black Culture Magazine*), she began writing science fiction in 1993. In 1995 she attended the Clarion Science Fiction and Fantasy Writers Workshop at Michigan State University.

Hopkinson's first novel, *Brown Girl in the Ring* (1998) is set in a near future version of a burned-out section of Toronto. Based in part on the author's extensive studies of Orisha worship, it follows a young Afro-Caribbean woman, Ti-Jeanne, as she confronts the leader of a gang who uses the power of dead souls trapped in his duppy bowl to control the living. To stand up to him, Ti-Jeanne must learn to accept her own visions as part of her gifted heritage. It won the Warner Aspect First Novel prize in 1997, whose lead judge, C. J. Cherryh, cited its combination of urban fantasy, science fiction, and Caribbean folklore.

Midnight Robber (2000), Hopkinson's second novel, is based in part on the Jamaican trickster figure Three-Fingered Jack. Beginning on the Caribbean colonized world of Toussaint, *Midnight Robber* follows its young heroine, Tan-Tan, who is forced to flee with her father to an exile world, New Half Way Tree. Assaulted by her father, she kills him, and must take on the identity of the legendary Midnight Robber to confront her stepmother. Like its predecessor, *The Midnight Robber* was lauded for its creative mixture of Caribbean folklore and science fiction. Hopkinson followed this up with *Skin Folk* (2001), a collection of stories drawing heavily on Caribbean folklore; a common theme is a focus on people whose skin conceals rather than reveals their true identity. *The Salt Roads*, her 2003 novel, continues in this Caribbean vein, focusing on three women from different points in history (one of them, Jeanne DuVal, is the Black mistress of Charles Baudelaire) who are linked by Ezli (or Iwa) of the **voodoo** pantheon, who travels across time to use each of them.

Hopkinson has also edited a collection of Caribbean fabulist fiction, *Whispers from the Cotton Tree Root* (2000), and maintains a personal web page at http://www.sff.net/people/nalo/index.html. She has taught widely at Canadian and U.S. universities.

Resources: Jennifer Burwell and Nancy Johnston, "A Dialogue on SF and Utopian Fiction Between Nalo Hopkinson and Élisabeth Vonarburg," *Foundation: The International Review of Science Fiction* 81 (Spring 2001), 40–47; Dianne Glave, "An Interview with Nalo Hopkinson," *Callaloo* 26 (Winter 2003), 146–159; Nalo Hopkinson: *Brown Girl in the Ring* (New York: Warner, 1998); "Dark Ink Science Fiction Writers of Colour," *Nalo Hopkinson: Science Fiction and Fantasy Author*, http://www.sff.net/people/nalo/writing/writrs.html; *Midnight Robber* (New York: Warner, 2000); *The Salt Roads* (New York: Warner, 2003); *Skin Folk* (New York: Warner, 2001); Nancy Johnston, "Nalo Hopkinson," *Dictionary of Literary Biography*, vol. 251, *Canadian Fantasy and Science-Fiction Writers*, ed. Douglas Ivison (Detroit: Gale, 2001), 134–138; Gregory E. Rutledge, "The Urban Jungle and Nalo Hopkinson's Speculative Fiction: How Capitalism Underdeveloped the Black Americas and Left a *Brown Girl in the Ring*," *Foundation: The International Review of Science Fiction* 81 (Spring 2001), 22–39.

Thomas J. Cassidy

Horne, Frank Smith (1899–1974). Poet and public administrator. Frank Horne's poetry and public administrative work both embodied the struggle against the prejudices and limitations facing African Americans. Horne graduated from City College of New York in 1921, Northern Illinois College of Optometry in 1922, and the University of Southern California in 1932. Horne practiced optometry from 1922 to 1926, and in the latter year became the Dean and acting President of Fort Valley High and Industrial School. In 1936 he started his career in public administration when he went to work for the U.S. Housing Authority. He worked for several of its agencies, including the Office of Race Relations, in both **Washington, D.C.**, and New York City. In 1956 he took a job as the Executive Director of the New York City Commission on Intergroup Relations; in 1962 he became a consultant for the New York City Housing Redevelopment Board. While in Washington, Horne was a member of President Franklin Roosevelt's Black cabinet, a forum for brainstorming solutions to problems in the administration. He also founded the National Committee Against Discrimination in Housing.

Horne's administrative work produced a number of pamphlets and other publications related to his ongoing work in fighting housing discrimination. His activist stance is also present in his poetry, although the poems often have a private, lyrical voice. In 1925 Horne, using the pseudonym Xavier I, won the Amy Springarn Contest in *The Crisis* for his poem "Letters Found Near a Suicide." The eleven-part poem is addressed to various people who had an effect on Horne's life, and seven additional poems were added in 1929. "Letters" established Horne's reputation as a poet, and in some of his other poems, such as "Harlem," "Nigger, A Chant for Freedom," and "On Seeing Two Brown Boys in a Catholic Church," he takes up the political themes of racial pride and/or discrimination. Horne is generally considered a minor poet of the **Harlem Renaissance**; his poetic corpus is relatively small, but he has been included in a number of important African American anthologies, such as **Langston Hughes** and **Arna Bontemps**'s *Poetry of the Negro, 1746–1949*.

Resources: "Frank (Smith) Horne," in *Contemporary Authors Online* (Detroit: Gale, 2002), http://galenet.gale.com; Frank Horne, *Haverstraw* (1963); Langston Hughes and Arna Bontemps, eds., *The Poetry of the Negro, 1746–1949* (Garden City, NY: Doubleday, 1949); Ronald Primeau, "Frank Horne and the Second Echelon Poets of the Harlem Renaissance," in *Remembering the Harlem Renaissance*, ed. Cary D. Wintz (New York: Garland, 1996), 371–391.

Sarah Antoinette Miller

Horror Fiction. The primary intent of horror fiction is to frighten the reader by inducing feelings of terror and/or dread. This fear is often brought about by the evocation of a supernatural source or cause of the terror. The fear may also be of a psychological or emotional kind, however, and need not spring from a supernatural source. The work may also focus upon instilling a feeling of suspense rather than utter dread.

The supernatural element at work in much horror fiction is often a monster or another kind of strange being: werewolf, ghost, mummy, or vampire. Vampires especially have been a favorite topic for writers of horror fiction. These creatures are usually the undead corpses of human beings (sometimes they are animals). They are immortals brought back from the dead by the bite of another vampire. They must suck the blood of humans in order to survive. Since the publication of Bram Stoker's *Dracula* in 1897, vampires have been a staple of horror fiction.

The modern horror fiction novel has its origins in the **gothic literature** of the late eighteenth and early nineteenth centuries. In America, Edgar Allen Poe, with short stories such as "The Tell-Tale Heart," "The Masque of the Red Death," and "The Black Cat"; Henry James with his novel *The Turn of the Screw* (1898); and Ambrose Bierce were pioneers in the field. H. P. Lovecraft, who called his works "weird tales," was also an important figure in the foundation of modern horror.

Perhaps the three most important classic works of horror fiction were produced during the nineteenth century: Mary Shelley's *Frankenstein; Or, The*

Modern Prometheus (1818), Robert Louis Stevenson's *The Strange Case of Dr. Jekyll and Mr. Hyde* (1886), and Bram Stoker's *Dracula* (1897). These three novels had an enormous impact on the works that followed, and continue to do so today. Stoker's Count Dracula has become an archetypal symbol of the vampire. Numerous films and books have been made and written about these works.

It is not surprising that African Americans did not begin exploring the genre of horror fiction until relatively recently. For much of the nineteenth century, during the years of **slavery**, it was illegal to teach a slave to read or write. What we do have from this time period are **folktales** that often contain horrific elements such as ghosts. These stories were passed down orally and served as a way of transferring information, and tales with horrific elements were used as a way of frightening people into a proper way of acting, in essence "scaring them straight."

Slave narratives relating the daily sufferings of African Americans often contained horrific elements as well, although we certainly would not classify them as horror fiction as it is known today. Writers of slave narratives cataloged the injustices and often the daily terror of life as a slave, but they certainly began to pave the way for all African American writers, including the horror writers of today. In the twentieth century, we have tales of **lynchings** in **the South**, and beatings and murders during the **Civil Rights Movement** of the 1950s and 1960s—all frightening to the reader—but it is only during the later portion of the twentieth century that we begin to see African American writers producing works of horror in the modern sense.

The popularity of the gothic novel began to decline during the mid-nineteenth century, and by the beginning of the twentieth century, much horror fiction was published mainly in inexpensive "pulp" magazines prevalent during the time period between the two world wars. In 1923 a pulp devoted specifically to horror fiction was introduced. *Weird Tales* published works by H. P. Lovecraft and reprinted works by Poe. There was a decline in interest and popularity in the pulps, and most of them were out of business by the time of **World War II**. In the 1960s the horror novel began to gain popularity again, due in part to the writer Ira Levin. In 1974 the publication of Stephen King's first novel, *Carrie*, ushered in a boom in the horror publishing industry.

Only in recent years has the genre of horror fiction begun to be explored by African American writers. Currently, the most popular African American writer working in the genre is **Tananarive Due**. Due began her writing career as a journalist with the *Miami Herald* and began her career as a novelist in 1995 with *The Between*, in which the protagonist, Hilton, attempts to deal with nightmares and the fear of his own death. Due shies from the label of "horror writer," instead saying that she wants to write stories about African Americans. In a 1998 interview with Lee Meadows she said that she "wanted to write the books [she] couldn't read," meaning stories with supernatural elements and about African Americans. *The Between* was followed in 1997 by *My Soul to Keep*, dealing with the love story of the immortal David, or Dawit, and the secret he has been keeping from his mortal wife, Jessica, a investigative reporter. Other novels by Due include *The Living Blood* (2001), which won a 2002 American Book Award, and *The Good House* (2004), Due's take on a haunted house story. She has also written a historical novel, *The Black Rose* (2000), and the memoir *Freedom in the Family: A Mother-Daughter Memoir of the Fight for Civil Rights* (2003), which she authored with her mother, Patricia Stevens Due.

L. A. Banks (the pseudonym of **Leslie Esdaile Banks**) is another prominent voice within the genre. Her Vampire Huntress series deals with an African American woman named Damali Richards who is a spoken-word artist as well as a powerful vampire huntress called a Neteru. The three novels in the series thus far are *Minion* (2004), *The Awakening* (2004), and *The Hunted* (2004).

Linda Addison was winner of the Bram Stoker Award for her collection of poems, *Consumed, Reduced to Beautiful Grey Ashes* (2001).

In recent years, there have also been a few important anthologies of African Americans working in speculative/horror fiction. Sheree R. Thomas edited the popular speculative fiction collection *Dark Matter: A Century of Speculative Fiction from the African Diaspora* (2000) and *Dark Matter: Reading the Bones* (2004).

Brandon Massey is the editor of the short story collection *Dark Dreams* (2004), one of the few anthologies that has been published thus far dealing exclusively with horror fiction written by African Americans. He has also written two novels, *Thunderland* (2002) and *Dark Corner* (2004).

Other African American writers who have produced works of horror fiction in recent years are Robert Fleming, Christopher Chambers, and Chesya Burke.

Resources: Primary Sources: Linda Addison, *Consumed, Reduced to Beautiful Grey Ashes* (New York: Space and Time, 2001); L. A. Banks: *The Awakening: A Vampire Huntress Legend* (New York: St. Martin's Griffin, 2004); *The Hunted: A Vampire Huntress Legend* (New York: St. Martins's Griffin, 2004); *Minion: A Vampire Huntress Legend* (New York: St. Martin's Press, 2004); Tananrive Due: *The Between* (New York: HarperCollins, 1995); *The Good House* (New York: Simon and Schuster, 2004); Interview with Lee Meadows, *Book Beat*, WPON (Detroit, Nov. 4, 1998); *The Living Blood* (New York: Pocket Books, 2001); *My Soul to Keep* (New York: HarperPrism, 1997); Brandon Massey, *Thunderland* (New York: Dafina, 2002); Brandon Massey, ed., *Dark Dreams: A Collection of Horror and Suspense by Black Writers* (New York: Dafina, 2004); Mary Shelley, *Frankenstein; or, The Modern Prometheus* (London: Lackington, Hughes, Harding, Mavor & Jones, 1818); Robert Louis Stevenson, *The Strange Case of Dr. Jeckyll and Mr. Hyde* (London: Longman's, Green, 1886); Bram Stoker, *Dracula* (Westminster, UK: Archibald Constable and Co., 1897); Sheree Thomas, ed.: *Dark Matter: A Century of Speculative Fiction from the African Diaspora* (New York: Warner Books, 2000); *Dark Matter: Reading the Bones* (New York: Warner Books, 2004). **Secondary Sources:** Roger Abrahams, *African American Folktales: Stories from Black Traditions in the New World* (New York: Random House, 1985); Harold Bloom, ed.: *Classic Horror Writers* (New York: Chelsea House, 1994); *Modern Horror Writers* (New York: Chelsea House, 1994); David Pringle, *St. James Guide to Horror, Ghost & Gothic*

Writers (Detroit: St. James Press, 1998); Jack Sullivan, ed., *The Penguin Encyclopedia of Horror and the Supernatural* (New York: Viking 1986).

Lakiska Flippin

Horton, George Moses (c. 1797–c. 1883). Poet and orator. George Moses Horton, a self-taught professional poet, was the first African American to publish a book in **the South**. Born on William Horton's tobacco farm in Northampton County, North Carolina, Horton learned to read from Bibles and hymnals, and absorbed the rhythms of the **spirituals** and **sermons** at church and camp meetings. His education was never supported by his master, and was actively opposed by other youths, who mocked and bullied him. Nevertheless, by the time he was a young man, Horton had begun to take advantage of his relative freedom of movement to travel to Chapel Hill to sell not only fruit but also his poems.

Horton made his start on the University of North Carolina campus, reciting poems aloud and selling impromptu love lyrics to students who wanted to court women. The university was at the time an impoverished institution with a wealthy, brash student body, and Horton was as much taunted and abused as he was admired. While his skills at public speaking and debate were valued, and while he enjoyed the friendship of the university president, Horton was also keenly aware of the patronizing attitude that many White students took toward him. The title by which he became known, "The Black Bard of North Carolina," was at least partly a joke at Horton's expense.

During this period, and with the encouragement of the students at the university, Horton began to drink. His battle with alcoholism was lifelong, and he wrote frankly about the miseries of drink, poverty, and other hardships in his later poetry.

Despite his great skill with language, Horton did not learn to write until about 1832. In 1828, however, his verses were printed with the assistance of his friend and patron Caroline Lee Whiting Hentz. Hentz was an author in her own right, and a dedicated transcriber of Horton's poetry. She sent two of his poems, "Liberty and Slavery," and "On Poetry and Music," to the *Lancaster* (Massachusetts) *Gazette*, which published them. The publication of these poems led to literary celebrity for Horton, and gained him some allies in his ongoing bid for freedom, literacy, and publication. The African American newspaper *Freedom's Journal* took up his cause and asked for donations toward his manumission; meanwhile, Horton's poetry continued to be published in other newspapers. In 1828 arrangements were made to publish a book of Horton's poetry, *The Hope of Liberty*, and to use the proceeds to purchase his freedom. The book was published in 1829, but did not earn enough to buy his freedom.

Horton continued to publish poems, battling alcoholism and depression as his struggle for emancipation continued without much hope of success. *The Hope of Liberty* was reissued twice, as *Poems by a Slave* in 1837 and, together with some of **Phillis Wheatley**'s verse, in 1838. Not until 1845 did Horton publish a new book, titled *Poetical Works of George M. Horton, the Colored Bard of North-Carolina to Which Is Prefixed the Life of the Author Written by Himself*.

For another twenty years Horton lobbied unsuccessfully for his freedom. In 1865, at the age of sixty-eight, he traveled to Raleigh, North Carolina, to meet the advancing Union troops. He came under the patronage of Capt. William H. S. Banks of the 9th Michigan Cavalry Volunteers, and collaborated with Banks on the publication of his third book, *Naked Genius*, in 1865. He gained his freedom that same year.

After becoming a free man, Horton migrated north to **Philadelphia, Pennsylvania**, after which little is known of his life or movements. He never published a promised fourth volume, to be titled *The Black Poet*, and the place and exact date of his death are not known.

Resources: Tonya Bolden, "Horton, George Moses," in *African-American Writers: A Dictionary*, ed. Shari Dorantes Hatch and Michael R. Strickland (Santa Barbara, CA: ABC-CLIO, 2000); George Moses Horton, *The Black Bard of North Carolina: George Moses Horton and His Poetry*, ed. Joan R. Sherman (Chapel Hill: University of North Carolina Press, 1997); Lonnell E. Johnson, "George Moses Horton," in *African American Authors, 1745–1945*, ed. Emmanuel S. Nelson (Westport, CT: Greenwood Press, 2000); Sondra O'Neale, "Roots of Our Literary Culture: George Moses Horton and Biblical Protest," *Obsidian* 7, no. 2/3 (1981), 18–28.

Karen Munro

Howard University Press (1972–present). Formally established in 1972, Howard University Press (HUP) became the first scholarly press owned and operated by a historically Black college or university. HUP's mission is to publish scholarly books about the "contributions, conditions, and concerns of African Americans, other people of African descent, and people of color around the world" (HUP Mission Statement). The press has published more than 150 scholarly books dedicated to advancing knowledge on African Americans, American minorities, and Blacks throughout Africa and the **diaspora**. HUP publications appear as supplemental texts for courses at 160 colleges and universities in North America and the Caribbean. Although the press has published some fiction and poetry, the majority of its titles contribute to research in African American literature, education, communications, political science, and social and religious studies. Some of the press's early titles played an important role in advancing the critical study of Black culture at a time when there were few academic presses publishing in this area.

Although HUP was formally established in 1972, its imprint began appearing nearly a century prior. For example, the 1892 memorial address for the clergyman, abolitionist, and author Dr. George Barrell Cheever by his brother Henry Theodore Cheever bears the Howard University Press imprint (Muse, 2000). Even though the HUP imprint frequently appeared on **newspapers**, periodicals, pamphlets, and books, it was not considered a fully operational publishing house because many of the production duties were fulfilled by outside contracts. Nonetheless, on February 7, 1919, the Howard board of trustees passed a resolution making HUP an official unit of the university. By 1926, new machinery, type, and supplies were purchased to support its growing publishing demands. The university's archival records indicate that by 1933 the trustees had closed the press, and its equipment and supplies had been sold (Muse, 2000). All university publications were then contracted to commercial printers and publishers. In 1959 the trustees reestablished HUP and developed its bylaws, but the press still existed in name only from 1959 to 1972; none of the publications appearing during this period used the press's resources. In 1971, Charles F. Harris, who later founded Amistad Press, was recruited to create and manage a fully functioning scholarly press. HUP was once again reactivated in 1972 and new bylaws were developed, this time making it an in-house press prioritizing scholarly research about African Americans and other peoples of African descent. Harris served as HUP's first director and chief executive officer of publishing operations, a position he held for fifteen years. The official launch of the new Howard University Press occurred on April 8, 1974, and within four years it published thirty-seven new titles. In 1979 the press was admitted to the American Association of University Presses.

For most of the 1970s and the early 1980s, HUP continued to publish Black scholarship. Walter Rodney's *How Europe Underdeveloped Africa* (1972), **Arthur P. Davis**'s *From the Dark Tower: Afro-American Writers (1900 to 1960)* (1974), Sylvia Lyons Render's *The Short Fiction of Charles W. Chesnutt* (1974), and **Woodie King**'s *The Forerunners: Black Poets in America* (1975) were among some of the early titles that helped to open up the store of information on Black scholarship and culture from voices that were previously ushered to the margins. Even though there was a steady increase in Black scholarship at other university presses, HUP continued its commitment to publishing exclusively on some of the little explored aspects of Black culture. Although the press did not focus as much on literature, it established the Howard University Press Library of Contemporary Literature, which included **Barry Beckham**'s *Runner Mack* (1983), **John Oliver Killens**'s *And Then We Heard the Thunder* (1983), George Davis's *Coming Home* (1984), **William Melvin Kelley**'s *Dancers on the Shore* (1984), and **Junius Edwards**'s *If We Must Die* (1985). The press was also responsible for fulfilling three journals: *Journal of Negro Education*, *Journal of Religious Thought*, and *Howard Journal of Communication*. By the time Harris left the press in the mid-1980s, several of HUP's titles were best-sellers and had received several honors and awards. In 1980, under Charles F. Harris's leadership, HUP established its Book Publishing Institute with a grant from Time, Incorporated. The annual five-week summer program was the only one of its kind operated by an academic press at the time. Until its closing in 1995, the Book Publishing Institute was widely credited with increasing the exposure and interest of people of color to the publishing industry.

The 1990s was a particularly trying period for the press: there was a sharp decline in university funding, the academic publishing market suffered a low growth period, and **Black Studies** titles were frequently appearing on mainstream publishing lists. By 1995, the press was forced, in accordance with budget mandates, to reduce its publication to only a few titles per year. Nonetheless, it published several important contributions, including Richard Jackson's *Black Writers and Latin America: Cross-Cultural Affinities* (1998), which was selected by the editors of *Choice*, a publication of the Association of College & Research Libraries, as one of its Outstanding Academic Books. In 2000, after a two-year hiatus, HUP resumed production with the appointment of a permanent director, D. Kamili Anderson. In February 2004, HUP launched the Classic Editions Series, which features a select list of some of the older and out-of-print titles that helped the press establish itself as a frontrunner in Black academic publishing in the 1970s and 1980s. The library print on demand (POD) series includes many of the titles that were in high demand when first published, such as Chinweizu, Onwuchekwa Jemie, and Ihechukwu Madubuike's *Toward the Decolonization of African Literature* (1983), William Leo Hansberry's *Africa and Africans as Seen by Classical Writers* (1977), and P. Olisanwuche Esedebe's *Pan-Africanism: The Idea and Movement, 1776–1963* (1982).

Resources: D. Kamili Anderson, "Howard University Press," in *Encyclopedia of African-American Education*, ed. Faustine C. Jones-Wilson et al. (Westport, CT: Greenwood Press, 1996), 218–219; Angela Dodson, "Ebony Accents in the Ivory Tower," *Black Issues Book Review*, Sept. 2001, 66–69; Donald Franklin Joyce, *Gatekeepers of Black Culture: Black-owned Book Publishing in the United States, 1817–1981* (Westport, CT: Greenwood Press, 1983); Clifford L. Muse, Jr., "The Development of the Howard University Publishing Program," *Howard University Archives Net* (Feb. 2000), http://www.huarchivesnet.howard.edu/0002huarnet/hupress.htm.

Dara N. Byrne

Hubbard, Dolan (born 1949). Literary critic, editor, and university professor. Hubbard grew up in the Piedmont area of North Carolina, in the town of Granite Quarry, where he was encouraged to pursue his interest in writing and literature by his teachers at the segregated "colored" school, and where his spiritual self was nurtured, in his own words, "in the loving arms of the black church" (*The Sermon*, xi). He completed a Ph.D. in English at the University of Illinois at Urbana–Champaign in 1986. His dissertation concerned the African American folk sermon and its influence on Black America in general and the writers **Frederick Douglass**, **Jean Toomer**, **Ralph Ellison**, and **James Baldwin** in particular. The dissertation was later revised as his first book, *The Sermon and the African American Literary Imagination* (1994), which was selected as an "outstanding academic book for 1995" by *Choice*. Since completing his doctorate, Hubbard has served on the faculties of the University of Tennessee at Knoxville, the University of Georgia, and Morgan State University in **Baltimore, Maryland**, where he currently is Chair of the Department of English and Language Arts.

Hubbard has described himself as a "cultural formalist" whose interpretations emerge not merely from within texts but "from the content of black life" (Fischer, 901–902). For example, in *The Sermon and the African American Literary Imagination*, he treats the Black preaching tradition not only as a stylistic or structural influence on African American writing but also as a sociopolitical force that has been essential to the formation of Black American identity and, thus, to a Black American literature. Just as the sermon itself helps to articulate a communal Black identity that has been historically suppressed, so does the appropriation of sermonic rhetoric by such fiction writers as **Zora Neale Hurston** and **Toni Morrison**. Similarly, in his own literary criticism Hubbard strives to articulate what it means to be Black in America and to do it in accessible, unpretentious language.

In addition to writing the book on **sermons**, Hubbard has served as editor or coeditor of four other books, each of which has made an important contribution to the study of African American literature and culture: *Recovered Writers/Recovered Texts: Race, Class, and Gender in Black Women's Literature* (1997), *The Collected Works of Langston Hughes*, vol. 4, *The Novels: Not Without Laughter and Tambourines to Glory* (2001), *The Souls of Black Folk: One Hundred Years Later* (2003), and *The Library of Black America Collection of Black Sermons* (2004).

Resources: "Dolan Hubbard," in *Contemporary Authors Online* (Detroit: Thomson Gale, 2004), http://galenet.gale.com; Rebecca Bartlett Fischer, "Choice Interviews: Dolan Hubbard," *Choice* 33, no. 6 (1996), 901–903; Dolan Hubbard, *The Sermon and the African-American Literary Imagination* (Columbia: University of Missouri Press, 1994); Dolan Hubbard, ed.: *The Collected Works of Langston Hughes*, vol. 4, *The Novels: "Not Without Laughter" and "Tambourines to Glory"* (Columbia: University of Missouri Press, 2001); *The Library of Black America Collection of Black Sermons* (Chicago: Lawrence Hill, 2004); *Recovered Writers/Recovered Texts: Race, Class, and Gender in Black Women's Literature* (Knoxville: University of Tennessee Press, 1997); *"The Souls of Black Folk": One Hundred Years Later* (Columbia: University of Missouri Press, 2003).

Clay Morton

Hudson-Smith, Linda (born 1950). Novelist. Born in Canonsburg, Pennsylvania, Hudson-Smith grew up for the most part in Washington, Pennsylvania. After studying business at Duff's Business Institute in **Pittsburgh, Pennsylvania**, she was employed as a public relations and marketing administrator with several firms. She began writing **romance novels** after she married an Air Force meteorologist, who was away from home for extended periods, and after she was diagnosed with systemic lupus, a chronic illness that has made it difficult for her to continue working. Ironically, her prolific output as a novelist—some thirteen novels in less than six years—suggests someone with tremendous stores of energy, not someone dealing with a debilitating condition.

For her debut novel, *Ice Under Fire* (2000), Hudson-Smith won the Gold Pen Award for Best New Author from the Black Writers Alliance. *Romance in Color* selected her as its Rising Star for the January 2000 issue. In addition, she received *Shades of Romance* awards as the MultiCultural New Romance Author of the Year and MultiCultural New Fiction Author of the Year.

Hudson-Smith has traveled widely internationally and within the United States, and by last report on her Web site, she has fallen just seven states short of her goal of visiting all fifty states by age fifty. Her firsthand experience of the diverse locations in which she has set her novels has allowed her to describe those settings with a vivid immediacy that is unusual in the genre. Indeed, starting with *Ladies in Waiting* (2002), a novel concerning the wives of men who are imprisoned, Hudson-Smith has begun to move, at least in some of her work, out of the romance genre and into mainstream fiction.

Her novellas have been published with those by several other authors in the thematic collections *Love in Bloom* (2002) and *Give Love* (2003).

Resources: Linda Hudson-Smith: *Above the Clouds* (New York: Kensington, 2005); *Desperate Deceptions* (Washington, DC: Arabesque/BET, 2001); *Fearless Hearts* (Washington, DC: Arabesque/BET, 2004); *Fire Beneath the Ice* (Washington, DC: Arabesque/BET, 2001); *Ice Under Fire* (Washington, DC: Arabesque/BET, 2000); *Island Interlude* (Washington, DC: BET, 2002); *Ladies in Waiting* (Washington, DC: BET, 2002); *One Moment in Time* (Washington, DC: Arabesque/BET, 2002); *Sass* (Washington, DC: BET, 2003); *Soulful Serenade* (Washington, DC: Arabesque/BET, 2000); *Tomorrow May Never Come* (Washington, DC: BET, 2003); *Top-Secret Rendezvous* (Washington, DC: Arabesque/BET, 2003); *Unaccustomed to Waiting* (Washington, DC: Arabesque/BET, 2004); Lillian Lewis, "Review of *Island Interlude*," *Booklist*, May 1, 2002, p. 1512.

Martin Kich

Hughes, Langston (1902–1967). Poet, short story writer, playwright, novelist, essayist, librettist, and editor. Langston Hughes emerged as one of the greatest of all African American writers. He is known for bold innovations in the poetics of the dream and for preserving the historical memory of racial freedom. His deceptively simple language represents a spiritual power that infuses lyrical landscapes such as those of daybreak in Alabama. Through political retorts about the imperative of civil rights expressed within a continuum—the consciousness and conscience of the nation—he redefined "American." His poems, short stories, novels, dramas, translations, and seminal anthologies of works by others, spanning the period from the **Harlem Renaissance** of the 1920s to the **Black Arts Movement**'s reorientations in the 1960s and 1970s, helped reshape the national identity. In the United States, he paved the way for the new female voices, including **Margaret Abigail Walker, Gwendolyn Brooks,** and especially **Alice Walker**. Internationally he inspired francophone visionaries such as the **Négritude** poet Léopold Sédar

Senghor and the Haitian novelist Jacques Roumain. Intrigued by Spanish, as well as by English, German, and French—he was an easy hook for new languages and cultures—he found a kindred spirit in a Cuban, Nicolás Guillén, whose literary artistry has proved crucial to a twenty-first century renaissance in African Latino studies. Hence, Hughes was a writer for the homeland and the world. Perhaps most significantly, he was the unofficial poet laureate of the African American people, whose memory lives on in his poetry.

Between 1921 and 1967, Hughes became both famous and beloved. Even before he had helped young Blacks gain entry to the major periodicals and presses of the day, his experiments in literary **blues** and **jazz** were acclaimed. He worked to introduce new forms that encapsulated confidence and racial pride. In his fictional characters and technical mastery, he displayed social awareness. Hughes, a product of the African American and American 1920s, helped to shape four subsequent decades of literary history. In addition to the decade of the

Undated portrait of Langston Hughes. Courtesy of the Library of Congress.

1920s—in which his innovative poetry of blues and jazz emerged—the 1930s marked his lasting insight into the class inequities of the United States. By the war decade of the 1940s, some of his finest lyrics had appeared as artistic relief for the racial **lynching** that was common at the time.

James Langston Hughes was born to Carrie Langston Hughes and James Nathaniel Hughes on February 1, 1902 in Joplin, Missouri. Carrie's father, Charles Howard Langston, known as Langston, had moved to Kansas in search of greater racial and financial freedom. His penchant for the literary and his desire to transcend the farm and the grocery store in Lawrence, Kansas, were passed on to Hughes. Charles's brother, **John Mercer Langston**, the poet's great-uncle, contributed to the family's literary efforts by penning an autobiography, *From the Virginia Plantation to the National Capitol* (1894). The financially secure John Mercer Langston willed to his descendants a big house as well as stocks and bonds.

In 1907 Langston's mother took him with her to a library in Topeka, where he fell in love with books, in part because he was impressed that the library was publicly maintained. Through the double perspective of boy and man, he recalled: "Even before I was six books began to happen to me, so that after a while there came a time when I believed in books more than in people which, of course, was wrong" (*BS*, 26).

In July 1920, on the train to visit his father in Mexico, while crossing the Mississippi River to **St. Louis, Missouri,** Hughes wrote the short lyric "The Negro Speaks of Rivers" (*CP*, 23). Through the images of water and pyramid, the verse suggests the endurance of human spirituality from the time of ancient Egypt to the nineteenth and twentieth centuries. The muddy Mississippi made Hughes think of the roles in human history played by the Congo, the Niger, and the Nile, down the waters of which the early slaves once were sold. And he thought of Abraham Lincoln, who was moved to end **slavery** after he took a trip on a raft down the Mississippi River. The poem that emerged from a draft he first wrote on the back of an envelope in fifteen minutes has become Hughes's most anthologized poem (Roessel, "Process").

Hughes lived with his father, who had left Hughes and his mother some years before, in Mexico until September 1921. He agonized over his father's desire for him to attend a European university and his own preference to attend Columbia University in New York City. To escape, he went to bullfights in Mexico City almost every weekend. He was unsuccessful in writing about them, but he did write articles about Toluca and the Virgin of Guadalupe. *The Brownies' Book*, a magazine just begun by **W.E.B. Du Bois**'s staff at *The Crisis*, published two poems by Hughes in the January 1921 issue, and *The Gold Piece*, his one-act play for children, in the July 1921 issue. **Jessie Redmon Fauset**, the literary editor, accepted one of his articles and the poem "The Negro Speaks of Rivers" for the June 1921 issue of *The Crisis*.

During the winter of 1923, Hughes wrote the poem that would give the title to his first volume of poetry. "The Weary Blues," about a piano player in **Harlem, New York,** captures the flavor of the nightlife, people, and folk forms that would become characteristic of the experimental writing of the Harlem Renaissance (Barksdale; Tracy).

Hughes's poetry during this period is youthfully romantic. "As I Grew Older" (*CP*, 93) blends reflection and nostalgia as the speaker, framed by light and shadow, seeks to rediscover his dream. In "Mexican Market Woman" (*CP*, 25), Hughes's narrator uses simile to create a dark mood of weariness and pain. And through the persona in "Troubled Woman" (*CP*, 42), the narrator portrays humanity bowed but unbroken. "Mother to Son" (*CP*, 30), a dramatic monologue, shows how **dialect** can be used with dignity. The image of the stair as a beacon of success inspires hope in the son. All of the poems appeared in *The Weary Blues*, which was published in January 1926. Also in 1926 Hughes published the essay "The Negro Artist and the Racial Mountain" in *The Nation*; it is considered one of the main aesthetic statements of the Harlem Renaissance.

Hughes met Charlotte Mason (who liked to be known as "Godmother") on a weekend trip to New York in 1927. A friend introduced him to the elderly White lady, who delighted Hughes immediately and who, despite her age, was modern in her ideas about books. She became his literary patron, a title both disliked. She was also well acquainted with **Alain Locke,** an early supporter of

Hughes, and **Zora Neale Hurston**. With her support, he began work on his first novel, which he envisioned as a portrait of a typical Black family in Kansas. The work, *Not Without Laughter*, which was accepted for publication and appeared in 1930, captures the folk flavor so vital to Hughes.

In the early winter of 1930, Hughes broke irreparably with Mason. Certainly, he had loved her kindness and generosity, including her sincere support for Black advancement and liberal causes. But the two of them disagreed on political philosophy and **race**. She believed that Blacks linked American Whites to the primitive life and should concern themselves only with building on their cultural foundations. Hughes rejected such a simplistic view of the role of Blacks in the modern world. Though he did not openly criticize her, he became psychosomatically ill following his final meeting with her.

Hughes's first volume of stories, *The Ways of White Folks* (1934), appeared during the **Great Depression**. An interface between history and fiction occurred on October 29, 1929, the day the stock market crashed, ending so many opportunities for publication and artistic performance that the **New Negro** Movement had created. In his first **autobiography**, *The Big Sea* (1940), Hughes, writing about Mrs. Mason, also refers obliquely to the fateful year of 1929–1930:

> I cannot write here about the last half hour in the big bright drawing-room high above Park Avenue one morning, because when I think about it, even now, something happens in the pit of my stomach that makes me ill. That beautiful room, that had been so full of light and help and understanding for me, suddenly became like a trap closing in, faster and faster, the room darker and darker, until the light went out with a sudden crash in the dark. (*BS*, 325)

During his travels in Russia in 1932, Hughes had learned well the relationship between writing and mythmaking. The representative of a leading American newspaper had intentionally printed a story in New York claiming that the film company with which Hughes was traveling was stranded and starving in Moscow. When the filmmakers showed the reporter the clippings, he merely grinned. But Hughes praised the many positive changes in post-Revolution Russia that Americans were ignoring, particularly the open housing and the reduced persecution of Jews. Eventually the poet figuratively turned away from Russia because he refused to live without jazz, which the Communists banned.

Determined to confront worldwide fascism and racism, Hughes returned to **San Francisco, California**, by way of Asia in 1933. His trip home demonstrates his headstrong personality. Though Westerners in Shanghai had warned him that the watermelons were tainted and potentially fatal there, he ate well, enjoyed the fruit, and lived to write the story. Warned to avoid the Chinese districts, he visited the areas and found the danger illusory. In Tokyo, the police interrogated, detained, and finally expelled him. In the Japanese press's inflated stories of Korean crimes, he read the pattern of racism so familiar to him in the United States. Aware that victims become victimizers in turn, he understood the Japanese debasement of the Chinese, and, on the way back to the United States, he warned that Japan was a fascist country.

In 1933 and 1934, Hughes retired temporarily from world politics. In Carmel, California, at Noel Sullivan's home "Ennesfree," he completed a series of short stories that were later included in The *Ways of White Folks*. There he became acquainted with the poet Robinson Jeffers and his wife, Una. He also wrote articles, including one on the liberation of women from the harems of Soviet Asia. Grateful to Sullivan for the time to write, Hughes worked from ten to twelve hours a day, producing at least one story or article every week and earning more money than he ever had. He sent most of his earnings to his mother, who was ill. Having broken with his father in 1922, Hughes learned, too late to attend the funeral, that his dad had died in Mexico on October 22, 1934. He traveled to Mexico and remained there from January to April 1935, during which time he read Cervantes's *Don Quixote*.

Shakespeare in Harlem (1942), Hughes's next book of poems, was well crafted. His *Fields of Wonder* (1947) appeared in a United States still full of racial strife but with a promise of social and artistic progress. However modern he was, Hughes would never abandon Black folk life for Western imagism. In *Montage of a Dream Deferred* (1951), his first book-length poem, dramatic and colloquial effects amplify his lyricism. Numerous projects in the writing of history and short fiction, such as *The First Book of Negroes* (1952) and *Simple Takes a Wife* (1953), drained his poetic energies. His style became more sophisticated. Through monologue and free verse, he stressed dramatic situations and mastered the apostrophe for blending content with form, fusing poetic narrative with sound effects.

By the time the book of stories *Laughing to Keep from Crying* was published in 1952, the color line had begun to fade. In 1953 Hughes was called to testify to the Senate subcommittee chaired by Joseph McCarthy, as part of its investigation into the purchase of books by subversive writers for American libraries abroad (*see* **McCarthyism**). Hughes read a statement about his own political views but did not discuss anyone else's (Ostrom, *Encyclopedia*, 239–240; Rampersad). For several years subsequently, Hughes received fewer offers to read his poems. He continued to hone his fiction. When *The Best of Simple* (1961) appeared, it presented a comic veneer and lightness that artfully concealed its complex symbolism. He had developed the character Jesse B. Simple in a column he began writing for the **Chicago Defender** in the 1940s, and he ultimately filled several volumes with the Simple stories (Harper). Another recurring comic, deceptively wise character in his writing is Madame Alberta K. Johnson, who appears in eighteen poems (Ostrom, *Encyclopedia*, 229–230).

In 1960 Hughes visited **Paris, France**, for the first time in twenty-two years; he had first visited the city and was employed there as a waiter after having worked on a transatlantic freighter in the 1920s. Subsequently, he would make many trips on cultural grants from the State Department—an irony indeed, since until 1959 he had been on the "security index" of the FBI's New York office. The year

1961 saw the publication of his crowning achievement, *Ask Your Mama* (1961), which expresses a satiric response to the rising anger of the 1960s. By the time of publication, Hughes had lived from one great movement of African American culture in the twentieth century—the Harlem Renaissance—to the second great one, the Black Arts Movement of the 1960s and 1970s.

Until four years before his death, Hughes avoided any controversy over what might now be called gay rights. By exploring the complexity of sexual orientation in "Blessed Assurance," a story about a boy singing in church, he reveals that a sacredness of God-given talent transcends sexual orientation. Despite the church audience's discomfort with a boy singer—especially the troubled father's anxiety—the uniqueness of the boy's voice compels the female audience to suspend their normal conformity to assumptions about gender. The girls, in other words, make an exception for his extremely high voice for a male and still appreciate the way he sings. Hughes's own sexuality has been a point of contention among scholars and critics.

Hughes was a writer of almost incredible versatility. He helped to establish the Harlem Suitcase Theatre, was active in theatrical circles in **Chicago, Illinois**, and wrote numerous plays. With Elmer Rice and Kurt Weill, he collaborated on the opera *Street Scene* (1946); he worked with Jan Meyerowitz and **William Grant Still** on other operas. He also wrote **gospel** song-plays, including *Black Nativity: A Christmas Song Play* (1961), which is still regularly produced. He edited *The Best Short Stories by Negro Writers: An Anthology from 1899 to the Present* (1967), as well as *Poems from Black Africa* (1963). Several of his children's books are still in print at this writing. On one of them, *Popo and Fifina* (1932), he collaborated with his lifelong friend **Arna Bontemps**. With Zora Neale Hurston, he collaborated on the ill-fated dramatic project *Mule Bone*, which was not produced until long after both writers had died. With Clarence Muse, he wrote the screenplay for the motion picture *Way Down South* (1939). With Milton Meltzer, he collaborated on *A Pictorial History of the Negro in America* (1956) (Miller, *Art and Imagination* and *Langston Hughes and Gwendolyn Brooks*; Ostrom, *Encyclopedia*).

Langston Hughes was both sympathetic and prophetic in a variety of ways. The 1980s marked a timely renaissance in his reputation. A Langston Hughes study conference held in March 1981 at Joplin, Missouri, helped inspire the founding of the Langston Hughes Society in **Baltimore, Maryland**, on June 26 of the same year. After a joint meeting with the **College Language Association** in April 1982, the Society became the first group focused on a Black author ever to become an affiliate of the Modern Language Association, in 1984. In the winter of 1983, at the City College of the City University of New York, **Raymond Patterson** directed "Langston Hughes: Art International Interdisciplinary Conference," one of the most satisfactory tributes ever paid to the author. Later, a public television production, *Voices and Visions*, included a program on Hughes and reaffirmed his place among the most celebrated national poets. **Arnold Rampersad**'s authoritative two-volume biography of Hughes appeared in 1986 and 1988.

Hughes's impact on American literary history is clear. He introduced some of the most experimental forms of African American music into the poetics of the twentieth century. During the despair of the Great Depression, he presented many deceptively simple stories that would endure beyond his time. He proved, during the late 1940s, that lyricism would prosper, despite the despondency of history. Neither the pessimism of the **Cold War** nor the mainstream backlash to the **Civil Rights Movement** of the 1960s—satirized by him in his final volume, *The Panther and the Lash* (1967)—disillusioned him completely. He discerned a disturbing cycle of inhumanity within history, but not without laughter. A man for all seasons, he was especially a voice of the mid-twentieth century. His work embodied a measured declaration on behalf of a most optimistic future. Thus, his words outlived his own century. He read the vicissitudes of history, often revealing their implications to those who experienced them with him (Miller, "Brief," 61).

Today it would be an unpardonable neglect to discuss either the Jazz Age or the Harlem Renaissance without mention of Hughes. The year 2001 began a steady stream of eighteen volumes, *The Collected Works*, from the University of Missouri Press. The publication is one of the most momentous in African American literary history. By the turn of the twenty-first century, at least four cities—Joplin, Missouri; Lawrence, Kansas; Cleveland, Ohio; and New York City—claimed Hughes as an honored citizen. Cleveland kicked off the national celebration early in June when the Case Western Reserve Historical Society and the **NAACP** reminded the nation that he had spent his high school years there. Soon major conferences took place at Lincoln University in Pennsylvania, the site of his undergraduate years; Yale University; and the University of Kansas, so close to the home of Mary Langston, the poet's maternal grandmother.

Indeed, the Kansas conference was a watershed moment in Hughes research. Outside the auditorium were long lines of local protesters who were angry that Langston Hughes—who was nearly as guarded about his sexual orientation as he was about his perception of God—may have been a gay Black male.

Nonetheless, the approval of Hughes by hundreds of academics and creative writers was indisputable, as was his acceptance by the general public: a U.S. postage stamp honoring Hughes was unveiled at the conference during a reading of his works by the actor Danny Glover. Inside the building were hundreds of intelligent laypersons from all walks of life who reaffirmed the legacy of the writer. Today Hughes still has the power to arouse strong emotions in people of varying aesthetics and ideologies. Few have been indifferent to his persistent belief in human freedom. Gwendolyn Brooks said his vision would last "until the air is cured of its fever." He voiced a celebration of survival and beauty that outlived his century. His writings are for all time. (*See* **Children's Literature; Langston Hughes Society; Marxism;** *Messenger, The*; *Opportunity*; **Protest Literature; Van Vechten, Carl.**)

Resources: Primary Sources: All of the primary sources are now available in Langston Hughes, *The Collected Works*, 18 vols., ed. Arnold Rampersad (Columbia: University of Missouri Press, 2001–2004). In text citations, *BS* = *The Big Sea* and *CP* = *Collected Poems*. **Secondary Sources:** Richard K. Barksdale, *Langston Hughes, the Poet and His Critics* (Chicago: American Library Association, 1977); Faith Berry, *Langston Hughes, Before and Beyond Harlem* (Westport, CT: L. Hill, 1983); Tish Dace, *Langston Hughes: The Contemporary Reviews* (New York: Cambridge University Press, 1997); Christopher C. De Santis, ed., *Langston Hughes and the Chicago Defender Essays on Race, Politics, and Culture, 1942–62* (Urbana: University of Illinois Press, 1995); Donald C. Dickinson, *A Bio-Bibliography of Langston Hughes, 1902–1967* (Hamden, CT: Archon Books, 1967); Susan Duffy, ed., *The Political Plays of Langston Hughes* (Carbondale: Southern Illinois University Press, 2000); James A. Emanuel, *Langston Hughes* (New York: Twayne, 1967); Donna Akiba Sullivan Harper, *Not So Simple: The "Simple" Stories by Langston Hughes* (Columbia: University of Missouri Press, 1995); Onwuchekwa Jemie, *Langston Hughes: An Introduction to the Poetry* (New York: Columbia University Press, 1976); Isaac Julien, *Looking for Langston* (experimental documentary) (New York: Waterbearer, 1999), VHS format; Peter Mandelik and Stanley Schatt, *A Concordance to the Poetry of Langston Hughes* (Detroit: Gale Research, 1975); Joseph McLaren: "Langston Hughes and Africa: From the Harlem Renaissance to the 1960s," in *Juxtapositions: The Harlem Renaissance and the Lost Generation*, ed. Loes Nas and Chandré Carstens (Cape Town, South Africa: University of Cape Town, 2000), 77–94; *Langston Hughes Folk Dramatist in the Protest Tradition, 1921–1943* (Westport, CT: Greenwood Press, 1997); Thomas A. Mikolyz, comp., *Langston Hughes: A Bio-Bibliography* (Westport, CT: Greenwood Press, 1990); R. Baxter Miller: *The Art and Imagination of Langston Hughes* (Lexington: University Press of Kentucky, 1989); "A Brief Biography," in *A Historical Guide to Langston Hughes*, ed. Steven C. Tracy (New York: Oxford University Press, 2004), 23–62; "Café de la Paix: Mapping the Harlem Renaissance," *South Atlantic Review* 65, no. 2 (2000), 73–94; *Langston Hughes and Gwendolyn Brooks: A Reference Guide* (Boston: G. K. Hall, 1978); Edward J. Mullen, ed., *Critical Essays on Langston Hughes* (Boston: G. K. Hall, 1986); Ifeoma Nwanko, "Langston Hughes and the Translation of Nicolas Guillién's Afro-Cuban Culture and Language," *Langston Hughes Review* 16, no. 1–2 (2001–2002), 55–72; Therman B. O'Daniel, *Langston Hughes: Black Genius* (New York: Collier Books, 1971); Hans A. Ostrom: *Langston Hughes: A Study of the Short Fiction* (New York: Twayne, 1993); *A Langston Hughes Encyclopedia* (Westport, CT: Greenwood Press, 2002); Arnold Rampersad, *The Life of Langston Hughes*, 2 vols. (New York: Oxford University Press, 1986–1988); David Roessel: "The Letters of Langston Hughes and Ezra Pound," *Paideuma: A Journal Devoted to Ezra Pound Scholarship* 29, no. 1–2 (Spring/Fall 2000), 207–242; "Process of Revision and Hughes," in Hans Ostrom, *A Langston Hughes Encyclopedia* (Westport, CT: Greenwood Press, 2002), 327–333; Steven C. Tracy, *Langston Hughes & the Blues* (Urbana: University of Illinois Press, 1988); C. James Trotman, ed., *Langston Hughes: The Man, His Art, and His Continuing Influence* (New York: Garland, 1995); *Voices and Visions: Langston Hughes* (New York: Winstar Home Entertainment, 2002), VHS format; Jean Wagner, *Black Poets of the United States from Paul Laurence Dunbar to Langston Hughes*, trans. Kenneth Douglas (Urbana: University of Illinois Press, 1973).

R. Baxter Miller

Hull, Akasha [Gloria T.] (born 1944). Scholar, poet, and literary critic. Akasha [Gloria T.] Hull is a feminist scholar and poet who was an early architect and promoter of contemporary Black Women's Studies and **Black feminist literary criticism** and feminist theory, a discipline and an approach that validate African American women's literature. Hull is also a prominent scholar and critic of the **Harlem Renaissance** writer **Alice Moore Dunbar-Nelson**.

Gloria Teresa Thompson was born in 1944 in Shreveport, Louisiana, to Jimmie Williams Thompson, a domestic worker, and Robert T. Thompson, a laborer. Hull married Prentice R. Hull in 1966. They were divorced in 1983 and have one son, Adrian L. Prentice. Hull legally changed her first name from "Gloria" to "Akasha," a Sanskrit word for "light," in 1992.

Hull received her B.A. in English from Southern University in 1966, her M.A. in English from Purdue University in 1968, and her Ph.D. from Purdue in 1972. She was an instructor (1971), an assistant professor (1972–1977), an associate professor (1977–1986) and finally full professor (1986–1988) of English at the University of Delaware, Newark. In 1988 she became a professor of Women's Studies at the University of California, Santa Cruz, where she was chairperson of the Women's Studies Department from 1989 to 1991. Hull is currently a professor emerita at the University of California, Santa Cruz.

Hull was an editor of the landmark anthology *All the Women Are White, All the Blacks Are Men, but Some of Us Are Brave* (1982). In the introduction to the text (written with **Barbara Smith**), Hull asserts the importance of African American women and promotes the careful, scholarly study and self-definition of African American women's experience and work. She acknowledges the political nature of Black Women's Studies while celebrating the vibrant intellectual life of Black women that is often expressed through literature. Hull links the intellectual work of African American women with their social empowerment and freedom. The book includes a section of critical essays about African American women's literature, bibliographies of African American women writers, and course syllabi from African American women's literature classes from various universities.

Hull's mother, who had little formal education, enjoyed the poetry of **Paul Laurence Dunbar** and shared this joy with her daughter. Subsequently, a significant portion of Hull's scholarship came to be focused on the work of poet, writer, teacher, public speaker, clubwoman and activist Alice Moore Dunbar-Nelson, the widow of Paul Laurence Dunbar. After being introduced to a niece of Dunbar, Hull gained access to large cache of unpublished manuscripts, novels, journals, pictures, assorted newspaper clippings, and other documents. Inspired to recover and make available part of the literary tradition of African American women, Hull helped produce two key texts on and about Alice Dunbar-Nelson, *Give Us Each Day: The Diary of Alice Dunbar-Nelson* (1984) and *The Works of Alice Dunbar-Nelson* (1988).

Hull provided a critical examination of the life and literary accomplishment of Dunbar-Nelson and two other writers in *Color, Sex and Poetry: Three Women Writers of the Harlem Renaissance* (1987). In this text, Hull explores issues of gender and sexuality as they related to the lives and work of Dunbar-Nelson, **Georgia Douglas Johnson** and **Angelina Weld Grimké**.

Hull's own poetry is collected in *Healing Heart*, published by **Kitchen Table/Women of Color Press**. Her latest work has centered on spirituality and the metaphysical dimension of the lives and experiences of African American women. Her book *Soul Talk* (2001) presents some of her scholarship in this area.

Resources: "Gloria T. Hull," in *Contemporary Black Biography*, vol. 45 (Detroit: Gale, 2004); "Gloria T. Hull," in *Notable Black American Women*, vol. 1 (Detroit: Gale, 1992); Gloria T. Hull: *Color, Sex and Poetry: Three Women Writers of the Harlem Renaissance* (Bloomington: Indiana University Press, 1987); *Healing Heart: Poems, 1973–1988* (Latham, NY: Kitchen Table: Women of Color Press, 1989); *Soul Talk: The New Spirituality of African-American Women* (Rochester, VT: Inner Traditions, 2001); Gloria T. Hull, ed.: *Give Us Each Day: The Diary of Alice Dunbar-Nelson* (New York: Norton, 1984); *The Works of Alice Dunbar-Nelson*, 3 vols. (New York: Oxford University Press, 1988); Gloria T. Hull, Patricia Bell Scott, and Barbara Smith, eds., *All the Women Are White, All the Blacks Are Men, but Some of Us Are Brave: Black Women's Studies* (Old Westbury, NY: Feminist Press, 1982).

Kimberly Black-Parker

Humor. Humor in the African American tradition can be found in the **vernacular** speech, songs, **folklore**, and literature of and by Black Americans. African American humor reflects a mixture of cultural influences and forms, many whose origins can be traced to Europe and Africa.

Ostensibly, African American humor shares many forms with the Western tradition of comedy that spans from antiquity to the present day. According to J. A. Cuddon, Aristotle defines comedy as that which "deals in an amusing way with ordinary characters in rather everyday situations" (149). While many histories of the tradition of comedy in the West do not usually include the contributions of writers of African descent (with the exception of Jean Genet, a dramatist whose work *The Blacks* is often considered within the tradition of the theater of the absurd), forms of comedy, such as farce, **satire**, **parody**, and tall stories characteristic of the European tradition are unmistakably evident in African American humor. For example, plantation sayings and stories told by slaves that mimicked the speech, manners, and mores of their masters and mistresses contain elements of both parody and satire.

The origins of **minstrelsy** in the United States, beginning in the nineteenth century, can be traced back to minstrels who traveled throughout Europe during the thirteenth and fourteenth centuries, singing traditional stories

(Cuddon). However, the use of racial stereotypes became the standard in American minstrel shows in the early 1820s after the success of Thomas D. Rice's blackface act and song "Jump Jim Crow." Jim Crow, the character in Rice's show who was played by a white performer who applied burnt cork makeup to blacken his face, set in place the "comic darkie" stereotype in American popular culture, one that caricatured Blacks as slow, childish, shiftless, happy-go-lucky, watermelon-eating, and, contradictorily, as John Lowe writes, "stupid but crafty, humble but scheming, cowardly but reckless, innocent but lascivious" (Lowe, "Humor," in *Oxford Companion to African American Literature*, 371). This stock character, as an object of Whites' derisive humor, helped perpetuate stereotypes of African Americans and found its way in the works of such nineteenth-century American writers as **Harriet Beecher Stowe** and **Mark Twain**.

African storytelling practices that were transported with slaves as they crossed the **Middle Passage** to the Americas influenced African American humor. According to Mel Watkins, African American humor can be traced to African griots, or storytellers, who traveled throughout western African singing traditional stories. Other elements of African American humor have their roots in Africa. Harold Courlander has traced and recorded the use of animal tales, such as Brer (or "Buh") Rabbit and Brer Fox, shared by many peoples of African descent throughout the Americas. **Henry Louis Gates, Jr.**, in *The Signifying Monkey*, locates the origin of the Signifying Monkey—a **trickster** figure similar to other animal characters such as Brer Rabbit and a central character and trope of the oral tradition, verbal play, and folklore of African Americans—in Esu-Elegbara, a trickster figure in Yoruba culture (*see* **Signifying**; **Thompson**, **Robert Farris**). What is characteristic of African American humor is its roots in "an oral tradition that esteemed dramatic colorful speech, imaginative storytelling, irony, and libelous verbal satire" (Watkins, xvii).

The reasons for and uses of humor by African Americans are several. During the nineteenth century, blacks used humor as a way of coping with **slavery** and racism. The slaves' plantation sayings, rhymes, animal and trickster tales, riddles, and songs evince deliberate uses of irony that served to "free" the slave from his or her subservient position. Daryl Cumber Dance notes that "folk riddles" are the earliest known forms of folklore (Dance, *From My People*, 538).

The animal and trickster tales that slaves told featured a cast of weaker animal characters (Brer Rabbit, the Signifying Monkey) who always managed to outwit the stronger (Brer Fox, the Lion). The slaves no doubt identified with the cunning ways in which Brer Rabbit and the Signifying Monkey were able to "trick" Brer Fox and the Lion, respectively. As Jennifer Andrews notes, the trickster, as a purveyor of the comic element, offered "a way to cope with and laugh at the strictures of white American culture" Joel Chandler Harris published many of these tales in *Uncle Remus, His Songs and His Sayings* (1880) and was responsible for preserving these early examples of African American humor. Another early example of African American humor that draws on the tradition of oral storytelling and pokes fun at the institution of slavery is **Charles Waddell Chestnutt**'s *The Conjure Woman* (1899) (*see* **Conjuring**).

While minstrel shows of the nineteenth century made Blacks the butt of racist humor, many plantation stories appropriated the stereotypical "darkie" and imbued him with subtle wit. Among them are the "John and Ole Massa" tales, in which John, the slave, is cast as dim-witted and slow. However, as each tale unfolds, John, who is associated with the legendary High John de Conquerer (Watkins, 46), emerges as a trickster hero, deftly demonstrating mastery of Massa's language in a subtly dazzling display of verbal play, out-witting him each and every time (*see* **John the Conqueror**).

The animal and trickster tales and other early forms reveal some of the aims of humor. The objects of African American humor are often Whites who occupy positions of power; some of the humor, however, is self-reflexive—as in the appropriation of the stereotypical "darkie" in the "John and Ole Massa" tales. Self-reflexive humor is most confusing to people outside the group, in that a negative stereotype is seemingly embraced and laughed at by members inside the group. This type of humor is called "corrective comedy" (*Encyclopedia of African American Culture*, 370). Corrective comedy is evidenced not only in early African American humor but also in later forms of the twentieth and twenty-first centuries.

After emancipation and into the early part of the twentieth century, African American humor transformed significantly as many Blacks moved from rural to urban and industrial centers in the Northeast and the Midwest. While influences of the folklore of the old, rural **South** were still part of modern African America, the new brand of humor reflected the milieu of urban America.

What is characteristic of modern African American humor is bolder and more audacious use of language and verbal play. Signifying, joning/joaning, cracking, specifying, and bookooing are just a few of the terms used to refer to a type of verbal sparring called "playing the dozens." Playing the dozens is a game of verbal one-upmanship in which the players attack each other with insults, most commonly scathing remarks about "yo' mama." According to Daryl Cumber Dance, while some scholars maintain that the labels mark differences between these verbal games, most practitioners do not recognize such distinctions (*From My People*, 539). Boasts, toasts and **ballads** were also part of the growing repertoire of forms of African American humor. One famous ballad is the "Sinking of the Titanic," which tells the tale of the only Black passenger, a man named Shine, of that ill-fated ship. Tales of the city reflected the activities there, from gambling and other vices to street preaching and faith healing.

Animal tales were still widely told and circulated; but the city gave birth to a new cast of characters, some of them bad Black men such as Stackolee and Jack Johnson. Stackolee, based on a real man who allegedly killed another man in **St. Louis, Missouri,** for stealing his white Stetson hat, epitomized the "bad Negro" and was the subject of many a ballad. **Jack Johnson**, the first Black heavyweight boxer to win the championship (1908), became a character in many a humorous tall tale because of his extravagant lifestyle and his blatant disregard for the illegality of interracial relationships. (He was allegedly refused passage on the *Titanic* because he was Black, and this ironic circumstance became the stuff of humorous folklore; see "Jack Johnson and Titanic," *Folknet Discussion*).

The twentieth century welcomed a growing corpus of literary works written by African Americans who incorporated these new forms of humor and took the opportunity to correct negative stereotypes of Blacks made popular in the previous century. The goals of the **Harlem Renaissance**, beginning in 1925, were most notably expressed in **Alain Locke**'s seminal essay "The New Negro" (1925). Locke's call for revision of representations of the Negro in literature and art brought new challenges to modern writers in terms of how to depict African American humor. The use of **dialect** was a big concern in the new literature because it was reminiscent of the nineteenth-century caricatures of Black slaves. Harold Courlander questions the use of dialect in expressing "wit and humor" because these can be easily translated from one language (or culture) to another (Courlander, 259).

Many writers were, of course, divided on this issue. **Zora Neale Hurston** was criticized for her representation of Black speech in her writing. Nonetheless, Hurston's research on folklore and vernacular speech allowed her to produce memorable moments of parody and verbal play in her novel *Their Eyes Were Watching God* (1937). Other novels by Hurston that showcased her skillful blending of Black Southern folklore and elements of humor include *Jonah's Gourd Vine* (1934), *Moses, Man of the Mountain* (1939), and *Seraph on the Suwanee* (1948).

Langston Hughes, who was a contemporary and good friend of Hurston, was legendary in his own contributions to humorous literature by African American writers during this period. Hughes is most famous for the creation of Jesse B. Simple, an urban folk character noted for his hilarious solutions to, and "simple" but ironic wisdom regarding, an array of issues from race relations to house cleaning. Hughes's Simple stories, first published in the **Chicago Defender**, were enormously popular. Hughes penned other humorous works— *Not Without Laughter* (1930) and *Tambourines to Glory* (1958), a novel that blends traditional folk culture and religion with jive and vice—and he edited *The Book of Negro Humor* in 1966 (Ostrom, 56).

Other **Harlem, New York**, writers produced work that incorporated Black vernacular humor, parody, and satire. These writers and their works are **Rudolph John Chauncey Fisher** and his comedic detective novel *The Conjure-Man Dies* (1932), **Wallace Thurman** and his ribald send-up of the Harlem Renaissance in *Infants of the Spring* (1930), **George S. Schuyler** and his lampoon of Blacks' and Whites' preoccupation with skin color in *Black No More* (1931), and **Carl Van Vechten** and his controversial satire on Harlem nightlife in *Nigger Heaven* (1926).

Much of the literature after **World War II** was steeped in Social Realism. However, humor in African American literature, while at times obscured by the social and political milieu of 1950s America and the push for civil rights, still thrived. **Ralph Ellison** gleaned elements from Southern Black folklore and rural and urban Black humor in writing *Invisible Man* (1952). Ellison played on the comedic traditions of "old" and "new" Negroes through his creation two trickster characters, Trueblood and Rineheart, in his novel.

Other notable examples of literature by Black writers that uses elements of African American humor from the 1960s to the present day are **Chester Himes** and his comedic detective novel *Cotton Comes to Harlem* (1964), **Alice Walker** and her use of Black vernacular speech in *The Color Purple* (1982), **Ishmael Reed** in his novel that takes up a dizzying array of folk practices from hoodoo to signifying, *Mumbo Jumbo* (1971), **Ntozake Shange** and her tale of women and magic in *Sassafrass, Cypress and Indigo* (1982), **Toni Morrison** in the tales, gossip, and jokes shared by the women in *Jazz* (1992), and **Percival Everett** in *Erasure* (2001), a tour de force play on the question of who is Black, in which he deftly combines elements of satire, parody and verbal play. Humor is also a significant element of **rap, hip-hop**, and **performance poetry**, and **blues poetry** also can be quite humorous.

Resources: Jennifer Andrews, "Reading Toni Morrison's *Jazz*," *Canadian Review of American Studies* 29, no. 1 (1999), 87–107; William L. Andrews, Frances Smith Foster, and Trudier Harris, eds., *Oxford Companion to African American Literature* (New York: Oxford University Press, 1997); Arna Bontemps and Langston Hughes, eds., *Book of Negro Folklore* (New York: Dodd, Mead, 1958); Harold Courlander, *A Treasury of Afro-American Folklore* (New York: Marlowe, 1996); J. A. Cuddon, *A Dictionary of Literary Terms and Literary Theory*, 4th ed., rev. C. E. Preston (Malden, MA: Blackwell, 1998); Daryl Cumber Dance, *From My People: 400 Years of African American Folklore* (New York: Norton, 2002); Daryl Cumber Dance, ed., *Honey, Hush! An Anthology of African American Women's Humor* (New York: Norton, 1998); Alan Dundes, ed., *Mother Wit from the Laughing Barrel: Readings in the Interpretation of Afro-American Folklore* (Englewood Cliffs, NJ: Prentice-Hall, 1973); Henry Louis Gates, Jr., *The Signifying Monkey* (New York: Oxford University Press, 1998); "Jack Johnson and Titanic Song," *Folknet Discussion*, http://www.folknet.org/_disc3/000002e3.htm; Langston Hughes, ed., *The Book of Negro Humor* (New York: Dodd, Mead, 1966); John Lowe, *Jump at the Sun: Zora Neale Hurston's Cosmic Comedy* (Urbana: University of Illinois Press, 1994); Hans Ostrom, *A Langston Hughes Encyclopedia* (Westport, CT: Greenwood Press, 2002); Mel Watkins, *African American Humor: The Best Black Comedy from Slavery to Today* (Chicago: Lawrence Hill, 2002).

Patricia E. Clark

Hunt, Marsha (born 1946). Novelist, actress, model, biographer, and auto-biographer. Hunt's writings engage the broad issues of **race**, class, **gender**, and oppression historically and within a contemporary context. Much of her work provides a thoughtful, personalized, and sympathetic view of the specific struggles and strengths of African American women in the United States and in Western society as a whole.

Hunt was raised in an extended matriarchal family consisting of her grandmother, Edna Mae Graham Robinson; her aunt Thelma; her mother, Inez Robinson Hunt; and an older brother and sister. Hunt's father, Theodore Hunt, Jr., lived apart from the family in **Boston, Massachusetts**, where he was a student, during her early life; later he became a psychiatrist and eventually committed suicide. Hunt was born and spent her early years in North **Philadelphia, Pennsylvania**. In 1951, her family moved to Germantown, Pennsylvania, and to Mt. Airy in 1955. In 1960, her family moved to Oakland, California, because her siblings were attending college.

Hunt attended the University of California at Berkeley in the mid-1960s and was active during student protests and took part in the Free Speech Movement there. In 1966, she dropped out of college and abruptly moved to Europe. She arrived in London with $1.83 in her pocket and a small list of telephone numbers of friends of her friends from Berkeley. She worked as an au pair and eventually served as a backup singer in British blues bands. Concerned about being deported, Hunt married a musician named Michael Ratledge in 1967, in order to stay in Great Britain. In 1968, Hunt landed a role in the British production of the stage musical *Hair*. Though she did not have a major role, Hunt became strongly associated with the play and was an overnight celebrity. She began modeling and recording music as a solo rock-and-roll artist.

When Hunt appeared as a model in a publicity photo for the Rolling Stones, she met the lead singer, Mick Jagger. The two became friends and lovers, and had a child together—Kharis, born in 1970, Hunt's only child. In her **autobiography**, *Real Life* (1986), Hunt describes her struggles as a young, single mother caring for her child while working in the entertainment industry in Europe. She confronted the issues that many young working mothers face—concerns about making adequate income, obtaining child support, finding appropriate child care, and establishing a schedule that accommodates a child's needs. Hunt held several different jobs in entertainment in Great Britain and throughout Europe, from being a solo performer to actress to hosting her own radio talk show.

In addition to an autobiography, Hunt wrote a biography of her paternal grandmother, Ernestine. She speculates that Ernestine was wrongly committed to a mental institution for over fifty years. In *Repossessing Ernestine* (1996), she attempts to uncover Ernestine's story, but, as is true of the mentally ill in many families, it is hidden, suppressed, ignored, or lost. Hunt describes her personal attempts to discuss Ernestine's story openly in her family, to uncover the issues leading to her commitment, to remove Ernestine from degrading institutional settings and to provide for her care.

Hunt began writing fiction in the 1990s. Although permanently living abroad, she engages African American culture and life in her fiction. Her characters are African American and the settings in her fiction are American.

Her first novel, *Joy* (1990), is presented from the viewpoint of "Baby" Palatine Ross, a former cleaning woman who becomes a friend to the Bangs, a young family of three girls headed by a single mother. Baby Palatine lives vicariously through the Bangs, her favorite of whom is the middle daughter, Joy. The story is set at Joy's funeral and the histories of the families are told through flashbacks—their rise from poverty and obscurity to become celebrated musical performers and an eventual return to obscurity. Baby Palatine, in attempting to understand the untimely death of Joy, must confront the often huge divide between perception and truth in human relations.

Hunt's second novel, *Free* (1992), is a moving **coming-of-age** story that deals with the aftermath of **slavery**, racism, classism, oppression, longing, homosexuality, and ultimately personal liberation and transcendence. Set in Germantown, Pennsylvania, at turn of the twentieth century, *Free* is the story of "Teenotchy" a quiet, introspective African American stable boy. Teenotchy struggles psychologically to deal with his mother's murder many years earlier, as well as with the development of a friendship and love affair with a young aristocrat, Alexander, that transgresses social taboos of race, class, and sexuality.

Her third novel, *Like Venus Fading* (1998), has a protagonist who is an entertainer—Irene O'Brien, who seeks to survive and transcend childhood sexual abuse and impoverishment during the **Great Depression**, a contentious and abusive marriage, a child who is cognitively "abnormal" and her struggles as a rising African American film star and bombshell under the studio system in Hollywood of the 1940s and 1950s. Irene deals with racism, sexism, poverty, and the vagaries of fame as she seeks to come to peace about her life.

Resources: Marcia Hunt: *Free* (New York: Dutton, 1992); *Joy* (New York: Dutton, 1990); *Like Venus Fading* (New York: Flamingo, 1998); *Real Life* (London: Chatto & Windus, 1986); *Repossessing Ernestine: A Granddaughter Uncovers the Secret History of Her American Family* (New York: HarperCollins, 1996); *The Way We Wore: Styles of the 1930s and '40s and Our World Since Then* (Fallbrook, CA: Fallbrook, 1993); "Marsha Hunt," in *Contemporary Authors*, 3rd ed. (Detroit: Gale Group, 1999).

Kimberly Black-Parker

Hunter, Travis (born 1969). Novelist. Born in Florence, South Carolina, Hunter grew up there and in **Philadelphia, Pennsylvania**. After serving in the U.S. Army, he attended Clark Atlanta University and then transferred to Georgia State University, where he pursued a degree in psychology.

Hunter began writing while he was still in the military. At first, he wrote song lyrics, but when he discovered that he had a facility for telling stories in those lyrics, he gradually shifted his emphasis to writing fiction. He has published one novel each year since 2001.

Hunter's first novel, *The Hearts of Men* (2001), focuses on the conundrums facing three African American men. Winston "Poppa Doc" Fuller is an influential father figure to many African American men in his community, but he can't communicate with his own son, who, though in his thirties, shows no inclination to lead a responsible life. A diagnosis of terminal cancer makes Poppa Doc desperate to reach his son. Raised in an impoverished household, Bernard Charles is obsessed with providing everything that his family needs or wants, but the time and energy he has devoted to being the provider have placed his marriage in jeopardy. Prodigy Banks is a womanizer who discovers that he can transform himself into a man devoted to one woman but still cannot escape his libidinous past. These three stories are circumstantially connected in a manner that provides a broad perspective on suburban African American life.

Hunter's second novel, *Married But Still Looking* (2002), focuses on Genesis Styles, a friend of Prodigy Banks who is less successful in transforming himself from a "player" to a faithful spouse. In *Trouble Man* (2003), Hunter juxtaposes the stories of two young men, Jermaine Banks and Calvin Sharpe, whose lives have reached crisis points. Banks is a street thug and Sharpe is a yuppie, but both have unsettled family situations complicated by their own indiscretions and impending legal problems.

Hunter's fourth novel, *One Woman Man* (2004), chronicles the escalating, interconnected troubles in the personal lives of Dallas Dupree and his married sister Carmen, and the eventual intervention of their older brother, Priest. Dallas has become a highly regarded, civic-minded teacher, but his life starts to come apart when his wife, to whom he has been devoted, dies giving birth to their daughter. By the time the daughter is an adolescent, Dallas's personal life has become so distressingly complicated and his daughter's behavior has become so incorrigible that he sends her to live with Carmen. But Carmen, now an established physician who has just recently married, finds her niece's indiscretions and impudence to be more than she can handle. Although Priest provided for and protected his younger brother and sister as they were growing up, he has become the black sheep of the family, making his money from enterprises that seem to have involved a series of disreputable business partners. Nonetheless, when Dallas and Carmen turn to Priest for help, many of this family's unresolved issues, past and current, are gradually solved.

After the success of his debut novel *The Hearts of Men*, Hunter established the Hearts of Men Foundation in **Atlanta, Georgia**, where he now resides. This nonprofit foundation offers support to disadvantaged adolescents in the areas of health, education, and the arts.

Resources: A. J. Bowser, "Review of *The Hearts of Men*," *New York Amsterdam News*, Sept. 12, 2002, p. 36; Travis Hunter: *The Hearts of Men* (New York: Random House/Villard, 2001); *Married But Still Looking* (New York: Random House/Villard, 2002); *A One Woman Man* (New York: Ballantine/One World, 2004); *Trouble Man* (New York: Random House/Villard, 2003); Victoria Christopher Murray, "What Do Those Big Publishers Want Anyway?" *Black Issues Book Review* 6 (Sept. 2004), 34; "Review of *A One Woman Man*," *Black Issues Book Review* 6 (July/Aug. 2004), 17; "Take Note," review of *Trouble Man*, *Essence* 34 (Nov. 2003), 150; Glenn Townes, "Review of *Married but Still Looking*," *Black Issues Book Review* 4 (July/Aug. 2002), 35;

Ahmad Wright, "Review of *The Hearts of Men*," *Black Issues Book Review* 3 (July/Aug. 2001), 33.

Martin Kich

Hurston, Zora Neale (1891–1960). Novelist, short story writer, playwright, folklorist, and anthropologist. Hurston is best known for novels and short stories that make use of the **vernacular** and display a rich, complex sense of rural African American life, particularly in **the South**. She was born in Notasulga, Alabama, on January 7, 1891, to John Hurston, a preacher and carpenter, and Lucy Potts Hurston, a retired schoolteacher. Hurston was the fifth of eight children. Shortly after her birth, the Hurstons moved to Eatonville, Florida, the first incorporated Black city in the United States, a city alive with opportunity. Whenever Hurston spoke of "home," she meant Eatonville.

Growing up in Eatonville profoundly shaped Hurston's worldview. As a child there, she attended the Robert Hungerford Normal and Industrial School, modeled after **Booker T. Washington**'s Tuskegee Institute. At this school, her industry and intelligence won her the praise of White philanthropists, along with her fair share of books, which she read voraciously, and clothes. Along with her formal education, Hurston learned the craft of storytelling by listening to the ribald stories told by men on the porch of Joe Clarke's store (*Dust Tracks*). Hurston used many of these stories in her later writings, particularly in her 1937 novel *Their Eyes Were Watching God*; in short stories, such as those collected in *Spunk* and *Sweat*; and in *Mule Bone*, the play she wrote with **Langston Hughes**.

Hurston's mother died on September 18, 1904, when Hurston was thirteen years old, and her death was a great blow. While Lucy Hurston always encouraged her daughter to "jump at de sun," John Hurston attempted to squelch Zora's bodacious spirit, believing that his daughter was heading to a world of trouble if she did not humble herself to supposed authority (Hemenway; Boyd). With the loss of her mother, Hurston found herself alone in a community that frowned upon her wild stories and her lively spirit.

John Hurston wasted little time in sending his daughter off to the Florida Baptist Academy in Jacksonville, Florida. Already motherless, Hurston essentially became fatherless as well. John Hurston stopped making the tuition payments at Florida Baptist, and as a result, Hurston was forced to scrub floors and perform other menial tasks to pay her way. Later, John Hurston put Hurston up for adoption, but there were no takers. She excelled academically her first year at Florida Baptist, but her return home after her first year was a failure.

Hurston was shocked to find that her father had remarried. For his new wife, he had chosen Mattie Moge, who was younger than his oldest son, and only six years older than Zora, who never got along with her new stepmother. Hurston caused a tremendous uproar over Lucy's featherbed, the bed Lucy had died on and upon which Mattie now slept, for Lucy had bequeathed the bed to her. The tensions in the home escalated to the point that John Hurston pulled a knife on his daughter, and Hurston left home (Hemenway; Boyd).

Hurston's dream of completing her formal education was put on hold as she worked menial jobs, fending off sexual and physical violence—as she learned all too soon, a Black teenage girl had few rights, if any, in a world run by White men. In 1912, she left Florida, living first with her brother Bob and his wife in the Black Bottom section of **Nashville, Tennessee**, and later in a middle-class neighborhood on Scott Street in **Memphis, Tennessee**. In 1914, Hurston returned to Jacksonville, and lived with her brother John before landing a job with a traveling Gilbert and Sullivan theater troupe.

With the troupe, Hurston worked as a wardrobe girl and a maid for the lead singer. She left the group when it reached **Baltimore, Maryland**, and began life anew. In September 1917, she enrolled in Morgan Academy, an elite all-Black prep school of what is now Morgan State University. To be eligible for Morgan, Hurston lied about her age, making herself ten years younger than she actually was. To pay her way through school, she worked in the home of Dr. Baldwin, a White clergyman and school trustee whose wife had a bad hip. In exchange for performing domestic chores, Hurston had all tuition waived, received room and board, gained access to a well-stocked library, earned a stipend of $2 a week, and was free to study during the day. At Morgan, she excelled in her English and history classes and, at times, taught the history classes (Hemenway).

In June 1918, Hurston withdrew from Morgan to pursue her dream of attending Howard University. She moved to **Washington, D.C.**, and, waiting tables at the exclusive Cosmos Club, earned the fees for Howard. When she went to enroll, however, Hurston learned that her work at Morgan was incomplete and did not qualify her for admission to Howard. Hurston attended Howard Academy, earning her high school diploma in May 1919. In the fall of that year, she began her undergraduate studies at Howard University, studying part-time from 1919 to 1923, while waiting tables and working as a manicurist in a barbershop.

An English major at Howard, Hurston worked with the philosopher **Alain Locke**, one of the framers of the **Harlem Renaissance**, and began her career as a writer in earnest. Hurston was a member of the Howard literary club, the Stylus, and in May 1921, she published her first poem, "O Night," and her first short story, "John Redding Goes to Sea," in its literary magazine, The Stylus (Hemenway; Boyd). Hurston's literary pursuits ranged off campus as well. She published two poems in **Marcus Garvey's Negro World**, the official organ for his Universal Negro Improvement Association, and attended the salons of the African American poet **Georgia Douglas Johnson**. At Johnson's literary salons, visitors included **W.E.B. Du Bois** and **James Weldon Johnson**, the writers **Jean Toomer** and **Rudolph John Chauncey Fisher**, and the poets **Sterling A. Brown** and **Angelina Weld Grimké**. During the fall of 1923, Hurston's last term at Howard, she excelled in what interested her and failed courses that did not. After the holiday break, she did not enroll for the spring term of 1924.

That year she published two short stories, "Drenched in Light" and "Spunk," in **Charles Spurgeon Johnson**'s *Opportunity*. Her writing career off to an auspicious start, Hurston left Washington for New York City in 1925. In New York, she took her place among other writers and artists of the Harlem Renaissance. Her story "Spunk" was anthologized in Alain Locke's foundational anthology of the Harlem Renaissance, *The New Negro* (1925), and in May 1925 she received two second-place prizes at the *Opportunity* awards dinner. At that awards dinner, among meeting prime movers of the Harlem Renaissance such as Langston Hughes, **Countee Cullen**, Fannie Hurst, and **Carl Van Vechten**, Hurston met Annie Nathan Meyer, a trustee of Barnard College who was impressed with Hurston's vivacity to the extent that, despite Hurston's less than impressive Howard transcript, she helped Hurston find scholarship money to attend Barnard College, beginning in the fall of 1926. During her first term at Barnard, Hurston worked as a secretary and chauffeur for the novelist Fannie Hurst. This position earned Hurston the esteem of some of her classmates, as well as of Virginia C. Gildersleeve, the dean of Barnard College. Despite access to White literary circles, $12.50 a week, and clothes, Hurston did not keep the job, but decided to wait tables and do housework for friends of Meyer.

The only Black student at Barnard, Hurston studied anthropology with Franz Boas and collaborated with Aaron Douglas, **Wallace Thurman**, and Langston Hughes on the avant-garde journal *Fire!!*, which was a kind of response to Locke's anthology and aimed to support and celebrate what the editors perceived to be fresher work by younger artists. African American art, Hurston believed, was defined through traditions such as oral history and **folklore**. As a result, Black art and culture, according to Hurston, were not necessarily obligated to respond to racist stereotypes. This belief forms one of the core principles of Hurston's body of work in which the "White" world is at the margins, never asserting a dominant influence over the humanity of her Black characters.

In 1927, Hurston, with the support of a fellowship from the Association for the Study of Negro Life and History, published her first field report, "Cudjo's Own Story of the Last African Slaves," in the *Journal of Negro History*. That same year, she met Charlotte Osgood Mason, a White philanthropist whose interest had turned from the Southwest American Indians to the **"New Negro"** of **Harlem, New York**. Mason supported a range of Black artists, writers, and intellectuals, including Langston Hughes, and she insisted that those in her pay call her "Godmother." For this work, Hurston received a stipend of $200 a month, with the understanding that all of the folklore she collected belonged to Mason.

In 1928, Hurston became the first African American to earn a B.A. from Barnard College. Barnard degree in hand and Mason's monthly stipend in pocket, Hurston traveled the South, gathering stories and folklore that she would fashion into novels, plays, and academic papers. In 1931, she published a 100-page scholarly article, "Hoodoo in America," which concerned what is commonly known as **voodoo**, in the *Journal of American Folklore*. That same year she began collaborating with Langston Hughes on a play, *Mule Bone*, that was to move beyond the minstrel images of Black people on stage. For a variety of reasons, including different views toward Mrs. Mason, the relationship between Hughes and Hurston disintegrated and collaboration ceased on *Mule Bone*, which was not produced until 1991 (*Mule Bone*; Taj Mahal), long after both writers were dead (*see* Beaufort). The controversy surrounding *Mule Bone* is recounted in detail in the 1991 edition, as well as in Rampersad's biography of Hughes, Hemenway's and Boyd's biographies of Hurston, and Hughes's autobiography, *The Big Sea*.

The relationship between Hurston and Mason became increasingly frayed as they clashed over the idea of folklore ownership; for Hurston, African American folklore was not something that could be owned, only shared. She left Mason's payroll in 1932, and began folklore concerts at which she dramatized life in railroad camps, using folk and work songs. In May 1934, Hurston published her first novel, *Jonah's Gourd Vine*, which became a Book-of-the-Month Club selection. The 1934 recipient of a Julius Rosenwald fellowship, Hurston published *Mules and Men* the following year, the first book of African American folklore written by an African American. With two solid books to her credit, Hurston was awarded a Guggenheim fellowship in March 1936 that took her to the West Indies to study obeah practices. In **Haiti**, she wrote her finest novel, *Their Eyes Were Watching God*, in seven weeks. In September 1937, Hurston returned to the United States and published *Their Eyes*. In that novel, the protagonist, Janie Mae Crawford, gains an independence of voice and attains an ideal, though short-lived, romantic love that Hurston herself never attained.

Zora Neale Hurston, 1935. Courtesy of the Library of Congress.

With a life filled with writing and traveling, Hurston was never married for long. Her 1927 marriage to Herbert Sheen, a medical student she met at Howard in 1921, was annulled in 1931, although they had separated four months after their wedding vows. In 1939, Hurston tried marriage again, this time with Works Progress Administration playground director Albert Price III, fifteen years her junior. After eight months, divorce papers were filed, and the divorce became official in 1943.

In 1938, the fieldwork Hurston had done in Haiti while on Guggenheim fellowships was published as her second collection of folklore, *Tell My Horse*. In June 1939, Morgan State

College awarded Hurston an honorary Doctor of Letters, and in November she published her second novel, *Moses, Man of the Mountain*, in which she explored the figure of Moses and African oral traditions. In November 1942, Hurston published her autobiographical memoir, *Dust Tracks on a Road*, her sixth book in eight years, and her greatest commercial success.

After this flood of writing, along with a range of short stories and essays, Hurston continued to write, but not at the same pace, publishing stories and articles in the *Saturday Review*, the *American Mercury*, and the **Negro Digest**. In fact, her stature as a writer began to wane, partly because **Richard Wright**'s *Native Son* (1940) brought **protest literature** into vogue. Nevertheless, Hurston continued the work that was important to her. In May 1947, she traveled to British Honduras (now Belize) to study Central American Black communities. In March 1948, she returned to the United States, and in October published her last novel, *Seraph on the Suwanee*. That same year, she was falsely accused of molesting a ten-year-old boy, and the charges were dropped in March 1949 when Hurston turned over her passport, which proved she was in British Honduras at the time of the accusation.

In the winter of 1950, Hurston moved to Belle Glade, Florida, and throughout the 1950s, she worked as a substitute teacher and as a domestic worker, while contributing to local Florida newspapers. Her income was never steady, but she never asked relatives for help. Even after a stroke in early 1959, Hurston remained fiercely independent, while her condition worsened financially and physically. In October 1959, Hurston was forced to enter the St. Lucie County Welfare Home, where she died on January 28, 1960 of "hypertensive heart disease" (Hemenway). She was at work on a biography of Herod the Great.

When Hurston died, none of her books was in print, although she was the most prolific Black woman writer in America. Buried in an unmarked grave in Fort Pierce's African American cemetery, Hurston's body lay in obscurity until August 1973, when **Alice Walker** found her unmarked grave and placed a tombstone on it. On this tombstone, Walker named Hurston a "genius of the South," a phrase from one of Jean Toomer's poems in *Cane*, and a phrase that situates Hurston as one of the preeminent writers of the Harlem Renaissance as well as a progenitor of Black women writers following in her wake. Since the publication of Walker's "Looking for Zora" in the March 1975 issue of *Ms.* magazine, Hurston has become a significant figure in the canon of American and African American literature, and her work has been widely republished.

Resources: **Primary Sources:** Zora Neale Hurston: *The Complete Stories* (New York: HarperCollins, 1995); *Dust Tracks on a Road* (1942; repr. New York: HarperPerennial, 1996); *Jonah's Gourd Vine* (1934; repr. New York: Perennial Library, 1990); *Moses, Man of the Mountain* (Philadelphia: Lippincott, 1939); *Mule Bone: A Comedy of Negro Life*, written with Langston Hughes, ed. George Houston Bass and Henry Louis Gates, Jr. (New York: HarperPerennial, 1991); *Mules and Men* (1935; repr. New York: Perennial Library, 1990); *Seraph on the Suwanee* (New York: Scribner's, 1948); *Spunk: Selected Stories of Zorah Neale Hurston* (San Francisco: Publishing Group West, 1997);

Sweat, ed. Cheryl A. Wall (New Brunswick, NJ: Rutgers University Press, 1997); *Their Eyes Were Watching God* (1937; repr. New York: Perennial Library, 1990). **Secondary Sources:** John Beaufort, "*Mule Bone* Debuts after 60 Years," *Christian Science Monitor*, Feb. 26, 1991, p. 13; Valerie Boyd, *Wrapped in Rainbows: The Life of Zora Neale Hurston* (New York: Scribner's, 2003); Robert E. Hemenway, *Zora Neale Hurston: A Literary Biography* (Urbana: University of Illinois Press, 1977); Karla Holloway, *The Character of the Word: The Texts of Zora Neale Hurston* (Westport, CT: Greenwood Press, 1987); Nathan Irvin Huggins, *Harlem Renaissance* (New York: Oxford University Press, 1971); Langston Hughes, *The Big Sea* (New York: Knopf, 1940); Carla Kaplan, ed., *Zora Neale Hurston: A Life in Letters* (New York: Doubleday, 2002); Carla Kaplan and Ralph E. Van Raaphorst Luker: "Hurston, Zora Neale," *American National Biography Online* (Feb. 2000), http://www.anb.org/articles/16/16-00817.html; "Hurston, Zora Neale," in *African American Women: A Biographical Dictionary*, ed. Dorothy Salem (New York: Garland, 1996); Hans Ostrom, "*Mule Bone: A Comedy of Negro Life*," in his *A Langston Hughes Encyclopedia* (Westport, CT: Greenwood Press, 2002), 261–262; Arnold Rampersad, *The Life of Langston Hughes*, vol. 1, *1902–1941* (New York: Oxford University Press, 1986); Taj Mahal, *Mule Bone* (Santa Monica, CA: Grammavision/Rhino Records, 1991), compact disc; Wallace Thurman et al., eds., *FIRE!! A Quarterly Devoted to the Younger Negro Artists* (facsimile reproduction) (New York: Fire Press, 1985); Alice Walker, *In Search of Our Mothers' Gardens* (San Diego: Harcourt Brace Jovanovich, 1983); Cheryl A. Wall: "Hurston, Zora Neale," in *The Oxford Companion to African American Literature*, ed. William L. Andrews, Frances Smith Foster, and Trudier Harris (New York: Oxford University Press, 1997); *Women of the Harlem Renaissance* (Bloomington: Indiana University Press, 1995); Steven Watson, *The Harlem Renaissance: Hub of African-American Culture, 1920–1930* (New York: Pantheon Books, 1995).

Delano Greenidge-Copprue